The Douglas B-18 and B-23

This labor of love and respect is dedicated to the men and women who designed, built, tested and, above all, went to war in these wonderful machines and who, until now, have been largely forgotten.

The Douglas B-18 and B-23

America's Forsaken Warriors

Dan Hagedorn Sr and Dan Hagedorn Jr

www.crecy.co.uk

Crécy Publishing Ltd

www.crecy.co.uk

First published in 2015 by Crécy Publishing

A CIP record for this book is available from the British Library

ISBN 9780859791786

Printed and bound in Slovenia by GPS

Crécy Publishing Limited
1a Ringway Trading Estate, Shadowmoss Road,
Manchester M22 5LH

www.crecy.co.uk

Front cover main image
R32 was a B-18A assigned to the 38th Reconnaissance Squadron (L/R), 19th Bomb Group and sported black and yellow chequered engine cowls. *via Ted Young*

Front cover small image
B-18 AC36-294 is a long way from home station, shown here on the tarmac on the Galapagos Islands. The camouflage shown here, including the almost white under surfaces, was unique to aircraft of the Sixth Air Force. *via John Woram*

Front flap top
The original DB-1 had been long since accepted by the Air Corps and designated as a B-18X with serial number AC37-51. *NARA RG342 Sarah Clark collection*

Front flap bottom
A B-18A assigned to the Air Corps Advanced Flying School, Bombardier Course, at Albuquerque, NM, as of 3 February 1942. *NARA RG342FH 4A-17097 via Dana Bell*

Back cover main Image
This early production B-18, marked BG 7, with Field Number 1 (probably the 7th Bomb Group Commander's aircraft), shows the two-color engine cowlings and early configuration of the cooling aperture. *Wright Field*

Back cover small images clockwise from top
The earliest known photo of the complete DB-1, dated 29 June1935. with a retractable tail wheel, a feature later deleted. *Boeing Archives SM-8168 and 8164*
'Satan's Chariot' was B-18C AC37-473, and shows evidence of the removal of most of her camouflage. *Peter M. Bowers via The Museum of Flight*
A rather spiffy looking B-18A, N56847 at Compton, California in August 1959, the former AC37-469. *via Al Hansen*

B-18 Barclay artwork by Rich Dann

Table of Contents

Publishers Note: Detailed appendices including a production list are available to download. Please contact enquiries@crecy.co.uk

Foreword

The B-18 grew out of a Douglas proposal to meet the Army Air Corps specification for a bomber to replace the obsolescent Martin B-10, which was the mainstay of the tiny US Army bombardment force in the 1930s.

In 1934, major US aircraft manufacturers, including Boeing, Martin, North American and Douglas, submitted proposals to the Air Corps. Douglas proposed the DB-1, which was powered by two Wright R-1820 engines of 930hp. The wings, tail and landing gear, according to common folklore, seemed to leave no doubt as to its Douglas Commercial (DC-1 and DC-2) ancestry. After testing, the Air Corps flight test board accepted the DB-1 for production as the B-18. The Boeing entry in the competition was the Model 299, a much larger and four-engine design, which was clearly superior – but the Army General Staff considered it too expensive and ordered ninety-nine B-18s in 1936 and thirty-five more in 1937.

At first glance, the B-18 did not appear to present any dramatic performance advancements. It was, however, a stable and honest aircraft. The closed cockpit was a great improvement over the B-10, as was the crew arrangement, and met with immediate approval by the air crews. There was also a comfortable cabin above the bomb bays that allowed for carrying passengers and where crews could rest on long hauls.

The B-18A was an improved version with a larger compartment for the bombardier, which gave the aircraft the distinctive 'shark nose' appearance, and full-feathering Hamilton Standard propellers. A total of 217 B-18A aircraft were purchased in the 1937-39 period.

The B-18 was generally regarded as underpowered, with corresponding performance, and by 1941 it had become the 'ugly duckling' of the bombardment community – but during the war that soon involved the United States it found a mission that it fulfilled admirably, that of anti-submarine warfare. As the Axis submarine threat developed, the B-18s were immediately available and, as the authors will show, were soon deployed seemingly everywhere along both coasts of the United States and deep into the Caribbean. A significant number of the surviving B-18s and B-18As were purpose-modified for the anti-submarine role by adding Air to Surface Vessel (ASV) radar – the first such US application of the new technology – as well as magnetic anomaly detection (MAD) gear. These became the B-18B and B-18C variants.

There were B-18s in Hawaii and the Philippines when the Japanese attacked the US, and they also served in other, remote overseas locations, seldom recorded by historians.

Often compared unfavorably to much later designs, like its pursuit stable mate the Curtiss P-40, the Douglas B-18s were what we had to go to war with and, on closer scrutiny, provided service to the country far in excess of their cost and total numbers. Indeed, the B-18 was one of the few pre-war US designs that served in numbers completely through the war years.

To the designers, craftsmen and crews who breathed life into these lumbering, reliable airplanes, who often flew into harm's way in solitary, remote actions, all honor.

Colonel Harry Goldsworthy, USAF (Ret)
2,000-plus hours in B-18s.

Acknowledgments

The project leading to this book commenced in the 1960s when, while serving a first tour in what was then the Panama Canal Zone, Lloyd Young, the Command Historian of the US Air Forces Southern Command (USAFSO), over a period of some three years, managed to interest the elder Hagedorn in the general history of Army aviation in defense of the Canal and the Caribbean area.

Although an avowed student of the history of Latin American aviation, Hagedorn gradually gained an interest in US service aviation in the region as well, as it became clear that the two interests not only were inextricably linked, but that precious little attention had been bestowed upon the subject. Lloyd Young has long since made his last flight, but to his everlasting credit and honor, by gentle prodding and poking, he caused Hagedorn to pursue the study of US service aviation in the region, and this led to the publication of *ALAE SUPRA CANALEM: Wings Over the Canal* by the Turner Publishing Co in 1995. To this day, the elder co-author of this book regards this as one of his most satisfying contributions.

Out of that title, likewise, was gained an acute appreciation for the officers and men of the Sixth Air Force and the associated Antilles Air Command, and in particular for the unsung anti-submarine war that they carried to the Axis powers during the first crucial eighteen months of the United States entry into that greatest of world wars. The role played by the B-18 and its crews in this campaign has, at best, been only briefly cited in countless studies of the overall war effort, and usually not at all. So, first and foremost, our profound thanks to Lloyd Young, for his mentorship and to the unnamed thousands of B-18 designers, builders and certainly crewmen who brought the lady to life and unheralded glory.

Sincere thanks are also due to Mr Chris Chatfield and the Monographs Committee of Air-Britain, the International Association of Aviation Historians, for recognising the righteousness of producing this history, hard on the heels of the magnificent two-volume history of the seemingly immortal relatives, the Douglas DC-1, DC-2 and DC-3 series, to which the emergence of the B-18 was inextricably linked – but not quite in the manner that has become almost the stuff of folk legend.

Readers of previous works by the elder Hagedorn will note that, for the first time, a very similar name has been added to the masthead, that of Dan Hagedorn Jr, now in his third decade and joining his old man in this effort by doing a considerable percentage of the footwork, and all of the original layout. There can be few things in life more gratifying than 'building' something worthwhile with a son.

Similarly, a cast of familiar characters has once again stepped up to support this project, many of them for the umpteenth time. Chief amongst these has been David W. Ostrowski, priceless friend and editor of the journal *Skyways*, who once again opened his vast personal collections of aircraft negatives to aid this project. Oldest aviation friends Dr Gary Kuhn and John M. Davis both provided their energies, time and resources, and helped keep the target in focus.

Mr Mike Lombardi, Historian and Archivist of The Boeing Company Archives, enabled the priceless Patricia M. McGinnis, Historian at the Long Beach, California, archival unit where virtually all of the former Douglas archives are maintained, to open the resources of that invaluable collection, the fruits of which made this work comprehensible beyond our most optimistic expectations.

Perhaps not surprisingly, there aren't many enthusiasts who specialise in the Douglas B-18. 'Lumpy' Lumpkin of Tucson, Arizona, is the exception, however, and it was through his devotion to the aircraft that the Pima Air and Space Museum completed the magnificent restoration of its B-18 in B-18B anti-submarine configuration. His personal collection of materials relating to the B-18, and his understanding of the evolution of the series, were of great help in sorting out some nagging problems.

Other enthusiasts have also stepped forward to assist this effort. These include Gustavo Arias of Colombia, who delved into the Colombian civil aeronautics records to aid in the identification of some of the post-war conversions registered there, and Brian R. Baker, who provided prints of those superb photos from the 1950s for which he is well known. William H. 'Bill' Bartsch came through with no fewer than twenty-two priceless images, and his work on Army aviation in the Philippines has been unquestionably of great importance to this project. Dear friend Kevin Grantham, Archivist of the American Library for the Photographic History of Aviation (ALPHA), endured never-ending updates on the status of this project, and provided several one-of-a-kind images from that collection. Special mention must also be made of the contributions of John Woram and Gilbert L. Hallquist, the latter having served with the little-known 1st Bombardment Squadron on Trinidad. Certainly the premier historian on Canadian Digby operations, Carl Vincent, provided extremely valuable data and images from his extensive research for this project on those RCAF aircraft.

The archivists at the National Archives at College Park, including Dave Giordano, endured our never-ending quest for details of B-18 development there, and assisted us in navigating through the so-called Sarah Clark Collection (RG342), which provided many unique insights into the day-to-day use of B-18s in extensive test activity. Likewise, David Schwartz, a former colleague and staff member at the Archives (Building 12) Unit of the National Air and Space Museum hefted many 80-pound boxes of manuals and documents from the Wright Field Air Technical Documents Library Collection for us.

Dennis Parks and his staff at the Museum of Flight in Seattle, including Photo Archivist Katherine Williams and Ted Young, assisted with wonderful images from the Peter M. Bowers and Norm Taylor Collections, and provide outstanding services.

Peter J. Marson at Air Britain provided information for the production list and Dave Menard, lately of the US Air Force Museum (where he is sorely missed), provided many tips, suggestions and contacts, as did his replacement at the now renamed National Museum of the United States Air Force, Bret Stolle and Jeff Duford, Research Historian there.

Although B-18 crewmen, their surviving family members and veterans were an invaluable source for data and photos, they are far too numerous to list individually here; instead we have cited them in the text, primarily in connection with the units with which they served. We have to make several exceptions, however. First, Colonel Harry E. Goldsworthy and Colonel Ole Griffith, both USAF (Ret), were great friends of this long-standing project, and their experience and counsel were invaluable. Robert L. Taylor, a Sixth Air Force veteran and editor of *The Caribbean Breeze II*, faithfully directed B-18 veterans our way, and our old friend and Canal Zone veteran Jim Dias made some of his superb prints available to this project. Ward Burhanna, son of a B-18A skipper who received the DFC for a successful submarine attack in the Caribbean, also provided invaluable assistance regarding his father's nearly forgotten wartime contributions.

Former NASM staff member, USAAF colors and markings historian and old friend Dana Bell was most helpful, as was the legendary Mrs Yvonne Kincaid of the USAF Command History Office Library at Bolling Field. John D. Weber, Command Historian of the USAF Materiel Command at Wright-Patterson AFB, provided valuable direction and resources. Jana L. Hammer of the FAA at

Oklahoma City helped confirm some of the post-war civil B-18s, and enthusiasts Guido E. Buehlmann (who has aided so many of our projects over the years), Brian R. Baker, Paul Bridgford, Ted Young, Dick Phillips, J. P. Rybarczyk (who produced the magnificent study of B-18 dispositions as of 7 December 1941), Ole Griffith, Dr Erik D. Carlson of the History of Aviation Collection, Kenneth T. Wilhite Jr, George Redheffer, John M. Fitzpatrick, Anne M. O'Conner of the USAFHRA, Mark Aldrich, August T. Horvath, the late Richard W. (Dick) Kamm, Leo J. Kohn, William T. Larkins, Mat Rodina, Dick Phillips, Doug MacPhail, Bill Stewart, and Robert F. Dorr also came through with some spectacular images and commentary.

The authors made a concerted effort to contact every repository in the United States that might conceivably hold material relating to the B-18 and B-23, and often were amazed at the extent to which the often volunteer and unpaid staffs of these institutions would go to assist us. These folks included Stacey Gatten of the American Airpower Heritage Museum in Midland, TX, and, a genuine bonanza on the early B-18Bs, Frank J. Conahan, Curatorial Assistant at the MIT Museum. A concerted effort was also made to 'visit' each surviving example, and only the aircraft at Castle AFB was missed. The restoration crew at McChord AFB was especially hospitable, and our sincere thanks to team leader Herb Tollefson, his son, and Ray Burgess.

Widely known and highly respected aviation artist and aero-historian Captain Rich Dann, USNR, volunteered to join this project and contribute both his wonderful drawings and side views, generated especially for this volume, as well as complete access to his own very considerable archive. His friendship, advice and support throughout it all have been a warmth beyond measure.

Finally, to son Dan Junior (DJ), of whom his old man is so proud, and our families, chief amongst whom is my sweetheart, wife, mother and stepmother, Kathleen, who has once again learned to accommodate yet 'another woman' in my life with never-ending support, patience and tolerance.

Dan Hagedorn Sr

Introduction

Throughout the lengthy period of research leading up to publication of this book, with the exception of the complete enthusiasm shown by former B-18 crew members, the response shown by nearly everyone to the fundamental idea of a book devoted to the Douglas twin-engine bomber ranged from total lack of recognition, through bewilderment, to frequent incredulity.

'Why on earth,' came the most common refrain, 'would anyone want to write, publish or read a book on the B-18?'

Your scribes, father and son, in the very beginning of the idea, on more than one occasion posed the fundamental question: why had this aircraft series been the subject of such bad press to the point that, with few exceptions, it was almost unanimously dismissed in the minds of even the most casual observers?

In the mid-1960s, when Dan Hagedorn Sr was first starting to conduct formal research into the origins and evolution of US Army aviation in defense of the vital Panama Canal, he was repeatedly confronted by the fact that the United States, between the two World Wars, had devoted a major percentage of its extremely limited defense funding, and the best equipment it could muster, to the aerial defenses of the Canal. As the 1930s unfolded, and the situation in Europe and the Far East continued to deteriorate, those defenses were bolstered and repeatedly reinforced. Throughout the record of the final approach to Pearl Harbor and the first, crucial eighteen months following the Japanese attack, one aircraft type repeatedly surfaced as central to the defenses of the Canal and the defeat of the Axis submarine threat in the Caribbean: the Douglas B-18.

Yet nearly every printed word that has been produced by the aviation media since that time has been nearly unanimous in condemnation of the design, one front-page banner headline going so far as to announce the lead article on the aircraft as 'The Bomber that Nobody Wanted'. A 1966 account, authored by an anonymous writer who identified himself only as 'Enyedy', was entitled 'Douglas' Reluctant Warriors'. One paragraph alone, quoted directly from this

decidedly opinionated historian, sums up the prevailing popular attitude regarding the initial decision by the Air Corps to acquire the B-18 versus, initially, the B-17:

'In 1935 … the Air Corps Procurement Section decided that the primary role of the airplane was to support the Army in the attack. As a consequence, development of the B-17 languished and it was only because of the dedicated work of a few men who believed in heavy bombardment as a strategic weapon that the program was kept alive. On the other hand, chairborne experts were deciding what shape the bomber of the future would take. From their Olympian heights they decreed that two-engined aircraft would be the standard. They saw aerial warfare in the form of interdiction and attack bombers and great emphasis was put on a new shape that was coming off the drawings boards at Douglas … the B-18.'

Yet another post-war, popular periodical ran an article entitled 'The Great Bolo Boondoggle', while even an otherwise outstanding 1982 four-part series, published in a Canadian publication, which was highly complimentary to their twenty Digbys, was introduced by the rather unfortunate title 'Distended Douglas'.

But even pre-war aeronautical journalism often oversimplified the nature of the aircraft and prejudiced otherwise reasonably well-informed readers. One fairly early account was headlined 'An Airliner Turns Bomber' and, in the accompanying caption for a 9th Bombardment Squadron B-18, informed the reader that the photo showed '…the sturdiness and size of Uncle Sam's latest "death angel"', which carried a '…formidable bomb load, and is heavily armed.' Even the highly regarded *Royal Air Force Flying Review* for January 1960, a staple of your co-author in his youth, in its usually highly reliable 'Technical Gen' feature, confidently replied to a reader that '…the Douglas DB-1, or B-18, was a medium-heavy bomber evolved from the Douglas DC-3.' The very highly regarded *The Army Air Forces in World War II*, an official publication, in the chapter devoted to 'AAF Aircraft of World War II', devoted precisely one sentence to the B-18, which read as follows: 'The B-18, then the standard two-engine bomber, was equal to any mission assigned the Air Corps and was much less expensive.'

B-18 AC36-323 MSN 1711 probably at Benedict Field, St. Croix between March and October 1942, bearing the 'cloud' splattered camouflage unique to Sixth Air Force anti-submarine aircraft during this period. When photographed, was probably being operated by the 12th Bomb Squadron. *via Rich Dann*

How, we asked, could so many otherwise well-read and serious observers, airmen and historians be so wrong? Or were they?

The answers to these questions proved a most challenging research journey, the sum of which have resulted in this volume.

A careful survey of the literature, pre-war, wartime and post-war, revealed that the aircraft had, in fact, received highly favorable commentary before the war and barely any at all during the war, and only commencing in the mid-1960s – more than twenty years after the last aircraft had been struck from active service – did writers commence bashing the aircraft, repeatedly.

As with so many facets of the comparatively brief history of aviation, the B-18 and its several developments appear to have suffered, unusually so it seems, at the hands of rapid changes in technology and operational philosophy, and, in no small measure, circumstances. But human memory and the media glorification of 'big name' campaigns and aircraft have also played a part and, inevitably, the B-18 was relegated ever further to the 'back 40' of historical recordation. In no small measure, the operational time span in which B-18s were actually engaged in very active combat, especially in the Caribbean, also played a pivotal part in the dearth of accurate recordation. The first twelve months of America's war, during which time we were scrambling to meet threats at nearly every turn, was not an ideal period for the creation of accurate records. Indeed, retrospectively, and in view of the difficulty that your co-authors have encountered in documenting what follows, this may in fact have been the primary reason that the B-18 never received its just due: the Allies were just too busy, everywhere.

But official security considerations may have been another reason. In late 1943 and early 1944 the wartime Commander of the Sixth Air Force, the major theater of actual combat experienced by wartime B-18 crews, like his counterparts elsewhere, was obliged to remind members of his command that '…private photography of radar equipment is strictly prohibited, and any photographs indicating that radar equipment is installed on any aircraft are likewise prohibited.' This service-wide prohibition effectively denied, especially B-18B and B-18C crews, the by then common custom of taking snapshots of their combat mounts, with the consequence that historical photos of these aircraft, so common of 'line' B-17, B-24, B-25 and B-26 bombardment units in Europe and elsewhere, are virtually non-existent.

But even earlier, in 1935, and indeed as late as 1940, in spite of the 'bomber mafia's' nearly prescient forecasts, no one in the extremely isolationist United States could have envisioned the war that was to come to the nation on 7 December 1941 – the fall of France and most of continental Europe, and most of China. The mighty Eighth Air Force, with its huge formations of B-17s and B-24s, and other large-numbered overseas air forces, which launched exceptionally courageous and intrepid mass heavy bombardment missions against Axis bastions, were only very poorly formulated dreams in the minds of a few visionaries in those years.

While it must be fairly noted that your co-authors have more than once stated that it was their joint ambition to '…rcdccm thc honor of the B-18 and its crews', this account, we believe the record will show, has been assembled with objectivity and care, and the failings – as well as the triumphs – of the series are recorded as accurately as possible. The aircraft were certainly not without fault, a reality that should be equally obvious of any aircraft of the period, Allied or Axis in origin.

But on balance we believe that the record will show that the American taxpayers certainly got their money's worth out of the B-18 series, and perhaps to a greater degree per capita than with any other contemporary bomber design.

This, then, is the story of the B-18 and its developments, an unassuming memorial to her resolute and gallant crews.

CHAPTER ONE

Development of the DB-1

Starting at the very beginning, we need to put one very nearly universally believed 'fact' to rest. It is usually phrased something like this: 'The B-18, oh, yes, that would be the bomber version of the DC-3.'

This is absolutely not correct.

As most aviation enthusiasts will know, the nearly legendary Grand Sire of the immortal Douglas Commercial series, the DC-1 (X-223Y, Douglas Manufacturers Serial Number 1137), made her first flight in California on 1 July 1933, followed by the definitive first DC-2-112, NC-13711 for TWA (MSN 1237), actually delivered on 14 May 1934.

A careful search of nearly every existing Douglas photographic negative in the Boeing Archives in California revealed that Douglas had prepared a wind-tunnel mock-up of an aircraft described at the time as the Douglas DC Bomber as early as 1 February 1934. This design, as shown by the accompanying photographs, clearly had the slender bomber fuselage that eventually evolved into the Douglas Bomber 1 (DB-1), as well as an empennage (fin, rudder, horizontal stabilisers and elevators) that shared virtually nothing with the DC-1 or DC-2, and a wing plan form that was similar, yet modified, from those designs as well.

Above: Every previously published account has declared that the 'B-18 was a development of the DC-2'. This Douglas image, dated 14 February 1934 – three months before the first DC-2 was delivered to TWA – shows the 'Douglas DC Bomber' wind-tunnel mock-up, strongly suggesting that the company had a bomber in mind from the beginning. *Boeing Archives SM-5665*

Right: The empennage of the 'Douglas DC Bomber' wind-tunnel mock-up was virtually identical to that of the DC-1, although the fuselage – which included nose and dorsal turret positions and 'port hole'-style skylight apertures for the forward crew positions, was very different. *Boeing Archives SM-5666*

The commercial success of the DC-2 had fully occupied the firm through the remainder of 1934, but by 19 January 1935 the very first Douglas image identified as the DB-1 (Image Number 7358) clearly showed the empennage of the definitive aircraft, and these photographic records substantiate the fact that the DB-1 and DC-2 series were developed separately, concurrently and intentionally, even though, as of January 1935, there was no official, announced requirement from any potential customer for such a bomber.

As of that time, the US Army Air Corps bombardment establishment, the only realistic potential customer for such an aircraft, was in a state of transition. From the end of the First World War the Army Air Service (renamed the Army Air Corps in 1926) had established requirements for bombardment aircraft for both day and night operations, primarily for eastern and western coastal defense of the Continental United States, and the overseas garrisons in the Commonwealth of the Philippines, the Territory of Hawaii and the Panama Canal Zone. These forces, usually consisting of, at best, one up-to-strength bombardment squadron in each location, were stretched very thin indeed, and operated, for the most part,

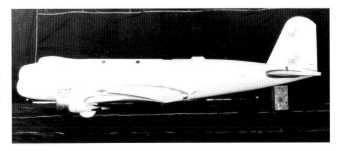

This top view of the 'Douglas DC Bomber', which reveals the project locations of seven 'port holes' and a dorsal hatch, clearly reveals that the DC-1 wings and empennage were fully exploited in the development of the design. *Boeing Archives SM-5667*

A bit less than one year after the wind-tunnel mock-up of the 'Douglas DC Bomber', Douglas was fairly well along with a detailed mock-up of what it was describing, by 8 January 1935, as the Douglas DB-1. *Boeing Archives SM-7280*

a succession of Martin, Curtiss, L.W.F. and Aeromarine NBS-1 biplane, twin-engine, heavy night bombers (definitive Army designation for the MB-2), Keystone B-3A, B-4A, B-5A and B-6A biplane, twin-engine heavy bombers, a small experimental batch of seven Boeing YB-9, Y1B-9 and Y1B-9A monoplane, twin-engine bombers, and the survivors of 103 Martin B-10B monoplane, twin-engine bombers – the latter the largest single Army between-the-wars contracts to that time. With this assortment of biplanes and monoplanes, with a few experimental and service test articles thrown in for tests, the Army gradually evolved its nascent 'bombardment philosophy' and the minority, so-called 'bomber mafia' fraternity within the Army officer corps cut its teeth.

Army Air Corps aircraft procurement as of 1936

It is central to the history of the evolution of the DB-1 and the B-18 to understand the evolution of Army bombardment philosophy and aircraft procurement. This, apparently, has been widely misunderstood, and contrary to many accounts the Army clearly had a better understanding of its responsibility to national defense, as defined by the several inter-war governments, than is often appreciated. As early as May 1926, for instance, the Army Air Corps, which was utterly dependent on the budgetary constraints and denouements of the War Department, recognised that '…the tactical utility of an aircraft is determined by the character of enemy equipment.'[1] As of that date, of course, it was nearly impossible to conceive of a foreign aviation threat to the United States – Charles Lindbergh would not make his transatlantic, non-stop flight from New York to Paris for another full year – and perhaps not surprisingly every informed thought turned to threats to the coastal regions and overseas possessions by foreign naval forces.

The War Department's Special Committee on the Army Air Corps published a report on 22 July 1934 that recommended an increase in the size of the Corps to 2,320 aircraft and a corresponding increase in the number of air crew to man them. This legislation, the so-called 2,320 Act, was actually signed by the President on 24 June 1936, but it is difficult to determine, from the existing records, whether Congress established this as an actual ceiling, based on War Department requests, and as being adequate. Whatever the actual situation, this number remained the 'official' ceiling on the size of the Air Corps until 1939, when the rush of world events once more forced a reopening of the entire question.

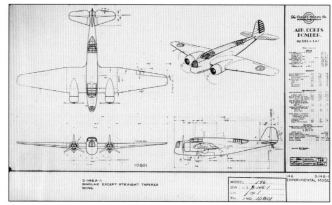

Above: Almost invariably referred to in most previously published sources as the Martin Model 145, SB-16 or XB-16A, the aircraft that actually competed with the DB-1 was the Model 146 as detailed here. *Martin Museum via Stan Piet*

Left: A first for a projected US bomber, the DB-1's unpowered, fully retractable dorsal defensive gun turret configuration was, in the production variant used in the B-18, very similar to the mock-up shown here on 28 February 1935. Note the 'sling' seat for the gunner, which persisted into the later, refined B-18A dorsal turret as well. *Boeing Archives SM-7593*

The standard Air Corps bombardment aircraft at the time of Circular Proposal 35-26 was the Martin B-10, and Martin – perhaps lulled into complacency by its superiority – only modestly upgraded the aircraft as the Model 146 to compete with the Douglas and Boeing entries. It did have side-by-side pilot and co-pilot enclosures, but a decidedly awkward rear gunner's position. Note the US Civil Experimental licence number, X-15550, in this 10 September 1935 image. *Martin Museum No 9678 via Stan Piet*

Earlier, as of August 1933, the so-called Drum Board was instructed to prepare for air operations by USAAC elements in the event of hostilities by the War Plans Division in conjunction with the 'color plans', which envisaged operations in areas that were viewed, at the time, as likely zones of foreign aggressive intent.

The very small Air Corps of the day, and its tiny planning element, struggled to present a meaningful aviation element to support these realistically formulated but unfunded defense plans for the nation. Incredible as it may seem in retrospect, the planners were tasked to craft their preparations on the basis that not fewer than 1,800 aircraft would be available for assignment – when, in fact, the Air Corps of 1933 would be hard-pressed to muster a fraction of that number. These plans were centered on the continental US itself, Panama and Hawaii, but not, significantly, as time would show, on the Philippines – although the Board recognised that air support for the latter would be considered '…should the national policy ever change'.

The Drum Board's concept for deciding on air strength of the Army went something like this: US Naval aviation should be about equal to, or perhaps greater than, any anticipated enemy force. Army Air Corps strength in Hawaii and Panama should be '…strong enough to meet a sudden emergency' and to maintain operations until such time as they could be, hopefully, reinforced from the continental US. Finally, they proposed the creation of what would come to be called the General Headquarters (GHQ) Air Force, which would be of sufficient size and content to ensure dominance in combat zones where action important to the defense of the nation might take place. The GHQ Air Force was conceived as, essentially, a self-contained organisation, capable of strategic missions against any enemy's economy as well as, inevitably, operations in direct support of Army ground forces. This force was to consist of 980 aircraft and at least 1,700 officers. The actual size of the entire Air Corps as of January 1936, however, was 360 aircraft of all types – of which only 165 could be regarded as 'first-line' combat aircraft – and the service could muster only 635 qualified pilots of all ranks.

The GHQ Air Force concept and evolution is important to our story, as the requirement eventually formulated for the B-18 was in direct response to the need to equip the bombardment element of that force. The Air Corps proposed a total of five Bombardment Groups with 215 aircraft and 645 officers, as well as four Pursuit Groups and two Long Range Observation Groups, and miscellaneous transport, cargo and headquarters aircraft, for a total of 980 aircraft and 1,728 officers – still far short of the recommendations made in 1934.

Created during 1935, the GHQAF, which, in the minds of most liberal Air Corps officers, was to constitute the first great concentrated striking force of strategic air power at the direct command of the high command, was created not as a subordinate section of the Chief of the Air Corps but rather as a virtually independent command reporting directly to the Army's Chief of Staff. This placed the Chief of the Air Corps, which was responsible for procurement of aircraft, in a difficult spot.

The Army's Chief of Staff and the Secretary of War recommending acquiring 800 aircraft each year until the expansion program was completed. This number was needed not only to flesh out the new Groups contemplated, but to replace obsolete equipment already fielded to existing units. But the only way this could be legally accomplished at the time, and assuming that Congress appropriated the required funding, was through the system of competitive bidding that had been initiated by the depression-era-constrained new government in December 1933. This system, while appearing fair and equitable on paper, had been so disastrous that, in the sixteen months preceding November 1935, the Army Air Corps, by Herculean efforts, had succeeded in obtaining not one single combat aircraft. After nearly two years of the competitive bidding system, a few were just beginning to be delivered. Indeed, insufficient aircraft had even been acquired to cover normal attrition, to say nothing of the 1,800 aircraft that had been authorized by the Act of 2 July 1926, commonly known as The Air Corps Act. This was the infamous plan that was to have given the Army 1,800 serviceable aircraft within five years, or by 1931.

Under the system that obtained as of the advent of the DB-1, this was fundamentally how the procurement cycle worked. It was first assumed that the Air Corps wanted the latest, fastest and most capable type. The service planners then arrived at a minimum number of these that would be required to equip the authorized Groups and Squadrons. The service dispatched a Circular Proposal for a design to meet the requirement for that type of aircraft to the entire US aircraft industry in being. It then sat back to wait. It usually waited from six to twelve months before it came time to open the bids submitted by industry and to learn – hopefully – what the several firms that felt they could meet the requirements had designed. The service then evaluated the various bids and advised the manufacturers that met the requirements – on paper at least – to show up at Wright Field with their evaluation article by a required date.

The Air Corps leadership, however, must also bear, in retrospect, some of the responsibility for the manner in which the procurement of the B-18 was handled. In this instance, they appear to have learned from Congressional example, by stressing the appearance of strength rather than the real thing. During Fiscal Year 1938, as will be seen, the Air Corps experimented with aircraft procurement by lumping two years' supply of B-18s in one year – while buying no pursuit aircraft – then reversing the procedure the following year, buying all pursuits and almost no bombers.

USAAC Circular Proposal No 35-26

The evolution of the DB-1 and B-18, and cutting of actual metal leading to these aircraft, can be directly attributed to Army Air Corps Circular Proposal No 35-26, which was for 'Airplanes, Bombardment' and was initially issued on 28 September 1934 – much earlier than often cited – and which was widely circulated to the US aviation industry of the time, as noted in the procedure outlined above.

The actual design submissions and bids for this competition were to be opened by the Contracting Officer, Air Corps Materiel Division, at Wright Field at 2pm on 22 August 1935[2], some eight months after Douglas had already formulated the design of the DB-1.

The competition was more intense than is commonly reported. Martin proposed what is often described as an 'upgraded B-10', its Model 146[3]. This aircraft, issued with US Department of Commerce Experimental License X-15550 (Manufacturers Serial Number 662), had a nearly 5-foot greater wing-span that the B-10B, then the current standard USAAC bomber, and was 7 feet longer.[4] It boasted two Wright SGR-1820-G5 engines (ironically, the same type of engines, of 850hp, often ascribed to the prototype DB-1), and identical armament and bomb load to the DB-1. Unlike the B-10B, however, it featured a wider fuselage, to accommodate a side-by-side pilot and co-pilot arrangement, with a total crew of six, and a very different rear dorsal gun position.

Boeing, taking a different tack, produced the Model X-299 (MSN 1963), grandfather of the B-17 series, and of course Douglas submitted its DB-1. To most latter-day observers, comfortably equipped with at least a working knowledge of the merits of the B-17 series, as it evolved, the selection of the Boeing submission seems on the surface of it to have been an obvious choice. On closer examination, however, and bearing in mind the limitations in funding and infrastructure that the Army Air Corps was laboring under at the time, it might be more appropriate to congratulate the Air Corps for deciding to order thirteen service test examples at all. Often termed the 'XB-17' (which it was not), the Model X-299 had a wing-span of 103ft 9 3/8in, and a length of 68ft 9in. In other terms, it would require a hangar with doors of at least that width

to accommodate even one aircraft (whereas the DB-1 and Martin 146 could easily be accommodated in existing hangars), and had two additional engines to service and fuel, and very real purchase costs for same per aircraft. The following chart graphically portrays the challenges that this factor alone presented to Air Corps planners.

With four 750hp Pratt & Whitney S1EG Hornets, the X-299 provided a maximum speed only 16mph faster than the DB-1, and mounted but two additional defensive machine guns (also of but .30 rifle caliber). In only two measurements was the X-299 more attractive: it had a range, at 140mph cruise (actually 33mph slower than the DB-1) of almost 3,101 miles and could lift a combined bomb load of 4,800lb, or 800lb more than the DB-1 or Martin 146.[5] As of 1936, however, aside from the sheer size of the aircraft, the two constraints that concerned the evaluation board more than any other considerations were the number of required crew members (totaling eight) and the cost-per-unit. Douglas, which could confidently boast that it had a production line 'in being' for the DC-2 and DC-3 that could easily accommodate a large order for B-18s, could offer its DB-1 at $58,500 per article[6], whereas the Model X-299 would cost a whopping $99,620 each. The reactions of serving officers of the day, the best remunerated of whom probably made less than $500 per month, to this total cost must have seemed a totally unrealistic demand to place before the budget folks.

But in reality, the clash of ideas between advanced thinkers in the Air Corps and Congress, who held the purse strings, placed the Air Corps leadership, who had to deal with the people's elected representatives, between a rock and a hard spot. An incident in April 1937, reported in the Congressional Record, vividly illustrates this day-to-day dilemma. None other than the chairman of the Appropriations Subcommittee at the time, which handled War Department estimates, confessed that he possessed '...no great familiarity with military matters'. Nevertheless, he made a matter of record his protest against what he perceived as an 'unwise' tendency within the Air Corps to build ever larger and more expensive bombers – such as the B-17. Less than two months later, the political fallout of this type of open criticism

	Martin B-10B	Douglas B-18	Boeing Y1B-17
Quantity	103	82	13
Total Cost Per Aircraft	$72,000	$105,000	$302,100
Airframe Cost Per Aircraft with Changes	$45,450	$72,243	$246,030
Cost of Government Furnished Equipment Per Aircraft	$13,650	$16,957	$23,261
Engine Cost Each Per Aircraft	$6,500	$8,200	$8,200
Engine Cost Per Aircraft	$13,000	$16,400	$32,800

The sad remains of the first of a legendary breed, the Boeing X-299 at Wright Field following its totally unnecessary crash on take-off. Note that, like the Martin entry, the X-299 carried a Department of Commerce Experimental licence on the tail (X-13372), as it was company owned. To what extent the loss of the X-299 influenced the decision in favor of a small quantity of Y1B-17s and a major contract for B-18s is imponderable. *Wright Field No 52785*

became clear. The estimates submitted for Fiscal Year 1938 called for 177 B-18s and thirteen Y1B-17s. The General Headquarters Air Force 'strongly recommended' to Congress that '…only the B-17' be procured. However, to buy the more expensive aircraft would be to buy fewer bombers and, in the face of Congressional criticism, the Air Corps leadership felt that it just wasn't practical to do so unless the Secretary of War himself was willing to '…accept the responsibility to Congress' for decreasing the total number of aircraft in the 1938 budget. Estimates for further B-17s were thus deferred until Fiscal Year 1939.

Most accounts of this competition also include the North American NA-21, which is incorrect; the NA-21 did not materialise for some time to come, and was instead the North American competitor to the Douglas B-18A (qv), and received the Air Corps designation XB-21.[7] It is not generally known that two other manufacturers also submitted paper proposals to this competition, namely Bellanca and Burnelli.

The Air Corps procedure used to evaluate the aircraft submitted to meet this Circular Proposal, although occasionally cited in some previous publications in passing, has never been fully described. Many accounts of the competition leave the impression that the reviewing Board was somehow preordained in favor of the DB-1, and that they viewed the comparatively huge Boeing Model X-299 with prejudice and highly skeptical misgivings. In fact, the competition criteria were remarkably even-handed and, taking the actual stated specifications and requirements into account, fair.

As one might expect from a military document, it was exacting and precise in terminology, and stipulated that the evaluation was predicated on aircraft that met all of the desired performance criteria set forth in the Type Specification, which was No 98-201 (see below). Figures of Merit were awarded and, in awarding these, the Air Corps specifically stated that '…additional weight is not provided for attainments which exceed those enumerated as desired, since any airplane having all of these characteristics is considered satisfactory for the purpose intended.' It also stipulated that no aircraft would be evaluated that did not conform to the strength requirements derived from a detailed stress analysis submitted by the manufacturers, that did not meet the minimum performance, armament and crew requirements of the Specification, and that did not meet characteristics *essential for safety* (emphasis added by authors). The Maximum Figure of Merit Points that could be awarded by the Board are shown in the accompanying table below.

Factor	Max Figure of Merit (Points)
Speed	150
High Speed	100
Operating Speed	50
Endurance (in Hours) at Operating Speed	100
Time of Climb	50
Service Ceiling	50
Structure and Design	100
Power Plant Installation	50
Armament Installation	50
Equipment/Misc. Installations	50
Maintenance and Repair	50
Landing Characteristics	100
Utility as a Type	250
TOTAL	1000

These Maximum Figures of Merit were governed by the following additional criteria that the officers making the evaluations could consult:

(1) Speed – The high speed and operating speed listed in the Type Specification were regarded as the desirable attainments, for that time, of an aircraft meeting the requirements of a bombardment type. An aircraft having a high speed of 250mph and an operating speed of 220mph would be given the maximum figure of merit. Two points would be deducted, without exception, for each Mile per Hour less than the *desired specified high speed* (emphasis added by authors). One point would also be deducted for each Mile per Hour less than the desired operating speed as well.

(2) Endurance – The endurance listed in the Type Specification was the desired attainment as related to the operating (cruise) speed. In order that the maximum range could be realised within the limits indicated for the factors of operating speed and endurance, an operating speed was selected within the limits listed that resulted in the greatest range. The Board deducted 25 points from the maximum figure of merit for each hour less than the desired endurance listed in the Type Specification. A proportionate number of points was deducted for any fraction of an hour less than the desired attainment, which was a rather optimistic (and possibly unattainable) 10 hours. As an example, an aircraft with an endurance of 7 hours 12 minutes received 70 points less than the maximum.

(3) Time of Climb – The Type Specification listed the desired time of climb as 5 minutes to 10,000 feet. The rules dictated that 10 points would be deducted for each minute greater than 5 minutes to that altitude. A proportionate number of points were deducted for each fraction of a minute more than desired. For example, a contender which had a time of climb to 10,000 feet of 8 minutes 30 seconds received 35 points less than the maximum allowable.

(4) Service Ceiling – The Specification listed 25,000 feet as the desired attainment for the service ceiling of the Bombardment aircraft desired, which, at the time, seemed reasonable. One point would be deducted for each 100 feet less than that desired.

(5) Structure and Design – These were obviously highly subjective, and as a result the rules were rather complex. The maximum points that could be awarded for this Figure of Merit were fixed on the basis of an aircraft that met all of the requirements of the Specification, coupled with the then extant edition of the 'Handbook for Airplane Designers', which nearly all US manufacturers viewed as 'the Bible'. They also represented an aircraft that was viewed, by the Board, as '…an article which was equivalent to the best aeronautical practices.' In determining the points to be awarded under this criteria (or those deducted), consideration was given to the following specific factors:

a   The potential characteristics of the airplane as a type.

b   Specific Design features, including (1) Body Group, (2) Wing Group, (3) Tail Group, (4) Landing Gear, (5) Engine Mounts and (6) Engine Cowlings

c   *Adaptability of the design to quantity production* (emphasis added by authors)

The Board members were cautioned that any entry found deficient in any one of the features noted above was sufficient to require deduction of the total number of points allocated to this factor.

(6) Power Plant Installation – The maximum number of points for this criterion were predicated on an aircraft that met all requirements of the Type Specification and the Handbook for Designers, and which represented an aircraft equivalent to the best current aeronautical practices. In determining deductions, Board members considered accessibility, fuel and oil systems, engine and fuel controls, as well as miscellaneous accessory installations. Again, any entrant that was found deficient in any of these features required deduction of the total number of points allocated to this factor.

(7) Armament Installations – Once again, the Board was instructed to base their score on aircraft that met the Specification, Handbook and best current practices. In awarding points, they were instructed to consider the suitability of the design, as well as accessibility for servicing of the bomb equipment, defensive machine guns and any associated pyrotechnics. Again, any single deficiency could result in the deduction of the total points allocated for this factor.

(8) Equipment Installations – Again, point allocation was based on the Specification, Handbook, and best current practice. Criteria included the suitability of the design, and accessibility for servicing of a number of specific systems, including the entire electrical system, the communications gear, navigational equipment (called Avigational equipment in the original document) and miscellaneous systems.

(9) Maintenance and Repair – Under this criteria, the Board was directed to pay particular attention to the fuselage and wings, the chassis (including the landing gear system), flight controls and surfaces, engine cowlings, engines and propellers and the overall ease of repair and replacement of equipment installations.

(10) Landing Characteristics – Under this criterion, a most unusual procedure was directed. A special Board of Officers was appointed to determine the points to be deducted (if any), and they were instructed to measure the length of the take-off run, the length of the roll-out on landing, the glide angle, the ability to side-slip, climb angle (without danger of stalling), directional stability during the take-off run and landing roll, lateral stability during glide and climb, ability to taxi without porpoising or 'bouncing' of the tail, and visibility to the crew on landing and take-off.

(11) Utility as a Type – This was unquestionably the most demanding of the tasks set before the Board, and it was specifically stated that the '…purpose of this factor was to afford the bidders an opportunity to actually demonstrate the worthiness of their airplane and also to permit the Air Corps to evaluate the true merit of the aircraft from a Service point of view.' Since this criterion involved the highest potential total score of any of the others, the factors to be taken into account were much more specific. They included:

a Military suitability of the aircraft, including operation of tactical equipment

b Airworthiness of the aircraft, with specific emphasis on manoeuvrability, stability and controllability

c Visibility required for military operation of the aircraft under tactical conditions

d Safety of the crew, including entry and egress, and associated criteria

e Adaptability of the aircraft to provide for interchangeability of the items of design load, with specific references to the alternate bomb loads included in the Type Specification.

Finally, and perhaps most revealing, the instructions stated that '…in considering the desired attainments of the Type Specification, it is realised that all of the characteristics can not be equalled at the present state of the art.' Further, it noted that it was also realised that individual aircraft characteristics, such as endurance, could only be obtained at the specific sacrifice of other characteristics. The Army enjoined the bidders to take into consideration that '…a balanced design is essential and that many of the aerodynamic requirements enumerated were conflicting' and that the Army expected them to achieve an effective compromise in order to obtain the greatest efficiency. But the most significant sentence in the entire document was this: 'Bidders should take into consideration that the Bombardment airplane is an integral part of the Air Force and must be coordinated with respect to speed and range with other units.'

The actual Air Corps Specification, often simplified in most accounts, was actually amended several times. The root document was US Army Specification 98-201, as noted above, but this was amended as No 98-201-A on 5 April 1935 and, definitively, as No 98-201-B on 14 January 1936. It called for a '…multi-engine, four-to-six place bombardment airplane' that met the General Specification for Airplanes (US Army No 98-1800), and the only specific requirement was in Section IV.2, which stated that '…the size and arrangement shall be consistent with the design useful load to be carried, the performance requirement, and the mission to be performed.'

At no point in any of the evaluation process was unit cost a factor, although many writers, looking back on the contest, have made much of such a consideration. The officers at Wright Field considered only the relative merits of the designs submitted, posted against the Specification issued.

Given all of the above, and the entries that were actually sent to Wright Field, it can, in the opinion of the authors, no longer be regarded as a surprise that the Air Corps selected the DB-1 for the major contract, while allowing – even after the disaster with the Boeing Model X-299 – a service test quantity of Y1B-17s.

The DB-1 described

The DB-1 (cited initially, internally, as the DS-135) was completed by Douglas in April 1935, not quite one year after the Army took delivery of the first of fourteen YB-10s, the service trials version of the B-10, in June 1934. Douglas photos reveal that a full-scale mock-up of the aircraft was nearly complete as early as 28 February 1935. It is interesting to note that, in a Circular Proposal (C.P.35-356) issued subsequent to the definitive publication cited above, Douglas had in fact proposed the DB-1 as an alternative aircraft to internal design DS-147, which was also cited by the enigmatic and completely undocumented Air Corps type specification 'X-202'.

A comparison of the DB-1 and the initial service YB-10 aircraft reveals the remarkable pace of advancement in aviation technology that was taking place in the mid-1930s. Boasting a sustained high speed of 196mph, the YB-10 was one of the most advanced bombers in the world as of the date of entry into service and, indeed, was faster than any of the standard USAAC pursuit aircraft then in service. It did little to improve upon crew interoperability over its predecessors, however, although it did provide canopy protection for the single pilot

By April 1935 the mock-up DB-1 had been translated into a genuine aircraft and, in its configuration as of the time of this 29 June 1935 image, the main undercarriage retraction mechanism included a streamlining cuff, which was very quickly dispensed with as a maintenance burden of little genuine value. *Boeing Archives SM-8163*

and rear gunner, and a rudimentary gun turret in the nose for the dual-purpose bomb-aimer/gunner. The production B-10B offered even more speed, and on a good day could turn 215mph flat out; also, in maximum load configuration, it could lift 2,260lb of bombs 1,240 miles (round trip). All of this was accomplished with a crew of only three and on two 700hp Wright R-1820-33 Cyclone engines.

By comparison, the DB-1 was a crew delight. For the first time, pilot and co-pilot shared a fully instrumented, enclosed and comfort-fitted station, and all of the other four crew positions, which included a gunner/bomb-aimer in the nose, a dedicated radio operator (who also doubled as a gunner), navigator and a dorsal turret/ventral hatch gunner, could be reached in flight from anywhere in the aircraft.

Although numerous publications have quoted performance characteristics for the DB-1, and almost without exception quoted the engines used as two 850hp Wright R-1820-G5 engines, in fact the actual engines used on the AAC performance test at Wright Field on 20 December 1935 were Wright SR-1820G-12s, also rated at 850hp with a 10:1 blower at 9,000 feet. Douglas had tested the aircraft extensively in California for at least four months before flying it to Wright Field, and it was probably initially fitted with the R-1820-G5s during the first part of that period. However, the Douglas Detailed Specification, dated 14 August 1935, described the aircraft as a '…six place, mid-wing cantilever monoplane of the bombardment type equipped with two Wright Cyclone SGR-1820-G12 engines, each rated at 830hp at 1,200rpm at sea level or, as an alternate, two Wright Cyclone SGR-1820-G5 engines as listed in addendum No 1.' Precisely how Douglas was enabled to conduct these flights without benefit of a Department of Commerce, Civil Aeronautics Authority experimental licence is not clear (the Boeing Model X-299, for instance, owned very similarly by the manufacturer, carried X-13372 and the Martin Model 146 carried X-15550), as the aircraft was still very much Douglas property at the time. The solitary clue that speaks to this anomaly was a 'Departmental Communication' from Project Engineer C. C. Pearson dated 29 May 1935 to Mr Webster, entitled 'Markings DB-1 Airplane'. In this two-paragraph memo, he stated that 'Standard Air Corps markings should be stencilled on the left hand side of the bomber's nose, except it shall be Douglas DB-1, no serial number, Crew Weight 1200lb; size of letters to be in accordance with Air Corps Specification 98-24105. The words US Army shall not appear on the wings as called

These two images, dated 8 May 1935, clearly show the DB-1 wings – and the fact that they have clearly had paint applied, but not all the way to the extremities of the wings, as well as USAAC national US insignia. It has been speculated that the color was yellow, but the rationale for truncating the painted area to make an apparently smaller wing 'shape' is unknown. The aircraft apparently did not have this paint when it arrived at Wright Field for the evaluations. *Boeing Archives SM-7943 and 7944*

for in above Specification. Insignia shall be as per previous communication.' There is also photographic evidence that, for some reason, the wings and horizontal tail surfaces (and possible the rudder) were painted chrome yellow – but the wings were painted in such a way as to show the yellow only to within about 2 feet of the wing tips, and applied in such a manner that it made it appear that the wing was smaller from a distance.

As of 25 June 1935, prior to going to Wright Field, the aircraft had a retractable tail wheel, a first for US bomber aircraft but not a feature retained on subsequent developments.

Test Reports and Analysis conducted by Douglas prior to the Wright Field competition, numbering more than forty-nine in number, reveal that the company did an extremely thorough job in preparing the aircraft for the competition, and nearly all of these had been accomplished by 17 August 1935. Never mentioned before, these included studies detailing the floatation equipment, which became a standard – and oft-cited – virtue of the production aircraft (although this was not incorporated into the DB-1 itself, initially), auxiliary bomb bay fuel tanks, as well as a study of ski installation, a capability hard to imagine on the Boeing Model 299.

Initially issued with Douglas Manufacturers Serial Number 1353, which fell between the first DC-2-115E for Fokker in the Netherlands (PH-AKH) and Pan American DC-2-118A NC-14292, the aircraft was referred to within the Douglas plant as D.S. Number 148, Shop Order 475, 'Proposal for US Army'. It was usually referred to on most Douglas internal engineering documents as the DS-148.

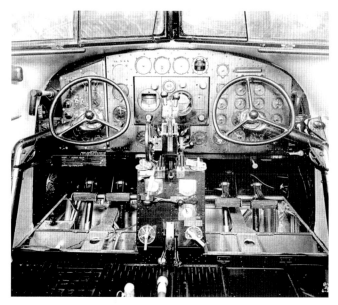

The 'front office' of the DB-1, as it appeared on 26 June 1935, was very sophisticated for its day, and heralded a new epoch for US bomber crews. Note that the two lowest central instruments on the right, for the co-pilot, are canted to the right a full 90 degrees, a practice continued throughout the B-18 production series. The pilot, on the left, had only flight instruments, while the co-pilot was responsible for these as well as engine instruments. The idea was to have the indicator needles all lined up neatly, probably during cruise. *Peter M. Bowers Collection, Museum of Flight*

The manually operated nose turret of the DB-1, as of 29 June 1935, was very similar to that mounted in its predecessor, the Martin B-10. The bomb aimer (the Air Corps had not yet adopted the term 'bombardier') doubled as a gunner, and the turret could only be entered or vacated when it was turned fully to the starboard (right) side. Note the wind compensator on the forward gun sight of the .30 caliber machine gun. Although it appears ungainly, the turret was actually very effective and afforded excellent visibility. *Boeing Archives SM-8147*

The late December 1935 official USAAC performance tests at Wright Field listed the aircraft with an empty weight of 14,806lb and a gross of 20,159, allowing 1,200lb for the crew, 254lb for equipment, and 2,532lb for armament, etc. The wing was an NACA 2215-2207.6 airfoil section, which gave a lift capability of 21lb per sq ft. Length was 57ft 3in, height 15ft 4in and span 89ft 7in. The maximum speed, at full power and at 10,000 feet, was 220.5mph (Douglas had guaranteed 215mph[8]). It landed, with flaps, at an incredibly docile 62mph and had a measured endurance, at a cruise speed of 173.5mph (Douglas had guaranteed 170mph), of just slightly short of 6 hours (Douglas had guaranteed 6 hours). The measured distance from a standing start required to clear a 50-foot obstacle, a very important consideration, given the nature of AAC operating stations at the time – and a completely unheralded measurement in the decision to acquire the B-18 over the Boeing 299 – with 20° of flaps, was 1,490 feet. The landing run out, with 55° of flaps, was 1,590 feet.

Armament was standard for the day, consisting of three flexible M-1 .30 caliber Model 1918 machine guns, one of each in a Douglas-designed nose turret, a fully retractable dorsal turret, also designed by Douglas, and a ventral hatch installation, each with 500 rounds per gun. The normal bomb load could consist of one 2,000lb weapon (actually 2,121lb), two 1,100-pounders, up to four 600-pounders, eight 300lb or twenty 100lb bombs. However, seldom noted, the DB-1 also had the capability of hefting a maximum bomb load, which could consist of two 2,000lb bombs, four 1,100-pounders, six 600-pounders, twelve 300-pounders or as many as thirty-two 100lb bombs – or various combinations of these weapons. The aircraft also had a bomb hoist included as a standard item of ancillary equipment.

The bomb bay in the DB-1 was divided into two halves by a center keel, with the center bomb racks attached and racks on each side, opposite the center racks. Two complete sets of racks were installed under the center wing proper, and the third set of racks aft of the rear center wing beam. This section of the bomb bay to the rear of the center wing beam extended up above the level of the center wing and provided room for the M-3 2,000lb bomb on each side, carried on a steel tubular structure that was removable for other bomb loadings. Fittings were also provided, it is seldom noted, under the center wing for carrying the Mark I, IMKI or IMII 2,000lb bomb on each side. The racks were designed to accommodate any combination of bomb loading within the limits specified. The bomb load could be released by salvo from the bombardier's compartment, or from the pilot's cockpit, and electrical release of the bombs could be accomplished automatically by contacts within the bombsight or manually. Considering that Douglas had never been faced with an engineering challenge like this, the installation was a credit to the engineering staff.

As for the defensive gun installations, the Douglas-designed nose turret included an adjustable back rest, a feature seldom noted. The gun truck was adjustable up and down on two tracks and curtain followers were provided both above and below the gun to protect the gunner from slipstream blast. A seat was provided for the gunner. The dorsal turret was, as noted, fully retractable to fit flush with the outer contour of the fuselage when not in use, a first on a US service type. When extended, the turret was about 18 inches above the top of the fuselage, and although rather ungainly in appearance, actually gave outstanding visibility and firing angles for the gunner. The turret could be raised about 4 inches, if desired, when the gun was not in use, and a canvas seat was provided for use during normal missions – in reality a sort of sling. The turret was bungee-loaded to facilitate quick deployment, and to compensate for air loads. The so-called 'tunnel gun' or ventral installation was of the folding type, and when the gun was not deployed, the doors formed a smooth contour on the lower side of the fuselage. The door was raised by use of a hand-crank and the pyralin window opened very quickly. The door was also bungee-loaded to compensate for air loads.

Above: The earliest known photo of the complete DB-1, dated 29 June 1935. Note that the paint on the wings, which had been present as of 8 May, has been removed, and that the US national insignia on the wings is canted outboard at the base. The aircraft was still Douglas property at this point and should have been wearing a US Department of Commerce Experimental Registration number, like the Boeing X-299 and Martin 146. There is no record of any such number being assigned. The aircraft had a retractable tail wheel at this point, a feature later deleted. *Boeing Archives SM-8168 and 8164*

Right: Taken the same day, this view of the DB-1 reveals details of the initial empennage arrangement and the fact that the long exhaust stacks were elevated above the rear engine nacelles by a small tripod device. The aerodynamic efficiency of the retracted dorsal turret is also evident. *Boeing Archives SM-8168 and 8164*

Seldom noted was the bombardier's window in the lower nose, which also folded and, when not in use, formed a smooth contour. During attacks, the window could be raised by means of a hand-crank, thus giving the bombardier the required angles of vision for the bombsight.

The DB-1 was fully equipped with both a Command and Long-Range Liaison radio and fully instrumented for 'avigation'. A most useful table was fitted aft of the co-pilot in this and all subsequent B-18 series aircraft, and included a drawer for maps. A bunk was also fitted in the left rear cabin, which could be adjusted to a level position when in flight or at rest on the ground – another very popular feature for future crews! Three additional bunks were stowed on the right-hand side of the rear cabin, opposite the port-side entry door. It had a parachute flare installation, flare pistol, and drift signals. The pilot, co-pilot (who Douglas decided would also double as bombardier and 'avigator') and radio operator all enjoyed the benefits of cabin sound-proofing, a first on US heavy bombardment aircraft, and the entire crew (which originally included three gunners as well) rejoiced that an extremely robust heating and ventilation system was incorporated into the aircraft. The original DB-1 did not have de-icer boots.

The DB-1, like all subsequent developments, featured a single collector exhaust system that exited over the top of the engine nacelle to the rear, a novel feature at the time, intended to not only shield exhaust flame from the crew but also to minimise the exhaust signature of the aircraft during night operations. Early photos show that Douglas experimented with a number of different configurations for this feature, and experienced some development challenges in finding the best solution.

Virtually every account of the DB-1 published to date has blithely referred to the aircraft as a '…bomber version of the DC-2', or some similar statement. While the aircraft unquestionably owed much to the DC-1 and DC-2, an examination of the vertical stabiliser of the actual DB-1 alone provides ample evidence that Douglas engineers had basically to redesign the entire aircraft to meet military specifications. Although the vertical stabiliser of the DB-1 was described by Douglas as '…similar in design and construction to that of the DC-2', the company went on at some length to point out that, while the stabiliser on the DC-2 had been designed to test out at 823lb in the Pull-up Condition and 1,348lb in the Steady Dive Condition, the DB-1 vertical stabiliser tested out at 958lb in the Pull-up Condition and only 1,208lb in the Steady Dive Condition. The loads applied in the tests of the DC-2 stabiliser were 86% and 112% of the design loads on the DB-1 surface respectively; a proof test of the latter surface to 60% of its design load was considered unnecessary. Douglas concluded that, even on the DB-1, the surface was '…obviously over-strength'.

The company did, however, stress the obvious benefits of utilising as many standard DC-2 components as possible in the aircraft. In a letter to the Materiel Division at Wright Field dated 3 May 1935, it stated that:

'…this airplane uses a large number of parts that are standard on the Douglas DC-2 transport, either in identical or slightly modified form. The center section, outer wings, tail surfaces, nacelles, landing gear, engine mounts and surface controls are either identical with the corresponding parts on the DC-2 or are so nearly so that they can be built on the same jigs. This not only eliminates the experimental status of these parts and reduces the cost of the airplane, but will also enable very early delivery schedules to be met.'

This is the nearly definitive form of the rear dorsal turret on the DB-1, as of 21 June 1935. Although the gunner sat on a sling, he was afforded a metal back brace, just visible, and was also provided with a wind-compensating sight. The turret could only be fully retracted when facing directly aft, and had two 'open' positions: full extended or half extended, for observation purposes. The design of the B-18 and later B-18A dorsal turret was the same with the exception of the upper cover. *Boeing Archives SM-8079*

Following the actual competition at Wright Field, Douglas engineers who accompanied the aircraft sent a long letter back to A. E. Raymond, Chief Engineer at Douglas, dated 24 August 1935, one week after the formal tests. Because this letter gives a unique insight into the process – as well as a bit of up-close-and-personal examination of the competition – it is quoted here at length:

> 'As you know, the DB-1 is now all weighed and is going through 689 inspection. So far the adverse comments have been few and far between, and we have managed to prevent a number of them from going down in writing by being on hand to explain and to sell what we have. I am sure Warren will be glad to know that the electrical system has been found very nearly perfect. The power plant installation was not quite so free from criticism, but I am certainly glad that we got in before the Boeing because I believe that we would have made a much poorer showing if the Inspectors had had a chance to look at the remarkably clean and accessible installation on that ship. I have not yet had a chance to go through the Boeing but have been able to inspect it carefully on the outside and look through the doors. It is, without a shadow of doubt, the most outstanding airplane in the world today, both from the standpoint of design and workmanship.'

The report went on to describe, in detail, various components of what was obviously the Boeing X-299, in particular the gun turret installations. With regard to the Martin Model 146, the Douglas crew was not nearly as generous:

> 'The Martin bomber is really quite disappointing – thank heavens. It seems to be nothing but an old B-10 with a fuselage about two or three times as wide. The front turret and bomber's window seem to be almost identical with the B-10 and there is no rear turret, just a wide gun track around the sides and back of the rear cockpit.'

The winner

The so-called 'Demonstration Article', the DB-1, contrary to the poorly informed comments of some of the previous accounts noted earlier, was selected for acquisition by the Air Corps Evaluation Board that convened at Wright Field on 2 December 1935. Described by some latter-day aero historians unflatteringly as 'chairborne' bureaucrats, the Board actually consisted of the following noteworthy panel:

Lieutenant Colonel Harold L. George, Chairman
Lieutenant Colonel Charles B. Oldfield
Major Eugene L. Eubank
Major Westside T. Larson
Major John F. Whitley
Captain Franklin O. Carroll

The DB-1 and the other aircraft in the competition were each flown by Board members, as well as members of the Wright Field Flight Test Section. Board members completed 18.5 hours in the DB-1, during which forty-seven bombs of various sizes, totaling 7,000lb, were dropped, and 3,000 rounds of .30 caliber ammunition was fired as well. They concluded, after the selection was announced, that '… the DB-1, as submitted and flown in the competition, is suitable for procurement as bombardment tactical equipment without changes.' However, they did note that the following changes were desirable:

(1) More vision laterally and forward beyond the horizontal for the bombardier

(2) More spacious working area for the bombardier himself

(3) Improved ease of operation of the defensive machine guns

(4) When the guns were fired only through openings of the window or sliding door in the fuselage, a mechanism for closing them should be rigged

(5) Built-in floatation gear, which Douglas had already envisaged, could be provided

Although Douglas had clearly flown the DB-1 from the factory to Wright Field in 1935 (again, without any known experimental licence or authority), its first '…extended cross-country flight', presumably with an Air Corps crew, was accomplished circa 9 January 1936 – again, without any known airworthiness certification.

The prestigious *Jane's All the World's Aircraft* 1936 issue, which covered Calendar Year 1935, managed to squeeze in a two-paragraph description of the DB-1 and the information that the design had won the bomber competition, one of the earliest international mentions of the type. Similarly, the January 1936 issue of *US Air Services* reported that the Air Corps had ordered ninety of the aircraft, with the additional editorial comment in the accompanying Air Corps photograph that the aircraft '…can cruise with a heavy load at more than 250 miles per hour', which must have brought on some smiles at Douglas. It opened its considerable commentary with the words:

> 'Billy Mitchell must begin to feel a little encouraged by reason of the character of the contracts made by the War Department, in the latter part of December, covering fighting aircraft. Surely, it won't be long now until General Mitchell must admit that this country possesses at least one airplane capable of meeting an enemy of the first class in the air.'

This is something of a mystery image, circulated amongst aviation enthusiasts of the day, and invariably referred to as the 'Douglas XB-14' – undoubtedly encouraged by an entry in the 1935 issue of the prestigious *Jane's All the World's Aircraft*. The rudder and central portions of the horizontal tail surfaces had been painted a dark color (possibly red), the long exhaust stacks had been removed, and a large sign had been posted beside the port-side entry door to 'Keep Out'! It is believed to have been photographed at Santa Monica, CA. *John Mitchell via David W. Ostrowski collection*

Compare this view of the DB-1 with the previous image. Purported to have been photographed at an air show in Chicago in 1938, the aircraft was now sporting rudder stripes once again, but was still without the long exhaust stacks, and now had a portion of the nacelle aft of the engine cowl painted black. *David W. Ostrowski collection*

The DB-1 again with a dark rudder, without the long exhaust stacks, and with what appear to be modified forward engine nacelles and engine cowlings. Note the very tall radio mast and the abbreviated cockpit windows, characteristic of only the DB-1. *David W. Ostrowski collection*

The earliest known image of the DB-1 taken after the aircraft had been formally acquired by the Air Corps in July 1936, but before it was 'accepted' in February 1937 as the 'first' B-18. It is noted here at March Field, CA, soon to be home to the first wave of production aircraft, on 2 October 1936, with the definitive vertical fin and rudder configuration, still minus the long exhaust stacks, and wearing a Wright Field 'arrow' on the rear fuselage. *NMUSAF*

The article went on to describe the Air Corps order for 115 Northrop aircraft (that would become A-17s, in a contract valued at $2,560,074), ninety Douglas aircraft (valued at $6,498,000, which of course would become the initial batch of B-18s), and Boeing (in a contract rounded off at 'about $3.75 million') for thirteen Flying Fortresses.

Some students of aviation history have been confounded for years by the entry in the earlier 1935 issue of *Jane's All the World's Aircraft* that described the '…XB-14, a twin-engined Army bomber and an adaptation of the well-known Douglas DC-2 transport', which the prestigious annual noted had two 700hp Pratt & Whitney Twin Wasps. Indeed, your scribes point to this, the earliest public pronouncement of a 'Douglas bomber developed from the DC-2', as the very genesis of the widely held belief.

To say that the US taxpayer received value for money from the DB-1 would be an understatement.

Although often cited, upon acceptance by the Army as the 'XB-18', in fact this designation was never officially assigned nor adopted. The aircraft that had been at Wright Field for the competition was formally accepted by the Army, according to most sources, on contract W535-ac-8307 at a cost of $83,790.04[9]; it became Army property on 28 January 1936 and was assigned Air Corps serial AC36-262. This was not accomplished until after a ten-day 'eastern states' flight, visiting numerous Air Corps installations, which was on-going as of 9 January 1936. During this series of flights the aircraft was observed to be suffering from '…excessive leakage of oil from the oil tank to the engine when the aircraft has been standing idle for some time,' not a Douglas but rather a Wright engine concern. Army red tape apparently did not catch up with the aircraft before 24 April 1936, however, as official correspondence as of that date continued to refer to the aircraft as type DB-1, and quoted it

Comparison of this 9 February 1938 view of the vertical fin and rudder of the DB-1 (which by this time was actually a B-18, but which had been returned to Douglas for further developmental work) with those of earlier configurations – and with that of the production B-18s – reveals that Douglas was trying to find the best mix, as described in the text. *Boeing Archives SM-12562*

By 1938 the former DB-1 – now designated as a B-18 (and often cited erroneously in some publications as type 'XB-18') – was being utilised intensively at Wright Field, OH, for a variety of special tests, including various radio and antenna installations. This interesting close-up shows a loop antenna and various smaller antennae atop the forward fuselage, the aircraft being minus engines and exhaust stacks at the time. *Wright Field*

as bearing Army serial number AC36-1, an obvious error or perhaps a temporary expedient, as indeed the aircraft was arguably the first aircraft known to the Air Corps officials on the spot to have been purchased with FY36 dollars. Paperwork apparently caught up with events, however, as AC36-1 was subsequently recognised to have been properly assigned to the Douglas XC-32 (Douglas MSN 1414, which was delivered on 30 September 1935), a cousin of the DB-1.

Interestingly, the actual Operating Instructions for the DB-1 (which were authored by Douglas and were dated 19 September 1935) were handed over to the Army at the same time by Mr Raymond and Mr Collbohm of Douglas.

At this point, however, an administrative anomaly enters the history of the DB-1. The official Army description of the procurement

of the B-18 series states, contrary to the oft-repeated citation of Contract W535-ac-8307 noted above, that the DB-1 was acquired on a Special Purchase Order (Change Order), No 2087, and this was dated 29 July 1936. This may account for the difference in Manufacturers Serial Numbers quoted for the aircraft, as the Douglas Order Book clearly cites MSN 1353 for the DB-1 as of the time submitted for the competition. The aircraft is known to have been returned to Douglas following the Wright Field evaluation, where, according to most accounts, it was brought '…up to B-18 production standard' and was then re-delivered to the Army on 28 February 1937. It is believed that it was at this point that the MSN was changed to 1650.

What had actually happened is that the aircraft had been flown to Langley Field for 'accelerated service tests' and, upon notification that the award had gone to Douglas, the Materiel Division obtained orders for the test crew to fly the aircraft to various points in the southern part of the US for accomplishment of the first 50 hours of these proposed tests. These orders were never accomplished, however, as procurement of the DB-1 was held up when Douglas would not accept the price that the Army was willing to pay for it. In fact, even though Change Order No 2087 noted above was dated 29 July 1936, the aircraft did not formally become Army property until 12 August.

Tinkering with the aircraft continued unabated, however, and about the time of the Change Order actually transferring ownership to the Army, the Materiel Division had acquired two Chandler-Groves carburetors for installation and test in the aircraft, but these suffered difficulties and were shortly replaced.

In fact, contrary to many accounts, the aircraft was *not* retrofitted to B-18 standard, and remained rather a hybrid aircraft. Amongst other things, the Army was advised by Douglas that '…the 16.00-16

Details of the inspection doors and cover plates of the DB-1, showing the wing plan form to very good effect.
USAF B-18 Engineering Drawings Microfilm, NASM

Bearing the unique Air Corps Headquarters designator insignia on the rear fuselage, and Field Number 2, these nearly identical poses of the DB-1 after being accepted by the Air Corps as the first B-18 show the aircraft with the distinctive tall radio mast, dorsal turret extended and retracted, and, in one view, with propeller spinners. *NMUSAF and Ted Young*

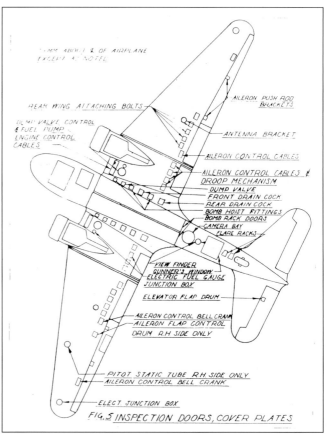

wheels, tires and brakes on the DB-1 are not standard production items, and spares could not be procured "off the shelf".' It is known, for instance, to have been dispatched to Langley Field, VA, for extended service tests on 8 December 1936, well before the alleged 're-delivery' commonly cited, and Douglas records show it as having been 're-delivered' on 23 February 1937. While at Langley, it was referred to repeatedly as a 'B-18' and cited as Air Corps serial number AC37-51. Reports from Langley also indicate that the bomb racks and bomb release controls in the aircraft were unlike the system that was to be standard in the production B-18. When it in fact arrived at Wright Field earlier that month, the logs showed that it had amassed a mere 22 hours flight time, of which 12 had been accumulated on the delivery flight from California. Yet the Board that had evaluated the aircraft at Wright Field between December 1935 and January 1936 had amassed not less than 18.5 hours on the aircraft alone! Clearly, following the return of the aircraft from that competition to Douglas, and following the revisions that Douglas carried out, the company felt justified in both issuing a 'new' manufacturers serial number to the aircraft and 'zero-timing' the airframe concurrently.

By 28 January 1937 the aircraft was being extensively flown by Air Corps crews, and was used to photograph the devastating Ohio River floods at the time, using five-lens cameras, between 25 and 28 January. Interestingly, the aircraft was repeatedly cited during this period as type YB-18, and the crew during the photographing of the flood included none other than Lt Benjamin S. Kelsey as pilot, with Capt L. C. Craigie as co-pilot, photographer Capt B. Talley of the Corps of Engineers, and four others on board.

By 27 May 1937 for the first time Army documents recorded AC36-262 as type TB-18. At this juncture this did not imply a 'training' status but rather a 'test' function. It was, therefore, used at Wright Field to conduct the formal Official Performance Test on 21 June 1937, and suffered an accident the next day at Wright Field due to an engine failure.

By early January 1938 the aircraft was still at Wright Field, where it was detailed to the Equipment Branch to test navigation equipment,

Compare this view of the definitive B-18 dorsal turret with that shown earlier as installed on the DB-1. Although essentially the same turret, the gunner's compartment had now been brightened by the addition of large windows on either side of the fuselage just after and below the turret. In this 9 February 1937 photo, probably showing the former DB-1 thus modified, the fuselage appears painted, but it was not.
Boeing Archives SM-10621

Still being referred to as type DB-1 by Douglas at the time of this 8 February 1938 view, the interior looking forward over the bomb bay reveals the myriad of special test equipment installed in the aircraft at that time.
Boeing Archives SM-12555

The earliest known image of a B-18 designated as such is this detailed close-up view of AC36-262 – which of course was the former DB-1 – taken on 22 February 1937, the day before it was formally handed over. Note that the antenna array and cockpit enclosure had been extensively modified, and additional windows added aft. *T.O.No.01-40E-2*

then being cited as type B-18. Douglas, however, in spite of all of these clear Army references to the airplane, referred to it as late as 31 January 1938 as the DB-1, when it apparently returned to the factory for dump valve tests, apparently in connection with required changes on the production B-18s. The aircraft was once again cited as a TB-18 by 15 April 1939, but had been redesignated as a B-18M by 1 April 1940, indicating that all armament and bomb racks had been removed. It became a more or less permanent feature at Wright Field as late as 25 January 1942, when it was transferred to Fort Dix, NJ, before going to Mitchel Field, NY, in February. It then returned to Wright Field again until July when it was sent to the San Antonio Air Depot for the fitting of special equipment associated with the Army's urgent need to develop radio searching equipment, the earliest such installations being cited as 'the Farnsworth equipment'. Apparently fitted with this device, it was sent to Lowry Field in August 1942, but returned once again to San Antonio where it was, incredibly, converted to B-18B status with a radar nose. (For a full account of the odyssey of this unique aircraft, see the Individual Aircraft Summaries in Annex 1 at the end of this volume.) It ended its days as a Class 26 instructional airframe by February 1944.

The Douglas DB-1A

While the basic DB-1 was being developed and marketed to the Army, Douglas and its design team did not remain idle.

As early as 15 August 1935, three days after the basic DB-1 specification was issued, the company had formulated an alternative design to the basic DB-1, with three differing engine installations, known as the DB-1A, also for posting against Army Specification No 98-201-A. So far as can be determined, these have never been published before. The accompanying table shows what Douglas calculated as the potential of these three combinations.

In fact, the Army selected the basic design, but stipulated Wright R-1820-45 engines of 930hp each, which rendered all of the earlier calculations academic, and the B-18 was born.

The DB-1 differed from the DB-1A design fundamentally in that the DB-1 had 5 feet less wing span, slightly less drag (due to the reduced span) and 370lb less gross weight in the normal useful loaded condition.

The advent of the B-18 (Douglas Specification DS-148)

The official Douglas account of the evolution of the B-18 said the following about the 'Development of the DB Series' in Report No 1647:

'The B-18 airplane, 132 of which are being manufactured for the Air Corps, first took form as the DB-1, submitted as a demonstration article under Circular Proposal 35-26 which opened August 22, 1936. The DB-1 utilised in much of its structure and a number of its installations experience gained in the manufacture of 126 DC-2 commercial transports. Production B-18s contain many of the improvements made in the DC-3, 50 of which have been manufactured. These improvements reflect themselves particularly in the flying, landing and taxiing characteristics, but throughout the B-18 are assemblies which have been perfected as a direct result of experience extending over a period of four years since the design of the original DC-1, a total quantity of airplanes of 200, and an accumulated flying time of over 500,000 hours.'

Perhaps no other statement has spoken so directly to the nature of the B-18 and the evolution of the type as stated so simply by the manufacturer.

The Army first described the B-18 in Technical Order No 01-40E-1, and announced that it was a:

'...six-place, mid-wing monoplane of all metal construction and retractable landing gear, built in accordance with Air Corps Specification 98-201A. It is powered with two engines, Air Corps designation R-1820-45. The all metal, full cantilever wing consists of three main sections, namely: the center section with engine nacelles attached and two outer sections with detachable wing tips. The ailerons are fabric covered and the right aileron is equipped with a tab to compensate for unsymmetrical loading. The horizontal and vertical stabilisers are full cantilever units and the elevators and rudder are fabric covered and are equipped with trim tabs which may be adjusted from the pilots' compartment while in flight. The elevator trim tabs provide adjustment of the longitudinal balance of the airplane while the rudder trim tab provides adjustment for the variation of engine torque with either or both engines running. The fuselage is of semi-monocoque construction. An escape hatch is located on the right hand side of the bomber's compartment and it may be opened from the inside or outside. When it is lowered, it may be used for entrance and exit. The cabin is located between the pilots' and the tail compartments. Access to the compartment is through the main entrance door on the left hand side of the fuselage. The hinge pins of this door are removable for emergency exit by pulling the cable attached to the pins. A door on the ceiling on the right hand side is for the removal of the life raft.'

The technical description of the aircraft in cold, military terms could hardly describe the interest and excitement of the Air Corps bombardment crews who would soon be receiving the new aircraft. While veterans of the war that would follow, and post-war aviation history enthusiasts, almost invariably have looked back on the B-18

Performance Characteristics	Air Corps Specification 98-201-A		Wright *Cyclone* G-5 Engines		Wright *Cyclone* G12 Engines		Pratt & Whitney *Twin Wasp* SB-G Engines	
	Minimum	Desired	Normal useful load	Desired useful load	Normal useful load	Desired useful load	Normal useful load	Desired useful load
(1) High Speed at 10,000 ceiling	200mph	250mph	211mph	209mph	215mph	213mph	211mph	209mph
(2) Operating Speed at 10,000 feet	170mph	220mph	170mph	170mph	170mph	170mph	170mph	170mph
(3) Endurance at Operating Speed at 10,000 feet (with 1/2 of fuel as an overload)	6hrs	10hrs	6hrs	8hrs (no overload)	6hrs	8hrs (no overload)	6hrs	7hrs (no overload)
(4) Service Ceiling	20,000ft	25,000ft	26,100ft	23,800ft	24,300ft	21,900ft	23,800ft	21,800ft
(5) Time-to-Climb to 10,000 feet	10min	5min	10.6min	13.3min	10min	12.2min	10min	11.8min
(6) Ceiling with One Engine Out	3,000ft	7,000ft	7,000ft	3,000ft (less 220Gal)	7,000ft	3,000ft (less 200Gal)	7,000ft	3,000ft (less 100Gal)
(7) Take Off over 50 Foot Obstacle with Designed Useful Load	2,400ft	2,000ft	2,120ft	2,770ft	1,830ft	2,360ft	1,860ft	2,310ft
(8) Landing over a 50 Foot Obstacle with Designed Useful Load	2,400ft	2,000ft	1,920ft	2,110ft	1,920ft	2,110ft	1,950ft	2,110

The definitive form of the production B-18 is shown to very good effect in this 23 February 1937 overhead view. This was probably the former DB-1, AC36-262, since the first 'production' B-18 was not accepted until 25 May. *Boeing Archives SM-10731*

as an 'obsolete' or, at best, obsolescent design meriting little thought or reflection, as of 1936 and 1937 it was the wave of the future and an eagerly anticipated piece of equipment. In this same vein, it is equally illuminating to examine, at this juncture, the B-18's peers around the world.

Right: The definitive standard B-18 nose turret, with .30 caliber gun deployed with flash suppressor attached, is seen on 30 June 1937, by which time acceptances by the Air Corps had commenced. *Boeing Archives SM-11456*

Below: This early production B-18, marked BG 7, with Field Number 1 (probably the 7th Bomb Group Commander's aircraft), shows the two-color engine cowlings and early configuration of the cooling aperture. *Wright Field*

The potential foreign competition

For all intents and purposes, as of the conclusion of the 1936 Wright Field bomber competition, the Douglas DB-1 and Boeing Model X-299 were unquestionably the most advanced bombardment aircraft in the western hemisphere, and could arguably lay claim to being the premier aircraft of their class on the planet.

Only seven other nations possessed aviation industry assets capable of producing heavy bombardment aircraft comparable to the DB-1, and none came even close to the Boeing Model X-299 as of 1936. These were, in order of relative capability, Germany, Japan, Great Britain, France, the Soviet Union, Italy and the Netherlands. Several other nations had industry capable of producing heavy bombers, but invested comparatively little in such direction, mainly due to political considerations. These included Sweden, Czechoslovakia, Yugoslavia and Austria.

All of these nations had a requirement for a bombardment aircraft of roughly the same class as the B-18, but to these were attached very different performance criteria and mission capabilities. With the exceptions of Great Britain and Japan, these nations looked to their bombardment aircraft in much the same way as the US Army – as adjuncts to ground forces for defense or, in a few cases, clandestine offensive operations.

Although some of the foreign contemporaries never attained production status or entered operational service, it is interesting nonetheless to compare the capabilities of these aircraft with that expected of the DB-1/B-18 as of 1934-36. The accompanying tables present the primary characteristics as compared to the same for the DB-1/B-18.

Nearly all of the aircraft represented in the tables were produced in some numbers and saw action during the war in some developed version, save the German four-engined Dornier Do 19, which failed to mature.

Douglas B-18

Type	Engines	High Speed	Range	Bomb Load	Defensive Guns
Douglas B-18-DO	2 x 815hp (at 10,300 ft.)	217mph	2,900 miles (with maximum bomb at 56% power)	4,400 miles	3 x .30cal guns or 2 x .30cal and 1 x .50cal guns

German Aircraft

Type	Engines	High Speed	Range	Bomb Load	Defensive Guns
Dornier Do 17E-1	2 x 1000hp	255mph	721 miles	1,102lb	3 x 7.9mm guns
Dornier Do 19	4 x 715hp	196mph	994 miles	3,527lb	2 x 7.9mm guns and 2 x 20mm cannon
Heinkel He 70E	1 x 750hp	223mph	776 miles	661lb	1 x 7.9mm gun
Heinkel He 111B-1	2 x 880hp	230mph	1,030 miles	3,307lb	3 x 7.9mm guns
Junkers Ju 52/3mg3e	3 x 725hp	171mph	808 miles	1,102lb	2 x 7.9mm guns

Japanese Aircraft

Type	Engines	High Speed	Range	Bomb Load	Defensive Guns
Mitsubishi Ki-2-I Louise	2 x 750hp	140mph	400 miles	600lb	2 x 7.7mm guns
Mitsubishi Ki-21-1a Sally	2 x 850hp	250mph (approx)	1,678 miles	2,205lb	3 x 7.7mm guns and 2x20mm
Mitsubishi G3M1 Nell	2 x 910hp	250mph (approx)	3,871 miles	1,764lb	4 x 7.7mm guns and 1 x 20mm cannon

British Aircraft

Type	Engines	High Speed	Range	Bomb Load	Defensive Guns
Armstrong Whitworth A.W.23 (became the Whitley series)	2 x 840hp	230mph	1,650 miles	7,000lb	5 x .303cal guns
Bristol Type 130 Bombay	2 x 750hp	180mph	2,230 miles	2,750lb	2 x .303cal guns
Bristol Type 143 (became the Blenheim series)	2 x 500hp	250mph	1,250 miles	2,000lb	None fitted
Fairey Hendon	2 x 480hp	155mph	1,360 miles	1,660lb	3 x .303cal guns
Handley Page Heyford	2 x 575hp	142mph	920 miles	2,660lb	3 x .303cal guns
Handley Page H.P.51 (became the Harrow)	2 x 830hp	200mph	1,250 miles	3,000lb	4 x .303cal guns
Vickers Wellesley	1 x 925hp	264mph	2,590 miles	2,000lb	2 x .303cal guns
Vickers Wellington I	2 x 1,050hp	245mph	3,200 miles	4,500lb	2 (later 4) x .303 cal guns

French Aircraft

Type	Engines	High Speed	Range	Bomb Load	Defensive Guns
Amiot 143-M	2 x 870hp	193mph	746 miles	1,764lb	4 x 7.5mm guns
Bloch M.B.200	2 x 870hp	177mph	621 miles	2,646lb	3 x 7.5mm guns
Farman F.222.2	4 x 920hp	224mph	1,367 miles	3,900lb	3 x 7.5mm guns
Lioré-et-Olivier LeO451	2 x 1,140hp	308mph	1,429 miles	3,307lb	2 x 7.5mm guns and 1 x 20mm cannon
Potez 540	2 x 690hp	193mph	777 miles	900lb	3 x 7.5mm guns

Soviet Aircraft

Type	Engines	High Speed	Range	Bomb Load	Defensive Guns
Ilyushin DB-3	2 x 800hp	400km/h	3,100km	2,500kg	3 x 7.62mm guns
Tupolev SB-2-M-100A	2 x 860hp	424km/h	1,500km	1,600kg	4 x 7.62mm guns
Tupolev ANT-42	4 x 850hp	444km/h	3,600km	4,000kg	2 x 7.62mm guns, 2 x 12.7mm guns and 2 x 20mm cannon

Italian Aircraft

Type	Engines	High Speed	Range	Bomb Load	Defensive Guns
Cant Z.1007bis	3 x 1,000hp	280mph	1,242 miles	2,600lb	4 x 7.7mm guns
Caproni Ca 133	3 x 460hp	174mph	839 miles	1,100lb	4 x 7.7mm guns
Caproni Ca 135/P.XI	3 x 1,000hp	273mph	1,242 miles	3,520lb	3 x 12.7mm guns
Fiat BR.20	2 x 1,000hp	267mph	1,863 miles	2,200lb	3 x 12.7mm guns
Savoia-Marchetti SM.79-I	3 x 1,350hp	267mph	2,050 miles	2,750lb	3 x 12.7mm guns, 2 x 7.7mm guns
Savoia-Marchetti SM.81	3 x 750hp	214mph	1,242 miles	2,640lb	5 x 7.7mm guns

The primary difference between the DB-1/B-18 series, when initially acquired and on entry into active service, and nearly all of these designs is that in the US the next generation of bombardment aircraft were already being developed, and resulted in war-winners, represented by the North American B-25 Mitchell, Martin B-26 Marauder, Boeing B-17 Flying Fortress, Consolidated B-24 Liberator and the Boeing B-29 Super Fortress series. The Douglas B-18s and B-18As procured between 1936 and 7 December 1941 could not have come at a more propitious time, and truly bridged the gap between the middle war years and the advent of the 'greatest generation' of US heavy bombers.

As of June 1938, however, despite the breathing room and time bought with the acquisition of the B-18 series, USAAC planners very soberly ranked the United States fifth out of the seven major nations in terms of high-speed twin-engined heavy bombardment capabilities, and seventh in high-speed four-engined heavy bombers. That ranking, drawn by the Office of the Chief of the Air Corps, and seldom cited in historical analysis, is demonstrated in the accompanying table, and was based on the best intelligence available at the time.

Comparison of World Heavy Bombardment Aircraft as of June 30, 1938

Ranked	Nationality	Type	On Hand	On Order
I (2-engine)	France	Lioré-et-Olivier LeO-45	1	242
I (4-engine)	France	Farman F.223/4	8	1
II (2-engine)	Great Britain	Vickers Wellington	8	242
II (4-engine)	Germany	Dornier Do 19	Unknown	Unknown
III (2-engine)	Germany	Heinkel He 111	1,700	Unknown
III (4-engine)	Italy	None known	None known	None known
IV (2-engine)	Soviet Union	Tupolev ANT-40	528	No Data
IV (4-engine)	Japan	None known	None known	None known
V (2-engine)	United States	Douglas B-18A	3	252
V (4-engine)	Great Britain	None known	None known	None known
VI (2-engine)	Japan	Type 97	70	50
VI (4-engine)	Soviet Union	Tupolev TB-6	420	No Data
VII (2-engine)	Italy	Fiat BR-20	134	45
VII (4-engine)	United States	Boeing Y1B-17	13	39

Air Corps units wasted little time in converting to the new B-18s. This view, looking forward from the dorsal turret, reveals the off-set of the loop antenna and the complexity of the wire radio antenna leading off from the masts. *William F. Yeager collection, Wright State University*

Although not stated, it is *assumed* that the reasoning behind ranking the US below nations that were not even known to have four-engined, high-speed heavy bombers, was based on intelligence that these nations were assumed to have such capability, such as Great Britain, which indeed would shortly field the classic Short Stirling and Avro Lancaster series as well as others.

The B-18 enters service

Differing from the DB-1 competition article in being powered by two 930hp Wright R-1820-45s, driving props with wider blades and mounted in revised engine cowls, a total of 131[10] production B-18s were ordered by the Air Corps in three distinct batches. These were assigned Air Corps serial numbers as follows:

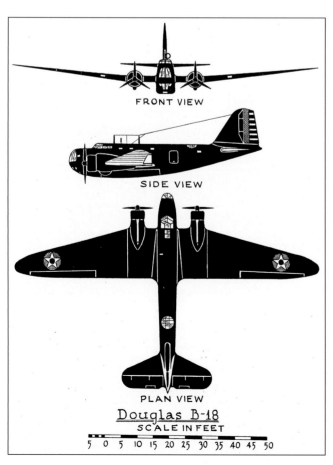

FRONT VIEW

SIDE VIEW

PLAN VIEW

Douglas B-18
SCALE IN FEET

5 0 5 10 15 20 25 30 35 40 45 50

AC36-262 to 36-343 (MSN 1650 to 1731) on Contract W535-ac-8307 with the first delivery on 23 February 1937 at a unit cost of $83,790.04[11]

AC36-431 to 36-446 (MSN 1732 to 1747) on Contract W535-ac-8307 with first delivery on 10 April 1938 at a unit cost of $83,790.04

AC37-1 to 37-33 (MSN 1748, 1749 and 1864 to 1894) on Contract W535-ac-8307 with first delivery on 15 April 1938 at a unit cost of $83,790.04. This contract was amended by Change 4 to include AC37-34. The reason that these last two sections of the order for a total of fifty aircraft were split between Fiscal Years 1936 and 1937 serial numbers was really very simple: Air Corps funding for those two Fiscal Years dictated that they could pay for sixteen of them with 1936 funds, and the balance of thirty-four with 1937 funds.

These also had a nose cone that was 7 inches shorter than the DB-1, and which incorporated the additional lateral window panels that had been specifically mentioned in the evaluation board recommendations as well as a bombardier's window modified to the request of the board.

The Air Corps dispatched the first production B-18, AC36-262 (in fact the reconfigured DB-1), to Wright Field, where the Acceptance Performance Tests were carried out on 21 June 1937. These reported that the aircraft had two Wright R-1820-45 engines of 815hp (rated as right engine s/n 36-395 and left 36-393) at 2,100rpm with a 10:1 blower. They turned three-bladed, constant-speed Design 6105A-18 props and had a fuel consumption rate of 65.7 gallons per hour. The empty weight was listed as 15,719lb, with a gross of 21,130lb, and allowed for a crew weight of 1,200lb, equipment totaling 270.4lb, fuel at 1,254lb, oil at 142.5lb and armament at 2,544lb. Maximum speed at 10,000 feet was clocked at 214.1mph at 2,100rpm with a time-to-climb to this altitude of 9.1 minutes. Time-to-climb to 20,000 feet was 25.3 minutes at 2,100rpm. The aircraft landed at 63.5mph with 59° of flaps and endurance was given as 6.36 hours on 418 gallons of fuel (the total fuel capacity being 822 gallons). Operating speed (best cruise) was 170mph at 10,000 feet. The aircraft could take off over a 50-foot obstacle with 15° of flaps in 1,460 feet, and total landing distance with 59° of flaps, also over a 50-foot obstacle, was 1,360 feet.

Most observers of the evolution of the B-18 assumed that all of the B-18s and B-18As procured were essentially identical. This was not the case. For example, Change 6 to Contract W535-ac-8307, dated 20 May 1937, directed that B-18s with serial numbers AC36-294 to 36-343 and AC37-1 to 37-50 (the last seventeen of which were not built, in favor of funding the initial procurement of B-18As) specified that Douglas furnish and install in these 100 aircraft the necessary equipment to provide for thirteen passengers in addition to the normal crew complement of six. These modifications were to include padded seats to seat three men in the bombardier's compartment, one in the navigator's position, five (along the side walls) in the rear bomb bay, and four more in the rear fuselage on the side floors.

Other changes directed by the Air Corps, by Change 7 dated 3 March 1938, reflected the following unique equipment installations and changes to the airframes:

AC36-262 to 36-343, AC36-431 to 36-446 and AC37-1 to 37-33 (131 aircraft) had dump valves installed in the two main fuel tanks, including operating mechanisms and outlet chutes to the center wing trailing edges

From AC36-275 onward, and later retrofitted to all B-18s, the aircraft had long exhaust stacks installed over the tops of the upper engine nacelle fairings. This three-view, issued December 27, 1939, is interesting when compared with similar views of the B-18s cousins, the DC-2 and DC-3. (Wright Field Image 66223)

AC36-262 to 36-342 as well as AC37-34 (82 aircraft) had the SCR-AG-183 Command Radio Set.

AC36-262 to 36-343, AC36-431 to 36-446, AC37-1 to 37-3 and AC37-34 had SCR-242-A had Radio Compasses installed.

AC36-262 to 36-343, AC36-431 to 36-446, AC37-1 to 37-33 and AC37-34 (102 aircraft) had the loop antenna, located on top of the fuselage, retractable, while those on the 30 aircraft AC37-4 to 37-33 were non-retractable.

AC36-275, AC36-316 to 36-343, AC36-431 to 36-446 and AC37-1 to 37-33 all had a new instrument wiring harness installed, to include lights for the flight instruments.

AC36-275, AC36-343, AC36-431 to 36-446 and AC37-1 to 37-33 had long exhaust pipes installed, and the same modification was later incorporated on 80 other aircraft, AC36-262 to 36-274 and AC36-276 to 36-342. This was intended to help reduce exhaust glare during night flight, and was a distinctive recognition feature for these aircraft.

AC36-343, and AC36-431 to 36-446 as well as AC37-1 to 37-33 (50 aircraft), were to be provided with curtains at the rear of the pilot's cockpit area, in order to prevent glare due to the main cabin lights – the radio operator and navigator needed lights to function during night flights. AC36-262 to 36-342 were later provided with the same equipment.

AC36-343, AC36-431 to 36-446 and AC37-1 to 37-33 (50 aircraft) had SCR-AH-183 Command Radio Sets.

AC36-343, AC36-431 to 36-446 and AC37-1 to 37-33 (50 aircraft) had roller curtains installed over the side windows of the navigator's and radio operator's compartment. Later, sufficient parts were acquired to do the same on AC36-262 to 36-342 (81 aircraft).

AC36-343, AC-36-431 to 36-446 and AC37-1 to 37-33 (50 aircraft) had metal visors installed in the forward part of the cockpit enclosure to prevent instrument light glare onto the cockpit windows.

AC36-343, and AC36-431 to 36-446 as well as AC37-1 to 37-33 (50 aircraft) were to have the inboard sides of the engine cowlings and nacelles painted a flat bronze green color (Shade No 9 on Color Card Supplement 3-1) as a means of preventing glare from reflected light off the otherwise highly polished, natural metal cowls and engine nacelles.

AC36-343, AC36-431 to 36-446 and AC37-1 to 37-33 had blind flying curtains added, and this change was also incorporated into AC36-262 to 36-342 later.

AC37-4 to 37-33 (30 aircraft) had SCR-242-B Radio Compasses installed.

AC37-9 to 37-33 (25 aircraft) had the engine instrument rheostat relocated to the co-pilot's side of the instrument panel and the exhaust gas analyser indicator light connected into the engine instrument rheostat circuit; these were to have sufficient dimming capability.

AC37-9 to 37-33 had an oil dilution system installed to facilitate engine start-up.

AC37-9 to 37-33 had an Army-supplied Type B-3 Stabilised Drift Sight installed, in lieu of the special Gatty-type drift sight.

AC37-9 to 37-33 had a refueling system installed that allowed these aircraft to be refuelled from 50-gallon drums in the field.

AC37-9 to 37-33 (25 aircraft) had the window in the pilot's floor removed and faired over, in order to prevent excessive light from entering the bombardier's compartment.

AC37-10 to 37-33 were to be provided with tow target equipment (less impellers and windless assemblies, which were provided by the Army).

AC37-458 to 37-594 had pilot instrument panels and a control pedestal that were different from those on AC37-595 and subsequent examples.

The fuselage, wing and vertical stabiliser stations on a standard production B-18. *Authors' collection*

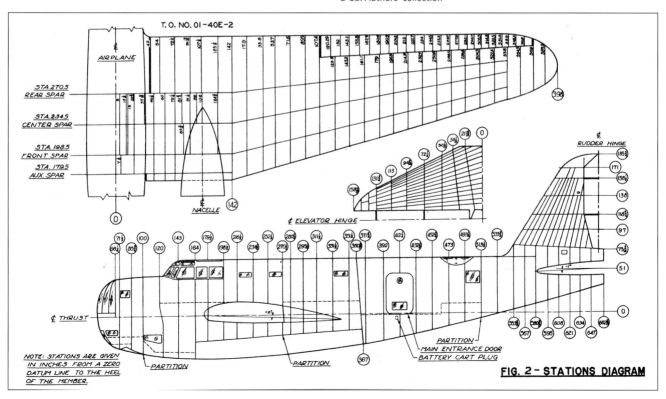

The evaluation crew's comments were revealing. There were very few negative comments. With regard to handling, the pilot-in-command noted that '…the plane executes all allowable maneuvers excellently, without buffeting or burbling' and that the aircraft was '…very stable under all conditions.' He did note that the aircraft was difficult to side-slip, but rated each of longitudinal, lateral and directional stability as 'excellent'. He noted that the nose was too high for vision by the pilot on the opposite side, but counted on the co-pilot to aid in that capacity. He also noted that the windscreen tended to frost up badly during cold-weather flights. Both pilot and co-pilot noted that the control wheels tended to sit a bit too close to the legs while at the controls, and recommended a better sliding seat arrangement. A 9 November 1937 Air Corps report, however, added a note of caution for single-engine operation of the basic B-18: single-engine flight could indeed be maintained so long as the fuel load on board was 800 gallons or less and provided that the basic load was no more than that used in the tests, which was not stated.

All in all, Douglas had delivered on its performance guarantees with the DB-1 competition article and the initial production B-18s.

The first three genuine production B-18s, however, accepted in May and June 1937, perhaps predictably, went to Chanute Field, Illinois (AC36-263), home of the Air Corps Technical School, Aberdeen Proving Ground, Maryland (AC36-264), and Maxwell Field, Alabama (AC36-264), home of the Air Corps Tactical School. These were followed by the next nine off the line going to Hamilton Field, California, the first station to see the type in any numbers.

The initial distribution of the 132 B-18s, which had been forecast by the AAC as early as 14 July 1936, is described as follows, and vividly depicts the thinly spread character of even this, the largest single bombardment aircraft order ever placed by the Army for one type:

This excerpt from actual Douglas engineering drawings depicts the close working relationship and crew stations on a standard B-18, including all but the rear gunner. Note that the 'Avigator' (as they were termed at the time) sat immediately behind the co-pilot, followed by the radio operator at a common work table. *NASM EDM37*

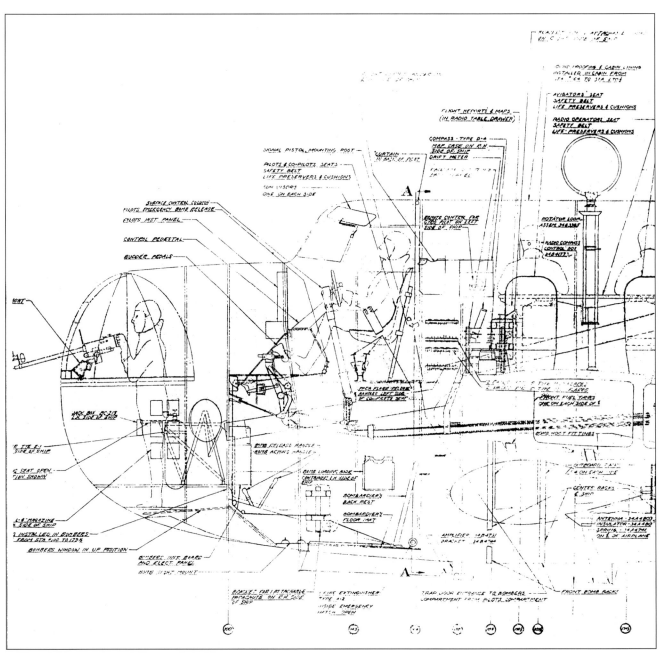

Wright Field, Ohio	1
Chanute Field, Illinois	1
Aberdeen Proving Ground, Maryland	1
Maxwell Field, Alabama	1
Hamilton Field, California	35
March Field, California	26
Mitchel Field, New York	40
Kelly Field, Texas	4
Langley Field, Virginia	5

The entry of an aircraft of the complexity of the B-18 into the Air Corps inventory has almost invariably been reported as a rather routine delivery matter, but in fact it required considerable up-front preparation and personnel reassignments, and an entirely new Table of Organisation & Equipment (TO&E), the fundamental manning document for any organised Army unit. Note that this array of specialists does not include the actual officer crew members of the aircraft (pilot, co-pilot), as of the effective date of the table was 24 March 1937, and was structured on a typical squadron of nine aircraft operating from a 'squadron aerodrome' with one ground radio station, less one flight (the other flight was a 'mobilisation flight' only added to the TO&E if the nation mobilised).

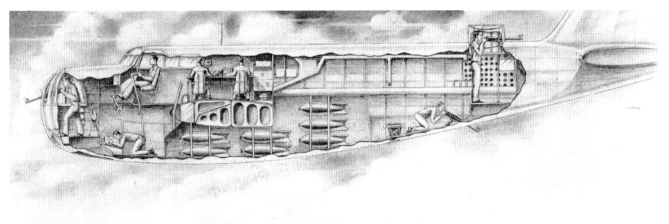

Although this artist's cutaway drawing does show the crew positions relative to one another, it actually shows two more crewmen than was standard. The bomb aimer doubled as the nose turret gunner, and the dorsal turret gunner was also responsible for the so-called ventral 'tunnel gun'. *Authors' collection*

The 'front office' of a production B-18 on 3 March 1937, with callouts for the various instruments and controls. This was undoubtedly the most sophisticated instrument panel introduced into an Army Air Corps cockpit to this time. *Wright Field 56303, 13282AC*

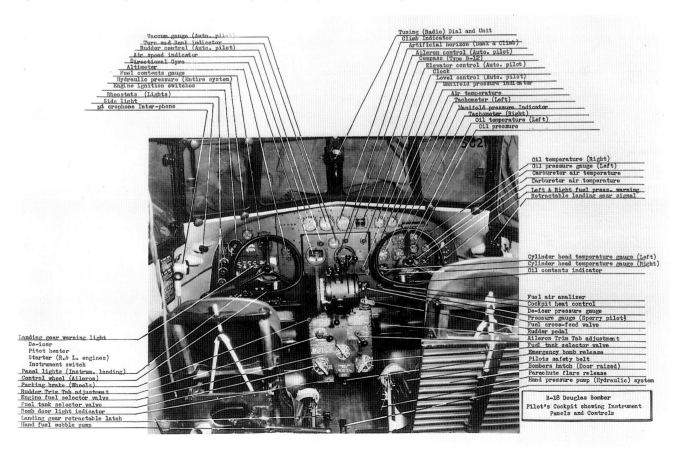

B-18 Squadron Table of Organisation

In addition to the accompanying table, these personnel were further broken down within the Squadron by specific functions as follows:

Headquarters and Headquarters Section
1 – First Sergeant
1 – Clerk, Administrative, 1st Class

Supply Section
1 – Clerk, Technical, 2nd Class
1 – Clerk, Technical 3rd Class

Mess Section
2 – Cooks, 1st Class
2 – Cooks, 2nd Class

Section Headquarters, Service Section
1 – Clerk, Administrative 1st Class
1 – Clerk, Administrative, 2nd Class

Engineering Section
1 – Master Mechanic, Airplane
1 – Aircraft Engine Mechanic, 1st Class
1 – Aircraft Engine Mechanic, 2nd Class
1 – Aircraft Instrument Mechanic, 2nd Class
1 – Aircraft Instrument Mechanic, 3rd Class
1 – Aircraft Metal Worker, 2nd Class
1 – Aircraft Metal Worker, 3rd Class

Armament Section
1 – Chief, Armament, Aircraft
2 – Aircraft Armament Specialists, 1st Class
2 – Aircraft Armament Specialists, 2nd Class
2 – Aircraft Armament Specialists, 3rd Class

Communications and Ground Radio Section
1 – Chief Mechanic, Aircraft Communications
1 – Aircraft Radio Operator, 1st Class
1 – Aircraft Radio Operator, 2nd Class
1 – Aircraft Radio Operator, 3rd Class
1 – Aircraft Radio Mechanic, 1st Class
2 – Aircraft Radio Mechanics, 2nd Class
1 – Aircraft Radio Mechanic, 3rd Class

Technical Supply Section
1 – Clerk, Technical, 1st Class
1 – Clerk, Technical, 3rd Class

Operations and Intelligence Section
1 – Clerk, Administrative, 1st Class
1 – Clerk, Administrative, 2nd Class
1 – Clerk, Administrative, 3rd Class

Squadron Commander's Crew
1 – Chief Mechanic, Airplane
2 – A&P Mechanics, 1st Class
1 – Aircraft Radio Operator, 1st Class (Combat Crew)
1 – A&P Mechanic, 2nd Class
1 – Aircraft Radio Operator, 2nd Class (Combat Crew)
1 – Aircraft Armament Specialist, 2nd Class (Combat Crew)

Flight Sections
2 – Master Mechanics, Airplane
8 – Chief Mechanics, Airplane
16 – A&P Mechanics, 1st Class
8 – Aircraft Radio Operators, 1st Class (Combat Crews)
4 – A&P Mechanics, 2nd Class
8 – Aircraft Radio Operators, 2nd Class (Combat Crews)
2 – Aircraft Armament Specialists, 2nd Class (Combat Crews)
4 – A&P Mechanics, 3rd Class
6 – Aircraft Armament Specialists, 3rd Class (Combat Crews)

Miscellaneous
20 – Privates First Class and Privates (Duty Soldiers and Guards)

B-18 Squadron Table of Organization

Specialties	Grades							
	1	2	3	4	5	6	7	Total
Master & Chief AP MECS & AP Mechanics	3	9	18	5	4			39
MR & CH Mechanics, Aircraft Communications		1						1
Aircraft Armorers		1	2	5	8			16
Aircraft Engine Mechanics				1	1			2
Aircraft Instrument Mechanics				1	1			2
Aircraft Metal Workers				1	1			2
Aircraft Radio Operators				10	10	1		21
Aircraft Radio Mechanics				1	2	1		4
First Sergeant		1						1
Clerks, Administrative				3	2	1		6
Clerks, Technical				1	1	2		4
Stewards and Cooks					2	2		4
Miscellaneous							10	10	20
TOTALS	3	12	36	30	21	10	10	122

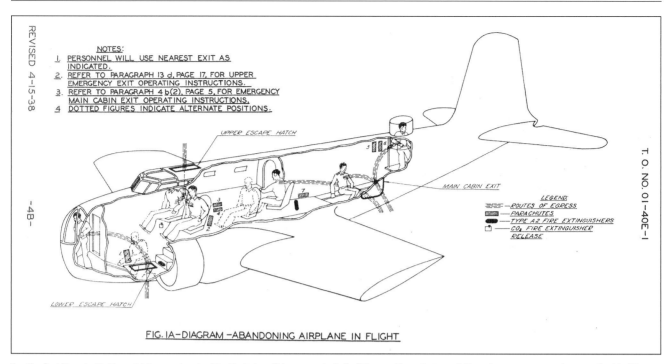

NOTES:
1. PERSONNEL WILL USE NEAREST EXIT AS INDICATED.
2. REFER TO PARAGRAPH 13 d, PAGE 17, FOR UPPER EMERGENCY EXIT OPERATING INSTRUCTIONS.
3. REFER TO PARAGRAPH 4 b(2), PAGE 5, FOR EMERGENCY MAIN CABIN EXIT OPERATING INSTRUCTIONS.
4. DOTTED FIGURES INDICATE ALTERNATE POSITIONS.

REVISED 4-15-38

-4B-

UPPER ESCAPE HATCH

MAIN CABIN EXIT

LEGEND:
ROUTES OF EGRESS
PARACHUTES
TYPE A2 FIRE EXTINGUISHERS
CO₂ FIRE EXTINGUISHER RELEASE

LOWER ESCAPE HATCH

T. O. NO. 01-40E-1

FIG. IA—DIAGRAM —ABANDONING AIRPLANE IN FLIGHT

For the first time in Air Corps history, a standard tactical aircraft incorporated all of the positions that would later become accepted as standard in US heavy bombers, and this necessitated new Tables of Organization & Equipment, as well as more practical day-to-day considerations, such as this crew escape chart for the B-18. *T.O.No.01-40E-1*

Permanent Air Corps facilities in California, not far from the manufacturer, were initially the greatest beneficiaries of the new aircraft, and the first of these arrived at Hamilton Field to great fanfare during the week of 16 July 1937, even as squadrons with the paper organisation shown above were being brought somewhere near at least operating strength.

Meanwhile, the General Headquarters Air Force, with its headquarters at Langley Field, Virginia – the east and west coast units of which received by far the greatest numbers of the new aircraft – and the Materiel Division at Wright Field were extremely concerned about the technical training of crews for the B-18s and Y1B-17s that were being delivered to the force.

In a letter to the Commander of the 1st Wing, GHQ Air Force at March Field dated 29 January 1937 the commands expressed the view that '…the greatest care be exercised in the preliminary instruction of Air Corps personnel in connection with flying and ferrying the B-18 and Y1B-17 airplanes.' They specifically mentioned that it had been the experience of the Materiel Division and, oddly, that of Pan American Airways that:

'…the actual flying of airplanes of this size is no more difficult and requires no more flying skill than the smaller airplanes which are in general use in the service. The probability of accident in these airplanes is primarily due to the fact that there are a number of duties to be performed by the crew, which in the case of smaller aircraft are performed by the pilot alone. It is essential that the Air Corps personnel to be assigned to these airplanes become accustomed to the idea that these are not "one man airplanes", but are operated by a crew that functions as a team, and thorough knowledge of the duties of each member of the crew and practice in team work prior to and during flight is essential.'

The GHQAF commander proposed that all members of each crew reporting to the Douglas or Boeing plants to take delivery of one of the new aircraft be given a technical examination by the Air Corps representative at each plant, based on the Handbook of Instruction with

which they had (supposedly) been provided before being sent to bring home the aircraft. They levied ultimate responsibility on each aircraft commander, however. Copies of these exceptional documents survive, and possibly mark the very first time that a US manufacturer provided such in-depth instruction to all members of a sophisticated aircraft. The School for B-18 Crew Chiefs at the Douglas Santa Monica plant unquestionably served as a model for such future preparatory courses.

Press releases extolled the virtues of the new aircraft, and pointed out that '…they have a sufficiently large enough radius to adequately protect the entire Pacific Coast,' a factor that certainly figured largely in the decision to acquire the type. The release went on to predict that the Army was going to acquire 177 of the aircraft, which, at the time, was the publicly announced number. Reports relating to the B-18 very quickly lost ground to a veritable barrage of press coverage on the Y1B-17s, however, as both the popular and aviation press of the country could not seem to resist the virility of the popular name that had been coined for the aircraft, the Flying Fortresses. Boeing, not surprisingly, also bought extensive advertising space for the Y1B-17s in the aviation press, while Douglas went about the workaday business of delivering a much larger number of very capable aircraft without the glamour of a glitzy popular name.

In the months that followed, the shiny new aircraft – the first in memory at the time that were not painted with Army blue fuselages and yellow wings – were seen in increasing numbers over the major population centers of the west and east coasts of the nation, but hardly at all in the heartland. Civilian newsmen waxed far more poetic about the aircraft than had the rather straightforward Army press releases, and the *Los Angeles Times* for 14 March 1938, in announcing the National Aircraft & Boat Show that was to open at the Pan-Pacific Auditorium on 2 April, opened its news item by describing the B-18 that was to be present as '…the mighty new Douglas bomber, the largest addition to United States Army flying service', which was to make its first public viewing there.

Selection controversy

Inevitably, the large B-18 order placed at the time soon resulted in a press whirlwind of allegations surrounding the choice, and the special relationship that was said to exist between Donald Douglas Sr and General Henry H. 'Hap' Arnold, Chief of the Air Corps. In particular, the prominent columnist and Washington, DC, pundit Drew Pearson seemed to make much of this procurement in his syndicated columns.

The two had been friends for many years, dating from Arnold's Air Service assignments in California in the 1920s. Much later, political pundits and syndicated columnists made much of this relationship, and pointed to the fact that Arnold's son, Bruce, was emotionally linked to Barbara, daughter of Donald Douglas Sr. Indeed, they were married during the war. Some went so far as to suggest that Arnold had 'thrown' the Air Corps decision to buy large numbers of B-18s at least in part because of these relationships.

Murray Green, who conducted one of the most extensive series of interviews with key personalities who knew Arnold, between 1969 and 1974[12], probed these allegations intensively, and in fact even interviewed Donald Douglas Sr himself. One of the key exchanges in this interview had to do with the competition that resulted in the selection of the B-18. That exchange is quoted here[13]:

> **Murray Green:** 'You know, one of the criticisms in his association, his friendship with you, was the fact that he went ahead with the B-18 production. The B-18 wasn't much of an airplane.'
>
> **Donald Douglas:** 'At the moment, it looked like it might be.'
>
> **Murray Green:** 'It was two-engine and it couldn't even get to Hawaii. Guys like Knerr, who wanted to go all out on the B-17, felt that Arnold was not aggressive enough in pushing the B-17s.'
>
> **Donald Douglas:** 'Well, I don't know. Hap was the only one that was pushing it.'
>
> **Murray Green:** 'Well, Andrews was pushing it. Andrews was pushing it harder than Arnold was. But Arnold was sort of the organisation man and he had to live with the War Department General Staff. At that time, the War Department General Staff had a conception. We had a program for 2,320 planes. Their idea was to make it all single-engine or twin-engine planes, so they would get more planes for the same dollars. And Andrews was then [Commander of] General Headquarters Air Force at Langley Field. And Knerr was his Chief of Staff. And they felt – Knerr says that they felt, Andrews felt – that Arnold was not aggressive enough in pushing the four-engine bomber. Do you remember any static on that score? I'm talking about 1937.'
>
> **Donald Douglas:** 'No, I don't. I'm trying to think back on why we went ahead with the B-18. I don't remember except we thought this was what the Air Corps wanted, and I guess they thought it was the best they could get at the moment.'

The truth was, of course, that although General Arnold was the Chief of the Air Corps at the time, and had ultimately to either endorse or disapprove the recommendation for the Board of Officers who had dutifully observed the very precise rules under which the selection of the B-18 was made (and which also, it must be said, saw the wisdom of allocating some of the available funding for the test batch of Y1B-17s – when they could have opted for more B-18s), he would have had little or no grounds for not approving the recommendation that was in fact forwarded to the War Department. Donald Douglas, who was certainly vitally interested in this process at the time, in his own words, as quoted above, clearly enunciated what everyone involved felt at the time: the DB-1/B-18 was the best aircraft that could be had

for what needed to be done as of 1935-36.

Green also interviewed Brigadier General Franklin Carroll at Boulder, CO, on 1 September 1972. It will be recalled that Carroll, as a Major, had been one of the members of the Board of Officers that had selected the DB-1 in the May 1937 competition with the Boeing and Martin entries. The following excerpts from this interview are pertinent:

> **Murray Green:** (Referring to Arnold and Douglas): 'Did Arnold give any preference to Douglas in procurement?'
>
> **BG Carroll:** 'My general opinion is that he wouldn't give Douglas any special favors over anyone else.'

In yet another interview, with Brigadier General Turner Sims at Washington, DC, on 26 August 1971, the following exchange was noted:

> **Murray Green:** 'Arnold and Douglas were close.'
>
> **BG Sims:** 'Arnold's son married Douglas's daughter. In fact, my wife played golf with Barbara yesterday.'
>
> **Murray Green:** 'Was there any feeling in Washington or Dayton that Arnold, being a close friend of Douglas, influenced procurement of the B-18?'
>
> **BG Sims:** 'That never bothered us.'
>
> **Murray Green:** 'Could Arnold have influenced the purchase of the B-18, if he wanted?'
>
> **BG Sims:** 'There was a Board that made a decision on all these planes. The Board didn't have the say in it. The Board made a recommendation. The Chief of the Air Corps was the one who made the decisions. Douglas was a damn good company at that time.'
>
> **Murray Green:** 'Did Andrews oppose the B-18?'
>
> **BG Sims:** 'I don't recall that much detail, as to whether he did nor not.'

The Alleged 100-Mile Limitation on Army Aviation in Coastal Defense, 1931-1939

Historians of bombardment aviation and the relative responsibilities of Army and Naval aviation to the coastal protection of the Continental United States have, for many years, alleged that the Army Air Corps responsibilities for this function were driven by some vague understanding that had been reached between the leadership of the Army and Navy after the First World War, when aviation started to come of age as a potentially useful defensive weapon. When the strident exhortations of the visionary Brigadier General William 'Billy' Mitchell are thrown into the controversy, the wording and arguments become nearly evangelistic.

The authors of this work, to the extent that this policy ever existed, could locate no evidence whatsoever of any Army-Navy agreement between 1931 (the Pratt-MacArthur air agreement) and 1936 (when the B-18 contract was let to Douglas) that in any way placed a limit on Army coastal defense aviation to an arbitrary area of within 100 miles of the coastline of the United States.

The oft-quoted Pratt-MacArthur agreement of 9 January 1931 said this:

> 'The Army Air Forces will be land-based and employed as an essential element to the Army in the performance of its mission to defend the coasts both at home and in our overseas possessions, thus assuring the Fleet absolute freedom of action without any responsibility for coast defense.'

Commenting on this, Major R. G. Hoyt stated to General 'Hap' Arnold on 11 March 1936 that:

'This appears to be the only concession ever made by the Navy in connection with Coast Defense. It was, allegedly, promptly repudiated by Admiral Pratt's successor, as Chief of Naval Operations (CNO), although no evidence of this repudiation as a matter of record has been located. Any effort made to make one service, either Army or Navy, responsible alone for Coast Defense has been to no avail.'[14]

In 1933 the so-called Drum Board, already cited in this account, in its 'Report of the Special Committee of the War Department General Council on the Employment of Army Air Corps Under Certain Strategic Plans' dated 11 October 1933, spoke of plans to employ Army aircraft 250 to 300 miles, and 200 to 300 miles out from the coastline, not in any restrictive sense, but as a practical distance of this particular war plan. The Drum Board recommended that 'The strategical and tactical employment of the units of the Army Air Corps after M-Day [Mobilisation Day] is governed by the Army Strategical Plan covering a specific situation. Such plans may provide for missions by these units over land or sea areas, either under Army command or Navy command.' By 1942, as events actually unfolded – and in particular as it involved our subject, the B-18 – these were extremely prophetic words.

The Joint Board approved the above recommendation, as well as many others suggested by the Drum Board on 26 September 1934, and stated in its interpretation that:

'...the Army Air Corps operates along the coast under the same conditions as in other operations, except that occasions may arise when the GHQ Air Force or units thereof may operate in conjunction with Naval air forces under temporary direction of Naval commanders; or similarly, when Naval air forces may operate in conjunction with and under temporary direction of Army commanders.'

Nowhere in these elaborate discussions did the Joint Board state, or imply, any limitations on the distance out from the coast.

All of this had to do, of course, with what Army planners intended for its bombardment aircraft to be capable of doing, should the need arise. In 1936 these planners could not possibly have conceived of an eventual need for heavy bombers to be able to operate in formations of hundreds and even thousands of planes from foreign bases, flying to and attacking such places as Berlin or Tokyo. Hindsight, in examining the decision to acquire both the B-18 and the Y1B-17s, reveals that a better combination at that particular juncture could not have been made. Both types evolved and met crucial needs. The evolution of the B-17 is legendary and well understood. The metamorphosis of the B-18 is not.

As early as August 1936 the Engineering Section of the Air Corps Materiel Division at Wright Field conducted a little-known comparison of the performance – and expectations – of the then current first-line bomber, the Martin B-10B, as compared to the new B-18 and Y1B-17s. This analysis sheds significant light on how the Air Corps regarded these aircraft at the time, and makes for extremely interesting reading. The accompanying table shows the normal and maximum loads (including armament, bombs and fuel) for all three types, with the resulting speed, endurance and range at 75% power. In the case of the B-10B, to make it even competitive, they allowed a 250-gallon bomb bay auxiliary fuel tank, which rendered no internal stations for bombs. In the case of the Y1B-17s, of course, the total fuel load was carried in the wings, although an auxiliary bomb bay tank of about 400 gallons had been designed and could have been carried in half of the bomb bay, still leaving space for internal bombs. This would have enabled the Y1B-17 to accomplish a range of approximately 2,140 miles at 75% power while carrying the same bomb load of 1,200lb that the B-18 could carry for maximum range. It should be noted that, perhaps not surprisingly, the Y1B-17s were 26mph faster while carrying twice the bomb load of the B-18 over approximately the same distance. Even at that, the statistics rendered by this study reveal that, at cruise, the B-18 could range further and longer than even the mighty Y1B-17.

Ironically, these early comparisons very quickly became obsolete, as the numbers of B-18s and B-18As procured became fixed, and the coming of war very quickly accelerated procurement of updated versions of the B-17 – all with ever heavier armament, crew composition, defensive gun installations and ancillary equipment. As most of the static numbers of surviving B-18As morphed into B-18B and B-18C configuration, the debates of the late 1930s quickly evaporated in the press of more urgent requirements, and the very real pre-war requirements for bombardment aircraft changed as well.

Loading and Speed	Factors	B-10B	Y1B-17	B-18
Normal Loading	Bombs	2,260lb	2,500lb	2,260lb
Normal Loading	Fuel	226 gallons	850 gallons	640 gallons
Normal Loading	Gross Weight	14,600lb	35,000lb	23,200lb
Normal Loading	Load Factor	5.5	5.5	5.5
Operating Speed	Speed	188mph	217mph	170mph
Operating Speed	Endurance	3.25 hours	5 hours	9.2 hours
Operating Speed	Range	611 miles	1,085 miles	1,570 miles
Maximum Loading	Bombs	0	2,500lb	1,200lb
Maximum Loading	Fuel	702 gallons	1,700 gallons	1,170 gallons
Maximum Loading	Gross Weight	15,320 lb	40,100lb	26,000lb
Maximum Loading	Load Factor	5.23	4.8	4.9
Maximum Operating Speed	Speed	188mph	210mph	170mph
Maximum Operating Speed	Endurance	10 hours	10 hours	16.2 hours
Maximum Operating Speed	Range	1,880 miles	2,100 miles	2,750 miles
Cruising Speed	Speed	130mph	150mph	150mph
Cruising Speed	Endurance	16.7 hours	17.4 hours	19 hours
Cruising Speed	Range	2,160 miles	2,600 miles	2,850 miles

A truly historic photo. Field Number 112 was actually, at the time of this photo, still officially designated as a B-18A. However, it was the first such aircraft to be converted to B-18B configuration This is actually AC38-599, which suffered an engine fire on take off from Wright Field on June 3, 1942, while under the command of CPT Elmer E. McKesson. It served out its useful life as a Class 26 instructional airframe. *Boeing Archives DAC-12431*

This organisational adjustment to the world situation in which the United States found itself in December 1941 is a credit to the foresight of the small group of Air Corps thinkers who sorted it all out during the five years between 1935 and 1940.

Medium versus Heavy Bombers

We cannot depart from the intense discussion that was ongoing around the time of the selection of procurement of substantial quantities of B-18s and a test batch of Y1B-17s without examining the very definition of bombardment aircraft that was swirling within Air Corps decision-making circles during the critical decade of the 1930s.

The designations that Army aviation gave to bombardment-type aircraft up to about 1930 were indefinite and often confusing. Such terms, and combinations of terms, as 'Day Bomber,' 'Night Bomber,' 'Heavy Bomber' and 'Long Range Bomber' were used quite generally. The 'Night Bombers' were usually the largest and heaviest of the aircraft used for bombing purposes, and could typically carry a bomb load of between 2,000 and 2,500lb, while the 'Day Bombers' were faster and lighter with a bomb capacity usually in the range of 1,200lb.

In 1930 the Air Corps Tactical School, nearly a magnet for the most talented thinkers in the service at the time, then at Langley Field, suggested that, because of the uncertainty of these various terms and the meanings of same, they should be discontinued. The Chief of the Air Corps agreed. The Commandant of the School pointed out, for instance, that the so-called 'Day Bombers' might be needed for missions at night, and the 'Long Range Bombers,' for short-range missions. The final decision was to use just one designation for aircraft used exclusively for bombardment work, and this would be indicated by the simple letter 'B' prefix before a numeric sequential designator. The terms 'light,' 'medium' and 'heavy' still continued to be cited, but only in a general way. The definitive Second World War-era Army Air Forces' definitions and general characteristics and purpose for minimum aviation requirements in these three categories is shown in the table on the next page.

The variety of designations that had, up until that time, been given to bombardment aircraft indicated the existence of a variety of ideas concerning their function and use. During the period between 1935 and 1939 the twin-engine (or 'medium' bomber) held the advantage in development and procurement simply because the views of the United States War Department were that the major function of the military aircraft was to support the ground forces, since the overwhelming body of opinion was that battles were 'won by the Infantry', and not by bombardment ahead of the ground forces. This philosophy, grounded basically in Great War experiences, prevented procurement of truly long-range bombers (such as the XB-15 and the definitive B-17) in any quantity except for the initial test batch we have discussed. The question was also discussed at this time as to whether the protection of the United States against possible air attack was the function of the Army or the Navy.

Despite this prevailing wisdom, the Air Corps managed to request a total of sixty-five early B-17 series aircraft from funds appropriated in Fiscal Year 1936 although, as we have seen, in fact only thirteen Y1B-17s were actually ordered. The Air Corps tried again in the 1937 Fiscal Year budget, when sixty B-17s were requested, but none were procured. In 1938, initially, it was decided to include the purchase of twenty long-range, four-engined bombers, obviously B-17 variants, but the Secretary of War eventually decided that it would be better to acquire forty-four twin-engined bombers instead. Yet again, sixty-one B-17s were requested by the Air Corps from 1938 funds, but the procurement of 177 B-18s and only the thirteen Y1B-17s was favored by the War Department.

But another factor, seldom cited in most discussions of the B-18 versus B-17 debate, was a requirement circa 1936 stipulated by the new Chief of Staff of the Army, General Craig, and his Deputy Chief of Staff, Major General Stanley Embick, which pushed for a significant reduction in what were viewed as excessive Research & Development expenditures. In June 1936, for instance, the War Department turned down heavy bomber advocate Westover's request for authority for a pre-production batch of Boeing's XB-15, as well as enough B-17s to equip at least two line Groups. At the General Staff's so-called 'bombardment conference' held on 28 August 1936 both Westover and Andrews argued passionately for four-engine bombers, but the War Department General Staff argued successfully that '...the bulk of bombardment aviation operating with a mobile Army should be the size and capacity of the standard B-18 medium bomber.'[15]

As late as October 1938 the Army's Adjutant General, speaking for the War Department, informed the Chief of the Air Corps that four-engined bombers were not to be included in the procurements from the 1940 and 1941 funds, and that the Air Corps, likewise, was not to be expanded in personnel and equipment, as recommended by the Woodring Program (March 1938), but that it should look to the Reserve Corps and civilian aviation in case of war. This heavy-handed and, in the face of world events, ill-advised attitude on the part of the

Type	Minimum Useful Radius	Minimum Ferry Range	Minimum Top Speed	Minimum Useful Bomb Load	Purpose
Heavy Bomber/ Long Range Recon	2,000 miles	3,000 miles	300mph	2,000lb	Designed as long range bomber but adaptable to use in long-range strategic recon over either land or sea
Medium Bomber/Recon	1,000 miles	–	350mph	2,000lb	Somewhat lighter, more readily procurable and cheaper aircraft designed to meet many requirements and not requiring the extreme range of the heavy bomber. Should be capable of adaptation for medium range recon
Light Bomber/Recon/Photo	300 miles	–	400mph	1,000lb	Readily procurable designed primarily to meet the needs of ground troops for offensive combat aviation

War Department at this stage of world affairs did not change significantly until events in Europe made it abundantly clear to even the most steadfast adherent to earlier policies, in 1939.

The B-18, central to this discussion, was therefore the result of the decision, in 1934, to encourage the development of an entirely new series of twin-engined bombers. It was desired to secure '…an advanced type, having increased bomb-carrying capacity, greater range of operation and a larger crew complement.' As a result of the competition described earlier, the Douglas DB-1 won, although as it developed the company decided not to deliver the first example for the amount offered by the Army.

A Utility Board, created by the Materiel Division at Wright Field specifically for the purposes of evaluating bombardment aircraft, recommended that the following specific changes be introduced into the design, in addition to those mentioned earlier as being recommended by the Board of Officers who selected the DB-1 as winner:

[1] Reinforce the fuselage for crash landing

[2] Strengthen the tail surfaces

[3] Install a visual indicator showing the position of the landing gear

[4] Add an automatic oil temperature control

[5] Install an Air Corps specified fuel signal system

[6] Add de-icing equipment

[7] Change the rear upper turret to a power-operated type (which was in fact adopted in the B-18A)

[8] Install an oil dilution system

Early reports from operating units indicated that crews regarded the type as 'well liked', and specific items of note included the heated interior, which eliminated the need for heavy flight clothing and gave a greater freedom of action.

Subsequently, innovations and changes were extensively tested or installed for permanent use in B-18 series aircraft, as will be seen. In particular, the incorporation of the power-operated turret in the B-18A[16] was the culmination of several years of effort on the part of the Materiel Division to secure a satisfactory power-driven gun mount or turret – and was the first such installation in a production US bomber. As of 1939, B-18s were fitted with M-1 bombsights and automatic flight control equipment, suitable for tactical use. A mechanism for a 'train' release of the bomb load was first tested in a B-18, but was discontinued as impractical at the time.

Even though the B-18s had been considered 'unusually satisfactory' as a new type, certain difficulties and desires for improvements inevitably developed with introduction into service units. Some initial difficulties were experienced with the engine cooling systems and with oil dilution; extensive corrosion and formation of sludge was sometimes found in the fuel tanks; and the auxiliary bomb bay fuel tanks often failed to release as advertised, which in at least one instance caused a spray of fuel to be thrown back into the rear of an aircraft for some 20 minutes, while an emergency landing was miraculously made. A number of complaints were also received from pilots concerning the crowded conditions of the cockpits and the arrangement of the instruments, but these came mainly from pilots who had never flown B-10Bs!

Ironically, the Air Board, at the end of the 1930s, once again recognised that world events necessitated the introduction and definition of various classes of bombardment aircraft to meet anticipated demands on the Air Corps, and, as the war that followed would demonstrate, this mix of types was a winning combination. That the B-18 and its developments met, almost perfectly, the Medium Bomber/Reconnaissance definition was more accidental than intentional, but was nonetheless the result of the very deliberate process that led to its procurement in the first place.

CHAPTER TWO

The Douglas DB-2 and B-18A (DB-5)

The final aircraft on the initial contract, W535-ac-8307, AC37-34, to have been Manufacturers Serial Number (MSN) 1895, was actually completed entirely out of sequence with the other production B-18s, and thus actually became the thirty-sixth B-18 to be delivered when it arrived at Wright Field on 8 November 1937.

This aircraft, which was Air Corps property, was accepted by the Army from Douglas on 30 September, but was designated by Douglas as the DB-2, and differed substantially from the stock B-18s then entering service.

The aircraft was fitted with a totally unique nose, which featured a power-operated gun turret and a more extensively glazed lower bombardier's position. This did not, however, prove satisfactory to the Air Corps.

The paper trail on this aircraft is, at best, confusing, and much more complicated then has been previously reported. Douglas records, for instance, indicate that the aircraft was changed from MSN 1950 to MSN 1895 when it became the 'reworked' DB-2. However, another note found in Air Corps documents at the National Archives stated that MSN 1950 was the DB-2, and that the Air Corps, at least initially, assigned it serial number AC36-302 and that '…this ship takes the place of Ship 1895 [with 1690 crossed out] which will not be built.' This leaves us with the very real question of whether or not the DB-2 was in fact Air Corps or Douglas property at the time of

construction, as the Douglas Order Book throws yet more fuel on the fire by stating that the aircraft was delivered to the Air Corps on 28 February 1937! The actual Air Corps serial number for this aircraft was AC37-34. Douglas's development of the aircraft at this date is supported, however, by the fact that the Guggenheim Aeronautical Laboratory at the California Institute of Technology did wind tunnel tests on the DB-2 design as early as 10 March 1937, and three-view drawings of what was fundamentally the DB-2 were dated as early as 21 December 1936.

Ironically, Boeing asked both the Army and Douglas on 3 August 1937 for permission to permit two of its engineers, Mr Murray and Mr Kylstra, to examine the DB-2. Neither Douglas nor the Air Corps objected, although it is difficult to imagine what prompted this unusual request. Although not acquired by the Army until October, the aircraft was definitely at Wright Field by 5 August 1937, as it was reliably reported to have been tested there on that date while fitted with Wright GR-1820-G115 engines.

The first specific Army mention of the procurement of the DB-2, however, was dated 8 October 1937, and was entitled 'Proposed Procurement DB-2 Aircraft as B-18 s/n 37-34 Contract AC-8307', which would appear to settle the ownership of the aircraft as of that date.

The earliest Army records indicate that the aircraft was assigned to Wright Field and the Armament Branch by 23 November 1937, which seems to agree with the original contention. The aircraft was described as '…a non-standard B-18, in that it has incorporated the power operated gun mount and resultant difference in the nose section.' It was used to thoroughly test the power-operated nose turret, for which the Air Corps had such high expectations, apparently

This is the earliest known image of the Douglas DB-2, dated 18 February 1937, ten days before Douglas turned it over to the Air Corps. The entire nose section had clearly been completely revised to accommodate a power-operated gun turret and improved bomb aimer's position.
Boeing Archives SM-10685

Taken the same day, this rear quarter view also reveals that the shape of the dorsal gun turret had been revised, and a port hole and window had been added to the port-side (left-hand) main entry door as well. *Boeing Archives SM-10687*

Above: The DB-2 after arrival at Wright Field around 4 March 1937 for extensive trials. *Wright Field 56362, NARA RG342FH*

Right: The DB-2 was subjected to a number of specialised tests and modifications. Here it is shown with Curtiss fully feathering props and, just above the .50 caliber gun in the nose turret, a telescopic gunsight can just be seen. The nature of the large oval port hole on the lower starboard nose is unknown, but may have provided a camera port to observe the function of the starboard prop while in flight. *Wright Field 58534, NARA RG 342FH*

Below right: The DB-2 was also used by the Air Corps to test a wide variety of aerial camera equipment, as shown in this 12 June 1939 view at Wright Field. Note the crew entry step just visible under the wing and the very lengthy bomb bay doors, common to all B-18 series aircraft. *Wright Field 64201, NARA RG342FH*

Below: The DB-2 has rarely been depicted in flight, and it presented a rather handsome and businesslike appearance for its day. *NMUSAF*

By February 1939 the DB-2 retained most of its original configuration, but a special dorsal turret had been installed that has not been identified, as seen here. The aircraft had also been fitted with propeller spinners, had the Wright Field logo on the rear fuselage and, by this time, the last two digits of her Air Corps serial number, AC37-34, on the vertical fin. *David W. Ostrowski collection*

with both .30 caliber and .50 caliber weapons. The subsequent Utility Board, however, considered the power-operated turret as 'very desirable', but stated that '…they were too experimental to justify incorporation into the 177 production aircraft.' The DB-2 was also used for various bomb tests as late as August 1938, and for icing tests into late December 1938.

Some sort of 'special turret', which has eluded identification, was installed in the dorsal position in February 1939, but was replaced by the original power turret. By April 1939 it had been cited, for the first time, as type TB-18 (indicating use for tests, not as a trainer), but was redesignated as B-18M, indicating elimination of all armament and bomb racks, on 1 April 1940. The aircraft survived a series of wartime assignments to be scrapped in August 1945.

The Air Corps had convened another Board of Officers at Wright Field on 3 May 1937 to consider the DB-2, which was a direct result of the recommendations made by the initial DB-1 selection board, and the B-18 Utility Board cited earlier. The Board consisted of the

An excellent close-up of the radical new nose configuration of the DB-2, as of 18 February 1937. The power-operated turret could mount either a .30 caliber or .50 caliber weapon (as shown here), and was a much more efficient position for the bomb aimer. *Boeing Archives SM-10690*

following officers:

LTC Howard C. Davidson, Chairman

Major Franklin O. Carroll

Major Eugene E. Eubank

Major John F. Whitley

Captain Stanley M. Umstead

The Board members flew a stock B-18 and the new DB-2 for a total of 42hr 50min in direct comparisons, and these tests resulted in the following specific recommendations to Douglas for incorporation into production B-18A aircraft:

[1] Reinforcements for landing with the gear retracted, a feature already common on Douglas DC-3 aircraft

[2] Strengthened tail surfaces

[3] Propeller de-icer slingers

[4] Provisions for refueling the aircraft in the field away from permanent station

[5] Interchangeability of the .50 caliber gun in the nose and lower gun positions

The Air Corps in fact procured a total of 217 B-18A aircraft by Contract AC-9977, modified twice, and, in order to facilitate this, had to stretch the order over three Fiscal Year budgets, as noted earlier. There just was not enough money to purchase the entire order in one Fiscal Year. This accounts for the anomaly of what appears to be three separate orders; in fact, they were continuously procured on the same line, with the resulting serial numbers:

AC37-458 to 37-634	177 aircraft ordered in June 1937
AC38-585 to 38-609	25 aircraft using FY1938 funds
AC39-12 to 39-26	15 aircraft using FY1939 funds

The most apparent difference between the B-18 and B-18A series aircraft was the definitive change in the configuration of the bombardier's position in the nose, and the nose gun 'blister'. Additionally, the definitive engine selection was the 1,000hp Wright R-1820-53, with fully feathering hydromatic propellers – a marked improvement over those on the earlier B-18s. The first production B-18A flew on 15 April 1938, and was delivered to the Air Corps on 1 June 1938.

Forgotten designs:
The Douglas DB-2A, DB-3, DB-3A, DB-3B, DB-3C, DB-3D, DB-4, DB-5 and 'B-18E'

Even as Douglas was pushing through the production B-18s and B-18As, as was so common throughout the aircraft industry at the time, the engineering staff continued to tinker with the fundamental design, as a combination of suggestions, recommendations and industrial intelligence reached the factory. This resulted in the proposed evolutionary designs, never before described, the DB-2A, DB-3 series, DB-4 and DB-5 (DS-223, DS-224 and DS-225). The DB-5 was, in fact, the Douglas in-house designation for the 177 B-18As (serials AC37-458 to 37-634).

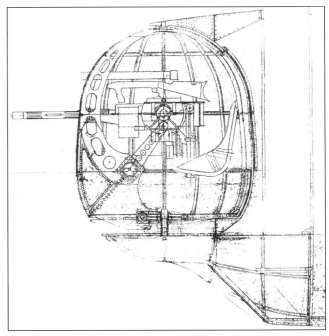

Above right: Douglas was well aware of the need to improve the defensive armament capabilities of its DB family. This rather large unit, very similar to that actually mounted on the DB-2, was proposed for installation in any of the DB-3, DB-4 or DB-5 variants. *NASM EDM37*

Middle right: This proposed dorsal turret appears to be similar to the one actually tested on the DB-2 at Wright Field in May 1939. Note the dorsal fin fillet just aft of the turret leading to the vertical stabiliser, which would have certainly been a problem operationally. *NASM EDM37*

Bottom right: Douglas suggested that any of the basic designs of DB-3 through DB-5 (sometimes cited as DB-223, 224 and 225) could be fitted with tricycle undercarriages, as shown here. *NASM EDM37*

Below: The DB-3 through DB-5, with a host of potential sub-variants, reflected efforts by Douglas to prepare alternative designs for domestic as well as export customers. They differed mainly in engine, cowling, engine nacelle and armament arrangements. *NASM EDM37*

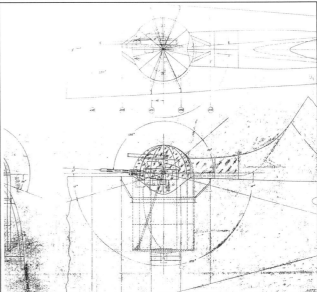

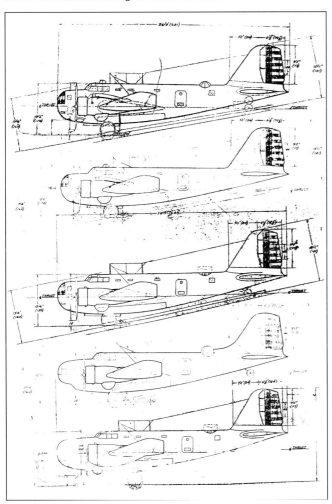

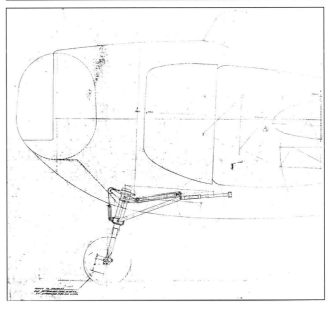

Upon winning the competition, Douglas felt that it was in a commanding position to provide the Army with the full advantages of large-scale, uninterrupted production of what it viewed by this point as a proven design that required only further refinements to meet changing requirements. They could, because of the established contract and relationship with the Air Corps, promise rapid delivery, low price due to volume and commonality of components, '...freedom from "grief"', as the company worded it, and simplification of field servicing due to commonality of basic design.

Since Douglas could quite rightly view its position as unique in nearly all of these respects, the company reasoned that improvements to the basic B-18 were all that was necessary, since to opt instead for an entirely new experimental aircraft, built to the same specifications that were evolving, would result in little more than a copy, without the background that the B-18 provided.

Douglas felt that it could provide an improved aircraft that could incorporate the following basic characteristics:

10-hour endurance at 220mph, or a 2,200-mile range, with a bomb load consisting of:

1 – 2,000lb bomb or

2 – 1,100lb bombs or

4 – 600lb bombs or

8 – 300lb bombs or

20 – 100lb bombs

with a defensive armament increased to five .30 caliber guns

The Army Circular Proposal No 36-545 had been issued at about this time, which called for a 'multi-engine bombardment airplane' with the following desired characteristics:

An exceptionally heavily armed version of the proposed B-18E included rear fuselage side blisters as well as power-operated ventral and dorsal guns. The aircraft would have been tricycle-geared in this configuration and rather larger dimensionally than the standard B-18 or B-18A. Boeing Archives

12-hour endurance at 230mph, or a 2,760-mile range, with a bomb load consisting of:

2 – 2,000lb bombs or

4 – 1,100lb bombs or

8 – 600lb bombs or

16 – 300lb bombs or

40 – 100lb bombs

with a defensive armament consisting of six .30 caliber guns

Douglas assumed, based on the above Circular Proposal, that the Army desired aircraft in the twin-engine category large enough to meet the desired characteristics of the multi-engine Circular Proposal, and that the two proposals would have to be combined, since the minimum requirements were identical. This assumption was reinforced by the wording of the description of the evaluation procedures that the Army would use, which stated, in part that '... the procedure for evaluation ... is predicated upon an airplane that meets all the desired attainments ... of Type Specification No 98-204.' The Army went on to state that, with the above in mind, no advantage would be gained, so far as the twin-engine circular was concerned, by just enlarging the aircraft basically to meet the additional desired characteristics of the multi-engine specification. However, Douglas observed that, during the intervening period, there had been a number of developments in engines, armament, provisions for high-altitude flying and the like, which it felt confident it could apply to the basic B-18 design. The company pointed out that it had already incorporated some of these in the DB-2, which it felt provided evidence of the company's ability to expand and improve the root design.

The DB-2A was a proposal of the basic DB-2 but with Wright Cyclone engines.

The DB-3 that was proposed appeared to fulfil the function, as Douglas viewed it, of submitting one bid that met all of the requirements of both the Specification and the Handbook. Douglas also described the DB-3 as '...the demonstration airplane; that is, the B-18 with the new

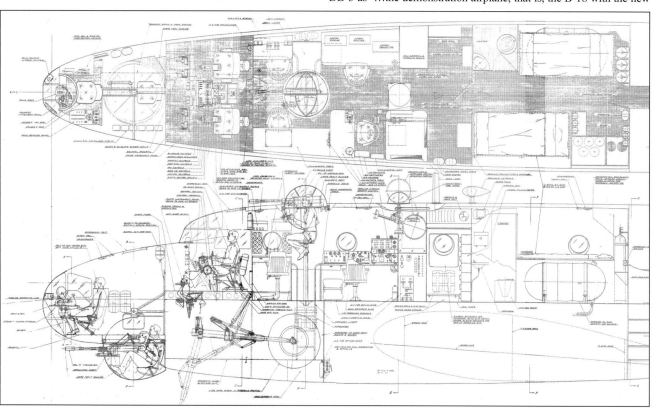

nose and advanced Cyclones.' The DB-3A was a development with turbo superchargers, while the DB-3B was to have had R-1830 engines, the DB-3C R-2180 engines, and the DB-3D R-2600s[17]. The proposed DB-5 was essentially identical, except for a few very minor additions, to the B-18, and was suggested only to provide a design that could be produced for the lowest possible price – and, most importantly, in the least time. The proposed DB-4, on the other hand, was the same as the DB-5 but incorporated a number of the requirements included in the Type Specification and the Handbook that Douglas felt offered better solutions. Douglas concluded by suggesting to the Air Corps, therefore, that it focus its attention on the proposed DB-4.

Specifically, the DB-4 included the following specific features not organic to the production B-18:

[1] Two additional guns in the bombardier's compartment, providing a complete intersection of fire of two or more of the guns within 100 yards

[2] All gun emplacements on the aircraft would be capable of mounting either .30 caliber or .50 caliber guns

[3] The addition of a 'turret' in the main cabin, aft of the pilot and co-pilot station, for celestial observations by the navigator

[4] Exhaust silencers to reduce noise and eliminate glare for night operations

[5] Propeller de-icer slingers

[6] Complete provisions for field refueling

[7] The ability to host any set of up to five different engine types including:

    a. Two Wright R-1820-45s (as on the production B-18)

    b. Two Wright G-117 series engines (as used on the DB-2)

    c. Two Pratt & Whitney R-1830-Cs

    d. Two Pratt & Whitney R-2180s

    e. Two Wright R-2600

Douglas observed that, of the proposed engine installations, the R-2600s would require the use of larger-diameter props than existing engine nacelles would permit and, consequently, a revised and wider center section wing would be required; either that or the standard wing section would suffice for the R-2180s, and in any case all would be fitted with fully feathering props of either Curtiss or Hamilton Standard design.

The DB-4 would also offer a bomb bay arrangement designed to provide wide flexibility of both bomb load and auxiliary fuel. It was to consist of a front rack, a center rack and a rear rack, the first two of which were grouped together to consist of sixteen stations. The rear rack, by itself, contained sixteen stations. The front and center racks were to be designed to accommodate the following:

    2 – 1,100 pound bombs or

    2 – 600lb bombs or

    8 – 300lb bombs or

    16 – 100lb bombs

The rear rack, by itself, could hold:

    2 – 1,100lb bombs or

    4 – 600lb bombs or

    6 – 300lb bombs or

    16 – 100lb bombs

These loads could be carried simultaneously. Additionally, the bomb bays could accommodate either two of the so-called 'long' 2,000lb weapons, carried on the front-center racks, or two of the 'short' 2,000-pounders on the rear rack. When the two 'long' projectiles were carried, no other weapons could be mounted, but with the two 'short' 2,000-pounders on the rear racks (or equivalent in smaller bombs), two 1,100-pounders could be carried on the front racks.

Wing tanks could hold a total of 805 gallons of fuel, but this could be increased to 1,570 gallons by the installation of integral tanks. In addition, two droppable tanks of 186 gallons each could be carried on the front and center bomb rack combination, and two identical tanks of

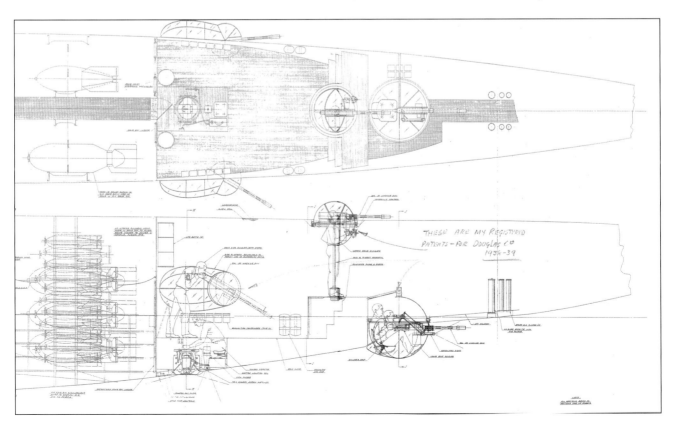

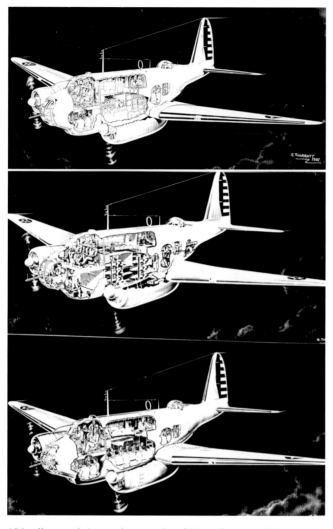

The proposed B-18E was intended primarily for the export market, and was shown in concept form here as early as 1937. It bore an uncanny resemblance to the North American XB-21 in concept. *Boeing Archives*

[8] Turbo-supercharger installation

[9] A complete oxygen system for the crew

[10] A Douglas perfected system for manufacturing integral fuel tanks

World events overtook the DB-3 and DB-4, however, and the Air Corps, which was receiving outstanding design proposals from every quarter for alternative designs, including Douglas, quickly moved on to the selection of root designs from North American and Martin to meet the basic Specification, and these became the B-25 and B-26 series. Had fascist aggression not accelerated as it did between 1937 and 1940, one can only speculate as to whether the Army might not have found the Douglas proposal to further 'stretch' the DB-1/DB-2 design to a tricycle gear development economically attractive.

Finally, on 20 May 1938, Douglas published the first of what became at least two distinctly different designs, which were labelled as B-18E, for 'Export'. The first, under Specification SS-234-A, was what appeared to all intents and purposes to be the DB-1 offered with alternative engine installations. These could be either Wright GR-1820-G102 Cyclones rated at 1,100hp for take-off; Pratt & Whitney GR-1830-SCGs, GR-1830-S1CGs or Wright GR-1820-G105s. Douglas predicted a maximum speed of 236mph, a range of 2,900 miles and a 6,316lb bomb load with three defensive guns. The company produced a 42-page sales brochure for the aircraft, which included illustrations of how the aircraft could be crated for shipment on a surface vessel – including actual images of a tarp-covered fuselage on a freighter and wings in crates! Clearly, following the Air Corps clearance of the type for export, the company pursued the possibilities. Somewhat earlier, in 1937, yet another evolution of the 'B-18E' was conceived, at least to the stage of artist's concept drawings, and this was a much larger aircraft, with tricycle undercarriage, very heavy defensive armament (including 20mm or 37mm guns in three turrets), as well as dedicated cargo and troop transport versions. Needless to say, none of these evolved to even mock-up stage.

The B-18A enters service

Like the B-18s that preceded them, nearly all of the B-18A production aircraft were delivered from the factory, initially, to units of the General Headquarters Air Force.

The first optional order for the revised B-18A was produced so rapidly that the Air Corps, immersed concurrently in the opening stages of a snowballing personnel expansion program, could not locate enough qualified crews to travel Temporary Duty (TDY) to Douglas to attend the conversion course and ferry the new aircraft to their initial stations. As a result, for some time the aircraft were lined up neatly after completion outside the factory awaiting minimum crews.

It is seldom recognised that the entire production run of B-18 and B-18A aircraft, 351 aircraft (including the DB-1 and DB-2), were handed over to the Air Corps between May 1937 and February 1940 – a scant thirty-four months. The vast majority of these were being crewed, both in the air and on the ground, for the first time by officers and enlisted ranks who, for the most part, were fresh from the Air Corps training establishment, fleshed out with more experienced cadre in leadership positions. Very few of these crews had any experience in aircraft requiring such a coordination of skills, the closest being the former Martin B-10B-equipped units where small flight crews of a single officer pilot and two enlisted ranks suddenly expanded to, at least on paper, as many as six to seven crew positions per aircraft.

186 gallons each (or two larger tanks of 287 gallons) could be installed in the rear bomb bay. Douglas observed that one of the advantages of the removable tanks was that, should the main tanks be hit by gunfire, the auxiliary tanks could be installed and the aircraft operated.

The company proposed the use of the same power-operated nose turret as mounted in the DB-2, and a similar turret in the dorsal position, as well as an electric bomb hoist.

As if this was not enough, Douglas proposed an Amendment XI to the DB-4 that would have incorporated a tricycle undercarriage, further facilitating loading. The company regarded the aircraft as being well adapted to his configuration, and claimed that the gear installation had already been tested by it on a Douglas OA-4A.

Douglas also promoted the use of the DB-4 as a reconnaissance aircraft, without reducing its value as a bomber. There were also a host of other minor improvements listed, and these included:

[1] Douglas method of flush riveting, which the company felt had been perfected

[2] Alcohol windscreen de-icers, which were being used successfully on the DC-3

[3] The so-called Inconel exhaust system

[4] An improved oil dilution system

[5] A dedicated accessory drive unit

[6] Retractable landing lights

[7] Hydraulically operated gun mounts with 'eyelid'-type gun mounts

Excellent detail is visible in this factory view showing the nose of a production B-18A being mated to the rear fuselage. The aircraft had a well-deserved reputation for being very rugged and extremely well built.
NARA RG342FH 134110AC

Production B-18A series aircraft saw a series of differing engine cowling, exhaust and nacelle changes, seldom reflected in accounts of the type. This view, showing a port-side engine on 7 December 1938, reveals a prop spinner, the de-icer boots, the closely fitted exhaust stack over the nacelle and the segmented paint on the cowling. *Boeing Archives SM-14266*

Production-line B-18As being assembled right alongside commercial DC-3 series aircraft at Santa Monica on 11 November 1939. The dorsal turret of the nearest aircraft, turned sideways, is shown to good advantage in this view.
NARA RG342FH 14145AC

A look at the starboard installation on a B-18A on 19 January 1939, with good detail of the Hamilton Standard propeller logo as a bonus.
Boeing Archives SM-14485

The challenges to the Air Corps system in preparing crews for this new experience were enormous, and had it not been for the help of the brief Douglas conversion course they would have certainly been much more protracted.

Although available in scattered form, a word about the basic configuration of the B-18A version may be prudent at this juncture. As can be deduced, it was normally a seven-place, mid-wing monoplane of all-metal construction, incorporating full retractable landing gear, hydraulically operated brakes, an Type A-2 auto-pilot (but only on airplanes AC37-458 to 37-594 inclusive), wing flaps of the split-trailing edge type, complete de-icer equipment (initially, including props and anti-icers) and soundproofed pilot's compartment. An escape hatch was located in the floor on the right side of the nose gunner's compartment, and could be opened from either inside or outside. When lowered, it could be used for entry and exit. The navigator's seat was located on the port (left) side of the aircraft just aft of the pilot, while the radio operator was also on the port side opposite the liaison radio set. The bomb bay doors were hydraulically

operated and were controlled from the bombardier's position, although the pilot also had an emergency, salvo bomb release control.

Like the B-18, initial B-18A deliveries saw individual aircraft being dispatched direct from the factory to Wright Field (the first B-18A, AC37-458), Mitchel Field, NY, Langley Field, VA, Chanute Field, IL, Lowry Field, CO, and Aberdeen Proving Ground, MD. This particular aircraft, AC37-458, was by 12 August 1939 at Wright Field being converted for the exclusive use of General Arnold; it was by that date designated as the B-18AS and was noted as having what 'Hap' Arnold described as '…Peruvian cowlings and an additional chair installed'. Precisely what this type of cowling looked like remains a mystery, as does the placement of the chair.

The first substantial concentration of B-18As was at yet another permanent California station, March Field, where three aircraft arrived on 29 September 1938 for the 19th Bombardment Group, and Mitchel Field, NY, which received no fewer than eighteen new B-18As between 30 September and 28 October for assignment to the 9th Bombardment Group and 18th Reconnaissance Squadron. Detailed

At least one B-18A was designated as type B-18AS for the exclusive use of General Arnold as a special staff transport with 'Peruvian cowlings'. It is believed that this might be that installation on AC37-458 on 12 April 1939. Compare this with the other cowling images. *Boeing Archives SM-14850*

When fitted with twin bomb bay fuel tanks, the range of the B-18A as a reconnaissance aircraft was extraordinary. This view shows the very large bomb bay, as well as the twin tanks and rather complex doors, looking aft on 28 December 1939. *Boeing Archives SM-16709*

The B-18A, with its much improved bombardier's station, proved very popular with crews. The nose gun relocation to the lower blister, shown here, while a seemingly poor design at the start, proved ideal for the mission that subsequently evolved in the anti-submarine and maritime patrol function. *via David W. Ostrowski collection*

Both the B-18 and B-18A could be fitted with a variety of cameras for dedicated photo reconnaissance and strike imagery and had this special position, near the ventral 'tunnel gun', for that purpose, complete with a swing-away seat for the camera operator and – more importantly – room to work! *Museum of Flight 10633*

emotionally and politically isolationist at the time, the spanking new bombers must have seemed a comfort and source of confidence to both those in uniform and the occasional citizenry that chanced to see them. The Air Corps leadership was relentlessly pushing training and readiness to the best of their ability, as the political leadership grudgingly provided the financial resources to do so. Significantly, on 8 September 1939, exactly seven days after Germany invaded Poland, General Arnold sent a high-priority telegram to the Air Corps Western District Procurement Officer, Major Lowell H. Smith, instructing him to '…contact Douglas Aircraft Co., Inc., and report without delay what steps they can take immediately to expedite the production and delivery of B-18s,' even though only fifty-four aircraft remained yet to be delivered to the existing contracts.

information on all individual aircraft assignments, throughout their service lives, is available from www.crecy.co.uk, and in the detailed discussions in subsequent chapters, as war arrived.

The delivery of the mix of B-18s and B-18As to operational units during that hectic thirty-four-month period paralleled the seemingly inevitable unraveling of world events, and in a nation that was

As will be seen in a careful reading of the individual operating unit summaries, the Air Corps was shifting its meager bombardment aircraft fleet hither and yon to try to meet every demand, and as rapidly as an under-strength squadron became minimally proficient,

Although vastly overshadowed during the war years and in post-war literature, at the time they were being introduced into service the B-18 and B-18A series were regarded by their crews as world-class aircraft, and a vast improvement over previous equipment. This fully attired pilot, with his mission kit, poses for the cameraman at the easy-access port-side door. *via Dana Bell, USAAF 2510AC*

B-18s only rarely show up in pre-war advertising, and even then for only a brief period, as advertisers swarmed to be associated with the B-17 Flying Fortress instead – by a ratio of more than 10 to 1! Eclipse starters used this example, however, a number of times. *Eclipse, Bendix Corp*

After entering the main crew door on the port (left) side of the fuselage, this was the view looking forward over the bomb bay of a B-18A. Imagine being a crewman weaned on Martin B-10s entering for the first time and spotting those dual bunks! *Boeing Archives SM-14509*

the cadre was splintered and aircraft reassigned to create yet more new units and cadres. Throughout it all, the B-18s and B-18As seemed almost omnipresent, and a foreign agent could have easily gained the impression that there were far more of the aircraft than in fact were on hand, and initial overseas deployments to America's bastions in the Panama Canal Zone, the Commonwealth of Puerto Rico and the Territory of Hawaii had already been completed. As of 31 March 1940 all contracted B-18 and B-18A aircraft (and the initial B-23s) had been turned over to the Air Corps, and the B-18 production line was completed. The United States Army Air Corps, as of that date, could count a total of one Boeing XB-15, thirteen Y1B-17s, one B-17A and thirty-nine B-17Bs in its inventory, as well as some B-10Bs and B-12As, and its primary bombardment strike force, consisting of 135 active B-18s and 214 active B-18As. As of that date, these aircraft were deployed as in the accompanying table.

Incredibly, the service had lost only a small number of aircraft between initial delivery and this date, despite very heavy utilisation and overseas deployments. A total of ten B-18s, twenty-six B-18As and one B-23 had been lost to a variety of causes, but none attributed to materiel failure.[18] Only a few of the stations shown, obviously, could muster B-18s in squadron strength and, not surprisingly, these were located on the east and west coasts, in Hawaii, the Canal Zone, Florida and Puerto Rico. The largest concentration, at Barksdale Field, Louisiana, all but three of which were B-18As, were seeing intensive service there in training and forming the cadres for yet more nascent units that would be quickly deployed.

By 30 September 1940, as the Air Corps continued its rapid expansion and the world situation further deteriorated, the B-18, B-18A and B-23 force was further redistributed, although some assignments remained essentially unchanged, and the dispositions were as in the accompanying table.

31 March 1940		Active
Variant	Station	on hand
B-18	Aberdeen Proving Ground, MA	2
B-18	Langley Field, VA	5
B-18	Mitchel Field, NY	2
B-18	Chanute Field, IL	2
B-18	Maxwell Field, AL	6
B-18	Scott Field, IL	1
B-18	Selfridge Field, MI	1
B-18	Wright Field, OH	3
B-18	Barksdale Field, LA	3
B-18	Brooks Field, c	1
B-18	Kelly Field, TX	4
B-18	Randolph Field, TX	5
B-18	Hamilton Field, CA	3
B-18	March Field, CA	4
B-18	Moffett Field, CA	1
B-18	France and Albrook Field, CZ	33
B-18	Territory of Hawaii	53
B-18	Middletown Air Depot, OH	1
B-18A	Aberdeen Proving Ground, MA	1
B-18A	Bolling Field, DC	11
B-18A	Langley Field, VA	24
B-18A	Mitchel Field, NY	28
B-18A	Chanute Field, IL	2
B-18A	Maxwell Field, AL	6
B-18A	Wright Field, OH	5
B-18A	Barksdale Field, LA	49
B-18A	Lowry Field, CO	5
B-18A	San Antonio Air Depot, TX	1
B-18A	Hamilton Field, CA	20
B-18A	March Field, CA **	43
B-18A	Miami, FL	9
B-18A	Borinquen Field, PR	9
B-23	Wright Field, OH	2

* Note: As will be described later in this account, by this time, a number of B-18 and B-18A aircraft had their bomb racks and guns removed in order to fully equip all of the B-18s and B-18As that had been deployed overseas, and these aircraft had the seldom seen "M" suffix applied to their designations temporarily.

** 1 condemned aircraft.

The pilot (left) and co-pilot (right) were within easy arm's reach of the 'Avigator' in the B-18A, and crew communication was excellent. *Eighth Air Force Museum*

30 September 1940		Active
Variant	Station	on hand
B-18	Langley Field, VA	5
B-18	MacDill Field, FL	2
B-18	Mitchel Field, NY	2
B-18	Orlando, FL	1
B-18	Wright Field, OH	1
B-18	Barksdale Field, LA	2
B-18	Hamilton Field, CA	2
B-18	March Field, CA	3
B-18	McChord Field, WA	2
B-18	Moffett Field, CA	1
B-18	Salt Lake City, UT	4
B-18	France and Albrook Field, CZ	28
B-18	Territory of Hawaii	53
B-18M	Orlando, FL	1
B-18M*	Chanute Field, IL	2
B-18M	Maxwell Field, AL	3
B-18M	Scott Field, IL	1
B-18M	Selfridge Field, MI	1
B-18M	Wright Field, OH	3
B-18M	Barksdale Field, LA	1
B-18M	Brooks Field, TX	1
B-18M	Kelly Field, TX	4
B-18M	Randolph Field, TX	5
B-18A	Aberdeen Proving Ground, MA	1
B-18A	Langley Field, VA	17
B-18A	MacDill Field, FL	8
B-18A	Mitchel Field, NY	27
B-18A	Orlando, FL	1
B-18A	Selfridge Field, MI	1
B-18A	Wright Field, OH	3
B-18A	Barksdale Field, LA	42
B-18A	Lowry Field, CO	19
B-18A	Hamilton Field, CA	7
B-18A	March Field, CA	16
B-18A	McChord Field, WA	22
B-18A	Salt Lake City, UT	6
B-18A	Borinquen Field, PR	9
B-18A	France and Albrook Field, CZ	4
B-18M*	Miami, Florida	7
B-18M	Bolling Field, DC	12
B-18M	Chanute Field, MI	2
B-18M	Wright Field, OH	3
B-18M	Brooks Field, TX	1
B-23	Aberdeen Proving Ground, MA	1
B-23	Bolling Field, DC	1
B-23	Orlando, FL	11
B-23	Maxwell Field, AL	2
B-23	Wright Field, OH	2
B-23	Lowry Field, CO	1
B-23	March Field, CA	1
B-23	McChord Field, WA	17
B-23	Pratt & Whitney, Hartford, CT	**
B-23	Douglas Aircraft Co., Santa Monica, CA	1

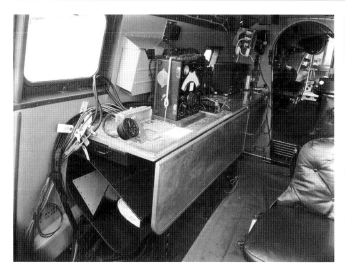

A veritable dream come true for 'Avigators' and radio operators, both the B-18 and B-18A were equipped with dedicated work stations (with a fold-down unit that could make it even larger), as well as windows. The door on the right in this view is towards the aft and bomb bay area. The two seats, one visible on the left, were on tracks that could allow movement fore and aft. *Walter 'Matt' Jefferies collection, Wright State University, #5543*

Unlike other contemporary designs, the B-18 and B-18A, because of their very roomy interior area, could be used as both transports and ambulances. Here, two stretcher cases are easily accommodated, with room for an attendant to function. *NARA RG342FH 21310AC*

The chairs for the 'Avigator' (nearest) and radio operator on the port side of the main cabin, looking aft. The radio operator had equipment for which he was responsible on both sides of the cabin. Note the shades that could be lowered on the two windows.
Walter 'Matt' Jefferies collection, Wright State University, #5544

The bombardier on his elevated perch, as viewed from just aft of the nose gun position and near the lower crew entrance hatch. Getting up there required some dexterity, but once there, what a view! *USAF via Dana Bell*

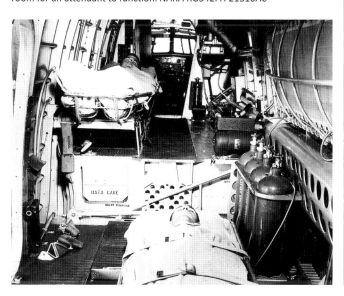

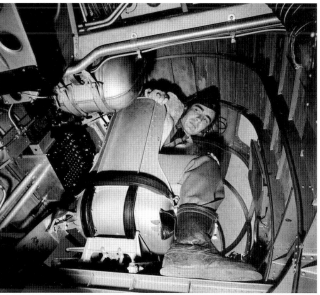

As of the above date, the Air Corps could muster, in addition to its widely dispersed B-18, B-18A and B-23 fleet, the single Boeing XB-15, the thirteen Y1B-17s, one B-17A, thirty-eight B-17Bs, seventeen B-17Cs and the first Consolidated XB-24, as well as assorted B-10Bs, B-12As and B-12AMs.

The Air Corps also came to the realisation on 24 October 1940 that the B-18s, B-18As and new B-23s entering the operational units could no longer be regarded as Heavy Bombers, and effective from that date reclassified all existing examples as Medium Bombardment aircraft.

By the end of 1940, nine months after the above report of distribution, the B-18 and B-18A force had experienced radical redistribution, and the aircraft were being utilised extremely heavily

The controls, pedestals and instrument arrays on B-18A series aircraft experienced changes throughout the production process. This shows the array on B-18As AC37-458 to 37-594, inclusive, as of 20 May 1938. *T.O. No 01-40EB-1*

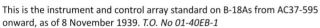

This is the instrument and control array standard on B-18As from AC37-595 onward, as of 8 November 1939. *T.O. No 01-40EB-1*

This cockpit array was dated 8 May 1939, and is slightly different from the others shown in some details. The cockpit afforded good visibility for the pilots. *Boeing Archives SM-15027*

These overhead silhouettes, perhaps better than any other means, show the relative planform differences between the C-39, C-47, B-18, B-18A and B-23. *USAAF*

CARGO (TRANSPORT)		TRANSPORT		BOMBER (HEAVY)	
C-47 SKYTRAIN	S. 95' 0" / L. 64' 6"	B-23	S. 92' 0" / L. 58' 2"	B-18	S. 89' 6" / L. 56' 8"
CARGO (TRANSPORT)		BOMBER (MEDIUM)		BOMBER (MEDIUM)	
B-18 A	S. 89' 6" / L. 56' 8"	C-39	S. 85' 0" / L. 61' 6"	B-10B	S. 70' 6" / L. 44' 8"
BOMBER (MEDIUM)		CARGO (TRANSPORT)		BOMBER (MEDIUM)	
B-25 C & D MITCHELL	S. 67' 6" / L. 54' 0"	B-34 PV (NAVY) VENTURA	S. 65' 6" / L. 51'2½"	C-56 C-60A LODESTAR	S. 65' 6" / L. 49' 4"

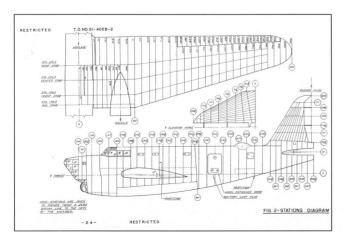

FIG. 2-STATIONS DIAGRAM

– 24 –

Major Command of Assignment	B-18	B-18A
General Headquarters Air Force units	25	124
Various Training Activities	18	7
Other Miscellaneous Activities	4	19
Territory of Alaska	–	9
Territory of Hawaii	53	–
Panama Canal Zone	28	24
Commonwealth of Puerto Rico	–	23

The stations callouts for the B-18A. Compare these with those for the earlier B-18. *NASM EDM37*

to train bombardment crews for the next generation of medium and heavy bombers just starting to leave the factory doors. So vital to this effort were these aircraft that General 'Hap' Arnold, in reviewing the distribution of the aircraft, noted in pencil at the bottom that he '… recommended approval. Training Centers must function or the whole set-up falls down and GHQAF does not get trained combat crews.' The breakout reflected forty-seven B-18s and 150 B-18As in the Continental United States and eighty-one B-18s and fifty-six B-18As stationed overseas. See table on page 50.

Arming the B-18 and B-18A: pre-war standards and early experiments

Previously published accounts of the B-18 series have invariably cast aspersions on the armament suite of the series, and invariably take the hindsight view that the aircraft were not adequately fitted with either offensive or defensive armaments.

In fact, the aircraft were armed as dictated by the wisdom current at the time of their specifications and, what is more, were in nearly every case on a par with both domestic and foreign contemporaries in mounting primarily rifle-caliber, .30 caliber Type M-1 weapons. The absence of self-sealing fuel tanks is also often cited when, in fact, not a solitary contemporary had such installations, foreign or domestic. Even the vaunted Boeing X-299, arguably the most advanced bombardment aircraft on the planet at its first flight in July 1935, with nearly twice the crew complement of the B-18, carried only five .30 caliber weapons (two more than the B-18) and eight 600lb bombs, only 800lb more than the B-18.

The dorsal turret on a B-18, shown stowed and looking aft. Note that the .30 caliber M-2 machine gun is standing vertically and, when stowed, the upper portion of the barrel protruded above the turret, a feature seldom captured in photos. *Museum of Flight 10620*

The B-18 did introduce features in defensive armament that had not been standard on any previous US bombardment aircraft, with the solitary exception of the semi-enclosed nose turret installed on late Martin B-10B aircraft. It had a spacious, easily controlled nose gun turret, and a semi-retractable dorsal turret, as well as the inevitable ventral 'tunnel gun', which seems to have enjoyed a psychological favor, if not demonstrable efficacy, in the minds of designers of virtually every pre-war bombardment and reconnaissance aircraft.

It will be observed that, on the standard production B-18 and B-18A aircraft, the front and rear turrets were, in fact, completely different designs. On the B-18 they were composed of sheets of pyralin riveted rather lightly onto supporting frames. A section was left open in each for extension of the guns, which revolved with the turrets. The rear turret slid up or down so that, when not in use, the aircraft would be free of this obviously drag-producing protuberance. The dorsal turret could be latched in a position 8 inches above the fuselage for observation purposes.

The actual gun mount on the nose turret of the B-18 was located on the turret directly below the gun port itself. It was designed so that the gun could be withdrawn into the turret entirely when not in use. Seldom noted, flexible trailing windshields were provided, which attached both above and below the guns, covering the gun port when the gun was not in use. A retractable seat was provided for the gunner and rings were provided in the flooring of the gunner's compartment for the attachment of so-called 'Monkey Tail' safety belts, as well as on the turret, for the attachment of a standard safety belt. The turret could rotate, contrary to popular belief, through a full 360º, but its latch could be set, as desired, to allow a movement of only 2½ inches if desired. To stow the gun, the gunner removed the upper flexible windshield, latched the gun into place, then rotated the turret until the actual gun port was inside the fuselage on the port (left-hand) side. The turret was never stowed on the starboard (right) side, as this would block the gunner's exit from the turret.

A detailed drawing of the B-18A dorsal turret. The operating mechanism, manual, was the same as the older turret used on the B-18. Note that when stowed and retracted, the gun barrel protruded into the slipstream above the 'tortoise-shell' housing. *NASM EDM37*

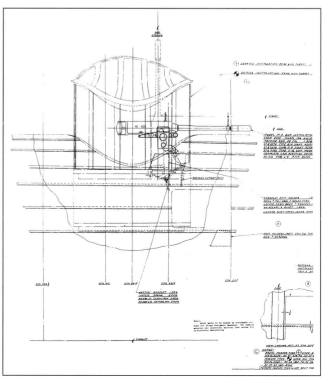

By contrast, this is the dorsal turret of B-18A AC38-592 when stowed. Note the apparatus affixed to the fuselage just aft of the turret, to the right, designed to prevent the gunner from shooting into the tail group! This is seldom seen in period photos. This aircraft survived the war as an RB-18A. *Walter 'Matt' Jefferies collection, Wright State University, #5525*

Details of the 'chin' forward nose turret as standard on B-18As, and one of the most noticeable changes from the older B-18. The housing was much more versatile in practice than it appears, although it required the gunner to be kneeling while using the gun. *Boeing Archives SM-13918*

The dorsal turret on the B-18 was extended by pulling upward on two latches. The turret had two extended positions, as noted, either 8 inches above the fuselage for observation purposes or fully extended for use of the gun, and the latches could be locked at both positions. The sliding door in the top of the turret had to be opened to get the gun into firing position. The turret could rotate through a full 360°, but a latch to the right of the gun mount could be set to prevent firing into the empennage. A retractable seat was attached to the turret, with the same safety belt provision as that in the nose turret. Sharp-eyed observers will quickly note that the dorsal turret as fitted to both the DB-1 and production B-18 aircraft was of a very different configuration from that fitted to the DB-2 and production B-18As. The DB-1/B-18 turret, when retracted, fitted almost completely smoothly into the contours of the rear fuselage, while that of the DB-2 and B-18A protruded in a streamlined manner, often referred to, even in official correspondence, as a 'clamshell' or 'tortoise-like' configuration. This latter turret was significantly improved, and enabled observation in flight without having to extend the turret 8 inches, with virtually no drag penalty.

The so-called 'tunnel gun' in both the B-18 and B-18A was located in the floor of the rear lower compartment, just aft of the camera bay, and enjoyed only two positions: stowed and firing. It was composed of two hinged sections, one metal and the other glass. A hand-crank was provided on the left side so as to enable the gunner to locate his target rearward or, when extended, downward. The glass section, which was divided and hinged together in the center, slid inward, making an opening for the barrel of the weapon, which, contrary to popular wisdom, could be either a .30 caliber gun or a .50 caliber weapon at this position. This gun could only be fired in an aft direction. Provision was also made for the installation of 500 rounds of ammunition within easy reach of each of the rear gunners, while the nose turret gunner had 600 rounds within easy reach.

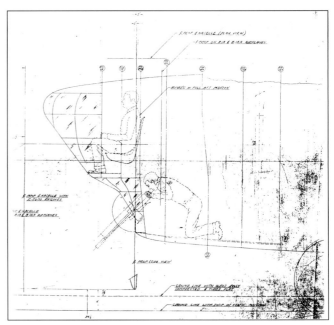

Above: This cutaway view shows the relative position of the bombardier when seated at his upper station and the gun position he was also expected to man in combat below. Movement from one to the other would have required some exertion. *NASM EDM37*

The nose or 'chin' gun position of the B-18A viewed from inside. The position was described as 'a bit draughty' while in actual use, and would probably have been of marginal defensive utility in a conventional sense. Once B-18As started performing maritime reconnaissance and anti-submarine patrols, however, it was very nearly the perfect design. *Boeing Archives SM-13917*

The so-called 'tunnel gun' or ventral gun position on a B-18 on 13 July 1937. Contrary to many reports, this position could accommodate either a .30 caliber or .50 caliber weapon, although in the event, due to the shortage of .50 caliber guns, the heavier weapons were only rarely installed. Note the frame across the opening designed to limit the track of the gun so as to avoid damage to the aircraft, and the fact that the hatch is actually angled upwards towards the rear. The dorsal turret frame can just be seen above and to the rear. *Boeing Archives SM-11571*

The 'tunnel gun' installation in the B-18A series was different in detail from that in the earlier B-18s. In this 31 May 1938 view the hatch is shown closed and the weapon secured in a special muzzle restraint device. *Boeing Archives SM-15480*

A schematic of the 'tunnel gun' installation on B-18s, which reveals that the hatch was not 'flat' on the bottom of the fuselage as is usually assumed, but rather angled upwards to the rear to facilitate use. It came into its element when anti-submarine missions commenced. *NASM EDM37*

Although much has been made of the bomb load of the B-18 and B-18A over the years, it is seldom noted that the aircraft could in fact be loaded in either Design Useful Load or Overload conditions, depending on tactical necessity. The Design Useful Bomb Load could be any one of the following:

    1 – 2,000lb weapon:

        Type M-34, MK-I, MK-IMII or MK-IMI

    2 – 1,100lb weapons:

        Type M-33, MK-III

    4 – 600lb weapons:

        Type M-32, MK-IMI or MK-III

    8 – 300lb weapons:

        Type M-31, MK-I or MK-IMI

    20 –100lb weapons:

        Type M-30, MK-I, MK-IMI or MK-IMII

These bombs had to be loaded on their respective stations as indicated by number plates on the bomb racks themselves. Alternatively, the B-18A could be loaded as follows, with a commensurate reduction in fuel load, or as a genuine war overload condition:

    2 – 2,000lb weapons:

        Type M-34, MK-I, MK-IMI or MK-IMII

    4 – 1,100lb weapons:

        Type M-33, MK-III

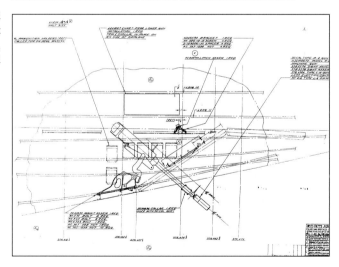

    6 – 600lb weapons:

        Type M-32, MK-IMI or MK-III

    14 – 300lb weapons:

        Type M-31, MK-I or MK-IMI

    32 – 100lb weapons:

        Type M-30, MK-I, MK-IMI or MK-IMII

The controls for dropping the bomb load consisted of electrical selective release by means of either electrical contacts, which could be automatically closed within the bombsight, by means of a momentary

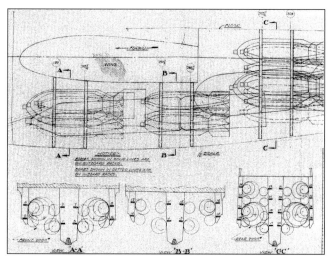

The B-18 and B-18A had nearly identical bomb bays, and could be configured to carry an extensive combination of weapons on both inboard and outboard racks. The bay was much longer than that on a B-17. *NASM EDM37*

Both the B-18 and B-18A featured a retractable bomb winch system, which could be manually or electrically operated; integral to the aircraft, it facilitated loading at dispersal stations. Here is the manual system installed under the port (left) wing, which could hoist a 2,000lb bomb. *Boeing Archives SM-10617*

contact switch manually operated, or as a manual salvo release of all bombs simultaneously. The manual emergency release handle for opening the bomb bay doors and salvoing the bombs was located at the bottom of the engine control quadrant in the cockpit, and could be accessed by either the pilot or co-pilot.

The question of bombsights in B-18 and B-18A series aircraft is seldom addressed. In fact, they did not become equipped with Norden

series sights until they had entered into dedicated service as bombardier trainers well after the US entered the war. However, extensive pre-war trials with Norden and a variety of other experimental bombsights were made by the Armaments Branch, and by 31 July 1940 they had even experimented with a comparison between glide bombing and low-altitude bombing versus the prevailing wisdom of '...high-altitude, precision bombing', experiments that have nearly always been placed much later in time. 'O' Series bombsights were, for example, fitted to B-18A series aircraft serial numbers AC37-555 to AC37-594 inclusive, and these had a glide-bombing feature incorporated. No other pre-war USAAC aircraft had this feature. The resulting tests, comparing the accuracy of this type of attack with that proposed by the so-called 'bomber mafia', were most revealing, as they clearly indicated that glide-bombing attacks by B-18 aircraft were vastly superior in terms of accuracy.

With all of that, as early as 14 July 1938 the Air Corps had devoted considerable thought to the problem of defending its new, standard heavy bomber. Extensive studies of 'field of fire' diagrams, together with numerous functional tests of the defensive armament installations on both B-18s and the new B-18A resulted in '...a belief that defense to the rear is inadequate. Action has been taken to determine the best arrangement for protection against attack from the vulnerable area for both B-18 and B-18A aircraft without radically affecting the tail structure or interfering with other equipment.' In short, the Air Corps recognised the reality of this shortcoming, especially in view of scattered reports that the Materiel Division was receiving from, of all places, the Spanish Civil War. By 16 May 1940 the Armaments Branch actually conceded that '...it is generally accepted that [the] existing gun mounts in B-18 and B-18A series aircraft are unsatisfactory, because guns are thrown off target by overturning [the] moment of firing.'

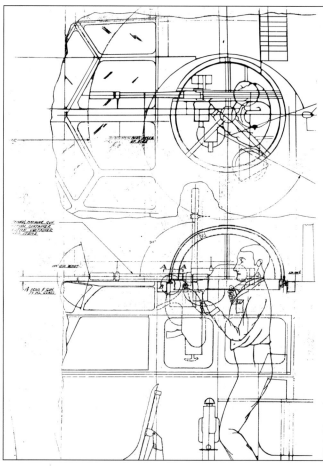

This drawing shows details of the proposed forward dorsal turret for B-18As, which was apparently to have been manually operated and non-retractable. Note that the gun muzzle extends over the cockpit, which might have been an issue during night operations. *Boeing Archives*

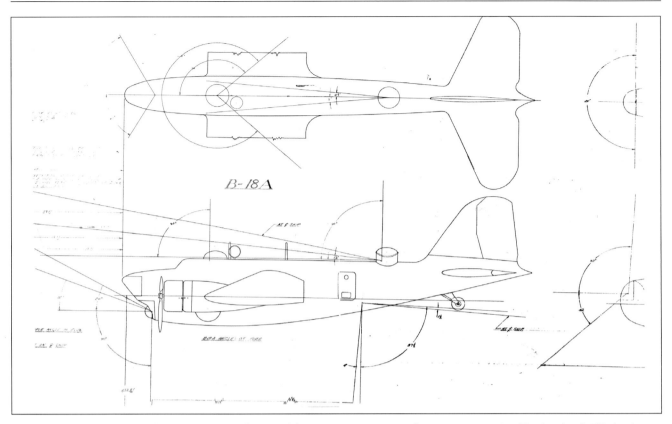

By 1941 Douglas was well aware that the B-18A was deficient in defensive armament compared to contemporary US and foreign aircraft. This drawing reveals that serious consideration was given to installation of a forward dorsal turret in place of the upper hatch, but this would have been at the expense of the work station for the 'Avigator'. The drawings also shows the angles of fire of the various gun positions. *Boeing Archives*

This study resulted in the Air Corps actually assigning B-18 AC37-34 to the Armaments Branch of the Materiel Division at Wright Field for very extensive tests and development of a number of novel solutions to the defensive problem. These included:

(a) the installation of a power mount in the nose turret (which has to date eluded identification)

(b) a stabiliser that was attached to the dorsal turret to counter-balance the air forces that were clearly affecting the operation of the flexibly mounted gun in that turret

(c) installation of an experimental Curtiss turret (also not identified) procured under FY37 Program funding

(d) a large number of miscellaneous tests involving various bomb sights

By 13 August 1938 the Armaments Branch had commenced an extensive study into the possibility of installing a remotely controlled tail gun in the B-18 and B-18A series aircraft, as it had concluded that this was the only sure means of covering a zone to the rear of the aircraft that simply could not be covered by the dorsal turret or tunnel guns. Although the merits of such an installation were abundantly demonstrated, it was regarded as impractical from an engineering as well as funding standpoint to retrofit the production aircraft with such an installation. Such an installation was in fact tested on AC37-34 circa 7 March 1940, but no illustrations of this installation have been located. It is, however, clear that this study influenced the Douglas decision to make such an installation in the B-23, the first modern-era US production aircraft to feature a dedicated tail gun installation as a standard feature.

Elsewhere, Air Corps commands had addressed problems with the defensive gun installations on their own initiative. It is generally not known, for instance, that nearly every B-18 transferred to Hawaii (and thus to the Philippines) had its front gunner's compartment doors

modified locally, and was different from all other Air Corps B-18s. The impetus for this modification has not been identified, but may have had something to do with egress from the turret area in the event of a forced landing at sea, the probabilities of which were obviously higher in the islands.

Study was also given to modifying the original rear dorsal turret on B-18A series aircraft to accommodate the heavier .50 caliber gun. This would have required that the turret be hoisted even further into the windstream, however, and that the gunner perform a balancing act while manning the weapon. The proportions of the rear fuselage shown here are smaller than they actually were. *Boeing Archives*

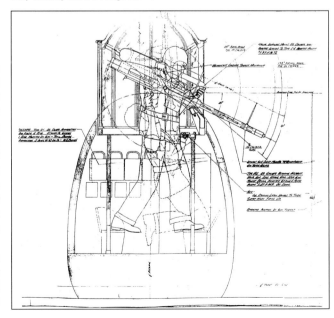

The original DB-1, by the time of this image dated 22 September 1939 at Aberdeen Proving Ground, Maryland, had been long since accepted by the Air Corps and designated as a B-18X with serial number AC37-51 and radically converted to mount a M1897 75mm howitzer in the former bomb bay area. Note the simple ring-and-bead-type gunsight used by the pilot to aim the weapon just ahead of the cockpit. *NARA RG342, Sarah Clark collection*

That 75mm Howitzer

But unquestionably the most bizarre pre-war armament experiment involving the B-18 was the experience of the venerable B-18 AC37-51, none other than the prototype DB-1 uniquely configured, and which, during the following tests, was often cited in official correspondence as type B-18X.

Although this aircraft has been reported upon previously, the impetus behind this installation has been poorly understood, and even incorrectly reported. While it may be true that the Air Corps gave some thought to developing such an aircraft as a dedicated ground attack aircraft, the official reason for the installation was to test the concept for use in the very heavily armed and exotic Curtiss-Wright XP-71 bomber interceptor.[19]

By 29 August 1939 the Fairfield Air Depot had extensively modified AC37-51 to incorporate a standard 75mm Field Artillery howitzer on a T-1 Aircraft Gun Mount, and, contrary to many previous reports, extensive ground and aerial firing trials were carried out. Indeed, it was used to fire against towed aerial targets at Valparaiso, Florida, with surprisingly good results. Although the initial ground trials resulted in some fracturing of cockpit glass, this was quickly adjusted for, and the overall results were as follows:

(1) A total of 50 rounds was fired statically while on the ground. The first two rounds fired resulted in the failure of the gunner's compartment windows. After three rounds, however, no additional failures were noted. The cockpit windows cracked after four rounds, however, at 75% of normal pressure.

(2) Subsequent rounds caused distortion of the nose plate immediately forward of the end of the steel blast plate, distortion of the inboard engine cowling fasteners, and there was distortion of the cover plates along the leading edge of the wing over the fuel line. In fact, they were so badly distorted inward that piping clamp bolts punched holes in the doors.

(3) After this, the blast deflector was removed. During the firing of the next ten to fifteen rounds, a spectacular muzzle flash was noted and there was some additional damage to the cowlings and fairings as noted above.

(4) Repairs were made, including some strengthening of the damaged parts and introduction of some rubber cushioning, and twenty-six rounds were fired in flight at 130mph indicated air speed at 5,000 feet. The aircraft, to the surprise of the flight crews, remained completely stable under all conditions while being fired in flight. In fact, the pilot, who actually aimed and fired the gun using a Type M-2 gunsight in his windscreen area, released his hands from the control column when one round was fired and the aircraft was absolutely rock-steady.

As a result of these tests, the Air Corps concluded that a 75mm gun could in fact be installed in an aircraft of this approximate size in a satisfactory way, but observed that, in any such future installations, the muzzle of the gun should be '…forward of all parts of the primary structure, all windows adjacent to the cannon should incorporate sponge-rubber mountings for the glass, and adequate ventilation should be provided for the gunner's compartment.' These trials clearly did not benefit the still-born XP-71, but did in fact come into play during the conversion of North American B-25H Mitchell series medium bombers during the war years.

During the trials a Northrop A-17A was used as a 'chase' plane, and also had a mount for motion picture and still pictures to be taken. The trials continued well into April 1940 at Aberdeen Proving Ground, MD.

Additional aerial test firing trials with the 75mm gun were made around 9 May 1940, under the auspices of the Air Corps Tactical School at Maxwell Field, AL, using a B-18A with an A-5 windlass to tow the target. During these tests, only shrapnel ammunition was used, but attacks were also made on targets on the water. By this time the pilot had been furnished with a Type N-2 gunsight. Cited as Project 50, these late trials concluded on 27 June 1940, with the final

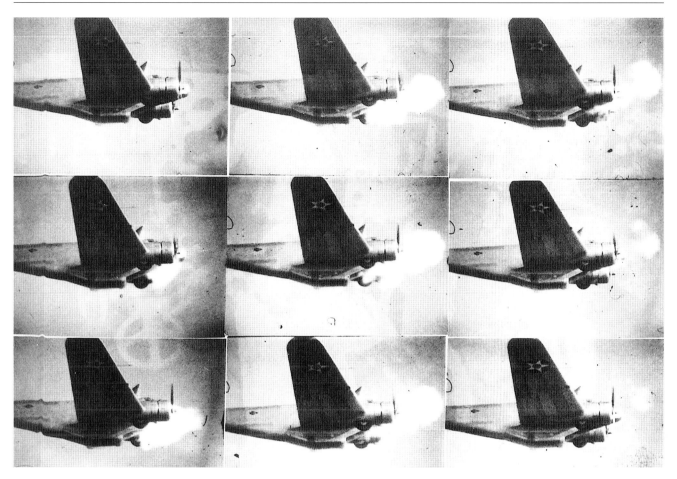

This series of nine time-sequenced views shows B-18X AC37-51 aloft while firing the 75mm howitzer twice in very rapid succession. The system proved to be remarkably accurate against both ground and towed targets, even with only a very rudimentary gunsight. The odd triangular structure above the cabin seen in the first image housed cameras to record the shots and trajectory, and remained on the aircraft in the flight tests as well. *NARA RG342, Sarah Clark collection*

report stating that firing tests concluded beyond any doubt the '… ability of this weapon to hit, effectively, single aircraft at ranges of 1,500, 2,000, 2,500 and 3,000 yards.'

This oddity was exhibited at an Air Corps open-house at Bolling Field, DC, with the 75mm gun installation partially shrouded, and bearing a most unusual camouflage scheme. Although considerable discussion ensued as to what should be done with the 'B-18X', including returning it to 'stock' B-18 configuration, it was not until 9 January 1941 that Master Sergeant Portor R. Bell of the Ordnance Department at Wright Field was sent to Chanute Field, IL, where the aircraft had ended up, to supervise the removal of the 75mm gun and sight. The pioneering aircraft ended its days innocuously as a Class 26 ground instructional airfield at Chanute's Technical School.

After-production modification

As with every production aircraft, as they entered line service operational crews found deficiencies and items of equipment that could be improved upon, and via a tortuous and often confusing series of 'through channels' recommendations, usually commenced by the feared Unsatisfactory Reports (U/Rs), these would sometimes find their way into directed modifications that could be accomplished at unit level in the field or by depot maintenance. The B-18 series was no exception, although the series proved to be remarkably free of really extensive post-production modifications, compared to wartime mass-production service types, with the exception of the elective modifications to become B-18Bs and B-18Cs.

One of the earliest modification was directed on 11 January 1938, conveyed by T.O. 01-40E-11, which instructed that all service B-18

aircraft then in the service (with the notable exception of the 'hybrid' AC37-51) be fitted with the RC-20 Marker Beacon Receiving Equipment, and that these units were being distributed to every operating unit without need to resort to requisition.

This was followed on 8 April 1938 by T.O. 01-40E-22, which pertained to B-18s serials AC36-262 to 36-332 inclusive and, for some reason, AC37-34. These aircraft were to be fitted with SCR-242-A Radio Compass gear.

One of the most recognisable changes was instructed by T.O. 01-40E-46 dated 5 August 1938, which stipulated the Installation of Long Exhaust Pipes, and this T.O. pertained to B-18s serials AC36-262 to 36-274 and AC36-276 to 36-342 inclusive.

T.O. 01-40-20 was the first Tech Order to pertain to both B-18s and B-18As, and was dated 10 October 1938. It directed the reworking of the bomb bay tank installations in B-18As AC37-458 to 37-460 and all B-18s to facilitate the installation and removal of bomb bay fuel tanks and their attachment fittings, a feature of the aircraft that dramatically extended its operational range. B-18As AC37-461 and all subsequent B-18As had these modifications built in at the factory.

On 24 October 1938 T.O. 091-40E-56 was issued, which covered the installation of SCR-242-B Radio Compass Equipment in B-18s AC37-4 to 37-33 inclusive. This was a depot-level installation.

On 13 January 1939 T.O. 01-40-67 was issued, which stipulated a mid-career change for a number of B-18s and B-18As, nearly all of which, remarkably, survived to be returned to normal combat configuration. This was the installation of C-4 Windlass Tow Target Equipment in B-18s AC37-10 to 37-33 and B-18As AC37-459 to 37-466. This vital but boring duty, interspersed with moments of

The initial ground shots of the 75mm cannon installation in the B-18X at Aberdeen were not without incident. The very well-travelled glass on the pilot's side sliding window was shattered, and there was some other minor damage, but the structure held up remarkably well overall. Note the pilot's gunsight just to the left in this 25 September 1939 view.
NARA RG342, Sarah Clark collection

terror as both aerial and ground gunners got a bit too close to the 'tow' aircraft rather than the drogue chute, usually marked the end of a service aircraft's career. In the case of the B-18s and B-18As affected, it was merely a momentary lull in their service lives.

A key recognition feature change, often commented upon by sharp-eyed observers of the B-18 series, was that dictated on 20 February 1939, which advised that B-18As AC37-540 to 37-569 were to have 'flared' engine ring cowls, designed to help reduce cylinder base temperatures.

A rather late Tech Order, T.O. 01-40E-100, applied to the reworking of the rear gunner's door window latch assembly, a seemingly minor 'fix', on all B-18, B-18M, B-18A and B-18AM aircraft then in the service – the first 'fleet-wide' change order. In fact, this was a rather important modification, as it prevented the rear (dorsal) gunner's window from opening accidentally in flight, which had caused numerous frightening (if not catastrophic) incidents up to that time.

A Tech Order issued on 12 February 1942 pertaining to all B-18 series aircraft appears to have been T.O. 01-40E-114, which had to do with a host of relatively minor internal radio equipment mounting and switch features.

The final B-18 Tech Order that could be located was issued on 26 June 1942 and, oddly, was T.O. 01-40E-101, which appears to have been out of order. It directed replacement of .30 caliber adapters and installation of blast tubes on all surviving B-18 and B-18A series aircraft.

Oddly, not a solitary Tech Order has been located pertaining to B-18B or B-18C series aircraft, and it is assumed that these were classified because of the nature of the sensitive equipment that they carried – a most unusual procedure for Technical Orders and Change Orders.

With these raw numbers in mind, let us now turn to the operational deployments of the new bombers, and an organisation that was destined to exist only briefly, but which contributed significantly to the rapid expansion of the Army Air Corps into the Army Air Forces. That organisation was the General Headquarters Air Force, most commonly cited as the GHQAF.

The B-18X was painted in a unique camouflage scheme and exhibited with other Air Corps equipment of the day at a special exhibition at Bolling Field, District of Columbia, just across the Anacostia from the National Capital building before the war. Note that a drape has been deployed to cover the 75mm gun installation. Note also what appears to be a spotting gun attached to the starboard (right) main undercarriage member! *NARA RG342FH 118196AC*

CHAPTER THREE

Operational Units

The General Headquaters Air Force (GHQAF)

The extremely rapid evolution of air power worldwide led, almost directly, to the creation of the Air Corps element known as the General Headquarters Air Force on 1 March 1935 – the same Federal fiscal year in which was formulated in C.P.36-25 the requirement for the aircraft that were to become the B-17 and B-18.

The first commander of the GHQAF was Major General Frank M. Andrews, and over the course of the following four years it achieved recognition – although often misunderstood – nationwide as a central element in the defensive forces of the United States.

In 1933 the Drum Board, noted earlier, made the initial analysis that led to the creation of this force. It was organised to fill a perceived need for a highly mobile and powerful striking force that could be moved quickly from one part of the country to another. The organisation evolved through a very deliberate service test period, including some of the largest maneuvers involving Air Corps elements to that time, in the immediate pre-war years.

For all intents and purposes, the GHQAF consisted of all of the operational combat squadrons in the Air Corps then located within in the Continental United States, some twenty-nine squadrons by 1940, organised into three tactical Wings. The 1st Wing, with headquarters

at March Field, California, consisted of two bombardment Groups, one attack Group and two semi-autonomous reconnaissance Squadrons. The 2nd Wing, on the east coast, had its headquarters at Langley Field, Virginia, but differed from the west coast organisation in that it included two bombardment Groups, the two semi-autonomous reconnaissance Squadrons, as well as two pursuit Groups. The 3rd Wing was headquartered at Barksdale Field, Louisiana, and was the smallest, with but one attack Group and one pursuit Group. The locations and constitution of B-18 operating units are detailed later in this chapter.

There is a tendency amongst students of US aviation history to think in terms entirely of combat squadrons – the fliers themselves and their airplanes – and neglect the very considerable system of services of maintenance and supply essential to support actual air operations. Within the GHQAF these services were provided by the Air Base structure, commands that consisted of the facilities and installations required for the operation, maintenance and supply of a specific air force. These Air Bases, names which by this time were etched into every day Air Corps life, had large geographical areas of responsibility, as well as scattered auxiliary airdromes that fell under their control. These were, essentially, 'housekeeping' organisations for the combat and maneuver elements, and saw to it that facilities at both the permanent stations and the auxiliaries were such that the combat units could move in and, in theory, start operations without undue exertions. By 1940 there were six such Air Bases specifically tasked to support the GHQAF. They were Langley Field, near Hampton, Virginia; Mitchel Field on Long Island, New York; Selfridge Field, Michigan; March Field, California; Hamilton Field, California; and Barksdale Field, Louisiana.

Only about thirty B-18s were assigned to domestic units of the General Headquarters Air Force (GHQAF) prior to the 15 November 1937 inauguration of the use of unit and aircraft-within-unit 'designators'. Prior to that date these aircraft were assigned arbitrary 'Field Numbers' at the whim of unit and base commanders, primarily at Hamilton, March, Langley and Mitchel Fields. Number 183, shown here, is otherwise anonymous, but nearly brand-new. *Fred C. Dickey Jr via George Steven*

Field Numbers 606 and 609 were 'straight' B-18s assigned to units of the GHQAF prior to 15 November 1937, and unfortunately very little information survives about this short-lived numbering system. No 609 was photographed in Missouri, probably at Robertson Field. *via David W. Ostrowski/Art Kreiger via Brian R. Baker*

Although throwing down the gauntlet to the 'bad guys', this postcard, sold at Air Corps PX outlets early in the Second World War, actually depicts a pre-war, GHQAF Langley Field-based B-18. The engine cowls were probably either red or blue. *Authors' collection*

The proud parents of young 2Lt Boardman C. Reed, Blanche and Phelps Reed, stand beside B-18A AC37-561 (coded 17B 47) of the 34th Bomb Squadron (M), 17th Bomb Group at Santa Barbara, CA, on 18 December 1940. This aircraft was later modified to B-18B standard and saw extensive anti-submarine service, surviving the war to become NC-66272. The father of 'B.C.' never flew once in an aircraft, but was very proud of his son, while 'Bunny' often flew with her son – once while wearing his officer's cap in the co-pilot's seat of a brand-new B-17E! *B.C. Reed*

UNCLE SAM'S AIR MEN
OUR DO AND DARE MEN
PROVE HUN AND JAP KNAVERY
NO MATCH FOR THEIR BRAVERY

One of the very first B-18As assigned to the GHQAF, Field Number 132, was operated by the Reserve Section of the GHQAF, probably at Langley Field. *via Robert L. Taylor*

BQ 32 was B-18A AC37-558, shown here with the GHQAF's 95th Bomb Squadron (M), 17th Bomb Group. The 'new' designators, such as BQ 32, started to be used in November 1937. This aircraft was destined to become a B-18B and B-18C and saw extensive service as such in the anti-submarine war, surviving the war as a Class 26 instructional airframe at Long Beach. *NMUSAF*

This 19th Bomb Group B-18 was probably assigned to the 30th Bomb Squadron (H) at March Field, CA, in 1940. The prop spinners are noteworthy, and are probably the same color as the engine cowls, probably black. Note the designator also painted under the port wing. *via Scott Swanson*

BS 31 was also a 19th Bomb Group B-18, and had an 'A' Flight Command Band around the rear fuselage. It was probably a 30th Bomb Squadron aircraft, and served as the camera ship for the classic movie *Test Pilot*. *via Al Hansen*

Wearing the insignia of the 32nd Bomb Squadron (H), 19th Bomb Group, BS 34 also displayed the designator on the upper left wing, just visible. It has a rudder clamp in place at the base of the rudder, tethered to a line running to the crew entry door. *via Rich Dann*

As of 1 March 1935, a little over two years before the first B-18s would arrive, the bombardment elements of the GHQAF, consisting for the most part of Martin B-10s, trained under the same general directive nationwide, but experienced diverse results in terms of proficiency, and it was quickly realised that combat units from different stations were unable to work together without a 'sorting out' period of combined training. Clearly this would not do, as the organisation of the GHQAF was intended to defeat this very tendency. As a consequence, intensive attention was focused immediately on uniform training directives and methods throughout all units of the GHQAF, and this augured very well indeed for the smooth introduction of the B-18 and other newer tactical aircraft into the force in the years that followed.

The GHQ Air Force has been described, especially by the very vocal strategic bombardment and separate service advocates of the day – the so-called 'bomber mafia' – as a '…step in the right direction'. This proved to be an apt description of the relatively short-lived organisation, which was principally handicapped by the inevitable split in existing air power between the Air Corps proper and the GHQAF, not having its own budget, Army Corps commanders retaining administrative control over airmen, and, ultimately, the War Department General Staff retaining authority over all air matters. Major General Frank Andrews, GHQ Air Force commander in 1938, speaking at the Army War College, stated unequivocally that the US could best defend her borders by attacking any enemy force '…as far from our shores as we can reach him,' and in those few words summarised the basic emphasis of the GHQ Air Force for the remainder of its existence.

The introduction of the B-18 and the successor B-18As into GHQ Air Force units between late 1937 and September 1939 reveals the turbulence that was impacting the force, as well as the transfer of early 'pug-nosed' B-18s to – mainly – overseas commands as more modern 'shark-nosed' B-18As became available. By 31 December 1937 the command could muster a total of forty-six B-18s. Three months later, on 31 March 1938, this had increased to fifty-six. After a busy summer, by 30 September 1938 a total of seventy-two B-18s and the first five B-18As had been distributed to units. Transfers of B-18s to other commands, mainly Hawaii and Panama, were reflected in the 31 March 1939 Order of Battle, when only thirty-two B-18s remained, but the census of B-18As had risen to eighty-four. The shift continued throughout that year, and by 30 September 1939 GHQ Air Force units had but twenty-one B-18s remaining, but 158 B-18As. This was to rise to a total of 191 B-18 and B-18A aircraft by 23 March 1940, when they were distributed as shown in the accompanying table.

GHQ Air Force B-18 Assignments 23 March 1940

Station	Aircraft Allocated	Aircraft Actually on hand and Notes
Langley Field, Virginia	22	38
Mitchel Field, New York	51	29
Selfridge Field, Michigan	0	1
Barksdale Field, Louisiana	47	52
Hamilton Field, California	23	24
March Field, California	45	46 (1 actually at Sacramento)
Moffett Field, California	1	1
TOTAL	189	192 (2 of which were surplus) (see Note*)

Note* Four of the B-18As at Hamilton Field, California were under GHQ Air Force orders for transfer to March Field at this date. A.C.37-51, equipped with a 75mm cannon at the time, was unallocated but regarded as a GHQ Air Force asset. One of the B-18s then at Wright Field (A.C.37-587) was equipped with an O-1 bomb sight and was actually on loan to Wright Field from a unit at Mitchel Field. Seven of the 12 aircraft then at Maxwell Field, Alabama, were on loan to the Air Corps Tactical School there from GHQ Air Force units at March Field (1), Hamilton Field (2), Mitchel Field (3) and Langley Field (1).

The provision of facilities and equipment was not a direct responsibility of the GHQ Air Force, a burden that the leadership was probably glad not to have. However, while relieved of the burden, the organisation still very much suffered from the effects of shortages resulting from the inability of the Air Corps to meet all of its needs. Shortages of equipment, together with shortages of personnel, were the main drag on the readiness of its units for combat – and for the program of expansion and training that was to overshadow combat readiness after 1938. The shortage of what were termed 'strategic airdromes', often compared to that of dedicated coastal Naval bases, was a serious problem, and was one of the seldom recognised impediments to mobility and the grandiose expansion plans that looked so great on paper.

A partial recognition of these problems was manifested in a decision, in March 1939, to place the GHQ Air Force directly under the Chief of the Air Corps, primarily to cope with the mammoth logistical problems the force was enduring. However, they were separated again in November 1940, but this time the split was essentially negated by the appointment of General Arnold to the War Department General Staff (WDGS) as Deputy Chief of Staff for Air, a position that enabled him to coordinate the two sections of the air arm rather effectively for the first time.

But out in the field, the numbers and types of aircraft assigned to the organisation, as late as August 1940, as can be seen in the accompanying tables, were an immediate and constant disability. Given, for example, the 2nd Wing's high density of proponents of long-range, very heavy bombardment (read B-17), the Wing commander bemoaned

Another pre-war 32nd Bomb Squadron (H), 19th Bomb Group B-18A, BS 36 appears to have yellow engine cowls and a watch dog painted on the lower window of the crew entrance door! *via Robert L. Taylor*

During the pre-war years reconnaissance squadrons were attached to Groups. R32 was a B-18A assigned to the 38th Reconnaissance Squadron (L/R), 19th Bomb Group, as of 28 July 1939, and sported black and yellow chequered engine cowls. The individual aircraft number, 32, was split on either side of the bomb aimer's window on the nose. *via Ted Young*

the B-18s assigned as '…the chief thorn: slow, weak, and short of range'. But the B-18 was, in fact, what they had the most of, and though its range was often decried by those who hadn't studied the numbers, its staying power was admitted to be enormous. The attitude of the 2nd Bomb Group was almost certainly shaded by the fact that, having been the first to receive and operate Y1B-17s in numbers, and regarding itself as 'the elite', by 1942 had been '…reduced to patrols of the Atlantic Coast, and looking forward to new, radar-equipped planes. When they arrived, they were old B-18s, dignified, because of the radar accessories, by the suffixion of B' – so read the official history of the unit.[20]

The chief focus of the GHQAF was in melding combat crews into flying teams. While on the surface not a new idea, it had not been routinely extended to aircraft crews until the training of tactical air units was centralised under the GHQAF. This contribution by the numerically prevalent B-18 and B-18As assigned to GHQAF units, as revealed in the following organisational breakdown, was unquestionably one of the greatest services performed by the Douglas twins, and has received scant attention from students of bombardment aviation. As one astute observer, Jim Rybarczyk, put it, '…many of the later B-17 and B-24 crews had to learn somewhere, and they started on the B-18.'

Besides the primary function of the type, bombardment aviation, by June 1938 B-18s were also the principal long-range reconnaissance aircraft within the GHQ Air Force, with four semi-autonomous squadrons devoted to this task. The importance of B-18s in this mix is obvious: of forty aircraft in the GHQ Air Force assigned to the reconnaissance squadrons, twenty-eight were B-18s, supplemented by eight assorted Douglas OA-4 Dolphin variants, three Sikorsky OA-8s and a single exotic Douglas OA-5. Each squadron averaged ten aircraft on strength. At the same time, the GHQ Air Force had an even 100 heavy bombers, of which eighty-eight were B-18s and the remaining twelve Y1B-17s assigned to eleven dedicated squadrons with an average of nine aircraft per squadron.

The creation of the GHQAF gave the Air Corps its first opportunity to test many of the theories of that hotbed of liberal air-minded officers, the Air Corps Tactical School. Three mass exercises and many smaller ones at Wing and Squadron level prior to December 1941 revealed progressive improvements and lessons that would be applied in the subsequent worldwide deployments.

But the central contribution of the GHQ Air Force to what was retrospectively viewed as part of the United States preparation for what evolved into the Second World War was training. By July 1939, with most assigned organisations more or less operational, the tactical units commenced intensive specialised training, for the first time in Air Corps history, for specific classes of combat crew personnel. This training included training of both pilots and co-pilots for heavy bombardment, attack, twin-engine pursuit and single-engine pursuit aircraft; training for bombardiers on both heavy bombardment and attack aircraft; training for navigators on heavy bombardment and strategic reconnaissance aircraft; so-called 'strategic observers' training on aircraft dedicated to this function; flight engineers on heavy bombardment and strategic reconnaissance; and gunners in all classes.

The world situation by this time, and the very heavy specialised training load placed on GHQ Air Force units – including preparation of crews for deployment to Panama, Hawaii and the Philippines – was constrained by a serious shortage of enlisted ranks, both trained and untrained. In fact, this shortage directly impacted the number of actual flight missions that could be carried out. At the same time, the existing bases were overcrowded, as recruiting of trainees accelerated, resulting in many of these having to be housed in tents and an amazing array of other 'temporary' cantonments.

Throughout this period, GHQ Air Force records, at nearly every level, consistently reported on the B-18 as having '…great value in giving specialised training for combat crews,' not only on B-17 and B-18s, but even for twin-engine fighter crews and transport crews as well. As a direct result, B-18 units were given the highest priority in assignment of operating personnel. It is interesting to note in this regard that the Commander of the 2nd Wing of the GHQ Air Force, based at Langley Field, VA, commented that:

> '…the B-18 and B-18A type airplanes are of great value for training combat crews, except pilots of heavy bombardment planes [e.g. B-17s]. Of course, if it is contemplated sending pilots with considerable flying time (but with little or no multi-engine time) to B-17 units for training, they must be given preliminary training on B-18 aircraft first.'

GHQAF units also took the opportunity to 'show the colors' throughout the hemisphere, reinforcing similar, seldom reported excursions carried out from Panama Canal Zone bases by other B-18 operating units (discussed in detail elsewhere). Outstanding amongst these were the flight of six of the new B-17s from Miami, Florida, all the way to Buenos Aires, Argentina, in 34 hours elapsed flying time, with a series of carefully arranged stops that unquestionably left an indelible impression on citizens and politicians of the region. Yet again, three B-17s flew from Miami to Bogotá, Colombia, in 8.5 hours, and the massive Boeing XB-15 flew from Langley Field, Virginia, to Santiago, Chile, a distance of 4,300 miles in 26.5 hours actual flying time. These long-range flights, through extremes of weather hazards and with navigational challenges that Air Corps crews had never faced before, were carried out with a precision that must certainly have impressed even the most skeptical friend or potential foe.

The leadership of the GHQAF lost few opportunities to stress the fact that the very backbone of the organisation was Bombardment Aviation (which it invariably capitalised in correspondence in just this way). Concurrently, it made rather astute use of the considerable news value of the aforementioned international flights by the massive B-17s, as well as the visual impact that they made in print, to promote the efficiency and capabilities of the service. The numerically more significant B-18s, on the other hand, were seldom featured, despite similar outstanding long-range flights and records, and this unquestionably contributed to the 'second-rate' image that slowly started to build around the type.

When first organised, as noted earlier in this account, the GHQ Air Force fell directly under the Chief of Staff of the War Department. However, on 1 March 1939 the chain of command, ostensibly to simplify peacetime procedure, was changed to place the GHQ Air Force directly subordinate to the Chief of the Air Corps – a decision greeted with enormous satisfaction within the Air Corps.

This nicely posed image of a 38th Reconnaissance Squadron (L/R) B-18A, R34, was probably taken at the time the unit deployed three aircraft to Fort Huachuca, AZ, in mid-February 1938. In this case the individual aircraft number is painted not only on the extreme nose under the bomb aimer's window, but on either side of the nose as well, and the yellow and black checks on the cowl are shown to good advantage. Note that the nose gun blister is covered to keep out the draught! *Museum of Flight*

The mission of the GHQ Air Force was very clearly spelled out in Training Regulations of the day, and it was authorized to engage in operations in close support of ground forces; in coastal frontier defense; in other joint Army and Navy operations; and, and most significantly, '…in independent operations beyond the sphere of influence of ground forces.'

The very first mention of the B-18 in connection with the GHQ Air Force was a 25 January 1937 document from the Commander,

B-18As of the 38th Reconnaissance Squadron (L/R), 19th Bomb Group, ranged far and wide prior to the war. Based at March Field, CA, R35 is shown here over the Grand Canyon on 29 March 1940, and did not have the distinctive chequered engine cowls at the time. The B-18A at the National Museum of the United States Air Force is painted in this unit's colors. *Lee Embree collection, Museum of Flight*

headquartered at Langley Field, and he was obviously counting the DB-1. His entire bombardment force as of that date – effectively the entire continental bombardment force of the United States – consisted of ten Martin B-10s, seventy-five Martin B-10Bs, six Martin B-12s, two B-17s – and two B-18s.[21]

By 15 August 1940, nearly a year after Germany had invaded Poland, and with most of Europe reeling from the Nazi onslaught, the GHQ Air Force was still very much 'under construction', although important structural and organisational details were fairly well developed, and the disposition of its very scattered elements are shown in the accompanying table.

Besides the organisational assignments of B-18 and B-18A aircraft within GHQ Air Force by this time, as shown in the table, by 15 March 1941 three B-18As were also assigned for staff use with the Headquarters and Headquarters Squadron at Bolling Field, DC, where it had just been moved from Langley Field, together with a Douglas C-39 and a Northrop A-17.

Many students of between-the-wars Army Air Corps aviation have been aware of the practice that the GHQ Air Force implemented with its Technical Order (T.O.) 07-1-1 dated 5 January 1938[22], which directed that each and every aircraft of the organisation be assigned a unique 'GHQ Airplane Number' (sometimes cited as the

Status of the GHQ Air Force and Readiness August 15, 1940

Unit and Station	A/C Authorized	A/C Actually on Hand	% of Auth. Equipment On Hand (less a/c)	Estimated Date at 100% Strength
7th Bomb Group (H), Hamilton Field, CA	26 – B-17	10 – B-17 10 – B-18	61%	January 1941
88th Reconnaissance Squadron (LR), Hamilton Field, CA	8 – B-17	1 – B-17 8 - B-18	72%	January 1941
8th Pursuit Group (Ftr), Langley Field, VA	80 – P-40	73 – P-40 30 – P-36	54%	January 1941
3rd Bomb Group (L), Barksdale Field, LA	44 – A-20	21 – B-18	65%	February 1941
9th Bomb Group (M), Mitchel Field, NY	44 – B-26	22 – B-18	36%	March 1941
20th Pursuit Group (Ftr), Moffett Field, CA	80 – P-40	28 – P-36 12 – P-40	52%	February 1941
19th Bomb Group (H), March Field, CA	26 – B-24	13 – B-17 8 – B-18	52%	January 1941
38th Reconnaissance Squadron (LR), March Field, CA	8 – B-24	2 – B-17 6 – B-18	62%	January 1941
2nd Bomb Group (H), Langley Field, VA	26 – B-17	10 – B-17 5 – B-18	73%	February 1941
41st Reconnaissance Squadron (LR), Langley Field, VA	8 – B-17	1 – XB-15 1 – B-15 3 – B-18	64%	March 1941
1st Pursuit Group (interceptor), Selfridge Field, MI	80 – P-38	36 – P-35	82%	August 1941
17th Bomb Group (M), McChord Field, WA	44 – B-25	21 – B-18 10 – B23	50%	April 1941
18th Reconnaissance Squadron (M), Mitchel Field, NY	13 – B-26	7 – B-18	66%	April 1941
31st Pursuit Group, Selfridge Field, MI	80 – P-44	25 – P-35 3 – P-36	59%	June 1941
25th Bomb Group (H), Langley Field, VA	26 – B-17	5 – B-17 7 – B-18	64%	May 1941
35th Pursuit Group, Moffett Field, CA	80 – P-39	27 – P-36	48%	August 1941
27th Bomb Group (L), Barksdale Field, LA	44 – A-20	21 – B-18	62%	April 1941
22nd Bomb Group (M), Mitchel Field, NY	44 – B-26	0	63%	June 1941
89th Reconnaissance Squadron (M), McChord Field, WA	13 – B-25	5 – B-23 3 – B-18	47%	April 1941
21st Reconnaissance Squadron (LR), MacDill Field, FL	8 – B-24	1 – B-17 7 – B-18	61%	April 1941
29th Bomb Group, MacDill Field, FL	26 – B-24	4 – B-17 8 – B-18	53%	September 1941
36th Pursuit Group, Langley Field, VA	80 – P-40	10 – YP-37 15 – P-36	48%	May 1941

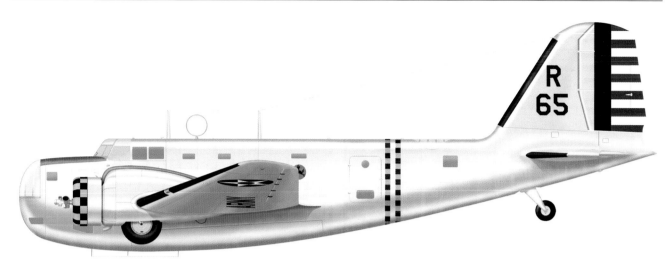

B-18 Checkers Artwork by Rich Dann

'Designator System'), usually painted on the vertical fin of each aircraft, and bearing no relationship to the actual Air Corps serial number of the aircraft. These often puzzling numbers are often seen in photos of Air Corps aircraft of the time, and while several attempts have been made to 'decode' them[23], they remain for many obstacles to a full understanding of their utility.

Basically, the system of numbers identified in the T.O., and necessarily amended several times as new aircraft and organisations joined the GHQ Air Force, was based on using the Group number as the airplane radio call sign when contacting airdrome control towers. This system was superseded by the system subsequently described in Circular 100-4 dated 27 May 1939. On 6 November 1939, however, the Chief Signal Officer of the GHQ Air Force recommended to the Chief of Staff that each aircraft, instead, be assigned a distinctive designation, which would consist of a combination of numbers and one or two letters. Basically, these would be assigned as follows:

a. The designator for aircraft assigned to the Headquarters Squadron, GHQ Air Force, was to consist of the letters 'HQ' followed (usually underneath this) by a number assigned by the squadron commander.

b. The designator for aircraft of the various Wings, Air Bases, Groups and separate Squadrons was to consist of the unit number, a letter or letters indicating the type of unit ('W' for Wing, 'AB' for Air Base, 'B' for Bombardment, 'P' for Pursuit and 'R' for Reconnaissance) and a number as assigned by the Wing, Air Base, Group or Reconnaissance Squadron commander.

Seldom illustrated, this B-18A, with Designator WB1, also bears the insignia of the 2nd Wing, General Headquarters Air Force. *via Robert L. Taylor*

For the record, as of 6 November 1939 the table overleaf shows a complete listing of these designators for all units of the GHQ Air Force assigned as of that date.

These numbers were to be painted on each side of the vertical fin of each aircraft, as well as on the top and bottom of the left wing of each aircraft. The letters and numbers were to be of the 'vertical type', not larger than 18 inches high, or strokes wider than 3 inches. On the wings, the designators were to appear on one line; on the vertical fins, the designator was to appear in two lines, the organisation number and letter or letters indicating the type of unit on the top line, and the individual aircraft number within the unit on the bottom. For example,

35P
77

indicated airplane number 77 within the 35th Pursuit Group. In addition, the individual aircraft number (in this case 77) was also to be painted on the engine cowl, or on the forward portion of the fuselage of each aircraft, so as to be visible from the forward hemisphere. Colors were to be black when on natural metal or against a light background, or yellow if shown against a dark background.

Unusual in sporting the distinctive 2nd Bomb Group insignia on the starboard side of the nose, B-18 BB 16 also had the three colors of the Squadrons of the group painted on the leading edges of the engine cowlings, as it was a Headquarters Squadron aircraft. Note that the prop spinners are yet a different color, probably black. It is pictured at Morrison Field, FL, in March 1938 with Frank and John Darling checking the undercarriage and Larry Heller (left) and Charles Darling posing for mother Marie Darling. *Marie Darling via Charles F. Darling*

GHQ Air Force Aircraft Designator 6 Nov 1939

Unit	Designators
Headquarters Squadron, GHQ Air Force	HQ1 to HQ_
Headquarters Squadron, 1st Wing	1W1 to 1W_
Headquarters Squadron, 2nd Wing	2W1 to 2W_
Headquarters Squadron, 3rd Wing	3W1 to 3W_
1st Air Base Squadron	1AB1 to 1AB_
2nd Air Base Squadron	2AB1 to 2AB_
3rd Air Base Squadron	3AB1 to 3AB_
4th Air Base Squadron	4AB1 to 4AB_
5th Air Base Squadron	5AB1 to 5AB_
6th Air Base Squadron	6AB1 to 6AB_
9th Air Base Squadron	9AB1 to 9AB_
17th Air Base Squadron	17AB1 to 17AB_
19th Air Base Squadron	19AB1 to 19AB_
26th Air Base Squadron	26AB1 to 26AB_
27th Air Base Squadron	27AB1 to 27AB_
2nd Bombardment Group (Heavy)	2B1 to 2B_
3rd Bombardment Group (Light)	3B1 to 3B_
7th Bombardment Group (Heavy)	7B1 to 7B_
9th Bombardment Group (Medium)	9B1 to 9B_
17th Bombardment Group (Medium)	17B1 to 17B_
19th Bombardment Group (Heavy)	19B1 to 19B_
27th Bombardment Group (Light)	27B1 to 27B_
29th Bombardment Group (Heavy)	29B1 to 29B_
1st Pursuit Group (Interceptor)	1P1 to 1P_
8th Pursuit Group (Fighter)	8P1 to 8P_
20th Pursuit Group (Fighter)	20P1 to 20P_
31st Pursuit Group (Single Engine)	31P1 to 31P_
35th Pursuit Group (Single Engine)	35P1 to 35P_
18th Recon Squadron (Medium Range)	18R1 to 18R_
21st Recon Squadron (Long Range)	21R1 to 21R_
38th Recon Squadron (Long Range)	38R1 to 38R_
41st Recon Squadron (Long Range)	41R1 to 41R_
88th Recon Squadron (Long Range)	88R1 to 88R_
89th Recon Squadron (Medium Range)	89R1 to 89R_
5th Transport Squadron	5T1 to 5T_
6th Transport Squadron	6T1 to 6T_
7th Transport Squadron	7T1 to 7T_

In addition to these identifiers, other coloring on unit aircraft also took on special significance, with white, yellow and red being the designated colors for most pursuit, attack and bombardment units, although in cases where a fourth squadron was attached to a Group the color blue was also used. This involved painting of the engine cowls of the respective aircraft, and the directives specified that '… a suitable depth of the front portion of engine nacelles' be painted with these colors. By 1940 Groups with three organic subordinate Squadrons were, essentially, given their choice as to how they wished to apply any of the four colors. Some readers will have noted in photos of B-18s of the period that, on some aircraft, cowlings were apparently divided into different colors. This was because aircraft assigned to Group Headquarters and Headquarters Squadrons (HHS) were divided into sections using the colors of each Squadron of the Group, while attached Reconnaissance Squadrons were assigned color combinations by respective Wing Commanders. The three Wing Headquarters, and the GHQAF command aircraft, on the other hand, were not allowed recognition colors for their organic aircraft, thus negating the possibility of elaborate schemes in these units.

Similarly, Command markings were also revised. A series of fuselage bands or stripes replaced the chevrons, diamonds and random bands of earlier periods, and were painted in the Squadron colors in 5-inch bands or stripes.

Where these identifiers or other codes have been positively linked, the reader will find references to them in captions, individual unit summaries, and in the comprehensive Production List in Annex 1. This is the first time that such an attempt involving the B-18 has been made, and should provide many readers with a convenient means to place an image that they may have or may have seen and connect it with a particular unit, or the exact Air Corps serial for the aircraft, or at a place and time.

By 30 April 1941 the force was in the midst of enormous expansion, and its B-18, B-18A and new B-23 aircraft were thinly spread throughout the organisation; some had been converted to the desultory but vital task of target-towing. The accompanying table shows the assignment of all GHQ Air Force B-18, B-18A and B-23 aircraft as of that date.

During that fateful summer of 1941, General Arnold grimly took stock of what appeared at the time to be potentially disastrous gaps

Below left: BB 16 of Headquarters and Headquarters Squadron, 2nd Bomb Group, home-based at Langley Field, VA, one of the premier operators of the B-18 series. Although quoted as AC36-311, this aircraft is not known to have been assigned to the 2nd BG. *via David W. Ostrowski*

Below: One of the first B-18As assigned to the 2nd Bomb Group at Langley Field, BB 17 was assigned to the Headquarters and Headquarters Squadron and features the three-color leading edges of the cowlings and the Group insignia on the port side of the nose. It is unusual in having the unit designator painted on the extreme outboard side of the lower port wing. *David W. Ostrowski collection*

GHQ Air Force B-18, B-18A and B-23 Deployment As of 30 April 1941

Unit and Station	B-18	B-18A	B-18 Tow Target	B-18A Tow Target	B-23
HHS GHQ Air Force, Bolling Field, DC		3			
2nd Bomb Wing Headquarters, Langley Field, VA		1			
2nd Bomb Group (H), Langley Field, VA		8	1	2	
22nd Bomb Group (M), Langley Field, VA	1	7			
41st Reconnaissance Squadron (H), Langley Field, VA	1	7		1	
18th Reconnaissance Squadron (H), Langley Field, VA	1	4			
6th Pursuit Wing Headquarters, Selfridge Field, MI		1			
6th Air Base Group, Selfridge Field, MI		1			
1st Air Base Group, Langley Field, VA	1				
2nd Air Base Group, Mitchel Field, NY	1	1			
2nd Air Force Headquarters, Fort George Washington, WA					1
5th Bomb Wing Headquarters, Spokane, WA					1
7th Bomb Group (H), Salt Lake City, UT	1	8	3		
17th Bomb Group (M), McChord Field, WA		6	1		11
88th Reconnaissance Squadron (H), Salt Lake City, UT	1	2			
89th Reconnaissance Squadron (M), McChord Field, WA		2			4
5th Air Base Group, Salt Lake City, UT	1				
19th Air Base Group, McChord Field, WA	1				1
3rd Bomb Wing Headquarters, MacDill Field, FL		1			
29th Bomb Group (H), MacDill Field, FL	1	12			
27th Bomb Group (L), Savannah, GA		13			
21st Reconnaissance Squadron (H), Miami, FL		6			
14th Reconnaissance Squadron (H), Miami, FL		1			
27th Air Base Group, MacDill Field, FL	1				
29th Air Base Group, Charlotte, NC		1			
35th Air Base Group, Savannah, GA	2				
16th Air Base Group, Maxwell Field, AL		1			
38th Air Base Group, New Orleans, LA		1			
41st Air Base Group, Tallahassee, FL		1			
4th Air Force Headquarters, Riverside, CA		1			
1st Bomb Wing Headquarters, March Field, CA			1		
19th Bomb Group (H), March Field, CA			1	1	
4th Air Base Group, Albuquerque, NM		1			
31st Air Base Group, Tucson, AZ		1			
32nd Air Base Group, March Field, CA	2				
TOTALS	**15**	**91**	**7**	**4**	**18**

between orders for the next generation of combat aircraft, actual deliveries, and his evolving air force – which, while appearing awesome and well-conceived on paper, was rather thin on the ground and in the air. The GHQ Air Force, supposedly the air arm's great offensive striking arm, could in fact muster only two groups of heavy bombers (about seventy aircraft on a good day), two groups of mediums (about 114 aircraft), two groups of light bombers (another 114 aircraft), and three pursuit groups, totaling about 225 aircraft – in other words, about nine groups, or a paper total of 523 aircraft all told. The small numbers of aircraft available to actual tactical units in the field was, in itself, alarming, but this was not the only danger. Even those aircraft noted in the accompanying table, often reported as 'available' on strength reports, were often not always really available. At one point during the summer, the Chief of the Air Corps

Above: The red center in the national insignia on HQ 2 indicates that this B-18A was photographed prior to 12 May 1942, yet after the application of olive drab camouflage topside and neutral gray undersurfaces. It is also unusual in having an RDF 'bullet' atop the forward fuselage, and was probably a command aircraft in the Headquarters of the 2nd Bomb Group at this time. *Harold G. Martin No A-3721, Kansas Aviation Museum*

Left: A very rare view of a 49th Bomb Squadron (H), 2nd Bomb Group quartet of B-18As at Dartmouth, Nova Scotia, probably en route to Argentia, Newfoundland, sometime after January 1942, with number '29' foremost. These aircraft were amongst the first USAAC aircraft to be placed potentially in harm's way, as they were tasked to support the so-called Neutrality Patrol. All three of the nearest aircraft have RDF 'bullets' atop their forward fuselages. *via Rich Dann*

Left: This is B-18A 41R 48 of the 41st Reconnaissance Squadron (H), probably at Langley Field, in 1941, bearing the unit insignia on the nose and cowling scalloping. The nose gun barbette is covered. *via Norm Taylor and Robert F. Dorr*

Below: The 41st Reconnaissance Squadron (H)), attached to the 2nd Bomb Group, had one B-18 and four B-18As, and all of these are shown here bearing the unit insignia on the nose and the distinctive cowl scalloping they wore, color unknown. *J. Meyer via Norm Taylor and Robert F. Door #000030*

The solitary B-18 assigned to the 41st Reconnaissance Squadron was 41R 46, pictured here with the portable equipment that the unit was destined to take with it to Newfoundland when it deployed there in August 1941 to take part in the Neutrality Patrol. *USAAC*

was forced to confess that two entire squadrons of B-17s and an entire Group of mediums (initial series B-25s and B-26s) were essentially grounded for want of parts or because of structural defects appearing after delivery. This placed the burden of responsibility on the now, evidently, too small force of airworthy B-18s and B-18As all too squarely. The ultimate irony in all of this, however, was a Memo issued by General Arnold on 5 August 1941, by then Chief of the Air Staff, entitled 'Airplanes Suitable for Tactical Purposes'. Neither the B-18 nor the B-18A appeared on that list.

On 20 June 1941 the War Department created the Army Air Forces, with the Air Corps and the GHQ Air Force, and the latter, for all intents and purposes, was redesignated as the Air Force Combat Command.

The GHQ Air Force, for the purposes of our story, had served its purposes well. It had effectively supervised the introduction of two radically new heavy bombardment aircraft into the national arsenal, the B-18 series and the first generation of B-17s. As it turned out, the GHQ Air Force tenure was the principal period during which B-18 and B-18A production aircraft saw service, in significant numbers, in their design role, within the framework of a conventional force. Few could predict that, in fact, the major contribution phase of the B-18 series still lay ahead, in a future role that not a single officer of the service could have predicted as late as the summer of 1941. This bridged the inevitable period of teething problems, represented by the Unsatisfactory Reports (U/Rs) dutifully submitted to Wright Field for fixes, and development of Tables of Organisation & Equipment (TO&Es), which stood the test of the Second World War basically unchanged, the sorting out of crew duties and responsibilities, giving the same crews the opportunity to work together in the manner that became the standard during the ensuing war, and perhaps most important of all, providing excellent training platforms. The only other services on the planet at the time that could say the same, ironically, were those of Germany, Italy and Japan, which had the added benefits of actual combat exposure of their bombardment aviators in the skies over Spain and China.

Following is a detailed discussion of all B-18 operating units of the GHQ Air Force, arranged by major subordinate element, then, within each organisation, individual B-18 operating units and organisations.

1st Wing, General Headquarters Air Force

One of the original Wing organisations of the GHQ Air Force, the 1st Wing was based at March Field, California, and was formally activated 1 April 1931 – even before the creation of the GHQAF in 1935. It became a formal component of the GHQAF on 1 March 1935. Although its area of responsibility and subordinate maneuver elements changed several times as the service expanded, it had basic area responsibility for the western regions of the US until 1941. It was redesignated as the

1st Bombardment Wing by 31 March 1941. The **Flight Section, Headquarters and Headquarters Squadron, 1st Bomb Wing**, had a single B-18 organic between April 1938 (and possibly earlier) and as late as 30 April 1941, AC36-323. This Wing existed during the crucial 'working up' period of B-18 (as well as B-17) deployment, and continued to play a key role in the history of the type until nominally, at least on paper, being transferred to the fledgling Eighth Air Force in England in July and August 1942. The Wing was headquartered at March Field, California.

An irony often overlooked by aero-historians is the fact that this Wing was commanded from 1936 by none other than (then) Brigadier General Henry 'Hap' Arnold, unofficial ranking man of the so-called 'bomber mafia', and who undoubtedly was deeply involved in the plans for fielding the new B-18s when they started to be assigned to subordinate elements of this major command. So far as can be determined, none of his thoughts on the advent of the B-18 into line service in his command have survived.

During the period central to our story, between 1935 and 1942, the Wing commanded the following subordinate elements, arranged in the following description by Group and, within Group, by Squadron or independent Squadron.

7th Bombardment Group, 1st Wing, GHQAF

One of the premier dedicated Bombardment Groups of the interwar period, this unit consisted of the Headquarters and **Headquarters Squadron, 9th, 11th, 22nd and 31st Bombardment Squadrons**, and **88th Reconnaissance Squadron**. This Group held the distinction of having transitioned through the entire series of pre-war USAAC monoplane bombardment types, including the Boeing Y1B-7, Martin B-10, Martin B-12 and Douglas B-18. It was stationed for most of the initial B-18 deployment period at the permanent and very well appointed Hamilton Field, California, and basically had responsibility for Air Corps bombardment coverage of the entire north-western US. On 7 September 1940 the unit was transferred to Fort Douglas (Salt Lake City), Utah, where it prepared for deployment. It was in fact on the way to reinforce the US garrison in the Philippines when Japan attacked, but by then it no longer operated B-18s.

Aircraft assigned to the 7th Bombardment Group during this period wore the 'BG' designator on their vertical fin, followed by a number beneath indicating the number within the Group. Although the Group was, for most of this period, almost completely equipped with B-18 and B-18A aircraft, by the time it had settled in at Salt Lake City at the end of March 1941 it could muster only three B-18s and seven B-18As, although it also had one B-18 fitted exclusively for target tug use and a B-18A similarly equipped, and its primary equipment consisted of twelve B-17Bs, four B-17Cs and three B-17Ds. By the end of April 1941 the Group had one B-18, eight B-18As and three B-18s equipped for target-towing, and ten B-17Bs, four B-17Cs and three B-17Ds. By 30 June 1941 the shape of equipment transition had been set, and the Group had but three B-18s remaining on strength, as well as eleven mixed B-17s.

Official and commercially published histories of this well-decorated unit, which went on to serve magnificently in the Dutch East Indies and the CBI later in the war, invariably focus on the wartime combat contributions of the organisation, which is perhaps as it should be. However, the fact is that between 9 July 1937, when the Group received its very first B-18 (AC36-266), it and its subordinate squadrons cut their crew-molding teeth on at least thirty-nine B-18s, following re-equipment commencing in November 1938, and forty B-18As. Virtually all of these were spanking-new aircraft, direct from the factory, and some accompanied the Group when it transferred to Utah in October 1941, by which time conversion to B-17s was well advanced. The role that these aircraft played in preparing crews to make that conversion has never been properly attributed.

9th Bombardment Squadron (H), 7
th Bomb Group, 1st Wing, GHQAF

The 9th Bombardment Squadron was one of the first USAAC units to receive B-18s, and operated the type exclusively between 1937 and 1940, transitioning in part to early B-17 variants in 1939. During most of this period it was stationed at Hamilton Field, California, but moved with the parent 7th Bomb Group to Fort Douglas, UT, on 7 September 1940. It operated both B-18 and B-18A aircraft, including BG11. Once the unit departed the US with the 7th Bomb Group in late 1941, it had no further association with the B-18, but earned a distinguished combat record in the SWP and CBI.

11th Bombardment Squadron (H),
7th Bomb Group, 1st Wing, GHQAF

Like its sister squadron, the 9th, the 11th Bombardment Squadron was assigned at Hamilton Field, CA, from 5 December 1934 until moving to Fort Douglas, UT, on 7 September 1940, then to Salt Lake City on 18 January until 13 November 1941. Prior to receiving its first B-18s in 1937, the unit had been equipped with Martin B-10s and B-12s, but commenced re-equipment with early B-17 variants in 1939. It was credited with flying some limited anti-submarine patrol missions off the California coast from 8 to 10 December 1941, but it is not clear if these missions were flown with B-18s or B-17s.

The unit, like nearly every pre-war B-18 operating tactical squadron, conducted intensive training exercises. In March 1938, on a long-range training flight to Barksdale Field, LA, four 11th BS B-18s completed the first leg of the flight from Hamilton Field to Bakersfield, CA, entirely on instruments, the elapsed time being about 1hr 30min. The flight had taken off and climbed to 3,500 feet until it reached the vicinity of Mt Diablo. The flight leader made the decision to attempt to fly over or through a front that, as it turned out, reduced visibility to nearly zero on the course to March Field. Throughout the flight, violent snow and rain squalls were encountered, which almost immediately broke all wing antenna wires, but aside from brief periods while flying through snow squalls, communication between the four aircraft was maintained. Icing was encountered, but to the pleasure of the crews the new luxury of leading-edge de-icers on the B-18s kept the wings free of ice. However, the crews did note that the command radio antenna masts vibrated rather badly at times, due to ice accumulation on these surfaces, which seemed to indicate that the de-icer boots on these masts was not as effective as hoped. At least one aircraft managed to open the navigator's hatch and a crewman hit the front mast, freeing it of ice.

Though in retrospect a seemingly routine exercise, this late 1930s cross-country flight by a quartet of line, fully manned and – for the time – modern heavy bombers epitomised the sense of urgency that the Air Corps was awakening to with its new mounts.

Two B-18As known to have been assigned to the 11th BS as of May 1940 were BG34 and BG38.

22nd Bombardment Squadron (H),
7th Bomb Group, 1st Wing, GHQAF

The 22nd Bomb Squadron did not join the 7th Bomb Group until 20 October 1939, when it was activated at Hamilton Field. Like its veteran sister units, it also moved with the Group to Fort Douglas, UT, on 7 September 1940 and on to Salt Lake City on 21 June 1941. When Pearl Harbor was attacked, the air echelon of the unit was deployed to Muroc, CA, on 8 December, but moved to Hickam Field, Territory of Hawaii, on the 18th, then on to Australia. The unit operated a mix of hand-me-down B-18s and single-engined Northrop A-17s from activation until 1940, when transition to early B-17s commenced.

The Squadron flew its B-18s intensively for proficiency training, and the directives for the period dictated that at least 50% of all crew flight hours must be night training.

The unit apparently did conduct limited coastal patrols from Muroc for three days, 8-10 December 1941, but it is not clear what aircraft were employed.

31st Bombardment Squadron (M),
7th Bomb Group, 1st Wing, GHQAF

Although one of the original subordinate squadrons of the 7th Bomb Group, the 31st Bomb Squadron was transferred to the 5th Composite Group (later 5th Bombardment Group) on 1 February 1938 at Hickam Field, TH, and took its thirteen organic B-18s, which it commenced receiving in 1937, to the islands with it. These were dismantled and shipped by surface freight aboard the USAT *Ludington* on 17 February, and the unit became the first bombardment squadron to be stationed at Hickam. It was eventually replaced in the Group by the 22nd Bomb Squadron, noted above.

For more on this unit, see the discussion of the B-18 in the Hawaiian Islands.

88th Reconnaissance Squadron (L/R),
7th Bomb Group, 1st Wing, GHQAF

Reconnaissance squadrons in the pre-war AAC were highly specialised units, and enjoyed a certain degree of autonomy. The 88th Recon Squadron was attached to the 7th Bomb Group from 1 September 1936, and later the air echelon was attached to the 31st Bomb Squadron from 10 December 1941 until 8 February 1942. The unit had been at Hamilton Field from 28 September 1935, and moved with the Group to Fort Douglas, UT, on 7 September 1940, then to Salt Lake City, where it remained from 15 January until 11 November 1941. It operated B-18s from 1937 well into 1940, but commenced re-equipping with early B-17s in 1939. As of 1 September 1940 the unit had eight B-18s and one brand-new B-17B, and had been transferred to Salt Lake City. It was consequently redesignated as the 88th Reconnaissance Squadron (Heavy) on 20 November 1940.

The Squadron dispatched two B-18s at 15-minute intervals from its home base at Hamilton Field in March 1939 via March Field to Kelly Field, TX, from where they made flights across the Gulf of Mexico to qualify their navigators in celestial navigation, a GHQAF requirement. Two navigators from the unit were assigned to each aircraft, with one performing the actual navigation while the other performed what was termed 'follow-the-pilot' navigation, whereby he plotted his landfall on his charts and computed his error independent of the other navigator. The aircraft landed successfully at the US Coast Guard base at St Petersburg, FL, a new experience for all concerned, and there the crews were entertained by both the Coast Guard and local townspeople. On return, the aircraft separated and successfully arrived over their objectives on the Texas coast, Corpus Christi and Rockport. The crews had successfully navigated more than 5,400 miles in slightly less than 34 flying hours.

It is seldom noted in published accounts that, as of 15 January 1941, the Squadron was assigned, at least temporarily, to Davis-Monthan Field near Tucson, AZ, but had moved to Salt Lake City by 31 March when the aircraft on hand very much reflected the re-equipment program that was ongoing. It had four B-18As and a tow-target-equipped 'slick' B-18, as well as two B-17Bs, a single B-17C and two B-17Ds. Within thirty days this had changed to a single B-18 and two B-18As, as well as single examples of the B-17B and B-17C and the two B-17Ds. By 30 June 1941 only one B-18 remained with the unit.

The unit made the headlines in December 1937 when it dropped food and other supplies to flood victims in central California, and it was B-17s of this unit that came under attack when approaching to land in Hawaii from the mainland on 7 December 1941. It went on to see action in the Pacific and was redesignated as the 436th Bombardment Squadron (H) on 22 April 1942.

17th Bombardment Group (M),
1st Wing and 5th Wing, GHQAF

Formerly the 17th Attack Group, this veteran organisation was redesignated as the 17th Bombardment Group (Medium) in 1939 and, following transition from primarily single-engined Northrop A-17s, operated Douglas B-18 variants in its subordinate Headquarters and Headquarters Squadron, 34th, 37th, 73rd and 95th Bomb Squadrons (M) from that year clear through 1941. The Group later converted in part to North American B-25s before eventually converting to Martin B-26 Marauders and deploying to North Africa. The Group was stationed at March Field, CA, for most of its pre-war existence, but moved to McChord Field, WA, on 24 June 1940 – although USAAC Order of Battle documents dated 1 July 1940 still showed it garrisoned at March Field. The Group was transferred from 1st Wing, GHQAF, to 5th Wing, GHQAF, on 16 January 1941. By 31 March 1941 the Group had a very cosmopolitan array of equipment, including eight B-18As (one of them fitted for tow target duty), one B-18 (also fitted for tow target duty), eleven B-23s and four B-25s. A month later, on 30 April 1941, the Group had six B-18As and one two-target-configured B-18, eleven B-23s and nine B-25s. It then moved to Pendleton Field, OR, on 29 June 1941 where it mounted twelve mixed B-18s, ten B-23s and nineteen B-25s, and to Lexington County Airport, SC, on 9 February 1942. The Group had participated in the famous Carolina maneuvers and was en route back to the Pacific Northwest on 7 December 1941 at March Field, by which time it had almost entirely been re-equipped with forty-one B-25Bs – all of which were dispersed by 1530 hours that infamous day after finally receiving official word of the Japanese attack around noon. The Group and its subordinate Squadrons carried out numerous coastal patrol and anti-submarine patrols along the west coast after Pearl Harbor as well as similar missions.

34th Bombardment Squadron (M),
17th Bomb Group, 1st Wing, GHQAF

Formerly the 34th Attack Squadron, the 34th Bomb Squadron (Medium) was redesignated as such on 17 October 1939, stationed at the time at March Field, CA. The Squadron trained intensively on B-18s under Major Eugene L. Eubank, and on 24 June 1940 moved with the Group to McChord Field, WA, when the unit partially re-equipped with Douglas B-23s. It later re-equipped with B-25s. The Squadron was credited with taking part in the food drops during the flood relief operations in Southern California between 2 and 5 March 1938, and with anti-submarine patrols with, initially, its fully armed B-23s and later its B-25s between 22 December 1941 and March 1942 in the Pacific Northwest. B-18s and B-23s assigned to the Squadron were distinguishable prior to 7 December 1941 by having insignia blue engine cowlings.

36th Bombardment Squadron (H),
28th Composite Group, 1st Wing, GHQAF

Something of an orphan organisation after constitution on 22 December 1939, the 36th Bombardment Squadron (Heavy) was stationed at March Field, CA, and was subordinated to the newly formed 28th Composite Group, also temporarily garrisoned there with its HHS. The unit was activated on 1 February 1940, and moved from March to Lowry Field, CO, between 9 August 1940 and 23 March 1941 prior to going, with the Group, to Elmendorf Field, AK, on 31 March, where it remained through the remainder of the war. For more on the unit and its association with the B-18, see the section on Alaskan operations.

37th Bombardment Squadron (M),
28th Composite Group and 17th Bomb Group,
1st Wing, GHQAF

Converted from the former 37th Attack Squadron, the 37th Bombardment Squadron (Medium) was activated on 1 February 1940, at which time it was assigned to the 28th Composite Group, which was headquartered at distant March Field, CA. The Squadron itself was at Barksdale Field, LA, at the time, and had been there since 6 December 1939. The Squadron was deployed Temporary Duty (TDY) to Lowry Field, CO, on 10 July 1940. It was reassigned to the 17th Bomb Group on 23 April 1941 and transferred to Pendleton Field, OR, on 19 June 1941 with nine officers and 217 enlisted ranks, and was thus not part of the 17th Bomb Group during its formative period in California. The Squadron converted from primarily B-18s to B-25s during the first months of the war.

73rd Bombardment Squadron (M),
17th Bomb Group, 1st Wing, GHQAF

Another former Attack Squadron, the 73rd was redesignated as a Medium Bomber unit on 17 October 1939 at March Field, CA. By 31 January 1940 the Squadron had eight B-18As and one Northrop A-17A on strength, and a year later had nine B-18As. This unit was reassigned to the 28th Composite Group for service in Alaska (qv) and its ground echelon departed Seattle for the frozen north on 10 March 1941 to Elmendorf Field, with the air echelon, consisting of nine B-18As, following on 27 March.

95th Bombardment Squadron (M),
17th Bomb Group, 1st Wing, GHQAF

Yet another former attack unit, the 95th was redesignated as a Bombardment Squadron (Medium) on 17 October 1939 at March Field. It moved with the Group to McChord Field, WA, on 26 June 1940, and to Pendleton Field, OR, on 29 June 1941. Throughout this period it progressed from B-18s through a mix of B-18s and B-23s into North American B-25s. Re-equipped with Martin B-26s, it deployed to North Africa in December 1942, but only after brief training stints at Lexington County Airport, SC, from 15 February 1942 and Barksdale Field, LA, from 24 June 1942 till 18 November 1942.

Although this image has been published previously, it has almost always been printed in reverse and described inaccurately. Field Numbers 7 and 8 are B-18s over Manila Bay in the Philippines on October 17, 1941, ferrying crews of the 17th Bomb Group (L) from Iba to Nichols Field. They were probably assigned to the 27th Material Squadron at this point.
M/Sgt William R. Wright via Bill Bartsch

89th Reconnaissance Squadron (M/R), 17th Bomb Group, 1st Wing, GHQAF

Designated as such on 22 December 1939, the 89th Recon Squadron was attached to the 17th Bomb Group from 1 February 1940 until finally assigned as organic from 25 February 1942, initially at March Field. The Squadron deployed with the Group to McChord Field, WA, on 26 June 1940, and to Pendleton Field, OR, on 29 June 1941 before returning to McChord around 30 December 1941, after the Japanese attack. It returned to Pendleton around 24 January 1942 before moving with the Group to Lexington County Airport, SC, on 15 February 1942 in preparation for movement to North Africa. Like other units in the 17th Bomb Group, the Squadron moved through a mix of B-18s and B-23s into B-25s before becoming a dedicated B-26 unit. For example, by 31 March 1941, while at McChord, the Squadron had a mix of two B-18As, five B-23s and one B-25, but within a month this had changed to two B-18As, four B-23s and four B-25s. By 30 June, however, only one of the B-18As remained, alongside six B-25s, and the B-23s were gone.

The unit was one of the first to really put the B-23 through its paces, and as early as 7 January 1941 commenced submitting a series of highly critical Unsatisfactory Reports on the type to the Materiel Division at Wright Field. As of that date, the Squadron had B-23s s/n AC39-41, 39-46, 39-56 and 39-60, and reported in restrained phrases that the novel new tail gunner's position, of which so much had been expected, had serious – if not potentially disastrous – shortcomings. It reported that the .50 caliber gun mounts and the gunner's compartment itself were of such basic design and construction as to make reloading of the single gun while in flight (let alone under potential attack) '…extremely difficult, if not impossible'. The averaged-size gunner, it was found, could physically not reach the feed mechanism of the M-2 gun in order to change ammo boxes due to the extremely close quarters and length of the gun. Additionally, the gun cover, it was found, could not be raised more than 3 inches while the gun was installed. This obviously prevented the clearance of second position stoppages that might (and often did) occur in the gun, as the cover hit against the yoke holding the gun. Furthermore, extra ammunition boxes were stored so far to the rear (towards the front of the aircraft) from the gunner, who obviously faced aft, that it was extremely difficult to obtain fresh boxes. The field of fire of the gun was also found to be seriously limited by the very small angles of elevation (about 20 degrees from the horizontal) and depression (about 15 degrees from the horizontal). Seldom, if ever, recognised as such, these very candid observations from a line unit in the field probably had more to do with the very sudden decision to withdraw these aircraft from tactical units and reconfigure them as high-speed transports under the UC-67 designation, than any other single factor.

Clearly, the decision to proceed with the relatively small batch of B-23s, heralded at the time as an 'improvement' on the B-18A, in closing out the B-18A production line, was in fact a case of wishful – rather than sound engineering – thinking. That the members of this Squadron and other units of the Air Corps actually carried out armed patrol missions in these aircraft and, as will be seen, apparently actually carried out at least one attack on a submarine, is a credit to the crews, as their mounts, although fiercely named and possessing pleasing lines and better-than-average performance for the time, would clearly have been a hindrance to protracted combat exposure.

19th Bombardment Group (H), 1st Wing, GHQAF

Nearly always identified exclusively with the December 1941 debacle in the Philippines, it is seldom recognised that the 19th Bomb Group enjoyed a significant pre-war existence in the United States, and was a key player in the fielding of the B-18. Designated as such in 1939, the Group and its subordinate Squadrons, the 30th, 32nd and 93rd

Bomb Squadrons, were stationed at March Field, CA, whence they deployed to Albuquerque, NM, between 7 July and 29 September 1941, prior to their eleventh-hour movement to Clark Field, Luzon, PI, around 23 October 1941. It was, consequently, the gestation of this Group from Martin B-10s, through Douglas B-18s and into early variant Boeing B-17s that enabled it to carry out the heroic although rearguard actions leading up to the surrender of the Philippines.

As early as 6 April 1938, the 19th Bomb Group possessed sixteen nearly brand-new B-18s at March Field although, as the countdown to war progressed, the conversion to B-17s, which was quite readily acknowledged by Group personnel and had been materially facilitated by the B-18 experience, continued.

A 19th Bomb Group B-18, piloted by the Group Commander, LTC Harvey S. Burwell, accompanied by 1LT A. G. Wilson (co-pilot), LT Raymond V. Swandeck (navigator) and three enlisted ranks, made history on 8 April 1938 when they flew non-stop from March Field to Langley Field, VA – the very first such non-stop transit of the Continental United States by a twin-engined bomber, and something of a jolt to B-17 enthusiasts, who had invariably disparaged the B-18 as being 'short-legged'.

Colonel Burwell, in fact, could best be described as one of the strongest Air Corps proponents for the B-18, and lost no opportunity to extol the virtues of the aircraft. At a ceremony at its home station on 21 September 1938, none other than Major General Oscar Westover himself, with the entire 19th Bomb Group on parade, presented the Group with both the coveted Colombian and Daedalian Trophies in recognition of the fact that the two line operational Squadrons of the Group (the 30th and 32nd – the 93rd had not yet been activated) had operated intensively for no fewer than 10, 942 flying hours without a solitary accident during Fiscal Year 1938. It was Colonel Burwell himself who, commencing in 1928, had orchestrated the so-called Army Maintenance System, a maintenance curriculum that he guided to perfection with his B-18s. This system, honed on B-18s, was essentially the same that carried on into the war years and which served the Army Air Forces so well in building the force that defeated the Axis powers.

Bob Fish, a 1940 Air Corps flight training graduate, was assigned directly from Randolph Field, TX, to the 19th Bomb Group at March Field, and recalled the B-18s 'with pleasure'. During the initial phase of his assignment to the Group, which was in the midst of converting to B-17s, he reported that '…first all new pilots assigned had to be checked out on the B-18 before checking out on the B-17. Therefore, I cut my bomber "eye-teeth" on the B-18.' He accompanied the Group to Albuquerque where, for all intents and purposes, the Group was split to form two additional Groups, the 30th and 41st. The two 'new' Groups inherited the B-18s that had previously seen such splendid service with the 19th, although the 19th still retained five.

By 31 March 1941 the 19th Bomb Group (H), still at March, still possessed only single examples of the B-18 and B-18A, both configured as tow target tugs for their two very early B-17s and nineteen B-17Bs by then on board. This was essentially the same complement as a month later, although the number of B-17Bs had declined to seventeen, and the Group even took its two trusty B-18s with it when it deployed to Albuquerque, where they were accompanied by a mix of thirteen B-17Cs and B-17Ds.

30th Bombardment Squadron (H), 19th Bomb Group, 1st Wing, GHQAF

One of the premier US bombardment squadrons, the 30th Bomb Squadron traced its origins back to the 30th Aero Squadron of June 1917, and evolved into the 30th Bomb Squadron (Heavy), so designated on 6 December 1939, by which time the unit had been operating B-18s for nearly two years – having been one of the very first units to receive the new monoplanes. Garrisoned at March Field from 25 October 1935, the Squadron sent nearly all of its crew chiefs to the Douglas plant for an unusual in-the-factory training course, and these NCOs later went on to form the core cadre for nearly all B-18 crews that followed. The Squadron took part in the large Air Corps maneuvers in central New York state, involving simulated attacks on metropolitan areas in 1938, and started transitioning to Boeing B-17Bs in 1939 – again, one of the first units to receive the latest state-of-the-art equipment. The Squadron moved with the Group to Albuquerque, NM, between June and September 1941, preparatory for its deployment to Clark Field, Luzon, in the Philippines, where it earned glory associated for the most part with the early B-17.

32nd Bombardment Squadron (H), 19th Bomb Group, 1st Wing, GHQAF

With a lineage nearly identical to its sister Squadron, the 30th, the 32nd Bombardment Squadron (Heavy) was so designated from 6 December 1939. Subsequently its movements were the same as its sister units, in particular the 30th Bomb Squadron as shown above, except that the air echelon was briefly attached to the IV Bomber Command circa 22 October 1941, and by 31 October was at Albuquerque with four early B-17s and one B-18 remaining. The Squadron was also nominally attached to the 7th Bombardment Group (for operations) in the Philippines (minus its air echelon) from 8 December 1941, but this assignment, often repeated in numerous accounts of this unit, was apparently provisional. In fact, its air echelon was at Hamilton Field, CA, under orders for movement to the Philippines at the time of the Japanese attack, and apparently moved, temporarily, to Muroc Dry Lake, CA, under extremely austere conditions, while its ground echelon departed San Francisco aboard ship on 6 December – but was ordered back to port on the 9th. In reality, therefore, the unit was thus thrown into the hastily organised Air Corps mix of transient and semi-formed units that were pulled together in California, Oregon and Washington state to prepare for Japanese moves against the west coast, and operated in a rather confused way from Bakersfield, CA, by 17 December. This situation existed only briefly, until things could be partially sorted out, however, and the air echelon, with its valuable early variant B-17s, departed for the Southwest Pacific in late December, effectively dissolving the Squadron for all intents and purposes, as its remaining stateside personnel were then assigned to other units. On paper, the Squadron, reorganised, was assigned to Geiger Field, WA, by 14 March 1942, then on to Alamogordo AAF, NM, by 27 May 1942, by which time its association with the B-18 had ebbed and flowed several times.

93rd Bombardment Squadron (H), 19th Bomb Group, 1st Wing, GHQAF

The third original Squadron of the 19th Bomb Group, the 93rd was activated as a Heavy Bombardment Squadron at March Field, CA, on 20 October 1939. It moved with the Group to Albuquerque between June and September 1941 and on to Clark Field, Luzon, in the Philippines, on 23 October 1941. During the period between activation and movement to Albuquerque, the Squadron was equipped with B-18s. However, by 9 December 1941 the Squadron, after arriving in the Philippines, was equipped with six early variant B-17s.

38th Reconnaissance Squadron (L/), 19th Bomb Group, 1st Wing, GHQAF

Yet another unit often overlooked in accounts of the GHQAF, possibly because another unit of the exact same designation was activated in March 1943 at DeRidder AAF, LA (by which time the original 38th

Recon had become the 427th Bomb Squadron (H), the 38th Recon was a rather well-known pre-war B-18 operator. The unit's association with the B-18 commenced in August 1937 when 38th Recon personnel were sent TDY to the Douglas factory at Santa Monica for an intensive course on the new aircraft. On 27 September 1937 the first B-18 arrived for the Squadron and, following the arrival of several more, the balance of the Squadron personnel who had not been to the Douglas factory departed for training as well. By December the unit had achieved partial operational readiness on B-18s, and was able to send two of its new aircraft to Hamilton Field to take part in maneuvers there. Besides the B-18s, the Squadron also received one of the five Sikorsky Y1OA-8 amphibians acquired by the Air Corps, a very exotic aircraft.

The Squadron sent three B-18s far afield between 17 and 19 February 1938, to Fort Huachuca, AZ, as part of a tactical exercise in long-range reconnaissance. A little-known deviation in the ongoing training of the Squadron occurred on 1 May 1938 when the entire aircraft complement of the Squadron was temporarily redesignated as the 1st Provisional Transport Squadron and, under the command of Major Paul R. Prentiss, commenced evacuating Air Corps personnel from March Field to several New England states for duty with various units of the 1st Wing taking part in GHQAF exercises. On 15 May the movement of troops and equipment was completed and the unit aircraft were then attached to other organisations for the actual maneuvers. The B-18s assigned to the Squadron enabled this operation, and it has largely escaped notice in historical accounts. No sooner had the Squadron recovered to its home station than it commenced a series of training missions to Valparaiso, Florida, Kelly Field, Texas, and other locations during June 1938.

The Squadron received its first new B-18A on 29 September 1938, and the crews were reportedly very pleased with both the 'modern' appearance of the aircraft and its improved systems. The Squadron had been alerted to deploy to the Philippines with the remainder of the 19th Group in September 1941, but at the last moment the movement orders were revoked. The Squadron commenced re-equipping with new Boeing B-17C and B-17E aircraft through to the end of the year and into early 1942, and served briefly with the so-called Sierra Bombardment Group after Pearl Harbor, although by this time the relationship with the B-18 was nearing an end.

2nd Wing, General Headquarters Air Force

The second of the original wings of the GHQAF, this organisation conducted much of the Army's pursuit, bombardment and observation operations in the eastern quadrant of the Continental United States, and was headquartered at Langley Field, Virginia, throughout the B-18 operating period. It was redesignated as the **2nd Bombardment Wing** in 1940. By March 1941 the **Headquarters and Headquarters Squadron** at Langley Field had one B-18A assigned, marked as WB1.

During the period that the Wing operated B-18 series aircraft, the major subordinate bombardment flying units were the **2nd and 9th Bombardment Groups**.

2nd Bombardment Group, 2nd Wing, GHQAF

Regarded by some historians as the premier Army bombardment Group, the Langley Field-based organisation had progressed from the biplane Keystone B-6A through the monoplane Martin B-10B by the time that it learned of the 1935 heavy bombardment aircraft competition at Wright Field, which led to the selection of the DB-1 to become the B-18. At practically the same juncture, the Group also learned that the Boeing Model X-299, which was ordered as the pre-production series of Y1B-17s, would almost certainly be assigned to the Group for operational testing. This suited the Commander and most of the crews, as the 2nd Bomb Group, for all intents and purposes, had been 'top-loaded' with Air Corps aviators who have, over the years, become rather inaccurately known as the 'bomber mafia'. In actuality, the officers and men of the 2nd Bomb Group knew little more about either aircraft than what could be gleaned from reading the same aviation journals of the day that were available to the average aviation enthusiast. There appears to have been a general sentiment, however, that a twin-engined aircraft could probably not meet the requirements of the so-called 'strategic bomber' that was the buzz-word of its day, but even so it was still probably better than the B-10Bs with which they had grown.

Facilities at Langley improved during the course of 1936 in anticipation of the arrival of both the Y1B-17s and the first of the B-18s, including the luxury of paved engine warm-up aprons in front of the permanent hangars.

Colonel Follett Bradley, at the time the Chief of Staff of the GHQAF, flew the first B-18 to the Group from Randolph Field, TX, in February 1937, and after arrival it was intensively exercised by 2nd Bomb Group crew – but deliveries of B-18s for line units at Langley did not commence until October 1937. Favorable tail winds at 9,000 feet had enabled Colonel Bradley to make the non-stop flight (which apparently amazed the Langley contingent, which had been led to believe that the B-18 couldn't make more than 850 miles) in a record time of 5hr 40min, averaging an incredible 275mph. This performance turned some heads amongst even the most ardent of the Y1B-17 proponents at the installation.

By 23 March 1939 the B-18s assigned to the Group were being used exclusively by the local navigator training course they had established, which was regarded as an excellent means of providing navigators for the B-17 crews. But by the third quarter of 1940 signs of changes to come were sweeping through the Group and increased from month to month until the Japanese attack. The 2nd Wing had grown by some 350% and the supply of aircraft to equip assigned units failed utterly to keep up with the pace. At the same time, the Wing and the 2nd Bomb Group were receiving larger and larger quotas from the Training Center; veteran officers and crews were transferred out, and Squadron training within the Group gave way to individual training.

In fact, by September 1940 the 2nd Bomb Group had, for all intents and purposes, become what the British would describe as an Operational Training Unit (OTU). It carried out a combination of both specialised ground and air training for no fewer than twenty-three student officers of Class 40-B, who had been assigned to the Group between 3 June and 23 August 1940. During that period the Group had committed nine of its prized B-17Bs, three B-18s, four A-17s and five North American BT-14s to the training program. Considering the trials that nearly all of these officers were to face in the following eighteen months, this preparation must be regarded as having been nothing less than invaluable, although it was nearly impossible for the Group to recognise at the time.

By December 1940, when the 2nd Group attempted to organise exercises under simulated combat conditions, it was forced to fall back, instead, on its achievements in this area of the preceding year, as the turmoil simply could not sustain any form of organised exercises. Finally, as war unforeseen approached, flow charts seemed to speed up and training schedules began to fill the days and weeks. As early as 8 October 1940 the 2nd Bomb Group was obliged to make the following melancholy entry in its organisational diary:

'Cool – overcast – ceiling 4,000 feet, visibility eight miles. This is a sad day for the 2nd Bomb Group as, on this date, Major George, leading a flight of 10 B-17B aircraft, departed for March Field, California, where the B-17Bs will remain on permanent assignment. This is a sad blow to the 2nd Bomb

Group, as the B-17Bs are to be replaced temporarily by B-18As. No definite information is available as to when this Group will again be equipped with heavy bombardment type aircraft. This was the first Bomb Group to be equipped with heavy, four engine type bombers.'

In fact, the Group was destined to go to war with B-18s, and flew numerous coastal patrol and anti-submarine missions with them, as will be seen later in this account.

By 30 April 1941 the 2nd Bomb Group (H) was drastically short of equipment, and could count only eight B-18As and three B-17Bs on strength, although it also had single examples of the B-18 and B-18A equipped for the all-important tow target function. By the end of June this had changed to seven mixed B-17 variants and just four B-18s, and by 31 October 1941, on the eve of the US entry into the war, the Group could muster a mix of fourteen North American B-25s, four B-18s, three B-17s and two brand-new Martin B-26s.

20th Bombardment Squadron (H), 2nd Bomb Group, 2nd Wing, GHQAF

The 20th Bomb Squadron was one of the veteran between-the-wars Air Corps bombardment units, and had operated from Langley as part of the 2nd Bomb Group since June 1922. It transitioned from Keystone B-6s to a few monoplane Boeing Y1B-9s between 1932 and 1936, when Martin B-10s arrived. Between 1936 and 1942 the Squadron saw the coming and going of an amazing assortment of equipment, including a few early B-17s, B-25s, Northrop A-17s, Douglas A-20s and B-23s, Lockheed B-34s and of course B-18s. The Squadron was one of the pioneer operators of the Y1B-17, and took part in mercy missions in relief of flood victims in Pennsylvania between 20 and 22 March 1936, and in the highly publicised Goodwill Flight to Argentina (15-27 February 1938), Colombia (3-12 August 1938) and Brazil (10-26 November 1939). While flying B-18s, the unit was engaged in intensive anti-submarine activities between 8 December 1941 and October 1942 (of which more later), at which time it was reorganised, re-equipped and deployed in preparation for the invasion of North Africa.

49th Bombardment Squadron (H), 2nd Bomb Group, 2nd Wing, GHQAF

Another of the veteran Air Corps bombardment units, the 49th Bomb Squadron joined the 2nd Bomb Group as a consolidated unit in 1936, although it had been garrisoned at Langley Field from 18 January 1928. Like the 20th Bomb Squadron, it had transitioned from Keystone B-6s through Boeing Y1B-9s between 1932 and 1936, and between 1936 and 1942 operated Martin B-10Bs, early B-17s, Douglas A-20s and B-23s, the solitary, massive Boeing XB-15 for a time, and B-18s. The unit used the XB-15 to make a spectacular mercy flight to Santiago, Chile, between 4 and 14 February 1939 to aid earthquake victims there.

The Squadron was also a participant in the 15-27 February 1938 Goodwill Flight with early B-17s to Colombia, another such flight to Mexico between 9 and 15 June 1939, and the flight to Brazil between 10 and 28 November 1939. It was a detachment of B-17s from the 49th BS that carried out the famous pre-war demonstration of the long-range capabilities of the B-17 when the unit intercepted the Italian liner *Rex* some 725 miles out at sea on 12 May 1938.

Although based at Langley from consolidation in 1936 until 23 November 1941, its air echelon was sent on a special deployment to Newfoundland Air Base and was en route there on 1 December 1941 at Mitchel Field, NY. The day after Pearl Harbor, however, the Squadron was ordered clear across the US to operate from Geiger

Field, Washington, in concert with the 12th Reconnaissance Squadron, until that echelon was dissolved in late December, a very little known deployment. In a rather confusing series of events, the Squadron was re-consolidated and sent on to Argentia, Newfoundland, in January 1942, but returned to Langley Field on 24 June 1942, whence it also took part in further anti-submarine patrols with B-18s. It became one of the very few Air Corps units that could, consequently, claim to have conducted coastal patrol and anti-submarine missions on both the Atlantic and Pacific coasts of the US. The unit was reorganised and re-equipped entirely as a B-17 operating unit and deployed to North Africa in April 1943.

96th Bombardment Squadron (H),
2nd Bomb Group, 2nd Wing, GHQAF

The round-out, third Squadron of the 2nd Bomb Group was the 96th Bomb Squadron, which was stationed at Langley Field from June 1922. Operating biplane Keystone B-6s from 1932 until 1936, it re-equipped with Martin B-10s, then into a mix of early B-17s, B-25s and B-18s between 1936 and 1942. Like the other bombardment squadrons of the 2nd Bomb Group, the unit participated in the Good Will flights to Argentina of 15-27 February 1938, Colombia (3-12 August 1938) and Brazil (10-26 November 1939) flying early B-17s. The Squadron received its first B-18As in September 1938, however, and was the unit tasked to evaluate them in comparison with the straight B-18s with which they were also partially equipped. Although having been exposed to the Y1B-17s, crews reported being impressed with the improved creature comforts afforded by the B-18As, although they bemoaned the fact that they did not become fully equipped at the time with early B-17s. Prior to the outbreak of war, the Squadron aircraft were distinguishable by having their engine cowlings painted chrome yellow.

The Squadron was reassigned to Spokane, Washington, some time prior to 1 October 1942, and on to Ephrata, Washington, on 29 October 1942, while still nominally part of the 2nd Bomb Group; there the crews found that their tent city living accommodations were more than a mile away from the rather austere flight line. They received a 'new' B-17E on 30 October 1942 while there, and could thus count a grand total of two aircraft on strength! It is not clear if the other airplane was a B-18 or B-17 at this point. The unit redeployed to Glasgow, MT, on 29 November 1942, where it was reorganised, brought up to strength and prepared for movement to North Africa as a strictly B-17 operating unit.

41st Reconnaissance Squadron (L/R),
2nd Bomb Group, 2nd Wing, GHQAF

Redesignated as the 41st Reconnaissance Squadron (Long Range) on 22 December 1939, and actually activated as such on 1 February 1940, this Squadron was immediately attached to the 2nd Bomb Group at Langley Field, VA. It was subsequently redesignated as the 41st Reconnaissance Squadron (Heavy) on 20 November 1940, and on 22 April 1942 became the 429th Bombardment Squadron.

Top right: The ten B-18As commencing with BI 73 in the line-up down the center of this parade at Bolling Field, DC, represent nearly every subordinate Squadron of the 9th Bombardment Group. The Group was home-based at Mitchel Field, NY, until the autumn of 1940 when it moved to the Caribbean. *via David W. Ostrowski*

Right: By the time the 9th Bomb Group (H) was reassigned from Mitchel Field, NY, to Rio Hato, Republic of Panama, where much of the Group is pictured in early 1941 not long after arrival, the unit designators on the vertical fins had changed to 24/9B, 4/9B, etc. Most of these aircraft were amongst those that saw the majority of the early anti-submarine efforts in the Caribbean. *Richard W. Spencer*

The Squadron had the distinction of not only operating Douglas B-18 variants, but also, briefly, the huge Boeing XB-15, early Boeing B-17 variants, and at least one Grumman OA-9 amphibian. By 31 March 1941 the unit had four B-18As (one of them fitted as a target tug) and a B-18 at Langley, but by 30 June 1941 had a mix of three B-18As and a small number of Boeing B-17Bs. The Squadron also had the distinction of being one of the very first USAAC units to 'go to war', when it was deployed to Newfoundland around 28 August 1941 to assist in 'enforcement' of the so-called Neutrality Patrols. It is thus fair to state that, by 30 November 1941, with a mix of six B-17Bs and one B-18A, the unit was the very first to take the B-18 series to a war footing and the potential of live-fire exchanges with Axis submarine and surface units in the North Atlantic. The Squadron, following redesignation as the 429th BS, moved to Ephrata, WA, on 29 October 1942, but by then was an all-B-17 operating unit.

9th Bombardment Group, 2nd Bomb Wing, GHQAF

Designated as such in 1935, this veteran organisation was redesignated as the 9th Bombardment Group (Medium) in 1939 and as the 9th Bombardment Group (Heavy) in 1940. Although assigned to the 2nd Bomb Wing, headquartered at Langley Field, the 9th was headquartered between 1922 and 6 November 1940 at historic Mitchel Field, NY. It was reassigned to the Caribbean Air Force on 12 November 1940, initially headquartered at remote Rio Hato in the Republic of Panama, but moved again to Waller Field, Trinidad, on 12 October 1940. For the purposes of this account, the 9th Bomb Group, and its subordinate Squadrons, was a major player in the B-18 epic, as will be seen later. Like so many pre-war units, the 9th Bomb Group had a 'later existence' in the Pacific theater as a Boeing B-29 operational unit, and as a direct consequence its earlier wartime exploits in the Atlantic and Caribbean theaters have been rather overshadowed. From an Air Force lineage standpoint, however, it was indeed one and the same unit. During its GHQAF phase, subordinate Squadrons included the 1st, 5th and 99th Bomb Squadrons. That part of their story that pertains to the Group prior to movement to Panama is summarised here; however, the bulk of the Group's very considerable early wartime story is recorded later, in the sections of this work devoted to the Caribbean war.

1st Bombardment Squadron, 9th Bomb Group, 2nd Bomb Wing, GHQAF

Lineally the oldest organised combat unit in the Army Air Corps as of this time, the 1st Bombardment Squadron was designated as such on 1 March 1935, being subsequently redesignated as the 1st Bombardment Squadron (Medium) on 6 December 1939 and the 1st Bombardment Squadron (Heavy) on 20 November 1940. Between 1936 and 1942 it operated, successively, Martin B-10s, Douglas B-18s and Boeing B-17s. Although stationed for many years at Mitchel Field, NY, it moved overseas with the Group to Rio Hato, Republic of Panama, on 13 November 1940, becoming an element of the Caribbean Air Force (later Sixth Air Force), then on to Piarco Field, Trinidad, on 24 April 1941. Subsequent movements are dizzying, as the unit responded to the nearly overwhelming Axis submarine threat in the Caribbean. After Waller Field was opened on Trinidad, to ease Allied congestion at Piarco, the unit moved there on 29 October 1941, then on to Edinburgh Field, Trinidad, on 23 August 1942, where it remained until returning to the Continental United States at Orlando Air Base, FL, on 31 October 1942. Some historians, with perhaps good reason, have often confused this organisation with the 1st Bombardment Squadron (M) (Provisional), part of the Headquarters, Chinese-American Composite Wing (Provisional), of October 1943, which served exclusively in the CBI, but they are completely unrelated.

B-18s of the 1st Bomb Squadron at Piarco Field, Trinidad – an operating station that was to become very familiar with the type during the war – were placed on alert as early as 1 July 1941, as the world situation deteriorated further and intelligence reports started predicting emergencies even in the Caribbean. *USAAF*

This is the Squadron insignia of the veteran 1st Bomb Squadron, 9th Bomb Group, which deployed to Rio Hato, Republic of Panama, on 13 November 1940, then on to Trinidad with a mix of B-18s and B-18As well into 1942. Although B-18s have been reported by former crew members as having worn this insignia, no photo evidence has been located. *USAF*

5th Bombardment Squadron, 9th Bomb Group, 2nd Wing, GHQAF

Designated as such on 1 March 1935, the 5th Bombardment Squadron became the 5th Bombardment Squadron (Medium) on 6 December 1939, in keeping with the Air Corps's effort to administratively describe the mission of assigned tactical units, but became the 5th Bombardment Squadron (Heavy) on 20 November 1940. Assigned

with its parent Group at Mitchel Field during the between-the-wars period, the Squadron also moved overseas on 13 November 1940 to Rio Hato, Panama, and onwards to Beane Field, St Lucia, one of the island bases acquired from the British in the famous 'Destroyers for Bases' arrangement of the immediate pre-war period in late September 1941. From there, as part of the Caribbean Air Force (later Sixth Air Force), it was equipped almost entirely with B-18s and was a central but unsung player in the early phases of the anti-submarine war. It also had a key role in the isolation and surveillance of the Vichy French fleet at Martinique in the Caribbean early in the war, all of which is described in detail later in this account.

This B-18, BI 47, was probably assigned to the 5th Bomb Squadron, 9th Bomb Group, while still at Mitchel Field, NY, before deploying to Panama in November 1940. *via Kev Darling*

The 5th Bomb Squadron, 9th Bomb Group operated a mix of B-18s and B-18As, and BI 48, being towed, bears the twin fuselage bands of the Squadron Commander's aircraft in this Mitchel Field, NY, image. Note that the prop spinners and forward portion of the engine cowls have been painted. *Authors' collection*

99th Bombardment Squadron, 9th Bomb Group, 2nd Wing, GHQAF

Another veteran unit, the 99th Bomb Squadron was actually one of the original units assigned to the 9th Bomb Group, commencing in February 1929, when it was still the 99th Observation Squadron. It was redesignated as a Bombardment Squadron on 1 March 1935 and successively as a Medium and Heavy squadron, in lock-step with its sister organisations, on 6 December 1939 and 20 November 1940 respectively. Also calling Mitchel Field home for much of the between-the-wars period, it moved to Rio Hato, Panama, with the Group on 13 November 1940, but was dispersed to distant Zandery Field, Dutch Guiana (Surinam), on 3 December 1941. This unit was also a key player in the B-18 anti-submarine war, and is dealt with at length later in this account.

This B-18, coded R 4 and bearing the insignia of the 99th Bomb Squadron, 9th Bomb Group on her nose, is something of a mystery. Being a dedicated bombardment unit, the code 'R 4' is inappropriate for this aircraft, and should probably have been BI 4. The men inspecting the aircraft appear to be West Point cadets. *Paul Bridgford*

Looking very sharp with Squadron Commander's fuselage bands, over which the distinctive charging buffalo unit insignia was superimposed, BI 70 of the 99th Bomb Squadron, 9th Bomb Group was a long way from home when photographed here at Seattle, WA. The leading edges of the cowlings were probably red. *Wright State University*

On 16 April 1940 2Lt Forman of the 18th Reconnaissance Squadron (M/R), attached at the time to the 9th Bomb Group, was forced to ditch AC37-480, coded R 5, off Coney Island, NY, when he and his crew became lost in very heavy fog and exhausted their fuel. The seaworthy qualities of the B-18A are evident and the aircraft was brought ashore. *USAAC, Base Photo Section, Mitchel Field, NY*

The clumsy recovery effort of AC37-480 inflicted more damage than the actual ditching, and the aircraft was a loss. Here she sits, still bearing the Flight Commander's fuselage band and unit insignia, forlorn and awaiting the scrappers. *Authors' collection*

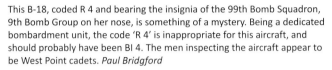

18th Reconnaissance Squadron (M/R), 9th Bomb Group, 2nd Wing, GHQAF

The semi-autonomous 18th Reconnaissance Squadron (Medium Range) was designated as such on 6 December 1939, and possessed a long and distinguished lineage. The Squadron was actually assigned to the 2nd Wing, but attached to the 9th Bomb Group, and based at Mitchel Field, LI, NY, from 1 September 1936 until it moved to Langley Field, VA, on 15 November 1940, after becoming attached to the newly formed 22nd Bombardment Group in September. By 31 March 1941, stationed at Langley Field, the Squadron had four B-18As and a single B-18 equipped as a target tug. By the end of April the first four B-26s had been received, but the aforementioned B-18As and B-18 were still on hand. The Squadron had a lengthy association with the B-18 series, from 1937 through to 1941, but also had small numbers of other so-called 'reconnaissance' aircraft, including at least one Sikorsky Y1OA-8. It transitioned into B-25s in 1941, then to Martin B-26s starting on 18 March 1941, although at least a few B-18s were still on strength as well, as noted. By 31 October 1941, however, the unit possessed fourteen B-26s, but still retained a single B-18. The Squadron was redesignated as the 18th Reconnaissance Squadron (Medium) on 20 November 1940, and subsequently as the 408th Bombardment Squadron (M) on 22 April 1942. It was credited with flying anti-submarine missions between December 1941 and January 1942, many on B-18s.

By August 1940 the 18th Reconnaissance Squadron (M/R), attached to the 9th Bomb Group, had changed unit designators as shown here by 7/18R. The wide, flat-black painted area aft of the long exhaust over the engine nacelle is unusual, and the ventral gun position traverse restraints are visible. *NARA, RG342FH, 118869AC*

22nd Bombardment Group (M), 2nd Wing, GHQAF

Constituted as such on 22 December 1939, but not actually activated until 1 February 1940, this was one of the expansion organisations of the pre-war Air Corps, and by 1 July 1940 was nominally based at Mitchel Field, LI, NY, but had no tactical subordinate squadrons there with it. These were stationed elsewhere: the 2nd Bomb Squadron (M) at Bolling Field, DC, by 1 February 1940, and the 19th Bomb Squadron (M) and 33rd Bomb Squadron (M) both at Patterson Field, OH, also from 1 February 1940. All operated B-18s. By 31 March 1941 the Group had consolidated at Langley Field, VA, and could count a total of nine B-18As and a single tow-target-equipped B-18 on strength at that time. Dramatic equipment changes took place starting as early as 30 April 1941, when the unit had received fifteen B-26s, although it still possessed seven B-18As and the single tow target B-18. By the end of June the unit still had six B-18As and, by 31 October 1941, with no fewer than fifty B-26s on hand, the Group could still muster three B-18As. The entire Group redeployed to the west coast (mainly to Muroc Dry Lake) from Langley Field, VA, by 9 December 1941, apparently leaving its last B-18s behind at that time, and was credited with anti-submarine patrols along the coast with the primary mounts, the B-26s. It then deployed to the Southwest Pacific.

Probably photographed at Langley Field, VA, after 31 March 1941, 22B/26 heads a line-up of 22nd Bomb Group (M) B-18As. The Group departed for the west coast in December 1941 and re-equipped with B-26s, leaving the comparatively short association with B-18s behind. *via Robert F. Dorr*

2nd Bombardment Squadron (M), 22nd Bomb Group, 2nd Wing, GHQAF

Although constituted on 1 January 1938 and redesignated as the 2nd Bombardment Squadron (Medium), this unit was not activated until 1 February 1940, and stationed initially apart from its parent Group at Bolling Field, DC, until moving to Langley Field, VA, on 14 November 1940, where it received two 'new' B-18As freshly overhauled by the Savannah Air Depot, a third following a week later. The unit did not start converting to Martin B-26s from B-18s until April 1941. It deployed to Muroc Dry Lake, CA, around 9 December 1941, after the Japanese attack, and apparently conducted anti-submarine patrols from there. It is believed that it had totally re-equipped with Martin B-26s by that time, however.

19th Bombardment Squadron (M), 22nd Bomb Group, 2nd Wing, GHQAF

This expansion unit was constituted on 22 December 1939 and activated on 1 February 1940, when it was assigned to the 22nd Bomb Group, but stationed apart from its parent Group at distant Patterson Field, OH. It moved with the Group and was consolidated at Langley Field, VA, on 16 November 1940, however, and had B-18s assigned throughout this period. It re-equipped with Martin B-26s in 1941 and deployed with the Group to Muroc Dry Lake, CA, then on to Australia.

33rd Bombardment Squadron (M), 22nd Bomb Group, 2nd Wing, GHQAF

This unit was created and activated exactly like its sister unit, the 19th Bomb Squadron (M), at Patterson Field, OH, and trained with B-18s before converting to Martin B-26s and ultimately moving to Australia in late February 1942.

25th Bombardment Group (H), GHQAF

The newest of the GHQAF heavy bombardment groups, the 25th was apparently assigned directly subordinate to the GHQAF rather than to the 2nd Wing, as were older organisations. Constituted on 22 December 1939 and activated on 1 February 1940, the Group trained intensively with Northrop A-17s and B-18s for the most part and moved to Puerto Rico from Langley Field a scant nine months after activation. It is frequently missed entirely as having been connected with the GHQAF at Langley. Subordinate Squadrons were the 10th, 12th and 35th Bombardment Squadron at this juncture. Ironically, this Group was destined to endure as one of the premier B-18 operating units of the war, and much more on its wartime activities will be found later in this account.

3rd Wing, General Headquarters Air Force

The last of the original major commands of the GHQAF was designated as such in 1935, and was redesignated as the 3rd Bombardment Wing in 1940. It was subsequently inactivated on 5 September 1941 in its final pre-war incarnation.

Although of marginal quality, this is one of the few known images of a Headquarters, 3rd Wing, GHQAF B-18A, Field Number 1 – and thus probably the Wing Commander's aircraft. The insignia on the rear fuselage is believed to have been that of the 3rd Wing, stationed then at Barksdale Field, LA. *USAF*

Between 1932 and 1941 the 3rd Wing had a total of five Bombardment Groups (as well as other units) subordinate, consisting of the 3rd, 13th, 27th, 29th and 44th Bombardment Groups.[24] The Wing was headquartered between February 1935 and 2 October 1940 at Barksdale Field, LA, but moved to MacDill Field in Florida, where it remained through till 5 September 1941. By March 1941 the Wing Headquarters at MacDill had one B-18A assigned to its Headquarters and Headquarters Squadron.

3rd Bombardment Group (L), 3rd Wing, GHQAF

Not normally associated with the B-18, the 3rd Bomb Group was stationed at Barksdale Field, LA, from 28 February 1935 until it moved to Savannah Army Air Base, GA, on 6 October 1940, where it remained until 19 January 1942, when it deployed to Australia. Subordinate units included the 8th Bombardment Squadron, 13th Bomb Squadron, 51st Bomb Squadron, 89th Bomb Squadron and 90th Bomb Squadron. Of these units, only the 51st Bomb Squadron never had B-18s assigned, and is thus excluded from the following brief discussion.

By 31 March 1941 the Group had three B-18As assigned for tow target duties at Savannah and was in the process of intensive re-equipment with Douglas A-24s and A-20s. By 31 October 1941 these attack types made up the bulk of the aircraft assigned to the Group and its subordinate units, with twelve A-24s and no fewer than forty-six A-20s on hand. However, three B-18s were still assigned. Although this Group was not a major B-18 operator, the type did figure significantly during its organisational and training phases, and thus rates inclusion in this narrative.

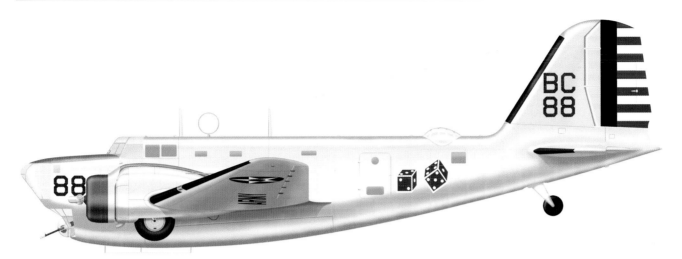

B-18 Dice. Artwork by Rich Dann

8th Bombardment Squadron (L), 3rd Bomb Group, 3rd Wing, GHQAF

The 8th Attack Squadron was redesignated as the 8th Bombardment Squadron (Light) on 15 September 1939 at Barksdale Field, LA, where it remained until transferred to Savannah, GA, on 8 October 1940. Equipped initially with Northrop A-17s, the Squadron received B-18As in September 1939, and later received eight of the exotic, twin-engined Curtiss A-18s in May 1940, but by the time it moved to Savannah these had been replaced by six B-18As. These were intensively utilised for training, and were handed off around 10 January 1941, when the first Douglas A-20As were received. By 3 September 1941 the Squadron had received A-24s, the aircraft with which it was shipped to Australia in February 1942.

13th Bombardment Squadron (L), 3rd Bomb Group, 3rd Wing, GHQAF

Formerly the 13th Attack Squadron, this unit was redesignated as the 13th Bombardment Squadron (L) on 15 September 1939 at Barksdale Field, LA, as a consolidated squadron and later became the 13th Bombardment Squadron (Dive) on 28 September 1942, by which time it had long since finished its brief engagement with the B-18. Along with the parent Group, it moved to Savannah Army Air Base, GA, on 10 October 1940, where it remained until 19 January 1942. During this period the Squadron operated a mixture of Martin B-12, B-18 and Douglas A-20A aircraft. It is credited with flying anti-submarine missions while stationed at Savannah with B-18s.

89th Bombardment Squadron (L), 3rd Bomb Group, 3rd Wing, GHQAF

This unit was a relatively new 'expansion' period organisation, initially formed on 20 November 1940 as the 10th Reconnaissance Squadron (L), but redesignated as the 89th Bombardment Squadron (L) on 14 August 1941 when it had a grand total of one officer and forty enlisted ranks on the rolls. Consequently, it never served with the parent Group at Barksdale, and saw US service with B-18s only at Savannah Army Air Base, GA, between 15 January 1941 and early 1942, although it started re-equipping with Douglas A-20As in August 1941. The unit subsequently deployed with the parent Group to Brisbane, Australia, where it saw extensive action throughout the remainder of the war. However, it is worth noting that three of the sixteen crews that took part in the immortal 'Doolittle Raid' on Tokyo were former 89th Bomb Squadron members, who put their training with their B-18s to good use.

90th Bombardment Squadron (L), 3rd Bomb Group, 3rd Wing, GHQAF

Formerly the 90th Attack Squadron, this unit was redesignated as a Bombardment Squadron (Light) on 15 September 1939, with the parent Group at Barksdale Field, LA. It also moved to Savannah Army Air Base, GA, on 10 October 1940 and deployment with the Group to Australia in February 1942.

13th Bombardment Group (M), 3rd Wing, GHQAF

The 13th Bombardment Group (Medium) was an expansion organisation, constituted on 20 November 1940 but not activated until 15 January 1941. It survived only through November 1942, by which time it had been transferred to the First Air Force and the Army Air Forces Antisubmarine Command. Its subordinate units included the 39th Bombardment Squadron (which became the 3rd Antisubmarine Squadron), 40th Bombardment Squadron (later the 4th Antisubmarine Squadron), and 41st Bombardment Squadron (later the 5th Antisubmarine Squadron). The Group was initially headquartered at Langley Field, VA, but moved to Orlando AAB, FL, around 6 June 1941, and later to Westover Field, MA, from 20 January 1942 until inactivation. Its units operated a mix of B-18, B-25 and A-29 aircraft. By 30 June 1941 the Group had a total of six B-18s at Orlando, increased to seven by 31 October.

39th Bombardment Squadron (M), 13th Bomb Group (M), 3rd Wing, GHQAF

Formed in June 1941, like so many cadre units, the 39th Bombardment Squadron (M) had only a handful of fairly inexperienced officers, just short of 100 enlisted ranks, and two B-18s, which they received on 2 June. Only two of the officers were qualified on B-18s, so the primary mission of the Squadron was initially to check out several co-pilots as first officers without delay. The unit moved from its initial station, Langley Field, VA, to Orlando on 4 June 1941 (although small detachments operated from Savannah AAB, GA, between 8 and 14 December 1941), and more officers trickled in; by August the unit could also boast a Boeing-Stearman PT-17! Typical of such cadre squadrons at the time, and with the world situation and Air Corps expansion in high gear, the Squadron was obliged to put its two B-18s on a 24-hour schedule as of 20 August 1941. Soon, new North American B-25s started to arrive, and by the end of December the unit had ten. We pick up the story of this unit once again after war is declared and it has moved to Westover Field, MA, later in the account.

40th Bombardment Squadron (M), 13th Bomb Group (M), 3rd Wing, GHQAF

Not to be confused with an entirely different unit with this designation, formed after the original unit was redesignated as the 4th Antisubmarine Squadron on 29 November 1942, the 40th Bombardment Squadron (Medium) was constituted on 20 November 1940 and activated on 15 January 1941. An air echelon of this unit was attached to the Caribbean Sea Frontier, a Navy organisation, between 30 August and 9 October 1942, as related later in this account in the section devoted to the anti-submarine campaign.

41st Bombardment Squadron (M), 13th Bomb Group (M), 3rd Wing, GHQAF

The lineage of this Squadron was nearly identical to its sister 39th and 40th Bomb Squadrons (M). It was initially stationed at Langley Field, VA, and moved to Orlando AAB, FL, on 7 June 1941, then on to Westover Field, MA, in January 1942. Like its sister squadrons, it was redesignated as an Antisubmarine Squadron and subsequently assigned to the 25th Anti-submarine Wing (qv). Additional details are included in the section of this book devoted to the anti-submarine campaign.

27th Bombardment Group (L), 3rd Wing, GHQAF

Often lost in the GHQAF accounting, due to the fact that it was much later redesignated as the 27th Fighter Group, the 27th Bombardment Group (Light) was constituted on 22 December 1939 and activated on 1 February 1940 at Barksdale Field, LA, consisting of the 15th, 16th, 17th and 91st Bomb Squadrons (L). The Group had been equipped with a mix of Douglas B-18As, Northrop A-17As and Curtiss A-18s as early as 11 March 1940 at Barksdale. The personal call sign of the Group Commander was 6MT, and the HHS, 27th Bomb Group, as of 11 March 1940, had three B-18As and a Northrop A-17A. Not normally associated with the B-18, the unit in fact had moved from Barksdale to Savannah AAB, GA, by 31 March 1941, and was equipped with not fewer than eighteen B-18As as well as three other B-18As fitted with tow target equipment. By the end of April 1941 the Group still had thirteen B-18As, but by 30 June 1941 it had commenced initial re-equipment with Douglas A-20s (twenty-one were on hand), but still retained nine B-18As. The unit sailed to the Philippines on 1 November 1941, and arrived at Manilla on the 20th. The aircraft for the organisation, which by this time had been changed to have been Douglas A-24s, had not arrived by the time of the Japanese assault, however, and were diverted to Australia. The Group CO and twenty pilots were flown from Luzon to Australia to retrieve the aircraft, but were unable to return before the situation in the PI became untenable. Some saw service in Java between February and May 1942 before they were reassigned. The members of the Group left on Luzon served as infantrymen in the battles for Bataan and Corregidor, and most were either killed in action or captured and taken POW. The 27th Group was transferred, on paper, from Australia to the US in May 1942 and re-equipped with Douglas A-20s, moving to North Africa in November 1942.

15th Bombardment Squadron (L), 27th Bomb Group (L), 3rd Wing, GHQAF

Constituted and activated along with the parent Group at Barksdale Field, LA, this unit was transferred to the V Air Support Command on 14 October 1941 and thus did not accompany the Group to the Philippines. It was redesignated as the 1st Pursuit Squadron (Night Fighter) on 1 April 1942, and by that time had long since ended its brief association with the B-18. As of 11 March 1940, however, the Squadron was very active at Barksdale and had six B-18As, two Curtiss A-18s

and a single (spare) Northrop A-17A on strength. It apparently did not transfer to Savannah with the remainder of the Group.

16th Bombardment Squadron (L), 27th Bomb Group (L), 3rd Wing, GHQAF

Organised and activated along with the parent Group at Barksdale, this unit was reassigned to Hunter Field, Savannah, GA, on 7 October 1940 together with the Group, and moved to Fort William McKinley, Luzon, PI, minus its aircraft, in October 1941, by which time it had been slated to become a Douglas A-24 operating unit. Prior to that movement, however, the Squadron had what was destined to be the first of two separate and distinct associations with the B-18.

While at Barksdale, and as of 11 March 1940, the Squadron had six B-18As, two Curtiss A-18s and a single Northrop A-17A (a spare) on strength, equipment identical to the other two Squadrons in the Group. The Squadron loaned one of its B-18As, AC38-600, to the Fort Wayne Army Air Base, IN, where the AFCE used it to install and test radio equipment in mid-April 1941. Following its arrival in the Philippines, however, and when it became evident that its complement of Douglas A-24s would never arrive, the Squadron was partially equipped with straight B-18s that had survived the Japanese onslaught (which the few pilots who managed to get to the controls described as being 'in rotten shape'), and it was with these aircraft that members of the unit managed to escape from Clark Field through Tarakan to Darwin, Australia, arriving on 22 December 1941, the same day that the so-called 'Pensacola Convoy' arrived in Brisbane.

Gustave M. Heiss Jr was one of the members of the 27th Bomb Group who flew out of Manila on the night of 17/18 December 1941 using two B-18s and a Douglas C-39 transport. He was Pilot in Command of one of the B-18s, with co-pilot Tim Timlin. When they landed at Batchelor Field, Northern Territory, with a planeload of men from the Philippines in one of the two B-18s, they were immediately ordered (by radio from the Philippines) to fly ammunition back to the islands. Without hesitation, they refuelled, loaded the cargo, and started the trek with the same aircraft back to the islands. They planned to retrace their route back to Borneo, then northward. However, Heiss and Timlin encountered a tropical storm off Borneo, which forced them back. They landed at Koepang and spent Christmas there. Shortly thereafter they returned to Australia, still with the cargo of precious ammunition aboard. This was unquestionably one of the B-18s, described later in this account, that continued to fly on in Australia for much of the war years with Transport Command out of Eagle Farm airfield in Brisbane.

17th Bombardment Squadron (L), 27th Bomb Group (L), 3rd Wing, GHQAF

This Squadron of the 27th Bomb Group had a service activation history identical to its sister Squadrons in the Group, especially the 16th BS. By 11 March 1940, while at Barksdale Field, it had six B-18As, two Curtiss A-18s and a Northrop A-17A on strength, and moved with most of these to Savannah AAB, GA, on 7 October 1940. It deployed, minus aircraft, to the Philippines, where it awaited its A-24s in vain.

91st Bombardment Squadron (L), 27th Bomb Group (L), 3rd Wing, GHQAF

This little-known unit, which had originally been constituted as the 11th Reconnaissance Squadron (L) on 20 November 1940, was in fact activated on 15 January 1941 (at which time it was attached to the 27th Bomb Group) and redesignated as the 91st Bombardment Squadron (L) on 14 August 1941. Consequently, it never served with the parent Group at Barksdale Field, LA, not joining until the Group arrived at

Above: B-18 series aircraft figured very prominently in the important massive domestic pre-war exercises held in 1940 and 1941. Here a B-18A, painted with water-based camouflage, becomes the very first aircraft to land on PSP (Perforated Steel Planking) laid down by Air Corps Engineers during the Carolina Maneuvers of 1941 – a system used extensively during the war. *NARA RG342FH 33552AC via Dana Bell*

Right; From left to right in the foreground, Major C. M. Berror of the 21st Engineers, Col Junius Houghton, 1Lt George E. Stewart (Corps of Engineers) and 2Lt J. S. McIntosh, pilot, pose for the cameraman after making the first ever landing of an aircraft on PSP on 25 October 1941 during the Carolina/Louisiana Maneuvers. The strip was about 3,000 feet long and 200 feet wide. *NARA RG342FH 3B40995 via Dana Bell*

Savannah AAB, GA, whence it had moved from Hattiesburg, MS, and was initially equipped with hand-me-down B-18s. It did move, minus aircraft (which were to have been A-24s), to the Philippines with the rest of the Group, where it suffered a similar fate, essentially ceasing to exist as a viable unit. From a lineage standpoint, the unit later became the 524th Fighter Squadron, and served as such in North Africa from December 1942.

29th Bombardment Group (H), 3rd Wing, GHQAF

Constituted as the 29th Bombardment Group (Heavy) on 22 December 1939, and activated on 1 February 1940, this tactical unit consisted of the 6th Bombardment Squadron, 29th Bombardment Squadron and 52nd Bombardment Squadron, and was initially assigned at Langley Field, VA, but moved to MacDill Field, FL, in May 1940. Its units were equipped with a mix of B-18 and B-17 aircraft and it was tasked with patrols in the Caribbean regions of Florida between December 1941 and June 1942. One of the few units that was more or less near strength, the Group had a total of thirteen B-18As and one B-18 (fitted for target tug duties) at MacDill by 31 March 1941. By the end of April this had decreased slightly to twelve B-18As and the single B-18. As of 30 June 1941 the unit had re-equipped with six mixed B-17s, but still retained two B-18As, and by 31 October the entire Group had but four mixed B-17s and one remaining B-18. After Pearl Harbor the hasty redeployment of available assets again altered the composition of the Group, and by 26 February 1942 the Group Headquarters and subordinate 6th, 43rd and 52nd Bomb Squadrons, together with the attached 21st Recon Squadron, all at MacDill, operated a heterogeneous collection consisting of one B-18, one Douglas A-20C, three B-18As and seven B-17Es. The 6th Bomb Squadron also had a small detachment at distant Ellington Field, TX, with another B-18A.

6th Bombardment Squadron (H), 29th Bombardment Group (H), 3rd Wing, GHQAF

Constituted on 22 December 1939, this unit was activated on 1 February 1940 at Langley Field, VA, and operated a small assortment of Y1B-17s (including the very first one taken into the Air Corps inventory), B-18s

and early B-17s. The Squadron transferred to MacDill Field, FL, on 22 June 1940 and carried out patrols, to the best of its ability, along the Caribbean west coast of Florida over the Gulf of Mexico all the way to the coast of Mexico. It became an operational training unit on 4 March 1942 and was transferred to Gowen Field, Boise, ID, before ultimately going to the Western Pacific as a B-17 and B-24 outfit.

43rd Bombardment Squadron (H), 29th Bombardment Group (H), 3rd Wing, GHQAF

The organisation and activation of this Squadron was identical to its sister 6th Bomb Squadron. However, following its move with the Group to MacDill Field, FL, on 21 May 1940, it was further reassigned to Pope Field, NC, on 7 December 1941, returning to MacDill by 1 January 1942. It operated a mix of B-18s and B-18As, and B-17Bs and B-17Es. This Squadron was apparently something of a throw-together unit, as, according to Air Force records, following its move to Pope Field, NC, it operated intensive coastal patrols from there and Charlotte to as far south as Miami, FL, with no fewer than twenty B-18s, making both daylight and night patrols.

52nd Bombardment Squadron (H), 29th Bombardment Group (H), 3rd Wing, GHQAF

The 52nd Bomb Squadron was activated on 1 February 1940, also at Langley Field, and its subsequent history was almost identical to that of the sister 6th Bomb Squadron. It is known to have operated both B-18s and B-17s between 1940 and 1943 and lost an aircraft under mysterious circumstances (given only as 'Number 97', probably a B-17) on a patrol out of MacDill in May 1942. Neither it nor its crew were ever found.

Activated in February 1940 as part of the 3rd Wing, GHQAF, the 52nd Bomb Squadron (H), 29th Bomb Group (H) was based at Langley Field, VA, and 29B/93 was one of its B-18As before it moved to MacDill Field, FL, in June. *Norm Taylor collection, Museum of Flight*

44th Bombardment Group (H), 3rd Wing, GHQAF

Constituted on 20 November 1940, this unit was activated on 15 January 1941. Most published histories of this distinguished unit do not link it with the B-18; however, as of 30 June 1941, while stationed at MacDill, it possessed two B-18s, operating alongside five early B-17s. By 31 October 1941, still at MacDill, it retained a single B-18 on strength, but B-17s had increased to seven. The subordinate Squadrons of the Group, the 66th, 67th and 68th Bomb Squadrons (H), commenced flying anti-submarine patrols from, of all places, Barksdale Field, LA, on Wednesday 28 January 1942, and by 26 February, still at Barksdale, the Group could muster a total of one Douglas A-20C, three Consolidated B-24C Liberators, five Consolidated LB-30 Liberators, and two B-18As. By this time the unit was part of the Air Force Combat Command (AFCC) (qv).

66th Bombardment Squadron (H), 44th Bomb Group (H), 3rd Wing, GHQAF

Activated at Langley Field, VA, this unit was almost immediately transferred to MacDill Field, FL, on 15 January 1941. It conducted its first cross-country flight on 19 April 1941, all the way to Kelly Field, TX, and from there to March Field, CA, to ferry back a new aircraft for the unit (assumed to have been a B-18), returning 'home' with it on 25 April. By 4 July 1941 the unit still had only a very small number of operational aircraft and, as a consequence, flying and training were described as 'very limited'. By 30 December 1941 the unit had a small number of B-18As, at least one North American BT-14 and two Boeing-Stearman PT-17 biplanes. The unit departed MacDill on 7 February 1942 and became an operational training unit at Will Rogers Field, Oklahoma City, OK, before deploying to England as a B-24 operating unit.

67th Bombardment Squadron (H), 44th Bomb Group (H), 3rd Wing, GHQAF

Like its sister units of the 44th Bomb Group, the 67th Bomb Squadron (Heavy) was constituted on 20 November 1940 and activated o 15 January 1941, but this Squadron was never, in fact, at Langley Field, first seeing existence as a unit at MacDill Field, FL. It moved to Barksdale Field, LA, on 9 February 1942, and from there became an OTU at Will Rogers Field, Oklahoma City, OK, before going to England as a B-24 outfit. It cannot be conclusively established that the 67th BS had B-18s assigned while at MacDill or Barksdale, but it apparently shared patrol duties with other Squadrons of the Group, probably pooling aircraft.

68th Bombardment Squadron (H), 44th Bomb Group (H), 3rd Wing, GHQAF

This history of this unit was identical to its sister 67th Bomb Squadron (see above), and it was also credited with anti-submarine operations between February and June 1942, but with unspecified aircraft. It is assumed to have used 'pool' aircraft with other Group units.

Pre-war B-18 assignments to non-GHQAF units and organisations

The bulk of the Air Corps combat strength was, obviously, concentrated in the Wings, Groups and Squadron of the GHQAF. Consequently, many historians, in describing the assignment history the B-18 series, have concluded that, prior to the creation of the Air Force Combat Command in mid-1941, *all* B-18s and B-18As within the continental limits of the United States were assigned to GHQAF. This is not correct.

A number of B-18 operating units, for one reason or another, were scattered throughout the United States, and served as either resources reporting directly to the Chief of the Air Corps, or as cadre units for the expansion program. Perhaps the prime example of this was the exotic 23rd Composite Group, which consisted of a Headquarters and Headquarters Squadron, the 1st Pursuit Squadron and the 24th and 54th Bombardment Squadrons. As this was, to say the least, an important B-18 as well as B-23 operator, it is described separately.

23rd Composite Group

This unusual organisation was formed by and served at the pleasure of the Chief of the Air Corps, while stationed to support the functions of the Air Corps Tactical School at Maxwell Field, AL. Although its existence was relatively brief, morphing from the original designation through **Air Corps Proving Ground Detachment** and, lastly, **Air Forces Proving Ground Group** between 1 December 1939 and 1 May 1942, the influence and service testing conducted by this unit was felt throughout the Air Corps and, in particular, the bombardment community. For example, the single 75mm cannon-equipped B-18 (originally the DB-1) was detailed to the unit around 29 February 1940, at which time it was referred to in official correspondence as the **23rd Composite Group (Demonstration Group)**. The unit moved from Maxwell Field to Orlando Army Air Field, FL, on 2 September 1940, and finally on to Eglin Field, FL, on 29 June 1941. It is worth noting that this Group was charged with finding a mission and measure the capability of the B-23 Dragon, and reported, rather pointedly, that by 28 November 1940 the unit was having 'difficulties' in keeping any significant number of the B-23s assigned to it operational.

The 23rd Composite Group was a very special unit that served the needs of the Air Corps Tactical School at Maxwell Field, AL. It was often referred to as the Demonstration Group. Here at Maxwell Field are nearly all of the aircraft of this unit, including at least two B-18s, three B-18As and two B-23s on 20 June 1940. *Curtis W. Oliver scrapbooks, Museum of Flight*

24th Bombardment Squadron (L),
23rd Composite Group

Originally constituted on 1 August 1939 as the **24th Attack-Bombardment Squadron** (the only known instance of such a designator), this unusual unit was redesignated as the 24th Bombardment Squadron (Light) on 28 September 1939 and was actually activated, at Maxwell Field, AL, on 1 December 1939. Apparently, aside from the exotic 75mm cannon-armed B-18 (DB-1), the Squadron did not receive any other aircraft until some time in 1940, probably after the Group move to Orlando AAF, FL. But from that point until it was disbanded on 1 May 1942, the Squadron possessed a truly amazing array of aircraft types. These included on 30 November 1941, by which time the unit had moved to Eglin Field, FL, four B-23s, three Boeing-Stearman PT-17s, a Lockheed C-36, a Curtiss A-18 and a Bell YFM-1A, as well as occasional use of single examples of the Curtiss A-12, Douglas A-20, Stearman XA-21, Martin B-10 and B-12, Douglas B-18 (as noted), North American B-25, Lockheed C-40, Douglas O-38, Consolidated PB-2 and, incredibly, at least one Navy Douglas SBD-1 Dauntless on loan!

54th Bombardment Squadron (M),
23rd Composite Group

Activated on 1 October 1939 as the 54th Bombardment Squadron, and redesignated as a Medium Bombardment unit on 6 December 1939, this unit moved with the parent Group exactly as did its sister bombardment unit, the 24th Bombardment Squadron (L) (qv). It differed somewhat from that unit in that it was apparently tasked specifically with conducting trials for the Tactical School and Air Corps Proving Ground with Medium Bombardment type aircraft, for the most part. By 6 August 1941 the unit was at Eglin Field, FL, and had no fewer than seven B-23s on strength, while by 30 November only one of these remained with the Squadron, the others having been replaced by three new Martin B-26 Marauders and a Grumman OA-9. By the time the Squadron was disbanded on 1 May 1942 it had also operated single examples of the Douglas B-18 (possibly the 75mm gun-equipped former DB-1), a Curtiss A-12, a Martin B-12, at least one Boeing B-17, a North American B-25, a Douglas O-38, a Consolidated PB-2, a Waco PT-14 and a Boeing-Stearman PT-17

Special assignments

We cannot leave the discussion of the GHQ Air Force phase of the B-18 saga without mentioning a number of special B-18 and B-18A assignments outside the organisation that had an impact on the course of other events out of all proportion to their number.

These were, initially, the first three B-18s, in serial number order, to come off the Douglas production line, alluded to briefly earlier in this account.

The Air Corps had the foresight to realise that fielding the new aircraft would require a mix of good training and evaluation. After all, the B-18 and B-18A were, technically, soon to become the most advanced and complex aircraft serving in sizeable numbers in the service at the time, and an entire new generation of air and ground crews would be required to augment the small cadre of veterans that would take the aircraft into service.

The first aircraft off the production line, as a direct consequence, AC36-263, was assigned to the Air Corps Technical School at Chanute Field, IL, arriving there on 27 May 1937, and remaining there until 7 March 1941. During that time this single aircraft, later augmented by another in February 1938, AC36-265, was polished, analysed and diagnosed by virtually every trainee that passed through the gates of the Technical School, and it was this fundamental and very intimate introduction to the B-18 that helped ease the transition of the rapidly expanding Air Corps bombardment

community from the B-10 to the B-17s and B-24s that were to follow. Previously, the men trained at Chanute had practised their training on Class 26 instructional airframes that included early B-10 and even elderly, 1932-vintage Keystone B-6A biplanes, hardly state-of-the-art training aids. The future Line Chiefs and senior maintenance chiefs of the Second World War era Army Air Forces, who saw promotions between 1937 and 1942 from Private to Master Sergeant, nearly all owed a special debt of gratitude to that pair of B-18s. Renamed the Air Corps Technical Center by 31 March 1939, the first B-18 was joined by two B-18As, and by September of that year the Center had no fewer than four B-18s and five B-18As assigned to handle the training load.

Certainly one of the most important but unsung B-18s in the Air Corps, AC36-263, the very first production aircraft off the line, was assigned to the Air Corps Technical School at Chanute Field, IL, on 27 May 1937, where it gained the unit's distinctive insignia and (initially) Field Number 50. It was probably the best-maintained B-18 in the service, and remained there through March 1941. *Franc Isla, via Houston collection and David W. Ostrowski*

Showing excellent details of the lower nose and retracted bomb aimer's station, these students load 100lb practice bombs aboard an Air Corps Technical School B-18 (probably AC36-263) at Chanute Field, IL. Note the bomb hoist mechanism deployed under the inboard port wing. *NARA RG342FH 19381AC*

Of almost equal importance was the next aircraft off the production line, AC36-264, which was immediately assigned to the Army's central test center at Aberdeen Proving Ground, MD. There it served the Air Materiel Command in an amazing series of nearly non-stop tests of the aircraft and its systems until finally being reassigned to Wright Field, OH, home of the Materiel Command, on 16 August 1940. Details of the tests conducted with this aircraft are given elsewhere in this account.

The third B-18 off the line, AC36-265, also provided yeoman service to the Air Corps through its initial assignment on 17 June 1937 to the Air Corps Tactical School at Maxwell Field, AL, where the staff wasted little time in exploiting the features of the new aircraft in developing tactics and operational procedures that soon became the norm not only for B-18 equipped units, but also for the four-engine heavy bomber squadrons, groups, wings and commands to come.

This B-18A, camouflaged with water-based paints, and with her nose gun blister sealed with what appears to be duct tape, was flying for the 'Blue Army' during a 'surprise' attack by paratroops of the 'Red Army' in the form of the 502nd Parachute Battalion at Fort Bragg, NC, on 19 November 1941, on the eve of the US entry into the world conflict. *NARA RG342FH 3B40992 via Dana Bell*

Left: Foreign observers were a fixture at pre-war US maneuvers. Here, left to right, LTC Guillermo Lopez of Chile, Col Miguel J. Neria from Colombia, Col Juan Jones Parra of Venezuela and LTC Guillermo Marin of Chile pose on 9 November 1941 before a B-18A with the odd, large placement of a Field Number on the nose, unit unknown. *NARA RG342FH 3B40989 via Dana Bell*

Few aircraft have had such a profound influence as these three on the transition, at a pivotal moment in both aviation and air force history, from the old to the new. Their joint contributions, at precisely the right moment, to the mighty evolution of AAF bombardment aviation that helped win the war that followed for the Allies have been forgotten.

Pre-war exercises and maneuvers

In the midst of the complex process of integrating the new B-18 and B-18A aircraft into Air Corps tactical units, expanding the size and depth of the service, and developing suitable tactics and operational plans for contingencies perceived at the time, the Air Corps conducted a series of extensive maneuvers in conjunction with ground forces units. Although these are frequently cited in many accounts, research has shown that they have often been confused and no clear picture of the aircraft and units participating has emerged. To understand how prominently B-18s figured in these exercises, conducted primarily by units assigned to the GHQAF and, subsequently, I Bomber Command, the accompanying chronological tables are presented.

Initial overseas deployments

A careful examination of the Production List in Annex 1, and the various charts presented in the GHQ Air Force discussion above, will quickly reveal that the numbers of B-18s, especially, and B-18As assigned to GHQAF units peaked, then apparently declined.

This happened because, while the United States as a nation was decidedly isolationist in the latter half of the 1930s, prudent Air Corps planners, watching world events perhaps more closely than the average man on the street, realised that, if the forces of totalitarianism continued to advance, the nation might well find itself surrounded on all sides.

Wargame B-18A. Artwork by Rich Dann

As a direct result, the decision was taken by the War Department General Staff (WDGS) to substantially reinforce America's traditional overseas bastions in first the Panama Canal Zone and shortly thereafter the Territory of Hawaii.

As new B-18As became available to GHQAF units, 'pug-nosed' B-18s were withdrawn and prepared for overseas movement, often with cadre crews accompanying them. The first three B-18s were flight-deployed to the Canal Zone on 22 July 1938 (being flown there by B-10B crews who had returned their weary aircraft to the United States), while the first examples shipped to Hawaii on surface transport arrived ahead of them, in February and March 1938. These assignments are dealt with in depth in the respective chapters. The import of these assignments, however, cannot be overemphasised: at a time when the US was struggling to prepare, fund and train an expanded air arm, it recognised the wisdom of placing forward some of the best that it had on hand at the time, as painful as this move must have been to the losing organisations. The aircraft deployed to Hawaii and Panama were to witness many adventures, as will be seen.

But now our story must return to the Continental United States, where the new Air Force Combat Command was about to take center stage.

Not to be confused with the current US Air Force major command of precisely the same title, which, in an instance of historical irony, bears an uncanny resemblance to the successor to the GHQ Air Force of the late 1930s, the Air Force Combat Command was created through the reorganisation of the entire Air Corps effective from 20 June 1941. As a consequence, some of the organisational arrangements shown in the earlier section devoted to the GHQAF, while accurately reflecting organisations actually planned under its aegis, do not necessarily reflect that some of the last of the Groups and Squadrons shown in fact did not become activated until after GHQAF ceased to exist as an authorized organisation.

Third Army Maneuvers (Louisiana Maneuvers) 22-24 May 1940

Unit	Aircraft	Base of Operation
Detachment, 2nd Wing Headquarters	2 B-18A	Barksdale Field, LA
Detachment, 1st Pursuit Group	24 P-35	Barksdale Field, LA
Detachment, 8th Pursuit Group	25 P-36	Barksdale Field, LA
Detachment, 31st Pursuit Group	18 P-35	Barksdale Field, LA
9th Bombardment Group, 3rd Wing (Provisional)	18 B-18A	Barksdale Field, LA
2nd Bombardment Group, 3rd Wing (Provisional)	9 B-18A	Barksdale Field, LA
2nd Bombardment Group, 1st Wing (Provisional)	12 B-17	Barksdale Field, LA

Third Army Maneuvers (Louisiana Maneuvers) 18-20 August 1940

Unit	Aircraft	Base of Operation
20th Bombardment Squadron (H)	3 B-17	Barksdale Field, LA
49th Bombardment Squadron (H)	3 B-17	Barksdale Field, LA
96th Bombardment Squadron (H)	2 B-17	Barksdale Field, LA
5th Bombardment Squadron (M)	6 B-18	Barksdale Field, LA
99th Bombardment Squadron (M)	3 B-18	Barksdale Field, LA
17th Pursuit Squadron	7 P-35	Barksdale Field, LA
27th Pursuit Squadron	7 P-35	Barksdale Field, LA
94th Pursuit Squadron	7 P-35	Barksdale Field, LA
41st Reconnaissance Squadron	3 B-18	Barksdale Field, LA

First Army Maneuvers (North East U.S.) 19-22 August 1940

Unit	Aircraft	Base of Operation
1st Composite Group HQ (2nd Bomb Group)	2 B-18A	Mitchel Field, NY (19-22 August)
1st Bombardment Squadron (M)	6 B-18	Mitchel Field, NY (19-22 August)
99th Bombardment Squadron (M)	3 B-18	Mitchel Field, NY (19-22 August)
18th Reconnaissance Squadron	3 B-18	Mitchel Field, NY (19-22 August)
33rd Pursuit Squadron	4 P-36	Municipal Airport, Syracuse, NY (20-22 August)
35th Pursuit Squadron	3 P-36	Municipal Airport, Syracuse, NY (20-22 August)
36th Pursuit Squadron	3 P-36	Municipal Airport, Syracuse, NY (20-22 August)
39th Pursuit Squadron	6 P-35	Municipal Airport, Syracuse, NY (20-22 August)
40th Pursuit Squadron	5 P-35	Municipal Airport, Syracuse, NY (20-22 August)

Second Army Maneuvers (North West US) 25-26 August 1940

Unit	Aircraft	Base of Operation
4th Composite Group HQ (9th Bomb. Group)	2 B-18	Municipal Airport, Madison, WI

Third Army Maneuvers (Louisiana Maneuvers) 1 September-3 October 1941

Unit	Aircraft	Base of Operation
HHS, 2nd Bombardment Wing	2 B-18A	Ellington Field, TX
22nd Bombardment Group (M)	2 B-18A	Ellington Field, TX
2nd Bombardment Group (H)	2 B-18A	Ellington Field, TX
34th Bombardment Group (H)	2 B-18A	Ellington Field, TX
43rd Bombardment Group (H)	2 B-18A	Ellington Field, TX
18th Reconnaissance Squadron	13 B-25	Ellington Field, TX
13th Reconnaissance Squadron	Unspecified	Ellington Field, TX

CHAPTER FOUR

Operational Units

Air Force Combat Command (AFCC)

The Air Corps's part of the reorganised Army Air Forces, a concept that even veterans of the war have trouble grasping (the Air Corps was part of the Army Air Forces in much the same way that the Signal Corps and Corps of Engineers were part of the greater US Army), briefly stated, was to tackle the responsibilities for training, procurement and supply, engineering and construction. Stated simply, the tactical units of the Combat Command were to do the fighting, while the Air Corps supplied the guns, planes, men and equipment to do the job.

The resulting organisational 'tree' chart, illustrated here, appears rather strange but, after brief study, helps clarify the direction that the service was trying to head.

Aside from Army Air Forces organisations stationed in Hawaii, the Panama Canal Zone and Caribbean bases and the Philippines, this was essentially the organisation that prevailed for domestic AAF activities as of the time of the Japanese attack on 7 December 1941.

By 31 October 1941, however, a scant thirty-seven days from the Day of Infamy in that fateful autumn, although it had inherited the tactical units molded and positioned through the exertions of its predecessor, the General Headquarters Air Force (GHQAF), the Air Force Combat Command had already adjusted these, and the incredible reshuffling of assets that ensued, as the AAF leadership

Often overlooked entirely by aviation historians, at least twenty-three B-18s and twenty-three B-18As were redesignated as B-18M and B-18AM because of the removal of their bomb racks and (in some cases) other armament capabilities. Photos of these are very rare. This B-18AM, with a Brigadier General's placard on the fuselage and the insignia of Bolling Field, DC (virtually identical to that of the 14th Bomb Squadron), has had the dorsal turret faired over completely, as well as a radically modified 'chin'.
Arthur Sutter via Robert L. Taylor

watched with increasing anxiety the seriously deteriorating world situation, is reflected in the bombardment aviation dispositions on that date, shown in the accompanying table.

The Command was obviously very seriously under authorized strength, and indeed some tactical units, although nearly up to authorized strength in terms of officers and enlisted ranks (although many were right out of training centers), had few aircraft on which to not only gain proficiency, but more to the point to meet aggression from potential enemies. Altogether the AFCC could count a total of 348 aircraft, of which seventy-one were a mix of B-18s and B-18As and an additional eight B-23s – against an authorized 'paper' strength of not fewer than 945 'modern' aircraft types, mainly B-17s, B-25s, B-26s and A-20s.

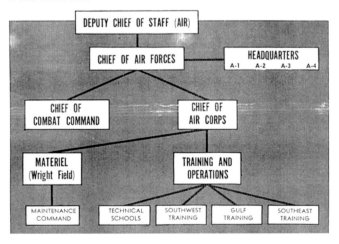

Air Force Combat Command Bombardment Unit Dispositions, Continental United States 31 October 1941

Unit	Location	Aircraft on Hand	Aircraft Required
2nd Bomb Group (H)	Langley Field, VA	3 – B-17 4 – B-18 14 – B-25 2 – B-26	27 – B-17
34th Bomb Group (H)	Westover Field, MA	4 – B-17 2 – B-18	27 – B-17
43rd Bomb Group (H)	Bangor, ME	4 – B-17 2 – B-18	27 – B-17
7th Bomb Group (H)	Salt Lake City, UT	6 – B-17 2 – B-18	27 – B-17
39th Bomb Group (H)	Geiger Field, WA	4 – B-17	27- B-17
29th Bomb Group (H)	MacDill Field, FL	4 – B-17 1 – B-18	27 – B-17
30th Bomb Group (H)	New Orleans, LA	3 – B-17 2 – B-18 2 – B-25	27 – B-17
44th Bomb Group (H)	MacDill Field, FL	7 – B-17 1 – B-18	27 – B-17
32nd Bomb Squadron (H)	Albuquerque, NM	4 – B-17 1 – B-18	8 – B-17
22d Bomb Group (H)	Langley Field, VA	3 – B-18 50 – B-26	44 – B-26
17th Bomb Group (M)	Pendleton, OR	57 – B-25	44 – B-25
42nd Bomb Group (M)	Gowen Field, ID	6 – B-18	44 – B-25
13th Bomb Group (M)	Orlando, FL	7 – B-18	44 – B-26
38th Bomb Group (M)	Jackson, MS	6 – B-18	44 – B-26
41st Bomb Group (M)	Tucson, AZ	6 – B-18	44 – B-25
45th Bomb Group (M)	Manchester, NH	2 – B-18	57 – A-20
46th Bomb Group (L)	Bowman Field, KY	9 – A-20 2 – B-18	57 – A-20
12th Bomb Group (L)	McChord Field, WA	3 – B-18 8 – B-23	57 – A-20
3rd Bomb Group (L)	Savannah, GA	46 – A-20 12 – A-24 3 – B-18	57 – A-20
47th Bomb Group (L)	Fresno, CA	3 – B-18	57 – A-20
48th Bomb Group (L)	Oklahoma City, OK	7 – A-20 2 – B-18	57 – A-20
1st Recon Squadron (H)	Westover Field, MA	1 – B-17	8 – B-17
13th Recon Squadron (H)	Bangor, ME	1 – B-18	8 – B-17
12th Recon Squadron (H)	Geiger Field, WA	1 – B-17	8 – B-17
14th Recon Squadron (H)	MacDill Field, FL	2 – B-17 1 – B-18	8 – B-17
2nd Recon Squadron (H)	New Orleans, LA	1 – B-17 1 – B-18	8 – B-17
38th Recon Squadron (H)	Albuquerque, NM	No aircraft	8 – B-17
21st Recon Squadron (H)	MacDill Field, FL	2 – B-18	8 – B-17
18th Recon Squadron (M)	Langley Field, VA	1 – B-18 14 – B-26	13 – B-26
16th Recon Squadron (M)	Gowen Field, ID	2 – B-18	13 – B-25
89th Recon Squadron (M)	Pendleton Field, OR	14 – B-25	13 – B-25
3rd Recon Squadron (M)	Orlando, FL	1 – B-18	13 – B-26
15th Recon Squadron (M)	Jackson, MS	2 – B-18	13 – B-26
6th Recon Squadron (M)	Tucson, AZ	2 – B-18	13 – B-25

USAAF Bombardment Aircraft Status 31 January 1942

Aircraft Type	Total Flyable on Hand	Total Grounded, All Causes
Martin B-10	7	6
Martin B-10B	27	10
Martin B-12	1	1
Martin B-12A	5	5
Boeing XB-15	1	
Boeing B-17	4	8
Boeing B-17B	29	6
Boeing B-17C	8	1
Boeing B-17D	21	
Boeing B-17E	159	13
Douglas B-18	65	25
Douglas B-18A	139	51
Douglas XB-19	1	
North American XB-21	1	
Douglas B-23	15	11
Consolidated B-24	1	
Consolidated B-24A	7	1
Consolidated XB-24B		1
Consolidated B-24C	8	
Consolidated B-24D	4	
North American B-25	2	20
North American B-25A	16	19
North American B-25B	41	63
North American B-25C	10	1

In fact, the US aviation industry was able to respond to nearly all of these in time, but the AFCC and the units portrayed in the accompanying table were not necessarily the primary beneficiaries. The evolution of the war on the fighting fronts after 7 December 1941 demanded that many of these units deploy to overseas destinations that could only be imagined in dreams a few months previously, and often minus any equipment at all – often having to await new aircraft once the surface contingents arrived in distant locations. By the end of January 1942 a look at the total numbers of bombardment aircraft by then actually in the USAAF inventory, regardless of assignment, is illuminating – and once again positions the numeric significance of the B-18, B-18A and B-23s in the force as of those very dark days.

While the table presents the overall numbers of medium and heavy bombardment aircraft actually available for operations worldwide, it does not adequately depict just how thinly spread these resources were by this time. The majority of the most modern and capable aircraft had been organised and dispatched to either Australia or the western Pacific, or to the Pacific coast of the United States, in anticipation of a possible Japanese attack there or up through Mexico. The remainder had been hastily organised at bases along the Atlantic and Gulf coasts, with the balance distributed to organisations forming in the interior and training centers. These raw numbers changed almost daily, and one can only imagine the mental balancing act that the AAF leadership must have endured during this period as daily loss reports due to enemy action, accidents and factory output of new aircraft were scrutinised. It was a very critical juncture, and an even more distressing outlook had the B-18 not been part of the overall picture.

By 26 February 1942, after nearly three months in which to sort things out, and with a growing realisation that German submarine depredations off the east coast and in the Caribbean posed a more immediate threat than any potential of a Japanese landing on the west

coast, the AFCC adjusted and, with a truly amazing array of domestically assigned aircraft (including still significant numbers of B-18s), deployed these as best it could to meet the new challenges to national defense. See Annex 2 for a complete breakdown of Air Force Combat Command units and aircraft assignments as of this crucial juncture.

At first glance the table in Annex 2 showing virtually every AAF aircraft then in the inventory in the Continental United States appears to suggest that B-18, B-18A and B-23 series aircraft had all but disappeared from the inventory, with only fifteen B-18s, five B-18Ms, fifty-two B-18A, seven B-23s and four C-67s being shown assigned in very diverse locations – and in far less than squadron strength.

Not represented in this overall picture, however, was the fact that the AAF had taken a decision in the spring of 1940 that was forced on the service by the rapid deterioration in world events, and the nearly concurrent demands for fully combat-ready B-18 and B-18A aircraft in overseas commands – and capable bombardier and crew trainers for the next generation of bombardment aircraft then on the near horizon. This resulted in the introduction of an entirely new designation suffix into the AAF system, one that has been poorly understood and often overlooked entirely to this day. This was the rapid demilitarisation of a substantial number of extant Martin B-10Bs, Douglas B-18s and B-18As for service in these roles as part of the rapidly growing training establishment.

In the midst of all of this, General Arnold and the War Department were struggling to arrange a leadership organisation for the burgeoning air arm and, spurred on by the so-called McNarney Committee, War Department Circular 59 was issued on 2 March 1942, to become effective a week later, which, for all intents and purposes, abolished the Army General Headquarters (GHQ). Army field forces remained under the control of the General Staff, and the War Plans Division (later renamed OPD) assumed planning and operational functions over all theaters of operations and the four domestic defense commands. To care for Zone of the Interior (later referred to as CONUS, or Continental United States) functions, three autonomous and coordinating commands were established directly under the Chief of Staff. These were the Army Air Forces (AAF), the Army Ground Forces (AGF) and the Services of Supply (later called Army Service Forces). The General Staff itself was also reorganised to include a more equitable number of air officers, which had far-reaching implications that served the nation well, as it turned out. This arrangement, once and for all removed a very long-standing grievance that the Army's airmen had frequently voiced by giving the now rapidly growing air arm equal status with the ground arm, if not, indeed, with the Army itself. It also brought to an end the rather confusing division of authority between the Office of the Chief of the Air Corps and the Air Force Combat Command. These entities were eliminated in the new AAF, and the functions of the former were divided between a reorganised Air Staff and a number of the subordinate commands shown in the table in Annex 2 in the Zone of the Interior. As for the AFCC, its very raison d'être had disappeared during the early months of the war. Of the four continental Air Forces previously assigned to it, the First and the Fourth had been turned over to the Eastern and Western Defense Commands respectively, and the Second and Third had essentially become huge unit training organisations.

Along with this organisation turmoil, perhaps not unexpectedly, came confusion in the field, and nowhere is this more evident than in the actual markings of aircraft. Many B-18, B-18A and B-23 aircraft continued to bear the former GHQAF codes, which had been so carefully developed prior to the huge expansion. These were quickly outstripped in many instances, however, by the press of events, and unit commanders were often left to their own devices to mark their aircraft according to their best understanding of what might seem appropriate. This probably accounts for some of the inexplicable codes and apparently random numbers that started to be seen on B-18 and B-23 aircraft throughout the United States between 7 December 1941 and mid-1942.

The Douglas B-18M and B-18AM aircraft

Few, if any, contemporary accounts of Army Air Forces designations credit the use of these designations – yet used they were, with appropriate records entries and changes to nomenclature as actually stencilled on the aircraft.

Between 1 April 1940, when Technical Order 01-40E-87 was issued, directing that the prescribed work be accomplished 'as soon as possible', no fewer than twenty-three B-18s and twenty-three B-18As were redesignated as B-18Ms and B-18AMs respectively. The language of the T.O. was unequivocal, and the reasons given ominous. The introductory paragraph said it all:

> 'In order to provide additional bomb shackles for carrying maximum bomb loads on B-18 series airplanes assigned to Panama, Puerto Rico, Hawaii and bombardment units of the GHQAF, the type D-3 and B-7 shackles now installed in certain B-18 series airplanes that are assigned within the continental limits of the United States for miscellaneous combat purposes will be removed.'

Once this work was accomplished, the D-3 and B-7 shackles were to be shipped by 'Extra Priority Air Transport' to a Control Depot, then on to the respective overseas commands. This work was, for the most part, completed between 1 April and 1 May 1940, a truly remarkable achievement, all things considered, as the order affected B-18s and B-18As all over the country. This order was clearly intended to be a permanent modification, since not only was the stencil detail below the port side of the cockpit of the affected aircraft to be altered, but also the actual serial number plates. However, a year later T.O. 01-40E-108, dated 3 April 1941, essentially reversed the original directive, and went so far as to order that when such retrofits were carried out, Wright Field was to be notified by radio, in each instance, of the aircraft affected.

In fact, only relatively few aircraft converted to B-18M and B-18AM status retained their 'toothless' configuration permanently, and most that did were older B-18s. The vast majority either reverted to B-18, B-18A or, in a chain of events that could not even be foreseen in April 1941, became B-18B or B-18C aircraft later in their service lives.

Nearly all of the aircraft thus impacted were assigned to training activities, where they saw intensive use as, mainly, crew trainers and bombardier trainers – minus the bomb racks, meaning that trainee bombardiers used the aircraft as training platforms to actually carry out their instruction to the point of actually dropping weapons. Later on, B-18s and B-18As with shackles continued in this role in considerable numbers, but by then had reverted to their original designations.

Every known instance of these redesignations is reflected in the several Annexes appended to this volume, including Annex 1, the detailed production listing.

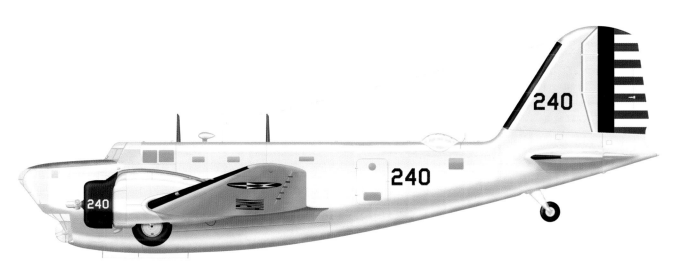

B-18A 240. Artwork by Rich Dann

CHAPTER FIVE

Canada's Digby

The Douglas DB-280 Digby

In 1982 Canadian aero-historian Carl Vincent published an outstanding four-part account of the acquisition and operational service of the twenty aircraft that were acquired direct from Douglas by the Royal Canadian Air Force (RCAF). Although entitled by the periodical 'Canada's Wings – High Flight', with the rather unfortunate title 'Distended Douglas', the piece followed an earlier April 1965 account in the serial *Roundel* by Flight Lieutenant H. A. Halliday, which, in part two of the three, presented an exceptional account of the primary RCAF Digby-operating unit, 10(BR) Squadron, and its very intensive anti-submarine campaign.

Although not generally available to most readers, the bulk of the details contained in these two historical accounts can be found in the Schiffer book by Dr William Wolf on the B-18, released in January 2007, together with a number of the illustrations, so they will not be repeated here.

What is generally not recognised is that, prior to the US entry into the Second World War, US aircraft manufacturers were constrained in their efforts to promote exports. When Italy had threatened impoverished Ethiopia in 1935, the resulting furore over arms manufacturers as warmongers and merchants of death had once again claimed the attention of the US Congress. The representatives promptly passed a neutrality measure that held out to the American public the promise that neutrality, in a warring world, could be had by legislation. The terms of the measure made it unlawful for citizens of the US to sell *or transport* arms to belligerents that had been

The third DB-280, RCAF No 740, delivered on 30 December 1939, is operating in typical Canadian winter conditions, probably not long after delivery. This aircraft survived the war. Wright State University

labelled as such by the President. In the years following, the policy influencing US exports, even as the US struggled to rise from the effects of the Great Depression, governing the release of aircraft and aircraft equipment to foreign governments, was minutely specified. The principles involved, however, can be stated rather simply: military aircraft purchased by the US *or designed to specifications of the military services* were not to be released for export until after a lapse of time, running up to as much as one year, following the start of production. In practice, this meant that no aircraft was in fact released until several years after it left the design stage and had already long since been compromised by public disclosure. Although the details of the policy changed from time to time, the basic principles involved remained constant well into 1939.

As a direct consequence, while Douglas was enjoying enormous success in selling numbers of commercial DC-2 and DC-3 variants overseas, and even though it had projected export versions of the DB-1 and DB-2, it was specifically prohibited from actively marketing these aircraft until 1939. This accounts for the nearly incredible fact that only one export customer for the series was arranged while the aircraft was evolving through Air Corps fielding from the DB-1, through the B-18, DB-2 and into the B-18A. While it is probably true that there were few potential customers for a bomber with these specifications, logic would suggest that several nations were potential prospects, notably China, the Netherlands East Indies, possibly Thailand, Brazil, Argentina, Chile, the British Commonwealth nations and even France, all of whom either purchased export versions of the Martin 139 or other twins, simply because nothing else was available. To date, no evidence has surfaced that any of these nations made overtures to Douglas regarding the DB-1.

The USAAC did in fact approve the Curtiss P-40, Douglas A-20A and Douglas B-18A or equivalent manufacturers' variants for sale to the Anglo-French Purchasing Commission around January 1940.

These were, however, the twenty aircraft acquired by Canada, which by 3 January 1940, in keeping with the British-inspired traditions adopted by the Commonwealth, had been identified by a popular name, 'Digby'[25], drawn from either the name of the small town in Nova Scotia that is the seat of Digby County, or after its founder, British Admiral Robert Digby, settled by Protestant Loyalists from the US. An RAF station in the United Kingdom, one of the oldest, also bore this name, and was populated by Canadians to a large extent, and it has also been suggested that this was the source of the popular name for the aircraft. No definitive rationale seems to have survived.

At the time of the Canadian purchase, officials of the USAAC could hardly imagine that, less than two years hence, they would be vitally interested in how these aircraft fared in northern climes – or that the US would be deploying substantial aviation assets to Iceland, Greenland, Newfoundland, Alaska and the Aleutians.

In January 1941 the USAAC came face to face with the difficulties that would be encountered in operating under Canadian winter conditions when nine B-18s were dispatched, under the command of Major H. H. George, to Quebec Province to cooperate with Canadian forces in an extensive search for some missing flyers. The irony was that the aircraft that was missing was a Canadian Digby, No 749, captained by F/O J. G. Richardson and his crew. Six of the USAAC aircraft were from the 2nd Bombardment Group based at Langley Field, VA, and the other three from the 18th and 41st Reconnaissance Squadrons. This exercise, one of the very first of its kind between the two neighbours, brought home to the USAAC leadership the '…considerable difficulties experienced [by the] US crews in operating under even moderate winter conditions.'

Returning home with these lessons fresh in their minds, and learning from their Douglas plant representative that the DB-280s had '…a much less robust cabin heat and ventilation ducting system' than even US B-18 series aircraft at that time, General Arnold asked the US Military Attaché in Canada to exert every effort to observe Canadian experiences in operating aircraft in these conditions. As a direct result, the Attaché forwarded a very detailed report (No 9545/786) to the Military Intelligence Division of the War Department General Staff on 27 October 1941, and this document served as the basis for US decisions that followed in providing for the deployment of substantial USAAC assets to Alaska and Iceland.

The report, in its entirety, follows, as these lessons had a profound and lasting impact on aircraft operations in the immediate years that followed, and even into recent times:

To ascertain the feasibility of operating and maintaining a number of Douglas Digby bomber aircraft during the winter months without hangar shelter, one Douglas Digby was operated during the winter of 1940-41 by a detachment of 10(BR) Squadron at RCAF Station Newfoundland. The report, which follows, deals with the following subjects:

(a) The removal of ice and snow from fuselage

(b) Covers

(c) Drifting snow

(d) Lubrication

(e) Cabin heater

(f) Engine operation

(g) Failure

The aircraft during the whole test was kept picketed in the open, and all maintenance and repair work was done with no shelter.

The scope of this test consisted of maintaining one Digby aircraft in good flying condition under the climatic conditions prevailing at RCAF Station Newfoundland, during the winter months. The temperature in this region was not what could be termed severe. The minimum temperature during the test period was -5.2°F. The average temperature was about 21°F. Changes of temperature are frequent and range from the minimum stated to approximately 45°F. Constant high winds seriously hamper maintenance of aircraft in the open. In this district falling snow is usually wet. Heavy snowfalls may occur, but freezing rain can be expected more frequently during the worst six months. The wet snow, accompanied by a driving wind, has two results:

(a) The freezing of snow on all exposed parts of the aircraft

(b) The driving of wet snow through unprotected openings in the airframe

In order to assess the value of the report properly, it is to be borne in mind that the primary function of the Detachment

The same aircraft is seen again probably just after completion and departure from California on delivery. The lacquer paints used were manufactured by W. P. Fuller. The significance of the sign marked '212' in the bombardier's aperture is unknown. The aircraft was Manufacturer's Serial Number 1632. *Douglas*

RCAF No 740 once again, viewed from the side on 18 December 1939, prior to hand-over, showing that the Canadian national insignia, in keeping with the Neutrality Laws, had been painted over. Strictly speaking, the aircraft should have had a temporary US Department of Commerce ferry licence. *Boeing Archives No 16700*

was a service operation, that the Detachment's Commander was burdened with a variety of duties, that the size of the Detachment was strictly limited by the accommodation available, and that the Detachment was a considerable distance away from town, where works such as the manufacture of wing covers, etc, could be done, and was therefore dependent upon the Halifax, Nova Scotia, area for most of such assistance. The communications by air were necessarily erratic due to weather and to operational requirements.

Under the conditions stated in the preceding paragraph, the Detachment was enabled to report upon the difficulties encountered, but was not able to devise, construct and experiment with the equipment to counteract the difficulties.

Removal of Ice and Snow

(a) Snow was removed from the wing surfaces by means of brooms. No difficulties were experienced.

(b) Ice – on several occasions an accretion of ice ¼ to ½ inch thick collected on the aircraft as a result of freezing rains. The most effective way of removing this type of ice was found to be the use of a rubber-covered rope. Gentle beating of the ice surface effectively removed the ice with no damage to the aircraft.

(c) Frost – white frost, if collection was heavy enough, was removed as detailed in paragraph (b) above. A light coat of white frost (i.e. approximately 3/16 inch or less) could not be removed in such a manner. Three methods were tried to remove this type of frost:

1. A wooden scraper
2. Various types of brooms
3. Use of anti-icer fluid

The wooden scraper was discarded due to the flaking of paint and possibility of scratching fuselage surfaces. A stiff bristle broom was found to remove the frost effectively only at temperatures of 30°F to 32°F. The most effective method of removal was found to be the use of anti-icer fluid. Approximately 3 to 5 gallons of this fluid is required to completely 'defrost' the Digby airframe. Removal of ice and frost would not have been necessary had proper wing covers been provided.

Covers

(a) Wing covers of 8oz duck supplied for test were completely unsatisfactory. Due to consistently high winds at the airport, these covers could not be fastened with sufficient tension to hold them in place. This type of cover billows and pulls away from the upper surfaces of the wing, resulting in severe chafing and strain in the ailerons and accumulation of snow and ice on the wing.

(b) This cover was supplied with tapes and lacing cord. These were found to be of no use due to stretching, and it was necessary to substitute one-quarter inch rope for ties. A further difficulty was that the covers were fitted only as far as the engine nacelles, and to be satisfactory this cover should extend over the whole wing area.

(c) Modified covers of heavier material were not obtainable, but it is believed that satisfactory covers could be made of 12oz duck and formed as an envelope to cover the whole wing area.

(d) In addition to wing covers, empennage covers are considered essential. These covers should be in such a form as to close the 'lightening' holes at the extreme rear of the fuselage, because the tail cone fills with damp snow and freezes, thus jamming the control units in the rear of the fuselage. It might be well to cover these holes permanently with doped fabric for winter operations.

(e) A considerable quantity of snow entered the aircraft around the gun positions. While this does not affect the operation of the aircraft, it unnecessarily increases the maintenance of the interior, and suitable covers are recommended for these positions.

(f) Tests by the Department some years ago indicated that lacing through grommets was unsatisfactory and hooks and laces were suggested. If the outboard ends of covers are pocketed to receive wing tips, fitting is facilitated in bad weather conditions.

Drifting snow

No difficulty was experienced as a result of drifting snow insofar as the wheel wells were concerned. The only difficulties are those mentioned in the paragraph above in the case of snow filling the tail cone and thus jamming the controls. The use of a stockade built 20 feet aft of the trailing edges of the aeroplane and about 6 feet high would reduce trouble from these storms.

Lubrication

Hydraulic fluid, lubricants and greases at present used for winter operation proved satisfactory. S.A.E.120 (A7) lubricating oil, and No 00 grease for grease gun fittings, and light oil, anti-freezing, were used.

Cabin heating

(a) It was found impossible to ensure that the steam cabin heating system would operate satisfactorily if water only were used. To prevent freezing, experiments were carried out with various proportions of glycol and water. One quart of glycol to three quarts of water was found to prevent freezing, but the boiling point of the mixture was too high to obtain steam for satisfactory operation of the heater. One-half pint of glycol in one gallon was found satisfactory when introduced into the boiler after starting the engines. This mixture was brought to a boil before the heater tank was filled.

(b) Various modifications have since been incorporated in this heater system, consisting of lagging of pipes, flexible hose window de-icer, the installation of a suitable funnel to permit filling the boiler directly, steam pressure gauge and increasing the size of the drain cock.

Engine operation

Engine oil was diluted after each flight or 'run-up'. No dilution was attempted until oil temperature dropped to a maximum of 55°F. Dilution was continued until oil pressure dropped to 20 to 25psi. The dilution system was entirely satisfactory and no difficulty was experienced in starting the engines under temperature down to -5°F.

Failures

(a) Two hydraulic pumps failed during the period of the tests, both immediately after starting the engines. The nature of the failure was a shearing of the shaft at the bearing. Both failures occurred at comparatively low temperatures. There is, however, considerable doubt whether the temperature condition was a contributing factor. The system was checked and found to be free from water and dirt. It is almost certain that the pump failures were due to over-small clearances upon original assembly. There is also now available a thinner hydraulic fluid.

(b) An excessive leakage of oil through the brake pistons was experienced. The cause of this leakage appears to be a contraction of the rubber gaskets on the pistons. The result of the leakage was that the fluid soaked the brake linings and the brake shoes developed a high polish. Combination of these two factors prevented proper braking. This condition exists only at freezing temperatures. No ready solution is offered except (a) one of replacing these gaskets each fall; (b) investigation to discover a more suitable material.

(c) Excess leakage of oil was also experienced in the case of propellers. Cause again would appear to be contraction of glands. No adverse effect on operation resulted from this condition. The thinning of the oil through dilution could also be a contributing factor.

(d) During the course of the test, the constant speed control units became very sluggish; examination showed an accumulation of sludge in the unit. Removal of this sludge restored the constant speed control to normal speed operation. This is considered to be an isolated case, possibly brought

about by the use of oil dilution, and would probably have cleared itself shortly with continued oil dilution.

(e) An excessive unserviceability of sparking plugs was experienced throughout the period of the test. This was attributed to condensation in excess of normal and the further fact that excess oil would not 'burn off' plugs. Numbers 5 and 6 cylinders required changes of plugs most frequently. A possible solution is the removal of all of the bottom sparking plugs when the engine is stopped and the substitution of unserviceable plugs kept for this purpose in adequate quantities.

(f) Difficulty was experienced in obtaining proper tappet clearances, due to personnel having to work in the open. The use of tarpaulins or nose tents properly heated would greatly facilitate maintenance work on the engines.

(g) It was found that under normal conditions experienced during the test it was impossible to properly patch fabric. Patches were sewn and doping was necessarily left until weather conditions permitted proper completion of the operation. The use of a heated blower unit [authors' note: this element was particularly checked off by USAAC authorities on the report] with a light fabric cage would permit the doping and repairing of fabric parts where necessary.

(h) One starter motor was rendered temporarily unserviceable by ice. Condensation freezing on the solenoid points of the starter motor formed a layer of ice .25 inches thick on the lower side, within the electrical junction box.

Conclusions

A number of Douglas Digby aircraft could be operated successfully under the winter conditions prevailing at RCAF Station Newfoundland, without hangar accommodations, provided the following facilities and assistance were made available:

(a) An adequate, well-heated workshop

(b) An increase of approximately 50% in maintenance personnel. Of this extra personnel, the greater part should be standard duties airmen, and only a small proportion need be aero-engine and airframe mechanics.

(c) Special snow removal equipment especially assigned to clear the vicinity of the parked aeroplanes without being in demand for clearing the airport runway.

(d) The supply of effective, endurable covers for the wings, tail surfaces and fuselage.

(e) The supply of at least one nose hangar per six engines. [Authors' note: this element was also specifically 'checked off' by USAAC authorities on the original report]

(f) The building of adequate snow fences to guard the park area from drifting snow. These fences may be of the portable locked pattern. [Authors' note: this element was also 'checked off' by USAAC officials on the original report]

(g) The posting of supervisory maintenance personnel who have had previous experiences in winter operation.

(h) The provision of suitable, portable heating units for use in the nose hangars and in the interior of the fuselage, to facilitate maintenance of the parked aircraft when it is not possible or reasonable to remove a component to the workshop.

Attaché's comment

By referring to the conclusions drawn, it seems apparent that the sum total of the precautionary measures that need to be taken to ensure satisfactory maintenance of aircraft parked out of doors during the winter months would in cost and effort about equal the construction of temporary hangars [underlining by USAAC officials, with the word 'Vulnerability?' penned in the margin]. Experience has taught that mechanics cannot perform satisfactory maintenance of aircraft operating out of doors at low temperatures. While emergencies may necessitate such operations from time to time, it is believed highly impracticable to accept such as an established policy.

Many commentators have often cited the Digbys as 'B-18As' supplied to Canada under Lend-Lease or as a form of Defense Aid.[26] This is absolutely not correct. The twenty aircraft were issued with Douglas Manufacturer's Serial Numbers that came even before those

of the first USAAC B-18s, and this seemingly insignificant and nearly universally overlooked fact, perhaps better than any other, points to the probability that these aircraft may, in fact, have served as the basis for the USAAC definitive B-18A configuration that followed later, rather than the other way around. Since Douglas is known to have issued its Manufacturer's Serial Numbers in more or less chronological sequence, it also suggests that the Canadian interest in the DB-280 may have dated from the April 1938 British purchasing party, known as the Weir Mission, which had actively considered the Douglas design as an alternative to the Lockheed Hudson series that was eventually selected instead.

The Royal Canadian Air Force sent its own procurement mission to the US in the fall of 1938, and used the findings of the Weir Mission to seek aircraft that were not only already 'approved' by the British, but which would be more or less immediately available. An extensive series of conferences ensued, and a tentative order for eight aircraft was finally settled upon with Douglas. The Canadians

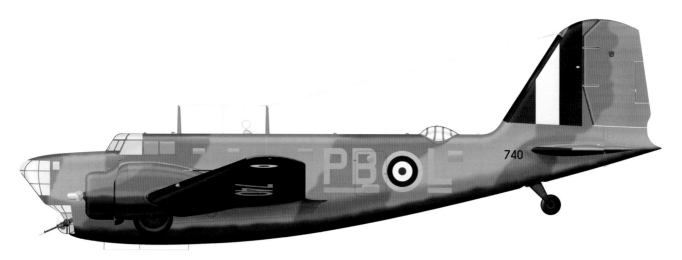

Early Digby *Artwork by Rich Dann*

Douglas DB-280 Digby, RCAF No 753, MSN 1645, was the sixteenth of the twenty-aircraft order, arriving on 2 May 1940. This aircraft crashed in bad weather near Gander, Newfoundland, on 26 March 1942. *Authors' collection*

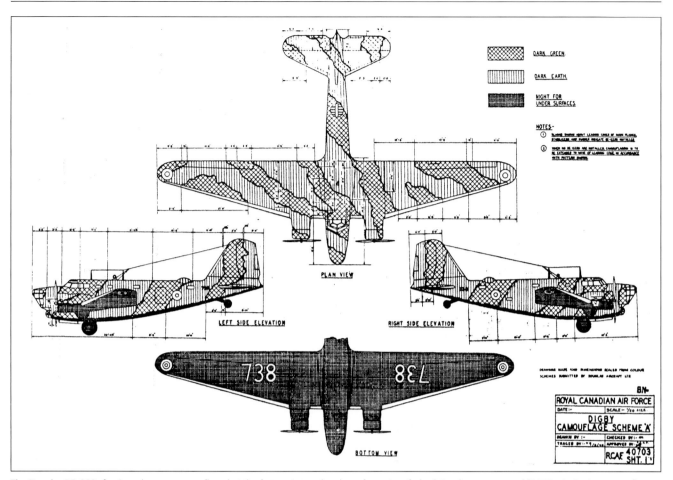

The Douglas DB-280s for Canada were camouflaged at the factory in two batches of ten aircraft, both in what was termed 'RAF Basic Design camouflage, each batch of ten being the 'Mirror Opposite' of the other. This is the scheme applied to the first ten. *Boeing Archives 40703 Sheet 1*

subsequently delayed the order, as the situation in Europe remained somewhat uncertain – the most often cited reasons being the appeasement of Nazi Germany by the French and British. Meanwhile, Douglas had apparently 'set aside' the serial numbers that it had identified for the British Commonwealth, and continued on with the large orders placed by the USAAC. This series of events may also, at least in part, explain why the Canadian DB-280s were initially delivered with what amounted to a British Royal Air Force-style European camouflage scheme. What is not generally recognised, however, was that the RCAF, in a memo dated 17 October 1939, instructed Douglas that, while the first ten aircraft were to be painted in the 'RAF Basic Design camouflage', the second batch of ten were to be painted in what was termed 'Mirror Opposite'. Douglas billed the RCAF $840 per aircraft for this special requirement. The Canadian order was actually signed on 31 August 1939 – the day before German forces surged across the Polish frontier. Since actual deliveries to the RCAF commenced on 29 December 1939, a scant four months later, there can be absolutely no doubt that some prior arrangement between Douglas and the Commonwealth must have been operative – especially in view of the positioning of the Douglas serial numbers for the twenty aircraft. The delivery of the first two aircraft was actually delayed two weeks because of the late RCAF camouflage requirement noted above, and the remaining eighteen were delayed one week each.

Although often quoted as being 'identical' to the B-18A, this is not true. The DB-280 differed in a number of details. The major differences involved features that would better suit the aircraft to a maritime reconnaissance mission, rather than as dedicated long-range heavy bombers as with the USAAC. These included two (rather than

one) auxiliary bomb bay fuel tanks and an auxiliary oil tank, as well as specially designed wing flotation compartments, and surface and propeller de-icing equipment. The formal Canadian 'popular' name for the aircraft, Digby, was not formally approved until 3 January 1940. Repeated suggestions and statements in many previously published accounts of the Digbys that the aircraft also carried the appellation 'Mk I' are completely erroneous; the aircraft were known officially in RCAF service, throughout, as simply Douglas Digbys.

It is fair to say that the Canadian taxpayers got their money's worth out of their new aircraft. Of the twenty acquired, and despite what can only be viewed as very heavy utilisation indeed, eleven survived long enough to be scrapped or sold as surplus at the end of the war, seven were lost to accidents – nearly all of which were attributed to the weather (except for three, which were attributed to the very same pilot!) – and two were lost without a trace on operational missions.

The Canadians were able to wring the most from their aircraft, and at least one mission was in the air for an incredible 12hr 45min. The aircraft was credited with a number of submarine attacks, and one confirmed sinking – while No 740, coded PB+L with 10(BR) Squadron, made the very first attack on the Axis powers by a North American-based aircraft on 25 October 1941 when, commanded by Squadron Leader C. L. Annis, it sighted a German submarine just east of the Strait of Belle Isle in 60-knot winds. In the subsequent attack two 600lb bombs were placed, one just short of the sub, and the other about 75 feet ahead of the swirl where the U-boat had crash-dived. The attack might have been successful had the crew not realised that the bombs had been disarmed by the bomb aimer without the knowledge of the aircraft commander.

RCAF Digby No. 745-?? (just visible on extreme nose) in a late-war anti-submarine color scheme, but oddly with an early-war fuselage roundel. *Carl and Elizabeth Vincent*

Late in their war, the surviving Royal Canadian Air Force Douglas DB-280 Digby's were nearly all repainted in a low-visibility, flat white color scheme, with what appears to be a pale blue anti-glare panel. The British Empire fin flash almost makes this appear a post-war view. The dorsal turret on this aircraft appears to have been faired or painted over. *via Carl Vincent*

It is noteworthy that at least a few of the Digbys were fitted with a primitive form of metric ASV equipment, at about the same time that the US was starting to mount ASV-10 in B-18s, a fact seldom recognised. Although temperamental and subject to sudden failure, the gear was highly prized by the few crews who enjoyed it, by all accounts.

Ironically, despite the exertions of the RCAF Digbys and their crews, the service had to wait until the third full year of operations to record a successful attack. On 30 October 1942, the same year that USAAF B-18s were so intensively engaged against the Axis submarine onslaught in the Caribbean, Flight Officer D. F. Raymes and his crew, in No 747, took off on a mission to escort inbound Convoy ON140. After being

relieved on station, and on the way home, the crew visually spotted a submarine on the surface due east of St John's, Newfoundland, with her decks awash. The Digby dived to the attack and, about 5 seconds after the conning tower disappeared, dropped a salvo of four 450lb depth charges along the track. The aircraft recovered to Gander at 2355 hours in darkness, thinking that the target may have been damaged. Not until after the war was it learned that U-520, with all hands, had gone to the bottom that day. This marked the seventh live-fire attack by 10(BR) Squadron.[27] The Digby had earned its spurs.

After the RCAF's surviving Digbys had received low-visibility anti-submarine camouflage midway through the war, at least a few were also fitted with an early form of metric ASV equipment, which has been seldom illustrated. These views show the bird-like antenna on the nose, which allowed the forward gun to be retained, and the wire antenna arrays under the wings – which were also mounted on the fuselage. *PA64314 and PA64050 via Jack Meaden*

Late Digby *Artwork by Rich Dann*

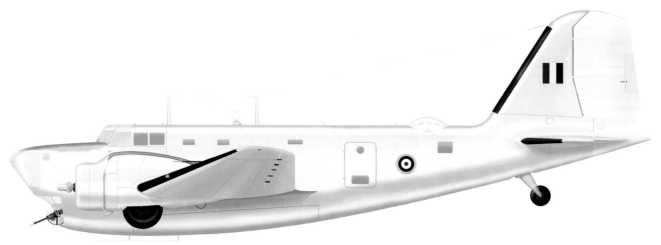

CHAPTER SIX

Reinforcing America's overseas outposts

The B-18 in Hawaii, Panama, Puerto Rico, the Antilles, Alaska, Newfoundland and the Philippines

Territory of Hawaii

By the end of the war no fewer than fifty-four of the total of 134 B-18s procured by the Army Air Corps saw service in the Territory of Hawaii – a testament to the importance attached to this Pacific bastion. Of this total, thirty-three were brand-new, factory-fresh aircraft, the first wave of which arrived as surface cargo on 24 February 1938. Of these, nineteen had arrived in the Hawaiian Department, as the Army's command there was titled at the time, by the end of March 1938. A year later, on 31 March 1939, the total complement had been delivered, and total strength in B-18s stood at fifty-two aircraft, two having been lost to accidents. One of these losses was made up by a new arrival by 31 March 1940 and the total on hand remained static at

USAAC bombardment units in the Territory of Hawaii commenced re-equipping with B-18s in March 1938. By 18 May 1940 the world situation had deteriorated to the point that black-out drills in major urban areas were being practised, and this Hawaiian based B-18, with an unknown insignia on the fuselage (and what appears to be a Brigadier General's placard in the gunner's window on the rear fuselage) was being used to load and drop leaflets announcing such a drill over Honolulu. *USAF 41007AC via Rich Dann*

fifty-three through till 7 December 1941. No B-18As were ever assigned to the Department. For a complete listing of the B-18s assigned to Hawaii, by unit, see the Annex on Stations.

The ultimate unit assignments of the B-18s sent to the islands was, practically, a roll-call of the Air Corps bombardment and reconnaissance squadrons that, for the most part, had been stationed there for many years. The challenges inherent in defining the mission and responsibilities of Army aviation in defense of the islands, with the possible exception of Air Corps elements stationed in the Panama Canal Zone, where a similar situation prevailed, occupied the thoughts of the Air Corps leadership there for most of the interwar period. For all practical purposes, the few Army Air Corps stations in the islands amounted to fixed, permanent 'aircraft carriers', surrounded by vast expanses of ocean in every direction. But this was not a concept that would withstand even casual discussion with Navy counterparts in the islands at the time. It was clear to even the most casual observer that the arrival of the new B-18 monoplanes, of which so much was expected, would enable the Air Corps to supplement, if not challenge outright, the Navy's view that it had first responsibility for ocean surveillance and reconnaissance. That this fundamental ability had not been fully understood and integrated into the defense preparations for the islands installations by 7 December 1941 is difficult to understand in retrospect. To conceive of the substantial Air Corps heavy bombardment force sent to the islands in traditional terms, which was apparently the prevailing wisdom, similarly, seems incomprehensible.

As of 30 November 1941 the Air Corps organisation within the Hawaiian Islands had been designated as the Hawaiian Air Force, and Headquarters and Headquarters Squadron, Hawaiian Air Force, had a single B-18 (and one North American O-47B) assigned.

An examination of the experiences of the B-18 operating units in the Hawaiian Islands prior to 7 December 1941 provides insight into the Air Corps philosophy of the period and, rightly or wrongly, how they arrived as they did on the Day of Infamy.

18th Wing

Originally constituted as the 18th Composite Wing on 8 May 1929, this 'capper' AAC organisation for the islands was activated on 1 May 1931, its title shortened to merely 18th Wing in 1937 and 18th Bombardment Wing in 1940. Headquartered initially at Fort Shafter, it moved to Hickam Field on 30 October 1937 and was inactivated within the islands on 29 January 1942, having been transcended by the Hawaiian Air Force, which was activated on 1 November 1940. This organisation thus gave birth to the great Seventh Air Force in February 1942. The major subordinate elements of the 18th Wing were the 5th and 11th Bombardment Groups and the 18th Pursuit Group.

The Wing Headquarters and Headquarters Squadron operated two B-18s by 30 November 1941 (as well as a single Boeing P-26A).

5th Bombardment Group (H)

The 5th Bomb Group had originated in the Territory of Hawaii in August 1919 as the 2nd Group (Observation), being redesignated as the 5th Group (Observation) in March 1921, 5th Group (Pursuit and Bombardment) in June 1922, and 5th Group (Composite) in July 1922. It was formally redesignated as the 5th Bombardment Group in March 1938, the 5th Bombardment Group (Medium) in December 1939, and finally the 5th Bombardment Group (Heavy) in November 1940.

Subordinate units during the B-18 operating phase of its existence consisted of its Headquarters and Headquarters Squadron (HHS), the 23rd Bombardment Squadron, the 31st Bombardment Squadron, the 72nd Bombardment Squadron and the 4th Reconnaissance Squadron.

As of 30 November 1941 the Group and its subordinate units could muster a total of eleven B-18s, four Boeing B-17Ds and a single Curtiss A-12.

The 5th Bomb Group (H) became the first major unit in the Territory of Hawaii to be re-equipped with B-18s starting in March 1938. The unit continued the GHQAF unit designator system, and BE 22 was probably assigned to the 23rd Bomb Squadron (H). Tarps have been thrown over the cockpit and dorsal turret to minimise the effects of the tropical weather. *via D. M. Davis*

23rd Bombardment Squadron (H)

Tracing its lineage clear back to the 18th Aero Squadron of June 1917, and redesignated as the 23rd Aero Squadron the same month, this unit was redesignated after an interlude as the 23rd Bombardment Squadron on 25 January 1923, the 23rd Bombardment Squadron (Medium) on 6 December 1939, and the 23rd Bombardment Squadron (Heavy) on 20 November 1940. It moved to Hickam Field from Luke Field on 1 January 1939 and, prior to receipt of its first B-18s in 1938, had been equipped with Martin B-12s.

The Squadron and, indeed, the entire Air Corps establishment in Hawaii received a shock on 14 November 1938 when a young Air Corps enlisted mechanic and Assistant Crew Chief, PFC Fliegleman, 'borrowed' one of the Squadron's B-18s, AC36-340 – the aircraft on which he crewed, for a completely solo hop. Somehow getting the aircraft started, and taking off by himself, he crashed about 5 minutes after taking off some 3 miles north-west of Waipalu (also given as Waipahu in some documents). Miraculously, he was only slightly injured, and actually walked away from the crash to face the consequences of his grand adventure. The aircraft was a write-off, but did not burn, and in fact survives to this day sitting tail-down in a ravine where the intrepid airman somehow pancaked it in. So far as your authors can determine, this was the one and only 'solo' flight ever made in a B-18 before the end of the Second World War.

Along with the remainder of the Hawaiian Air Force, the 23rd Bomb Squadron was placed on high alert for the entire month of April 1941, owing no doubt to the heightened tensions in the Pacific, although the crews were never told the reason.

The Squadron commenced training on a single B-17D received, much to the delight of all concerned, in April 1941, and by August the decidedly under-strength unit could count that aircraft, together with three B-18s and a Curtiss A-12, as their entire airworthy element.

BE 32 was probably also a 23rd Bomb Squadron (H), 5th Bomb Group (H), B-18 that somehow managed to come out of this forced landing on a sandy beach relatively unscathed in 1938. Note the exhaust stains aft of the long exhaust stacks over the engine nacelles, the bane of the Crew Chief. *Marvin Hawkins via NMUSAF*

31st Bombardment Squadron (H)

Compared to its sister 23rd Bomb Squadron, the 31st Bomb Squadron was a relative newcomer to Hawaii. Organised originally as the 31st Aero Squadron in June 1917 and not reconstituted after the end of the First World War as the 31st Bombardment Squadron until 24 March 1923, this unit spent most of the between-the-wars years at March and later Hamilton Field, California, before moving, lock, stock and barrel, to the islands on 8 February 1938. There it was redesignated as the 31st Bombardment Squadron (Medium) on 6 December 1939 and as the 31st Bombardment Squadron (Heavy) on 20 November 1940.

With thirteen nearly brand-new B-18s, a substantial boost to the Hawaiian garrison, as well as thirty officers and 180 enlisted ranks and their families, the Squadron left the comforts of Hamilton Field for Oahu's new Hickam Field, which turned out to be little more than a tent city when they arrived. It was the first B-18 heavy unit to occupy the new station, and remained so for some time, until the permanent installations, which became so familiar to so many, were hastily rushed to completion. The aircraft and most of the Squadron personnel departed together for the tropical paradise on the USAT *Meigs* on 12 February and the USAT *Ludington* on the 17th.

Until departing for Hawaii, the Squadron had been part of the 7th Bombardment Group at Hamilton Field.

The third Squadron making up the 5th Bomb Group in Hawaii was the 72nd Bomb Squadron (H), and BE 60, shown here, was the Squadron Commander's aircraft. This photo was taken from the USAT *Republic*, an Army transport vessel, en route from San Francisco to the islands in 1939. Unfortunately, the unit colors, worn on the cowls and the fuselage bands, are unknown. *John M. Fitzpatrick*

Rarely pictured, this B-18 sports the unit insignia of the 72nd Bomb Squadron (H), 5th Bomb Group, in pre-war guise – but no unit designators. This unit operated seven B-18s from Bellows Field as late as 16 April 1942. *NMUSAF*

The 31st Bomb Squadron (H), 5th Bomb Group (H), moved to Hawaii, along with its equipment, in February 1938, and BE 49, with painted engine cowlings, was one of the organic aircraft. The units of the 5th Bomb Group practised extensive over-water patrols around the islands prior to 7 December 1941. *SSG David Miller via Bill Stewart*

5B40 is a B-18 of the 5th Bomb Group's 31st Bomb Squadron, the Squadron Commander's aircraft as shown by the fuselage bands. The engine cowlings appear to be orange or faded red. *via Rich Dann*

moved into the tent city at Hickam on 18 April 1938, specifically for the purpose of transitioning completely to the B-18, and received five additional examples on 9 June 1938, which the Squadron was obliged to set up virtually on its own – a most challenging exercise.

4th Reconnaissance Squadron (M/R)

Originally organised as the 4th Aero Squadron in May 1917, and later reconstituted as the 4th Observation Squadron, this unit became the 4th Reconnaissance Squadron on 25 January 1938, the 4th Reconnaissance Squadron (Medium Range) on 6 December 1939, and the 4th Reconnaissance Squadron (Heavy) on 20 November 1940. The unit had been in the Hawaiian Islands since January 1922 and was attached to the 5th Bombardment Group on 12 October 1938.

The Squadron moved to Hickam Field from Luke Field on 1 January 1939 and, later in the war, was redesignated as the 394th Bombardment Squadron (Heavy).

On the eve of the Japanese attack, as of 30 November 1941, the Squadron was designated as the 4th Recon Squadron (Long Range), which does not appear in most accounts, and had a mix of four B-18s and two new Boeing B-17Ds.

72nd Bombardment Squadron (H)

Yet another Air Corps unit dating its lineage from the 72nd Aero Squadron of February 1918, with the end of the First World War, the unit was demobilised and not reconstituted as the 72nd Bombardment Squadron until 6 February 1923, and was then activated, at Luke Field, Territory of Hawaii, on 1 May 1923. The unit was redesignated as the 72nd Bombardment Squadron (Medium) on 6 December 1939, and as the 72nd Bombardment Squadron (Heavy) on 20 November 1940.

Like its sister 23rd Bomb Squadron, the unit was equipped with Martin B-12s between 1936 and 1938, before receipt of new B-18s, some of which were passed along by the newly arrived 31st Bombardment Squadron in March 1938 when the Squadron moved to newly carved-out Hickam Field for operations. The Squadron actually

The dedicated reconnaissance unit of the 5th Bomb Group was the 4th Reconnaissance Squadron (M/R), and a line-up of its aircraft is pictured here. *Hawaii Collections Folder, Museum of Flight*

11th Bombardment Group (M)

Part of the Air Corps pre-war expansion program, the 11th Bombardment Group was not activated, in Hawaii, until 1 February 1940, and became the 11th Bombardment Group (Heavy) on 1 December 1940. The Group was composed of the Headquarters and Headquarters Squadron, 14th, 26th and 42nd Bombardment Squadrons, and the attached 50th Reconnaissance Squadron. Initially equipped entirely with thirteen hand-me-down B-18s acquired from the 5th Bomb Group, the Group started to receive B-17s during 1941, and consequently, while training intensively on its B-18s, it had only a fairly brief exposure to the aircraft. By 30 November 1941 the Group mustered a total of nine B-18s, as well as four Boeing B-17Ds and a single Curtiss A-12.

14th Bombardment Squadron (M)

Originally organised as the 1st Aviation School Squadron in May 1917, this unit went through a number of permutations, usually associated with Bolling Field, DC, before being reactivated with the 11th Bomb Group at Hickam Field, TH, on 1 February 1940. It trained intensively on a relatively small number of B-18s until well into 1941, when B-17s started to arrive. The Squadron redeployed to Clark Field, Philippines, on 16 September 1941, where it arrived barely in time to be decimated by the Japanese onslaught. It left its B-18s in Hawaii.

26th Bombardment Squadron (M)

Another unit that could trace its lineage back to the 1st Reserve Aero Squadron of May 1917, this Squadron went through periods as the 26th Aero Squadron (from October 1917) and the 26th Attack Squadron (January 1923), until finally redesignated as the 26th Bombardment Squadron (Medium) on 6 December 1939, and the 26th Bombardment Squadron (Heavy) on 11 December 1940 at Hickam Field. The Squadron began to receive B-18s in May 1940, but started transition onto two B-17s on 21 May 1941. By 7 December 1941, the unit had five B-18s and two B-17s at Hickam.

42nd Bombardment Squadron (M)

Organised as the 42nd Aero Squadron in June 1917, this unit went through the usual between-the-wars, on-again/off-again existence until being redesignated as the 42nd Bombardment Squadron (Medium) on 22 December 1939. Redesignated as the 42nd Bombardment Squadron (Heavy) on 11 December 1940, the unit had actually only been activated on 1 February 1940 with the parent Group at Hickam Field.

Typical of the subordinate Squadrons of the 11th Bomb Group, the first officer of field grade, Major C. K. Rich, did not arrive as Squadron Commander until 20 March 1940, relieving Lieutenant Ohman, who became the Squadron Adjutant. Besides that essential task, the unfortunate Lieutenant was also detailed as the Squadron Technical Supply Officer, Communications Officer, Engineering Officer, Operations Officer, Armament Officer, Athletics Officer and Supply Officer! Apparently, the additional duties of Mess and Transportation Officer did not seem important enough to task him with as well.

From activation through to about 16 June 1940 the Squadron described itself as 'growing up'. Newly arrived, comparatively, it found that it did not have to endure the 'tent city' existence of the older garrison units, and its growing personnel roster was able to be quartered in the 'Big Barracks', newly completed just across the street from the hangar area.

Much has been made of the alleged pre-7 December 1941 'sabotage' reports that seemed to surface almost daily in Hawaii. But as a direct result the 42nd BS, together with nearly every Air Corps unit at Hickam, was placed on Alert Status, and the first hectic period of this stressful (and eventually boring) status did not end until 21 December 1940. The growth of the Squadron during its first six months following activation could not be called phenomenal. As of 31 July 1940 the roster comprised five assigned and two attached officers and 181 enlisted ranks, together with an additional twenty-five enlisted men in the Squadron on detached service. The Squadron received its first two B-17s in May 1941, joining five B-18s, and this remained the strength through November 1941.

50th Reconnaissance Squadron (H)

Another veteran unit, organised in August 1917 as the 50th Aero Squadron, this one went through the typical between-the-wars hiatus, and was not activated again until 1 November 1930; it was then redesignated as the 50th Reconnaissance Squadron on 25 January 1938 and assigned to the 5th Composite Group in October of that year. Redesignated as the 50th Reconnaissance Squadron (Medium Range) on 6 December 1939, the unit had been attached to the 5th Bombardment Group on 12 October 1938. It was relieved from that attachment and attached to the 11th Bomb Group on 1 February 1940, being assigned to Luke Field from 1 November 1930, but moving to Hickam Field on 9 October 1939. Like many former Reconnaissance Squadrons, the unit was redesignated as a Bombardment Squadron during the war, and thus lost its original numeric designator, becoming the 431st Bomb Squadron (H). This AAF practice, coincidentally, has also made research into the history of these units prior to these redesignations much more difficult.

The Squadron was typical in receiving new replacements right out of basic training and the recruitment process nearly every day as war approached. One of these was Lee Webster, who arrived in Hickam Field in 1939, and was shortly enrolled in the Aircraft & Engine School run for the Hawaiian Air Force by the 17th Air Base Squadron. He graduated in May 1940 as a PFC and was almost immediately assigned to the 50th RS, where he was advanced to Corporal, with assignment to become Crew Chief and Flight Engineer on one of the Squadron B-18s. His experience as holding a dual role as both Crew Chief and Flight Engineer on his aircraft was common practice at the time nearly service-wide.

He and his crew were on hand when the Kilauea volcano erupted on Mauna Loa on the island of Hawaii (also known as 'The Big Island'). His aircraft and two other B-18s were selected to fly a group of newsmen over the scene of the eruption. At 13,000 feet, orbiting near the eruption required the crew to go on oxygen, which, while still rather novel for all crew members, consisted of a pipe-stem-like object that was placed in the mouth and had a manually operated valve located at each flight station in the aircraft.

The crew experienced a tremendous updraught from the eruption while flying at 15,000 feet due to the heat being generated, and the aircraft shot upwards. The mission was terminated by the aircraft commander for fear that the extremely rapid ascent may have caused damage to the aircraft, so they returned to Hickam. The mission was, however, ruled a success, in spite of the early return, as the cameras that had been mounted in the open bomb bays had automatically exposed some spectacular images.

One of Webster's fondest memories of the B-18 was the common practice of having the Flight Engineers on each aircraft hoist themselves up through the overhead cockpit escape hatch, and sit with their legs dangling down in the cabin, to aid the aircraft commander during taxi, due to the nose-high attitude of the aircraft. This was accomplished both in departures and arrivals, and he often assumed that position during the landing roll-out.

Like other Hawaiian Air Force B-18 operating units, the 50th also did annual live-bombing exercises out of Morris Field on the Big Island. Typically, they would fly at varying altitudes and drop practice bombs on targets drawn on the black lava rock in a restricted area set aside for the military.

The Squadron was also actively engaged in towing sleeves for the Coast Artillery anti-aircraft crews near Fort Kamehameha, located on the western shoreline not far from Hickam Field, and Camp Maiakole near Ewa, where a Marine Corps airfield was located. These sleeve targets were attached to steel cables and reeled several hundred feet aft of the aircraft, as most of the anti-aircraft gunners were firing .30 and .50 caliber guns. On a number of occasions, the tow cable was severed by gun fire, much to the chagrin of the crews. The aircraft usually flew parallel to the beach gunnery range and from a point at sea, flying inland to give the ground forces an overhead shot. On one such mission Webster related that both engines quit at once, as the pilot had apparently forgotten to switch the tanks. The target sleeve was cut loose by the two crew members in the rear fuselage, using a pair of bolt cutters carried for just such an emergency – but not before being dragged for some distance across the thorny Kiave underbrush.

The unit approached war, as of 30 November 1941, in transition, having four B-18s and two new Boeing B-17Ds on hand.

The 50th Reconnaissance Squadron was attached to the 11th Bomb Group in Hawaii, and this was the Squadron Commander's aircraft at Hickam Field in 1940. *via Rich Dann*

Panama Canal Zone

When the first three B-18s, AC37-31/32, arrived in the Canal Zone at France Field on the Atlantic side, and 37-33 at Albrook Field on the Pacific side, on 22 July 1938, they were an instant sensation, representing the very latest in heavy bombardment aviation and seemingly tailor-made for conditions in the Canal Zone and the tropics. Little did anyone suspect on that hot and humid day that, by the end of 1942, these aircraft and their sisters would become one of the most important weapons in the US arsenal in that region against an enemy onslaught.

In this introductory section, however, only the use of the aircraft prior to 7 December 1941 will be discussed, although the utilisation they received was, to say the least, far more significant than hitherto recognised.

This was because, unlike the B-18s dispatched to Hawaii, the Philippines and even Alaska, aside from US personnel and close allies, and (perhaps) some Japanese agents, the aircraft had nowhere to go and no one to see them. The Panama-based B-18s, on the other hand, were used almost from the beginning to project US power and influence in Central America, South America and the Caribbean, while at the same time providing their far-ranging crews with invaluable operational experience in truly strange places.

Between July 1938 and 7 December 1941 a total of twenty-one B-18s were assigned to 19th Wing units at France Field, and eleven B-18s and two B-18As to Albrook Field – a modest investment considering the number allocated for Air Corps units in Hawaii not long before. But these thirty-two aircraft would be followed, in the months and years to come, by nothing less than the majority of airworthy B-18s and B-18As remaining with CONUS organisations by the end of 1942.

The introduction of the 'first wave' of B-18s into Panama was done is rather spectacular fashion. On 26 January 1939 Canal Zone-based units flew the last ten Martin B-10Bs to CONUS and the same crews returned with ten new B-18s so that by 12 June 1939 the command had received a total of thirty B-18s in this manner. Of these, ten were assigned to squadrons subordinate to the 16th Pursuit Group at Albrook Field, and twenty to the 6th Bomb Group at France Field. By 11 June 1941 B-18s (totaling twenty-seven) and B-18As (seventeen) were the most numerous combat type available in Panama, an arithmetic testament to their importance to the defense of the command.

By 30 November 1941 Headquarters and Headquarters Squadron, Panama Air Force, had one B-18A and a Douglas C-49 on strength.

19th Wing

The entire Air Corps establishment in the Canal Zone had been reorganised on 15 August 1937 and, compared to that in the Hawaiian Islands, was a rather modest assortment of units situated on two principal fields near the Atlantic and Pacific approaches to the vital canal. These consisted of the Headquarters and Headquarters Squadron, 19th Wing (formerly the 19th Composite Wing), the Headquarters and Headquarters Squadron 6th Bombardment Group (formerly the 6th Composite Group), which included the 7th Reconnaissance Squadron and 25th Bombardment Squadron at France Field, and the 16th Pursuit Group and all of its subordinate units, which was located at Albrook Field on the Pacific side. The 16th PG included a Headquarters and Headquarters Squadron, the 24th and 29th Pursuit Squadrons, the 44th Reconnaissance Squadron and the 74th Attack Squadron. These units, combined with the two Air Base Squadrons and the Panama Air Depot, were often cited locally as the Panama Canal Air Force (and this designation became official on 19 October 1940). All of these, as well as all other Air Corps assets in the Caribbean region, were combined together to form the Caribbean Air Force on 8 May 1941.

The B-18s assigned to the Wing got very heavy utilisation following arrival. This included some rather unusual activities not normally associated with Air Corps units anywhere else. For example, between 29 April and 4 May 1940 B-18s from the 6th Bomb Group took part in extensive tests of the Aircraft Warning Service, which was regarded as crucial to detect any inbound air attacks on the vulnerable canal

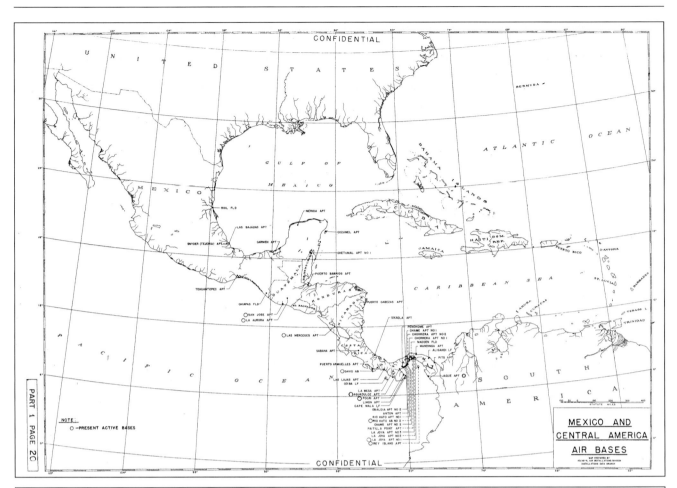

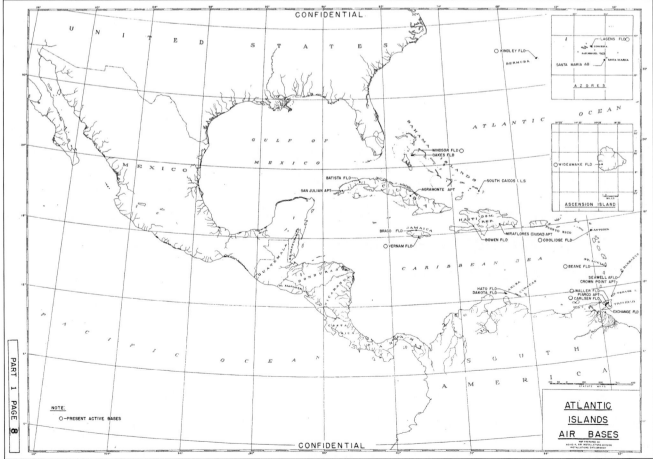

Taken at Albrook Field, Canal Zone, during President Roosevelt's pre-war inspection tour, these three B-18s, probably of the 44th Reconnaissance Squadron, display a surprising variety of camouflage schemes not seen elsewhere in the Air Corps at the time, as well as varying sizes of national insignia. *NARA via Dana Bell*

6B/16 of the 6th Bomb Group arrives rather ingloriously at France Field, Canal Zone, aboard a barge after being recovered from a crash site on the Atlantic coast of the Isthmus. The aircraft was returned to service. *via Ed Young*

installations. The following month the Wing became concerned about the dispersal of ordnance for its growing fleet of heavy bombardment aircraft and, in anticipating the arrival of the 9th Bomb Group in November, recommended that existing stocks of bombs, from 2,000lb down to 100lb weapons, be dispersed so that at least one full load per aircraft was available at each of the major operating bases – Albrook Field, France Field and Rio Hato – a prudent suggestion considering what followed in Hawaii and the Philippines. By 27 May 1940 the thirty-three B-18s assigned to the Command were distributed as follows:

The 'front office' of a 19th Wing B-18, unit designator '172', as viewed from the floor looking up and forward from the radio operator's position. Note that the glass in the upper hatch had already been distorted by the torrential rain and heat of the tropics. *Major Jesse W. Miller, USAF (Ret)*

Opposite page: The Army Air Corps operating command in the Caribbean and in defense of the Panama Canal was the Caribbean Air Force, which had far-ranging responsibilities. This airways map shows some of the locations and stations that became the 'stomping grounds' for B-18 series aircraft from the time the first examples arrived in July 1938 clear through to the end of the war. *USAAF*

19th Wing Headquarters	2
6th Bombardment Group	19
7th Reconnaissance Squadron	6
44th Reconnaissance Squadron	6
74th Bombardment Squadron (being reorganised from an Attack unit)	due to receive 6

Contrary to many criticisms levelled at Air Corps planners in the other two major US overseas bastions, Panama-based planners recognised full well by 23 July 1940 that, even with the dispersal base at Rio Hato, which was adequate and largely unknown to prying eyes, the 19th Wing's principal strength was vulnerable at the well-known Albrook and France Field bases. Accordingly, immediate steps were taken to identity Emergency Landing Field sites throughout the Republic of Panama, including David (two sites were selected near that far western city), Chame, Aguadulce, Garachine (San Miguel Bay), Jaque, Pocri, Las Lajas, La Chorrera, La Mesa, La Jolla (also known as La Joya or Pacora) and Changuinola (Almirante Bay area). Nearly all of these became at least occasional haunts for dispersed B-18s. It is worth noting that, had the Command received the coveted B-17s that it had wanted, it would have been difficult, at best, to operate from these stations during the critical early stage of the war. The B-18s had no trouble at all.

While the dispersal plans were prudent and good planning, given the information filtering in from Europe, they were not without day-to-day challenges. These remote sites were, to put it mildly, difficult to reach via surface transport – as anyone who has served in the interior of Panama can attest. That meant that the Air Corps had to depend on commercial oil companies in Panama to distribute fuel to the various locations (the service did not have enough trucks of its own at the time to transport oil and fuel from the single distribution center near Panama City), and they together had only fourteen tank trucks with a total capacity of 13,000 gallons and one barge with a 25,000-gallon capacity. Intensive air operations, as envisaged as of late October 1940, might necessitate at least twenty missions per month (which turned out to be a ridiculously low estimate) with a peak load of three missions in a 48-hour period, for a total of fifty-four B-18 aircraft and twenty-seven B-17s. The B-17s could operate only from the relatively 'hard-surfaced' Albrook Field, while the B-18s could operate routinely from Albrook, France Field, Rio Hato, Chame, Aguadulce and David. Since Albrook would almost certainly be a prime objective of any attacking force, the available B-17s would have been in a severe predicament, as there was *absolutely no alternative aerodrome that could take them at the time*. Howard Field, also on the Pacific side of the Isthmus, and which would eventually become known as 'the bomber base', was still under very slow construction as of 30 October 1940.

With the deteriorating world situation following the German advances in Europe and Japanese aggression in the Far East, the 19th Wing was reinforced in November 1940 when the entire 9th Bombardment Group (qv) departed Mitchel Field, NY, for assignment to the GHQAF, and moved lock, stock and barrel to the remote Rio Hato aerodrome about 70 air miles west of the Canal Zone in Panama, bringing with it twenty-two nearly brand-new B-18As, where it remained until moving again, on 30 October 1941, to Waller Field, Trinidad. This Group's fortunes, perhaps more than most, were inextricably linked with the B-18 series. With the arrival of the 9th BG, the 19th Wing's B-18 strength soared almost overnight from thirty-three aircraft to fifty-five. The 19th Wing had been led to believe that it would be receiving a Group fully equipped with the new Boeing B-17s and commented bitterly to the Air Corps leadership that, although glad to have the unit and the additional aircraft, the B-18As lacked '…the speed and range…and were in no wise suitable for the air mission in Panama.' This preliminary and rather covetous assessment was to change in the months that followed. Although still regarding itself as weak during what was recognised as a transitional period, no one could have predicted the expansion that would follow in the next 18 months.

But the 19th Wing's primary pre-war accomplishment, and one that is seldom recognised, was in the projection of US power and influence in the region. These so-called 'Good Will' flights, of which many did eventuate, were often more for the benefit of wavering regional governments and known agents of foreign powers stationed in the vicinity of the Canal Zone bastion. On 17 and 18 December 1940, for example, no fewer than twelve 19th Wing B-18s, accompanied by six P-36As of the 12th Pursuit Wing, flew from the Canal Zone over San Jose, Costa Rica, in formation for 15 minutes, before flying on to Managua, Nicaragua, where they circled twice before landing to take part in Pan American Aviation day there.

A month later, on 13 January 1941, two of the newly arrived 9th Bomb Group B-18As left Albrook Field for Lima, Peru, and returned with two Peruvian Army officers, who studied air defense and training methods then being used in the Canal Zone. Given that the entire Peruvian bombardment establishment consisted of Italian aircraft at this juncture, it takes little imagination to recognise the propaganda value of this exercise.

The following month, February 1941, 19th Wing B-18s, with stops en route at Maracaibo, Venezuela; Port of Spain, Trinidad, and Paramaribo, Dutch Guiana, flew all the way to Belém, Brazil, to deliver some rubber seeds to plantations there, which had been en route by surface vessel from the Philippines. The steamer missed its connection with a Brazilian-bound vessel and, as the seeds, of the Hevea species, were extremely sensitive to deterioration in the tropical environment, they needed to be speeded onwards. That same month, the Commanding General of the Panama Canal Department, Lt-Gen G. Daniel Van Voorhis, made a far-reaching inspection of some of the new bases in the region acquired via the 'Destroyers for Bases' deal with the British. Flying in a Douglas C-39 and accompanied by five B-18s, the General made calls in Maracaibo, Venezuela, Trinidad, Puerto Rico and Jamaica. The similar flights that followed, on practically a weekly basis, could easily have given the impression that the Air Corps establishment in the Canal Zone was much larger than it actually was at the time, an impression that must certainly have not escaped the notice of the planners.

The 19th Bomb Wing trained nearly all of its own bombardiers within the command at this point, and bombing trainers were available at both Albrook and France Field; each of the Squadrons of the 6th Bomb Group (the 3rd, 25th and 74th Bomb Squadrons and the attached 7th Recon Squadron) had a trainer for its exclusive use. Actual live bombing training was practiced by the 6th Bomb Group

on targets at Valladolid Rock in Panama Bay and, unique to the command, a sunken ship in Limon Bay, which was often the cause of considerable rumor amongst ships' companies transiting the Atlantic entrance to the Canal.

Gunnery schools were also conducted within the Squadrons of the command and, interestingly, these were run for both officers and all enlisted crew members, and it was not uncommon on a June morning in 1941 for Panamanian fishermen to have their eyes jerked skywards by machine gun fire from B-18s off Pina Point, or over Buenaventura Island.

Navigation training was conducted, for the most part, under Group direction, and the numerous long-distance 'Good Will' flights noted were all part of these exercises. Although celestial navigation was taught, the local emphasis was on dead-reckoning, for it was a common belief in the 19th Wing that the navigation schools in CONUS spent way too much time on celestial, and that it should be held in reserve only, as the prevailing weather conditions in the tropics were seldom conducive to this form of sophisticated navigation.

From time to time, B-18 formations, sometimes mixed with the few, highly prized B-17Bs recently arrived, made mock attacks on the Canal Zone's defenses, and these were invariably instructive. There were also numerous Army-Navy exercises, something that Air Corps units in the Hawaiian Islands and the Philippines seldom enjoyed.

By 25 August 1941 the 19th Bombardment Wing strength was, in actuality, rather dispersed, and only one unit was anywhere near statutory authorized strength. The accompanying table shows their dispositions.

One unusual 19th Wing training project was carried out on 13 September 1941 when twenty B-18s were used as troop carriers. It was assumed, for the purposes of the exercise, that friendly parachute troops had secured an 'enemy' installation, in this instance Howard Field. The mission of the B-18s was to transport the entire 550th Airborne Infantry Battalion from Rio Hato to Howard Field so that it could consolidate the positions being 'held' by the paratroopers.

As of 30 November 1941 HHS, 19th Bombardment Wing (as it was formally redesignated in 1940) itself had one B-18, one B-18A and an A-17 on hand. However, official USAAF documents state that the 19th Bombardment Wing was inactivated on 25 October 1941 having, for all intents and purposes, been replaced by VI Bomber Command, which was activated that same day.

Making use of the organisation shown in the accompanying table for 19th Bomb Wing, the magnitude of the effort expended by VI Bomber Command in carrying out its mission to defend the Canal Zone and its approaches is seldom fully appreciated. Between 7 December 1941 until the end of 1942, VI Bomber Command aircraft, including its sizeable B-18 component, flew 10,000,000 nautical miles on tactical missions, mostly patrols. This was the equivalent in distance of a formation of thirty bombers flying from England to Berlin and back every day of the year. Some 15,000 tactical missions were flown.

6th Bombardment Group (H)

Created in September 1919 specifically for service in the Panama Canal Zone as the 3rd Observation Group, and redesignated as the 6th Group (Observation) in 1921, 6th Group (Composite) in 1922, 6th Bombardment Group in 1937, 6th Bombardment Group (Medium) in 1939 and, finally, 6th Bombardment Group (Heavy) in 1940, this organisation was the premier bombardment aviation unit in the region. By 30 November 1941, on the eve of the US entry into the war, the Group and its subordinate Squadrons possessed a total of fifteen B-18s, two B-18As, a Northrop A-17 and three Boeing B-17Bs. It was subsequently disbanded in the Canal Zone on 1 November 1943, but went on, lineally, as a noted Very Heavy bombardment group in the Pacific flying B-29s later in the war. Subordinate units varied, but

19th Bombardment Group Disposition 25 August 1941

Unit	Aircraft on Hand	Aircraft with Full Military Equipment	Station
HHS 19th Bomb Wing	B-18A – 1	B-18 – 1	Albrook Field, CZ
	B-18A – 1	B-18 – 1	
6th Bomb Group (H)	B-18A – 1	B-18A – 1	France Field, CZ
	A-17 – 1		
3rd Bomb Squadron (H)	B-17B – 2	B-17B – ?	France Field, CZ
	B-18 – 6	B-18 – 5	
25th Bomb Squadron (H)	B-17B – 1	B-17B – ?	France Field, CZ
	B-18 – 5	B-18 – 5	
74th Bomb Squadron (H)	B-17B – 1	B-17B – ?	Howard Field, CZ
	B-18A – 1	B-18A – 1	
	B-18 – 4	B-18 – 4	
HHS 9th Bomb Group (H)	B-18A – 2	B-18A – 2	Rio Hato, RdeP
	A-17 – 1		
5th Bomb Squadron	B-17B – 1	B-17B – ?	Rio Hato, RdeP
	B-18A – 4	B-18A – 4	
99th Bomb Squadron	B-17B – 1	B-17B – ?	Rio Hato, RdeP
	B-18A – 4	B-18A – 4	
7th Recon Squadron	B-17B – 1	B-17B – ?	France Field, CZ
	B-18A – 1	B-18A – 1	
	B-18 – 5	B-18 – 5	
	A-17 – 1		
44th Recon Squadron	B-17B – 1	B-17B – ?	Howard Field, CZ
	B-18A – 1	B-18A – 1	
	B-18 – 5	B-18 – 5	
59th Bomb Squadron	A-20A – 12	A-20A – 12	

consisted of the 3rd Bomb Squadron from February 1940, the 25th Bomb Squadron, the 74th Bomb Squadron, the 7th Recon Squadron and the 44th Recon Squadron during most of its pre-war and wartime existence. The Group organisation within the successive Panama-based Air Corps establishment gradually lost importance as events unfolded, and although the various Squadrons remained nominally subordinate to the Group, they operated with a far greater degree of independence than almost anywhere else in the service.

3rd Bombardment Squadron (H)

An expansion organisation, this unit was not constituted until 1 January 1938, becoming the 3rd Bombardment Squadron (Medium) on 22 December 1939, but not activated until 1 February 1940 and immediately assigned to the 6th Bomb Group. The unit was redesignated as the 3rd Bombardment Squadron (Heavy) on 20 November 1940. The unit remained an element of VI Bomber Command, Sixth Air Force, for its entire Second World War existence.

Initially stationed at France Field, it deployed to Rio Hato, Republic of Panama, on 8 December 1941, and subsequently led an exceptionally far-ranging existence, about which more later, in the section of this book devoted to the wartime experiences of the B-18.

25th Bombardment Squadron (H)

Organised as the 20th Aero Squadron in June 1917 but redesignated as the 25th Aero Squadron the same month, this unit evolved into the 25th Bombardment Squadron in January 1923, after being posted to the Canal Zone on 30 April 1922. It became the premier bombardment squadron in the Canal Zone defensive establishment, and was redesignated as the 25th Bombardment Squadron (Medium) on 6 December 1939, then the 25th Bombardment Squadron (Heavy)

One of the premier overseas operators of the B-18, this is an original rendition of the unit insignia of the 25th Bombardment Squadron in the Panama Canal Zone. The unit operated B-18s between 1938-1942. *Author's Collection*

on 20 November 1940. Like its sister units of the 6th Bomb Group, it led a rather nomadic existence, although it was garrisoned at France Field from April 1922 until 8 December 1941, when it deployed to Rio Hato, Republic of Panama.

A pioneering Martin B-10B operator, the unit converted to the first B-18s to reach France Field in 1939. The Squadron used its new mounts in October and November 1939 to conduct extensive searches over vast stretches of the Pacific for two Peruvian airmen who had reportedly ditched at sea while ferrying new aircraft from the US to Lima. They were later found safe after a forced landing in Ecuador, however. The search had taken the B-18s along the 80th meridian to a distance of some 250 nautical miles seaward and, because of the shortage of trained navigators in the unit, the trio of B-18s engaged in the search stayed within sight of each other, with one trained navigator leading. These missions typically lasted 5 hours, and proved an excellent training exercise for the unit. The B-18s covered some 10,000 square miles of sea east to about 100 miles along the coast of Central America. They carried sufficient fuel for not less than 11 hours flying time.

Like other 6th Bomb Group units, the 25th took part in a large number of 'Good Will' flights to neighbouring nations, including three B-18s that flew to Guatemala City on 17 February 1941.

74th Bombardment Squadron (H)

Organised originally as the 74th Aero Squadron in February 1918, this unit was reconstituted and consolidated as the 74th Pursuit Squadron on 8 May 1929, but was not actually activated as such at Albrook Field until 1 October 1933. It then changed mission on 1 September 1937, when it became the 74th Attack, and, one of the few squadrons to make such a transition, became a dedicated Medium Bombardment Squadron on 6 December 1939. It finally became the 74th Bombardment Squadron (Heavy) on 20 November 1940. It remained at Albrook Field until 14 July 1941, when it became one of the first units to move to the new bomber base on the Pacific side of the Isthmus, Howard Field. It was also one of the first units to deploy on change-of-station to the satellite aerodrome at Aguadulce, Republic of Panama, on 8 November 1941 and on to Rio Hato around 11 December 1941.

The Squadron received its first B-18, AC36-283, in early February 1939, the first of a long relationship with the type. The Squadron was unusual in also having a Grumman OA-9 amphibian on strength by December 1939.

Prior to becoming a Medium Bombardment Squadron and transitioning to B-18s, the unit had been assigned to the 16th Pursuit Group (Interceptor) at Albrook.

The Squadron deployed to Rio Hato in July 1940 for eight days of intensive bomb and gunnery training at the remote aerodrome, including extensive bomb training, some 635 practice bombs, thirty-six 300lb weapons and six 600-pounders being expended. The unit took this opportunity to train eleven enlisted bombardiers, being in the air not less than 138 hours on actual bomb missions.

The empennage of a 19th Wing B-18, unit designator '152' (probably a 25th Bomb Squadron aircraft) is just visible on the left in front of a new hangar being constructed at the Rio Hato aerodrome, some 80 air miles west of the Panama Canal, in 1941. *Frank Hohmann*

A veteran Canal Zone unit, the 25th Bomb Squadron (H), 6th Bomb Group, converted from Martin B-10Bs when the first new B-18s arrived at France Field in 1939. Unit designator '152', shown here sporting red leading edges on the engine cowlings, apparently collided with something hard! *Frank Hohmann*

Formerly an Attack Squadron, the 74th Bomb Squadron (H) was redesignated as such on 6 December 1939, having received its first B-18s in February 1939, even before it had been formally redesignated. Here, four unit aircraft bear the squadron insignia and 6th Bomb Group unit designators at the Rio Hato aerodrome on deployment. *Frank Hohmann*

This quartet of 74th Bomb Squadron (H) B-18s of the 6th Bomb Group is pictured at the Rio Hato aerodrome and includes 6B/55, a Flight Leader's band on the rear fuselage. *Frank Hohmann*

74th Bomb Squadron B-18 6B/55 at Rio Hato aerodrome in 1941 after receiving olive-drab 'war paint'. *Frank Hohmann*

7th Reconnaissance Squadron (M/R)

Another veteran Canal Zone organisation, the 7th Reconnaissance Squadron owed its existence to the original 7th Aero Squadron formed in March 1917 at Ancon, Canal Zone. Redesignated as the 7th Observation Squadron in January 1925, and the 7th Reconnaissance Squadron in September 1937, it became the 7th Recon Squadron (Medium Range) on 6 December 1939, and the 7th Recon Squadron (Heavy) on 20 November 1940. The lineage of the unit is often submerged in the fact that it was redesignated as the 397th Bombardment Squadron (H) in April 1942. It was attached to the 6th Bomb Group from 1 February 1940 (having formerly been regarded as a Panama Canal Zone Department asset), and formally assigned to the Group on 25 February 1942.

The Squadron had become one of the first Canal Zone units to acquire B-18s, having six by the end of 1939 (alongside a single Northrop A-17), and shortly thereafter also acquired a Sikorsky OA-8. By July 1940 the unit, stationed at France Field, had honed its skills on the new aircraft through participation in a number of the far-ranging 'Good Will' flights so familiar to AAC crews in the Canal Zone. Also, in October 1939, it made use of three of its B-18s to take part in the search for a missing schooner, the *Resolute*, which had been bound for the San Andres Islands from Cartagena, Colombia. The vessel had damaged her rudder and was floating at the mercy of the currents. This and similar exercises proved an invaluable source of highly practical training for the B-18 crews for the wartime sea searches that would soon fall to them. The three unit B-18s covered some 10,000 square miles of sea to a distance of about 100 miles along the coast of Central America in searching for the *Resolute*, and an equal distance to sea. Each aircraft operated independently, maintained radio contact with the home station at half-hour intervals, and carried sufficient fuel for an incredible 11-hour mission, although in the event only 4-hour missions were necessary.

The Squadron was ecstatic to be designated as one of the units to receive one of the brand-new Boeing B-17Bs in June 1941, which joined its five B-18s and single B-18A. By November the unit had received four B-17Bs, but this was reduced to just one by the end of the month, as area Commanders reassessed the assignments of these wonderful new weapons; by the time the Squadron moved to Howard Field on the Pacific side of the Isthmus by 26 November, the Squadron had five B-18s, one B-18A and an A-17.

9th Bombardment Group (H)

Cited earlier in this account in connection with its long existence as a part of the GHQAF at Mitchel Field, NY, from August 1922 until November 1940, this Group was specifically reassigned to Rio Hato, Republic of Panama, to nearly double the heavy bombardment force guarding the vital Panama Canal.

This Group, if remembered at all, is usually connected with its much later Second World War experience as a dedicated Very Heavy Bombardment Group operating B-29s in the Pacific. Indeed, its brief Caribbean interlude has been, at best, confused and fragmented by the administrative reassignments and attachments that the Group experienced from practically the beginning of its service there.

Besides the subordinate squadrons that had accompanied the Group to Panama, the veteran 44th Reconnaissance Squadron, which had been stationed at Albrook Field for some time, was also attached to the Group as of 20 November 1940, which, besides bringing along its five B-18s, also added the very first four-engine B-17B to the Group.

The Group, at least on paper, subsequently relocated in a series of reassignments and became the premier anti-submarine units in the theater, mainly by virtue of events as they unfolded, rather than by conscious design. The subordinate 1st Bomb Squadron moved to Piarco Field, Trinidad, some 1,400 miles distant, on 24 April 1941, followed by the 5th Bomb Squadron, which departed for Beane Field, St Lucia, in the Antilles, north of Trinidad, on 28 September 1941. The Group headquarters itself finally moved to the new US-built airfield on Trinidad, Waller Field, on 30 October 1941, where it was joined shortly by the 1st Bomb Squadron. The attached 44th Recon Squadron moved to Atkinson Field, British Guiana, a further 400 air miles around the north-east 'hump' of mainland South America, on 4 November 1941, and the 99th Bomb Squadron moved to even more isolated Zandery Field, Dutch Guiana, on 3 December 1941. The 9th Bomb Group thus found itself, on the eve of war, one of the most dispersed – if not *the* most dispersed – USAAC operational unit anywhere, a circumstance that became the norm for B-18 operating units in the region as the war unfolded. With all of those dispersal challenges, however, as of 30 November 1941 the Group could show a grand total of only six B-18As, and was very much being eviscerated to the benefit of the veteran 6th Bomb Group, which was much closer to authorized strength (qv).

The attached 44th Recon Squadron was formally assigned to the Group on 25 February 1942, and was redesignated as the 430th Bomb Squadron on 22 April 1942. The 9th Bomb Group Headquarters was disbanded on 22 July 1942 and, for the moment, the veteran 9th Bomb Group ceased to exist as a tactical unit. The formerly subordinate 1st Bomb Squadron lived on, changing stations to Edinburgh Field (a British facility) on Trinidad on 23 August 1942, and the remnants of the Group were reassigned to the little-known Antilles Air Task Force (AATF) on 18 September 1942, where it continued anti-submarine activities intensively, as will be detailed later in the text, as well as (nearly) taking part in the planned seizure of the Vichy French fleet anchored at Martinique. The remaining subordinate units of the 9th Bomb Group were transferred to the 25th Bomb Group in October 1942.

Commonwealth of Puerto Rico

The story of the Army Air Corps and USAAF involvement with the Commonwealth of Puerto Rico dates from 1 February 1940, when world events prompted War Department planners to regard the island of Puerto Rico, midway down the Antilles chain from Florida to the 'hump' of mainland South America, as vital to US defense interests.

The War Department directed that the Army Air Corps take immediate steps to increase and reorganise the nearly non-existent AAC presence on the island and at nearly the same stroke created the 13th Composite Wing as the local AAC command to facilitate that expansion.

13th Composite Wing

It is important to recognise that, as of the date of creation, the new 13th Composite Wing was not associated with the Panama Canal Zone defense establishment. That did not happen until somewhat later on, as will be seen.

By 31 December 1940 the 13th Composite Wing had tactical control of the following organisations, which had been hastily reassigned to Borinquen Field, Puerto Rico:

25th Bombardment Group (H), with elements of the 27th Reconnaissance Squadron

40th Bombardment Group (H), with elements of the 27th Reconnaissance Squadron

4th Observation Squadron

36th Pursuit Group

24th Air Base Group (Reinforced)

48th Air Base Group

Although impressive on paper, these organisations were nearly all under-strength and, what is worse, were crowded onto the minimal base facilities that were still under construction on the island. As it developed, these organisations and the 13th Composite Wing enjoyed only a very brief relationship, as the command structure of the US forces in the Caribbean morphed through a truly Byzantine series of changes in the months and years that followed. Most of the above units, although remaining in the theater, were accordingly reassigned. Following, for the first time, is a chronological sequence of the Command changes that eventuated, all of which impacted B-18 operations and the anti-submarine campaign that became central to its primary wartime contribution.

13th Composite Wing (from 3 September 1940)

Caribbean Interceptor Command (from 3 June 1941)

Caribbean Air Force Interceptor Command and Caribbean Air Force Bomber Command (from 18 September 1941)

6th Bomber Command (also cited for a time as **VI Bomber Command**) and **6th Interceptor Command** (from 25 October 1941)

Caribbean Naval Coastal Frontier (from 19 December 1941 – the entire **Panama Region, 6th Interceptor Command** was detached from the parent organisation at this point)

6th Interceptor Command (from 14 December 1941 – and which also commanded all Army Air Forces units in the **Caribbean Naval Coastal Frontier** at this time)

Army Air Command, Caribbean Coastal Frontier (from 26 December 1941 – with the **6th Interceptor Command** still subordinate, but for supply and administration only)

Caribbean Sea Frontier (from 27 January 1942)

6th Interceptor Command, Caribbean Sea Frontier

Headquarters, 6th Interceptor Command, Antilles Air Task Force (from 16 February 1942)

Headquarters, VI Fighter Command, Antilles Air Task Force (from 4 June 1942)

Headquarters, Antilles Air Task Force and VI Fighter Command

Antilles Air Task Force (from 20 May 1943)

Antilles Air Command (from 27 May 1943)

This series of shifts in command of anti-submarine and B-18 operating units had some unusual side-effects. Amongst these was the practice of citing Army Air Forces units, while nominally under Navy operational control, using Navy-style acronyms. Thus, it was not at all uncommon to see the 10th Bombardment Squadron cited in both AAF and Navy activity reports as the 10BOMRON.

As of 30 November 1941 there were a total of twenty-one B-18As stationed on Puerto Rico proper (one B-18A, alongside a P-36A, with HHS, 13th Composite Wing; seven B-18As as well as one P-36A and one A-17 with the 25th Bomb Group; two B-18As and one P-36A with the 27th Recon Squadron; three B-18As and one P-36A with the 5th Recon Squadron; seven B-18As and one P-36A with the 40th Bomb Group; and one B-18A assigned to the 48th Air Base Group) as part of the Caribbean Air Force, with others scattered in Trinidad (eight, plus two B-17Bs of the 9th Bomb Group), distant British Guiana (five B-18s, one B-18A and one B-17B with the 44th Recon Squadron), and the Windward Islands (two B-18As and one B-17B of the 9th Bomb Group).

25th Bombardment Group (H)

Although activated at Langley Field, VA, on 1 February 1940, as early as 2 December 1939 the Group had been identified for permanent station on Puerto Rico. The Group was organised from personnel formerly assigned to the 20th Bombardment Squadron, 2nd Bomb Group at Langley. The Group consisted of a Headquarters and Headquarters Squadron, as well as the 10th, 12th and 35th Bomb Squadrons (H) with the 27th Reconnaissance Squadron (H) attached.

The Group was originally equipped with a mix of seven new Boeing B-17s and B-17Bs, alongside six B-18As at Langley, with which the crews were quite smitten. One can only imagine their chagrin, therefore, when they were obliged to transfer all of the B-17s to March Field, CA, on 8 October 1940, in return for which, a week later, they received seven Douglas B-18As. No sooner had the B-18As arrived, and hasty transition training carried out, than the ground echelon of the unit deployed to Puerto Rico on 26 October 1940 aboard the USAT *Hunter Liggett*, followed by a reinforced air echelon, boosted to a total of fourteen B-18As and two Northrop A-17s on 3 November 1940, taking up rather crowded residence at the newly constructed Borinquen Field.

By 31 January 1941 the Group could muster a total of fifty-three officers and 818 enlisted ranks, but, as was the custom at the time, surrendered a substantial number of these officers and men on 1 April 1941 to form the cadre of the 40th Bombardment Group (M) (qv).

The Group also organised its own Bombardment School for enlisted bombardiers at Borinquen Field on 3 March 1941, with 1Lt Herbert Morgan Jr and 2Lt Charles E. Leffingwell, trained bombardiers, as the solitary faculty members. The Group recruited nine enlisted students, with three others being detailed from the attached 27th Recon Squadron (H). The students were required to have at least one year of active service in the Air Corps, with preference being given to trained Armorers and to those who were junior NCOs or Privates '…possessing the characteristics desirable in Non-Commissioned Officers'. This type of unit training of enlisted bombardiers became very common in the Sixth Air Force and Antilles Air Command as the organisation expanded and evolved, and resulted in probably the highest concentration of enlisted bombardiers anywhere in the AAF.

The Group also enjoyed a most unusual auxiliary when, on 16 August 1941, two NCOs assigned to the Group HHS, SSG Wallace Hess and John G. Gostomczik (the latter, by then, assigned to HHS 40th Bomb Group) bought a used, two-place Rearwin Model 7000, powered by a 70hp LeBlond engine. The aircraft was apparently rented out for pleasure flying by officers of the units, excursions over Puerto Rico, and some student flight training. The fate of the aircraft is unknown.

This B-18A, unit designator BY11, was assigned to Headquarters and Headquarters Squadron, 25th Bomb Group, at Langley Field, just before deploying to Borinquen Field, Puerto Rico, in October 1940. This unit became one of the premier anti-submarine units with these same aircraft by early 1942. *NMUSAF*

After arriving in Puerto Rico in October 1940, the 25th Bomb Group set about becoming familiar with its operational neighborhood. This Headquarters Squadron aircraft, 25B/12, by then wearing the new-style unit designators, is pictured at St Thomas, British Virgin Islands, a challenging operating station with which the unit was to become very familiar. *Herman C. Wood*

10th Bombardment Squadron (H)

Initially, along with the parent 25th Bomb Group, a GHQAF asset, the Squadron was activated 1 February 1940 at Langley Field, VA, under the command of Capt Alva L. Harvey. At the time of activation, the Squadron had most unusual quarters at Langley, being domiciled in the Lighter-than-Air Hangar, which it shared with its sister Squadrons, the 12th and 35th, as well as the Group HHS. The enlisted ranks were quartered in two-storey temporary barracks and, upon activation, had nine officers and 160 enlisted ranks – as well as a grand total of four aircraft, two B-17Bs and two B-18As. On 26 October 1940 the Squadron, by then consisting of eight officers and 143 enlisted ranks, left the relative comforts of Langley Field for Newport News, VA, sailing from there on the USAT *Hunter Liggett* for San Juan, PR, making a brief stop in Charleston, SC, to bring aboard the 24th Air Base Group, also destined for Borinquen Field, PR. The Air Echelon arrived without incident on the afternoon of 3 November 1940, after brief refueling stops at Miami and Camaguey, Cuba.

At Borinquen Field, the Squadron was quartered in four single-storey temporary barracks, and equipment consisted of four B-18As and an A-17.

The subsequent organisational history of this unit, which was destined to become one of the premier anti-submarine organisations in the Caribbean, is rather unusual. It was transferred, on paper, to Edinburgh Field, Trinidad, minus personnel circa November 1942, about which more later.

12th Bombardment Squadron (H)

Constituted on 22 December 1939 and activated along with the parent Group on 1 February 1940 at Langley Field, the 12th Bombardment Squadron became one of the truly unsung units that operated B-18 aircraft almost exclusively for its entire active service existence.

The unit moved from Langley to Borinquen Field, PR, on 1 November 1940, then commenced a migratory existence up and down the Antilles chain, starting with deployment to Benedict Field, St Croix, the day after the Japanese attack on Pearl Harbor.

Bearing unit designator 25B/54, this B-18A is probably a 12th Bomb Squadron (H), 25th Bomb Group, aircraft. Note that the entire inboard side of the engine nacelles has been painted matt black and that the crew escape hatch atop the cabin is ajar, providing good ventilation to the crew in the tropics. *NMUSAF*

The Squadron was redesignated as a Medium bombardment unit later, on 7 May 1942, and will be noted in much further depth as this narrative unfolds.

35th Bombardment Squadron (H)

Yet another 'expansion' unit that shared an identical constitution and activation cycle with the sister Squadrons of the parent 25th Bomb Group, the 35th Bomb Squadron was destined to see perhaps more action with B-18 series aircraft than any other USAAF unit, and taken collectively, the story of this forgotten unit ranks amongst the greatest chronicles of the untold story of its primary mount, the B-18.

Ironically, although in nearly continuous action against the Axis submarine threat from the entry of the US into the war until disbandment in June 1944, the unit never adopted a unit insignia – one of the very few USAAF bombardment squadrons not to do so. One former member said the reason wasn't lack of interest: – they were simply too busy and constantly on the move.

The Squadron moved with the Group from Langley to Borinquen Field, PR, on 31 October 1941 and, after barely settling in, on to the new base at Coolidge Field, Antigua, on 11 November. The trek of this unit throughout the Caribbean in the years that follows reads like the diary of a rum-befuddled itinerant, and very much more anon. Like the Group headquarters as noted earlier, the Squadron found time while at Borinquen to form (briefly) a 35th Squadron Flying Club, and actually collected enough money to acquire an Aeronca K, NC-19321, from a former Puerto Rican owner. The sudden deployment to Coolidge Field ended that, however, and the aircraft was sold to the 29th Squadron Flying Club at Borinquen Field on 3 November 1941.

Rarely illustrated, this B-18A, unit designator 25B/71, bears the distinctive unit insignia of the 35th Bomb Squadron (H), destined to become one of the most distinguished anti-submarine units early in the war. The crewman shown is unidentified, but the image was taken at Borinquen Field, PR, on 12 June 1941. *Herman C. Wood*

27th Reconnaissance Squadron (H)

Ironically, the 27th Recon Squadron appears to have fallen off the edge of the earth, as even the monumental USAF monograph *Combat Squadrons of the Air Force – World War II* by the redoubtable Maurer Maurer does not index the unit. One must search manually until locating the successor organisation, the 417th Bombardment Squadron (H) (qv).

Constituted and activated on the same day, 16 September 1939, and designated from the very beginning as an asset of the Puerto Rican Department, the unit was actually formed at Langley Field, VA.

Chronologically, the 27th Reconnaissance Squadron (Long Range) arrived at the port of San Juan, PR on 21 November 1939, and was thus one of the pioneer USAAC units to arrive and form the original 13th Composite Group. The USAT *Chateau-Thierry* is alleged to have literally tipped sidewise on arrival and, according to legend, dumped eight officers and 160 men with '…untold gobs of equipment on the dock, and then sailed blissfully away, seemingly quite unaware of the historical significance connected with the venture' (quoted from the official unit history). Whatever the reality, the 27th had arrived and, early on the morning of same day, set out by a rather motley collection of surface conveyances for Punta Borinquen which, at that stage, was a place name only, being cited on most 1939 documents simply as Air Base No 1. It turned out to be a hastily carved swathe through a mongoose-infested cane patch. Upon arrival on the 22nd, the first order of business was to set up the unit Mess and try to feed everyone, which, as it turned out, did more for morale than 'a three-month furlough'.

The next morning, the Squadron woke to reveille played rather clumsily by a Private who had played trumpet in high school (he apparently got most of it about right), and shortly its members were introduced to mosquitoes, centipedes and, also seemingly in the millions, local Paisanos – all of whom were apparently very hungry. Shortly, train loads of unit equipment started to arrive.

The first unit aircraft – and almost certainly the first of a very long series of B-18s to follow – arrived on 25 November 1939, with Major Palmer and Lt Ballard at the controls. The Squadron Commander and one other officer then departed in the same aircraft shortly thereafter to return to Langley Field to gather the remainder of the unit air echelon and guide it to its new station. One wag recalled that the first inventory of the tented 'Post Exchange', conducted shortly after the CO's departure, counted a grand total of six razor blades, seven tubes of toothpaste, seventeen cartons of cigarettes and '8,000 cases of beer' – although this latter count may have been exaggerated.

On 5 December 1939 the Air Echelon returned from Langley with nine B-18As. Work continued on what became known as Borinquen Field, and the 27th literally paved the way for the 25th Bomb Group

that followed. The unit was cadre in other ways as well, surrendering many of its 'veteran' enlisted men and officers to units of the 25th Bomb Group and, later, the 40th Bomb Group as well. The Squadron was attached, as was the custom with Reconnaissance Squadrons at the time, to the 25th Bombardment Group some time in November 1940.

Finally, after being featured in numerous aviation publications of the day, the unit was split up in 1941 and formed the newly organised 5th Reconnaissance Squadron, which was activated on 1 April (see under 40th Bomb Group). For several months the 5th and the 27th worked together as a sort of composite Reconnaissance Squadron, but finally, on 1 September 1941, were formally separated and commenced operating independently. At about this same time the personnel of the 27th moved into their first 'permanent' quarters in nearly two years, including tiled floors, individual rooms for the NCOs, and indoor kitchens.

One of the highlights of the pre-war period in the history of the 27th was on 22 November 1940, when Sgt Thomas F. O'Malley was awarded the Distinguished Flying Cross. He received this award, rarely presented to enlisted men in the pre-war period, as the result of his actions while serving as Crew Chief on a unit B-18A that had been en route from San Juan, PR, to St Thomas, Virgin Islands, on 5 March 1940. While the aircraft was trundling along over the spectacular mountainous Caribbean vista at 2,500 feet, both engines suddenly quit. While frantically trying to identify the problem, the Pilot in Command ordered O'Malley and the four officer passengers on board to jump, using their parachutes. O'Malley released the emergency door hinges, saw to the adjustment of the chutes of the four passengers, assisted them overboard, then, instead of jumping himself, re-joined the pilot and provided assistance to him in the crash landing that followed. As this aircraft is not otherwise identified in loss reports of the period, it is assumed to have survived and been repaired – a further testament to the pilot and O'Malley.

December 1940 also saw the change of the unit designation from Long Range (L/R) to Heavy (H). Although the Squadron entered the war in a very splintered fashion, with detachments literally all over the Caribbean, it did not finally surrender its identity until May 1942, when it was redesignated as the 417th Bomb Squadron (H) – and this accounts for the difficulty in researching this pioneering Caribbean unit.

The cadre nature of the unit is best illustrated by the fact that, although almost up to statutory authorized strength in aircraft and personnel in 1939 and 1940, by September 1941 the Squadron had only three B-18As remaining.

Above: The 27th Reconnaissance Squadron (Long Range) was the first Air Corps unit to be deployed to Puerto Rico, arriving on 21 November 1939. R1, shown here, was the Squadron Commander's aircraft, shown on the hard-standing at Borinquen Field (then known as Air Base No 1) not long after arrival. The unit was attached to the 25th Bomb Group in November 1940. *Marvin Mayo*

Left: Operating from Borinquen Field, Puerto Rico, the 5th Reconnaissance Squadron was immortalized in a wartime series of Hearst-produced "Postamps" which included a Disney-designed logo. It is not clear if the insignia was ever painted on any of their B-18s. *via Lumpy Lumpkin*

A 27th Reconnaissance Squadron (L/R) B-18A inspects the USAT *American Legion* at sea somewhere in the Caribbean on 26 December 1940. The squadron became expert at locating ships at sea, and personnel trained in this manner served as cadre for the anti-submarine units that still lay in the future. *NARA RG342FH 35465AC*

40th Bombardment Group (M)

A latecomer, compared to other B-18 operating units in the Caribbean, the 40th Bombardment Group (Medium) was constituted on 22 November 1940 but not formally activated, as an expansion asset of the defenses of Puerto Rico and the Antilles, until 1 April 1941, owing much to the cadre of the 25th Bomb Group (qv). Indeed, the entire commissioned complement of the Group was drawn from the 25th Bomb Group, while the enlisted cadre was reassigned from a combination of the 24th Air Base Group, the 25th Bomb Group and the 27th Reconnaissance Squadron. The Group consisted of the 29th, 44th and 45th Bombardment Squadrons (M) and the attached 5th Reconnaissance Squadron (but the latter for only several months), prior to the outbreak of war, and was supplemented by others as time moved on. The unit moved to Howard Field, CZ, on 16 June 1942, from its initial station at Borinquen Field, PR, and its wartime Caribbean contributions will be covered in detail later.

29th Bombardment Squadron (M)

Constituted and activated with the parent Group, this Squadron was poorly documented prior to the outbreak of war. Initially stationed with the Group at Borinquen Field, PR, it moved to Aguadulce, Republic of Panama, on 16 June 1942, and until that time was probably severely under strength in both aircraft and personnel. Primary mounts were B-18As, although at least one Northrop A-17 was on hand at one point. The Squadron also organised a 29th Squadron Flying Club while in Puerto Rico, and acquired the Aeronca K, NC-19321, formerly owned at Borinquen Field by the 35th Squadron Flying Club, on 3 November 1941. The fate of the aircraft is unknown.

44th Bombardment Squadron (M)

Sharing an identical formative experience with the other Squadrons of the 40th Bomb Group, the 44th Bombardment Squadron (Medium) was little more than a paper organisation for the first three months of its existence, and had no aircraft during that time. The unit then received a solitary B-18A in Puerto Rico and, before departure by boat to Balboa, Canal Zone, and on to Howard Field, CZ, had apparently received two. Indeed, during those first three months of existence, from activation on 1 April 1941, the unit was actually attached to the 10th Bombardment Squadron for flying, a source of no little friction between the two organisations, as aircraft and equipment were scarce. More on this unit after the outbreak of war later in this account.

45th Bombardment Squadron (M)

The third, round-out Squadron of the parent 40th Bomb Group was activated concurrently with its sister units, and had five officers and 146 enlisted ranks, composed primarily or raw recruits with almost no training.

Stationed at Borinquen Field, PR, from creation until moved to France Field in the Canal Zone on 7 June 1942, the unit flew numerous training missions throughout the Caribbean, often using borrowed B-18s. It went on to experience many adventures with the B-18, as will be recounted later.

5th Reconnaissance Squadron (M)

Activated concurrently with the 40th Bomb Group, to which it was attached initially, this unit was formed, as mentioned previously, by a split of the veteran 27th Reconnaissance Squadron (qv), and every single member of the new 5th Recon Squadron came from that organisation. The original officer staff consisted of fifteen officers (ten of them brand-new 2nd Lieutenants just out of flying school) together with two Master Sergeants, five Technical Sergeants, fifteen Staff Sergeants, eleven Sergeants, four Corporals and ninety-seven Privates. On activation day, twenty-five recruits from Charleston, SC, joined the Squadron, and by 17 October 1941 additional infusions brought the unit to authorized strength at last.

For actual flight purposes, however, the 5th Recon Squadron shared aircraft with the 'parent' 27th Recon Squadron between activation and 1 September 1941, and used, primarily, three aircraft,

R-2, R-3 and R-5. Although nominally on the strength of the 27th, the 5th actually maintained and operated them with the result that nearly all of the flying hours and training achievements of the 5th during this period were actually attributed to the 27th! On 1 September 1941, however, the Squadron started operating completely independently, and inherited half of Building T-112 at Borinquen Field – and the three B-18As mentioned from the 27th. By 14 October 1941 the Squadron could count a total of seven complete combat crews for its three aircraft – although none of its Aerial Gunners were qualified by AAC standards.

The unit was later redesignated as the 395th Bomb Squadron (on 25 May 1942, after movement to the Canal Zone), and this accounts for the dearth of details concerning its early existence.

Territory of Alaska

Although seldom thought of in pre-war days as a threatened American frontier, Air Corps planners more familiar with geography and the vast, unpopulated reaches of Alaska realised that, when the resources became available, the territory would need, as a minimum, a garrison capable of skirmishing for delay on the northern flank.

For reasons not as yet clear, the very first B-18A to reach Alaska was AC37-466, which was assigned there, at Fort Richardson, in September 1940, arriving from McChord Field in Washington. It was not, however, the first Air Corps aircraft assigned to the remote region; that honor fell to a lowly Douglas O-38F biplane, which had arrived in April 1940 specifically for assignment to the infant Cold Weather Test Detachment at Ladd Field. It is possible that the B-18A was detailed to Alaska for the same purposes. It was not followed by Squadron-size elements until March 1941, as Japanese escapades in Asia grew ever more ominous.

Initially organised, as in Puerto Rico, under the umbrella of a Composite Group, the Air Corps establishment in the territory faced challenges of weather, distance, resupply and the simple details of day-to-day existence radically different from what crews had been accustomed to in the peacetime Continental United States garrison environment. Although the B-18 force in Alaska was never large, the total number of aircraft eventually deployed involved one solitary B-18, eighteen B-18As and one B-18B (in fact, one of the former B-18As assigned there, and the solitary B-18B assigned anywhere in the Pacific theater).

28th Composite Group

Constituted on 22 December 1939 and activated on 1 February 1940 at March Field, CA, then moving to Moffett Field, CA, between 10 December 1940 and 12 February 1941, the 28th Composite Group was destined for dedicated service in Alaska, and finally moved there, to Elmendorf Field, on 23 February 1941. The organisation eventually grew into the wartime Eleventh Air Force.

The establishment of the Air Corps in Alaska was, to say the least, faltering and difficult and, despite the best efforts of the small detachment sent north to pave the way for the arrival of tactical units, the approach of the first winter found the infant organisation with a partially completed temporary hangar and construction only just beginning on three permanent hangars, obliging the ill-equipped crews to work outdoors to maintain aircraft. They were also left with responsibility to maintain the single runway and, as no markers had as yet been received, resorted to using cut spruce trees to line the runway edges.

As of the eve of the US entry into the growing world war, on 30 November 1941 Headquarters and Headquarters Squadron, 28th Composite Group, had one B-18A and a Curtiss P-36A on strength. Besides the tactical units noted below, the 23rd Air Base Group also had a B-18A as of that date (in addition to a Martin B-10BM, a Stinson O-49, a Douglas OA-5 and four Beech AT-7s). Additionally,

The Squadron Commander's aircraft of the Headquarters Squadron, 28th Composite Group (probably shared with the Group Commander), arrives ignominiously at Patricia Bay, British Columbia, in 1941 after an incident en route to its new and very difficult station in Alaska. *PAC PBG792 via Carl Vincent*

Very rarely illustrated, B-18A 28MB/46, bearing the pre-war Unit Designators of the 28th Composite Group, was probably on the books of the 73rd Bomb Squadron (M) at the time. A unit insignia is on the mid-fuselage side, but cannot be defined. Most Alaska-based B-18s had yellow engine cowls until after the war started. *Fred Turner via David W. Ostrowski*

the Ladd Field Detachment had a single B-18A, together with an exotic Curtiss YP-37, for arctic tests, although strictly speaking these were not assets of the 28th Composite Group.

The 28th Composite Group eventually received three squadrons that were equipped in whole or in part with B-18s: the 36th, 73rd and 77th Bombardment Squadrons.

36th Bombardment Squadron (H)

Constituted and activated concurrently with the parent Group at March Field, CA, the 36th Bombardment Squadron (Heavy) moved to Lowry Field, CO, on 8 July 1940, and on 23 March 1941 commenced the long transfer to Elmendorf Field, Alaska.

At activation, the Squadron was very much under-strength, with but four B-18s, but this had increased to eight (as well as two early B-17s) by 8 July 1940. The unit regretfully left the B-17s behind when it departed Lowry, and moved to Alaska with but six of its B-18As, arriving at Elmendorf on 26 May 1941. Apparently, Air Corps planners, anticipating the extremely limited radio facilities and the vast distances involved in this deployment, arranged to replace the Squadron's low-power, short-range SCR-183 radios with brand-new Lear T-30s, and reportedly also had other winterisation equipment added at the Sacramento Air Depot before deployment, although the precise nature of this equipment is not known.

The ground element of the 36th arrived on 17 March 1941 aboard the SS *Chirikof*. Not long after arrival, on 1 April, the Squadron commenced a seemingly never-ending series of lonely coastal patrols extending from Seward to Point Barrow. By 30 November 1941, however, the Squadron could muster only four serviceable B-18As. More on this unit later, following 7 December 1941. It turned out that this unit was the final tactical unit to be deployed to Alaska in 1941.

73rd Bombardment Squadron (M)

A veteran Air Corps unit, tracing its lineage back to the 73rd Aero Squadron of February 1918, this unit had been, successively, a Pursuit Squadron (from 8 May 1929 until 1 March 1935), then a dedicated Attack Squadron, until redesignated as a Medium Bombardment Squadron on 17 October 1939 at March Field, when it was still regarded as an element of the 17th Bombardment Group. As of 31 January 1940 the unit was very nearly up to statutory strength, with eight B-18As and a single Northrop A-17A. While at McChord the Squadron suffered a tragic loss when one of its B-18As, AC37-523, crashed into Deschutes Peak, WA, with the loss of all on board. By 31 January 1941 the A-17A had departed, but B-18A strength had increased to nine aircraft. It was reassigned to the 28th Composite Group on 3 May 1941.

The Squadron transferred from March Field to McChord Field, WA, on 26 June 1940, and remained there until 10 March 1941, when it, too, was ordered to Alaska. The unit had in fact been alerted for this movement as early as 23 September 1940, and in fact arrived ahead of the 36th Bomb Squadron noted above.

In fact, it was a B-18A from the 73rd, crewed by Lt Joe G. Schneider and Lt Frank L. O'Brien, that had the honor of becoming the first permanently assigned B-18 (unit No 9) to arrive in the territory, when it landed at Elmendorf on 19 February 1941 to make arrangements for the remainder of the units to arrive. The aircraft had departed McChord two days earlier and, upon arrival in the vicinity of Elmendorf, was guided to a landing by a Master Sergeant using the radio in a Martin B-10, since the control tower at the field was not yet built! The B-18 was followed two days later by the first elements of the 18th Pursuit Squadron, and the Air Corps build-up of a modest defensive force had commenced.

The ground echelon of the Squadron arrived on 14 March 1941, followed by eight more Squadron B-18As on 30 March, making the trip from McChord in three days uneventfully and, once again, guided in to land by the Master Sergeant using the B-10's radio.

The flight of the unit's B-18s through Canadian airspace was a sensational event for the municipalities where they stopped for refueling and overnight stays. One of these was Prince George, BC, which had never before witnessed the like. The city newspaper, the *Prince George Citizen*, remembering that Canada was very much a nation that, by this time, had been at war for more than nineteen months, described the experience as follows:

'A few days ago, a fleet of bombing airplanes flew over Prince George. There was no air raid shelters, no caves of safety, no sirens ululating, no wardens rushing to put out fires. But a mad rushing along the streets occurred. Cars were dashing along to the limit of all speed laws. Pedestrians were hurrying at the double quick. Children played truant from school, and the newsboys who always before came on time to the *Citizen* office to get their papers failed to appear. And we thought as we heard the thunder of the engines of the big bombers and saw the flight of our citizens to the airfield: what a contrast to the rushing of our friends and kin in England when bombers come over there.

Here, we rushed to the airfield to meet these bombers and their crews of fine, healthy young men. For they were our friends from what our geographers say is a foreign land. But to us they were doves of friendship, no eagles of prey.

It was a fine sight to see these planes fly over here. Finer still to meet such a splendid group of men, so like our own sons and brothers we could tell no difference. Yet finer still to ponder over was the thought that, though they were ships of war from another land and nation, they could come as pals and use our

humble airfield all they wanted as if they were their own. To their station, they have gone on duty and on guard for their country. And we know that, in the final vigil they will keep, they guard us, too. And when they return on furlough to their own country in the course of time, we hope that none will be missing. We hope, too, they will need refueling or something so that they may again spend a period with us and renew the friendships they made here.'

One of the first orders of business after arrival was to paint new unit designators on the vertical fins of the B-18s, which consisted of an individual aircraft number (e.g. 9, 22, etc) over the Group designator, which was 28MB. They also had their engine cowls painted yellow, a characteristic of all B-18s in Alaska prior to Pearl Harbor.

The Squadron had the dubious distinction of being the first Air Corps permanent party unit to suffer the loss of an aircraft when, on 3 July 1941, 2Lt P. Clark's aircraft, AC37-466 – which, ironically, had been the very first B-18A to arrive in the theater – experienced a runaway starboard propeller and was forced down into the water near Prince Rupert, British Columbia, although the crew survived unscathed. On the eve of war the 73rd Bomb Squadron, as of 30 November 1941, could count a total of five B-18As combat-ready. The unit re-equipped with Martin B-26s by 28 February 1942, and consequently passed its B-18s to its sister unit, the 36th Bomb Squadron, seeing only limited 'wartime' flying with them.

77th Bombardment Squadron (M)

Constituted on 20 November 1940 but not activated until 15 January 1941 at Salt Lake City, UT, as an element of the 42nd Bombardment Group, the 77th Bomb Squadron was reassigned to the 28th Composite Group after Pearl Harbor on 2 January 1942, but by then had been completely re-equipped with Martin B-26 Marauders. The Squadron's existence at Salt Lake City was barely more than a 'paper exercise', as it had but one officer and twenty-seven enlisted ranks. It is seldom noted that the Squadron was formally transferred to Boise, ID, on 3 June 1941 and, for the purposes of this account, had a grand total of one B-18A as of that time. Not long afterwards it added another B-18A and, of all things, a Boeing-Stearman PT-17 biplane, mainly to enable the pilots assigned to maintain at least some flying proficiency. Consequently, the association of this unit with the B-18 was formative, but brief.

Commonwealth of the Philippines

The decision to, rather tardily, reassign at least one squadron-sized element of B-18s to be based in the Commonwealth of the Philippines has often been attributed to have come about as a direct consequence of the most consequential meeting, in early August 1941, in foggy Placentia Bay, on the bleak southern coast of Newfoundland, between President Franklin D. Roosevelt and British Prime Minister Winston Churchill.

In fact, however, the first of an eventual total of nineteen B-18s, drawn down from active-duty Squadrons of the 5th and 11th Bomb Groups in Hawaii, arrived at Clark Field via rather tortuous surface shipment on the SS *Washington* and subsequent vessels, between January and July 1941. It is seldom noted that this transfer was covered by the Air Corps code 'Project X'. Officially, the first aircraft, AC36-341, arrived in January 1941, followed by seven in May 1941, five in June 1941, four in July 1941, and, inexplicably, one in January 1942 (AC37-16). All but two went directly to Clark Field, care of the Philippine Air Depot, where they were rather laboriously reassembled one at a time and issued to the operating unit. After assembly, the former Hawaiian aircraft retained their former 5th and 11th Bomb Group Field Numbers for a brief interval, which has led some historians on a merry chase. These included 2/5B, 4/11B, 21/11B, 84/50R and

The B-18s from Hawaii arrived in the Philippines still bearing the unit designators and unit insignia of their former operators, such as 5B/2, here having its rudder reattached. Note the rare North American A-27 in the left background. *G. O. Idlett via Bill Bartsch*

The USAAC made the decision to reinforce the garrison in the Philippines and selected nineteen Hawaii-based B-18s from the 5th and 11th Bomb Groups to be surfaced-shipped to the Far East between January and July 1941. Here, one of the last two to arrive at the Philippine Air Depot in June 1941 was Field Number '3'. *John L. Brownewell via Bill Bartsch*

Much of the final reassembly of the ex-Hawaiian B-18s after arrival in the Philippines took place in the open, as with this mix of former 11th and 5th Bomb Group examples at Nichols Field in June 1941. *Forrest Hobrecht via Bill Bartsch*

The Philippine Air Depot, although faced with a daunting challenge in reassembling such large aircraft, wasted little time in putting the ex-Hawaiian B-18s in airworthy condition. Here, Lt Roy D. Russell poses before Field Number '8' in July 1941 at Clark Field. *Roy D. Russell*

Unit designator 11B/21 identifies this B-18, pictured at Nichols Field in mid-1941, as a former 14th Bomb Squadron, 11th Bomb Group, aircraft. *A. H. Reynolds via Bill Bartsch*

One of the last of the ex-Hawaiian B-18s to arrive, Field Number 58B, awaits her wings and tail surfaces. This designator is rather puzzling and the significance is unknown. *Albert J. Bland via Bill Bartsch*

others. The other two were assigned directly to Nichols Field.[28] Thus, while the monumental discussions in Newfoundland were under way, B-18s had already been in the islands for some six months or more, and the decision to send them there was probably taken by the Air Corps in 1940. It certainly predated the Japanese invasion of French Indo-China in late July 1941, and the nearly concurrent announcement by General George Marshall, Army Chief of Staff, that it would henceforth be the US policy to defend the islands.

Army Air Corps Aircraft in the Philippines as of 30 November 1941

Performance	Martin B-10B	Boeing YB-17	Douglas B-18
Operating Speed	188mph	210mph	170mph
Operating Endurance	10 hours	10 hours	16.2 hours
Operating Range	1,880 miles	2,100 miles	2,750 miles
Maximum Bomb Load	0	2,500 pounds	1,200lb

A number of writers have challenged the wisdom of sending B-18s to the islands, and have invariably claimed, in so many words, that the aircraft were incapable of reaching Formosa, the most likely source of trouble, as of the date of their arrival. This is, quite simply, incorrect. As evidenced earlier in this account, a detailed Engineering Section Memorandum Report dated 6 August 1936 and entitled 'Comparative Performance of B-10B, YB-17 and B-18 Airplanes', clearly established that, although slower at Operating Speed by 40mph than the YB-17, the conditions as detailed in the accompanying table obtained.

Thus, while the YB-17 (B-17C and B-17D variants could do somewhat better) could carry more than twice as much ordnance and reach Formosa easily, the B-18 could actually reach further and, at operating speed, remain in the air more than 6 hours longer. If at cruising speed, this improved even more to an incredible 19 hours and 2,850 miles. In other words, if necessary the B-18 could have even reached the home Japanese islands and returned to the Philippines. The B-10Bs still in the Philippines could reach Formosa, but only as reconnaissance aircraft, because in order to achieve maximum range they had to delete bomb loads altogether. Since there were no B-17s in the islands when the B-18s arrived, offensive plans had to involve them exclusively. The performance of the B-18 and B-18A in terms of endurance and range has, invariably, been either omitted entirely or misrepresented in nearly every other account over the years, and its subsequent long-range performance in the anti-submarine role in the Caribbean, as will be detailed subsequently, confirmed this ability repeatedly.

Inevitably, however, in the time-honored traditions of the service, the nineteen aircraft that were identified by Air Corps officers in Hawaii (all from Hickam Field assets) for dispatch to the Far East were the highest-time aircraft in the command, and included those with the most Unsatisfactory Reports (U/Rs). Even so, they were not the 'hangar queens' often depicted by the legions of detractors of the type and, as of the date of arrival, according to the Individual Aircraft Record Cards, the oldest amongst them, AC36-326, had but 786 hours total time on the airframe and, having been turned over to the Air Corps on 26 January 1938, was only 29 months old. These aircraft, collectively, represented the most distant deployment of the type from US soil and, until the arrival of early Boeing B-17C and B-17D variants, were unquestionably the most potent offensive tool available to US planners in the area.

The Air Corps establishment in the Philippines, even as late as 30 November 1941, deserves examination in detail, as it has been widely misunderstood, and so far as can be determined has never been described in print in this detail. The entire on-hand Air Corps aircraft strength in the islands, at that pivotal date, amounted to not more than 317 aircraft. While this seems like a substantial number, the actual tactical deployment and composition of the force presents a somewhat different picture, as shown in the accompanying table.

Organization	Aircraft on Hand
Headquarters and Headquarters Squadron, 4th Composite Group	1 Seversky P-35A 2 Curtiss P-40B
Headquarters and Headquarters Squadron, 7th Air Force	1 Stinson O-49 1 North American A-27 1 Curtiss P-40E 1 Douglas C-49
14th Bombardment Squadron (H)	8 Boeing B-17D
24th Pursuit Group (3rd, 17th and 20th Pursuit Squadrons)	2 Martin B-10B 4 North American A-27 15 Boeing P-26A 49 Seversky P-35A 25 Curtiss P-40B 6 Curtiss P-40E 3 Douglas O-46A
28th Bombardment Squadron (M)	2 Martin B-10B 15 Douglas B-18
20th Air Base Group	1 Martin B-10B 2 Douglas B-18 1 Douglas C-39 1 Grumman OA-9 2 Stinson O-49 1 Seversky P-35A
2nd Observation Squadron	3 North American A-27 3 Douglas O-46A 10 Curtiss O-52 4 Martin B-10B
Tow Target Detachment	3 Martin B-10B 1 Douglas B-18 1 Thomas-Morse O-19E 1 Douglas O-46A
19th Bombardment Group (H) (14th, 28th, 32nd and 93rd Bomb Squadrons)	4 Boeing B-17C 19 Boeing B-17D
Not Yet Assigned to Tactical Units (and in some instances, still in transit to the Philippines and later diverted elsewhere)	2 Boeing B-17C 2 Boeing B-17D 13 Bell P-39D 1 Curtiss P-40B 106 Curtiss P-40E

Clearly, the primary offensive weapons at this point were the B-17s, which totalled six B-17Cs and twenty-nine B-17Ds, for a total of thirty-five aircraft. It has seldom been observed, however, that the 28th Bomb Squadron, with fifteen B-18s on hand, constituted nearly 50% of the US bomber strength in the islands.

As it turned out, and as will be detailed later in this account, a combination of exceptionally poor preparation by the US leadership in the islands, coupled with arrogance and a nearly total lack of appreciation for the capabilities of the Japanese Army and Naval aviation forces, led to the well-documented decimation of this modest force before it was ever able to be brought to bear, for the most part, against the sudden enemy.

The principal – but not solitary – B-18 operating unit in the Philippines prior to the Japanese attack was the 28th Bomb Squadron.

28th Bombardment Squadron (M)

This veteran unit traces its lineage back to the 28th Aero Squadron of June 1917, which saw action in France during the First World War. After the war it was reactivated on 1 September 1922 specifically for service in the Philippines, where it was formally designated as the 28th Bombardment Squadron on 25 January 1923 at Clark Field. It constituted, for many years, the solitary Air Corps bombardment unit in the islands, and certainly the most distant from the US. The unit transitioned through a veritable lexicon of Army bombardment aircraft, ranging from the de Havilland DH-4, through the Curtiss NBS-1, Keystone LB-5 and B-3, Martin B-10 and finally B-18s and B-17s.

The unit had commenced camouflaging their aircraft, in accordance with a USAAC directive issued in October 1940, after their arrival in the islands from Hawaii. Most received the standard olive-drab upper surfaces over neutral gray undersides common throughout the Air Corps, and this had been applied by 17 October 1941 – much earlier than most sources suggest. However, photographic evidence exists that seems to indicate that at least several received the mixed dark gray/olive-drab upper surfaces treatment experimented with elsewhere, and also had rather large US national insignia on both fuselage sides, upper left wing and lower right wing. They also received individual numbers, in yellow, on the vertical fin, and these appear to have been strictly sequential from '1' to at least '15'. One aircraft carried the Field Number '70' after being camouflaged, but was not thought to be a 28th BS aircraft. The aircraft assigned to the Tow Target Detachment was apparently not camouflaged and no Field Number for it is known.

The Squadron was stationed at Clark Field as of 7 December 1941 and, of the total organisational strength as of that time, only twenty-five officers and twelve enlisted ranks survived to reach Australia after the Japanese attack. The odyssey of the Philippines B-18s, their crews, and the 28th Bomb Squadron will be detailed later, once open warfare was joined.

Right: Field Number 13 (in yellow on the nose of this camouflaged aircraft) of the 28th Bomb Squadron undergoes engine work on the line at Nichols Field near Manila some time between 20 November and 8 December 1941. Are those war clouds overhead? *William Marrocco via Bill Bartsch*

Below: This excellent October 1941, pre-Pearl Harbor view of Philippines based B-18 Field Number 70 reveals that, even though only recently camouflaged for the tropics had already started eroding the paint. *M/Sgt William R. Wright via Bill Bartsch*

Although the majority of the nineteen B-18s received from Hawaii for service in the Philippines were assigned to the 28th Bomb Squadron (M), at least two were assigned to the 20th Air Base Squadron, including 20AB/178 pictured here at Nichols Field. Note that the third B-18 in this line-up has been camouflaged. *Roy Speir via Bill Bartsch*

By 17 October 1941, not long after the last aircraft arrived from Hawaii, nearly all of the Philippines-based B-18s had been camouflaged, apparently in a rather casual way, and over-size US national insignia applied on both sides of the rear fuselage, such as Field Number 12 (in yellow on the vertical fin and nose) of the 28th Bomb Squadron shown here at Makati. Although the undersurfaces appear dark, the lower side of the engine cowl reveals that neutral gray was in fact applied to the undersides.
Major Mike Campos collection via Bill Bartsch

By 17 October 1941, when this photo was taken, Field Number 7, formerly of the 28th Bomb Squadron, had been passed to the 27th Materiel Squadron, which was using it to ferry pilots and crews of the 17th Pursuit Squadron from Iba back to Nichols Field when photographed. The dorsal turret appears to have a large-format camera in place of the .30 caliber gun! The two- or three-color camouflage used in the Philippines is just barely discernible on this aircraft. *R. LaMar Gillett via Bill Bartsch*

Newfoundland

Where the so-called 'Neutrality Patrol' left off and war began is difficult to determine with other than strictly legal meaning. But well before 7 December 1941 an element of Langley Field's 2nd Bombardment Wing, flying out of the Newfoundland Air Base, was actually engaged in combat with German submarines in the frigid waters of the North Atlantic – an aspect of the US approach to war that is usually, if mentioned at all, attributed to US Navy surface units.

Stated simply, President Roosevelt had ordered that the US would cooperate with Canadian forces in defense of Newfoundland against Axis attack, whether by land, sea or air.

This had not been the Air Corps first exposure to Newfoundland, however. As noted earlier in this account, in November 1940 an RCAF crew had been forced to abandon a Digby while en route from

Right: Air Corps enlistees wrote many post-cards home during the build up leading to the U.S. entry into the war. This one post-marked October 19, 1942, shows a pre-war rendition of a well-known photo of five 21st Reconnaissance Squadron B-18As in Neutrality Patrol markings. *via Paul Minert*

Below: Seen on 5 April 1940, four B-18As of the 21st Reconnaissance Squadron, including the Squadron Commander's aircraft on the extreme right, sweep low off the Atlantic coast of Florida. On 29 April 1941 these same aircraft transferred to St John's, Newfoundland, to take up combat missions as part of the Neutrality Patrol, at which time they had a large US national insignia painted on either side of their nose. *NMUSAF 19851AC*

Newfoundland to Montreal. Langley Field's 2nd Wing had dispatched a flight of nine B-18s, commanded by Major H. L. George, to assist in the search for them – in fact, a rather weakly concealed opportunity to both expose US crews to operating in the area and display US sympathy for the British Commonwealth, which, by that time, was standing alone against the Axis powers. The experience of operating suddenly across an international border and in ugly weather was, to say the least, a revealing experience. The B-18s arrived at St Hubert's airport, as directed, at dawn on 20 November 1940, only to find that not a soul was expecting them, which, needless to say, raised consternation locally. Though having had little or no sleep, the crews were unable to find accommodation to rest until 1500 that afternoon. The senior RCAF officer in the area advised them that '…he had nothing to do with the project and could provide neither transportation nor guidance,' hardly the welcome that had been anticipated. With the aid of local Canadians, food was finally available – two days later – and, since no hangar or shop space of any sort was available, the crews had to contrive whatever expedients they could with their own wits. An airline waiting room, which had been reluctantly made available, had to be vacated at odd moments to make room for paying airline passengers, and locating 100 octane fuel for the aircraft was exceptionally challenging. These experiences, combined with nine days of icy searching, led Major George to rather pointedly comment that '…there is every likelihood that units of the General Headquarters Air Force will be operating in this area in the future' but that they would require supporting ground staff and infrastructure to relieve the flying crews of these many administrative and logistics burdens. His final recommendation, while not acted upon, was a portent of things to come: 'Operations in the area are so peculiar and difficult that we should detail men to work three or four weeks with the RCAF units at Newfoundland and Halifax for familiarisation.'

AC3:—ARMY BOMBERS FLYING IN PERFECT FORMATION.

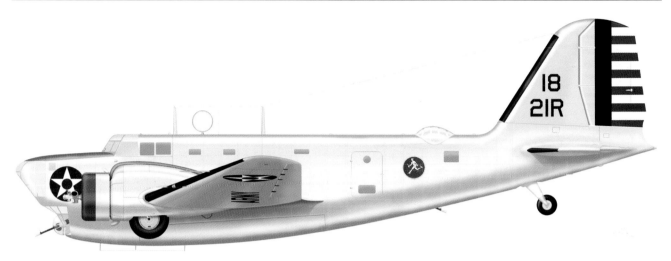

21st Recon Artwork by Rich Dann

Thematically, the subsequent story of B-18 operations in the area commenced once again, without benefit from Major George's recommendations, on 29 April 1941, when the first of nine B-18As of the 21st Reconnaissance Squadron, transferred to St John's, Newfoundland from the comforts of Miami, no less, arrived. It would be difficult to conceive of a more profound climatic transformation, and was certainly in keeping with the common wisdom regarding 'GI' assignments and dart boards! The Ground Echelon, consisting of 208 enlisted ranks, was accompanied by Major Jarred V. Crabb, the CO, one First Lieutenant and two Second Lieutenants. Their arrival was a portent of things to come; fog delayed going ashore until the following day, 30 April.

The problems that faced the Squadron, how they were dealt with, and the activities of the unit and its replacements can best be recorded by quoting directly from Major Crabb's Progress Report to the local leadership, the recently styled Newfoundland Base Command.:

> 'The simplest activities were performed without adequate vehicles, trucks or other equipment, and were constantly hampered by the most incredible mud and foul weather. Operation of the one aircraft now present [apparently B-18A 37-597] has been extensive when weather permits. Flights have been made to acquaint pilots and crews with the entire area of Newfoundland.'

Mosquitoes were apparently a nagging problem, as one of the highest priorities was locating screen materials for the existing barracks, mess facilities were shared with Royal Canadian Air Force personnel, and laundry facilities were completely non-existent.

The 21st, with little regret, returned to Miami in the latter part of August 1941, and took all but two of the B-18As with it. The unit association with the B-18 had commenced as early as 6 October 1938, while still at Langley Field, VA, when two new B-18s (AC36-284 and 36-315) were received. The unit had transferred, with considerable glee, to Miami's Municipal Airport on 9 September 1939, in response to the German invasion of Poland and the commencement of hostilities in Europe. The Squadron was still nominally home based at Langley as of 30 April 1941, with one B-18, seven B-18As and one other B-18A fitted as a target tug, but which was actually operating from Miami with six of the B-18As. After returning from Newfoundland, they moved to MacDill Field, FL, around 3 September 1941, by which time the unit had only two B-18s remaining, and on to Gowen Field, ID, on 25 June 1942. Much later, the unit lost its identity and became the 411th Bombardment Squadron. It was relieved at the Newfoundland Base by the 41st Reconnaissance Squadron (H). It is worth noting that the Intelligence Officer for this unit, for a time, was Elliot Roosevelt.

Although formerly a B-18 operating unit, by the time the Squadron deployed from attachment to the 2nd Bomb Group it had re-equipped with six Boeing B-17Bs, although it retained one B-18A and briefly gained the use of one of the former 21st Recon Squadron B-18As.

One of the 41st Recon Squadron's B-17Bs made history on 26 October 1941 when an aircraft commanded by Captain P. A. Sykes carried out an attack on a German submarine, the first such attack by a US aircraft.

Iceland

Many readers will be surprised to find the B-18 associated, in any way, with Iceland – an assignment that did in fact occur and which, incidentally, qualifies the type as having experienced a European theater assignment – but only just!

Often overlooked entirely in studies related to the opening stages of the Second World War, Iceland was, as of 1940 and 1941, regarded by both Britain and the US as absolutely vital to guarding the flank of the British lifeline of surface convoys bound back-and-forth across the dangerous North Atlantic. While a massive 'aircraft carrier' and potential bastion in its own right, it was equally important to deny Germany the same ground. That Germany, and Hitler in particular, recognised the strategic importance of Iceland and had intentions towards it is well documented.

The solitary B-18 series aircraft to serve in the European theater before and during the war was B-18A AC37-540, shown being unloaded from the SS *Delta* at Reykjavik, Iceland, on 13 January 1942 – although, inexplicably, reports show it as having been on the island nation as early as 30 November 1941. *via Ragnar Ragnarsson*

Manhandling the B-18A through the narrow streets of Reykjavik from the dock areas to the Iceland Base Command's operating base in the Arctic night involved putting the aircraft on its main gear, and employing two men in the cockpit to operate the brakes! *via Ragnar Ragnarsson*

Iceland had been regarded as semi-independent and neutral, but under the protection of Norway until the eyes of the world became riveted on the seemingly inexorable march of German arms into the Low Countries, Denmark and Norway in May 1940. The British, upon seeing the fall of Norway, wasted no time in mounting its own small occupation of Iceland on 10 May 1940. As the United States expanded its own role in the so-called Neutrality Patrol into the hot and hectic summer of 1941, a little-known US force was also dispatched to Iceland to form the basis for what became known as the Iceland Base Command.

The British plans for the defense of Iceland assumed that the primary threat was from an invasion by German forces, an operation that Hitler had in fact considered as early as June 1940 as a preliminary to the invasion of Britain itself, but which the German Naval Staff flatly opposed. Iceland was, however, just within range of Luftwaffe long-range bomber units in occupied Norway, and the *Bismarck*'s ill-fated foray into the Atlantic had shown what might happen if Hitler transferred other units to Norwegian bases, as he constantly suggested doing.

By August 1941 the British had, based on Reykjavik, No 1423 Flight with single-engined Fairey Battles[29], a detachment of eight or nine Hawker Hurricane fighters, and the Norwegian No 330 Squadron, equipped with six unique Northrop N-3PB single-engine, float-equipped patrol bombers, and some thirty other mixed utility aircraft. A Detachment of No 221 Squadron did move to Reykjavik from 29 September until 4 October 1941, but the home base for this short-lived deployment was Limavady, Ireland. At Kaldadharnes, about 35 miles south-east of Reykjavik, the RAF stationed No 269 Squadron, consisting of twenty-six Lockheed Hudsons, with two additional utility aircraft, while another detachment of Norwegian Northrop N-3PBs, with three aircraft, was at Akureyri and three more at Búdhareyri. These were joined, between 15 December 1941 and 18 August 1942 by No 612 Squadron with a B-18 contemporary, the Armstrong-Whitworth Whitley.

To this the US added a US Navy unit flying PBY Catalinas from Reykjavik and the 33rd Pursuit Squadron (F) and the 8th Pursuit Group (F) with, initially, thirty Curtiss P-40Cs and two Boeing-Stearman PT-17s – and a solitary Douglas B-18A.

Of this seemingly potent force, only the P-40Cs of the 33rd Pursuit Squadron and the solitary B-18A fell under the direct control of the US commander of the Iceland Base Command, and the only aircraft on the island available for medium-range reconnaissance in support of the ground-based defenders of the island with the Northrop N-3PBs of No 330 Squadron – and the B-18A. The Whitleys and Hudsons were fully occupied in the extremely intense anti-submarine campaign.

Although the 33rd Pursuit Squadron and the single 'unassigned' B-18A were shown on Air Corps reports as being physically in place in Iceland as of 30 November 1941, B-18A AC37-540 was not lifted off the SS *Delta* until 13 January 1942 and, after a rather protracted reassembly, was not flown for the first time until 5 March. More about this protracted and rather strange odyssey of this lonely aircraft follows later in this account.

To summarize, as noted in the foregoing discussions, by the critical date of 30 November 1941, of the total of 134 B-18s (including the DB-1 and DB-2) and 217 B-18As built and delivered to the Air Corps, seventy-five B-18s and fifty-seven B-18As had been deployed to foreign stations, constituting more than 45% of the most numerous bombardment aircraft, after losses to accidents, in the US inventory.

Other assignments prior to 7 December 1941

Besides the wide dispersal of the B-18 and B-18A fleet throughout tactical units in the United States and overseas described above, other examples ended up in rather unusual assignments prior to Pearl Harbor and, for the record, these were as follows.

The US Army's **3rd Corps Area**, which had command jurisdiction over Air Corps activities at Baltimore Municipal Airport (Dundalk, MD), the Air Corps Detachments at Pittsburgh's Allegheny County Airport as well as Air Corps Reserve elements, had one B-18 assigned for the use of the Commanding General between 31 December 1937 and 30 September 1939. It was supplemented in March 1939 by a single B-18A.

Likewise, the **6th Corps Area**, which had jurisdiction over Air Corps oriented as well as ground forces at Camp Skeel (Oscoda, MI), Chicago's Air Corps Detachment and Reserve Flying, and Scott Field's 7th Air Base Squadron, Air Corps Technical School Branch, the 15th Observation Squadron and the 93rd School Squadron, had a single B-18 as of September 1939, probably based at Fort Sheridan, IL.

The Army's **8th Corps Area**, which encompassed vast areas and installations in Texas and Arizona, had one B-18 assigned as of 30 September 1939, probably based in San Antonio, as the 8th Corps Headquarters was at Fort Sam Houston.

With the huge pre-war build-up and expansion of the Air Corps, the **First Air Force**, born out of the Northeast Air District, was redesignated as such in early 1941. This organisational element was important in the history of the B-18, as it gave birth to **I Bomber Command**, about which much more in the chapter following. The First Air Force was headquartered initially at Mitchel Field, Long Island, NY. **Headquarters and Headquarters Squadron, First Air Force** had one B-18A assigned as of 31 March 1941.

Likewise, on the Pacific Coast, the Air Corps created the **Second Air Force**, born out of the Northwest Air District, early in 1941, headquartered at McChord Field, WA. **Headquarters and Headquarters Squadron, Second Air Force**, had single examples of the B-18A and B-23 at Fort George Washington as of 31 March 1941, but had lost the B-18A by 30 April.

In California, the **Fourth Air Force**, born out of the Southwest Air District, was redesignated as such in early 1941 and by 31 March 1941 had one B-18A assigned for staff use based at Riverside, CA.

Thus, besides B-18, B-18A and B-23 aircraft assigned for staff use by the leadership of the Air Corps, by November 1941 the above-named organisations accounted for an additional three B-18s, four B-18As and one B-23.

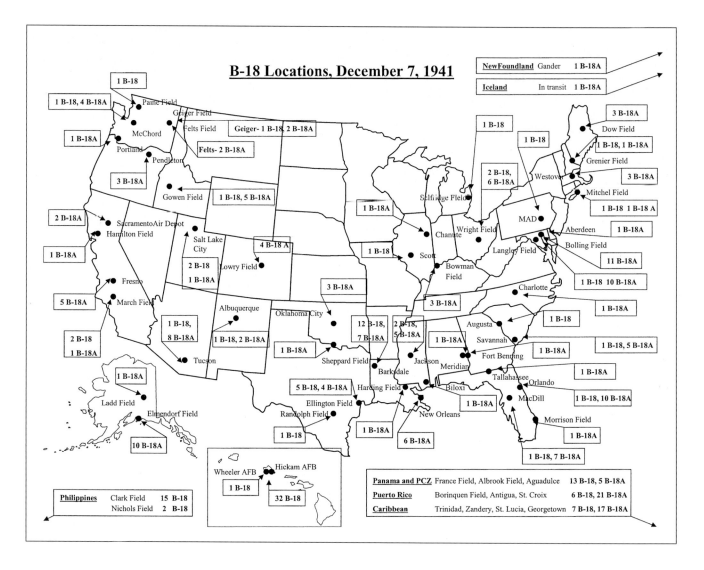

B-18 Locations, December 7, 1941

NewFoundland	Gander 1 B-18A
Iceland	In transit 1 B-18A

1 B-18

1 B-18, 4 B-18A — Paine Field

Geiger Field

1 B-18A — McChord

Felts Field — Geiger- 1 B-18, 2 B-18A

Portland — Felts- 2 B-18A

Pendleton

3 B-18A

Gowen Field — 1 B-18, 5 B-18A

2 D-18A — Sacramento Air Depot

Hamilton Field

1 B-18A

Salt Lake City

4 B-18 A

2 B-18 — Lowry Field
1 B-18A

Fresno

5 B-18A — March Field

Albuquerque

3 B-18A

2 B-18 — 1 B-18, 8 B-18A
1 B-18A

1 B-18, 2 B-18A

Tucson

Oklahoma City

1 B-18A

Sheppard Field — 3 B-18A

5 B-18, 4 B-18A — Harding Field

Ellington Field

Randolph Field

1 B-18

1 B-18A

6 B-18A

1 B-18

2 B-18, 6 B-18A

1 B-18A

Chanute — Wright Field

1 B-18 — Scott

Bowman Field

Selfridge Field

MAD

12 B-18, 7 B-18A — 2 B-18, 5 B-18A

Barksdale — Jackson — Meridian

1 B-18A — Fort Benning

New Orleans — Biloxi

Tallahassee — Orlando

MacDill

1 B-18A

3 B-18A — Dow Field

1 B-18, 1 B-18A — Grenier Field

3 B-18A — Mitchel Field

1 B-18 1 B-18A

Aberdeen — 1 B-18A

Langley Field — Bolling Field

11 B-18A

1 B-18 10 B-18A

Charlotte

1 B-18A

1 B-18

Augusta — Savannah

1 B-18A — 1 B-18, 5 B-18A

1 B-18A

1 B-18, 10 B-18A

Morrison Field

1 B-18A

1 B-18, 7 B-18A

1 B-18A — Ladd Field

Elmendorf Field

10 B-18A

Wheeler AFB — Hickam AFB

1 B-18

32 B-18

| Philippines | Clark Field | 15 B-18 |
| | Nichols Field | 2 B-18 |

Panama and PCZ	France Field, Albrook Field, Aguadulce	13 B-18, 5 B-18A
Puerto Rico	Borinquen Field, Antigua, St. Croix	6 B-18, 21 B-18A
Caribbean	Trinidad, Zandery, St. Lucia, Georgetown	7 B-18, 17 B-18A

CHAPTER SEVEN

The B-18 goes to war, 1941

Hawaii

Although much of the world had been involved in open hostilities since the German invasion of Poland in 1939, and the United States had enjoyed an interlude of some two years, during which time the vast majority of the population of the nation was overwhelmingly isolationist, the military leadership of the nation had been laboring strenuously for what lay ahead.

An examination of the pre-7 December 1941 deployments of B-18, B-18A and B-23 aircraft active in the Air Corps inventory, and noted in detail in the preceding chapters, clearly depicts the burden of expectations that had been placed on these aircraft and their operating units – even though the vast majority of them were under authorized strength in terms of both hardware and manpower.

That US military planners anticipated American entry into the war, in spite of popular and political opinion, is obvious, and it must be said, to their credit, that they executed upon these grim forecasts as best they could, given the prevailing climate. That the overburdened intelligence apparatus of the country failed utterly to predict the circumstances of the commencement of hostilities is also well established, and so will not be summarised here.[30]

The US leadership in the Pacific bastions of Hawaii and the Philippines had been alerted on numerous occasions throughout 1941,

Above and tables page 122-124: Prepared by James P. Rybarczyk

but were concerned more with espionage and sabotage than the aerial onslaughts that appeared suddenly and in totally surprising efficiency.

Ironically, the solitary US Army Air Corps aircraft airborne at the time of the Japanese attack on Pearl Harbor and USAAC installations in the Hawaiian Islands was none other than an unarmed B-18, and this flight had been decided by the flip of a coin.

On Saturday 6 December 1941 Major Gordon Austin, at the time Commanding Officer of the 47th Pursuit Squadron (F) at Wheeler Field, and his Deputy Commander, Bob Rogers, were discussing whether or not to instruct squadron personnel to report for duty on Sunday the 7th. They in fact flipped a coin, and decided to give the hard-worked crews the day off. Austin and Captain Sherwood E. Buckland, a friend, then climbed into a duty B-18, borrowed from a unit at Wheeler, and, with two other artillery officers from Schofield Barracks, as well as fourteen or fifteen enlisted men, flew the aircraft to Molokai, where they spent the remainder of the day deer-hunting as guests of Chung-Hoon, a Chinese-American merchant who 'knew everybody', as well as scouting out a planned firing range – the actual 'official' justification for the flight. They were on Molokai on the fateful morning when they learned that Oahu was under attack. Austin and the other officer then flew the B-18 back to Oahu, arriving over Hickam Field near the end of the second wave of Japanese attackers, just in time to '…see the last end of the Japanese airplanes', and arrived in the midst of total confusion there. With US Navy anti-aircraft weapons firing at them, Austin related that '…I never got scared like that in the rest of the war. I turned the control wheel of the B-18 and headed for the mountains. We got out of these, and then we called the Wheeler tower. Wheeler tower said the field had been under attack and there were live bombs and bomb craters on the field.'

Austin said to Buckland, 'We'd better get out of here and go somewhere else.' But he said, 'No, we'd better land right here.' That turned out to be a wise decision. After making a quick pattern around Wheeler, they landed with the flight lines ablaze. They then taxied past the tower, going in an easterly direction, way off the field by the old Group headquarters. Once there, Brigadier General Howard Davidson showed up in a staff car and told Austin to get the B-18 serviced and take it immediately to Hickam. Buckland then turned to Austin and said, 'Gee, I don't think that's a very good idea. Do you?' They waited until the General left and quietly deplaned. The aircraft in question

was used as a 'hack' by the 18th Pursuit Group crews stationed at Wheeler and was probably B-18 AC36-325, which had been the solitary B-18 stationed at Wheeler from June 1940.[31]

Like the 31st Bomb Squadron B-18 pictured, the 18th Wing Command aircraft, 18W/1 (probably AC36-272), caught outside, also had the undersides painted neutral gray in preparation for a complete camouflage paint job when the 7 December 1941 attack occurred. This aircraft was damaged beyond repair. *via Rich Dann*

Unfortunately, while the 28th Bomb Squadron in the Philippines had camouflaged all of its B-18s and assigned Field Numbers to them, no cross reference to actual Air Corps serials survived. Number '5' shown here, although having suffered damage and stripped of some parts (including the rudder and ailerons), appears intact, and was captured by the Japanese. It is not believed to have been returned to airworthy condition.
Ua Tagaya via Bill Bartsch

Easily missed, the B-18 shown here, 5B/2 (AC36-333), had apparently had the undersides painted neutral gray, preparatory to a full upper camouflage scheme being applied. The aircraft was repaired. Note the insignia of the 31st Bomb Squadron, 5th Bomb Group. *NARA RG342FH 59986AC*

B-18 & B-18A :   ASSIGNED LOCATIONS IN CONTINENTAL U.S.,   DECEMBER 7, 1941

TOTAL	42 B-18	= 15 M's with no Bomb Racks
		2 DAM, long term more than 2 months
TOTAL	135 B-18A	= 15 M's with no Bomb Racks
		4 DAM, long term more than 2 months, PLUS 2 being repaired long-term at SAD

GRAND TOTAL   177 in Continental US
- **8 Long Term Repair**

TOTAL USABLE   169 Usable in Continental US (40 B-18 + 129 B-18A)
- 30 Bomb Gear removed (quickly reinstalled in 29 a/c by 1-13-42)

BOMBERS   139 Usable as Bombers in Continental US (25 B-18 + 114 B-18A)

NORTHEAST, 1st Air Force

Location	B-18	B-18A	
Bangor, Maine, Dow Field, 43 BG(H)	0	3	A 37-605, -612 (DAM), -614
Manchester, NH, Grenier Field 45 BG(L)	1	1	36-292 A 38-596
Westover Field, MA 34 BG(H)	0	3	37-475, -485, 39-017
Long Island, NY, Mitchel Field 8 & 33 PG's	1	1	36-316 A 37-550
Langley Field, VA 2 BG(H), 22BG(M)	1	10	37-028 A 37-470, -482, -507, -517, -538, -593, -613, 38-591, -594, -607
Selfridge Field, MI 1 & 52 PG's	1	0	36-274M
Louisville, KY, Bowman Field 46 BG(L)	0	3	A 37-619, -622, 38-598
Wash DC, Bolling Field	0	11	A 37-458M, -483M, -487, -489, -490M, -491, -492M, -502M, -544M(DAM), -546M, -551M
Aberdeen Proving Ground, Aberdeen MD	0	1	A 37-463
MAD, PA	1	0	36-286 (ex NACA)
Rantoul, IL, Chanute Technical School	0	1	A 37-527
Scott, IL	1	0	36-273
Dayton, OH, Wright Field	2	6	36-262M, 37-034M A 37 -469M, -476M, -477M, -511, -528M, -587
	8	40	(3 M's) A (12 M's, 2 DAM, long-term)

NORTHWEST, 2nd AF

Location	B-18	B-18A	
Tacoma, WA, McChord 12 BG(L)	1	4	36-297 A 37-557, -569, -570
Spokane, WA, Geiger Field 39 BG(H)	1	2	37-014 A 37-508, 39-020
Everett, WA, Paine Field 54 PG	1	0	37-025
Portland, OR 55 PG	0	1	A 39-018
E. Spokane, WA, Felts Field	0	2	A 37-594(DAM) -625
Pendleton Field, OR 17 BG(M)'	0	3	A 37-499, -519, -602
Boise, ID, Gowen Field 42 BG(M)	1	5	36-279 A 37-500, -505, -542, -564, 39-021
Denver, CO, Lowry Field	0	4	A 37-462, -504, -595, 39-024
	4	20	A (1 DAM)

SOUTHEAST, 3rd Air Force	B-18	B-18A	
Charlotte, NC, Douglas F. 56 PG	0	1	A 37-571
Savannah, GA 3 BG(L)	1	5	37-017 A 37-459, -525, -552, 38-599, 39-015
Lawson Field, Fort Benning, GA	0	1	A 38-593
Augusta, GA	1	0	37-029
W. Palm Beach, FL, Morrison Field 49 PG	0	1	A 37-541
Tampa FL, MacDill F, 29 & 44 BG(H)s	1	7	36-296 A 37-460(DAM), -486, -493, -545, -585, -634, 39-013
Orlando, FL, 13 BG(M)	1	10	36-284 A 37-473, -495, -497, -530, -533, -534, -589, -592, -597, 38-597
Tallahassee, FL, 53 PG	0	1	A 37-512
Meridian, MS	0	1	A 37-609
Jackson, MS, 38 BG(M)	2	5	36-285, 37-030 A 37-484, -566, -606, -617, -620
Biloxi, MS	0	1	A 37-461
Shreveport, LA Barksdale F,	12	7	36-263M, -266M, -271M, -278M, -287, -289(DAM), -290M, -303, -305, -313M, -314M, -445 A 37-494, -556, -615, 38-588, -592, 39-019, -025
Baton Rouge, LA, Harding Field 58 PG	0	1	A 37-539
New Orleans, LA, 30 BG(H)	0	6	A 37-472, -496, -611, -618, 38-586, -590

18   47   (7 M's, 1 DAM)

A (1 DAM)

SOUTHWEST, 4th AF			
Randolph Field, TX	1	0	36-298
Wichita Falls, TX, Sheppard Field,	0	1	A 37-555M
Ellington Field, TX	5	4	36-264M, -267M, -268M, -276M, -277M A 37-471M, -506M, -631, 39-016
Oklahoma City, OK Okla Air Base 48 BG(L)	0	3	A 37-474, -510, -559,
Albuquerque, NM	1	2	37-026 A 37-572, 38-601

Tucson, AZ 41 BG(M)	1	8	36-322
			A 37-501,
			    (7 to Fresno, 12-7-41) 37-575, -603, -607, 38-606, -589,
			    - 609, 39-014

Salt Lake City, UT	2	1	36-320, 37-022, A 37-573
Riverside, CA, March Field 14 & 51 PG's	2	1	36-304(DAM), -306 A 37-560
San Fran, CA, Hamilton Field 7 BG(H), 20 PG	0	1	A 37-562
Fresno, CA 47 BG(L)	0	5	A 37-558, -561, -563, -574, -596 (+7 from Tucson 12-7-41)
Sacramento, CA, SAD	0	2	A 37-627, 39-026 both from Elmendorf, Alaska

12   28   (5 M's, 1 DAM)

A   (3 M's)

	B-18		B-18A		
Northeast, 1st AF =	8	+	40	=	48
Northwest, 2nd AF =	4	+	20	=	24
Southeast, 3rd AF =	18	+	47	=	65
Southwest, 4th AF =	12	+	28	=	40
	42	+	135	=	177

B-18 & B-18A:　ASSIGNED LOCATIONS OVERSEAS,　DECEMBER 7, 1941

TOTAL　　75 B-18　= 5 DAM, long term more than 2 months

TOTAL　　56 B-18A　= 5 DAM, long term more than 2 months

TOTAL　　131 Based Overseas

- 10　Long Term Repair

TOTAL BOMBERS USABLE　　121 Usable as Bombers Overseas　(70 B-18 + 51 B-18A)

HAWAII,	B-18	B-18A	
Hickam,　5 & 11 BG	31	0	36-270L -272, 288(DAM), -310, -327, -328L, -329, -331L, -333L, -334, -336, -337, -339, -342(DAM), -433, 436, 438, 442L, 37-001, -002, -003L, -004, -005, -006, -007L, 011L, -012L, -015, -018, 019L, -020　　　　　　　　　　L = 10 Lost in Pearl Harbor Attack
HAD	1	0	37-335(DAM)　Lost at HAD in Pearl Harbor Attack
Wheeler, 17 AB Sq	1	0	36-325　???perhaps landed at Wheeler during PH Attack, on trip back from Hilo
	33	0	3 DAM, long term

PHILIPPINES			
Clark F	15	0	36-326, -330, -332, -338, -341, -343, -431, -432, -434, -439, -440(DAM), -441, -443, -444　　37-023
Nichols	2	0	37-008, -016 (survived till 1944)
	17	0	1 DAM, long term

PANAMA & PCZ, 6th BG(H)			
France F,　3 BS = 6 a/c, 25 BS = 5 a/c	8	2	36-282, -291, -299, -309, -318,　　37-010, -027, -032 A 37-624 , -628
Aguadulce, Panama 74 BS (A/C assigned to Howard F)	4	1	36-294, -300, -302, -315 A 37-633
Albrook F	1	2	37-009, A 37-526, -590
	13	5	

PUERTO RICO, 40 BG & 25 BG			
Borinquen F, 40 BG(H)　29 BS = 4 a/c 44 BS = 3 a/c 45 BS = 3 a/c 5 RS = 3 a/c 25 BG(H)　10 BS = 3 a/c 27 RS = 3 a/c	6	15	36-269, -275, -280, -295, -312, -321 A 37-464, -465(DAM), -479, -514, -548, -567, -568, -598, -599, -601, -610, -621, -623,　　38-587, -605,　　　　39-012
Antigua B.W.I. 35 BS = 3 a/c	0	3	A 37-478, -547 + 1 of above
St. Croix, V.I., Benedict F, 2 BS = 3 a/c	0	3	A 37-516, -532, -600
	6	21	A 1 DAM, long term

CARIBBEAN FRONTIER, 9 BG(H)			
Trinidad, Waller F 1 BS = 5 a/c Zandery, Surinam 99 BS = 6 a/c	1	13	37-031 A 37-467, -481, -513, -524, -543, -577, -578, -579, -580, -591, 38-602, -604(DAM), -608
St. Lucia, Brit W. I., Beane F, 5 BS = 5 a/c	1	4	36-308 A 37-582, -585, -588, -629
Georgetown, British Guinea, Atkinson F,　44RS = 5 a/c	5	0	36-323, -324, 37-013, -024(DAM), -033
	7	17	
TOTAL CARIBBEAN	**26**	**43**	1 DAM, long term　+　A　1 DAM long term

ALASKA			
Anchorage, Elmendorf F	0	10	A 37-522(DAM), -529(DAM), -531, 536(DAM), -537, -549, -554, -626, -630,　　39-023 (PLUS, 2 A/C at SAD for long-term repair…counted there in US Total)
Fairbanks, Ladd F	0	1	A 37-535
	0	11	A 3 DAM, long term

NEWFOUNDLAND			
Gander	0	1	A 38-600
	0	1	

ICELAND			
In transit, NY or N England?, transfer from Langley	0	1	A 37-540
	0	1	

76 +　56　= 132 - 10 DAM = 122 Available

GRAND TOTAL:　　Continental US = 40 B-18 + 129 B-18A (+ 8 in long term repair)

Overseas　　　= 71 B-18 + 51 B-18A (+ 10 in long term repair)

TOTAL AVAILABLE　= 291 a/c = 111 B-18 + 180 B-18A (+18 in long term repair) = 309 TOTAL B-18 & B-18A

The Japanese naval air attacks on Hawaii at Hickam Field, Wheeler Field, Bellows Field, Pearl Harbor, Kaneohe, Ewa Field and Fort Kamehameha had commenced at 0755 hours and the second wave, during which the B-18 trundled onto the scene, came at 0945 hours, and consisted for the most part of strafing and some dive-bombing attacks. The third wave, consisting of almost entirely high-altitude bombers, hit Navy targets at Pearl Harbor once again. According to a Seventh Air Force report, as a direct result of the attack the air strength of the Hawaiian Air Force before and after the attack was as shown in the accompanying table.

Clearly, the Japanese had severely injured the Air Corps effective strength during the attack, but the B-18s on hand remained, numerically, the most significant long-range aircraft still capable of mounting offensive action until 9 December, when, as of 1000 hours, the Hawaiian Air Force reported that it had been reinforced to bring the total bombardment and attack element on hand to twelve airworthy B-17s, eight A-20As and ten B-18s.

B-18 losses on 7 December in Hawaii immediately reduced the Air Corps inventory by twelve aircraft as total losses, although several of these were at first thought repairable. For the record, this was the B-18 status report for that and the following day.

Although the Japanese attack on Hawaii has been exhaustively documented, very little has been published regarding the immediate aftermath, when US forces hastily shook off their wounds, organised, and launched search missions in a frantic effort to both forestall a subsequent attack force, but equally to locate the source of the initial attack and, if possible, inflict some damage in return.

As noted earlier, the first offensive aircraft to get airborne after the attack were four Douglas A-20As and two B-17s at 1140 hours. It is not clear what their assigned mission was, other than to search the ocean areas around the islands for any possible sight of the attack force.

General Rudolph, Commander of the 18th Bomb Wing, had scheduled a B-18 orientation flight for the morning of 7 December for '…some of the youngsters who had not completed a B-18 training.'

He found that he had more pilots than airworthy aircraft prior to the attack, and the relative quiet of a Sunday morning provided an opportunity to give them an extra hour of training. Some twenty-four enlisted men and officers were in the Wing hangar, moving the B-18s out for an 0800 take-off, when the Japanese attacked – and twenty-two of them were killed outright, with two others of the group seriously injured. Outside the hangar Master Sergeant Dave Jacobson was changing the main tyre of a unit B-18 on the ramp. He disappeared without trace when a bomb made a direct hit on the aircraft. 18th Bomb Wing airmen and B-18s thus became amongst the very first US casualties of the war.

Not far away, a Private First Class (PFC), assigned as an Orderly Room Clerk and described as '…a very mild-mannered soldier', somehow managed to open a Squadron arms room, locate a .30 caliber machine gun and ammunition, lug it out to one of the B-18s on the line, and properly mount it in the nose turret of the aircraft. Not familiar with the mounting procedure, he braced the unstable gun, which turned out to be an infantry .30 caliber gun, against his shoulder and managed to maintain a steady rate of fire at the low-flying Japanese aircraft. A Japanese aircraft apparently spotted the defender, strafed the offending B-18, and set it afire. The PFC was apparently absorbed by his work and failed to notice the aircraft was afire and perished with it. This incident probably constituted the very first time that a gun position of a B-18, however improperly, had been engaged in earnest against a live-fire enemy.

The same line-up in which this unnamed but gallant young soldier gave his all soon became a target of preference for the strafing Japanese aircraft, and the majority of the B-18s destroyed that day were in that same line-up. The order was passed from man to man, in shouts and screams, to get the aircraft dispersed, and scores of men, regardless of speciality or rank, rushed out on the Hickam flight line to do so, heedless of the strafing aircraft. An unidentified General's aide-de-camp was seen trying to taxi one of the B-18s when attackers shot one of the engines lifeless. It was no easy task to taxi a B-18 solo

Aircraft Type	On Hand 7 December	On Hand After Attack	Airworthy After Attack
Boeing B-17D	12	8	4
Consolidated B-24	1	1	1
Douglas B-18	33	21	11
Douglas A-20A	13	10	6
Martin B-12A	5	4	1
Curtiss P-40C	12	7	2
Curtiss P-40B	87	50	25
Curtiss P-36A	39	35	16
Boeing P-26A	11	9	9
Boeing P-26B	7	3	3
North American O-47B	12	5	7
Curtiss A-12	3	2	1
Curtiss A-12A	2	2	2
Stinson O-49	3	3	3
Grumman OA-9	3	3	3
Sikorsky OA-8	1	1	1
North American AT-6	4	3	3
Douglas BT-2	2	0	0
Douglas BT-2BR	2	2	2
Douglas BT-2CR	1	1	1
Douglas C-33	2	2	2

B-18 Losses

Field Number	Unit	Air Corps Serial	Status	Status as of 1845 8 December 1941
5B80	4th RS, 5th BG (H)	37-1	Hole in left wing and rudder	In commission
5B81	4th RS, 5th BG (H)	37-2	Undamaged	In commission
5B31	23rd BS, 5th BG (H)	36-339	Undamaged. At Hilo	In commission
5B62	72nd BS, 5th BG (H)	36-342	Undamaged	In commission
5B63	72nd BS, 5th BG (H)	36-329	Undamaged	In commission
5B64	72nd BS, 5th BG (H)	36-433	Left wing, vertical fin and rudder damaged	In commission
92	5th BG (H)	?	Not to be confused with another B-18 with Field Number 92 of the 11th BG	In commission
5B2	31st BS, 5th BG (H)	36-333	Right wing and elevator damaged	Repairable
5B83	HHS, 5th BG (H)	36-310	Right engine damaged, many bullet holes	Repairable
5B33	23rd BS, 5th BG (H)	36-438	Left wing, ailerons and elevators, many bullet holes, left tire damaged	Repairable
5B35	31st BS, 5th BG (H)	36-337	Right engine prop damaged	Repairable
5B36	31st BS, 5th BG (H)	36-334	Vertical fin and right tire badly shot up	Repairable
5B3	4th RS, 5th BG (H)	37-4		Destroyed
5B82	4th RS, 5th BG (H)	37-3		Destroyed
5B32	23rd BS, 5th BG (H)	37-11		Destroyed
5B37	31st BS, 5th BG (H)	37-19		Destroyed
?	31st BS, 5th BG (H)	36-331		Destroyed
?	4th RS, 5th BG (H)	37-18		Initially thought repairable but condemned
11B50	HHS, 11th BG (H)	36-327	Undamaged	In commission
11B52	26th BS, 11th BG (H)	36-336	Undamaged	In commission
11B53	26th BS, 11th BG (H)	37-20	Required air line patching materials	In commission
11B94	50th RS, 11th BG (H)	37-5	Undamaged	In commission
11B54	26th BS, 11th BG (H)	36-328	Complete empennage metal work, replace all wheels	Initially reported destroyed, but later repaired
11B77	42nd BS, 11th BG (H)	36-436	Needed new vertical stabilizer and rudder, left wheel and right aileron	Repairable
11B78	42nd BS, 11th BG (H)	36-437	Major work required	Repairable
11B79	42nd BS, 11th BG (H)	37-15	Patching for vertical fin, right wheel, right elevator and oil leak on right engine	Repairable
11B76	HHS, 11th BG (H)	36-288	At HAD for complete repair	Repairable
11B93	50th RS, 11th BG (H)	37-6	Originally thought to be a complete loss, but repairable	Repairable
11B4	HHS, 11th BG (H)	37-7	Major metal work, entire right landing gear assembly	Repairable but in fact condemned
11B51	11th BG (H)	36-335		Destroyed
92	50th RS, 11th BG (H)	36-270		Destroyed
11B95	14th BS, 11th BG (H)	37-12		Destroyed
1	HHS, Hawaiian Air Force	? (probably 36-442)		Destroyed
1	HHS, 18th Bomb Wing (H)	? (probably 36-272)		Destroyed

with only one engine turning, but he finally managed to do so by fire-walling the one good engine until it pulled that side of the aircraft forward, then slamming that brake on hard, which forced the other wing up. Waddling and crawfishing along in this manner, all the while under enemy fire, he finally brought the aircraft across the landing mat to comparative safety.

While the attack was still in progress, Air Corps personnel at Hickam, Wheeler and Bellows Fields began to prepare available aircraft for search missions to locate the attack force. Captain Russell L. Waldron, who had hastily been appointed as 'Provisional Commander of all B-18s', joined in the search with two fully loaded B-18s, taking off at 1330 in, as it turned out, the correct direction – north-west. The aircraft had been loaded quickly with the first bombs to arrive, six 100lb weapons, but only two .30 caliber guns each (the tunnel guns were not mounted), and although a provisional assembly of personnel, most of the crews were from the **31st Bombardment Squadron**. Two other 5th Bomb Group B-18 aircraft were apparently piloted by Captain B. E. Allen and Major L. G. Saunders with volunteer crews, and were the first off the ground from Hickam Field. Waldron later commented that it was probably just as well that they did not locate the Japanese force, but given the adrenalin flow of the day there is little doubt that they would have pressed home an attack – and the rest would have been history. On their return, perhaps not surprisingly, the two aircraft encountered absolutely withering anti-aircraft fire and, although they had been instructed to observe radio silence, he was finally compelled to come up on the radio and broadcast, 'This is Gatty, your friend! Please let us land!' This continued for some 45 minutes to an hour – before they finally got clearance to land.

In all, and contrary to many reports, the few available A-20A, B-17D, B-18, P-40, P-36 and O-47B aircraft flew a total of forty-eight sorties in a fruitless search for the enemy carriers.

During the period immediately after the attack, every aircraft of the **5th Bomb Group** that could be made airworthy was put to work in an endless series of long-range searches. Offensive action against the Japanese and revenge for the attack were thirsted for by all concerned, but targets failed to materialise, despite nearly feverish efforts. Slowly, as new B-17s arrived from the US mainland, the 5th Bomb Group converted to these aircraft, and within months participated in the pivotal Battle of Midway.

Within the Group, the **23rd Bomb Squadron** suffered the loss of its only B-17 and one of its B-18s when the Squadron hangar was hit and destroyed. Another B-18 was disabled and the only other unit B-18 was away at Hilo. The Squadron suffered thirteen casualties, nearly all of them in the unit barracks. By 10 December the unit had four B-17s and by the 21st ten B-17Es, ending its association with the B-18.

The **31st Bomb Squadron** reportedly engaged enemy aircraft at 0755 on 7 December according to the unit history, but the exact nature of that engagement has eluded identification. The Squadron lost two enlisted men in action that day.

A Japanese officer inspects the remains of Field Number 12, which has sustained enormous damage – some undoubtedly from the Japanese, but the missing cockpit almost certainly from a US charge placed to deny the carcass to the invaders. Upon close inspection, the aircraft reveals some of its camouflage details. *via Kirby J. Key and Bill Bartsch*

The **72nd Bomb Squadron**, on the other hand, suffered only one B-18 seriously damaged and this was returned to airworthy status within three days of the attack, and the Squadron's hangar was unscathed. Squadron B-18s were ready to sortie within 60 minutes of the first attack but, due to a complete lack of intelligence as to the direction of the attack force, none took off until 1400. At that time two aircraft launched fully loaded but returned late, after dark, having found nothing.

On the morning of 8 December the 72nd Bomb Squadron began conducting regular search-and-attack missions 350 miles to seaward, carrying an overload of 1,200lb of bombs, auxiliary fuel tanks and full crew. At that time the unit had only two airworthy B-18s, as its B-17s had been transferred to the 23rd Bomb Squadron. The Squadron was attached to Bellows Field from 11 December, where it was assigned additional B-18s that had been at Hickam and had been undamaged. On 19 December 1941 Lieutenant H. M. Campbell and his crew dropped a 600lb bomb on an oil slick that was sighted some 250 miles from Oahu while on a patrol. This was the first known instance of a USAAC B-18 dropping an offensive weapon in earnest. Another oil slick then appeared, leading the crew to believe that a hit had been scored on a Japanese submarine. Because Japanese submarine records were destroyed at the end of the war, this attack has unfortunately eluded verification.

The Squadron history had this intriguing entry:

'One afternoon after the attack, at about 1400, several B-18s, less navigators or complete navigational equipment, had been dispatched with orders to search their assigned sectors until sunset, then to return home. This would never have been recorded had it not been for the fact that, about the same time the pilots started their return flight to Oahu, the weather started moving in – and won the race to the islands. Most of the pilots were fortunate in that their guesses as to course and wind direction were sufficiently accurate to enable them to hit the completely blacked-out islands, locate Hickam Field, and land. Lieutenant Kacmarcik and Lt. Healy, pilot and co-pilot of one of the B-18s, were not so lucky. After they were positive that their ETA had passed, they broke radio silence for "fixes" to be taken on their aircraft. Fixes were taken, but for a time proved to be inaccurate. A patrolling Navy PBY Catalina had been 'fixed' instead of the B-18. Some 30 search lights around the home island were turned on and pointed into the night sky. To make a long story short, a nearly correct heading was given the plane and, after a few minutes, the crew sighted the shaft of lights. Lt Kacmarcik approached the island via Kainae Point and his last radio report on his fuel supply stated simply "Almost gone". Not certain he had sufficient fuel to reach Hickam, he landed at Ewa which, on orders from Hickam, had the runway edged with smudge pots. The plane, without bomb bay tanks and with full bomb load, had been in sustained flight for nearly nine and a half hours. This was believed to have established a record for the B-18 at the time.'

For a few weeks after the above incident, the old 2,600-foot runways at Bellows Field, which had been a feature of the station for years, was used for routine operations by the B-18s with full war loads, which, to say the least, was rather sporty. This made it necessary for the aircraft, with 2,400lb of bombs aboard, to open throttles with brakes locked, release them, run to the end of the runway and literally yank the aircraft into the air – and pray. This condition was corrected, even as the B-18s continued to operate, but during the 'winter' months, when rain and overcast skies prevailed. The 72nd retained the distinction of being the only bombardment unit to operate from the field while basically a fighter strip.

The **11th Bomb Group** started the transition to B-17Ds on 2 October 1941, and had lost its **14th Bomb Squadron**, which had been transferred to the Philippines on 2 September. The **Headquarters and Headquarters Squadron** suffered more casualties on 7 December than any other unit at Hickam Field. Of 350 men, 245 were casualties, including sixteen fatal and another fifty permanently disabled. The majority of these were suffered while in their barracks.

The Group's **26th Bomb Squadron** at Hickam had two B-17Ds and five B-18s as of 7 December, and one of the B-18s, 11B54, was initially thought completely lost, but was later repaired after considerable exertions. The Squadron moved to Wheeler Field several days after the attack and completely converted to nine new B-17Es that had just arrived, ending its nineteen-month association with the B-18.

The war diary of the **42nd Bomb Squadron** for 7 December 1941 was terse: 'Hickam Field, T.H. Squadron withstood air attack; moved by marching to area across mat from hangars. Command Post established at head of by-road, 29 casualties.' Of the unit aircraft only two – a B-17 and a B-18 – could be repaired and returned to operational status. The unit lost one other B-17D and four B-18s damaged beyond repair.

Also at Hickam Field, the **50th Reconnaissance Squadron** was only able to save one B-18 from its strength of two B-17Ds and four B-18s on hand before the attack. By 0820 most of the enlisted men of the unit had reported to the unit hangar, which probably accounted for the relatively low casualty rate experienced by the unit compared to others. As trained, by 0825 they had set up and actively manned several .30 caliber machine guns and this apparently attracted some of the strafing Japanese aircraft away from other targets on the flight line, and probably saved lives. At 0900, however, horizontal bombers, flying at an estimated 12,000 feet, released bombs, two of which made direct hits on the unit hangar and two NCOs were wounded. Orders were given to clear the hangar and the shocked airmen started across the landing mat, but almost immediately were set upon by nine strafing aircraft, although miraculously no one was hit.

The Squadron did not manage to dispatch its only airworthy aircraft, B-18 11B94, until 0400 hours on 8 December, with Lt Trent in command, but the long search was fruitless. This was apparently the only mission flown by the unit during the initial alert period. On 18 December five B-17Es and a B-17C arrived for the unit from the US mainland, to the rejoicing of all concerned, and combat crews were immediately assigned and oriented. The unit apparently converted entirely to B-17s at this point.

By 31 December 1941 the Hawaiian Air Force had managed to stabilise its strength through a rush of reinforcements from the mainland, but the B-18s in the Command, in spite of their perceived shortcomings, remained on first-line strength into 1942, as will be seen.

The Philippines

The Japanese attack on Hawaiian installations, hindsight and reason suggests, should have allowed the US defenders of the Philippines at least a brief interval in which to brace themselves for what surely must be next.

In fact, at his Headquarters near Manila, General MacArthur received word of the attack several hours before dawn on 8 December. General Brereton, Commander of what was called the **Far Eastern Air Force**[32], effective from 4 November 1941, headquartered at Clark Field, was immediately informed. Both he and MacArthur, from existing records, apparently considered the possibility of getting the jump on the Japanese by sending their heavy bombardment force of some thirty-five mixed Boeing B-17Cs and B-17Ds on a raid against known Japanese staging fields on Formosa. However, in order to do so effectively a current reconnaissance of the targets would be necessary. One source, found at the US Air Force Historical Research Agency, claims that one long-range recon mission to Formosa was flown by a

B-17 piloted by Captain Purcell before the commencement of hostilities, but this has eluded absolute verification. While one of the B-17s was fitted with cameras (which were flown to the operating base by a B-18), MacArthur authorized Brereton to make the attack as soon as he was ready. Early that same morning, General Henry Arnold made a rare long-distance telephone call from Washington to warn Brereton to be fully alert and prepared for a Japanese air attack – from Formosa.

The next morning USAAC patrol aircraft, including at least two B-18s, took off to conduct a search to the north and north-west for the anticipated Japanese formations. During most of the morning the majority of these aircraft conducted successive searches while most of the remaining combat-ready aircraft were dispersed or were in the air to avoid being caught on the ground. Only a few Japanese reconnaissance aircraft were encountered, however, and these quickly turned tail.

The US forces did not know that the Japanese had, indeed, planned an early-morning attack, but that their heavy bombers and escorts had been grounded at their Formosa bases by early-morning fog. By 1000 hours local time, however, the fog had lifted and nearly 200 Japanese aircraft sortied towards Luzon.

The American crews, perhaps overconfident in their circumstances and rookies at the business of combat, having expended their adrenalin in the early morning hours with little to show for it, returned to their stations to refuel, have lunch, and rest a bit – leaving many of their

aircraft lined up on the aprons, positioned for a quick take-off if necessary. Coincidentally, in the time-honored manner of the Philippines, perhaps a majority of the elaborate air warning service spotters and runners who had been organised went off to lunch as well and, as in Hawaii, early warning radar reports of the approaching Japanese armada did not reach Clark Field, where the majority of the FEAF was based. To his eternal regret, Brereton and his subordinate commanders had issued no specific instructions for dispersal or for a standing air patrol during the lunch hour.

When the Japanese aircraft appeared over Clark Field, according to first-hand accounts, they were astonished to find the USAAC aircraft lined up on the field. They quickly seized the moment, and in short order eighteen of the highly prized B-17s and at least fifty-three P-40s were destroyed or rendered inoperable where they stood. Nearly every other aircraft on the field received at least some damage. Only seven Japanese aircraft were downed in the attack, which, in itself, was something of a minor miracle. Nearly 50% of the FEAF was in flames.

Some accounts have reported that, by the end of that fateful day, nine of the ten B-18s at Clark Field had been either destroyed or rendered not airworthy. Precisely how this information has been arrived at is unknown, as, despite intensive first-hand research in known USAF and National Archives collections, no such information has come to light. The truth appears to be that no firm estimate of the numbers of B-18s that survived the first wave of attacks seems to exist. Other reports refute the oft-published account.

What is known is that at least one of the B-18s managed to take off, under fire and with its own gunners returning fire (a first in the history of the B-18 series, and possibly one of only two occasions that this form of air-to-air action can be positively documented) and managed to divert to one of the alternate, deployment aerodromes at Rosales, about 100 miles north-west of Clark Field. Some sources claim that it managed to land there, but was subsequently declared a 'write off' due to the battle damage that it had suffered, while others state that it was pushed off to the side of the field, camouflaged, and later patched up and placed into limited service in the defense of the islands.

At Nichols Field, where only two of the B-18s were stationed, both have been reported as having been destroyed when Hangar 4, in which they were housed, was hit. This is open to question, as at least one of the Nichols Field B-18s was operating later in the month, although it is possible that this may have been an aircraft flown in from another location. A subsequent night-time attack on Nichols, according to the same source that reported both aircraft as destroyed in the first raid, is claimed to have destroyed Hangar 4 (again) and that another B-18 was also damaged. This appears to conflict with known deployments.

Although the date of this image cannot be verified, it is probably after 20 November 1941 at Clark Field, and shows at least four B-18s on the line, including Field Number '13' nearest – a number normally skipped in many Air Corps units! The B-18s assigned to the Philippines received two-tone upper-surface camouflage, not just olive-drab. *Erickson via Bill Bartsch*

The highest Field Number known for a Philippines B-18 was '15', which is shown in the background here at Clark Field as Japanese officers inspect the remains of another aircraft. The B-18 appears relatively unscathed, but the cabin area has been destroyed, suggesting that retreating US forces may have blown it up to deny it to the advancing enemy. *Rico Jose collection via Bill Bartsch*

It has been widely reported that all or nearly all of the Philippines-based B-18s were destroyed during the initial Japanese attacks. In fact, at least six or seven were deployed to the Del Monte auxiliary aerodrome by 17 December. This one, showing evidence of hard use aside from the obvious attack damage, was hit by four Japanese Navy Mitsubishi A6M series Zero fighters on 19 December at the near end of the field on the first pass. *Monty Montgomery via Bill Bartsch*

Clearly a different B-18, this aircraft was also destroyed on the first pass by the same group of marauding Japanese aircraft on 19 December 1941, just as a truck was backed up to it to unload vital ammunition being flown to Del Monte from elsewhere. *Monty Montgomery via Bill Bartsch*

At least two B-18s, nominally assigned to the 5th Air Base Group, had been flown earlier to Del Monte, where one of them, camouflaged on the periphery, acted as a mobile radio command post, tuned to the Clark Field frequency. The other was actively engaged in long-range reconnaissance missions, including at least two missions to the Davao area to check on reported Japanese landings. S/Sgt Hays H. Bolitho of the 5th Air Base Group, after the war, related that one of these B-18s was used to fly back to Clark Field to bring small arms back to the local defenders at Del Monte, as the personnel there did not have enough weapons to go around. The aircraft returned stuffed with mostly Enfields, but also had located one case of new Garands. He also said that there were definitely two B-18s at Del Monte as late as 19 December.

It is known with accuracy that a number of B-18s were employed well after most of the B-17 force had been all but decimated, although the number engaged is difficult to establish. They are known to have made a substantial number of armed flights between bases on Luzon (including Clark Field, Nichols Field, Iba aerodrome and Del Carmen aerodrome) and Mindanao (Del Monte aerodrome). These 650-to-700-mile one-way flights were accompanied by a very high 'pucker factor' for the crews, and were usually made at very low altitude, in the hope of eluding Japanese patrols. They usually planned to arrive at dusk or after dark, refuel, return to Luzon or Mindanao and sometimes return in the morning twilight. The crews of these aircraft have never received recognition for these vital missions and, indeed, it has proven nearly impossible to identify most of them, a sizeable percentage of whom appear not to have survived the campaign.

On 12 December 1941, four days after the first attack, Major David Gibbs was instructed to assume command of the Del Monte aerodrome from Major Emmett O'Donnell, who was transferred to Clark. Gibbs decided to make the flight to Del Monte in one of the B-18s and, after an 1800 departure, was never heard from again.

There was also a secret US operating field on the island of Mindoro, operated by a detachment of seventy-five men from Clark Field, and it is believed that a number of B-18 reconnaissance missions were staged out of this base.

At Del Monte the US forces did not lose a single aircraft because of Japanese attack, that is until General Royce's raid in the early spring of 1942 when one B-17, flown by Captain Bostwicke, which the General insisted be left on the open field in daylight, was destroyed by Japanese dive-bombing. Until 18 December this was the only US operating base capable of taking B-17s, but after that date engineers had managed to build a number of auxiliary strips and put them into operation until the total was raised to an astonishing twenty-one. Many of these were not far from Del Monte itself. Crews took care that, during the daylight hours, none of the aircraft were left on Del Monte, flying them to one of the auxiliaries, many of which were cut out of the surrounding cane. Filipino trucks, furnished by Mr Crawford, Manager of the Del Monte Corporation, were used to cart camouflage material from cocoanut trees, which were used to cover the aircraft during daylight hours. As a result, the Japanese never did discover where these aircraft were.

In one raid on 17 December, however, according to one survivor, six or seven B-18s were definitely still in the Del Monte operating area, and 'several' of them were destroyed. This seems to agree more with the facts than the previously published accounts, which had them all destroyed on the opening day of hostilities.

Early on the morning of 19 December, eleven days after the attack, Brigadier General Clagett, whose 5th Interceptor Command had been all but annihilated, departed Nichols Field with his staff in two B-18s for Del Monte, where four remaining B-17s were hidden, and were to be used to shuttle his staff to Australia. It is believed that one of these was the one piloted by O'Donnell, which made the non-stop flight to Darwin, a

The wide expanse of the so-called Del Monte auxiliary aerodrome allowed for wide dispersal of the available aircraft – a necessity learned at huge cost – but afforded precious little for camouflage from enemy aircraft. At least five B-18s and two B-17Ds are visible in this 15 December 1941 photograph, and the B-18 in the right foreground is Field Number '14'. *Col Ralph L. Fry via Bill Bartsch*

distance of more than 2,000 miles. Japanese air units had apparently finally discovered Del Monte, however, and not long after the B-18s arrived four Japanese aircraft (most often identified as Mitsubishi A6M2s, but possibly other types) suddenly appeared out of nowhere and strafed the aircraft, setting one of the B-18s afire and hitting two of the B-17s as well.

The B-18s did in fact fly missions from Del Monte, but only armed reconnaissance as far as can be ascertained, not dedicated bombardment missions. They were also used on several occasions to fly out to recover the crews of B-17s and other aircraft that had been forced down at various locations due to enemy action or mechanical failure.

As the Japanese forces consolidated their landings on Luzon and pushed south, the B-18 force continued its nightly missions, when virtually every other form of USAAC activity had all but ceased.

Due to the series of debacles that followed in rapid succession, the role played by the comparatively small FEAF B-18 fleet is, at best, poorly understood. As noted previously, it has been widely recorded that all but four of the nineteen aircraft, which had only been in the Command since May 1941, fell victim to the initial onslaught at Clark Field. Fragmentary evidence, however, laboriously assembled by the Air Force from survivor accounts after the war, seems to suggest otherwise.

What can be reported, based on the official record, is that no fewer than thirteen of the nineteen aircraft are listed, officially, as Destroyed by Enemy Action and stricken from the inventory effective from 18 January 1942. This is probably a fairly reliable number. What happened to the aircraft between 8 December 1941 and 18 January 1942 – more than forty days – is, however, another story entirely.

Perhaps the first known exposure of a B-18 to an enemy aircraft in flight actually took place prior to the Japanese attack. Concerned that his pursuit pilots had little practical experience at night-time interceptions, Major Orrin Grover, Commander of the 24th Pursuit Group, arranged with the FEAF Tow Target Detachment[33] to provide an aircraft as a 'target' for such training. The aircraft selected turned out to be the Detachment's solitary B-18. Operating in conjunction with a Coast Artillery searchlight unit, the idea was to illuminate the B-18 by searchlight so that the P-40s could locate and make practice intercepts on the aircraft. During one of the drills on the third morning, a P-40 flight was in attack formation on the target B-18 when an aircraft described as a P-35 clearly dived between them and the B-18. Later, when being debriefed, the P-40 pilots complained about the intrusion of what was believed to have been one of the fifty-seven Seversky P-35As then in the command – only to learn that, at least officially, no P-35s had been airborne at the time. It was concluded that the aircraft may well have been a Japanese intruder, although the possibility of a practical joke by an 'unauthorized' P-35 pilot could not be ruled out. In the opinion of this writer, the possibility of this having been a Japanese aircraft is remote in the extreme, as to have so recklessly endangered the operations then being planned by the Japanese leadership would have been a most unlikely action for a Japanese reconnaissance crew.

Previously published reports that the 28th Bomb Squadron's B-18s were relegated to transport and reconnaissance duties prior to the outbreak of hostilities tell only half of the story. In fact, nearly every bombardment aircraft in the command was exercised in this way, as there were only a handful of dedicated transports in the Philippines. That the B-18s were in fact used in this manner after hostilities commenced is in no way demeaning; it just made good sense at the time, and constituted a competent expression of military prudence.

Commencing on 23 October 1941 the **19th Bombardment Group (H)**, cited earlier in this account, started arriving in the Philippines from Albuquerque, NM, with its nearly brand-new Boeing B-17Cs and B-17D aircraft. With its arrival, the **28th Bombardment Squadron** with its B-18s was reassigned from the **4th Composite Group** to the 19th BG and was at least partially re-equipped with a small number of the Group's thirty-five B-17s.

Between the time of the arrival of the 19th Bomb Group and the end of December 1941, records pertaining to aircraft assignments within FEAF are, at best, very sketchy. It is known that, as of 8 December 1941, the deployments of the FEAF bombardment aircraft were as shown in the accompanying table.

The table seems to clearly suggest that the vast majority of FEAF losses on 8 December were suffered by the 30th Bomb Squadron at Clark Field but, more importantly for our narrative, that only seven B-18s had been lost during the initial Japanese attack, rather that the 'all but four' that have been so frequently recorded in earlier accounts.

In the midst of all of the initial turmoil of the Japanese attack, the **27th Bombardment Group (L)**, also noted earlier during its working-up phase at Savannah, GA, had sailed for the Philippines on 1 November 1941 – minus their Douglas A-24s, which were to follow the personnel of the Group, but most of which eventually ended up in Australia. The Group Commander, Colonel John H. Davies, together with twenty pilots, had actually been en route to Australia from the Philippines, shortly after arrival, to return with some of their A-24s, but only got as far as Java because of the rapidly deteriorating situation in the Philippines. The 27th BG had considerable experience with B-18s, having honed its skills on B-18As at Savannah, where it also had a few Curtiss A-18s '…thrown in for general Hell-raising'. The unit subsequently received Douglas A-20s at Savannah, which it enjoyed immensely until August 1941, when the Group's pleasure was '…suddenly interrupted by the arrival of the Douglas Dauntless, or the A-24 dive bomber – more familiarly known as the Blue Rock Clay Pigeons,' according to the official unit history.

At this point the path of the hapless 27th Bomb Group and the apparently 'unassigned' B-18s that had been almost gleefully abandoned by the 19th Bomb Group when the giant 'modern' B-17s arrived, become intertwined. The tenor of the hectic interlude experienced by the Group is perhaps best described by a literal transcription of their unit history for the period, which miraculously survived, and which, prior to this telling, has never been associated with the B-18.

FEAF deployments

Unit	Location	Aircraft Type	Number on Hand
HHS, 19th Bomb Group	Clark Field	None	None
93rd Bomb Squadron	Del Monte	B-17D	12* (shared with 14th & 28th BS)
14th Bomb Squadron	Del Monte	B-17D	*
28th Bomb Squadron	Clark Field	B-17D	*
30th Bomb Squadron	Clark Field	B-17D	18
Unassigned	Clark Field, Nichols Field, Neilson Field	B-18	10*
Unassigned	Del Monte	B-18	2

'We have all been speculating on our move from Fort McKinley to San Marcelena. San Marcelena was over on the west coast, north of the Bataan Peninsula, and so far as we could find out, it didn't have anything for us in the way of water, food, runways, houses or any of the essentials necessary to maintain a Group. The last two days of November, we borrowed four old and very decrepit B-18s from the 19th Group at Clark Field. None of us had enjoyed flying time for the month, so the Group arranged a schedule with these four aircraft so we could all fly our necessary four hours apiece. As stated before, the ships were in extremely sad shape – parts were held together with baling wire and other parts held together with what appeared to be only gravity. Backus was an old airline pilot by the way. He and a pilot from the 19th took off together with a load of 19th pilots. The 19th was skeptical of our flying ability and they had arranged that one of their pilots was to be co-pilot every time we flew. On this particular take-off, Ed Backus's co-pilot forgot to pull up his wheels, and as a result they didn't gain much altitude on account of the load. They asked Backus to let them fly from then on – he hit the roof, naturally. Schmidt blew out a tire and Hipps ground looped again. Stephenson and McAfee clipped the tops out of the trees for 100 yards after a scrogged-up take-off. But back to San Marcelena, we looked the field over while we were getting our flying time in. It looked sort of wild and woolly so we decided to rent a house in Manila for an Officer's Club. We planned on flying men down for the weekend and officers could sleep and eat at the Club.

Lancaster was given the job of Club Officer and commissioned to rent us a house. He naturally had to collect 10 pesos off every officer before he could start his work, but Bert found a fine house with furnishings which he rented for 50 pesos a month. Most all of the officers put their wool clothing and uniforms in the Club for storage.

The Army-Navy Game on November 29th was certainly a fine event, for it gave everyone in Manila a chance to fill up on grog and be very fraternal down at the Army-Navy Club. McAfee was a cheer leader for the Army along with Horace Greeley and Wynekeep. Colin Kelley was supposed to have been the fourth cheer leader, but he was on alert at Clark Field that night. Stephenson worked the lights on the score board. It was a good game, so they say – we didn't hear it on account of static interference. The Army lost. Herman Lowery took off cross-country in a jeep going home from the Club; he, Walker and Ruegg ended up in a rice paddy with mud up to their ears, almost sober.

On the 7th of December, we were at peace on account of the difference in Hawaii and PI times, the 27th was challenged to a soft ball game by the Manila Polo Club. An all-star team was chosen from all the Squadrons and the Group left at 1pm for the Polo Club. The game began at 2pm and by 4pm the score was 19 to 2 in favor of the Polo Club. Hipps and Schmidt had a fine argument over who made the most errors, and that little tiff was finally fairly well settled. The game gradually shifted to the bar at the club where everyone got stiff in preparation for the dinner the Group was giving in honor of General Brereton, who was the C.G. of the FEAF.

The day was started in the Philippines (December 8th, as we were across the International Date Line), most of the Headquarters and Headquarters Squadron, 27th Bomb Group, was in quarters at Fort McKinley. Later on, when the air raids started, Headquarters was transferred to a tent in the ravine back

of the quarters. Here, George Kane, the Group Adjutant still managed to keep all the paper work going, in spite of the war.

To be as mild as possible, it was a Hell of a situation. No planes, no weapons except a few pistols, and let's condense it and just say "no nothing". Right here was where the 27th had their first run-in with that all-powerful chunk of paper called the T.B.A.[34] The T.B.A. said no rifles and no machine guns and that the Materiel Squadron at an Air Base was supposed to do our protecting for us. What Materiel Squadron and what Air Base wasn't specified, and that ended that. We learned fast, though, and with a little aid and some fast paper work that was never proven, 450 rifles appeared on the scene and the Group started training. Some of the wilder souls next suggested hand-grenades. But on due consideration (after ducking every five minutes when some simple bloke decided that grenades were an inhuman weapon and not for use by the Air Force) this idea was quietly forgotten.

The first afternoon, the Group was asked to furnish three B-18 crews for night bombing of Formosa. They never got to bomb, but were later used as transports. We also furnished personnel to run Neilson Field for the big shots and for the Interceptor Command. I never was quite sure what there was to run at Neilson, but anyway we ran it. We were also called on to furnish men to man anti-aircraft guns at Nichols Field, and a detail of 10 officers was sent to Clark Field. Everyone wanted to be on the last detail, because they thought they would fly P-40s. Too bad they didn't get to, we would have shot down the first Nip sooner.

Just before the war started, the Group had been bust filling sand bags and building revetments at Neilson[35] for our planes when they came (they were always coming around the mountain). We filled 100,000 and Ed Backus went down to draw another 150,000. Less than 500 were available. This was two days before the war started. Ed went to see the Colonel in charge of the Depot and asked if they couldn't be procured for us. The Colonel laughed, and said, "Well, we have authority to buy them locally and local manufacturers can furnish us about 100,000 a week. But I don't think there's enough of an emergency now to justify spending Government funds for that purpose." Ed was always sort of outspoken, so we will omit his reply, but the Colonel doesn't like us anymore. To get back to Neilson, though, we had the first revetments half built when war was declared and that is as far as it got. The next morning, there was a truck backed up against it and they were loading the sand bags on to stack around the Headquarters building.

On December 8th, the **16th Bomb Squadron (L), 27th Bomb Group (L)**, was peacefully sleeping in various buildings and tents on the pleasant campus of Fort McKinley as well. Our A-24s had not yet arrived, and we had fully enjoyed our brief stay in the Philippines, seeing the sights and trying to tell a taxi driver where we wanted to go in our fluent Tagaley dialect. At 0430, Major Davies, our CO, got the phone call that Pearl Harbor had been bombed. We couldn't believe it. And all we could do was sit tight and hope our ships arrived. So we went back to bed. At 0800, reports started to arrive of other raids, and most of them in the Philippines. Clark Field and Iba were hit the hardest. Nobody knew what to do. The only thing we knew how to fight with was aircraft, and we had none. Captain W. H. Hipps, the 16th Bomb Squadron CO, started the men off on small-arms drill and we went about unimportant details in a daze.

Around noon on the 8th of December, three B-18s were assigned to our Group. Ruegg, Peter Beuder and Salvatore were to take the first mission. Crews were assigned and we waited for the word to go. It didn't come, and the next day, another Squadron took over the B-18s and we didn't see them again for 10 days. The rest of the day was taken up with digging fox holes and camouflaging. By nightfall, we were more or less used to the idea that the war was here, and spent hours cussing whoever was responsible for shipping the 27th BG to the PI without aircraft. We went to bed ready for anything. And it came. About 0100, we had an air raid alarm which got everyone up but nothing happened. At 0200, we had another false alarm. And at 0430, we were sound asleep when a terrific blast shook all the buildings, followed by a weird display of fireworks. And 1,000 men more or less made a desperate dive for the comparative shelter of a ravine 50 yards away. A 12-foot drop into the ravine was no obstacle, and we all piled up neatly at the bottom. Total casualties: one sprained ankle. Sleep was out of the question from then on.

Detachments of men were sent to Nichols and Neilson Fields for duty and the Japs struck Nichols Field. The first casualty of the Group was PFC Chitwood of the 16th Bomb Squadron, manning a machine gun and a bomb got him. Hipps was transferred to Headquarters at Neilson, along with McAfee, Stevenson and Ruegg. Those on day shifts couldn't sleep much at night because of the constant fear of night raids, and on the night shift, sleeping in the daytime was taboo because of the heat and air raids. So most of us went without. Peter Bender was flying a B-18 somewhere on the island and we would get reports of incredible achievements, but little detail. The **17th Bomb Squadron (L)**, 27th Bomb Group was at Nichols Field on the 8th. One bomb came close to where the 17th was stationed and hit the P.A.A. radio station, not a mile distant. The Squadron moved from the parade ground to the jungle nearby. The next morning, the Squadron was issued small arms, ammunition and gas masks. Major Davies had the Squadron Commanders in for a short meeting and standing by for orders. Crews were formed to man the B-18s and they had us stand by.

The next day, the 9th, found the 17th BS with some of the crews manning machine gun posts at Nichols Field and with flying crews standing by to man the B-18s. Tom Gerrity and Ed Townsend had one, Pete Bender and Harry Roth of the 16th had the second, and Gus Heiss and F. E. Timlin of the 17th had the third. All had it easy on the 9th, but on the 10th, all were called out. Tom and Ed were down at Nichols preparing for a bombing mission when shortly after noon, the Japs staged a huge raid. Tom and Ed ran for cover as the Zeros began to strafe the B-18 that they were to use on their mission. Tom unfortunately was hit in the hand by a piece of shrapnel and Ed got to cover just as the B-18's load of bombs blew up.'

Although some recently published accounts suggest that the 27th Bomb Group was equipped entirely with B-18s in the Philippines, based on the foregoing this appears to be only partially correct. While it may in fact have become the intended organisation for the B-18s remaining in the Islands, only about half of the aircraft appear to have actually reached any of the subordinate squadrons and crews formed.

Using at least four of these aircraft, a number of 27th BG crews did in fact manage to fly out of Clark Field, via Tarakan, and on to Darwin, Australia, arriving on 22 December 1941 – which just happened to be the same day that the so-called Pensacola Convoy, with its A-24s and the remainder of its crews, arrived in Brisbane.

Earlier, Gustave M. Heiss Jr was one of the Group members who flew out of Manila on the night of 17/18 December 1941 in two B-18s and a single Douglas C-39 transport. Heiss was piloting one of the B-18s, with Tim Timlin as co-pilot, and one of his passengers to Tarakan, Koepang and Darwin was Colonel Davies, the Group Commander. When their B-18 arrived at Batchelor Field in the Australian Northern Territory, loaded with men from the Philippines, they were almost immediately directed to fly ammunition back to the Philippines, and as soon as this was loaded they departed. They had intended to retrace their route back via Borneo, then northward. However, Heiss and Timlin flew into an intense tropical storm off Borneo that forced them to turn back. They landed at Koepang and spent Christmas on the airstrip there. Shortly thereafter, they returned to Australia, having been unable to delivery the badly needed munitions.

At the end of December 1941 the leadership of the FEAF had concluded that the command could no longer realistically function effectively from Manila. Nearly all ammunition and spares were, by that point, being diverted to Australia, and the rally point for reforming shattered units was also taking place there. By the last week in December, withdrawal of all ground units onto the Bataan Peninsula and Corregidor started to take place, and forces from South, North and Central Luzon were retreating there as rapidly as they could manage. Captain Floyd Pell of the FEAF staff was dispatched to Australia aboard a B-18, and arrived there on 18 December. He was followed by General H. B. Clagett, who was sent to Australia specifically to take charge of the mountain of supplies arriving there and, if possible, to organise Air Corps elements for the relief of the Philippines. It is not clear if he travelled on one of the B-18s, but it appears that this was the case.

By 6 February 1942, in addition to the special air section of Headquarters, US Air Forces in Australia (**USAFIA**), an **Air Transport Command** was created under it, and none other than the legendary Captain Paul I. 'Pappy' Gunn was assigned as Commander of this rather cosmopolitan force at Amberley Field, Brisbane. His unit consisted of the following aircraft:

Douglas C-53	6
Beechcraft	3
Consolidated LB-30	3
Douglas B-18	3
Boeing B-17C	1 (not in combat commission)

Joined by ten North American O-47s on 12 February, the unit was intensively engaged in transportation of personnel and equipment in support of the defense of Java, in leading flights of Curtiss P-40s along the ferry route both within Australia and over the water route from Darwin to Java and, ultimately, in the evacuation of personnel from Manila. The B-18s, unquestionably the survivors of the nineteen aircraft assigned to the FEAF in the Philippines, were in the thick of this, but precise records of their involvement have not survived. These three B-18s were joined by a fourth aircraft, probably from Java, and eventually passed to the custody of the **21st Troop Carrier Squadron** at Amberley Royal Australian Air Force Station, near Brisbane, the very first formal USAAF unit formed in Australia out of the ATC USAFIA. This most unusual unit was the US component of what was known as the **Allied Directorate of Air Transport** (ADAT or, more often, simply DAT), which had been thrown together to attempt to coordinate all Allied air transport in the ravaged Southwest Pacific area. These extraordinarily well-travelled aircraft led something of a charmed existence for some time, but must be counted as amongst the very few B-18s actually lost in aerial combat to enemy air units. The accompanying table provides a summary capsule history of these aircraft.

Aircraft Summary Capsules

Serial	Unit	Fate
36-338	28th BS; 27th BG; ATC USAFIA; 21st TCS	Certainly one of the two B-18s that departed Nichols Field, PI in December 1941, arriving at Darwin 21 December 1941 crewed by Geiss and Timlin. This is the aircraft that was shot down in action by Japanese aircraft over Java 4 February 1942, 30 miles west of Surabaya with the loss of the entire crew, including MAJ Austin A. Straubel, CO of the 7th BG and COL Murphy, a communications expert.
36-343	28th BS; 27th BG; ATC USAFIA; 21st TCS; DAT NFI	Departed Nichols Field, PI 22 December 1941 and arrived Darwin via Tarakan, Balikpapan, Macassar & Koepang and arrived Amberley Field 25 December 1941. Interesting recorded locally as "N36343". To 3 SFTS 21 February 1942, ATC USAFIA and named Julie 3 April 1942. To 21st TCS 5 July 1942 and "VHC CB". Transferred to DAT NFI and thought to have crashed around October 1942. One B-18 was known shot down at Buna, and may have been this aircraft.
36-434	28th BS; 27th BG; ATC USAFIA; 21st TCS	Two B-18s departed Nichols Field, PI in late December 1941 and arrived at Darwin 21 December and this was certainly one of them, probably with 36-338 above. This aircraft crash landed into the sea on 7 March 1942 when "Hoot" Horrigan attempted to fly it out of Bandoeng.
37-16	28th BS; 27th BG; ATC USAFIA; 21st TCS	Arrived from Clark Field, PI at Darwin via Tarakan, Balikpapan, Macassar, and Koepang, probably on 21 December 1941. To ATC USAFIA January 1942. On 14 January 1942, departed Amberley for Darwin via Charleville and arrived at Pearce 13 March 1942. To 21st TCS named Goober Dust as "VHC-WB" 3 April 1942 and formally converted to transport 5 July 1942 by 21st TCS. Transferred out of 21st TCS for use by General Connell circa 1945 and was still in service at Townsville in that year. May also have used local Australian radio call signs "VHC-BR" and "VHC-DX".

Between January and July 1942 the ADAT flew a staggering five million miles (that can be accounted for) and, as readers will note from the table, the aircraft assembled flew using Australian civil registrations as radio call signs. These were painted white over the camouflage of the various aircraft, or on the rear fuselages. Though some disagreement on the presentation of these call signs as worn by the B-18s persists, those shown here and in the detailed production list are believed correct.

It is interesting to note that the official USAAF *Fifth Air Force Month End Inventories of Aircraft – November 1941-May 1944* shows that the inventory of B-18s dropped from eighteen in November 1941 to just three by the end of December 1941, then to just two by February 1942, and remained at zero until July 1945, when one magically reappeared on the listing – probably 37-16 noted below. The aircraft had long since been stripped of its camouflage, and wore late-style US national insignia. In actuality, this listing is fairly accurate as, for all intents and purposes, the B-18s that survived in Australia well into 1942 and beyond were not, strictly speaking, assigned to the Fifth Air Force.

It is known that joint Allied operations in the defense of Java, by which time the decimated and scattered FEAF had been redesignated as the **Fifth Air Force**, included at least two of the former Philippines B-18s, both of which were on hand and reported as 'in commission for combat' as of 25 February 1942. The activities of these aircraft have been utterly lost in the collapse that followed. One is known to have been lost in aerial combat, as noted elsewhere, with all hands. The other apparently escaped to Australia.

On Mindanao, until the end of March 1942, US forces kept flying from Del Monte and vicinity, mainly through the aid of small, inter-island steamers. Then the Japanese finally started concentrating on these vessels and communications were finally cut, isolating each island, and the situation became untenable. It is known that on the day that the Japanese landed at Davao, a mission was run by a B-18 to the west of Mindanao, but the actual invasion force was not located. This may have been the final B-18 combat mission in the islands.

Although some sources have suggested that the invading Japanese forces captured a number of B-18s abandoned in the Philippines, this is something of an academic exercise, since, unlike the P-40s and B-17s, the Japanese appeared to have little or no interest in them. At least two (including No 15) were more or less intact, minus their engines, although it appears that retreating US crews may have placed charges or hand grenades in the cockpits.

Panama

Perhaps as a result of extensive defensive preparations, and possibly also because of its distance from practical Axis operating bases, the vital Panama Canal and its installations were not targeted like Hawaii and the Philippines during the opening days of the war for the US.

In retrospect, this was unquestionably a tactical error of immense proportions on the part of the Axis powers, and one that would come back to haunt them as the war progressed.

The threat of such an attack, however, did require the US to obligate significant resources to the continued defense of the region, and the Axis submarine offensives of 1942 and 1943 – the closest that

Air Corps Canal Zone-based units adopted the same Unit Designator system as used by the GHQAF in the Continental United States, and 44R/1, a B-18A, is the 44th Reconnaissance Squadron Commander's aircraft in this view from inside a unit tent at Albrook Field in 1941. Panama based B-18s were camouflaged very gradually as the year wore on. *Authors' collection*

The 44th Reconnaissance Squadron, based at Albrook Field, was a veteran outfit, and had taken part in a large number of wide-ranging 'Good Will' flights throughout Latin America prior to the war. By 1941 it was operating a mix of B-18s and B-18As, including 44R/6 shown here. *via Robert J. Karrer*

The 44th Reconnaissance Squadron, stationed at Albrook Field on the Pacific side of the Panama Canal, stands on parade with all nine of its B-18s, which at this time had Field Numbers in the 100s, No 112 being nearest. The B-18 was, numerically, the most significant aircraft in the Canal defenses as of 7 December 1941. *Walter 'Matt' Jefferies collection, No.9202, Wright State University*

any Axis unit came to the Canal, so far as can be determined – required that these defenses be far-flung and in depth.

As early as 28 November 1941, however, the leadership of the US Caribbean defense establishment, the Caribbean Defense Command (CDC), had sent the following message to the Trinidad Base Command:

'The current Diplomatic Conference in Washington, with envoys from Japan, is at a standstill. Armed conflict is not improbable. Sabotage and the like will probably follow. This information must be kept restricted to the fewest possible number at this time.'

As noted earlier in the pre-war discussion of Caribbean Air Force assets, the B-18s and B-18As were, as of 7 December 1941, numerically the most significant US warplane types in the entire Caribbean area.

Although augmented by relatively small increments of Boeing B-17E and Consolidated LB-30 and B-24D aircraft, B-18s continued to bear the brunt of long-range patrols designed to provide not only early warning, but a dedicated strike force against any Axis surface threat to the Canal.

By 24 July 1942, with the advent of the radar-equipped B-18B, the newly redesignated Sixth Air Force had worked out a plan with Headquarters, Army Air Forces, which provided for every seventh B-18

An immaculate B-18 of the 44th Reconnaissance Squadron, 44R/5, runs up at the secret Rio Hato aerodrome, 80 air miles to the west of the Canal, in 1941, next to a 32nd Pursuit Group Curtiss P-36A, also still bearing pre-war markings. The unit colors, painted on the engine cowls by this time, are believed to have been red. *Jim Dias*

After 7 December 1941 those B-18 and B-18A aircraft assigned to units in the Caribbean that had not already been camouflaged quickly received war paint. They rarely operated in formation, however, but this trio of what are believed to be 12th Bomb Squadron B-18As wings along at standard patrol altitude over the trackless jungles of the region in 1942. *NARA RG342FH 21363AC*

While serving with the 1st Reconnaissance Squadron out of its base at Rio Hato, Panama, this B-18, AC36-291, became mired up to its wheels on the port side in mud landing at Bluefields, Nicaragua, after completing an Atlantic patrol early in 1942. It was later lost at sea operating out of Curacao with the 59th Bomb Squadron on 19 February 1943. *USAFHRA*

Fully armed, crews perform open-air maintenance on this 1st Reconnaissance Squadron B-18A at Rio Hato, Panama, in early 1942. Note the PSP planking used for the revetment and the underside camouflage, which extends very high up the fuselage sides, unique to the Sixth Air Force. *USAFHRA*

then in the Continental United States (CONUS) retrofitted as a B-18B to be assigned to the Command. The same plan called for Sixth Air Force to then return a standard B-18 or B-18A to CONUS for every B-18B received. By 9 August 1942 the Sixth Air Force was forecasting that twenty standard B-18As in the Command could be thus re-equipped, which would result in these aircraft augmenting thirty-eight B-18Bs that would be assigned to the Sixth Air Force under the plan.

The first three B-18Bs (described in teletype messages as 'B-18As with ASV') were received by the Sixth Air Force on 28 July 1942, and were immediately assigned to the 25th Bomb Group at Camaguey, Cuba.

Subsequent deliveries of B-18Bs to Sixth Air Force units followed by 7 September 1942 and the spread of assignments stipulated by the command indicates the urgency of the widespread need. Eight were flown directly to Edinburgh Field, Trinidad, with four more going to distant Zandery Field, Surinam. Two were assigned to Atkinson Field, British Guiana. Three others were to be based at least temporarily at France Field, Canal Zone, on the Atlantic side of the Isthmus and, in a previously unreported deployment, two went to Seymour Island in the Galapagos in the far Pacific approaches to the Canal, a testament to the fact that the Sixth Air Force was still alert to the possibility of Japanese submarine activities in that area.

By 26 September 1942 the Sixth Air Force could count a total of sixteen B-18s, twenty-two B-18As and thirteen B-18Bs on strength, of which eight B-18s were in the Panama Sector and eight others in the Puerto Rico/Trinidad Sector, five B-18As were in the Panama Sector, and seventeen in the Puerto Rico/Trinidad Sector; all thirteen B-18Bs were in the Puerto Rico/Trinidad Sector. It is important to understand that these were not the only B-18s operating in the region at this point, as the Antisubmarine Command was also deploying B-18B-equipped units to the region on a 'Fire Brigade' basis to aid in the campaign against the U-boats.

By 24 April 1943 the total numbers of B-18 series aircraft assigned to the Sixth Air Force had shifted dramatically. A total of twelve B-18s remained (four in the Panama Sector and eight in the Puerto Rico/Trinidad Sector), but only one B-18A remained in the Command, and this was assigned to the Panama Sector. But the command had no fewer than forty-five B-18Bs, all assigned to the Puerto Rico/Trinidad Sector.

By 3 March 1944 the lengthy primacy of the B-18 series in the Caribbean had past, and only fifteen aircraft remained in the theater. These included three RB-18s, a solitary RB-18A and eleven RB-18Bs, all of the latter assigned to the Antilles Air Command.

The pre-war exercise markings on this B-18A, marked 2/3ASC, indicates she is the number two aircraft of the 3rd Air Support Command, which, as of 26 February 1942, had two aircraft stationed at Savannah, GA. These were almost certainly AC37-495 and 37-510. *NMNA via Capt Rich Dann*

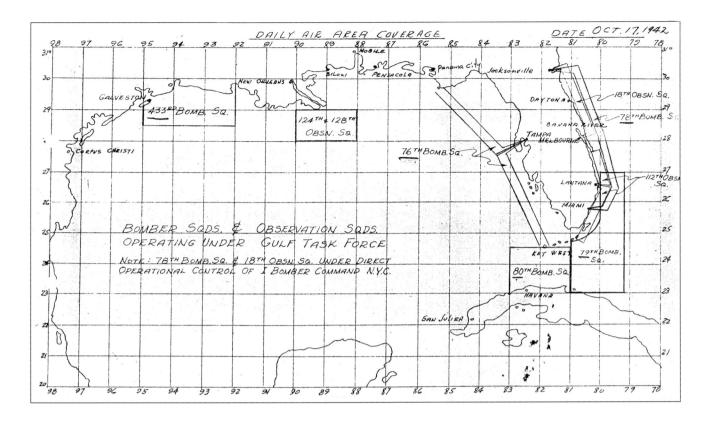

CHAPTER EIGHT

Defending the Continental US and the anti-submarine campaign

The B-18 evolves into the B-18b and B-18c

In nearly every account of the history of the B-18, some version of the foregoing record of their seemingly limited service at the very start of the war for the US in Hawaii and the Philippines has been presented as, for all intents and purposes, all that there was to the story, period. The otherwise authoritative 991-page *Combat Chronology 1941-1945*, part of the outstanding, multi-volume *The Army Air Forces in World War II* prepared by the Office of Air Force History and published in 1973, contains one solitary entry relating to the B-18. That entry, for 18 May 1942, states simply that the '… Seventh Air Force is placed on alert in anticipation of a possible attack on Midway. For the next 10 days, the old B-18s on hand are used on search to supplement the B-17s. VII Bomber Command receives an influx of B-17s during the period and the 72nd Bomb Squadron is converted from B-18s to B-17s.' And that is it.

At the time of the US entry into the Second World War, I Bomber Command of the USAAC assumed responsibility for the coastal and anti-submarine defenses for virtually all of the US Atlantic and Gulf coasts. By October 1942, unbeknown to the defenders at the time, the submarine onslaught had peaked, but the Gulf Task Force had meanwhile been organised to contend with attacks in that vital region. This map shows the breakdown of patrol areas. B-18-equipped units were handed the most critical areas. *USAFHRA*

One might easily conclude, from such official historical treatments, that this relatively little-known incident was as close to combat as the B-18 fleet ever came. In fact, as the account beginning in Chapter 9 will disclose, B-18s of numerous variants were involved in what can only be described as an amazing number of lonely patrols, incidents and attacks off the east and west coasts of the US mainland, and heavily involved in the Caribbean where, indeed, they bore the brunt of anti-submarine actions for nearly all of calendar year 1942 and well into 1943. Yet not a word of these actions made their way into official, published Air Force chronicles of the war.

Without question, the greatest naval confrontation of the war was the so-called Battle of the Atlantic, which without reservation can be described as a mortal struggle to prevent enemy submarines, surface units and raiders from severing the oceanic lifeline between Britain, the US and her dominions – not to mention her extensively scattered fighting forces all over the world. Winston Churchill himself, an historian of keen insights, said that the battle was '…the dominating factor all through the war… Everything happening elsewhere, on land, at sea, or in the air, depended ultimately on its outcome.' Any thorough study of the war will reveal the absolute truth of this assertion. The submarines, in particular, had been defeated not by the early British and US Eighth Air Force ineffective attacks on its bases in France and assembly factories, but rather by new advances in technology and tactics in anti-submarine warfare – which were largely pioneered by our hero subject, the lowly B-18.

The first six months of the war for the US were a virtual case study in crisis management, as the nation mobilised to face real as well as imagined threats from nearly every direction. The Army Air Forces, grappling with incredible expansion in every arm of service, quickly adjusted its organisational structure for the defense of the Continental United States, while at the same time responding to extremely urgent demands for reinforcement in the Far East, the mid-Atlantic, the Caribbean and Alaska.

On the east coast, a new organisation was born that, initially, had sweeping defense responsibilities, I Bomber Command.

I Bomber Command

As noted elsewhere in this account, and the subject of extensive discussion in the aviation history literature, the question of Army and Navy cooperation for the defense of the US coastal areas had been discussed for many years prior to 7 December 1941, but prior to 1940 such discussions had led to little in the way of actual, tangible planning.

In 1923 a Joint Army and Navy Staff Planning Committee was formed to discuss methods of cooperative defense along the US coasts and, on 23 April 1927, that Committee issued a plan for joint action of both services that was a general statement of principles for the command defense activities of both branches. This general statement of principles was apparently all that was agreed upon until the issuance, on 11 September 1935, of FTP-155. This document was really simply a revised copy of the 1927 statement, and was still couched in very general terms. It defined frontiers as geographical units established '…to ensure effective cooperation of the Army and Navy'. It drew no specific plan of action, but stipulated that defense plans for the Eastern Sea Frontier should be prepared by '…collaboration between the Commandant, Third Naval District, and Commanding General First Army.'

It was not until 1940 and 1941, however, that action was taken on the generalisations that had been made during the preceding seventeen years. In those years, coastal frontiers were given geographical limits and actual organisations were established. Provision was also made for liaison between the Army and Navy, but broad principles of cooperation were not specifically defined. On 26 March 1941 the first operation plan of the Eastern Sea Frontier was issued, and provided for the patrol of offshore areas by US Naval aircraft that were to be assigned to the Eastern Sea Frontier.

On 10 July 1941 the Commander of the Eastern Sea Frontier proposed a joint Army-Navy control and information center, to be established on the 14th floor of the Federal Building at 90 Church Street, New York City – an address that was to become imprinted on the memories of many anti-submarine warriors in the months to come. The Army accepted the proposal and operations were provided adjacent to the Headquarters of the North Atlantic Naval Coastal Frontier for the Northeast Defense Command, the First Air Force, a message center room, a coding room and a teletype room. The Navy also installed telephone and teletype facilities and a large operations room. This joint control and information center was completed just four days after the US declared war on Germany. It proved to be a valuable contribution to the war effort and, in fact, became a model for similar joint control rooms that were subsequently established in Miami and in foreign theaters.

On 7 December 1941 the matter of cooperation between the Eastern Defense Command and the Eastern Sea Frontier had been generally established as the result of discussions in previous months. In theory, the Navy was assigned to virtually all operations beyond the coastline but, in fact, it had no suitable aircraft capable of offshore patrols in that area at that time. As a result, the Commander of the Eastern Sea Frontier requested the Commanding General of the Army Eastern Defense Command to undertake this mission. This the Army Air Forces did, and began over-water patrols on the morning of 8 December – a mission for which the units involved had not been trained and had never expected to have to assume under pre-war doctrine.

Left: B-18 series aircraft operated from every single operating base noted on this map until 1 June 1943 at one time or another, with the exception of Kindley Field, Bermuda. *USAFHRA*

Below: I Bomber Command and its scattered subordinate operating units did a magnificent job of combating the submarine menace commencing on 31 December 1941. It was reconfigured as the Army Air Forces Antisubmarine Command (AAFAC) by 1 October 1942, however, in recognition of its highly specialised role. This map vividly displays the growth in coverage of the operational units. *USAFHRA*

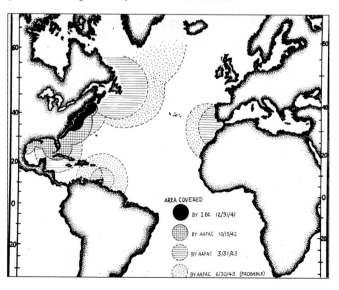

Available defenses at the time against an enemy submarine attack in the Eastern Sea Frontier were pitifully small at the outbreak of war. At that time the Commandant of the North Atlantic Naval Coastal Frontier had at his disposal four PT boats, four SC boats, one 165-foot Coast Guard cutter, six 125-foot Coast Guard cutters, two PG boats and three so-called 'Eagle' boats, or a total of twenty surface craft. In a letter dated 22 December 1941, from the Commandant of the North Atlantic Naval Coastal Frontier to COMINCH, it was stated: 'There is not a vessel available that an enemy submarine could not out-distance when operating on the surface. It most cases, the guns of these vessels would be out-ranged by those of the submarine.'

Naval air protection was equally small, and the total available aircraft amounted to only 103 assorted types, of which no fewer than ninety were trainers, scouts or transport aircraft, entirely unsuited for actual anti-submarine operations.

On 31 December 1941 a Coast Guard cutter reported sighting a periscope in the Portland Channel, and although this sighting was regarded as of dubious accuracy, it was followed by scattered reports of sightings by Army aircraft. On 7 January 1942 an Army aircraft made what was apparently a good sighting of a sub at 4055N 7048W and, on the same day, COMINCH reported that there were indications of at least sixteen submarines proceeding southward from the Newfoundland coast – although he added that the objective of this fleet was not clear. Any doubt as to enemy objectives were promptly clarified, however, by the sinking of the SS *Cyclops* on 11 January 1942 at 4150N 6348W, followed on the 14th by the sinking of the tanker *Norness* at 4028N 7050W. In the remaining seventeen days of that month, thirteen more ships were sent to the bottom in the territory that was the responsibility of the Eastern Sea Frontier.

The seriousness of the situation and the total inadequacy of the Naval defenses to cope with it were well summarised in a letter from Admiral Adolphus Andrews, Commandant of the North Atlantic Naval Coast Frontier, to COMINCH on 14 January 1942. In it, he confessed that:

'…there are no effective planes attached to the Frontier, First, Third, Fourth or Fifth Naval Districts capable of maintaining long-range seaward patrols. One Squadron of single-engine observation scouts, VS 1D1, is being formed at NAS Squantum [this unit had twelve Vought-Sikorsky OS2U-3s by 31 January] and Squadron VS 1D3 was commissioned at NAS New York 31 December 1941 [and had twelve OS2U-3s and three Grumman J2F-5s]. These units are suitable only for inshore patrol and have a relatively short radius of action when carrying two Mark XVII depth charges. Single patrols in unarmed Coast Guard amphibians or flying boats are being maintained at Salem, Floyd Bennett Field and Elizabeth City, NJ. Squadron ZP12 was placed in commission at NAS Lakehurst on 2 January 1942. Of the four ZNPs designated for this unit, two have been detached for duty on the Pacific Coast; consequently, daily patrols are limited at this time to two airships. The Army's First Air Support Command is operating patrols during daylight hours in single-engine land observation aircraft extending about 40 miles offshore from Portland, Main, to Wilmington, NC. These planes are not armed and carry only sufficient fuel for flights of between two and three hours. The pilots are inexperienced in the type of work they are endeavoring to do. Not more than 10 of these observation planes are in the air along the Coastal Frontier at any one time. I Bomber Command has been maintaining, since the week of 7 December 1941, patrols from Westover Field, MA, Mitchel Field, NY, and Langley Field, VA, and, as of 11 January 1942 are commencing patrols from Bangor, ME. These patrols, averaging three aircraft each, have extended, weather permitting and according to the type of aircraft, to a maximum distance of 600 miles to sea. Two flights each day are being made from the aforementioned fields. I Bomber Command has been utilising approximately half of its available equipment in order to maintain these patrols, at the expense of a striking force which could be called upon in case of enemy attack.'

The question is often raised as to why the Army became involved in Naval warfare in the form of hunting and destroying submarines. The above brief description of the events prior to the outbreak of the war for the US, and Admiral Andrews's letter, seem to provide a capsule answer to this question. Pre-war plans for Army and Navy cooperation had not contemplated any such activity on the part of Army aviation, but defenses were totally inadequate at the outbreak of war and the threat was so great that it was necessary to engage in this type of warfare until such time as the emergency had passed – or until the Navy finally became adequately prepared to assume its stated responsibilities.

As Admiral Andrews had candidly reported, the bulk of anti-submarine aircraft operations were carried out by the Army Air Forces via the units of I Bomber Command and, in fact, for many months I Bomber Command provided the backbone of the US air opposition to the Axis submarine assault.

It has been frequently charged that Army pilots were not properly trained for such work and that their equipment was inadequate. This charge is unquestionably accurate, since in none of the pre-war discussions had there been any indications whatsoever that the Army would be called upon for this type of work and, in fact, there had been severe restrictions placed on Army over-water flying, as noted earlier. On the bleak morning of 8 December 1941, when the Army started anti-submarine operations, the aircraft available were not suited to anti-submarine patrol. They were equipped entirely with demolition bombs rather than depth charges, and the air crews had been given little or no instruction in Naval identification or in the best methods of attacking submarines. The six months following the outbreak of war was, in reality, a training and organisation period. Equipment had to be obtained, a tremendous amount of experimentation and tactics development had to be worked out, and a system of centralised control had to be established – aided by an elaborate system of communications, both by wire and radio – built up along the entire Atlantic and Gulf coasts of the mainland US. The Army's centralised control under the Headquarters of I Bomber Command in New York City proved extremely advantageous and allowed that development and training work to go forward rapidly. The Navy's time-honored system of Naval Districts proved very cumbersome, and it was soon learned that the essence of successful anti-submarine operations required a centralised control that could rapidly dispatch aircraft to the scene of a sighting. Unfortunately, the enemy had accurately gauged the inadequacy of the US anti-submarine forces, and struck heavily between January and July 1942. Nearly 1,400,000 tons of shipping was sunk in the Eastern Sea Frontier and the Gulf Sea Frontiers during this period.

The history of anti-submarine warfare on our coasts is best illustrated in the May 1943 issue of the *Monthly Intelligence Report*, which concluded with a series of charts showing the sinkings of merchant vessels, and the lethal or damaging attacks on the submarines by six-month periods from the beginning of the war to that time. The attacks on the US coast between September 1941 and February 1942 are clear, and it is indicated that the subs operated very nearly without any risk to themselves whatsoever. In the six months following February 1942, however, attacks on submarines became much more numerous, and the enemy virtually abandoned the area by first leaving the Atlantic seaboard, and subsequently leaving the Gulf of Mexico, after defenses there had been organised in June 1942. The activities and aircraft available for use by I Bomber Command units are shown in the accompanying tables.

I Bomber Command Operations January 1942-October 1942

Month	Hours Flown	Subs Sighted	Subs Attacked	Ships Sunk	Total Tonage	Average Daily Sub Density
January 1942	3,134	11	7	13	92,955	3.4
February 1942	4,766	18	12	19	128,585	5.9
March 1942	7,247	35	26	30	193,478	5.7
April 1942	6,328	34	19	26	138,521	8.1
May 1942	6,618	23	12	47	249,741	11.1
June 1942	5,439	40	29	32	162,290	9.0
July 1942	6,799	24	16	18	73,700	14.9
August 1942	5,685	14	8	3	9,489	8.5
September 1942	6,822	5	2	1	6,511	4.7
October 1942	6,410	4	1	0	0	2.2

Tactical Army Bombardment Aircraft In Use – I Bomber Command December 1941-October 1942

Month	DB-7B or A-20B	A-29	B-17	B-18	B-24	B-25	B-34	Number with Radar
December 1941	–	15	12	20	–	13	–	0
January 1942	55	–	11	13	–	43	–	0
February 1942	55	17	12	9	–	26	–	0
March 1942	50	16	11	23	–	29	–	4
April 1942	50	26	5	23	–	31	–	16
May 1942	47	16	15	22	–	27	–	33
June 1942	45	25	14	26	–	40	–	22
July 1942	32	23	12	41	–	50	58	50
August 1942	31	22	12	30	–	52	48	40
September 1942	28	20	13	22	2	41	40	34
October 1942	22	19	12	14	3	35	43	27

The contributions that AAF aircraft, and particularly the B-18 series, made to the defense of Allied shipping on the US coasts during the period noted in the table cannot be measured adequately by bare statistics, or by the number of Axis submarines claimed sunk or damaged. The Douglas DB-7Bs, aircraft intended for Britain but taken over by the AAF, joined by some early A-20Bs, were arguably very inadequate as anti-submarine aircraft, as the single pilot was fully occupied flying a sophisticated aircraft and the rear gunner had very poor visibility downward. Although they could carry a third crewman in the bombardier nose, this was seldom done. It was the constant presence and patrols of these waters by aircraft – of any type – that forced submarines to submerge frequently and thus lose their targets, which was of unquestionably very great value.

Early in 1942 it became evident that the submarine could not be eliminated as a menace simply by throwing defensive patrols around shipping. It was clear that the mobility of aircraft must be used to the fullest extent possible and that arrangements should be made to shift aircraft to any threatened point without delay.

As of activation, I Bomber Command was, at least on paper, a formidable organisation, encompassing as it did nearly all of the tactical bombardment and many of the observation units stationed on the eastern seaboard. Units assigned are reflected in the accompanying table.

Although the equipment, as shown in the 'official' AAF table herewith, reflects essentially state-of-the-art equipment as of activation, within days after Pearl Harbor the equipment picture changed radically, as most of the B-17s, LB-30s and B-25s were bled off to the Pacific – and nearly all of these units were then provided with either a mix of repossessed Douglas DB-7Bs, A-20As or, significantly, more Douglas B-18s.

For the purposes of this study, reducing the deployment of active AAF I Bomber Command assets as of the declaration of war requires an almost day-by-day examination, which is beyond the practical limits of this volume. A record of the telephone exchanges between Major McCaffery of the First Air Force and Major Donald R. Lyon of I Bomber Command as of 0300 hours on 8 December 1941, illustrates this point. The orders issued were as follows: 'Direct that all airplanes on alert be prepared for over-water patrol. All B-25s to go to Mitchel Field as soon as possible and operate from there.' Major Lyon then relayed these orders to Major Paul C. Ashworth of the 2nd Bomb Group at Langley Field and arrangements were thrown together to '…get surplus pilots from the 18th Recon Squadron and the 22nd Bomb Group to augment the 2nd Bomb Group', which had just received two B-25s and five B-18s, but did not have enough pilots for the B-18s. A second call from the First Air Force, at 0345, notified the 2nd Bomb Group that '…a threat from the French Fleet exists'. Major Lyon promised that a patrol

I Bomber Command Units as of 14 January 1942

Parent Group	Subordinate Squadrons	Operating Station	Equipment
HHS, I Bomber Command 2nd Bombardment Group (H)*	20th Bomb Squadron (H)	Mitchel Field, NY Langley Field VA	Douglas B-18A – 2 North American B-25 – 2 North American B-25A – 1 North American B-25B – 8 Douglas B-18A – 2 Douglas B-18 – 5 Boeing B-17 – 2
	49th Bomb Squadron (H)** 96th Bomb Squadron (H) 41st Recon Squadron (H) (attached)***	 Mitchel Field, NY Langley Field, VA Langley Field, VA	 Boeing B-17 – 7 Douglas B-18A – 3 Boeing B-17E – 2
34th Bombardment Group (H)	4th Bomb Squadron 7th Bomb Squadron 18th Bomb Squadron 1st Recon Squadron (H) (attached)	Westover Field, MA Westover Field, MA Westover Field, MA Westover Field, MA	Consolidated LB-30 – 4 North American B-25 – 1 North American B-25A – 2 North American B-25B – 19 Douglas B-18 – 8 Consolidated LB-30 – 1
43rd Bombardment Group (H)	63rd Bomb Squadron 64th Bomb Squadron 65th Bomb Squadron 13th Reconnaissance Squadron (H) (attached)	Bangor, ME Bangor, ME Bangor, ME Bangor, ME	Consolidated LB-30 – 7 Lockheed A-29 – 6 Douglas A-20A – 1 Douglas B-18 – 1 Douglas B-18M – 3 Douglas DB-7B – 55

Notes: * The 2nd Bomb Group, at this point, in actuality had only one operating Squadron actually under its control at Langley, as the 20th Bomb Squadron, as shown, had been detached and was operating semi-autonomously out of Mitchel Field.

** The 49th Bomb Squadron, although shown as a 2nd Bomb Group unit at this point, was under a number of "conflicting movement orders, and it literally scattered all over the United States," so could not actually be counted as an effective organization at the time.

*** As recently as April 14, 1941, the 41st Recon Squadron, which at that time was at Langley Field as an element of the First Air Force Bomber Command, had been brought up to statutory strength with eight B-18s. Thus, within eight months, the unit, typical of the period, had lost five of these to other units and gained the two new B-17Es, the envy of their sister units.

would be accomplished and, incredibly, it was suggested that I Bomber Command move, lock, stock and barrel, to New York City, and that Major McCaffery would then start planning a patrol. Major Lyon then gave the First Air Force, while almost certainly trying to sort out exactly how such a move would be accomplished, a preliminary estimate of the aircraft status of I Bomber Command as of that moment. He reported that '…we have two B-17s and one B-18 at Bangor, two B-18s at Westover Field, twelve B-25s and eight B-18s at Langley', but that not all of these aircraft were in commission for action. The order of the day is exemplified at the subordinate command level by a telephone conversation between I Bomber Command and Major Howard Moore, CO of the 43rd Bomb Group at Bangor, ME, which took place at 1415 hours that day. I Bomber Command instructed the Group to:

'…conduct reconnaissance today over as much as possible of the area Portland – Cape Sable – 4140N 6530W – Cape Cod using one B-18 of the 43rd BG and one B-17A of the 13th Recon Squadron. Land at Westover upon completion of the mission. Both planes will be attached to the 1st Reconnaissance Squadron on their arrival at Westover. Take a full load of 300lb demolition bombs and land with bombs. Report enemy surface craft to Army Airways Communications Service (AACS).'

I Bomber Command settled down after the initial rush to action station and, by 11 January 1942, was maintaining patrols from Westover, Mitchel and Langley Fields and, from that date, commenced patrols from Bangor. These patrols averaged three aircraft each and had been

extended, weather permitting, to as much as 600 miles out to sea. Two flights each day were being made from these fields and about 50% of the available aircraft were being utilised, at the expense of a strike force that could be called upon in case of an actual attack. For all intents and purposes, during the entire month of December 1941 I Bomber Command had only three organisations that were actually engaged in patrols: the 1st Recon Squadron at Westover, which flew 117 missions; the semi-autonomous 20th Bomb Squadron at Mitchel Field, which flew the vast majority of missions with 152; and the mix of small squadrons of the 2nd Bomb Group at Langley, which could manage only eighty-six missions.

In January 1942 I Bomber Command had been reinforced to include the under-strength 43rd Bomb Group at Bangor (which turned in only seven missions), the semi-autonomous 13th Reconnaissance Squadron, also at Bangor, which managed eleven missions, the 1st Recon Squadron at Westover, which flew a very respectable total of eighty-one missions, the forming 13th Bomb Group at Westover (eighteen missions), the 3rd Recon Squadron at Mitchel (twenty-eight missions), the large 20th Bomb Squadron, also at Mitchel (ninety-seven missions) and the 2nd Bomb Group at Langley (sixty-seven missions).

By February 1942 I Bomber Command had been reshaped once again, and now was composed of the 45th Bomb Group, 13th Bomb Group and 2nd Bomb Group, with the semi-autonomous 92nd Reconnaissance and 3rd Reconnaissance Squadrons. These organisations completed a very respectable total of 591 patrol missions during that harsh winter month, with the 45th Bomb Group leading with no fewer than 285 missions.

The anti-submarine tempo continued to increase in March 1942, when essentially the same subordinate units as had been on hand in February completed 1,219 patrol missions, of which 150 were regarded as 'special' and the remainder 'routine'. It is significant that, as of 18 March 1942, I Bomber Command had yet to receive a single ASV-equipped aircraft – and it should also be noted that not a solitary aircraft in the Command had Identification Friend or Foe (IFF) equipment. The 40th and 80th Bomb Squadrons (M) were still nominally assigned to I Bomber Command as of 29 March, but had been formally designated as operational training units.

In April 1942 the composition of the Command was once again subtly transformed. The 45th, 13th and 2nd Bomb Groups all remained organic, but the 92nd Recon Squadron had been redesignated as the 433rd Bomb Squadron (M), while the 3rd Recon Squadron had been redesignated as the 393rd Bomb Squadron (M). These organisational shuffles have perpetuated numerous gaffs in historical references to these units. The operational tempo had also soared, with 1,960 patrols completed, of which 621 had been between Wilmington, NC, and Miami, one of the submarine 'hot spot' areas at the time. The 45th Bomb Group led with 576 'routine' patrols and six 'special' missions.

I Bomber Command subordinate organisations remained static through May 1942, but the total number of missions completed rose to 2,126 and, once again, the 45th Bomb Group performed the most, with 733 'routine' patrols and sixty-eight 'specials.' On 23 May 1942 a Detachment of I Bomber Command (sometimes cited as of this point as **First Bomber Command**), consisting of ten ASV-equipped Douglas B-18s, was dispatched on a rush basis to the Florida area, where they reported to the Commander of the Third Air Force for supply and administration and to the Commander, **Gulf Sea Frontier**, for actual anti-submarine operations. Three days later, nothing less than a direct order from General 'Hap' Arnold, via Col Sorenson, Director of Bombardment, instructed that five more ASV-equipped B-18s were to be rushed to I Bomber Command for '…Temporary Duty to the unit commanded by Col Dolan [this became the 1st Sea Search Attack Group, which was semi-autonomous, reporting directly to the CG, AAF, and was not a I Bomber Command organic unit]. These aircraft are to report to Col Dolan through the Commander, Gulf Sea Frontier in Miami.' This extraordinary order resulted from a telephonic plea from the Chief of Staff, First Air Force, who reported that all ten of Col Dolan's ASV-equipped B-18s, were '…engaged in exhaustive searches against two subs now in the Florida area. Additional submarines had been located and it was of the utmost importance that they be taken under an exhaustive search.' The five additional ASV B-18s came directly from the impromptu ASV School at West Palm Beach, FL, commanded by Col Monahan, and were supposed to be returned to the school after the crisis. This was the first and only I Bomber Command association with B-18Bs before the entire anti-submarine war changed, with the activation of the AAFAC.

Between June and August 1942 the major subordinate units of I Bomber Command remained the 45th, 13th and 2nd Bomb Groups, as well as the 393rd Bomb Squadron (M), but the 433rd Bomb Squadron (M) was merged with the 17th Bomb Group and a Detachment of the 2nd Bomb Group to form what was called the **Gulf Task Force** to adjust once again to a major shift in U-boat activity. This ad hoc, thrown-together organisation had temporary headquarters at Charleston, SC, but ultimately moved to Miami. Besides the I Bomber Command units detached, it also commanded all Civil Air Patrol units then engaged in anti-submarine patrols in the Gulf Sea Frontier as well as the **97th Observation Squadron, 66th Observation Group** at Miami. Seldom noted in 'official' records, this unit had four B-18s assigned at this time. The Detachments from the 2nd Bomb Group alone consisted of twenty B-18s. During this three month-period, and before morphing into the **Army Air Forces Antisubmarine Command (AAFAC)** in October 1942, units of the Command flew an astonishing 7,334 patrols, of which the majority were flown by the 45th Bomb Group once again, with 2,504 patrols.

During September 1942, the last full month of I Bomber Command anti-submarine activities, aircraft of the Command flew 1,842 missions, totaling 6,822hr 24min flying time with units operating from Westover Field, MA, to Galveston, TX. It is interesting to note that the Command A-2 Section (Intelligence) issued a special Policy Statement to all elements on the 25th of that month, stating that '…the use of the word "Radar" will not be used in reports to either higher or lower units. All special equipment will be referred to as SE (Special Equipment) in reports.' During the final full month of existence, I Bomber Command aircraft strength was reported as shown in the accompanying table.

The Army Air Forces Antisubmarine Command (AAFAC) was activated on 15 October 1942, and essentially absorbed all of the units and the mission of I Bomber Command. Students of the subject have frequently been confused by the fact that, after AAFAC had successfully completed its mission and anti-submarine responsibilities were returned to the Navy in the western hemisphere, AAFAC was again redesignated as I Bomber Command on 24 August 1943.

II and III Bomber Command

Like I Bomber Command, II Bomber Command and III Bomber Command were also activated on 5 September 1941. While the intent was basically the same as the rationale for creating their east-coast counterpart, these two commands were rather quickly diluted and their tactical units either dispersed or converted to intensive operational training.

For its part, II Bomber Command had responsibility for what was fundamentally the **Second Air Force** area of responsibility in the Pacific Northwestern part of the mainland United States, and was headquartered at Fort George Washington, in Washington state. Similarly, III Bomber Command, at least briefly, stretched from Savannah, GA, down through Florida and included the large fields at Drew Field, GA, and MacDill Field, FL. The bombardment element of the **Third Air Force** was headquartered at Drew, and the **Headquarters and Headquarters Squadron** there had single examples of the Douglas C-67, B-18A and

I Bomber Command Aircraft Strength

Type	Number Assigned	Number in Commission	% of Aircraft in Commission	Total Hours Flown by Type	Hours Flown by A/C in Commission
Boeing B-17E	13	10	77%	30	3:00
Douglas B-18	22	17	77%	35	2:04
North American B-25	41	35	85%	79	2:15
Lockheed A-29	21	17	81%	53	3:06
Lockheed B-34	33	22	66%	20	0:55
Douglas DB-7B	28	22	86%	51	2:03

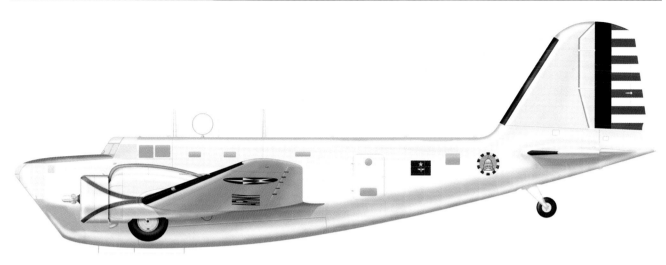

VIP B-18A Artwork by Rich Dann

C-49 for VIP transport purposes by 26 February 1942, while the **Headquarters and Headquarters Squadron, III Bomber Command**, with Headquarters at MacDill Field, FL, had one B-18A as well. The activities of III Bomber Command are often overlooked, but between 24 December 1941 and 18 August 1942 the Command flew no fewer than 1,000 anti-submarine missions.

Individual units and stations of both of these parent organisations were credited with anti-submarine campaign activities. As of activation, II Bomber Command included maneuver units, and those employing B-18s or B-23s are noted in the accompanying table.

In reality, although the elements of II Bomber Command looked very impressive on paper, in fact only a few of the subordinate squadrons were at anything approaching operational strength, and the 42nd, 7th and 39th Bomb Groups were, for all intents and purposes, operational training units awaiting deployments overseas to the fighting fronts.

In fact, II Bomber Command was turned over to the control of the **Fourth Air Force** just after Pearl Harbor. Eight aircraft of the 42nd Bomb Group were moved from Boise, ID, to Portland Air Base, OR, and Paine Field, WA, where they took part in very poorly coordinated (and poorly documented) anti-submarine and coastal patrol missions. At the same time steps were taken to move the bulk of the medium and light bombardment aircraft of Second Air Force to aerodromes west of the Cascades. The 17th Bomb Group at Pendleton Field, OR was directed to have all of its aircraft loaded

II Bomber Command Organization, September 1941

Parent Organization	Subordinate Units	Station	Aircraft Assigned
17TH Bomb Group (M)	34th Bomb Squadron (M)	Pendleton, OR	Douglas B-18A
			Douglas B-23
			North American B-25
			North American B-25A
	37th Bomb Squadron (M)		Douglas B-18
			North American B-25
	95th Bomb Squadron (M)		Douglas B-23
			North American B-25
	89th Recon Squadron (M) (attached)		Douglas B-18
			North American B-25
42nd Bomb Group (M)	70th Bomb Squadron (M)	Gowen Field, Boise, ID	Douglas B-18A
	75th Bomb Squadron (M)		Douglas B-18M
			Douglas B-18A
	76th Bomb Squadron (M)		Douglas B-18A
	16th Recon Squadron (M) (attached)		Douglas B-18
7th Bomb Group (H)	9th Bomb Squadron (H)	Fort Douglas Air Base, UT	Boeing B-17
	11th Bomb Squadron (H)		Boeing B-17
	22nd Bomb Squadron (H)		Boeing B-17
	88th Recon Squadron (H) (attached)		Boeing B-17
39th Bomb Group (H)	60th Bomb Squadron (H)	Geiger Field, Spokane, WA	Boeing B-17B – 13
	61st Bomb Squadron (H)		Boeing B-17D – 1
	62nd Bomb Squadron (H)		Boeing B-17E – 2
	12th Recon Squadron (H) (attached)		Douglas B-18 – 2
			Douglas B-18A – 2
			Douglas A-20C – 3

143

with bombs, to be as fully equipped as possible with machine guns and to be on the alert from 0300 hours on 9 December. However, anything near normal wartime bomb loads were only available at McChord Field, a well-established Air Corps station, and at Portland and Everett for one mission by available aircraft. The Group, incredibly, was also short of some 164 .30 and .50 caliber machine guns, which had been transferred to overseas units to try to bolster the rapidly expanding strength there. Groups and subordinate Squadrons were also dispersed to the maximum extent possible.

The advent of the B-18B:
the forgotten stop-gap weapon

Col Harry J. Halberstadt, USAF (Ret), in an interview with this writer in 1994, put it this way: 'Had Douglas set out to produce the perfect anti-submarine aircraft in 1934, they could not have arrived at a more perfect orchestration of qualities than the aircraft that had evolved into the B-18B of 1942.' With more than 1,000 hours on B-18s in lonely, often nocturnal combat patrols, Colonel Halberstadt – like every other crewman who served on B-18s contacted – sung the praises of the lumbering old girl.:

> 'It did not need to be fast. In fact, the ideal cruise speed also happened to be the ideal patrol speed. It did not need high-altitude capabilities, as the normal operating altitude for most of our patrols was between 300 and 500 feet. It offered room to rest, prepare meals, attend to bodily needs, move about with ease, a perfect platform for observers in all positions, extremely comfortable flight and handling qualities, with no unbearable vices and, above all other considerations for Caribbean patrols, if the old girl went down at sea in heavily shark-infested waters, she would float for ever!'

Rarely, if ever illustrated before, this B-18B wears the unique neutral sea gray over white anti-submarine scheme used for a period by anti-submarine units on the East Coast of the U.S. *via Dana Bell*

This latter characteristic, added with an utter sense of confidence that nearly every crew member recalled, was of inestimable value to crew morale.

The B-18A, as designed, and as Colonel Halberstadt described it, was an almost perfect mount for all manner of anti-submarine gear at precisely the moment that it was most urgently needed. Seldom in aviation history have so many elements of a complex equation come together so fortuitously.

From the time that Germany, Italy and the US declared war upon each other in December 1941, the character of the Axis submarine battle in the Atlantic, which had been ongoing against British and French assets for some time already, changed dramatically. As noted in the foregoing discussion of the ever-increasing activities of the pioneering I Bomber Command, the German U-boat high command ordered a step-up of activity in keeping with the increased ocean traffic, particularly turning attention to US coastwise routes, where the pickings were, initially, incredibly easy. At the start of the war for the US, unarmed and unescorted US and Allied ships died within sight of citizens on our own shores in very large numbers. The hard-strapped US Navy deployed all available odds and ends of patrol boats, planes and blimps to do battle, but it was nothing less than sheer improvisation. Deep in convoy defense, the British lifeline and urgent concerns in the Pacific, the Navy was privately relieved to get help from the Army land-based bombers.

But before commencing this detailed examination of the recorded actions of B-18s and their crews, it is necessary to discuss the evolution of the definitive B-18B (the second and 'official' USAAF aircraft variant to gain this designation) – and the little-known B-18C.

Nearly every standard reference book states that '...of the 217 B-18As built, 122 were converted to B-18Bs'. Precisely how this number was arrived at is something of a mystery, as not more than 112 were in fact formally converted and redesignated as B-18Bs by the USAAF. What is more, by the time the first of these conversions had been completed, the total USAAF inventory of B-18As had been reduced, by accidents and operational losses, from 217 to 181. Consequently, not less than 62% of the surviving B-18As went through this very extensive conversion, if not a total metamorphosis, one of the most extensive programs ever undertaken by the AAF to that time.

The US had, as a result of exceptionally close links with the British in the pre-Pearl Harbor period, been following the development of airborne radar technology by the Royal Air Force with great interest – and in particular the British adaptation of this gear to locating surface targets, especially surfaced submarines, which were a very serious threat to the prosecution of the war. Indeed, German submarines were often seen in action along the entire US east coast, and an urgent and coordinated response was vital. Although fraught with fierce doctrinal debates between the Army and the Navy, the so-called Arnold-McNarney-McCain Agreement was hammered out, which resulted in a workable compromise: anti-submarine operations were to be the Navy's, but, and vital to this account, control of all land-based, long-range air assets belonged to the Army Air Forces. Arnold himself was satisfied with this arrangement because it meant that, at least for the time being, his AAF would have complete and uncontested control over long-range attack planning and operations against the German submarine menace.

This entire process – including the selection of the B-18A as the aircraft of choice for the Army Air Forces program that followed – had actually got under way far earlier than previously reported. One B-18A, which had already been assigned to the Materiel Division at Wright Field for assorted tests, AC37-587, Materiel Division Field Number MD/119, had been sent to Boston and Mitchel Field as early as 25 April 1941 with a 'special Plexiglas nose' and a prototype ASV-10 device designed by Western Electric, where it was engaged in unspecified radar trials with a Royal Canadian Air Force (RCAF) Boeing 247D, No 7655. Following this, events moved very rapidly. By 31 December 1941 the Technical Executive of the National Defense Research Committee had already confirmed to the Chief of the Experimental Engineering Branch at Wright Field, LTC B. W. Chidlaw, that at least three repossessed British Consolidated LB-30 Liberators had:

'…already been fixed up. I am not so much worried about the dispositions of these as I am about what action we should take with the B-18s. We have already ordered Plexiglas noses for the B-18s, and if we want to get eight or ten of these airplanes fixed up by the end of February, we should know in the next two or three days so we can take necessary action to get the radio equipment changed.'

The urgency in these messages was nearly palpable, as is the clear implication that detailed engineering measurements to fit the aircraft with the British ASV-10 radar and Plexiglas radome noses had already been completed by 31 December 1941. The LB-30s held the honor of becoming the first US aircraft to mount the British radar, but these were being rushed to Panama and the Pacific as fast as they could be completed and crews trained, as the common wisdom at the end of December 1941 was that the Japanese might be contemplating attacks on the west coast or the vital Panama Canal, and the radar-equipped LB-30s were the only aircraft with sufficient range to provide limited 'picket duty' on the ocean approaches to vital installations in California and the Canal Zone.

It is clear from these deliberations that, within days of Pearl Harbor, very high-level decisions had been made to equip two aircraft types with the British ASV-10 radar: the windfall LB-30s, euphemistically 'repossessed' from British contracts, and the B-18As. In retrospect, the decision was little short of a textbook case of 'the right aircraft, at the right place, at the right time'. The LB-30s and later B-24s became submarine killers par excellence, and the aircraft that evolved into the B-18B held the line in the interim, and did so marvellously well. This central accomplishment of the B-18 series was not celebrated at all during the war, and, perhaps because of the singular lack of publicity, only recently celebrated since.

B-18A (it was apparently not redesignated as type B-18B until later) AC37-477 had been equipped with 'secret radio equipment' as early as 18 September 1941. In this view, however, showing what was termed AGL-1 equipment as of 10 June 1942, the aircraft is unusual in that it has not been camouflaged, has the abbreviated aircraft serial number on the nose, and the radar gear and Plexiglas radome is mounted on a metal 'balcony'. Note also that the lower nose gun blister has been replaced by a simple glass dome with no gun provision. *MIT Museum RL-142-2*

The Aircraft Radio Laboratory at Wright Field, Ohio, had provided the nucleus of interest in airborne radar that helped facilitate the process that followed, particularly with regard to the ASV aspects. The Lab had been in the process of developing fifteen radar units for the Northrop P-61 Black Widow night fighter, then under development, but these were, according to some sources, eventually installed in B-18Bs instead. The efforts at Wright Field were linked to those at the Massachusetts Institute of Technology (MIT). An organisation known as the 'Roof Group' had, as early as the spring of 1941, begun experiments to adapt an experimental Airborne Intercept (AI) 10 centimetre microwave radar apparatus for installation as an ASV (search) radar using, of all things, the experimental and exotic Lockheed XJO-3, a Lockheed 12-A with fixed landing gear (which had been acquired by the Navy in October 1938 to test carrier-deck performance of a twin-engine aircraft with tricycle landing gear). A similar system had been crafted for installation in an early Martin PBM-1 Mariner flying boat during the autumn of 1941, but did not actually fly in this configuration until 3 January 1942.

According to an account in Henry E. Guerlac's excellent *Radar in World War II* (Tomash Publishers, 1987) a conference orchestrated by the NDRC between MIT Radiation Lab staff and the AAF Radio Lab staff at Wright Field, shortly after Pearl Harbor, resulted in an urgent request by one of the officers present to make the new gear available for mounting in B-18 series aircraft '…or some similar type' on what was essentially a crash-basis program. Ironically, the original intent of this program was not to combat German submarines in the Atlantic or Caribbean but, rather, for Pacific patrol work, where the threat of a Japanese attack was regarded as imminent. The 10cm sets that were under discussion at the time were, with slight changes, very similar to those being installed in British Bristol Beaufighter night fighters.

The Air Corps Materiel Division wasted little time in acting on what became project CTI-446. A Technical Instruction was issued on 7 January 1942 ordering Air Force Combat Command (AFCC) to make ten B-18As on call to the Materiel Division for the express purpose of installing the Plexiglas noses to accommodate what was now termed ASV-10. The AFCC was further instructed to provide the Division with the Air Corps serial numbers of the aircraft selected, and the Division was tasked to perform the modifications, apparently in concert with MIT, at East Boston Airport, Massachusetts. Four of these aircraft were drawn from Eastern Defense Command assets and the other six from Western Defense Command.

A close-up of the non-standard, segmented Plexiglas radome and mount for the AGL-1 spinner on B-18A AC37-477 as of 2 June 1942. This aircraft was later redesignated as type B-18B. It was used extensively for tests of various installations and was lost in an accident at East Boston Airport on 15 June 1943. It ended its days as an Instructional Airframe (Class 26) at Grenier Field. *MIT Museum RL DR-13*

It is safe to say that the instrument array was not exactly the same on any two B-18Bs. This is AC37-600 (note the Radio Call Sign placard on the instrument panel), showing some of the scopes and instruments unique to tests of the AN/APG-1 gear. Note that several of the instruments on the right (the co-pilot's panel) turned 90 degrees to the right on the board. *MIT Museum RL-91-146*

This is the instrument panel on B-18A AC37-477 (it had not yet been redesignated as a B-18B), with the very non-standard array including the central panel for the AGL-1 scope as of 1 June 1942. *MIT Museum RL-AG-142-9*

Another view of B-18A AC37-477 looking forward, but this time showing the equipment operator. This was the location for most radar operators on operational B-18Bs, more or less the same location as the navigator's station on most standard B-18 series aircraft. *MIT Museum RL-AG-142-5*

Lt Holm, on the left, made history as the first pilot to fly a B-18 using the AGL pilot's indicator and range meter in B-18A AC37-477, installed at the MIT labs in great secrecy. This and similar wartime developments, rushed to operational status by an outstanding combination of the best scientific minds and military leadership, enabled the Allies to defeat the Axis submarine menace by early 1943. *MIT Museum RL-113-32*

The first two of the ten aircraft to be modified were completed at Wright Field starting on 2 January 1942. It was originally intended to convert all ten there, but in the event the other eight were completed at the San Antonio Air Depot. Following this, the plan had been to fly them to Scott Field, IL, for the crews to be trained on the equipment.

In February 1942 ten Army crews were ordered to San Antonio Air Depot (SAAD) and thence to MIT to witness the installation of ASV equipment in their B-18s and to be educated in its use. From the Fourth Air Force came six aircraft and crews, piloted by LTC W. C. Dolan, Capt A. K. Breckenridge, 1Lt Leo J. Foster, 1Lt Francis B. Carlson, 2Lt William J. Foley and 2Lt John F. Zinn. From Langley Field came four aircraft and crews: one pilot/commander remains unknown, but the others were 1Lt Moensch, 1Lt Lolley and 2Lt F. A. V. Hartbrodt. These crews then 'traded in' at SAAD the B-18As they had flown down for ASV-configured aircraft and flew on to Boston, wholly independent of each other. Colonel Dolan's trip was representative. He admitted that he was 'astounded' at the performance of the radar equipment. At supper, he was informed that a Navy observation aircraft had been lost at sea some 50 miles offshore. If the ASV equipment just installed in his aircraft was everything the lab men maintained, that plane could be located, reasoned the Colonel. A member of the MIT lab accompanied Col Dolan and his crew, as they were not yet adept in the fine points of the gear. Difficulties prevented take-off before 1300 hours, and the drift of the lost aircraft was estimated as being to the north of the area being searched by Navy surface vessels. At about 1500 hours the ASV set picked up an indication at 20 miles. They reached the area but could see nothing visually. A rising star shell assured them that they had located the missing aircraft, however. A destroyer was summoned and the crew was saved. Thus the very first use of a USAAF ASV equipped B-18B involved the salvation of a US Navy patrol aircraft crew, an irony not lost upon those involved.

Tests at New London with 'friendly' US submarines indicated that a decided advantage was held by ASV-equipped aircraft. The subs were usually caught in most instances before they could submerge – and this with conning tower lookouts who had been briefed to watch for the aircraft.

The original plan was to have each ASV-equipped aircraft return to its home station to carry on searches from there. Col Dolan, however, maintained that such a dispersion of the force so happily brought together at Boston would dissipate its effectiveness, and proposed that they be formed as a unit operating from the same base.

AC37-477 at East Boston Airport in June 1942 is still resplendent in pre-war, non-camouflaged finish. This aircraft served as a test platform for many anti-submarine systems and earned a place in aviation history for this contribution that has gone unheralded until now. *MIT Museum RL-AG-142-2*

Right: AC38-589 was one of the first ten B-18As converted to B-18B configuration, and this was very nearly the definitive configuration for the B-18B that resulted after the service decided on redesignating them. Note that the pre-war 'red ball' in the center of the national insignia is still in place and that the dorsal gun is in place in the retracted turret. The service life of this aircraft was cut short on 6 September 1942 when a ground-looping P-47B, AC41-5986, collided with it on landing at Mitchel Field, NY. *MIT Museum RL-AS-113-3*

Meanwhile, elsewhere within the Army bureaucracy, it was not until 21 February 1942 that the Chief of the Field Service Section, LTC J. H. Hicks, raised the question of changing '…the model designation of B-18 airplanes equipped with "special radio equipment" in order to differentiate them from other B-18 series aircraft.

Less than a week later, the Chief of the Materiel Division's Experimental Engineering Section, Col F. O. Carroll, reported that work on the ten aircraft covered by CTI-446 to modify them to carry Radiation Laboratory ASV-10 equipment had commenced. He went on to report that '…in order to make this installation, it is necessary to install a special upper Plexiglas nose, to move the bombsight and install a plate glass window in the lower nose section, to change the generator on the left engine to 200 amps, and to change the generator on the right engine to 100 amps, 12 volts. As of this date, the following B-18A airplanes have been modified at Wright Field and are now at the Boston Municipal Airport for tests of the equipment and training of crews:

AC37-517 & AC37-593'

A close-up of the nose configuration on the port side of B-18A (later B-18B) AC38-589. Compare this with later configurations illustrated herein. Only the first ten aircraft converted had this profile. *MIT Museum RL-AS-113-38*

The definitive form of the nose radome on standard B-18Bs is shown in AC38-599, Field Number 112, which had made a wheels-up landing at Wright Field on 3 June 1942 after an in-flight engine fire with Capt Elmer E. McKesson in command. The damage appears minimal, but the aircraft went to Class 26, had the radar gear removed, and was redesignated as an RB-18A. *Wright State University*

A good study of the definitive radome configuration on standard B-18B aircraft as shown on AC38-599 after a wheels-up landing on 3 June 1942 at Wright Field. Note that the central gun blister in the lower nose position was replaced by an optically flat panel, leaving no forward-firing guns. Although it appears to be repairable, the aircraft went to Class 26 and had the radar gear removed. *Wright State University*

He also reported that, following the virtually custom-made modifications to the first two aircraft noted above, that eight more B-18As were to be modified at the San Antonio Air Depot (SAAD), where all subsequent conversions were carried out. The other eight aircraft were AC38-586, 38-590, 38-606, 37-561, 38-589, 37-470, 37-538 and 37-574. The first four of these were completed by 6 March and the other four by the 16th.

In the meantime, the Air Service Command was pressing Wright Field for a decision on the recommended model designation change for these ten aircraft, as security issues and day-to-day communications regarding the aircraft demanded that some common definition needed to be applied. Referring to the aircraft repeatedly as 'B-18As with special radio equipment' was simply not working, and confusion was rampant.

Exactly a month after the Japanese attack on Pearl Harbor, the first Wright Field document devoted to this subject, and entitled 'Modification of B-18A for ASV-10 Installation', was assigned a project code, as noted above, of CTI-446.

Detailed drawings, probably of a British installation, had apparently been rushed to Wright Field as a complete suite of blueprints, around 9 January 1942, and attributed to General Electric, cited the program as 'Project AI-10'. Soon the MIT was asked to take the point on this

crash program and, for security reasons, both the aircraft selected to mount the equipment, and the equipment itself, were cloaked in deception language. The earliest mention of the specific aircraft to be converted was on 21 February 1942 when a Wright Field Cross Reference document entitled 'Model Change B-18 Airplane Equipped with Special Radio Equipment' was posted. Finally, on 17 March 1942 the Materiel Command issued the following, very brief TWX to all of the interested parties: 'To avoid confusion, AAMC has assigned model designation B-18-B to the ten B-18-As which have been equipped with special radio equipment SCR-517 (ASV).' This was also the first instance in which the US designation for the ASV-10 equipment, SCR-517, was mentioned in official documents located to date.

A measure of the urgency and priority attached to this program can be found in a message sent from the Technical Executive at the Materiel Command, instructing that the Chief of the Air Corps, General Arnold, desired a weekly report on the status of the ASV-equipped LB-30s and B-18s, as well as their location after completion at Patterson Field and SAAD, and the number of crews available, as training men in the use of the new equipment was a challenge seldom noted.

The wartime confusion surrounding the Top Secret project, especially in the crisis mode of the first three months of 1942, can be felt in a TWX sent from the Technical Executive on 17 March, in most 'un-military' language, concerning the whereabouts of two of the 'special' B-18s. It read as follows:

'While this is none of our business, perhaps, the Air Service Command informs us that two B-18As, AC38-586 and 606, have been ready since March 10th at SAAD for ferrying to Boston for the completion of ASV installation. The two crews that took these airplanes to San Antonio apparently came from Westover Field, left them at San Antonio, and departed to parts unknown. Due to the necessity of getting these airplanes into immediate tactical service, it is requested that your office contact LTC Dearmond, Hefley or other authorities and see that these two airplanes are on their way.'

By 3 April 1942 the Radiation Laboratory at MIT had developed an eight-page Instruction Manual for what was termed 'the B-18 Receiver', as the crews that were being instructed in the use of the new gear were, up till that time, being instructed individually and verbally.

Left: A side view of the veteran sub-hunter AC37-543, which appears to have had a nickname over the 'rooster' emblem on the port nose painted over, and the upper halves of the engine cowlings painted at some point. The aircraft had certainly earned a rest, after extensive anti-submarine patrols, but was sold as surplus. *Norm Taylor collection, Museum of Flight*

Below: This B-18B, AC37-543, was one of the first ten aircraft converted to the status, and is shown here standing surplus after the war with a 'rooster' emblem on the port nose – and the silhouettes of two submarines just under the cockpit coaming. It served until 14 July 1943 with the 12th Antisubmarine Squadron, and was surplused in July 1945 to become NC-56569. This would have made a great warbird, had anyone known of its wartime exertions. *Wright State University*

The installation of the ASV gear on the first ten aircraft was not without challenges. By 15 April fifty special Plexiglas noses for the conversions that were to follow had been ordered from Rohm & Haas in Philadelphia, PA, on Requisition 2906A.R.L.42 and assigned a '… special priority, by verbal order of General Arnold'. A week later, on 22 April, Arnold was able to report to the Secretary of War that the first ten ASV-equipped B-18Bs were in fact at stations on the east coast and in service, the first report attesting to the commencement of actual operations of the type. That same week, Col Dolan, who had been summoned to Washington for a conference with General Arnold also attended by Gen McClellan and Col R. G. Breene, the Director of Technical Services, submitted his proposal for a specialised B-18B operating unit, with a station at Langley Field. He was issued, initially, with verbal orders to form what was initially designated as the **Seasearch – Attack Development Unit (SSADU)**. On 8 June 1942 the Adjutant General circulated a letter constituting the organisation as the **Headquarters, 1st Sea Search Attack Group (M),** with its only subordinate unit, at the time, being the 2nd Sea Search Attack Squadron (M), and ordered its activation at Langley by the Commanding General, First Air Force. However, the Group was assigned directly to Army Air Forces rather than the First Air Force.

As noted, the first microwave ASV radar sets used by the AAF were those built by the MIT Radiation Laboratory and installed by that institution in the first ten aircraft. This gear was usually cited simply as the 'M.I.T. Radar', without any formal nomenclature. These aircraft were issued to the 2nd Bombardment Group, at the time an element of I Bomber Command at Langley Field, in April 1942 but, as noted below, very shortly thereafter went to other subordinate units. The MIT radar was, essentially, laboratory equipment, installed before production models became available. Although it was intended that it be replaced with production models as soon as feasible, in fact this did not take place until July 1943, so these first ten B-18Bs were virtually unique and recognisable. The MIT sets were also used in testing various associated radar devices, such as the Echo Box (SS #22), Radar Beacon (SS #27) noted elsewhere, and an Audio Indicator (SS #33), as well as providing for field testing of certain design changes, such as the cosecant squared antenna, which was designed to eliminate the necessity to tilt the antenna downward upon approaching a target, but this was not found satisfactory. The MIT radar sets gave remarkably good performance for prototype equipment, but required experienced maintenance personnel, as they were completely non-standard. With the experienced maintenance personnel of the 1st Sea Search Attack Group, the performance record for these sets actually compared favorably with that achieved later by 'standard' production types.

The activation of the 1st Sea Search Attack Group, noted above, at Langley on 8 June 1942, grew out of the special testing of the MAD and ASV system development noted above. The Group was charged with a three-fold mission: (1) to develop tactics and techniques for the employment of known destructive devices; (2) to develop new experimental apparatus (as noted later) and; (3) to train combat crews and technicians in the use of these instruments. Therefore, the primary mission – at least initially – of the Sea Search Attack Group was not in dedicated anti-submarine units, patrol work and attack, but rather the development of special detector equipment used in anti-submarine warfare. The 1st Sea Search Attack Group, under LTC W. C. Dolan, ultimately included the 2nd and 3rd Sea Search Attack Squadrons, which flew B-18Bs and B-24Ds, and the 4th Sea Search Attack Squadron, which joined the Group in November 1943 and flew B-17s. The Group played a vital role in the sinking of an enemy submarine off the Florida coast in August 1942, a probable sinking in September off the Virginia Capes, and the possible confirmation of two sinkings near Trinidad in October. The Group worked on more than sixty projects between June 1942

and July 1943 (qv). Unit aircraft also flew a very large number of armed patrols, and these are noted in Chapter 9.

During the 'incubation' period of the Group, five crews were sent to Miami and five to Key West on 22 May 1942. The organisation, when constituted, was often referred to in official correspondence as simply 'The Search' or 'The Sea Search'. Upon activation, it acquired six of the B-18Bs then at Langley. When crews were detached to I Bomber Command for combat duty off Trinidad on 15 August 1942, it was up to strength with ten B-18Bs and at no time before or after did it ever have that number again. The operating squadron, the **2nd Sea Search Attack Squadron**, was commanded by Capt Francis B. Carlson, who soon gained notoriety as one of the most experienced anti-submarine aircraft commanders, as reflected in the number of operations he became involved in. The **3rd Sea Search Attack Squadron (H)** was not activated at Langley until 9 December 1942, and operations did not commence until 1 January 1943 from Hangar 532-E at Langley with three RB-18Bs handed over from the 2nd SSAS. This unit soon transitioned into B-24Ds and, by the winter, was operating a mix of B-24Ds and RB-18Bs until June 1943, when it converted to B-24s entirely. During its first year of existence, the 1st SSAG flew 1,499.7 hours on patrols and searches, was credited with two confirmed submarines and probable destruction of three more. The unit had made forty-three sightings (twenty-two by MAD gear, eighteen by ASV and three visuals).

In addition to the early MIT-equipped B-18Bs, as noted, eight additional B-18Bs, fitted with SCR-517A radars, were assigned. These were the first commercially built microwave sets used by the AAF. They had originally been designed for aircraft interception, but had been modified for ASV or aircraft-to-surface-vessel work. The range on a given target was somewhat less than on the MIT radar, since the maximum range was only 30 miles. The overall weight was also greater, as they were much more ruggedly built. They were found, however, to be less reliable than had been expected. As a result of service tests on this equipment, it was definitely shown that during the first 50 hours of operation of a radar set, a much higher rate of failure was experienced than thereafter. This information was used in planning all operations, and a 'shake-down' period was specified. The SCR-517A sets were further field-tested on detached service in Florida and Trinidad, where they gave satisfactory performance. During the operations in Trinidad, it became apparent that the Sea Search SCR-517A ships could serve an extremely useful purpose in that high-intensity operational area, and as a result the aircraft so equipped were left there and assigned to the 9th Bombardment Group.

The aircraft that the 1st SSAG left behind in Trinidad, described above, were replaced by B-18Bs equipped with **SCR-517C** radars. This was a modification of the basic SRC-517A set to include a 100-mile range and beacon operation. These figures increased in usefulness for navigation, although the performance on targets having a detection range of less than 30 miles, such as a submarine, was effectively the same as the SCR-517A. Certain faults were found in the SCR-517Cs, however, which were corrected in later versions. One was inaccuracy in range calibration, which became very apparent when using the beacon for obtaining a navigational 'fix'. Errors of up to 25% were found. Another fault was the drift of indicator adjustments during flight. Frequent readjustments were always required by the operators.

The 1st SSAG also conducted extensive service tests with US Navy **ASG Radar** installed on one of its B-18s. This was very similar to the SCR-717B in terms of operation. Many features were different, however, and it had a lower power output. In spite of this, the ASG performance was only slightly less than that of the SCR-717B. Very little maintenance was necessary during about 100 hours of operation. Several features were found that were not as good as the SCR-717B. The remote indicator, for example, did not have a system of lights for showing which range scale was in use. Automatic frequency control

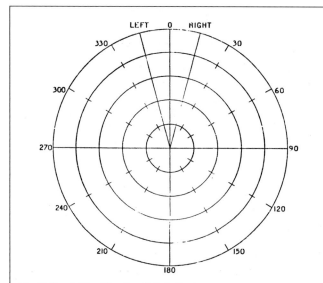

```
                    LEFT   0   RIGHT
              330                    30

         300                              60


    270                                        90


         240                              120

              210                    150
                         180
```

Figure 1 – Calibration for 717B indicator. Each circle represents 1 mile on the 4 mile range, 2 miles on the 10 mile range, 4 miles on the 20 mile range, 10 miles on the 50 mile range, and 20 miles on the 100 mile range. On the 4 mile range, zero distance (or the position of the airplane) is on the first circle rather than at the center. This allows one to read the azimuth angle with the same accuracy down to zero range.

The 1st Sea Search Attack Group, besides conducting a large number of operational missions, was also heavily involved in development of new weapons, devices and tactics. This shows the scope calibration of the SCR-717B radar, first fitted to B-18B AC37-533 on 6 April 1943. *USAFHRA*

was not used, and the expanded center for more accurate homing was not used. The Group had tested the SCR-717B on AC37-533, completing the tests on 18 February 1942 – much earlier than often reported. Maximum range had been found to be 25 miles, with the average closer to 18 miles. The test crew observed that the controls for this set were '…placed in such a location that the operator, when wearing winter flying clothes, almost invariably knocks the tuning out of adjustment if he holds his hand microphone in his left hand.'

Yet another radar type was the so-called **Light-Weight ASV** also developed by MIT. This gear, with a standard-size 'spinner', was also installed in a B-18, and service tests were conducted during June and July 1942. It was found that this set performed very reliably and that its size and weight were advantageous. However, since its range was only about half of that obtained on SCR-517C equipment, it was believed that this type of radar would be unsuitable for anti-submarine work.

The program was deemed a success, and orders went forth to convert more of the aircraft to B-18B configuration. By 30 June 1942 no fewer than thirty-one B-18Bs were in operation, including the ten that had been '…factory modified before delivery to the AAF' (the meaning of this phrase is not clear, as Douglas made no such conversions, and it thus almost certainly refers to the MIT/SAAD modified examples). Nearly all were operating from Langley Field, and the operating units, the 40th Bomb Squadron and the 2nd Sea Search Attack Squadron, had been authorized to further modify them locally to include a ventilation door.

B-18B AC37-533 was detached to the NACA at Langley Field around 14 August 1942, to investigate some of the aerodynamic and engineering problems that had been encountered in actual service with the aircraft to that time. They described the loading conditions for the B-18B as follows:

(1) normal crew of seven

(2) full fuel load at 802 gallons, no bomb bay tanks

(3) one .30 caliber gun in the dorsal turret

(4) all standard equipment, plus 'special radio equipment', under sea-search conditions, an additional load of four depth charges and one bomb bay fuel tank would be carried. The aircraft at NACA was a 2nd Sea Search Attack Squadron machine.

The NACA reported that the aircraft was '…unstable in flight due to the installation of radio equipment at Wright Field'. Oddly, no remedy for this condition was recommended, and since the conversions continued unabated it is assumed that the operating crews simply learned to deal with the new condition. This may, in fact, have been a comparison of the flight characteristics of a standard B-18A, which was regarded as very stable, to that of the B-18B conversions, the bulbous radome nose of which undoubtedly had some influence on the flight characteristics of crews accustomed to standard B-18As. As noted earlier, one of the challenges associated with the power-hungry radar gear was providing sufficient electrical current. The B-18Bs operating out of Langley, by 28 August, were powered by a P-3, 200 amp, 28 volt generator connected to the port (left) engine, the solitary load on which was the radar equipment, while the remainder of the aircraft operated on an E-8, 100 amp, 14 volt generator on the starboard (right) engine.

The entry of the B-18Bs into line service was not without further challenges. By 7 September 1942 distortions in the Plexiglas noses (Part No X41M484) on B-18Bs being converted to the latest version of the radar gear, SCR-517-A at SAAD, were being noted as occurring after about twenty days of operation. The Plexiglas had not been camouflaged when first installed, but of course was painted when the aircraft reached operating units. The camouflage paint apparently was sufficient to raise the temperature beyond what was termed the 'cold-flow point' or the 'hysteresis memory' of the Plexiglas, which induced the Plexiglas to return to a flat state! One can only imagine the chagrin of operating crews, and the rude comments that must have been voiced. This condition is known to have occurred on AC37-499 and 37-463 while in flight. Needless to say, the distortion rendered the SCR-517-A inoperative.

SAAD recommended the following corrective actions as fixes:

(1) use polystyrene ribs to retain the shape

(2) use plywood to form the nose radome instead of Plexiglas

(3) remove and reform the noses that were distorted

The classified nature of the SCR-517-A gear was considered of sufficient sensitivity that camouflage was required and a non-conducting nose section was vital.

As a temporary solution, plywood noses were to be mounted on the B-18Bs then at SAAD, but to date no illustrations of this temporary installation have been located.

SAAD performed modifications of B-18As to B-18B configuration for the remaining aircraft as follows:

March 1942	10
May 1942	4
June 1942	16
July 1942	14
August 1942	12
September 1942	15
October 1942	11
November 1942	14
December 1942	7
January 1943	2
March 1943	2
April 1943	1
May 1943	1
Unknown conversion month (but probably April 1942)	3

HK-519 was B-18B AC39-14, a combat veteran, MSN 2662 and was last operated by Colombian operator TACA in 1961. She had an extensively modified nose. Here she sits forlorn and derelict at Villavicencio, Colombia, in November 1972. *Guido E. Buehlmann 28268*

After the initial difficulties with the Plexiglas radomes deforming, the B-18B conversions were described as:

'…very satisfactory, with the exception of three areas:

a. The Transmitter/Receiver units and the antenna equipment are difficult to service. The transmitter receiver cans must be swung backwards to remove the units from inside. When swung backwards, they still do not allow sufficient room for the average size service technician to have access to the antenna equipment. As the antenna equipment must be serviced rather frequently, this is a considerable disadvantage. It is believed that, if the mounting rack was made so as to allow the cans to slide backwards as well as (or instead of) swinging backwards, this situation would be greatly improved.

b. The Radio Operator and the Radio Observer are in each other's way when both have to operate at the same time. Both of these men do need to work at the same time about 20 minutes out of every hour on an ordinary patrol mission. It would be desirable to mount the radio receiver in the rear of the aircraft. In one ship here, the radio receiver was mounted on a bracket in the rear, and the arrangement proved to be satisfactory. The Radio Operator must then stand to tune his receiver, but can sit down comfortably while operating.

c. The Synchronizer is mounted so low that adjustments on it are difficult, and the meters on it are hard to read. It would be much better to have the Synchronizer mounted above the radio compass rather than below it. There are few controls on the radio compass which are used by the Radio Operator, as it is generally operated by remote control from the Pilot's seat. It is very hard for the Radio Observer at present to adjust the Synchronizer, particularly at night and with a Radio Operator sitting beside him.'

The AAF became very interested, between May and July 1942, in the relative efficiencies of the various aircraft types that had been pressed into service by that time in the new mission of anti-submarine warfare, especially along the east coast of the US and in the crucial Caribbean area. In order to obtain a measure of the relative efficiency of these aircraft, even though the figures were open to variables and unique circumstances, a set of procedures were set down.

The Army set as the standard an average non-radar-equipped aircraft, and assigned these types the arbitrary value of 1.00 for efficiency. Based on the experiences of aircraft during the first four full months of the war for the US, such an aircraft would typically require no fewer than 869 patrol hours per submarine sighting less than 60 miles off shore, and 288 hours per sighting more than 60 miles from shore. It was then possible to calculate, from the actual number of hours flown inshore and offshore, an expected number of sightings. The ratio of the actual to the expected number of sightings was then a measure of the relative efficiency of the type of aircraft, which was deemed at least partially corrected for the range of the aircraft.

The relative efficiencies are shown in the accompanying table. It is obvious from this that most of the non-radar-equipped aircraft have efficiencies near 1.00, while radar-equipped aircraft had an average efficiency of 2.79, clearly indicating that the use of radar increased the number of sightings by at least that factor. This was regarded, at the time, as an actual underestimate of the value of the radar gear, however, since it did not take into account the fact that radar aircraft could search in all weather conditions and at night, when visual patrolling was little more than useless. This made radar-equipped aircraft especially valuable for convoy escort under poor visibility conditions.

A few words about the individual aircraft types cited is clearly in order, however. Among those equipped with radar, the figures for Boeing B-17 variants and B-18Bs were based, at the time, on such a small amount of actual operational flying that the figures had no statistical significance. This was shown by the large probable error in the last column of the table. For the other types, the order of decreasing efficiency was North American B-25 variants, Lockheed A-29 and Douglas DB-7. Apparently the high-speed aircraft were actually less efficient than the

Radar Efficiency Table

Type	Relative Efficiency	Probable Error
Lockheed A-29	.94	.28
Boeing B-17 (without radar)	1.92	1.29
Boeing B-17 (without radar)	2.79	.62
Douglas B-18 (without radar)	–	–
Douglas B-18 (with radar)	2.31	1.54
North Am. B-25	1.33	.28
Douglas DB-7	.58	.22
Consol. LB-30	4.76	2.24

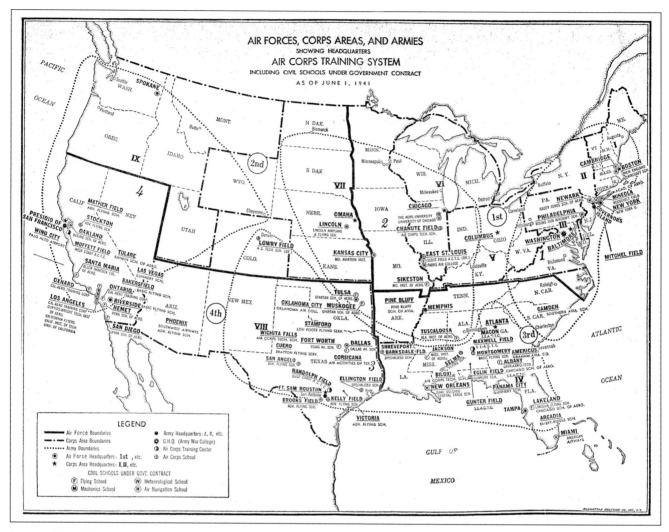

Between 1 June 1941, when this map was made depicting Army and Air Corps areas of responsibilities and major activities, and June 1942, by which time the US had been plunged into the war, the deployment of the surviving B-18s had undergone a radical transformation. The accompanying tables still reflected assignments of a number of aircraft at locations on this map.

low-speed types, probably because they required more attention on the part of the pilot(s), thereby giving them less time for meaningful observation. In the case of the Douglas DB-7, there was the added disadvantage that there was no co-pilot. Amongst the radar-equipped aircraft, the efficiencies differed by amounts less than the probable errors.

Between June and mid-October 1942 numerous Army Air Forces reports cited a number of B-18 aircraft as type 'B-18BR', including AC37-482 and 37-593. The precise significance of the additional 'R' identifier on the designation has not been determined but, where it was thus reported, this has been repeated in the chronological sequence of attacks and sightings that follows.

Additionally, contrary again to nearly every previously published account, of the total of 112 aircraft that were converted to B-18B status, no fewer than twenty-one were further redesignated as type B-18C, and it appears that this designation surfaced between December 1942 and July 1943. According to crew members who served on these aircraft, the solitary distinguishing feature between a standard B-18B and the B-18C was the addition of a .50 caliber machine gun fitted in the lower right fuselage, firing forward, and controlled by the pilot, who was also furnished with a simple ring-and-bead gun sight! This installation was demanded by B-18B crews when the Axis submarines began to remain on the surface to engage attacking aircraft with an ever-increasing number of machine guns and light flak weapons. More on this will be found in the chapter on armament.

Although it will be detailed at length later in this account, I Bomber Command, the initial USAAF contribution to combating the submarine menace, was activated in December 1941. It was made up of virtually every AAF bombardment, reconnaissance and observation unit on the east coast, and flew a conglomeration of available equipment, consisting for the most part of early variant Boeing B-17s, Douglas B-18s, North American B-25s, repossessed Douglas DB-7s, and Lockheed A-29s, some of them converted to carry SCR-521 radars, as noted. I Bomber Command, largely forgotten to historians of the period, stayed on the job until late in 1942, when it was inactivated to form a nucleus for the new **Antisubmarine Command**. However, in the meantime a second AAF organisation broke into the anti-submarine picture during the spring of 1942, and this was the all but forgotten **1st Sea Search Attack Group**, known at AAF Headquarters collaterally as the **Sea-search Attack Development Unit (SADU)**.

The SADU was formally activated, under the command of Col William C. Dolan, as noted elsewhere in this account, on 17 June 1942, when the U-boat depredations were at their worst, and was given a combined mission. This consisted of (1) development of tactics and techniques for using anti-submarine devices and (2) to conduct general sea search. Practically unique in the history of the wartime AAF, and not repeated until 1944 with the advent of the Boeing B-29-equipped XX Bomber Command, the SADU reported directly to the Commanding General, Army Air Forces. Operationally, however, it fell under the Navy.

The SADU was, initially, the sole operator of the first ten radar-equipped B-18Bs, mounting the practically hand-made, pre-production SCR-517s, as well as two of the first three ex-British Consolidated LB-30 Liberators, nicknamed within the unit as 'Dumbo I' and 'Dumbo II'. As of 30 May 1942 all fifteen ASV-equipped B-18Bs assigned to the Eastern Defense Command were transferred to the SADU as well as two Consolidated LB-30s (equipped with ASV-10) on loan from the British.

The SADU learned while fighting. Not large enough to join the I Bomber Command line units in day-in-day-out patrols, it became a sort of on-call, emergency 'fire brigade' unit. It sent frequent 'killer' detachments, hopping down the coast and as far afield as Trinidad, wherever U-boats concentrated, at the Navy's beck and call. From activation until 15 July 1943 SADU aircraft sank or damaged four U-boats and made eighteen confirmed sightings, involving 209 hunts/patrols and 1,274 flying hours.

By 22 September 1942, according to one of the weekly progress reports to General Arnold cited earlier, outlining the locations and status of radar-equipped aircraft, the following shows the relative numeric importance of the B-18B conversions in the anti-submarine campaign in two of the crucial theaters:

Eastern Defense Command

Douglas B-18B	47 (with ASV-10)
Boeing B-17E	11 (with Mark II)

Caribbean Defense Command

Douglas B-18B	22 (with ASV-10)
Consolidated LB-30	16 (with Mark II)
Boeing B-17E	18 (with Mark II)
Consolidated B-24D	7 (with Mark II)

By 29 December 1942 the situation had changed, as more and more B-18B conversions were pushed through the SAAD, and, with the reorganisation and emergence of the Antisubmarine Command, operating units reported the following radar-equipped, dedicated anti-submarine assets:

Antisubmarine Command

Douglas B-18B	63 (with ASV-S)
Lockheed B-34	39 (with Mark II)
Boeing B-17E	11 (with Mark II)

Caribbean Defense Command

Douglas B-18B	45 (with ASV-S)
Consolidated LB-30	16 (with Mark II)
Boeing B-17E	19 (with Mark II)
Consolidated B-24D	22 (with Mark II)

The B-18B: a study in versatility

From the foregoing, and combined with the sparse previously published descriptions, it would be easy to conclude that all of the B-18B conversions were identical. In fact, this was not the case at all, and besides the configuration of the basic ASV radar suite, which varied from unit to unit, a dizzying array of offensive submarine-killing weapons and systems were employed at one time or another.

The accompanying table, prepared by the 26th Antisubmarine Wing[36], which was activated at Miami on 20 November 1942 under the command of none other than Col Harry A. Halverson, shows the dispersion of the Wing, and the suite of radar gear, operating altitudes and mission load that the subordinate Squadron carried between creation of the Wing and 24 June 1943.

The various ASV radar developments were not the only specialised equipment fitted to B-18Bs. As early as 12 April 1942 one B-18 (ironically, AC36-262, the original DB-1 aircraft), flying out of Mitchel Field, NY, and piloted by Capt O. B. Hardy, was being used to test an entirely new weapon, a magnetic detector housed in a special 'stinger' boom protruding from the extreme end of the fuselage of the aircraft. While ASV-10 and ASV-S were very effective in locating submarines on the surface in all weather conditions and at night, the new Magnetic Airbourne Detector (MAD)[37] gear could multiply that effectiveness by enabling the aircraft to detect a submarine submerged. The device was developed by Dr Bowles of the National Defense Research Council, who recommended that at least 250 such units be ordered for use by the AAF at once. This was in addition to 275 units that had been ordered previously, fifty of which were being procured on the highest priority for fitting to B-18Bs.

That very first MAD 'stinger' on any USAAC/USAAF aircraft was removed from AC36-262 and installed on AC36-268 by 24 May 1942, also at Mitchel Field. These are believed to have been the only 'straight' B-18s ever fitted with MAD booms.

Columbia Laboratories, in conjunction with the NDRC, developed most of the MAD Mark IV gear and supervised the testing leading to entry into service. The so-called 'single' MAD Mark IV installation was tested on B-18Bs AC37-464, 37-464 and 38-587. The 'Dual' MAD Mark VI installation was tested on B-18Bs AC 37-470, 37-538, 37-561, 37-593, 38-590 and 39-21, while the 'O'-type MABS (Magnetic Airbourne Bomb Sight) was tested on B-18s AC37-470 and

Radar Equipment Operational Performance

Squadron	Type Equipment	Average Operating Altitude	Number of Missions	Operational Effectiveness of Equipment
7th ASRON	SCR-517A	1325ft	95	84%
	SCR-517C	1225ft	173	78%
8th ASRON	SCR-517C	1300ft	64	60%
	SCR-521	1300ft	16	50%
	SCR-717A	1300ft	97	81%
9th ASRON	SCR-517A	800ft	3	66%
	SCR-521	1400ft	25	67%
	SCR-717A	1800ft	29	79%
10th ASRON	SCR-521	1900ft	55	97%
15th ASRON	SCR-521	3300ft	100	98%
17th ASRON	SCR-517A & C	1550ft	100	62%

Pictured often, AC37-530 is shown here while serving with the 1st Sea Search Attack Group in the Caribbean by 15 July 1942, and was one of the first aircraft to also gain the MAD 'stinger', being often cited as such as type 'B-18B-R'. The aircraft has a nickname on the forward nose but it was apparently deleted by censors. After a very extensive war against the submarines this aircraft was wrecked at Trinidad on 16 August 1944 while being commanded by William W. Walmsley. *via David W. Ostrowski*

37-538. A single experimental 'T'-type MABS installation was tested on B-18B AC39-21 as well.

Because of the obvious proliferation of steel parts on an aircraft that might affect the performance of a weapon such as this, considerable work was done on magnetic compensation on B-18 series aircraft using the Mark IV-B2 and Mark VI MAD equipment. A system using vertical, lateral and transverse magnetic corrections was developed, and this pioneering work in ASW technology has never been acknowledged.

Ironically, it was during the first actual test flight of the MAD gear on the B-18B noted above that Bowles, who was on board, witnessed a ship off Barnegat Lighthouse actually in process of being torpedoed by a German submarine. The aircraft had a live situation in which to actually test the MAD gear under combat conditions, and it subsequently made twenty-two successful signal contacts and dropped two depth charges, which unfortunately failed to detonate. About 10 minutes after the torpedo attack, the MAD equipment picked up a signal about 1.5 miles from the sinking vessel. It became impossible to drop a flare because the senior pilot became so excited that he was completely distracted, issuing countermanding orders to his crew who, on his orders, had crowded forward into the control cabin area.

The MAD equipment was developed under CTI-690, and it is known that the AAF procured sufficient specialised tail cones for the gear to fit seventy-five of the B-18Bs with it, commencing after 2 June 1942. Three B-18s had been fitted with the MAD stingers by 14 July 1942, and ten by 15 August 1942. It is not clear if all seventy-five were in fact so modified, and evidence suggests that in fact only thirty conversions were carried out. Reports by some observers that

the addition of this gear qualified the aircraft for designation as type B-18C are not correct. The gear was developed by Columbia University Laboratories under the auspices of the NDRC and was initially designated as MAD Mark IV-B2.

Similar MAD units were also installed, commencing around 15 June 1942, in US Navy blimps and Consolidated PBY-5 Catalina series flying boats and amphibians. In most instances the gear was fitted in the tail of the aircraft, but in the case of the B-18Bs a special plywood 'tail cone' extension was built onto the extreme tail. The AAF B-18Bs fitted with MAD gear initially operated exclusively from Langley Field, VA. Within the first full month of operation, twenty contacts were obtained, resulting in two confirmed sinkings and two probables. The ASV/MAD combination was obviously the answer to the Axis submarine problem.

The MAD gear fundamentally gave an aircraft the ability to sweep a swathe about 700 feet wide and, if cruising at 150mph, an ideal B-18B operating speed, the aircraft could sweep 20 square miles per hour. The beauty of this method of searching was, of course, that the opposition could not possibly know that such a search was on. Apparently, from available sources, the German submarine command never did figure out how their subs were being detected.

The majority of the B-18Bs equipped with MAD gear were initially assigned to the 2nd Sea Search Attack Squadron based at Langley Field, VA, where, by 1 July 1942, a MAD Laboratory and Shop was set up in the Squadron hangar. Five unit B-18Bs were modified between 1 July and 1 September 1942, and the unit also trained 119 MAD operators for further assignment to other units equipped with the new gear, mainly the 12th and 18th Antisubmarine Squadrons.

MAD-Equipped B-18B Aircraft

Unit	Station	Total B-18B Aircraft On Hand	B-18B MAD Equipped	Not Equipped	Equipment Needed*	Tail Cones Needed
4th ASRON	Mitchel Field	11	8	3	4	2**
8th ASRON	Miami	2	2	0	1	0
9th ASRON	Trinidad	10	3	7	8	7
12th ASRON	Langley Field	12	12	0	1	0
18th ASRON	Langley Field	3	3	0	1	0

*One additional set was to be used for test bend and/or as a spare unit
**One airplane of this Squadron had a tail cone installed but no actual MAD equipment

At least two MAD Mark IV-C units were designed for installation on B-18s, and these were very unusual, consisting of streamlined housings for wing-tip installation, and both had been rushed to completion by 31 August 1942. Unfortunately, no photographs of this exotic installation have been located to date.

The original MAD Mark IV-B2 gear was eventually refined into the definitive wartime MAD Mark VI, which was about 150lb heavier than the original sets, and these were installed only on B-18Bs. A practical test of the combination of the MAD Mark VI and a retro-bomb-equipped aircraft (see the chapter on Armament) made off California using a friendly submarine and detonator caps on the Mousetrap bombs resulted in the first drop of four bombs achieving one hit. The second drop, also of four bombs, gave no hits, but the third, using eight bombs, gave two hits. The submarine was completely submerged at the time.

By 29 January 1943 the AAF Antisubmarine Command had requested that every single B-18B in the Command be retrofitted with the MAD gear. It is not clear if this was ever actually completed, however. The program is described in the table on page 154.

Giving the B-18B teeth:
armament and special weapons

Between June 1942 and July 1943 the 1st Sea Search Attack Group conducted extensive tests on no fewer than sixty distinct projects related to anti-submarine warfare, and in the process became unsung pioneers in this highly specialised form of combat. Although many of these will be discussed elsewhere in this volume in the sections detailing camouflage, weapons and radar, a brief outline is appropriate at this juncture. The project tests included the very earliest use of sonobuoys, and three progressively improved Magnetic Anomaly Detection (MAD) systems: the Mark IV-B2, the Mark VI and the Mark X.

The sonobuoy was revolutionary, and advanced forms of the same basic device are still in use worldwide today. Basically, after sighting a submarine the B-18B crew dropped the devices into the sea to pick up underwater sounds, and the buoys then relayed the signals to the aircraft or other aircraft in the area. With the Mark IV-B2 MAD mounted as a distinctive tail 'stinger' on some B-18Bs, the aircraft could search a 16.6-square-mile area in about 60 minutes. The Mark VI was tested on a B-18B, but was mounted operationally on B-24 Liberator anti-submarine aircraft, and had detectors on the tips of each wing. The Mark X MAD consisted of a 'bird' towed beneath a B-18B, and was developed in early 1943.

A brief synopsis of some of the first twenty-nine special tests, until 17 August 1942, may serve to illustrate the breadth of the involvement of this very special unit. Each project was identified by an 'SS' number (for Sea Search), and a brief descriptor:

SS #4 – Mortar Projection of Flare: Work on this fascinating project, never described before, began on 4 July 1942, and involved the use of nothing less than a 60mm mortar illuminating flare projected forward from a B-18's upper rear turret for the purpose of identifying a target at night. Construction of a suitable 60mm mortar was accomplished at the Rock Island Arsenal and differed from a standard Infantry 60mm mortar in that it had a longer tube, an installation to absorb recoil and could be opened at the rear (base) for loading and firing. Ground tests at Aberdeen Proving Ground with the weapon installed on a B-18 proved satisfactory. Flight tests on 16 November 1942 at Langley showed that slight modifications of the mortar support would be necessary. A modified mortar was ground- and flight-tested at Aberdeen on 17 December, after which it was decided to change the angle

of fire. Investigation of mortar and projectile characteristics were also carried out. Lack of ammunition delayed further testing and, as it was concluded that the immediate problem had been solved by a searchlight installation (SS #55), the project was dropped.

SS #5 – Low Altitude Radar Altimeter (AYB-1): The AYB-1 altimeter operated on the radar reflection principle, ranging from zero to 400 feet from ground level. B-18s, which operated almost exclusively in the anti-submarine environment at very low altitudes, could clearly benefit from such an installation, and hence the very low number assigned to this project. An AYB-1 altimeter was installed in a B-18 assigned to the 1st SSAG and tests commenced on 16 October 1942 in conjunction with the NACA. The results were favorable and the tests revealed that the AYB-1 was reliable within 6 feet from zero to 400 feet. However, maintenance problems were encountered. At least three 1st SAAG B-18Bs were subsequently equipped with this gear, however.

SS #9 (and SS # 56) – NDRC Rocket Flare – Reloadable Rocket Gun (see also SS #40): This device was tested extensively at Aberdeen Proving Ground commencing on 8 July 1942, and proved to be 67% satisfactory. The B-18 that was fitted with this equipment, which has eluded identification, was in fact transferred to Langley Field, where further tests were conducted. The purpose was to determine the feasibility of forward-firing rocket flares as a means of target identification and to establish optimum explosion height and time delay factors. The original installation consisted of two exterior rocket tubes mounted on the nose of a B-18. These were not reloadable in flight, and the rockets were fired by a switch in the cockpit. First lots of ammunition received were unreliable and difficulty was experienced with the tube installation due to rust and corrosion. As a result, it was recommended that a reloadable rocket gun should be built instead, and the project was changed to SS #56. The first model of this modified rocket gun was received at Langley in December 1942 and, after ground tests, was mounted through the bombardier's compartment on a B-18. While numerous flight tests were accomplished by the 1st SSAG, progress was delayed by the seeming inability of the development group to determine the optimum explosion height and time delay factors. The gun also suffered from excessive leakage of flame and gases and was determined to be unsafe for operations. A standard Star Shell Flare was fitted to a rocket motor and, when fired, shot about 1.1 miles ahead of the aircraft, and provided excellent illumination. The basic idea was to illuminate the target for at least enough time to establish the identity prior to the arrival at the bomb release line.

A new, improved rocket gun was installed, however, during the week of 8 June 1943, and was ground-tested at Wright Field with very good results. It was mounted, instead, in the rear of the B-18, opposite the side entrance door at an angle of 23° to the horizontal flight line of the aircraft. The front end of the tube projected 2 feet above the top of the fuselage, and the rear end extended 1 foot below the belly. This projector tube was loaded at the middle of the weapon by means of a 3-foot section of tubing, hinged at the front end, which was equipped with a latch to secure it during firing of the rocket flares. Flight tests of the installation were conducted at Langley on 16 June 1943, and the tube functioned satisfactorily except in one instance, when the loading door was not properly secured. As a result, a portion of the blast from the rocket escaped into the tilted part of the tube, forcing the tube back and tearing out two of the front supports. Further tests of this exotic device were discontinued by the 1st SSAG as of 15 July 1943, although it is believed that further tests were later conducted on another aircraft at Eglin Field, FL. A total of nineteen flights and 26hr 15min of flight time were expended in these tests. This weapon should not be confused with the Retro Flare Tubes that were fitted in the ventral gunner's hatch of some 1st SSAG RB-18Bs. These could be fired manually or automatically by means of the MABS unit (qv).

SS #10 – ASV Equipment: B-18B AC37-533 was fitted successfully with SCR-717B gear by 6 April 1943. This project also included the installation of lightweight radar on B-18B AC37-574, which was flown to Boston on 10 May 1943 to have the MIT-designed equipment installed.

SS #11 – Radar Marking Float: This device, developed by Dr Bowen of the Bell Laboratories, was just starting test applications, but had been shipped to Langley Field for actual tests.

SS #16 – Target Marking Slick Dropper: The Langley Sub-Depot constructed six of these odd devices and they were actually installed on B-18Bs AC37-470, 37-538, 37-561, 37-593, 38-590 and 39-21 on a priority basis. (See also SS #54)

SS #17 – High Altitude Radar Altimeter: The unit had conducted a photographic test of this device over land, in conjunction with the NACA, and was just about to commence additional tests over water.

SS #18 – Night Marker Float: This device was functioning very satisfactorily and, as many night missions were being flown, was given a high priority. It was developed by Columbia Laboratories. This project commenced on 10 July 1942 and was concluded on 28 August, but was regarded as a 'minor' system.

SS #19 and #21 – 'Fido' ('Mark 13 Mine'): To become widely used in Europe and elsewhere later in the war, tests by the 1st SSAG were conducted starting on 10 July 1942 using a B-18B as well as B-34, B-24 and B-17 series aircraft. This was, basically, a torpedo fitted with microphone equipment that operated controls to make the torpedo 'home' on any source of sound. Only test quantities were available prior to March 1943 and, in most communications, this system was noted as '…a very secret development' for obvious reasons. This system was developed in conjunction with the Navy.

SS #20 – Radar Bomb Sight: This project was initiated on 21 July 1942, and involved at least one B-18B, but jurisdiction for it was transferred to another agency on 18 January 1943.

SS #22 – Echo Boxes: This device remains somewhat mysterious, and apparently tests involving larger resonators were being conducted at the time, but it was apparently functioning as designed. The project started on 17 July 1942, and was rated of 'minor' importance.

SS #24 – Microphone-Radio (Sonic) Buoy: More popularly known as the 'Sonobuoy', this device was tested by the 1st SSAG for the first time between July and 13 August 1942 and was found to be 'highly useful'. Developed by the Columbia Division of War Research at the Naval Underwater Sound Laboratory, it consisted of a tubular float arranged with a hydrophone, which hung 20 feet below the water's surface and converted water sounds

to electric voltages. These were amplified and applied to a low-power frequency-modulated transmitter within the float. The job of the Sonic Buoy (as it was initially termed) was, obviously, to pick up sounds made by a submarine and transmit them in the form of radio waves that could then be received in the searching aircraft and used as another agent to help identify the source of the associated MAD signals. Tests made by the 1st SSAG showed that the maximum useful radio range of the device was 17.5 miles with the receiving aircraft operating at not more than 500 feet. Tests by the Group of this device at Langley included actual drop tests, experimentation on the most suitable type of antenna, and determining the proper location of the receivers in both B-18 and B-24 series aircraft. In addition, and this has seldom, if ever, been noted, tests were successfully completed to incorporate an aircraft's interphone system with the Sonic Buoy receiver so that all members of the crew could listen to the sonic sounds at one time.

The Group tested the device under actual combat conditions in Trinidad, employing four buoys, each using a different frequency to gain directivity, and these met with success. During the period July 1942 to July 1943 the 1st SSAG had eight B-18Bs and two B-24s equipped with Sonic Buoy receivers. During that same period 108 buoys were expended in actual sub searches.

SS #26 – 100-Mile 'B' Scope (SCR-520-B): Developed by Bell Laboratories, this device was apparently in need of additional development as of this time, based on the findings of actual tests conducted by the 1st SSAG commencing on 6 August 1942.

SS #25 – Recognition of Vessels by Ultra-Violet Reflection: The 1st SSAG, in conjunction with NDRC crews, conducted numerous tests with this exotic equipment in September and October 1942, in order to provide a recognition system that was entirely under the control of the search aircraft commander and, at the same time, invisible to enemy surface craft and surfaced submarines. An ultra-violet autocollimator was installed on a crash boat and an ultra-violet light source was mounted on one of the B-18Bs. Results showed that a satisfactory identification signal could be obtained for an aircraft flying at 300 feet. The average range at which the light was visible was 3,700 feet. Results of these trials were turned over to the Navy, but apparently no further development was forthcoming.

SS #28 – Camouflage: A high-interest item, B-18 AC37-475 was apparently the first of a number of B-18s used to conduct extensive tests on the best camouflage for aircraft engaged in anti-submarine work. Although the 1st SSAG commenced intensive experiments with camouflage as early as 6 August 1942, by 8 January 1943 this test work was transferred to Wright Field. AC37-464 is known to have had its undersurfaces painted insignia white camouflage enamel shade #46 while the side and top surfaces received enamel white over black camouflage to produce what was termed a bluish 'haze' effect. AC37-465 had all exterior surfaces painted camouflage enamel white, applied in a pattern of graduated light reflective values over black camouflage enamel, to also produce a bluish 'haze' effect. AC37-621 had the undersides painted with white insignia camouflage enamel, vertical control surfaces and sides of the fuselage neutral gray camouflage lacquer, and top surfaces were left in the original color of dark olive-drab. AC37-561 had all her undersurfaces painted neutral gray and side and top surfaces dark olive-drab. Finally, AC37-574 was left in her original finish, consisting of insignia white on all surfaces.

SS #32 – Magnetic Airborne Bomb Sight (MABS): B-18B AC39-21 was being used at Langley as of 30 March 1943 to release flares and sub-calibers in connection with the tests of this sight. B-18 AC37-470 was also apparently used to test this gear by 6 April 1943. Daily flights using both of these aircraft over Plum Tree Coil were made and by 12 April forty bombs and flares had been expended. There was an apparent tendency to overshoot the target with this gear. AC39-21 was subsequently flown to SAAD for radar modification. B-18 AC37-538 was also fitted with this gear by 29 April 1943. The 'O' Type MABS was an electronic device that automatically fired retro-bombs (qv) on the crest of the negative or positive magnetic poles of a submarine.

SS #33 – Audio Indicator: This device was installed on B-18 AC37-593 and a B-24 of the 1st SSAG, and tests were conducted satisfactorily with the indicator operating with both MIT and SCR-717A equipment by 29 April 1943.

SS #34 – Directional MAD Equipment: By 30 March 1943 Wright Field was so interested in this project that it detailed a Lieutenant Erickson to Langley Field to supervise the installation of this MAD Mark VI gear development on five 1st SSAG B-18Bs.

SS #40 – NDRC Retro-Flare and Tube: By 11 May 1943 retro-flare tubes were being installed on all 1st SSAG B-18s that also had vertical bombing equipment (Mousetrap) and Mark VI MAD gear. This gear was originally tested on AC39-21, and was mounted over the rear gunner's hatch.

SS #48 – Non-Magnetic Detector (MAD Mark X): B-18 AC38-590 was flown to NAS Quonset on 28 January 1943 and had this gear installed at the time.

SS #49 – Vertical Bombs: This project involved the installation of wing-tip MAD Mark VI installations on the retro-rail-equipped aircraft available to the 1st SSAG by 12 April 1943, AC37-593 and 37-561. The rails could normally accommodate a total of twelve 60lb Mark 20 contact bombs, and these could be rigged to fire in a ripple of two sticks of six each. They were fired rearward at a speed of 135mph (the 'ideal' B-18 airspeed!) and a timer device was provided in order that they strike the water at the point of release. They were set at an angle to spread the bombs in a pattern approximately 120 feet wide at a 100-foot altitude drop point.

SS #52 – Ship-to-Plane IFF: This was a high-priority project, designed to fit every aircraft assigned to the 1st SSAG by May 1943 or later with SCR-595 IFF (Identification, Friend or Foe) equipment. Apparently, Allied surface vessels had frequently been alarmed by the very aggressive, low-altitude 'attacks' made by B-18 series aircraft, and on occasion had been known to engage them with their anti-aircraft armament.

SS #54 – Marker Slicks: Apparently the tests conducted under SS #16 (see above) were sufficiently successful that this project, involving 500 fluorescein marker slicks in containers, had been received for tests from the manufacturer, Wilsonite Products Inc. They were tested using the slick droppers described in SS #16 on B-18 AC37-465 and three B-24s.

SS #56 – Reloadable Rocket Gun: This project was initiated on 8 July 1942 to determine the feasibility of forward-firing rocket flares as a means of target identification and to establish optimum explosion height and delay factors. The original installation (see SS #9 and SS #40) consisted of two exterior tubes mounted on the nose of a B-18. These were not reloadable in flight and were fired by a switch by the pilot. This weapon was found to have excessive leakage of flame and gases and was determined to be unsafe for operations. An improved rocket gun was tested during the week of 8 June 1943 and ground-tested at Wright Field. It was mounted in the rear of a B-18, opposite the side entrance door at an angle of 23° to the horizontal flight line. The front end projected 2 feet above the top of the fuselage and the rear end extended 1 foot below the belly. It was loaded in the middle by means of a 3-foot section of tubing at the front.

Other tests conducted included a B-18 fitted with what was called an **MIT Audio-Indicator.** This device produced an audio note in a pair of headphones when the ASV radar picked up an echo from some object on the surface, such as a surfaced submarine. An **Airborne Odograph** was also tested on B-18B AC37-561 circa 17 September 1942. This instrument automatically plotted the actual course of the search aircraft, which would have obvious benefit to an aircraft commander in determining an effective search pattern for a submerged submarine. Finally, experiments were conducted using a B-18B in what was termed **Recognition of Vessels by Visual Reflection** on 21 September 1942, using B-18B AC38-590. A Navy sea-going tug was used as the 'target' and the B-18 was fitted with three red-filtered landing lights. The B-18 made a standard ASV approach to the tug with the bombardier turning on these lights at 2,000 feet from the target. The results were apparently inconclusive. At least one B-18 was also fitted with a K-24 camera mounted in the bottom of the aircraft, inclined backward at a 30° angle, to record the results of submarine attacks. The angular coverage was approximately from straight down to about 60° to the rear of straight down. This therefore included both the point where a dropped depth charge struck the water and the point where it would explode, making exposures at the rate of three per second. It was operated by the bombardier.

During Sea Search Exercises at Key West around 7 June 1943, B-18Bs of the 1st SSAG also employed the **N-3A Low Altitude Optical Bomb Sight** and the **Gremlin Mark II Bomb Sight.** The **Mark VI Double Wing-Tip MAD** was also tested by RB-18Bs of the unit, and comprised two complete magnetic detectors, each having an approximate range of 600 feet on medium-size submarines. Each was equipped with a tape recorder, which kept a record of the MAD activities in chronological order.

But the experiments with electronic gadgetry and radar were not the only measures being investigated to make the B-18 an effective anti-submarine weapon. One of the most recurring complaints from operating crews on B-18As engaged in anti-submarine patrols, but especially on the B-18Bs, which had to forsake their solitary forward-firing flexible gun in order to accommodate the radar installation, was what was regarded as an urgent need for forward-firing armament. In a Memo dated 1 May 1942, entitled 'Proposed Installation of Fixed, Forward Firing Cannons in B-18A Airplanes', the Materiel Division at Wright Field received a consolidated Unsatisfactory Report (U/R No 42-4771) from Langley Field that essentially stated that the frontal fire power of the operational B-18A and B-18B aircraft, which were primarily engaged in anti-submarine work, was, at best, insufficient or non-existent. Wright Field accordingly initiated a project to install two fixed forward-firing cannon in the nose of a Boeing B-17C for test purposes. However, in view of the fact that the overwhelming use of

B-18s in anti-submarine work dominated the scene at that time, Wright Field recommended that the proposed installation of forward-firing cannon in the nose of B-18s be referred to the Director of Military Requirements for a decision, since such a retrofit would not only require extensive modifications but would also result in the withdrawal of the aircraft from the work at hand for intervals of time when they were crucially needed. The Director of Bombardment, perhaps to no one's surprise, replied on 4 May that he did not deem such an installation desirable. He reasoned that nothing less than 37mm weapons would be effective against submarines and, with the installation of ASV equipment in the noses of the B-18Bs, it was regarded as very doubtful if a suitable installation could be made.

This was not the end of the matter, however, as clearly the objective was not to disable subs but rather to clear their decks when on the surface so that their increasing anti-aircraft capabilities could not impede the attacking aircraft in carrying out their actions. Although no official records have been located describing the subsequent decision to install single .50 caliber weapons on the lower right forward fuselages of B-18C variants, this installation was clearly made in a sizeable number of aircraft, and apparently assuaged the hard-pressed crews.

But perhaps one of the most impressive weapons developed for use on B-18s was the so-called **Mark 20 (Mousetrap) bomb**.

This ingenious weapons system was initially developed exclusively for B-18 series aircraft, and the first operational use of the Mousetrap 'contact' bombs took place in the Trinidad arena.

Sometimes also cited as Vertical Bombing and Retro-Bombing, the Mousetrap was fired to the rear of the launching aircraft at a speed designed to compensate for the forward speed of the aircraft. The drop then became almost vertical, and the underwater trajectory, as noted, was practically nil. With a Mark 31 fuse, the bombs armed in 10 feet of water travel, then went off on contact. A smaller version, used only for training but with the same characteristics, was named 'Minnie Mouse'.

These weapons had a number of distinct advantages over the conventional bombs and depth charges that were the standard ordnance used up to that point. In the first place, a long 'lethal stick' of bombs could be dropped, using an intervalometer, which would allow for normal bombing errors. In the second place, the weapons exploded on contact at any depth greater than about 6 feet, thus trumping one of the major disadvantages of depth charges, which exploded at only one pre-set depth. Additionally, the sink rate of the Mousetrap bombs in water was very rapid (about 24 feet per second), which meant that a submarine had, for all intents and purposes, no chance of moving out from underneath these weapons once dropped.

Mousetrap bombs were originally designed, as noted above, as self-propelled (rocket) bombs, to be used on surface sub-chaser craft, and they showed great promise for such work. The bombs had an overall weight of about 60lb, and carried a 30lb warhead. As used on B-18s, the rocket charge was not used, although they were in fact tested with this. However, the long tail fins and the flat noses of the bombs gave it a highly desirable air and water travel characteristic when dropped from an aircraft. They travelled between 35 and 50 feet forward underwater before dropping vertically down. They remained unarmed until they reached a depth of 6 feet, and consequently provided only a very small chance of getting an explosion on a surfaced sub, and then only if one of the bombs hit the lower part of the sub after arming. Tests performed off Trinidad showed no ricochets up to speeds of 250mph when dropped from 75 feet.

Although it is not possible to state that the explosion of one Mousetrap bomb on contact with a sub would always result in a kill (it probably would not, for example, in the very unlikely event that the bomb happened to explode on one of the deck guns), tests on models indicated a very high probability of a kill.

Not long after the Mousetrap system was made operational on B-18s, US Navy Consolidated PBY Catalina series patrol bombers were also equipped with the system. The installations consisted of rails, running parallel to the fuselage on the undersides of the wings and, in the case of the B-18s, both inboard and outboard of the engine nacelles. Tests with 45° installations were also made on B-18s, but were apparently never perfected. They typically carried ten Mousetrap bombs, two Mk 17 and two Mk 29 depth charges. Typical

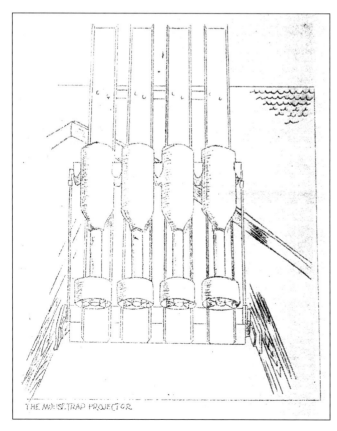

THE MOUSETRAP PROJECTOR

Left: One of the least known but most impressive weapons developed for the B-18Bs was the so-called Mark 20 Mousetrap bomb. An early version was configured, as shown here, to fire through the former ventral gun hatch of a B-18B. *USAFHRA*

Below: A more effective means of launching the Mark 20 Mousetrap retro-bombs was on rails under the wings of B-18Bs. Initially only twelve were mounted, but four more racks were added inboard of the engine nacelles as of 14 October 1942, as shown here. This proved to be a very effective weapon. *Boeing Archives SMFT 418*

tactics developed for both B-18s and PBYs using this system involving a fully surfaced submarine, were that when Mousetrap bombs were dropped the aircraft also dropped all on-board depth charge weapons as well, after which it would make a sharp turn back over the position of the sub and salvo the remainder of the Mousetrap weapons. If the target submarine was partially or completely submerged when the attacking aircraft first got into position to drop its bombs, the Mousetrap bombs and all depth charges were all salvoed, the depth charges being, ideally, placed alongside the center of the stick of contact bombs. The difference in forward underwater travel of the Mk 17 and Mk 29 depth charges gave satisfactory spacing of these bombs, even if all were released at once. The B-18B typically mounted sixteen Mousetrap bombs (although initially twelve was the maximum – four more racks were later added inboard of the engine nacelles), which they normally released in a long 'stick', and three Mk 17 depth charges. By 18 November 1942 at least five B-18s of the 1st SSAG had been fitted with these rails, as well as the MABS system. However, the Army Air Forces Antisubmarine Command formally requested that an entire squadron of B-18 aircraft be fitted with the underwing retro-bombing rails as of 19 April 1943 as well as the retro-flare gun, all of which, it stated, were already equipped with Mark IV MAD gear. It is not clear which squadron was so equipped. The request went on to state that the 1st SSAG had, at the time, a total of six B-18s equipped with the rails. The report went on to state that '…although the addition of rails may cut down the speed of the B-18s slightly, the decrease in weight, due to carrying twelve 60lb, as compared to the present load of four to six 325lb depth charges, should almost compensate for this installation.' This was the first indication that the retro-rails caused any noticeable effect on the aircraft performance. The request also noted that, as of that date, the system had 'never been tested against enemy submarines'.

The development of these weapons for use on the B-18 was not without incident, however. The Experimental Engineering Section at Wright Field, for instance, sent an urgent teletype to the 1st SSAG at Langley Field on 30 November 1942 stating that it was '…imperative that the four inboard wing rails on B-18s not be fired in forthcoming tests, as per latest information from the California Institute of Technology,' which spearheaded the development of the retro-bombs.

By 9 December 1942 B-18 AC36-262 was being used at Wright Field for the tests of a new Low Altitude Radar (LAR) bombing system, but this was apparently not actually installed on operational B-18Bs.

By 2 March 1943 at least one of the 1st SSAG B-18Bs, AC37-470, had a new version of the intervalometer installed, which allowed a train of more than eight bombs to be dropped at once, although it is not clear what weapons were involved.

Status of all Army Air Forces B-18 series aircraft, 30 June 1942

Although it is clear from the foregoing that, by June 1942, the Army Air Forces had diverted a significant number of the available B-18A aircraft for conversion to the vital task of combating the Axis submarine threat, the remainder of the extant airworthy fleet were also giving the US taxpayers their money's worth.

While the majority of the Army B-18 fleet that survived the Japanese onslaught was deployed to defend the east and west coasts of the US mainland, and many others were engaged in anti-submarine warfare in the Caribbean, a numerically small but utility valuable assortment were detailed to training. Here a B-18A assigned to the Air Corps Advanced Flying School, Bombardier Course, at Albuquerque, NM, as of 3 February 1942, illustrates how an instructor could work directly with a cadet trainee in the spacious bombardier's compartment. The B-18s assigned to Albuquerque (later to become Kirtland Field) had not yet gained Field Numbers, but had three-quarters of their engine cowls painted yellow. *NARA RG342FH 4A-17097 via Dana Bell*

In February 1942 Col Harold George of the Air War Plans Division, at AAF Headquarters, recommended to General Arnold the diversion of combat aircraft to the defense of the Continental United States. However, by March the shock of the submarine menace had changed the relative priorities of the moment in favor of the east coast of the US, rather than the west coast. While the west coast had received an initial secondary priority, next to reinforcing Australia, because of the vulnerable aircraft industry concentrated there, by March 1942 the emphasis had decidedly shifted to the east coast. None other than (then) Col Hoyt Vandenberg, then A3 (Air Operations) to General Marshall, Chief of Staff of the Army, called Marshall's attention to the dramatic increase in the number of successful submarine attacks along the US east coast and urged that air defenses along that coast be reinforced immediately. He requested a minimum of twenty-four aircraft suitable for ASW warfare and this action directly resulted in the rapid reassignment of eleven B-18s, including eight from west coast stations to the east coast.

By mid-1942 US production had finally enabled the Army Air Forces to move variants of the North American B-25 into the first place for most numerous Medium Bombardment type in the service, with nine B-25s, twenty-six B-25As, fifty-nine B-25Bs, 252 B-25Cs and fifty-two B-25Ds active in the inventory. However, a total of 245 assorted B-18s (eighty B-18s, 134 B-18As and thirty-one B-18Bs) were also reported, placing the series in the second position. The accompanying table shows the whereabouts of the scattered B-18 fleet as of 30 June 1942, as well as its operational status.

From the foregoing, it can easily be seen that the remaining B-18s in the inventory had, aside from overseas deployments and several Antisubmarine Command stations, been dispersed throughout the Continental US in support of anti-aircraft artillery training, glider corps training, regional headquarters support and, most importantly, training of bombardiers and cadre bombardment aircraft crews. Similarly, the remaining B-18As were likewise dispersed, although squadron-size elements were still very actively engaged in Alaska, Panama and the Caribbean, I Bomber Command stations, and, very significantly, Training Command stations.

The assignment of B-18s and B-18As to Air Training Command installations at this juncture, and especially bombardier schools, is highly significant to our story, and an aspect of the wartime contributions of the aircraft that have been seldom appreciated. It is true that great numbers of the highly trained, commissioned bombardiers streamed from training installations to the far-flung numbered overseas air forces, and took the war to the Axis in overwhelming numbers from 1943 onwards. Most of them were trained on purpose-built Beech AT-11 Kansan advanced trainers, designed

Variant Grid

Variant	Station	Operational	Non-Operational	Variant	Station	Operational	Non-Operational
B-18	Augusta, GA	1		B-18A	Floyd Bennett Field, NY		1
B-18	Bolling Field, DC	1	1	B-18A	INDIGO (Iceland)	1	
B-18	Charlotte, NC		1	B-18A	Langley Field, VA	2	
B-18	Cherry Point MCAS, NC		1	B-18A	Newfoundland		1
B-18	Columbia AAB, SC	1		B-18A	Westover Field, MA	12	4
B-18	Dover AAF, DE	1		B-18A	Mobile Air Depot, AL	1	
B-18	Fort Dix AAB, NJ		1	B-18A	Drew Field, IN	1	
B-18	Langley Field, VA	1		B-18A	MacDill Field, FL	3	
B-18	Mitchel Field, NY	6	5	B-18A	New Orleans, LA	2	
B-18	Drew Field, Tampa, FL	1		B-18A	Orlando AAB, FL	1	
B-18	MacDill Field, FL		1	B-18A	West Palm Beach, FL		1
B-18	Meridian, MS	1		B-18A	Savannah, GA	8	2
B-18	New Orleans, LA	1		B-18A	Fairfield Air Depot, OH	1	
B-18	Orlando AAB, FL	1		B-18A	Chanute Field, MI		1
B-18	Savannah, GA		2	B-18A	Wright Field, OH	3	1
B-18	Tallahassee, FL	5	3	B-18A	San Antonio Air Depot, TX	1	2
B-18	Baer Field, IN	1		B-18A	Albrook Field, CZ	17	9
B-18	Camp Williams AAF, WI	1		B-18A	Baton Rouge, LA	1	
B-18	Scott Field, IL	1		B-18A	Midland AAF, TX (Bombardier School)	8	3
B-18	Wright Field, OH	1		B-18A	Oklahoma City AB, OK	1	
B-18	San Antonio Air Depot, TX	1		B-18A	Post Field, Fort Sill, OK	1	
B-18	Alamogordo AAF, NM		1	B-18A	Randolph Field, TX (Training Command)	30	14
B-18	Barksdale Field, LA	1	1	B-18A	Felts Field, WA	1	
B-18	Randolph Field, TX	1		B-18A	Geiger Field, WA	1	
B-18	Sheppard Field, TX	4	2	B-18A	Lowry Field, CO	4	
B-18	Geiger Field, WA	1		B-18A	McChord Field, WA	1	
B-18	McChord Field, WA	1		B-18A	Salt Lake City AB, UT	2	
B-18	Wendover Field, UT	2	1	B-18A	Wendover Field, UT	10	2
B-18	Bakersfield, CA	3	1	B-18A	Bakersfield, CA	1	
B-18	BRONZE (Alaska)	1		B-18A	BRONZE (Alaska)	3	
B-18	Kern County Airport, CA		1	B-18A	Elmendorf Field, AK	5	
B-18	March Field, CA	1		B-18A	Kern County Airport, CA	1	
B-18	Victorville AAF, CA	5	3	B-18A	Kodiak, AK	13	
B-18	Puerto Rico Air Depot, PR	5		B-18A	Puerto Rico Ai Depot, PR	14	
B-18	Benedict Field, St. Croix, VI	1		B-18A	Benedict Field, St. Croix, VI	2	
B-18	Panama Air Depot, CZ	10		B-18A	Trinidad	12	
B-18	Hawaiian Air Depot, TH	18		B-18A	Panama Air Depot, CZ	4	
B-18	Atkinson Field, British Guiana	3		B-18A	Atkinson Field, British Guiana	2	
B-18	Salinas, Ecuador	4		B-18A	Beane Field, St. Lucia	5	
B-18	Fortaleza, Brazil	2		B-18B	Langley Field, VA	15	4
B-18A	Aberdeen Proving Grnd, MD	1		B-18B	Jacksonville, FL	2	
B-18A	Augusta, GA	1		B-18B	San Antonio Air Depot, TX	2	8
B-18A	Bolling Field, DC	5	2				
B-18A	Charlotte, NC	1					

specifically to mold the necessary skills. The AT-11 was an excellent training platform, but deliveries in significant numbers did not commence until well into 1942; in the meantime B-18 and B-18A aircraft – which provided trainee bombardiers with a much more 'realistic' mount and, it might be added, a much more spacious training environment – filled the gap. In fact, statistics show that, of the bombardiers that took the war to the enemy at the crucial turning points in 1942 and 1943, more than 60% had honed their skills on B-18s.

Actual transfers of B-18M and B-18AM aircraft, denoted as of 14 January 1941 as 'Limited Standard Combat Types', to Air Corps Training Centers from GHQAF tactical units was planned to see twenty-one reassigned in this way by 15 February 1941, thirty-two more by 22 March, and seventy-four by 3 May 1941. The GHQAF, as of 18 January 1941, however, only possessed a total of 139 B-18s of all variants, both serviceable and unserviceable. Of those, twenty-four were fitted with target-towing equipment for which there were

Above: This B-18A was also assigned to the Bombardier's Course at Albuquerque as of 3 February 1942, but was fully camouflaged. It wore Field Number 26, probably a hold-over from its previous line bombardment unit. Note that the censor has obscured the top-secret Norden bombsight in the bombardier's panel, and the cadet trainees are shown being escorted by pistol-packing instructors as they carry sights to their assigned aircraft in satchels. Dedicated Beech AT-11 bombardier training aircraft were just starting to arrive. *NARA RG342FH 4A-17118 via Dana Bell*

Right: By 7 May 1942 the B-18As assigned to the Bombardier Course at Albuquerque, like AC38-596 seen here, had acquired Training Command Field Numbers, this one being Q-111 for Albuquerque. The aircraft was reassigned to more bombardier training duties at Midland, TX, on 27 November 1942, and survived the war to be surplused as NC-67852. This may be the aircraft that was used in combat by the Caribbean Legion in Costa Rica in 1949 as TI-205. *NARA RG342FH 4A-17122 via Dana Bell*

Above: Two cadet trainees prepare to board B-18A Q-101 at Albuquerque on 26 May 1942 through the easy-access ladder-door under the nose. Although the aircraft is fully camouflaged, it sports yellow engine cowls, and the nose gun blister has been covered over. Beech AT-11 Q-4 in the background is unusual in bearing pre-war-style markings. Most cadets regarded the B-18As as better training platforms and far more akin to the actual bombardment aircraft in which they would serve in combat, B-17s and B-24s for the most part. *NARA RG342FH 4A-17174 via Dana Bell*

Between July 1941 and February 1943, two B-18s and twenty-four B-18As were assigned to the bombardier training squadrons at Albuquerque, and Field Numbers were in the range Q-101 to Q-135, the latter the highest known for a B-18. Note that Q-135 (AC38-585) has had the nose gun blister rather crudely sealed with what appears to be duct tape! This aircraft was assigned to Albuquerque on 21 January 1942 and went to Midland, TX, on 27 March 1942. It is known to have been engaged later in anti-submarine patrol work and survived the war to be salvaged. *via Harry Davidson*

AC38-597, assigned to Albuquerque on 31 December 1941, is unusual in wearing its abbreviated Air Corps serial number with pre-war-style national markings. It was assigned to the bombardier training school at Albuquerque and is seen here winging over the huge empty spaces of New Mexico that made it ideal for such work. This aircraft was lost in an accident at Albuquerque while commanded by David Grinnell on 14 March 1942. *via Harry Davidson*

absolutely no replacements, and the GHQAF averaged only eleven B-18s per tactical Group.

By 12 August 1941 the AAF had instructed that, as soon as sufficient 'modern' combat aircraft became available for tactical units, B-18s would be reassigned to the various training schools – but this did not include B-18s assigned to overseas units.

It is interesting to note that, effective from 21 May 1942, the Army Air Corps G-3 (Operations) Directorate granted an exception to AAFR (Army Air Forces Regulation) 60-24 to permit B-18s assigned to Air Force Flying Training Command to operate B-18s on 'local training flights at bombardier training schools' provided that a qualified Crew Chief be substituted in lieu of the normal co-pilot.

By 20 February 1943, by which time B-18As, B-18Bs and B-18Cs had been distinguishing themselves in combat against the Axis submarine threat for some time, AAF Training Command still had thirty-eight assorted B-18s assigned as follows:

AAF Western Training Command had one B-18 with 18 hours flown (it was the only B-18 in this Command and was used for flexible gunnery training).

AAFGCTC (Army Air Forces Gulf Coast Training Command) had thirty-five B-18s, which was by far the most numerous bombardment type available to it. All of these were assigned as bombardier trainers. This command also had one other B-18 employed in Basic Training duties.

AAFSETC (Army Air Forces South Eastern Training Command) had one B-18 assigned for administrative duties.

CHAPTER NINE

B-18 and Digby
operational chronology

As noted earlier, by the time that the Japanese attacked Pearl Harbor and the United States declared war on the Axis powers, the total number of B-18 and B-18A series aircraft remaining active in the inventory had been reduced by accident to a combined total of thirty-eight aircraft. Considering that they had been in service since first deliveries of production aircraft in May 1937, and flown intensively both domestically and overseas, this was a loss rate below the average for nearly any other type in the inventory.

When the losses in Hawaii and the Philippines in the opening months of the war are added, those left over were obviously what was left to continue in war service. The B-18s and B-18As, and their derivatives drawn from those ranks that shortly followed, constituted the oldest aircraft then in the active USAAF inventory still engaged in combat operations in squadron strength, an unheralded testament not only to the durability of the design but also to the urgency of the need.

While researching for this project the authors were progressively amazed at the emergence of two overwhelming conclusions. First, the sheer number of missions flown by B-18s, the youngest of which was two years old by the time intensive patrol operations commenced in February 1942, and second, the numbers of hours flown by individual crew members – pilots, co-pilots, bombardiers, navigators, radar operators, radio operators and gunners – some of whom measured their

flying time in these aircraft in the thousands of hours. In the Eighth Air Force, to which all honor is accorded, the commissioned officer with the highest number of completed missions achieved ninety-one over enemy territory in which hostile action could be expected. B-18 crew members, at every crew position, routinely exceeded this number of combat missions within one year of operations. True, they certainly did not have to face the combined fury of the Luftwaffe and the withering flak over occupied Europe. But on every single mission they faced the armed prospect of encountering a determined enemy, who outnumbered them five to one, with daunting anti-aircraft capabilities – while flying alone, without much hope of air-sea rescue if downed, often at night, and in shark-infested waters. The fact that these crews earned the exact same Air Medals for their missions as their major overseas air force comrades in arms is often forgotten entirely.

This volume, were all of their stories told in detail, would be beyond the bounds of economy. Consequently, a decision was made to summarise the operations of B-18 series aircraft chronologically, as follows, by war year. It is the sincere hope of the authors that this compromise will adequately convey to the reader the sheer weight of their number, and the incredible untold story that they depict.

1940

The first of the family line to go to war were, of course, the Royal Canadian Air Force DB-280 Digbys, initially bearing RAF-style European dark green and dark earth camouflage over black undersurfaces. They also sported blue and red 'B-type' roundels on the fuselage and extremities of both upper wings, but had conventional blue-white-red roundels on the undersides. The Digbys were the most modern bombardment aircraft in the RCAF inventory at the time, soon joined by Lockheed Hudsons. *AF PL797 via Carl Vincent*

15 July 1940: The Royal Canadian Air Force moved the first elements of No 10(BR) Squadron to Gander, Newfoundland, where they commenced operations shortly thereafter on patrols and convoy escorts. These were the first armed missions flown by Douglas DB-1 and DB-2 derivatives anywhere. 'A' Flight made two or three long patrols each day, as well as shorter reconnaissance missions, weather permitting.

Above: After initial deliveries in late December 1939, the RCAF issued most of the new DB-280 Digbys to No 10(BR) Squadron based at Winnipeg and St Hubert. By this time, the 'B-type' fuselage roundels had been altered to 'A.1-type' with the large-diameter outer yellow circle and yellow underlined unit codes – in this case apparently PB+G. The Lockheed Hudson Mk I aircraft in the foreground were assigned to No 11 Squadron RCAF between October 1939 and July 1942. *RCAF P.L.1173*

Left: The early camouflage scheme applied to RCAF Digbys did not hold up well to the harsh weather conditions of even the Canadian autumn, and No 751, shown here, which had been delivered on 8 March 1940, and was probably with No 12 (Communications) Squadron when pictured here in October 1940, already shows evidence of significant fading. *CAG PL 3940A via Carl Vincent*

28 September 1940: An RCAF Digby of No 10(BR) Squadron recovered to Dartmouth after being airborne on patrol for 12hr 45min – a portent of things to come, and an endurance routinely exceeded by both RCAF crews and USAAF B-18 crews as the war progressed.

6 November 1940: In a classic case of 'what might have been', three RCAF Digbys from their Gander, Newfoundland, base were sent to attack the German commerce raider *Admiral Scheer*, which was reportedly operating 600 miles off the coast. In fact, the cruiser was 800 miles off the coast, and the aircraft could not locate her.

1941

1 July 1941: The Commander of the 19th Bomb Wing, Caribbean Air Force, issued an order that all bombardment units (exclusively equipped with B-18s at this point) at Piarco Field, Trinidad (specifically, the 1st Bomb Squadron), would maintain one aircraft on high readiness or within '…such radius of the base that it could return to the field within 30 minutes of the receipt of an emergency radio call.' The provocation of these instructions is not known, but they apparently implied the expectation of some form of attack through the Caribbean. On the same day, Col Strong, at the time the US Military Attaché in Bogota, Colombia, transmitted to the Commander of the Panama Canal Department a report of 'doubtful reliability' that suggested that a torpedo attack against the Canal might take place between 1 and 15 July, adding '…while this sounds fantastic, take it for what it is worth.'

22 August 1941: The first actual alert involving armed USAAC B-18s was sounded in the Puerto Rico area. It was prompted by an urgent radiogram from the Department Headquarters to the 13th Composite Wing, informing it that the Navy had passed on intelligence that two German submarines, with a tender, appeared to be heading for the Puerto Rico area. As many aircraft as possible were to be held ready.

Nine B-18As were each loaded with six 300lb bombs and prepared for immediate take-off. The next day, the Department radioed that conditions had changed little, but that 3-hour readiness was to be maintained – but with no interference with on-going training. On 28 August the Wing was advised that three aircraft on readiness would suffice. On the 31st the Wing S-2 (Intelligence) was told by the Department G-3 that a Royal Canadian Navy cruiser had sighted the German cruiser *Koln* 800 miles east of Philadelphia on 27 August and that the USS *Wasp* had reported sighting the German cruiser *Hipper* 300 miles east of Bermuda on the 28th. On the night of the 30th the US Navy reported that a ship without lights passed through the Virgin Passage. The upshot of all of this was that nothing further was heard of the *Koln*, and the supposed *Hipper* turned out to be HMS *Rodney*. The vessel that had slipped through the Virgin Passage turned out to be a British freighter and the two submarines were finally believed to be somewhere in the South Atlantic.

30 September 1941: An RCAF Digby of No 10(BR) Squadron out of Gander was dispatched on the first known authenticated anti-submarine mission. The sub had disappeared by the time the aircraft arrived on the scene, however.

25 October 1941: The first known instance of contact with the enemy by a B-18 series aircraft involved a Digby of the RCAFs No 10(BR) Squadron. German submarines had sunk several Allied vessels off Newfoundland the night before and a maximum effort was mounted, with no fewer than seven Digbys involved. No 740, flown by Sqn Ldr C. L. Annis, a former unit member then on temporary duty at Gander, and his crew, sighted a U-boat just east of the Strait of Belle Isle in 60-knot winds and attacked with two 600lb bombs. One fell just short and the other 75 feet long amidst the swirl of the crash-diving sub. The bombs apparently failed to detonate, much to the chagrin of the bomb aimer, as he had disarmed them without the crew's knowledge.

A truly historic aircraft, RCAF Digby No 740, coded at the time as PB+L, of No 10(BR) Squadron, under the command of Squadron Leader C. L. Annis, attacked a surfaced U-boat on 25 October 1941 just east of the Strait of Belle Isle, Newfoundland, but the bombs apparently failed to detonate, as the bomb aimer had disarmed them without the crew's knowledge! It was the first attack on a submarine by a North American-based aircraft of the war. *via Carl Vincent*

27 October 1941: Headquarters, Caribbean Defense Command, Quarry Heights, Panama Canal Zone, issued CDC-S 381 'Authority to Open Fire'. This extraordinary document stated, in Paragraph 1, that: 'In the event German, Italian or Japanese airplanes definitely identified as such by an officer trained for such duty, or a flight of ten (10) or more planes that cannot be identified as United States Army or Navy planes should enter the area of Army defenses, both pursuit aircraft and anti-aircraft artillery are authorized to open fire.' In Paragraph 2, it brought home to one and all the seriousness of the document: 'In the event that the hostile targets come within range of the anti-aircraft artillery, the artillery is to keep up its fire regardless of the position of our own aviation.'

By November 1941 all of the B-18s in the Philippines had been camouflaged, and some deployments had been made. Although of marginal quality, this is one of the last photos known to have been taken of a B-18 in the islands before the Japanese attack on 8 December. It is believed to be at either Nielson or Nichols Field, with the tents of the 27th Bomb Group (L) in the background. *Olive Dorn via Bill Bartsch*

7 December 1941: The 43rd Bomb Squadron (Reinforced), an element of the III Bomber Command, was immediately transferred to Pope Field, NC, and given responsibility for performing three reconnaissance missions per day in an area north of Savannah, and also for maintaining nine B-18s on 1-hour readiness during daylight hours.

The 82nd Bomb Squadron (L), 13th Bomb Group (L), operating from McChord Field, WA, operated ten dedicated anti-submarine missions between this day and the end of the month using a mix of Douglas B-18As and B-23s over the Puget Sound area. The unit transitioned to B-25As in January 1942. Elsewhere, the 43rd Bomb Squadron, based out of Charlotte, NC, conducted both day and night coastal patrols all the way to Miami, FL, with a mix of twenty B-18s. The unit moved to MacDill Field, FL, on 1 January 1942.

In the far north, immediately after the Japanese attack, the 36th Bomb Squadron and the 73rd Bomb Squadron in Alaska commenced lengthy patrols, with flights being made on alternate weeks by each squadron south over Kenai into the Gulf of Alaska. When not flying, the units were on constant alert. At one time the Air Warning Service supposedly sighted some thirty enemy aircraft south of Kodiak on course towards Anchorage and the intrepid 36th Bomb Squadron immediately got four B-18As into the air to 'intercept' them! After several hours of futile searching they straggled back to base – the AWS had 'made a mistake'.

8 December 1941: B-18s assigned to III Bomber Command commenced continuous offshore patrols during daylight hours, while observation aircraft of the Command maintained an inshore patrol. These were continued unabated until the formation of the Eastern Theater of Operations. The Command was also ordered, as part of Navy Western Hemisphere Plan No 2, to maintain, on minimum 2-hour readiness, three Boeing B-17s at MacDill Field and three B-18As or B-24s at Orlando. As of this date AAF units and aircraft were conducting intensive over-water patrols and reconnaissance from domestic stations as follows:

Langley Field, VA
2nd Bombardment Group (H)
22nd Bombardment Group (H)
18th Reconnaissance Squadron (M)

Bangor, ME
43rd Bombardment Group (H)
13th Reconnaissance Squadron (H)

Westover Field, MA
34th Bombardment Group (H)
1st Reconnaissance Squadron (H)

Numerous other units equipped with B-18s throughout the US, in the Caribbean and Pacific, also commenced locally authorized patrols this day, including the 3rd Reconnaissance Squadron (M) flying an average of three missions per day through to 22 January 1942, when the unit re-equipped with B-25s and moved to Mitchel Field, LI, NY. The unit flew morning, midday and afternoon patrols of usually 4-hour duration, logging nearly 30 hours per week. Four B-18A crews of the 41st Bomb Squadron (H), commanded by Lts Horner, Frame, Ottinger

Pre-war color images of B-18 series aircraft are very rare, but in-flight views, in company with Curtiss P-36 aircraft of the 28th Composite Group in Alaska are even rarer. Here B-18A 28MB46, probably of the 73rd Bomb Squadron (note barely visible unit insignia on mid-fuselage) wing over the rugged territory in November 1941. *Fred Turner*

and R. L. Cox, were sent to Savannah, GA, on detached service late in the date for the specific purpose of patrolling the Atlantic coastline. Lt Busch was in nominal command of this special detachment, which eventually totalled nine B-18As. Four days later the detachment was moved to Fort Bragg, NC, then on to Morrison Field, FL. The same day, the solitary B-18 remaining with the 41st Bomb Group (M), still at Hammer Field, Fresno, CA, was immediately sent to Hamilton Field, thence to Sacramento, CA, for patrol duty on the Pacific coast. This aircraft, while its sisters were away at Savannah on the east coast, became part of a so-called Provisional Squadron – a pool of all aircraft at that time in the California area, patrolling the west coast until after 1 January 1942. This may have been the genesis for the so-called, and poorly documented, Sierra Group.

8 December 1941: In Hawaii, battled-scarred AAF units scrambled to prepare for what might come next. The 50th Reconnaissance Squadron, after working without rest all day maintaining and repairing its aircraft that could be made serviceable, got No 94 into commission and took off on a long-range patrol at 0400 with 2Lt Trent in command. They returned disappointed. This was the solitary aircraft this unit had salvaged from the raid, having lost two B-17s and three B-18s.

9 December 1941: The 17th Bomb Group (M) at Pendleton, OR, was ordered to have all aircraft loaded with bombs, to be as fully equipped with defensive guns as possible, and to be on alert from 0300 hours. However, sufficient bomb loads were only available at McChord Field, WA, Portland, OR, and Everett, WA, for one mission each by available aircraft. The Group was short of some 164 machine guns! The units of II Bomber Command, which had been turned over to the operational control of the Fourth Air Force just after 7 December were disposed to the maximum extent possible. Steps had been taken to move most of the medium and light bombardment aircraft of the Second Air Force west of the Cascades.

10 December 1941: A Detachment of the 43rd Bomb Squadron (Reinforced) was formed and sent to Morrison Field, West Palm Beach, FL, where it was ordered to maintain three B-18s on 30-minute readiness and to use its other three B-18s for very intensive operational training. The parent unit, still at Pope Field, NC, was by this time tasked to operate two patrols daily over the area between Cape Fear and Georgetown.

11 December 1941: The official history of the 6th Bomber Command, 25th Bomb Group, states that a B-18A, AC37-601, was 'lost in action' on this date while on a patrol mission over the Caribbean, with the loss of all hands, but the nature of this loss has eluded documentation. The crew consisted of pilot 1Lt Maurice M. Miller, 2Lt W. S. Walker, 2Lt J. A. Hutchins, S/Sgt Walter E. Brown, Sgt Todd Tilton Jr, Capt Vincent P. Papa, PFC John L. Hoffman, and PFC H. E. Gonzales.

12 December 1941: B-18s and other US Naval aircraft assigned to the Caribbean Air Force attacked the Japanese vessel *Alert* at Caldera at 1630 hours in Costa Rican waters. The Costa Rican Government requested that the attacks be stopped, as the Japanese on board had been taken into custody. This is the only known instance of a Panama-based USAAF element attacking a Japanese vessel during the war.

18 December 1941: In Panama the 6th Bombardment Group was ordered to send a detachment of six B-18As with ground crews to operate from Guatemala City – one of the very first 'foreign' deployments, not only of B-18s, but of any USAAF aircraft, to a foreign nation following Pearl Harbor. Starting on the 20th, this detachment was to dispatch three B-18As each day on a 'fan search' and reconnaissance of the sector to the west in the Pacific from the Guatemalan coast to the absolute limit of their endurance, with but a

200-gallon reserve. Considering that these aircraft were flying over a very empty Pacific Ocean sector, without a chance of air-sea rescue if they got into trouble, these were particularly courageous missions. Although carrying full combat crews and, oddly, four guns each, these aircraft were loaded with only two 300lb bombs each in order to achieve maximum range.

20 December 1941: Two Provisional Squadrons, the 85th Bomb Squadron and the 97th Bomb Squadron, were formed, and personnel from the 84th Bomb Squadron at Fresno, CA, incorporated into both – one with Douglas B-18As and the other with early B-24s. Both were engaged actively in anti-submarine patrols over the Pacific coast.

22 December 1941: The Panama Canal Zone-based 15th Naval District reported that a hostile submarine was detected at 1015 hours 2 miles off the entrance of Balboa Channel on the Pacific side of the Panama Canal entrance, and a destroyer made depth charge attacks. Destroyers continued to drop depth charges 5 miles east of Taboguilla light. A Caribbean Air Force Alert Force of B-18s was dispatched to the area but no target was sighted. The same day the Caribbean Defense Command established the Air Task Force, which included all bombardment aviation assets in the Panama Sector, as well as all Navy patrol bomber aviation assigned to defend the Canal. In effect, this meant all of the B-18s in the area. They were charged with establishing an aerial reconnaissance of the Pacific and Atlantic sectors of the Panama Naval Coastal Frontier and to locate, trail and attack any enemy force encountered.

This B-18, 44R/4 of the 44th Reconnaissance Squadron based at Albrook Field, Canal Zone, was apparently still awaiting camouflage when placed on alert to attack a submarine off the Balboa Channel on the Pacific side of the Isthmus on 22 December 1941. Note that the dorsal turret is being flown extended and armed. The unit insignia on the nose has been painted over, probably in anticipation of camouflage paint coming next.
Brigadier General Charles E. Williams Jr

23 December 1941: The Caribbean Defense Command Liaison Officer at Interceptor Command reported that a radio message had been received at 1320 hours from a 7th Reconnaissance Squadron B-18 reporting an unidentified submarine off Prieta Point heading inbound towards the Pacific entrance to the Panama Canal by 1640 hours at 0403N 9050W, and that it had submerged immediately. A Caribbean Air Force B-18 Alert Force was dispatched to the scene but found nothing. The same day, the 16th Reconnaissance Squadron (M), based at Astoria and Marshfield, OR, commenced flying anti-submarine patrols every day with a mix of ten B-18As, six Martin B-26s and two organic Boeing-Stearman PT-17s through to 4 May 1942, weather permitting. These patrols were flown under the supervision of the Navy.

Above: The 16th Reconnaissance Squadron (M), based at Astoria and Marchfield, OR, by 23 December 1941, was flying anti-submarine patrols over the Pacific from that date until 4 May 1942, with a mix of B-18As and Martin B-26s. *via Paul Bridgford*

Right: Although the Royal Canadian Air Force had come to appreciate the rugged qualities of its small force of Digbys by the winter of 1941, operating conditions, as this crewman can attest, were horrible and very hard on the aircraft. An RCAF Digby, No 744, was lost at sea on patrol under unknown circumstances on 29 December 1941, along with her six-man crew. *via Rich Dann*

26 December 1941: The 36th Bomb Squadron in Alaska continued flying inshore patrols south to Seward, flying to the maximum range of the B-18As. To enable them to search greater areas, flights occasionally landed at Yakutat to rest and refuel, returning to their home base at Elmendorf Field the following day. On this day Lt Ramouti and his crew of the 36th Bomb Squadron started a patrol that did not end until 6 January! Bad weather forced him to cancel his plans to return to Elmendorf and he landed at Yakutat. The same weather grounded him there until New Year's Day. The weather improved a little and he left the ground, intending to complete his flight to Elmendorf. North of Yakutat the aircraft ran into heavy cloud banks but continued flying on instruments toward the Elmendorf radio range. Because the pilot could not trust the range completely, he climbed to 18,000 feet and found that the range had faded completely. He turned back towards Cordova and initiated a let-down on the Cordova range. The aircraft broke out at 200 feet and he found that the beam had split in the storm and carried him some 20 miles north of the field. His B-18 landed at dusk with an estimated 15 minutes of fuel remaining. The aircraft remained at Cordova until 6 January, when the weather again cleared.

27 December 1941: A Detachment of the 43rd Bomb Squadron (H), Third Air Force, flew five 'combat missions' on B-18s and also observed and provided cover to the SS *President Adams*, which had been disabled by a submarine attack. They continued to provide escort to the vessel into the next day.

29 December 1941: RCAF Digby No 744 of No 10(BR) Squadron was lost without trace at sea under unknown circumstances with her six-man crew. The 43rd Bomb Squadron (H) flew at least three B-18A reconnaissance missions from Pope Field, NC, while a Detachment of the same unit, flying four B-18As, per verbal orders of the Commanding General, flew reconnaissance missions from Jacksonville to Key West in the morning and afternoon.

31 December 1941: The 43rd Bomb Squadron (H) at Pope Field, NC, flew nine missions on this date. On the fourth, at 1216 hours, a B-18A dropped bombs on a suspicious oil slick at 3222N 7534W, but no results were claimed.

1942

1 January 1942: The 43rd Bomb Squadron (H) Detachment at Jacksonville, FL, flew eight missions on this date, using twelve B-18As.

5 January 1942: Two missions, using two B-18As each, were flown by the 43rd Bomb Squadron (H) Detachment escorting the USS *Algorab* from south of Key West to 2150N in the Yucatan Channel. The main body, still at Pope Field, NC, dispatched no fewer than eight B-18As on long-range reconnaissance missions, but the first and fifth returned in 10 and 15 minutes respectively with engine trouble, and the second and third hit very dense fog near Cape Fear, with the former forced to land at Charleston.

6 January 1942: The 43rd Bomb Squadron (H) Detachment at Jacksonville, FL, sent out six B-18As on reconnaissance missions. The number three aircraft suffered failure of her hydraulic system on return and the landing gear was washed out on landing – a symptom of the very heavy utilisation the aircraft were experiencing since 7 December 7.

11 January 1942: The 6th Reconnaissance Squadron (M), attached to the 41st Bomb Group (M), transferred from Muroc Army Air Base, CA, to Mather Field, Sacramento, CA, and continued to fly anti-submarine patrols off the west coast, commencing on 8 December 1941, with a mix of Lockheed A-29s, Douglas B-18As and a few Consolidated LB-30s. Coastal patrols were conducted from Sacramento almost exclusively with B-18As, although the unit encountered frequent fog and rain. These patrols were continued until 10 March 1942, as well as transition and combat crew training until 8 April, when twenty-five officers and 153 enlisted ranks were moved to Naval Air Station Alameda, where they trained with a Navy Fleet Air Detachment. Coastal patrols were continued from Alameda from 10 April to 9 May 1942, the unit being redesignated as the 396th Bombardment Squadron (M) on 22 April.

15 January 1942: Lt Lolley of the 20th Bomb Squadron, flying a B-18A, sighted a diving submarine at 1653 hours but could not make an attack before the sub dived.

The seaworthy qualities of the basic design were illustrated early on when RCAF Digby No 738 – the very first Digby – while coded as PB+N with No 10(BR) Squadron, crashed in flames into Freshwater Bay, Newfoundland, on 2 January 1942, subsequently being towed ashore the hard way, as though she were a flying boat. *via Rich Dann*

Incredibly, the crew of RCAF Digby No 738 managed to swim ashore after the aircraft crashed. Here, RCAF crews salvage what they can after the remains were pulled ashore by brute force of manpower. *via Rich Dann*

By mid-January 1942, after a fighting retreat from the Philippines and Java, the surviving B-18s in the Far East had all arrived in Australia, where they were put to good use on a multitude of duties. These anonymous examples, possibly including AC37-16, which later gained Australian radio call sign VHCWB and was named 'Goober Dust', are seen here sharing a field with several Royal Australian Air Force Avro Ansons and a Consolidated LB-30 Liberator (AL570) at Maylands Aerodrome, Perth. *Gordon Birkett and Western Australia Aviation Museum via Buz Busby*

17 January 1942: A 20th Bomb Squadron, I Bomber Command, B-18, commanded by Major D. O. Smith, spotted a periscope at 1010 hours at 3920N 7328W and attacked with four 300lb demolition bombs. No results were claimed. This was regarded as Mission No 1 of the newly constituted Army Air Forces Antisubmarine Command (AAFASC). Post-war analysis concluded that this was almost certainly not a U-boat. It was, however, the first submarine attack claimed by a B-18 crew.

Meanwhile, in Hawaii, while he was eating lunch at 1230 hours, a note was passed to Lt G. L. Kelley. It contained the name of two geographic locations, Nohili and Makaha, and the information that a submarine had been seen lying on the surface at 1130 hours a mile off shore. Three B-18s took off at 1230 to search an area of some 150 square miles in formation (Areas 31-26-37 C-72) for a distance of 15 miles from the shore at 1,500 feet. They found nothing, discontinued the search and recovered to Kauai practice range to complete the mission.

19 January 1942: An RCAF Digby flown by Flt Lt J. M. Young, while on patrol east of Gander, sighted a submarine through snow squalls and attacked. The aircraft dropped a salvo of three depth charges as the sub crash-dived, followed by a second string of three on a second pass. No results were observed, but the aircraft continued to search the area to the extent of its endurance.

Meanwhile, in the far Pacific off Hawaii a submarine was reported near Blow Hole at 1720 hours local time and a B-18 from the 72nd Bomb Squadron was sent to attack. At 1800, what appeared to be the shadow of a submarine was in fact bombed, but due to darkness it was not known whether the bombing was effective. Navy dive bombers and two destroyers arrived and started depth charge operations and the B-18 returned to base.

20 January 1942: The Headquarters, 13th Bomb Group (M), and its subordinate 39th Bomb Squadron (M) transferred from Orlando AAB, FL, to Westover Field, MA, and commenced flying anti-submarine patrols immediately with a mix of B-18s and B-25s.

21 January 1942: The 16th Reconnaissance Squadron (M), attached to the 42nd Bomb Group, II Bomber Command, commenced flying anti-submarine and coastal patrols from Paine Field, WA, with a mix of B-18s, Martin B-26s and Lockheed A-29s, and sent a detachment, believed with B-18s, to Astoria, OR.

Much further south, and involving a deployment that has been completely ignored in historical accounts, the 25th Bomb Squadron (H), 6th Bomb Group, in Panama was dispatched from Rio Hato, Republic of Panama, to distant Salinas, Ecuador, where it commenced extremely lonely anti-submarine patrols along the far north-western 'hump' of

mainland South America in the obvious direction of the Galapagos Islands – key to the Pacific defense of the Canal. By 16 February the unit had been re-equipped with four Boeing B-17Es and retained only one of its B-18s. It was known during this deployment as Task Force 3.

22 January 1942: An RCAF Digby commanded by Flt Lt E. M. Williams attacked a sub on return from a convoy escort mission, the first attack being delivered while the stern was still above the surface. Two of the first three depth charges hung up, however, but the third exploded near the center of the sub. A full salvo might well have sunk her. The aircraft made two more attacks, dropping her remaining five depth charges then dropping flares to mark the spot, and did not leave the area until the weather closed down.

Yet another testament to the sea-handling qualities of the design, this B-18 appears to have become amphibious as it is winched ashore from the Essequebo River in British Guiana using a seaplane ramp on 23 January 1942. Although still bearing the codes for a 44th Reconnaissance Squadron aircraft, 44R/3, it was actually assigned at this time to the far-ranging 35th Bomb Squadron, which was destined to become a premier anti-submarine unit with B-18s. It had made a forced landing on the water while under the command of 2Lt Benson W. Munro. *USAAF*

25 January 1942: A Hawaii-based AAF aircraft, believed to have been a B-18 (unit unknown), spotted a large air bubble and green shadow about 5 miles east of Makapi Point at 2130 1571. It was ascertained to be a submarine and the aircraft dropped two 300lb bombs and claimed hits with both of them. No other details have been uncovered.

28 January 1942: The Third Air Force ordered III Bomber Command to maintain two strike units consisting of no fewer than two B-18As each at New Orleans and Corpus Christi, TX, for coverage of the Gulf of Mexico. At about this same time a Detachment of the 67th Bomb Squadron (H) of the 44th Bomb Group at MacDill Field, FL, was transferred to New Orleans to operate the two B-18As at the commercial airport there. The two aircraft at Corpus Christi moved to Ellington Field, near Houston, by 22 February, and were operated by a 6th Bomb Squadron (Detachment).

During January 1942 aircraft and units of I Bomber Command flew a total of 3,134 hours on anti-submarine patrols and sighted at least eleven submarines, of which seven were attacked. Thirteen Allied ships were sunk in the Command's area of responsibility during the month.

1 February 1942: the 75th Bomb Squadron, 42nd Bomb Group, II Bomber Command, commenced flying anti-submarine and patrol missions from Portland, OR, 300 miles out to sea in 'fan' patterns with Douglas B-18As, a few early Martin B-26s, and oddly, unarmed B-18Ms. It continued these missions until May, when the unit started to receive Lockheed A-29s.

3 February 1942: At 0745 hours an aircraft from the 42nd Bomb Squadron out of Hawaii (it is not clear if it was a B-17 or B-18, as the unit was operating a mix of both at the time), flown by 1Lt H. T. Hastings, sighted a submarine 1 mile off Diamond Head. It broke surface then submerged immediately but the pilot was unable to spot the sub thereafter, although he searched for 50 minutes.

5 February 1942: Two B-18As from the 29th Bomb Group (H), III Bomber Command, were dispatched on Mission A.O. #13 in search of a reported enemy submarine but, when unable to locate it, were obliged to land at Havana, Cuba.

6 February 1942: A single B-18A was launched by the 29th Bomb Group (H), III Bomber Command, to continue the search for a reported U-boat sighted the day before, but again it was not located.

In Alaska the entire 36th Bomb Squadron with its B-18As was transferred from Elmendorf Field to Kodiak. From there patrols were flown regularly west to Cold Bay and Umnak, east to Yakutat, and south deep into the Gulf of Alaska.

9 February 1942: The 78th and 79th Bomb Squadrons (M) of the 45th Bomb Group (M) commenced flying anti-submarine patrols with a mix of Douglas B-18s and DB-7s from Grenier Field, Manchester, NH.

12 February 1942: Lt Zumwalt, flying B-18 AC36-288 of the 4th Reconnaissance Squadron (H), Seventh Air Force, in Hawaii, while on an interception training mission at 0016 hours, sighted a periscope at 2249N 1560W and dropped six bombs on the course of the suspected submarine. There was no evidence of any damage after the attack.

16 February 1942: A German submarine was attacked at 0620 hours by a B-18 of the 59th Bomb Squadron (L), Caribbean Air Force, off Willemstad, Curacao, NWI, commanded by Lt James E. Lazenby. LTC Gerald E. Williams of the 9th Bomb Group (H) and his crew were also credited with B-18 action on this date. Six more B-18s arrived to help in the attack at 1040 hours and also claimed to have spotted a submarine and sunk it.

17 February 1942: LTC Gerald E. Williams and his 9th Bomb Group (H) B-18 crew were credited with engaging an enemy submarine in combat on this date.

18 February 1942: In one of the most bizarre B-18 actions of the war, a crew from the 40th Bomb Group, led by none other than the Group Commander, Col Ivan Palmer, who had just completed a 6-hour patrol escorting a small convoy of four shallow-draught tankers from Las Piedras, Venezuela, across the 50-mile stretch of water to Oranjestad, Aruba, were eating a cold lunch of 'C' rations at the gravel-surfaced operating field on the island. The story goes that the enlisted bombardier of the crew, Sgt James E. 'Buck' Dozier, happened to look seaward and screamed, 'Submarine in the harbor!' Incredibly, when the rest of the crew jerked around to look, a fully surfaced sub was clearly visible just off the west end of the runway, and crew members could be seen coming down the conning tower towards the 88mm deck gun. Unbeknown to the B-18 crew, the sub had already fired a torpedo, on the surface, at the crowd of tankers in the harbor, which beached it. After a shouted 'Let's go!' the entire B-18 crew sprinted across the runway some 200 feet to their B-18, where the Crew Chief, Sgt Bennie Slonina, busy pumping fuel into the plane, looked up in surprise. He was ordered to clear the bowser while the crew scrambled to their

positions. Sgt Dozier had the presence of mind to pull the pins from the four depth charges in the bomb bay. Col Palmer had not rejoined the crew, as he was away conferring with Dutch and US leaders on the island, so the command of the aircraft passed to Lt Ira V. Matthews.

As they quickly fired up the engines and turned onto the runway, the aircraft came literally face to face, at the end of the 3,500-foot stretch, with the sub. Just as the pilot was about to advance the throttles, the crew noticed a khaki-clad figure running in front of the aircraft – it was Col Palmer, who quickly boarded and resumed command of the aircraft – luckily so, as Lt Matthews was about to take off down-wind. The Colonel then calmly released the brakes and taxied directly towards the sub, down the strip. Lt Matthews then instructed the bombardier to use the nose gun to start firing at the surfaced sub, but Colonel Palmer instantly instructed him to hold on that, as they were about to turn for take off, and the Colonel was afraid he might hit a prop. By this time, the B-18 was less than 500 feet from the surfaced sub, and the crew could clearly see the Germans climbing the conning tower ladder, as at least four others manned the deck gun. Fearing a hit from the 88mm gun at any moment, the crew marvelled as the Colonel calmly went through normal mag checks, then took off and immediately executed a shallow right turn at 300 feet. Lt Matthews looked back and the sub was already slanting towards the harbor channel, bow submerged.

As the aircraft climbed to 1,000 feet, the bombardier gave the pilot instructions, called his pre-release angles from the fixed bomb sight, and the bomb bay doors opened. Moments later, all four depth charges were salvoed. The aircraft immediately banked into a steep left turn and soon after landed again at the airfield to rearm with more depth charges. This was almost certainly the shortest combat mission of the war. No claims were made, although the B-18 almost certainly saved a slaughter of the tankers anchored in the roadstead.

20 February 1942: The 3rd Bomb Squadron, 6th Bomber Command, in Panama was placed on alert to send one B-18 to search for and attack a submarine sighted at 0644N 8250W. This was very possibly the submarine attacked off Colon on the 24th (qv). A B-18 of the 45th Bomb Squadron (M) was also credited with engaging a submarine on this date, possibly the U-156.

21 February 1942: A composite organisation known as the Eastern Theater of Operations took over responsibility from the Third Air Force for air defenses from Virginia on the east coast all the way to Pensacola, FL. The organisation responded to reports from the Navy and from a number of Observation Squadrons conducting inshore patrols, and had a strike force consisting of two B-18s each at Charleston, SC, and Miami to answer calls. These responsibilities were eventually assumed by the Army Air Forces Antisubmarine Command (AAFAC).

The same day two B-18s of the 1st Bomb Squadron (H) in the Caribbean were credited with engaging a submarine on this date, probably the U-161.

23 February 1942: Four B-18As, in two separate flights of two each, and a single B-18 of the 29th Bomb Group (H) conducted an intensive search for a reported submarine between Daytona and Palm Beach, FL.

The same day, on the west coast, Imperial Japanese Navy submarine I-17 surfaced and fired no fewer than thirteen rounds of 140mm (5.5-inch) shells from her deck gun into an oil refinery and tank farm north of Santa Barbara, CA. AAF pursuit aircraft and bombers, believed to include a number of B-18s stationed in the area, responded but did not locate her. This attack accounts for the numerous deployments of B-18s to unusual stations in California in the early months of 1942 shown in the Production List of Individual Aircraft (Annex 1).

24 February 1942: The destroyer USS *Goff* engaged an enemy submarine not far off the breakwater of Colon – well within sight of the Atlantic entrance to the Panama Canal. At 2140 hours the 3rd Bomb Squadron was ordered to launch three B-18s due north of the Colon breakwater and to make absolutely sure of the identity of their target, as there was also a friendly submarine in the area. While en route, the leader of the trio of B-18s requested information as to whether the USS *Goff* could send homing signals, and they were told to go to 375 or 396kc. At 2153 the three B-18s were ordered to proceed to the so-called Fortified Zone – but not to engage the sub unless found to be in actual combat with the USS *Goff*. At 2210 France Field advised Lt McIheran, apparently leading the B-18s (the other two were commanded by Lt Wormwood and Captain Wallace), that the friendly submarine was at 1005N 7941W (this was very possibly the Free French super submarine *Surcouf*, which was lost in this vicinity and is assumed to have been rammed inadvertently by the SS *Thompson Lykes*) and that any other submarine in the area was to be sunk. They were apparently unable to locate a target, and struggled back to France Field, landing at 0355 on the 25th.

25 February 1942: 6th Bomber Command ordered three more B-18s from the 3rd Bomb Squadron off at 0455 in search of the submarine being engaged by the *USS Goff* (see above). They apparently did not find a target.

26 February 1942: The brand-new Eighth Air Force, at this time still part of Air Force Combat Command and with its glory days in England and over Axis Europe still in the future, is organised at Savannah, GA, and amongst its initial equipment are single examples of the Douglas B-23, B-18A and A-20A.

During February aircraft and units of I Bomber Command flew a total of 4,766 hours on anti-submarine patrols, sighted eighteen U-boats and attacked twelve of them. A total of nineteen Allied vessels were sunk during the month in the Command's area of responsibility.

By the end of February 1942 and into March, the remaining B-18s stationed in the Hawaiian Islands were heavily engaged in patrol work to the limit of their endurance around the islands, and all had been camouflaged and the red 'ball' in the center of the national insignia had been painted over with white. This B-18 has clearly suffered a severe ground loop as well as damage to the rudder, and the camouflage pattern is of interest. However, the serial code on the vertical fin, '002', cannot be explained, as it matched no known B-18 serial and must have been a unit code. *NARA RG342FH 62996AC*

3 March 1942: A B-18 operating from Waller Field, Trinidad, was credited with engaging a submarine on this date, possibly the U-161.

9 March 1942: A B-18 of the 45th Bomb Squadron was credited with engaging an enemy submarine on this date, possibly the U-69.

16 March 1942: Lt Walker, flying B-18 AC36-288 of the 4th Reconnaissance Squadron (H), Seventh Air Force, out of Hawaii, while returning from a special mission over Kauai, bombed a submerged submarine bearing 279°, distance 25 miles at 1855 hours. No results were observed.

20 March 1942: 2Lt Benjamin L. Parkinson, flying B-18 AC36-310 of the 4th Reconnaissance Squadron (H), Seventh Air Force, out of Hawaii, reported that while climbing over Ilio Point at 2,000 feet, bubbles just offshore west of the point were spotted. About 30 seconds after the bubbles were sighted, a periscope broke water very close to the bubbles and stayed above water for about 10 seconds, then submerged. He searched for the suspected submarine for 20 minutes, then continued on his scheduled mission.

23 March 1942: A 2nd Bomb Group B-18A, commanded by Lt Kush, spotted an oil slick 10 miles south of Cape Lookout at 1915 hours and dropped five depth charges. He had intended to drop only one, but all were salvoed accidentally.

25 March 1942: A 2nd Bomb Group B-18B, flown by LTC Smith, made a radar contact at 3615N 7515W at 1040 hours and dropped five depth charges, one every 10 or 15 minutes, but with unknown results.

The extremely harsh winter conditions in eastern Canada claimed yet another RCAF Digby, No 753 of No 10(BR) Squadron, on 26 March 1942, when it crashed in impossible flying weather near Gander, Newfoundland. By this time the aircraft had gained a reputation with crews for extreme ruggedness and the qualities necessary to get them home. *via Carl Vincent*

Artist Paul Goranson vividly portrayed the hardships of operating RCAF Digbys during the early winter months of 1942 in this drawing, which depicts crews struggling to load three 450lb Amatol-filled depth charges. The original of this evocative piece disappeared in the immediate post-war years, and only this black-and-white rendering survives at the Canadian War Museum. *CAF OL 13418*

27 March 1942: B-18As assigned to the squadrons of the 25th Bomb Group (H), as of this date under the operational control of the 6th Interceptor Command, Antilles Air Task Force, commenced continuous daylight patrols over the Mona Passage with two aircraft. Another aircraft was tasked to make daily reconnaissance flights over the area south of Puerto Rico for a distance of 50 miles, and between 6450N 68W. Two other B-18As, stationed at St Croix, commenced making daily reconnaissance flights over the area between 17N and 1810N and 6540 and 62W. Two other Group aircraft, based further south at Antigua, were to make daily reconnaissance flights over the area between 1810 and 1540N and 52 and 6050W, as well as make daily observations at 1100 hours and 2200 hours of the Vichy French cruiser *Jeanne d'Arc*, at that time anchored at Guadalupe. B-18s and B-18As of the 9th Bombardment Group, also under the control of the Antilles Air Task Force based at St Lucia, commenced daily reconnaissance flight with two aircraft between 1540 and 1320N and between areas 10 miles westward and 50 miles eastward of the entire Lesser Antilles chain. The bulk of the Group's aircraft, stationed on Trinidad, started making daily recon flights with two B-18s over the area between 1320 and 1050N and 62 and 60W as well as over the area 50 miles seaward from the east coast of Trinidad and the coast of mainland South America. They were also tasked with providing air cover for the vital harbor port of Port of Spain and bauxite shipping entering and leaving for 30 miles from the point of anchorage.

9th BG B-18s stationed at distant Atkinson Field, British Guiana, started making recon flights with two aircraft daily over an area 50 miles to sea between 59 and 5630W and twice per week, at irregular intervals, over the backlands of British Guiana itself – the most unpopular duty.

Group B-18s stationed at Zandery Field, Surinam, were charged with making daily reconnaissance flights 50 miles to sea between 5630 and 54W and twice a week, at irregular times, between Surinam and the coast of French Guiana. The B-18s on these missions were armed with all guns, full crews, and either four Mk 17 depth charges or four 300lb bombs with 1/10 second delay fusing.

The 44th Reconnaissance Squadron had finally camouflaged most of its aircraft by the time the unit moved to Atkinson Field, British Guiana, in November 1941, and a line-up of most of the unit aircraft is shown here. The unit operated a mix of B-18s and B-18As and was redesignated as the 430th Bomb Squadron (H) on 22 April 1942. They were on nearly constant anti-submarine alert and watched the Vichy French colony in French Guiana to the east as well. *Brigadier General Charles E. Williams Jr*

28 March 1942: A Sixth Air Force B-18A operated into La Paz, Bolivia, although the reason for this unusual mission is unknown. It is believed to have been the furthest south in the western hemisphere that any US-operated B-18 ever operated.

28-31 March 1942: The precise date for a mission flown by Lt Kush in a B-18B of the 2nd Bomb Group is not clear, but it is known that it was between these dates and that he and his crew dropped three bombs on a surfaced submarine at 3633N 7448W.

During March 1942 aircraft and units of I Bomber Command flew 7,247 hours of anti-submarine and convoy escort and sighted no fewer than thirty-five U-boats, of which twenty-six were attacked. During the same month, thirty Allied vessels were sunk in the Command's area of responsibility.

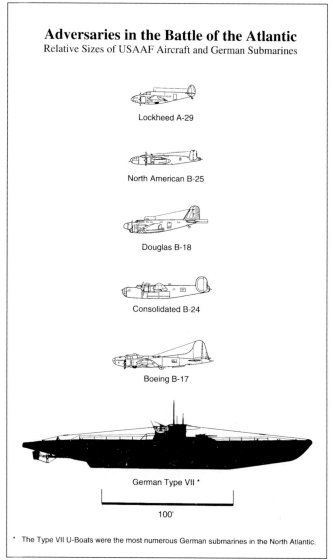

Adversaries in the Battle of the Atlantic
Relative Sizes of USAAF Aircraft and German Submarines

Lockheed A-29

North American B-25

Douglas B-18

Consolidated B-24

Boeing B-17

German Type VII *

100'

* The Type VII U-Boats were the most numerous German submarines in the North Atlantic.

This chart graphically portrays the principal combatants during the Battle of the Atlantic and the Caribbean, the standard German Type VII U-boat being by far the most numerous type engaged. *USAF*

April 1942: During the month the 6th Reconnaissance Squadron (M), attached to the 41st Bomb Group (M) based at Mather Field near Sacramento, CA, began operations from Naval Air Station Alameda, CA, flying anti-submarine patrols off the California coast with Douglas B-18As, Lockheed A-29s and a few Consolidated LB-30s. The unit was redesignated as the 396th Bomb Squadron (M) on 22 April.

In the Caribbean, the B-18-equipped 1st and 10th Bomb Squadrons were placed on alert this month and into May in connection with the ongoing crisis with regard to the Vichy French surface vessels, including an aircraft carrier, cruiser and a number of auxiliaries, at Martinique. A detachment of B-18s from the 10th under Col Harvey was dispatched for very specific patrols and probes of the defenses of the island.

1 April 1942: A No 10(BR) Squadron Digby was hit by anti-aircraft fire from a 'friendly' freighter, the first known instance of a B-18 series aircraft taking damage from surface fire, although happily the crew and aircraft survived with only one member wounded in the hand.

On the US north-west coast, the 16th Reconnaissance Squadron, 42nd Bomb Group, II Bomber Command, was flying intensive anti-submarine and coastal patrols from Paine Field, Everett, WA, with a mix of Douglas B-18As, Martin B-26s and Lockheed A-29s. A detachment was sent to Astoria, OR, but the unit was redesignated as the 406th Bomb Squadron on 22 April and ceased these activities preparatory to movement to Alaska.

2 April 1942: A 20th Bomb Squadron (H), 2nd Bomb Group B-18B, commanded by Lt Kush, carried out an attack on a surfaced submarine at 0318 hours at 3633N 7448W from 300 feet, dropping three 325lb Mk.17 depth charges in a salvo with a 50-foot setting. All apparently hit within 10 feet of the sub. The results were claimed as 'excellent' and it was thought that the sub was destroyed. This was the first officially recognised night radar pick-up of a surfaced sub by a B-18B with ASV. The ASV radar operator on this flight, T/Sgt John H. Wilson, was commended for his performance, and is believed to have been the first USAAF crewman so honored.

8 April 1942: A 3rd Recon Squadron B-18, flown by Lt Boylan, dropped one depth charge on the site of a Navy scout aircraft's flare at 1100 hours at 3912N 7335W, believing that the flare indicated the presence of a submarine. It turned out the naval aircraft was apparently marking the location of a sunken vessel. This was but one of numerous instances of exceptionally poor communication and coordination between USAAF and Naval aviation assets during this period.

9 April 1942: The 78th Bomb Squadron (M) of the 45th Bomb Group (M) transferred from Grenier Field, Manchester, NH, to Langley Field, VA, but continued to fly anti-submarine patrols without interruption during the move, with a mix of Douglas B-18s, A-20As and DB-7s.

18 April 1942: A B-18B of the 2nd Bomb Group flown by Lt Reynolds attacked a submerging submarine at 2250 hours at 3845N 7443W with one 325lb c/s set at 50 feet. There were no apparent results and the surface could not be seen due to the darkness.

19 April 1942: A B-18 of the 3rd Recon Squadron flown by Lt Fitzgerald dropped one 325lb depth charge set at 25 feet on a Navy signal at 1415 hours at 3901N 7356W at the location of a suspicious oil slick, where surface naval units were also attacking. It proved to be the location of a wreck, however. The same day, at 1640 hours, Lt Minette, flying a B-18 of the 13th Bomb Group, spotted a submarine periscope at 4050N 7115W. The scope, also seen by four other members of the crew, disappeared before the aircraft could make an attack run.

20 April 1942: A B-18B of the 20th Bomb Squadron, commanded by Lt Reynolds, attacked a submarine on the surface at 2250 hours at 3845N 7440W from 1,000 feet with one depth charge. Results were claimed as 'good'.

22 April 1942: Lt Kush of the 2nd Bomb Group made his second attack of the war at 0815 with a B-18B on a moving oil slick at 3605N 7500W, dropping three depth charges and claiming 'good' results. The same day Capt Hardy of the 3rd Recon Squadron, flying a B-18, dropped a single depth charge on a wake and oil bubbles at 1735 hours at 3815N 7435W with negative results.

24 April 1942: A B-18A using radio call sign '9RD5' of the 39th Bomb Squadron (M), 13th Bomb Group, flown by Lt Blakelock carried out an attack on a submarine from 75 feet at 0758 at 4112N 6658W with three depth charges, but the results were not noted.

27 April 1942: A B-18 of Headquarters Squadron, I Bomber Command, flown by Capt Hardy spotted a periscope at 1615 hours at 3935N 7355W but was unable to attack, as the aircraft was carrying unspecified 'special equipment' instead of bombs.

30 April 1942: A 2nd Bomb Group B-18B, AC37-517, operating out of Langley Field, VA, and commanded by 1Lt Francis B. Carlson, attacked a surfaced sub at 1950 hours at 3416N 7353W from 200 feet,

The solitary B-18 series aircraft to serve in the European theater was B-18A AC37-540, which was assigned to INDIGO (Iceland, TF-4) on 29 April 1942. It served a very useful service life in Iceland doing both close-in coastal patrols and target-towing for the island's anti-aircraft units, and survived the war to be salvaged there on 31 March 1945. *via Ragnar Ragnarsson*

dropping one depth charge. No results were claimed. The same crew, but reportedly flying a B-18A, made a second attack the same day at 2310 hours at 3429N 7427W from 300 feet, dropping three depth charges and claiming 'fair' results. Lt Carlson and his crew, 2Lt Donald L. McKay, 2Lt Clarence L. Harmon, 2Lt Junior M. Barney, T/Sgt Lawrence A. L. Craig, S/Sgt Walter S. Sloan and Cpl Edward M. Lemons were in fact credited with a sinking that day and awarded the Air Medal. The same day, at 1745, Lt Allen, flying a B-18 with radio call sign 'OB46' of the 13th Bomb Group, made an attack with four 325lb Mk 17 depth charges on a suspicious oil slick at 1745 hours at 4230N 6955W, but the target was apparently a large fish!

During the month of April 1942 aircraft and units of I Bomber Command flew a total of 6,328 hours of anti-submarine and convoy escort and sighted thirty-four U-boats, of which nineteen were attacked. A total of twenty-six Allied vessels were sunk by submarines and mines in the Command's area of responsibility this month.

1 May 1942: 1Lt Arthur J. Kush, commanding a 2nd Bomb Group B-18B, AC37-538, using radio call sign 'ZB17' and flying from Langley Field, attacked a submerging submarine at 1035 hours at 3408N 7241W from 500 feet with four depth charges and claimed the submarine sunk. Oil and air bubbles appeared immediately after the attack and large air bubbles 28 minutes later. Lt Kush and his crew, 2Lt Joseph P. Schilling, 2Lt Everett E. Haskell, S/Sgt Walter C. Ahrens, Sgt Gregory Bournazos and PFC Charles H. Torrence were credited with a sinking on this mission and awarded the Air Medal (this was Lt Kush's First Oak Leaf Cluster). The same day, Lt Carlson, flying another B-18B with radio call sign '6GC7,' also of the 2nd Bomb Group, sighted a surfaced sub at 1950 hours at 3416N 7353W on course of 180 degrees. An instrument pick-up was made at 18 miles but the sub disappeared at 3 miles. The same crew spotted a second sub on the surface at 2310 at 3429N 7427W and made an instrument pick-up at 22 miles, followed by a visual at 1½ miles, straight ahead. Two Mk 17 depth charges were dropped on the first attack and one on the second with a 25-foot setting and 30-foot spacing, and two detonations were observed, showing up the sub very plainly during the attack. On the first attack, the point of impact appeared to be 10 to 16 feet from the sub with the second straddling the sub. On the second attack, the point of impact was 50 feet ahead of point of impact and it appeared to have been dropped on the apparent location of the conning tower. This crew was relieved on station after 15 minutes.

3 May 1942: Another RCAF No 10(BR) Squadron Digby sighted a U-boat (probably U-455), but it escaped before an attack could be made. This crew, led by P/O E. J. Padden and S. S. G. Stubbs set an endurance record of an incredible 13hr 10min four days later and, as if that was not enough, increased it to just under 15 hours on 11 June. This same crew was the one lost on 14 July 1942.

B-18s stationed in British Guiana made frequent excursions southward in search of enemy submarines and other suspicious activities. This 44th Reconnaissance Squadron B-18 was photographed while at Boa Vista, Brazil, in May 1942. John Beyer, who took the photo, reported that '…two Japanese Navy personnel were captured near there operating a weather station … they were flown to Atkinson Field and turned over to the British.' *Col Johnson Beyer*

By mid-1942, B-18s, B-18As and B-18Bs were the major combatants engaging enemy submarines from British Guiana northward through the entire Caribbean basin. This 44th Reconnaissance Squadron B-18A, operating from Atkinson Field, has landed inland to inspect a possible Axis operating base, as it was still suspected that the Germans and Italians had 'secret' airfields in the interior of mainland South America. Note the canvas cover over the Norden bomb sight. *Col Johnson Beyer*

In the Caribbean, the 1st Bomb Squadron (H) was credited with engaging an enemy submarine, probably the U-66, with a B-18 on this date.

5 May 1942: A B-18 of the I Bomber Command operating from Miami damaged both main tyres on take off for a patrol, and the aircraft commander elected to jettison the four depth charges on board 20 miles east of Miami at 1645 rather than attempt to land with the tyres damaged. The aircraft returned, landed with minimal damage and was returned to service. The same day, the indomitable Lt Kush, flying a B-18B with radio call sign 'KT25' of the 2nd Bomb Group, spotted a surfaced sub via special equipment at 15 miles at 2256 hours at 3525N 7455W. It was a visual only, and there was not enough time for an attack.

6 May 1942: A B-18B using radio call sign '2RJ9'of the 2nd Bomb Group flown by Lt Wesche (also given as Weasch) caught a sub on the surface at 0417 hours from 1,700 feet following an instrument pick-up at 3605N 7505W (grid location CH4459), but for reasons not explained no attack was made. The crew did make a visual pick-up directly over the sub at 500 feet. On a second run, the sub was no longer visible on instruments or visually and did not reappear. The aircraft remained in the area until 0515.

9 May 1942: The question of the Vichy French Navy surface flotilla and the garrison at Martinique in the Caribbean neared crisis point. The US Commander on the scene, General House, detailed a group of

AAF assets, consisting of six B-18s, eight pursuit aircraft, four Marine aircraft and four Navy PBYs based at Antigua, north of Guadeloupe, with specific orders to sink the French cruiser *Jeanne d'Arc*. General House established his Command Post for the operation at St Lucia, and concentrated the 1st and 5th Bomb Squadrons, six Navy PBYs, four Marine aircraft and ten Army pursuit aircraft there. The plan of attack called for the initial assault to be made by five Army pursuit aircraft dive-bombing the Vichy French Navy's sole aircraft carrier, the *Bearn*, with 500lb demolition bombs. They were then to strafe such French seaplanes as were in the area, then pull off and spot and neutralise anti-aircraft positions on the island. The Navy and Marine pursuit aircraft were to follow with a dive-bombing attack on the same vessel. The 1st and 5th Bomb Squadrons with their B-18s were to attack the auxiliary cruiser *Emile Bertin* and the carrier *Bearn*, unless already sunk, in which case the 1st Bomb Squadron was to hit the cruiser *Barfleur*. The PBYs were to follow the B-18s and get the tankers and the *Barfleur*, following which all aircraft were to recover to St Lucia to reload. Fortunately, on 14 May word was received that negotiations for the 'neutralisation' of the fleet and garrison had been received and the operation was called off.

12 May 1942: A 2nd Bomb Group B-18B using radio call sign 'TZ94' flown by Lt Sproat spotted air bubbles at 1030 hours at 3614N 7531W and dropped four depth charges, but results were reported as 'negative'. The crew spotted one plank and small chunks of wood. They returned to the area at 1400 hours and one large oil slick was spotted.

15 May 1942: Lt Carlson, flying a 2nd Bomb Group B-18B with radio call sign '8SZ9', made an attack at 1900 hours at 3521N 7505W on a target given as a '…greenish object, about 150 long, 25 feet wide and pointed at both ends. Pilot believed it to be a damaged submarine lying on the bottom.' One 325lb Mk 17 depth charge was dropped but results were unknown. The crew checked the area for 15 minutes after the attack, then made land-fall to check their position; they returned to the area again at 1950, then returned to base.

17 May 1942: Lt C. J. Moench of the 2nd Bomb Group, flying a B-18B with radio call sign 'B459', spotted a sub on the surface at 2100 hours at 3605N 7452W but no attack was made. An instrument contact was made at 6 miles, 60 degrees right, and visual at 30 degrees right at less than a quarter of a mile. The crew reported that the conning tower appeared to be 'low and squat' in appearance. Ironically, no attack was made on the first sighting, as the aircraft was too close to the sub and, by the time he could come around, the sub had managed to crash-dive. The B-18 stayed in the area for 30 minutes but made no further contacts. Two Navy surface units north of the location were signaled with blinker light, and this was acknowledged by the destroyer, which then sent some message that the B-18 crew could not understand.

25 May 1942: Major Wallen, flying a B-18 with radio call sign '1FA6' of the 433rd Bomb Squadron (but also cited on some reports as Headquarters Squadron, I Bomber Command), made a sound contact with 'experimental equipment' at 1560 hours 3 miles off Barnegat Light (1410N 1735W) and dropped two Mk 17 depth charges, but both were duds. A tanker had just been torpedoed in the area and there was much oil and smoke on the surface with survivors on rafts a short distance from the sinking vessel. His crew dropped a raft to the survivors and radioed for surface help. They then patrolled the area for 3 hours until blimps and Navy aircraft arrived. This was in fact the first flight with the experimental MAD gear.

26 May 1942: A Detachment of I Bomber Command under the command of LTC Louis M. Merrick was designated as the core

This otherwise anonymous B-18A was photographed at Patricia Bay, Victoria, British Columbia, and is almost certainly AC37-630, which was destined to be assigned to the 15th Tow Target Squadron at Elmendorf Field, Alaska, as of 27 May 1942. It was one of the longest-serving Eleventh Air Force B-18As, not returning to the Continental US until 16 February 1944. *PBG 2032 via Carl Vincent*

element of the Gulf Task Force, consisting of an ad hoc composite unit with ten ASV-equipped B-18s.

A 5th Bomb Squadron (H) B-18, commanded by 2Lt Vernon D. Torgerson, was credited with engaging a submarine in the Caribbean on this date.

During the month of May 1942, I Bomber Command aircraft and units flew a total of 6,618 hours on anti-submarine and convoy escort and sighted twenty-three U-boats, of which twelve were attacked. A total of forty-seven Allied vessels were sunk by torpedo or mine action in the Command's area of responsibility during the month.

30 May 1942: All fifteen ASV-equipped B-18s at this time assigned to the Eastern Defense Command were assigned to the Sea Search-Attack Development Unit (see below).

2 June 1942: Wright Field issued CTI-690 entitled 'Tail Cones for MAD Equipment', which set down an immediate authorisation for procurement of seventy-five MAD tail cones for B-18 aircraft. This is the solitary document indicating the possible total of B-18Bs that could have been modified to carry the MAD tail 'stinger'.

3 June 1942: The first ten ASV-equipped B-18Bs became available from depots as of this date and remained attached to I Bomber Command until such time as a tactical unit was prepared to operate them. These were initially vested in what was temporarily designated the Sea Search-Attack Development Unit (SSADU) under the direct command of the CG, AAF, General Arnold. Operational control, however, was vested in the CG, First Air Force.

4 June 1942: Since 7 December 1941 the 36th Bomb Squadron (M) in Alaska had been flying almost non-stop coastal, anti-shipping and anti-submarine patrols along the enormous Pacific coast of Alaska, ranging far out into the Gulf of Alaska and from Yakutat to Unmak Island, using a combination of B-18As, six B-17s and one LB-30.

11 June 1942: A B-18B of the 20th Bomb Squadron, Gulf Task Force, piloted by 1Lt C. J. Moench, flying with radio call sign 'GS10', attacked a partially submerged submarine's conning tower at 0605 from 400 feet at 2240N 7815W with four Mk 17 depth charges with 25-foot fuse setting, claiming 'excellent' results.

Above: The very first B-18 to be fitted with the distinctive MAD 'stinger' was, ironically, AC36-262 – the original DB-1. Note the host of small antenna blades on the fuselage sides, the whip antenna, RDF bullet and large blade antenna on the forward fuselage, and the fact that the aircraft is still in natural metal, pre-war markings in this 1942 image. *NARA RG342 Sarah Clark Collection ARL B104S and B105S*

Right: By mid-1942 the RCAF had lost exactly half of its fleet of twenty Digbys to accidents and operational losses and had decided to eliminate the European-style camouflage in which the aircraft had operated since new in favor of an off-white scheme more suitable for its primary task of anti-submarine work. Here, an un-coded example taxies past a trio of RCAF Hawker Hurricanes. *via Carl Vincent*

Below: A few B-18As continued to serve the Eleventh Air Force in Alaska well into 1943, including AC37-535 shown here, which had arrived in the Territory on 31 March 1941 from McChord Field. It is seen here at Ladd Field at the Arctic Test Center, apparently testing a cold weather maintenance shelter. *NARA RG342FH 27482AC*

12 June 1942: Two B-18Bs of the 20th Bomb Squadron, Gulf Task Force, made separate radar contacts with a surfaced submarine at 2250 hours and 2345 hours, at 2330N 8128W and 2337N 8128W. Visual contact was made in the first instance, but too late for an attack, and in the second contact the sub disappeared before visual contact was made.

14 June 1942: Two B-18Bs of the 20th Bomb Squadron again made radar contacts at 0305 and 0502 hours at 2400N 8142W and 2356N 8158W, but again the contact disappeared before visual contact could be made.

15 June 1942: 2Lt Wayne Hall, pilot, and his co-pilot, Lt Howard E. Byers, as well as bombardier Sgt Phillip P. Thomas, Engineer Sgt W. Masyn and radio operator Sgt J. E. Richards of the 99th Bomb Squadron (H), were credited with engaging in combat with a submarine while commanding a B-18A on this date.

16 June 1942: The 40th Bomb Squadron (M), 13th Bomb Group (M), moved from Westover Field, MA, to Langley Field, VA, with B-18s and continued to fly intensive anti-submarine missions. The unit subsequently returned to Westover.

22 June 1942-15 July 1943: The newly formed 1st Sea Search Attack Group flew 2,497hr 24min on a very wide range of projects tests during this period, as well as 2,309hr 42min on actual combat patrols and killer searches.

23 June 1942: Six combat crews from the 20th Bomb Squadron were transferred to the 1st Sea Search Attack Group.

29 June 1942: A B-18B using radio call sign '1YJ7' of the 2nd Bomb Group flown by Lt Thomas and crew attacked a submarine following a visual sighting at 3533N 7458W at 0155 hours, and the conning tower and deck gun were visible above the surf. Four Mark 17 depth charges with 25-foot fuses were dropped and all detonated. Because of darkness, however, results could not be ascertained. A periscope was subsequently picked up by special instruments in the same area at 0230, protruding from the water about 10 feet, and appeared to be moving. It was eventually lost in the haze.

Elsewhere, in the Caribbean Capt Kenneth H. Hohlaus and his B-18 crew of the 12th Bomb Squadron (M) were credited with engaging a submarine in combat on this date.

30 June 1942: A B-23 using radio call sign 'Y584'of the 18th Observation Squadron, First Air Force (but also cited in some reports as Headquarters and Headquarters Squadron First Air Force), flown by Major W. A. Keenan and crew (including a Sgt Dorsey, the enlisted bombardier), apparently operating from Drew Field, FL, made two attacks on a submarine just surfacing at 3810N 6837W at 0545 and 0600 hours (at 3810N 6837W) from 1,000 and 500 feet respectively. The bow and conning tower were visible during the second attack. One of the depth charges (which turned out to be a dud) hit near the bow and the other three about 20 feet ahead of the submarine, and the crew observed a heavy oil slick and air bubbles for 3 or 4 minutes after the submarine disappeared. As the first submarine dived, a second was seen to surface. The aircraft stayed on-scene for 45 minutes. The aircraft claimed 'possible damage'. It appears that the tail gunner may have engaged the submarine with his .50 caliber gun, as a B-23 crewman received an award for such an action at about this time. This is the only known instance of a Douglas B-23 in action against the enemy.

During June 1942 aircraft and units of I Bomber Command flew a total of 5,439 hours of anti-submarine and convoy escort and sighted no fewer than forty U-boats, of which twenty-nine were attacked. A total of thirty-three Allied vessels were sunk in the Command's area of responsibility during the month.

July 1942: The 48th Bomb Squadron (M), 41st Bomb Group (M), Fourth Air Force, Western Defense Command, moved from Minter Field to NAS Alameda, CA, and continued flying anti-submarine and radar calibration patrols with a mix of Lockheed A-28s and Douglas B-18As.

4 July 1942: The US State Department intelligence apparatus forwarded to the Caribbean Defense Command the substance of a rumor that Japan intended to make either a submarine or surface raider attack on the oil fields at Talara, Peru, on this US holiday. The US base commander at Salinas, Ecuador, who had control over assets including a B-18 (AC36-294) and two B-18As (AC37-624 and 37-628) was directed to extend patrols to cover the area around Talara.

5 July 1942: A Panama-based US Navy Patrol Wing 3 report stated that a U-boat was sighted at 2215 hours at 1230N 7110W and was sunk. However, this report was amended to state that the sub was not sunk by Navy aircraft, but by a VI Bomber Command, 59th Bomb Squadron (L), B-18 commanded by Capt Norman H. Pederson and his crew, consisting of 1Lt M. F. Hooper (co-pilot), 1Lt D. J. Snow (navigator), Sgt J. C. Nadep (engineer), S/Sgt R. V. Klaver (radio operator), M/Sgt F. J. Poisker (bombardier) and Cpl W. H. Burnett (gunner). This action remains a mystery. Another crew from the same unit, commanded by Capt Thomas R. Ford, was also credited with engaging with a sub in combat on this date.

6 July 1942: A B-18B of the 20th Bomb Squadron, Gulf Task Force, piloted by Lt Minette and flying out of Opa Locka, FL, spotted a sub on the surface at 2237 (6 July), 0250 and 0400 hours (7 July) from 150 feet at locations between 2640N 7925W and 2650N 7920W, and attacked with four depth charges. Results were unclear, as some say that 'no action' ensued. Much later that same day, at 2237 and 2340 hours, Lt Price and Lt Cox, also flying 20th Bomb Squadron B-18Bs, spotted subs on the surface at 2620N 7913W and 2626N 7916W and, in the second spotting, dropped four depth charges fused at 25 feet, but results were 'negative'.

Deep in the Caribbean, 1Lt Marshall E. Groover and his B-18 crew from the 59th Bomb Squadron (L) were also credited with engaging a submarine in combat on this date.

7 July 1942: Lt Price, flying a B-18B of the 20th Bomb Squadron, Gulf Task Force, caught a sub in a crash dive at 0205 at 2548N 7921W, but was unable to make an attack before it escaped. Lt Kane of I Bomber Command was credited with a very effective attack on a submarine at 3452N 7554W the same day, but it is not clear if he was flying a B-18. The German submarine U-701 became the first confirmed submarine sunk by the USAAF on this date, but it is unclear if the above attacks were connected with this sinking.

10 July 1942: RCAF Digby No 739 of No10(BR) Squadron went missing on patrol over the north Atlantic (often reported as 14 July).

12 July 1942: Capt James M. Huntsman and his 417th Bomb Squadron (L) B-18 crew were credited with engaging a submarine in combat on this date in the Caribbean.

13 July 1942: The first reported attack by a B-18C in which MAD gear was actually employed in an area where an enemy submarine was known to be located was made by a 2nd Sea Search Attack Squadron aircraft commanded by 1Lt Donald L. McKay on a moving oil slick at 1857 hours at 3849N 7351W with one depth charge. The object of the search was to locate a sub damaged previously by a Douglas DB-7. At 1900 hours at 3849N 7351W the B-18C received an indication on MAD and, as the aircraft circled, a fresh oil slick approximately 2 miles long was noted, from north to south. The submerged object was noted to be at the southern extremity of the slick. On the fourth run the bombardier dropped a depth charge with no visible results. No claims were made and Lt McKay was of the opinion that the sub was traveling at far too great a depth to be affected by the depth charges.

15 July 1942: At 1615 hours at 3453N 7523W the SS *Bluefields* was attacked, and sank 20 minutes later. The SS *Chilore* and SS *J. A. Mowinkle* were also crippled by torpedoes. The CO of the 1st SSAG was notified of these actions at 1855 hours and two B-18Bs equipped with MAD were airborne by 1947. The Group CO, Col Dolan, flew AC37-475 while Lt Zinn was in 37-530. Both crews covered the area of the sinking in formation but only one of the aircraft had the MAD gear in operation. Reports were unfortunately negative. The gear operated satisfactorily, but the area of the search presented a unique problem: it was so crowded with wrecks that one target could not be distinguished from another. The Group CO was of the opinion that the sub may have been laying mines.

18 July 1942: Flt Lt Cundy, RAF, apparently attached to the 2nd Sea Search Attack Squadron and flying a unit aircraft (it is not clear if it was a B-18B), made what was believed to be a successful attack on a U-boat.

19 July 1942: 1Lt Julian Dendy Jr and his B-18 crew from the 417th Bomb Squadron (L) were credited with engaging a submarine in the Caribbean on this date.

20-21 July 1942: At 1710 a B-18 operating from Gallion Field, French Guiana – probably Capt Robert S. Lippincott and his crew, consisting of Lt Clarence C. Murphy (co-pilot), T/Sgt M. Bakalo (gunner) and Sgt William F. Murphy (gunner), of the 59th Bomb Squadron (L) – was dispatched to the area of a previous submarine attack at 0448N 4910W, and sighted a submarine on the surface at 8 miles distance. The B-18 started two attacks but was forced to withdraw out of range because of intense anti-aircraft fire from the sub, which kept turning continuously toward the aircraft. The B-18 circled out of range for 30 minutes when the sub suddenly started to dive. The aircraft dived at 140 knots and dropped five Mk 44 depth charges on the course of the sub from 25 feet, spaced at 100 feet with a 25-foot fuse setting. The first one fell 100 feet ahead of the swirl approximately 30 seconds after the sub dived, and all exploded. There were no visible results.

23 July 1942: RCAF Digby No 747 attacked a diving object believed to be a sub in the Strait of Bell Isle area. After dropping four of the new 450lb depth charges, an oil slick was observed, but this was later judged to be similar to that achieved when whales had been 'attacked' on previous occasions, a not uncommon event in anti-submarine warfare in these waters.

29 July 1942: 1Lt Luther O'Hern and his B-18 crew from the 417th Bomb Squadron (L) were credited with engaging a submarine in combat on this date in the Caribbean.

30 July 1942: Lt Reynolds and crew in B-18B AC37-482 of the 1st SSAG flew an 8hr 30min patrol with no results.

31 July 1942: Lt McKay and crew in B-18B AC37-482 of the 1st SSAG flew a 7hr 10min patrol with no results.

During July 1942 aircraft and units of I Bomber Command flew a total of 6,799 hours on anti-submarine and convoy escort, and sighted twenty-four U-boats, of which sixteen were attacked. A total of eighteen Allied vessels were sunk in the Command's area of responsibility during the month.

1 August 1942: Lt Uhle of the 80th Bomb Squadron, Gulf Task Force, flying a B-18B, made a visual pick-up of a submarine on the surface at 6 miles at 0113 hours at 2705N 7925W but was unable to close the distance and make an attack before it crash-dived. The radar gear on board the aircraft was not functioning properly but four crew members positively identified a submarine on the surface at 6 miles in the moon-path. The aircraft continued to orbit the area for an hour after the spotting, when the radar operator got his gear functioning again, then stayed on station another hour without success.

Elsewhere, Lt Herrick and crew of B-18B AC37-485 of the 1st SSAG flew a 3hr 20min 'killer search' with negative results.

2 August 1942: Lt Reynolds and crew in B-18B AC37-482 of the 1st SSAG flew a 5hr 5min patrol with negative results. Lt Hartbrodt and crew, in B-18B AC37-561 of the same unit, flew a 6-hour patrol the same day, also without result. Col Dolan, the Group Commander, and his crew flew a 3hr 50min patrol the same day in B-18B AC37-561 after Hartbrodt and his crew returned. This was followed by Lt Lehti and his crew in B-18B AC37-530 on a 6hr 30min patrol.

The same day, a B-18B of the 80th Bomb Squadron made an instrument pick-up at 0630 at 2535N 8002W and maintained a good contact until 2 miles from the target, which then faded.

Elsewhere, a 5th Bomb Squadron B-18, commanded by Capt Raymond E. Davis, was also credited with engaging a submarine this date, probably the U-160.

3 August 1942: Lt McKay and his 1st SSAG crew flew B-18B AC37-575 on a 7hr 55min patrol without results. This mission was followed by one of 7hr 10min by Lt Herrick and crew in AC37-561, and a 3hr 45min patrol by Lt Walker and crew in AC37-550.

The same day, the 40th Bomb Squadron (M), 13th Bomb Group (M), moved from Westover Field, MA, to Mitchel Field, NY, with B-18s and continued flying intensive anti-submarine missions.

4 August 1942: Lt Norton, flying a B-18B of the 80th Bomb Squadron, Gulf Task Force, I Bomber Command, made an instrument pick-up at 6 miles at 0330 hours at 2658N 7952W, but the sighting faded at 1 mile. The crew saw disturbed water at the contact point. Back at Langley Field, crews of the 1st SSAG flew two long patrols this day: Lt Hartbrodt and crew in B-18B AC37-563 did 6hr 25min and Lt Zinn and crew in AC37-485 did 7hr 45min.

5 August 1942: An unidentified B-18 operating from Trinidad attacked a surfaced submarine with .30 caliber machine gun fire at 1415N 6140W, as the aircraft was being ferried between stations with no bombs or depth charges on board. The sub crash-dived and escaped. At Langley Field the 1st SSAG flew two patrols: Lt McKay and crew in B-18B AC37-575 flew 4hr 30min with no result, and Lt Coleman in AC37-561 flew 4 hours.

6 August 1942: Lt Zinn and crew of the 1st SSAG flew B-18B AC37-563 on a 2hr 30min 'killer search' without result.

9 August 1942: Capt Charlie M. Ross (pilot), Capt Ernest N. Ljunggren (co-pilot), T/Sgt W. M. Wicker (engineer), Cpl J. E. Doughan (assistant engineer), T/Sgt L. J. Troy (bombardier), Sgt P. P. Thomas (gunner), Sgt S. Frankewich (radio operator) and Private W. A. Parker (assistant radio operator), while crewing a 99th Bomb Squadron (H) B-18A, were credited with engaging a submarine in combat on this date.

10 August 1942: A B-18B commanded by Lt Foley of the 1st SSAG conducted a 3hr 25min patrol out of Langley Field in AC37-530 without contact.

11 August 1942: Three 1st SSAG crews flew patrols. Lt Coleman in B-18B AC37-602 flew a 3hr 40min 'killer search', landed, then flew another 2hr 5min 'killer search' in AC37-561, both with high hopes but no results. Later, Lt Reynolds, in B-18B AC37-550, flew a 7-hour patrol, also without results.

12 August 1942: The 1st SSAG flew a total of three missions on this date, all 'killer searches' in B-18Bs. They were commanded by Lt Hartbrodt (a 6hr 30min mission in AC37-602), Lt Zinn (7hr 15min in AC37-482) and Lt Coleman (30 minutes in 37-485).

Unique to Trinidad, the 'divi-divi' trees reflected the long-term effects of the ever-present trade winds – a factor with which B-18 crews had to contend on a daily basis. Here B-18B AC37-472, assigned to the 40th Bomb Squadron, receives open-air maintenance on 12 August 1942, probably at Waller Field on temporary deployment from Mitchel Field, NY. The aircraft was redesignated as a B-18C on 11 May 1943, and was later named 'Satan's Chariot'. It survived the war to be scrapped. *USAAF*

15 August 1942: Col Dolan of the 1st SSAG received orders to detach six of his B-18Bs with crews to I Bomber Command. Within 6 hours seven RB-18Bs were ready to go led by Dolan, and were on station at Key West by the 17th, where they conducted twenty-four missions with five instrument pick-ups and three visual sightings by 23 August.

The same day a B-18B of the 80th Bomb Squadron made a positive sighting at midnight at 2400N 8154W at 16 miles, but it faded at 6 miles. The sky was very light, however, and the crew felt that the sub could have heard or seen the aircraft.

Deep in the Caribbean, Capt Harry E. Goldworthy and his B-18 crew of the 10th Bomb Squadron (M) were credited with engaging a submarine in combat on this date.

17 August 1942: Lt Curtis, flying B-18B AC37-512 with radio call sign 'W198' of the 40th Bomb Squadron, spotted a periscope at 1920 hours at 4021N 7340W but was unable to make an attack before it disappeared. The bombardier had spotted a periscope heading south, submerging from 400 feet, but they were in the midst of a tropical rain storm and visibility was less than a mile.

On this same date, an unidentified B-18A operating from Trinidad claimed a submarine as sunk at 1200N 6411W at 1942 hours. The aircraft dropped four bombs, two of which were near misses, with the third striking the submarine and forcing it over onto its side. The conning tower hatches were open at the time and water was seen to be entering the tower. The fourth bomb hit close to the stern. The crew saw 15 feet of the bow rise to about 80° out of the water. The B-18's rear turret gunner fired thirty to forty rounds of armor-piercing ammunition into the sub. This was most likely the aircraft of Capt R. M. McLeod, who spotted a submarine 20 miles from a convoy while assigned to the 1st Bomb Squadron (H). The sub then slipped backwards into a 50-foot-diameter oil slick and sank. However, Capt James D. Barlow, of the same unit, was also credited with engaging a submarine on this date.

Lt Reynolds, of the 2nd Sea Search Attack Squadron, 1st SSAG, on detached service in Trinidad, also flew B-18B AC37-485 on this date on a 6hr 30min 'killer mission' without result. Lt Kenneth V. Carlsen and his 99th Bomb Squadron (H) crew were also credited with engaging a submarine in combat crewing a B-18.

18 August 1942: Three crews from the 1st SSAG, on detached service in Trinidad, flew three 'killer searches' on this day. LT Lehti in B-18B AC37-602 flew 6hr 50min, while Lt Zinn, in the same aircraft, flew 6hr 50min same day! Lt Coleman, in AC37-558, flew a 6hr 55min mission, also without result.

Elsewhere, a B-18B of the 80th Bomb Squadron made a possible sighting at 2355 hours at 2405N 8100W at 6 miles, but lost the target while making a sharp turn. At 0015 on the 19th, at the same position, a radar sighting was once again made, but it faded at 3 miles.

19 August 1942: A B-18B, AC37-485 of the 2nd Sea Search Attack Squadron, commanded by Lt Franklin T. E. Reynolds and operating temporarily from Key West, made a strong ASV contact on a sub at 1600 hours at 2328N 8226W but made no attack as the target disappeared from radar at 7 miles. A second signal was noted at 1820 hours 12 nautical miles due west of the same position and the signal came in strong from a distance of 14 miles, but faded until about 12 miles, then completely disappeared at 11 miles. In this area there was a 2.5-knot current and, presuming the sighting was a submarine, its course was 270° and, if below the surface, it would have to head up the current. The ASV operator was fairly sure it was a sub.

The same day three other crews from the same unit also made 'killer searches' in B-18Bs AC37-482 (Lt McKay, 6hr 30min), AC37-550 (Lt Lehti, 6hr 40min) and Lt Foley (AC37-507, 7hr 20min) without result.

Elsewhere in the Caribbean Capt James D. Barlow, flying a B-18A of the 1st Bomb Squadron, sighted a partially surfaced sub at a distance of 5 miles while patrolling at 1,800 feet (the date of this action has also been given as 17 August). He released five depth charges, the third of which caused the sub to list away from the attack. A fourth depth charge was believed to have hit the stern about 20 feet below the surface. Capt Robert M. McLeod of the same unit was also credited with engaging a submarine on this date. Capt Kenneth T. Wilhite (pilot) and Capt Harry J. Halberstadt (co-pilot) of the 99th Bomb Squadron (H) were also credited with engaging a submarine (probably the U-155) in combat on this date, as was Capt Charlie M. Ross and his crew from the same unit. A B-18 crew commanded by 1Lt Richard A. B. Sheddon of the 59th Bomb Squadron (L) was also credited with engaging a submarine in combat on this date, as was that of Capt Murdoch W. Campbell of the same unit.

20 August 1942: Three crews from the 1st SSAG on detached service conducted 'killer searches' on this date. Lt Zinn in B-18B AC37-485 flew 7hr 5min; Lt Coleman in AC37-602 flew 6hr 20min and Lt McKay in AC37-482 flew 6hr 45min, all without result. Capt Ernest N. Ljunggren (pilot) and Capt Charlie M. Ross (co-pilot) and crew of a 99th Bomb Squadron (H) B-18 were also credited with engaging a submarine in combat on this date.

Elsewhere in the Caribbean, 1Lt Robert F. Swisher and his 417th Bomb Squadron (L) B-18 crew were also credited with engaging a submarine in combat. The U-155 reported being surprised on the surface by a B-18, believed to be from the 1st Bomb Squadron, east of Trinidad. The lookout was so late in making the alarm that the submarine commander, Piening, had to leave one of his men still on the conning tower when the boat crash-dived. The crewman was probably killed by the blast of the four depth charges going off as the sub dived. The detonations caused light-bulbs and glass fittings on the sub to shatter and the crew was severely shaken up, but the sub survived.

21 August 1942: A RB-18B, AC37-602 of the 2nd Sea Search Attack Squadron, 1st Sea Search Attack Group, flown by 1Lt Franklin T. E. Reynolds (with co-pilot Lt William Hafner, Navigator Lt Crowell E. Werner, Bombardier Lt H. B. Wise and ASV/MAD operator Sgt E. A. Kaszubski) radio call sign 'VL8' out of Meacham Field, spotted a sub on the surface with 'special instruments' at 28 miles at 0938 hours, followed by visual at 7½ miles at 0952 hours at 2428N 8313W. Four Mk 17 depth charges were dropped, two in train on the port side of the sub; one detonated approximately 25 feet off the port side of the sub abeam of the conning tower, and the second about 25 feet off the starboard bow, and all detonated. An oil slick was immediately observed and small air bubbles were seen. A very large oil slick had formed by 0956 and the aircraft departed the area at 1007 hours to rearm at Key West. The same aircraft and crew returned to the area at 1118 hours and an ASV signal was picked up at 3 miles, heading 30° true at about 2 knots. At 2 miles a periscope was sighted. The aircraft dropped smoke flares to mark the spot. A destroyer and SC boat arrived and dropped a large number of depth charges on the spot. The aircraft was able to verify by MAD that the sub was in fact in the area of the explosions. A relief aircraft arrived at 1324 hours.

The same day Lt Hartbrodt and his crew, also of the 2nd Sea Search Attack Squadron, made a strong MAD contact off Cape Henry and dropped bronze slicks and notified nearby patrol boats, which dropped depth charges. Results were unknown. This was a busy day for crews of the 1st SSAG, as in addition to these two missions four others were flown totaling 30hr 35min – one of them, Lt Zinn in B018B AC37-550, lasted 10hr 20min!

22 August 1942: A RB-18B, again AC37-602, of the 2nd Sea Search Attack Squadron, Gulf Task Force, flown by Lt Robert L. Coleman, operating temporarily from Key West, attacked a partially surfaced submarine at 0030 hours from 200 feet at 2350N 8355W with three Mk 17 depth charges and claimed a kill. The sub had been sighted after an 'instrument pick-up' at 18 miles. Lt Coleman, in his after-action report, stated that '…at first sighting, I could not turn fast enough to make an attack. After the attack was made, the bow raised to an angle of 30° to the surface and the U-boat then submerged stern-first.' The same day, at 1740 hours, Lt Reynolds of the same unit, flying B-18B AC37-558, spotted a sub on the surface at 2310N 8348W but it crash-dived before an attack could be made.

Meanwhile, back at Langley Field, home station of the 1st SSAG, a very interesting engagement the same day took place that made manifest the need for much closer liaison between the Army and Navy. At 1330 hours RB-18B AC37-563 took off from Langley Field on a MAD demonstration flown by Lt Hartbrodt with co-pilot Lt Rockwood, ASV and radio operator Sgt Kantowski, Dr Norman V. Webster (a MAD research engineer from Columbia University); Commander Hammond and Lt Merrill of the US Navy were observers. At 1441 hours a depth charge explosion was noted, this having been dropped by a Navy surface vessel. There appeared to be five vessels surrounding an area at about 3618N 7518W. The RB-18B immediately commenced to search with MAD at 100 feet and, at 1500 hours, MAD indicated they had passed to one side of a submerged object. The aircraft attempted repeatedly to establish radio contact with the Navy surface vessels as well as by Grimes light, but without success. The aircraft returned to base frustrated. Capt Pohan, also of the 1st SSAG, made a 2hr 40min 'killer search' on this date in B-18B AC37-563.

This same day, a 45th Bomb Squadron, 40th Bomb Group B-18A, operating from France Field, Canal Zone, caught U-654 on the surface 150 miles from Colon, Republic of Panama. At 2 miles the aircraft observed the U-boat beginning a crash-dive. Four depth charges bracketed the sub and it simply continued on down to the sea floor. The unit, which had previously been stationed in Puerto Rico, had arrived to find hand-me-down B-18s that had been in Panama since their initial deployment, and were flying a punishing schedule of 90 flying hours per pilot, per week. The crew of this aircraft is believed to have included aircraft commander Captain P. A. 'Chick' Koenig and bombardier Bill Lessin. This was claimed to be the first Axis submarine destroyed in the Caribbean. At least five other B-18s from this same unit soon joined in the attack, and these were commanded by Capt Eddie Glass, Capt Robert Moss, 1Lt Marvin Goodwyn, 1Lt Ira Matthews and 1Lt C. A. Woolsey. Oddly, and perhaps to divert Axis attention from the fact that one of its subs had

got this close to the Canal, not a solitary press release was issued to celebrate this accomplishment and, so far as can be determined, no awards were issued. It was not until after the end of the war that the unit was credited with sinking the U-654 with all forty-four hands. 1Lt Lyle G. Frost and his B-18 crew of the 417th Bomb Squadron (L) were also credited with engaging a submarine in the Caribbean on this date.

Yet another instance of the wonderful flotation qualities of the B-18 design. This 1st Observation Squadron, 6th Bomb Group, B-18, AC36-321, went down at sea on a night patrol 45 miles west of France Field, Canal Zone, while commanded by Capt Nester E. Cole with a crew of three. The crew at first intended to abandon the aircraft after it landed in the water but, when they discovered it was still well afloat, remained with it. When it lurched to a stop suddenly and the rocking of the waves stopped, they opened the crew door in the rear fuselage and stepped ashore without so much as getting their feet wet! *via Lee M. Sympson*

24 August 1942: Capt Richard H. Gunckel and his crew, aboard a 99th Bomb Squadron (H) B-18, were credited with engaging a submarine in combat on this date.

25 August 1942: Capt Kush of the 20th Bomb Squadron made a radar pick-up on a sub at 0720 hours at 3941N 6957W fully surfaced at 5 miles. It crash-dived before a run could be made.

In Alaska the 36th Bomb Squadron, although re-equipped for the most part with a mix of one B-17B, one B-17E and two LB-30s (by 1 June) was still operating at least one B-18A, on a mission to Dutch Harbor, as late as this date.

In the Caribbean, Capt Alden I. Robblee and his B-18 crew of the 10th Bomb Squadron (M) were credited with engaging a submarine in combat on this date. Capt T. I. Ramsay and his 25th Bomb Group (M) B-18 crew were also credited with engaging a submarine this day.

27 August 1942: 2Lt Harlan E. Murray and his B-18 crew of the 99th Bomb Squadron (H) in the Antilles were credited with engaging a submarine in combat.

28 August 1942: A B-18A of the 1st Bomb Squadron (H) claimed the sinking of the U-173, but in fact it was only further damaged after earlier attacks by RAF Hudsons of 53 Squadron. U-173 was ordered home.

30 August 1942: The air echelon (only) of the 40th Bomb Squadron (M), 13th Bomb Group (M), home-based at Mitchel Field, NY, started flying anti-submarine patrols on this day, a Sunday, from NAS Guantanamo Bay, Cuba, with B-18s.

In all, during August, the 1st SSAG flew twenty-one missions totaling 202hr 50min combat time, and another twenty-one missions, totaling 152hr 35min, on detached service – all on only ten aircraft!

Also during the month aircraft and units of the I Bomber Command flew a total of 5,685 hours of anti-submarine and convoy escort missions and sighted fourteen U-boats, of which eight were attacked. Only three Allied vessels were sunk in the Command's area of responsibility during the month, a marked decline since the previous seven months.

1 September 1942: A 'B-18BR' (AC37-485, but also given as 37-482 on some documents) of the 2nd Sea Search Attack Squadron, 1st Sea Search Attack Group, flown by Lt George M. Biddison, carried out an attack with three depth charges on the outline of a submerged submarine following a MAD contact at 1220 hours from 300 feet at 3603N 7454W. The 'killer search' mission lasted 7 hours. Results were not recorded. Another incident the same day by a B-18B of the 80th Bomb Squadron at 1754 hours at 2703N 7956W produced a weak radar contact at 8 miles, but it disappeared at 2 miles. Elsewhere, crews of the 1st SSAG flew three other missions this date. Lt Herrick in B-18B AC37-550 flew a 7hr 10min 'killer mission', while Lt Easterling, in AC37-475, flew the same mission in pair with him. Lt Walker and his crew, in B-18B AC37-561, flew a 6-hour 'killer search' as well.

2 September 1942: Lt Lehti and his crew from the 2nd Sea Search Attack Squadron, flying B-18B AC37-530, made both strong ASV and MAD contacts but could not close the target. Their mission lasted 4hr 35min. The same day, Lt Wood and crew of the 1st SSAG flying B-18B AC37-575 flew a 6hr 10min 'killer search' without result.

3 September 1942: F/O Sanderson and the crew of an RCAF No 10(BR) Squadron Digby, while on convoy escort, sighted a sub about 9 miles to the south and dropped four depth charges along the track as the sub dived. Another unit Digby and an escort vessel relieved this aircraft, but no claim was made.

The same day, much further south, a 2nd Sea Search Attack Squadron, 1st Sea Search Attack Group 'B-18B-R', AC37-530, using call sign '9C6' and flown by Lt Coleman, made a radar contact at 12 miles at 2130 hours at 3648N 7512W, but the signal faded at 3 miles. This patrol lasted from 1600 hours until 2310. Lt Easterling, in another B-18B of the same unit, made MAD contacts at 3646N 7513W but could not locate the target. Crews from the same unit flew three other missions on this date, two of them 'killer searches' and one a patrol, totaling 15hr 30min collectively. They were commanded by Lt Walker (in B-18B AC37-475), Lt Harris (AC37-575) and Lt Easterling (in AC37-485).

4 September 1942: A high-water-mark day for crews of the 1st SSAG, who completed no fewer than seven 'killer searches' on this date. Lt Foley, in B-18B AC37-561, flew 7hr 50min, Lt McIntosh and crew in AC37-475 flew 4hr 50min, Lt McKay flew 4hr 15min in AC37-507, Lt Herrick flew 2 hours in AC37-475, and Lt Hartbrodt flew 2hr 55min in AC37-530. The unit also flew its second Consolidated LB-30 Liberator 'killer search' on this date in AL596 commanded by F/LT Cundy of the RAF, lasting 9hr 20min.

5 September 1942: Lt Foley and crew of the 1st SSAG flew a 6hr 55min patrol in B-18B AC37-475 without result, and the Group Commander, Col Dolan, flew a 3hr 10min mission in AC37-530, also without result.

6 September 1942: Lt Coleman of the 1st SSAG and his crew flew a 4hr 15min patrol in B-18B AC37-475 without result.

7 September 1942: Lt Flowers, flying a B-18B of the 80th Bomb Squadron, Gulf Task Force, had a strong 'SE' ('special equipment') contact at 0525 hours at 2532N 7959W at 10 miles. He followed the track to the source but could not locate a target, although he remained

in the area until 0545. He had another strong 'SE' contact at 8 miles 20 minutes later at 2548N 7958W, but again could not see a target. The same day, Capt Coles, also of the 80th Bomb Squadron, flying a B-18B, had an 'SE' sighting at 1545hrs at 2335N 8112W on what appeared to be four separate targets at 18 miles. The sighting faded at 3 miles and, although three runs were made, no results were claimed. The same aircraft made another 'SE' sighting at 1840 hours at 2545W 7945W at 6 miles. Again, three runs were made without result.

9 September 1942: Lt Wood and crew, flying B-18B AC37-530 of the 1st SSAG, flew a 7hr 30min 'killer search' on this date without result.

12 September 1942: The 79th Bomb Squadron (L) commenced anti-submarine patrols from Miami, FL, using a mix of Douglas DB-7s and B-18s. The unit later became the 8th Antisubmarine Squadron.

13 September 1942: Lt Amend flying B-18B AC37-472 of the 40th Bomb Squadron with radio call sign 'MO67' made a radar pick-up at 2230 hours at map location '460558' on two objects at 25 miles from a convoy on a 295-degree course from the convoy. The objects were between a quarter and half a mile apart. Pick up was 28 miles from the aircraft. He approached to 16 miles, then the indications began to get dimmer until they disappeared, and could not be regained. The aircraft was operating at 1,000 feet.

Elsewhere in the Caribbean, 1Lt Johnson Beyer and his crew, flying a 430th Bomb Squadron (H) B-18, were credited with engaging a submarine in combat on this date.

14 September 1942: Lt Thorne, flying B-18B AC37-562 with radio call sign 'L431' of the 40th Bomb Squadron, made a radar pick-up at 0015 hours at map code '464533' at 6 miles, but it disappeared immediately. It was picked up again at 2 miles but again disappeared.

16 September 1942: Lt Reynolds of the 2nd Sea Search Attack Squadron, 1st Sea Search Attack Group, flying B-18B AC37-558, radio call sign 'S97', made no fewer than six MAD pick-ups at 1315 hours at 3507N 7530W at 16 miles, but they disappeared at 4 miles. A wedge-shaped wake followed by a swirl was seen at a distance where the pick-up faded. The sub was then picked up visually by the co-pilot and bombardier and three depth charges were dropped, but they all failed to detonate. His mission lasted 6hr 35min. The same aircraft, flown by Lt McIntosh, also flew a 'killer search' lasting 4hr 40min same day and made a radar contact at 2242 hours at 2549N 7933W, but no attack was made. Also on the 16th 1Lt Frank M. Wyman and 1Lt Vernon D. Torgerson and their crews of the 430th Bomb Squadron (H) and 5th Bomb Squadron (H) respectively were credited with engaging enemy submarines in B-18s.

17 September 1942: The 1st SSAG flew three 'killer searches' in B-18Bs. Lt Coleman, flying AC37-485, flew for 7 hours without result, while Lt Reynolds flew 6hr 45min in AC37-507 and Lt Lehti flew 6hr 15min in AC37-485, also without result.

18 September 1942: Lt Wood, flying B-18B AC37-507 of the 1st SSAG, flew a 5hr 30min 'killer search' without result.

Capt Eugene M. Berkencamp and 1Lt Randolph H. Seguine and their B-18 crews from the 5th Bomb Squadron (H) were credited with attacking the U-516 on this date in the Caribbean.

19 September 1942: A B-18B of the 80th Bomb Squadron, Gulf Task Force, I Bomber Command, while on a special search mission piloted by 1Lt Harold W. Norton, sighted a small boat under sail containing four people approximately 50 miles south-east of Key West, drifting in the direction of Cuba. Members of the crew dropped messages in bottles rigged with improvised parachutes and were able to ascertain that the occupants were survivors of a sunken ship and were in

During the autumn of 1942 the Fighter Command of the Antilles Air Task Force published its own mimeographed newsletter, and the very first cover, Volume 1, Number 1, for 1 September 1942, featured what was clearly intended to represent a B-18B going after an Axis submarine. *USAFHRAv*

distress. After having advised his home base, Lt Norton remained the area until dark, during which time he dropped survivor kits. The survivors were rescued and the entire crew of the B-18 received commendations.

Much further down the Antilles chain, a B-18 of the 5th Reconnaissance Squadron (erroneously cited as the 5th Bomb Squadron in some accounts), based at St Lucia, made a very nearly fatal attack on the U-516 on the surface. The B-18 crew dropped their depth charges so close to the sub that it was severely damaged, but survived.

20 September 1942: A Detachment of the 2nd Sea Search Attack Squadron (M), home-based at Langley Field, VA, began flying anti-submarine missions from Edinburgh Field, Trinidad, this Sunday, using RB-18Bs. They returned home on Wednesday 21 October.

21 September 1942: 1Lt Vernon D. Torgerson and his B-18 crew from the 5th Bomb Squadron (H) were credited with engaging an enemy submarine in combat on this date in the Caribbean.

22 September 1942: The 1st SSAG, home-based at Langley Field, VA, sent eight RB-18Bs and crews to the British West Indies to take part in extensive anti-submarine operations there. Col Dolan was based out of Trinidad from this date until 16 October, and while there on Temporary Duty his eight aircraft conducted no fewer than seventy-eight 'killer' searches and eight patrols. They made six sightings and carried out three confirmed attacks, the first on 1 October 1 (qv).

24 September 1942: Seven crews from the 1st SSAG, all on detached service, flew seven separate patrols totaling 34hr 15min. Aircraft involved were B-18Bs AC37-575, 37-530, 37-550, 37-485, 37-582 and 37-563 (two separate missions commanded by Lt Zinn).

25 September 1942: Crews of the 1st SSAG on detached service flew five patrol missions totaling 25hr 35min without result.

26 September 1942: A U-boat was sighted at 2612 hours at 1950N 7510W outside Guantanamo Bay, Cuba, and another at 2617 hours at 1810N 6430W in the Virgin Islands area. A B-18 from an unknown unit – probably Capt Cameron W. Lane's crew from the 5th Bomb Squadron (H) – attacked a sub painted white at 2612 hours 20 seconds after it had submerged at 1628N 5844W, dropping two depth charges. One of these fell 75 feet short and the second failed to explode. A third and fourth depth charge failed to release from the bomb racks and no claims were made.

27-29 September 1942: Crews of the 1st SSAG on detached service in the Caribbean flew a total of twelve missions, six patrols and six 'killer searches', all on B-18Bs and totaling 73hr 35min, the longest of which was an 8-hour mission on the 29th by Lt Easterling and crew in AC37-482.

29 September 1942: A B-18B of the 2nd Sea Search Attack Squadron, 1st SSAG, commanded by Lt McKay, picked up MAD contacts but had negative subsequent results.

30 September 1942: The 1st SSAG on detached service flew five missions this date, four 'killer searches' and one patrol. Lt Rockwood in B-18B AC37-563 was out for 7hr 30min, while the Group Commander, Col Dolan, was in AC37-485 for 3hr 45min, both on 'killer' searches. Lt Easterling in AC37-575 did a 6-hour patrol and the indefatigable Lt Reynolds flew 7hr 35min in AC37-473. Lt Zinn also did a 'killer' search in AC37-482 for 6 hours.

During September 1942, aircraft and units of I Bomber Command flew a total of 6,822 hours of anti-submarine and convoy escort missions, sighted five U-boats and attacked two of them. Only one Allied vessel was sunk during the month in the Command's area of responsibility. As of this date, an organisation known as the ASV Training Squadron was operating from Morrison Field, FL, with two B-18Bs, but had moved to Boca Raton, FL, by 13 November 1942.

Also during the month of September the 1st SSAG flew twenty-seven missions totaling 152hr 40min combat time.

1 October 1942: Lt Robert W. Lehti (with co-pilot Lt Hafner, navigator Lt Cothran, bombardier Lt Wilson and radar operator Sgt Hericsina), flying RB-18B AC37-550 of the 2nd Sea Search Attack Squadron, 1st SSAG, on temporary duty at Trinidad from Langley Field, VA, attacked a submarine that had sunk a freighter off the mouth of the Orinoco River. His ASV operator reported a target at 2007 hours at 12 miles and he attacked with two 325lb depth charges as the aircraft passed over the stern of the U-boat at 45° to course. There was no moon, but the B-18 crew could see the hatches open and lights from below deck, and men scrambling over the hatchway as the sub crash-dived. The interphone on the aircraft was not working, and the bombardier was not able to tell the pilot to turn quickly enough to make another attack. The B-18 circled the area for 45 minutes, then went ashore to get a navigational 'fix' before returning to the area. The ASV operator then picked up another signal at 8 miles and led the pilot to the target. The pilot saw the sub at a quarter of a mile and dropped his two remaining depth charges off the port side across the stern at 45° to the course of the sub. He claimed one hit.

The same day Lt Zinn and his crew, flying B-18B AC37-485 of the 2nd Sea Search Attack Squadron, picked up both ASV and MAD contacts between 0015 and 0121 hours that led to a visual sighting of a sub. One 650lb and one 325lb depth charge were dropped, followed by two more 325-pounders on a fully surfaced submarine. The same crew recovered to base and launched on a second mission, when they once again established a MAD contact, possibly on the same target, but with negative results.

Two 1st Bomb Squadron B-18s were also credited with attacking the U-175 on this day in the Caribbean and the sub was forced to crash-dive twice to escape. The sub did in fact sustain damage from each attack.

2 October 1942: 1Lt Franklin T. E. Reynolds (with co-pilot Lt Hickman, navigator Lt Frizzie, bombardier Lt Thiele and radar operator Sgt Hickman), flying RB-18B AC37-550 of the 2nd Sea Search Attack Squadron, 1st SSAG, on detached duty in Trinidad, made an ASV-directed attack at 0500 hours on a signal picked up at 16 miles, and spotted a submarine awash at 0905N 6020W. The sub was running at about 6 knots on a course of 170°. 1Lt Reynolds attacked from 200 feet directly from astern, dropping three depth charges (two 325-pounders and one 650-pounder) while the conning tower was still visible. He dropped a fourth 325lb depth charge and claimed another hit. The sub was seen sinking on its side and the B-18 crew spotted survivors in a life raft at 0730; they were later picked up by PCs and a freighter.

The same day Capt Pohan's patrol, in 2nd Sea Search Attack Squadron B-18B AC37-482, picked up an ASV contact, but had negative results. Their 'killer search' lasted 8 hours. The same unit flew four other missions the same day totaling 27hr 20min. Also, Capt Howard Burhanna Jr and his crew, flying B-18A AC37-579 coded 'B171' of the 99th Bomb Squadron (H) out of Zandery Field, Surinam, sighted a submarine at 1150 hours at 0550N 5225W at 15 miles on course 20 degrees true (ironically, some 20 miles off Devil's Island). He made a low-level attack from 50 feet at 180mph and dropped two 325lb and two 600lb depth charges with 25-foot fuses. Air bubbles came up immediately and kept coming up for 37 minutes. For 3 minutes air and oil spouted from the surface in large quantities and 5 minutes thereafter one survivor was sighted and a life raft was dropped to him. After 3 hours an oil slick 6 miles long was sighted. This submarine was claimed as sunk. Lt Burhanna and his crew, co-pilot Capt Lloyd L. Reynolds, T/Sgt William Ludkiewicz, S/Sgt Theron R. Jones, S/Sgt Alexander M. Bloshko, Sgt Albert K. Will, Sgt Jack Archer

Capt Howard Ward Burhanna Jr and his 99th Bomb Squadron (H) crew, operating B-18A AC37-579 out of Zandery Field, Surinam, were credited with sinking a German submarine on 2 October 1942 after a nearly 3-hour engagement! The entire crew was awarded the DFC and this is regarded as the first successful and confirmed combat action involving a crew of the Sixth Air Force, although by no means the first action of any kind. *Ward Burhanna*

and PFC John R. McNellis, were all awarded the Distinguished Flying Cross on 21 January 1943 for this action. This was the first successful combat action of a unit of the Sixth Air Force during the war. The survivor of this sub, later confirmed as the U-512, was subsequently picked up by the USS *Ellis* and turned over to British authorities after ten days on the raft that had been dropped by the B-18.

In yet another action on this historic day in the service life of the B-18, another 99th Bomb Squadron B-18B, commanded by Lt Lehti, took off at 2400 hours and patrolled eastward from Zandery Field, Surinam, to his assigned patrol area along the French Guiana coast. At 0400 the next morning his radar operator advised him of a contact at 12 miles. At 1 mile the aircraft was over the sub's wake heading northwest. As it crossed over it dropped two depth charges and the crew noted that the two deck hatches were open. One of the 650lb depth

The orders awarding the Distinguished Flying Cross to Capt Burhanna and his entire crew as the result of the action of 2 October. The victim was U-512, a Type IXC. *Ward Burhanna*

By early October 1942 B-18s continued to soldier on based in the Hawaiian Islands, including AC36-433, possibly assigned to the 860th Bomb Squadron at the time of this photo, shown releasing a carrier pigeon, in flight, from the topside hatch! The significance of the smaller number under the abbreviated serial on the vertical fin is unknown, and the camouflage scheme worn by this time is reminiscent of that carried by some USAAF aircraft during the Battle of Midway. *via Rich Dann*

charges entered the water ahead of the sub with another, a 325-pounder, 30 feet further on, and the sub, identified as U-512, disappeared. Lehti then turned for shore, 120 miles distant, to check his position. He recrossed the Cayenne lighthouse and returned to the scene of the action where he found U-512 once again on the surface, caught yet again by surprise. As he crossed the sub he dropped two 325lb depth charges simultaneously and they landed alongside the sub. There was no further sign of the sub. The unit was credited with sinking U-512.

4 October 1942: Capt Pohan and crew, flying 2nd Sea Search Attack Squadron B-18B AC37-563, picked up a MAD contact but were unable to locate the target. The 'killer' search lasted 7 hours.

6 October 1942: The air echelon of the gypsy 40th Bomb Squadron (M), 13th Bomb Group (M), still nominally home-based at Mitchel Field, NY, as part of the Eastern Defense Command, First Air Force, was operating from Vernam Field, Jamaica, but moved on this date to Edinburgh Field, Trinidad, with its B-18s. The unit moved to Zandery Field, Surinam, on the 9th.

7 October 1942: Two 1st SSAG crews on detached service flew patrols totaling 14hr 40min, Capt Pohan in B-18B AC37-482 and Lt Easterling in AC37-550.

8 October 1942: Two 1st SSAG crews on detached service flew patrols totaling 12hr 55min, Lt Lehti in B-18B AC37-563 and Lt McKay in AC37-550.

9 October 1942: Lt Zinn and crew of the 1st SSAG on detached duty flew a 7hr 30min 'killer search' with negative results in B-18B AC37-482.

Much further south, a 99th Bomb Squadron B-18, crew unknown, flying from Zandery Field, Surinam, spotted the U-332 300 miles south-east of Galeota Point, Trinidad, and attacked her on the surface. Three depth charges hit the water just as the conning tower went under in the crash-dive and the crew claimed severe damage. The sub survived, however, and surfaced an hour later to check for damage – and was attacked again by another B-18, although the unit and crew of this attack are not confirmed. This time the depth charges dropped were further off and did no damage. This could possibly have been the attack by 1Lt Frank M. Wyman and his crew, although they were actually assigned to the 430th Bomb Squadron (H) at the time. The submarine was probably the U-332, which was damaged.

10 October 1942: A 'B-18BR', AC37-593 of the 40th Bomb Squadron, commanded by Capt Mackall and flying with radio call sign 'L431', made a radar contact at 1045 hours at 3830N 7253W, but it faded at 7 miles out. Elsewhere, three 1st SSAG crews on detached service flew two 'killer searches' and one patrol totaling 17hr 45min.

11 October 1942: Lt Lehti of the 1st SSAG on detached service flew a 6hr 40min patrol in B-18B AC37-563 but without result. The same day, at 1818 hours, Lt Detjens, flying a 'B-18BR' of the 80th Bomb Squadron, made an instrument contact at 2410N 8200W at 16 miles. The signal was lost at 4 miles, but the crew felt sure it was a sub. The aircraft stayed on station for 4hr 20min but no further contact was made in the very deep water of the area.

12 October 1942: Lt Detjens, flying a 80th Bomb Squadron 'B-18BR', made a radar contact at 1818 hours at 2410N 8200W at 16 miles, but the signal faded at 4 miles.

13 October 1942: Lt Biddison (with co-pilot Lt Burghoff, navigator Lt Harmon, bombardier Lt Tressel and radar operator Sgt Robinson), flying RB-18B AC37-473 of the 1st SSAG on detached duty out of Trinidad, took off at 1715 hours in response to a report that the

freighter SS *Wildwood* had suffered an aborted submarine attack. At 1910 Biddison's ASV operator picked up a signal 14 miles out and sighted the sub visually at 300 yards, 45° starboard of the aircraft. The crew lost sight of the submarine in the gathering darkness, however, and went ashore to get a navigational 'fix'. The aircraft returned to the scene at 2137 hours and ASV got another signal at 12 miles, and sighted the sub visually at 0832N 5934W. The submarine was noted to be stationary. The aircraft made a 180° turn and at 2145 passed over the sub, dropping a 650lb depth charge across the beam. Results were not observed but the submarine was gone by the time the aircraft could turn around.

Elsewhere the same day Lt Reynolds and his crew, flying 2nd Sea Search Attack Squadron B-18B AC37-482, picked up a MAD contact on a moving oil slick. Navy PC boats were guided to the area and dropped nearly fifty depth charges, but it was ruled doubtful if this was an enemy submarine after all of the effort. Another crew from the same squadron, commanded by Lt Easterling, also in a B-18B, AC37-550, picked up a MAD contact and, again, Navy PCs were guided to the area and dropped about thirty depth charges; again, no results were observed.

The same day, far south in the Caribbean, the U-514 was sighted by a Consolidated PBY-5 of VP-53, then was subsequently attacked by a B-18 of the 99th Bomb Squadron out of Zandery Field, Surinam, without known result.

14 October 1942: Once again, Capt Pohan and his 2nd Sea Search Attack Squadron B-18B crew in AC37-50 picked up both ASV and MAD contacts that led to sighting of a swirl at 0137 hours. No attack was made. His mission lasted 6hr 50min. 2Lt G. M. Biddison and his B-18 crew from the same unit were also credited with engaging a submarine in combat on this date. A B-18 crew from the 99th Bomb Squadron was also credited with attacking the U-514.

15 October 1942: The Army Air Forces Antisubmarine Command (AAFAC) was activated. The same day Lt Reynolds of the 2nd Sea Search Attack Squadron in B-18B AC37-473 picked up an ASV contact that led to a visual sighting of an enemy submarine. The sub crash-dived, however, before an attack could be made. His mission lasted 8hr 20min. The same unit flew no fewer than five other missions that day, totaling more than 30 hours.

An incredible survival story: B-18 AC36-343 is shown here in Townsville, Australia, wearing US national insignia first authorised in August 1943, and by the date of this photo has returned to a bare natural metal color scheme. This was one of the aircraft that survived the Japanese onslaught in the Philippines in December 1941, and which served in Australia with the ad hoc 21st Troop Carrier Squadron until at least 10 October 1942. Although reported crashed during that month, it in fact clearly survived and was not salvaged until 3 September 1944! *via Buz Busby and Rich Dann*

16 October 1942: Two 1st SSAG crews on detached service flew an 8-hour 'killer search' (Lt Harris and crew in B-18B AC37-473) and a patrol of 8hr 15min (Lt Easterling in AC37-563) without result. This unit element, while on detached service, had flown seventy missions in the Caribbean during October alone, totaling 451hr 30min combat time.

25 October 1942: The 99th Bomb Squadron (H), Sixth Air Force, at this time stationed at Zandery Field, Surinam, exchanged four B-18As for four 'new' B-18Bs with ASV. The unit commander, however, noted that '…combat efficiency is being seriously affected by the difficulty in keeping the radar equipment in operating condition. No facilities for such maintenance at this station requires frequent trips to Trinidad in order that necessary work can be accomplished.'

30 October 1942: RCAF Digby No 747, commanded by Fg Off D. F. Raymes, while heading home after escorting Convoy ON 140 westbound about 140 miles away, and due east of St John's, spotted a sub on the surface with decks awash, and attacked. Four depth charges were dropped quickly and an explosion ensued after which a dark object appeared in the water, followed by oil and bubbles. Although assessed as 'damaged', post-war evidence confirmed that this was in fact U-520, which was lost with all hands. This was the seventh No 10(BR) Squadron attack, and more than justified Canada's investment in her twenty DB-280s.

During October 1942 aircraft and units of the USAAF I Bomber Command flew a total of 6,410 hours on anti-submarine and convoy escort missions and sighted four U-boats, of which one was attacked. Not a single Allied vessel was lost in the Command's area of responsibility during the month.

November 1942: The 10th Bomb Squadron, completely equipped with B-18s, completed nineteen convoy coverages, nine convoy sweeps, thirty-eight anti-submarine sweeps and hunts, and forty-five patrols and bauxite convoy escorts during the month.

2 November 1942: Headquarters and Headquarters Squadron, 25th Antisubmarine Wing, and Headquarters and Headquarters Squadron, 26th Antisubmarine Wing, were activated from personnel of the Headquarters, 1st Patrol Force (Provisional), Headquarters, Gulf Task Force and several other Group headquarters.

3 November 1942: RCAF Digby No 747 again, this time commanded by Fg Off Sanderson, attacked a crash-diving submarine, believed to be either U-106 or U-183, but without success.

8 November 1942: Capt Donald K. Brandon and his crew (Lt Lloyd A. Crumpton, co-pilot; S/Sgt Bien, engineer; Sgt Leonard G. Felder, radio operator; S/Sgt Herbert S. Skinner Jr, bombardier; and Sgt Huchzermeier (gunner) of the 10th Bomb Squadron, 25th Bomb Group (M), operating from Edinburgh Field, Trinidad, sighted a sub from 4,000 feet when they

spotted the wake of a periscope from, incredibly, about 20 miles. The sub dived before they could attack. Twenty minutes later, however, the crew again sighted the sub, which surfaced for about 40 seconds. The B-18A dropped four depth charges from 25 feet, then remained in the area for about an hour, but saw nothing more.

11 November 1942: A B-18 crew of the 59th Bomb Squadron (L) consisting of 1Lt Lawrence R. Jordan, 2Lt Ivan N. Bernson (co-pilot), Sgt Harold A. Fischer (bombardier), Cpl Veldor L. A. Kopiske (radar), Sgt William C. Russell (gunner), and S/Sgt Donald A. Winney (engineer) were credited with engaging a submarine in combat in the Caribbean on this date.

13 November 1942: Another 59th Bomb Squadron (L) B-18 crew, consisting of commander 1Lt Richard A. B. Sheddon, 1Lt Irvin M. Parsons (co-pilot), S/Sgt Edward Day (bombardier), Pt Wayne A. Brown (radar), Pt Cyril A. Michuda (gunner), Sgt Edward J. Noller (engineer) and Sgt Louis Stahl (engineer) were credited with engaging a submarine in combat in the Caribbean on this date.

15 November 1942: The itinerant 40th Bomb Squadron (M), 13th Bomb Group (M) air echelon, which had been all over the Caribbean but which was home-based at Mitchel Field, NY, finally ceased operations from Vernam Field, Jamaica, on this date and returned to Mitchel Field. The unit was redesignated as the 4th Antisubmarine Squadron (H) on 29 November.

17 November 1942: RCAF Digby No 751, operating from No 10(BR) Squadron's new station at Dartmouth, was engaged in an anti-submarine sweep around a convoy when a surfaced submarine was spotted. Although not immediately confirmed because of the haze, the target was attacked, but only after it had dived, and no claims were made. This was the last attack recorded by a No 10(BR) Squadron Digby during the war.

23 November 1942: 1Lt A. L. Majure, flying a 'B-18R' of the 40th Bomb Squadron, saw surface Navy vessels dropping depth charges at 1640 hours on a sound contact and assisted them to relocate the contact after they had lost it. On instructions from the lead destroyer in the action, he dropped four 325lb depth charges with 25-foot fuses and all exploded, but there were no visible results. He finally departed the scene after remaining on station for an hour, leaving three Navy aircraft and two vessels in the area.

Often erroneously credited as being photographed in Hawaii, AC37-465 was a singularly special RB-18B as of the time of this posed photo with a group of WACs. It had been heavily modified and assigned to the 1st Motion Picture Unit at Culver City, CA, by 13 March 1944, and had special modifications for aerial camera work. *NARA RG342FH 3A41256*

27-28 November 1942: Two 'B-18Rs' of the 40th Bomb Squadron, 25th Anti-submarine Wing, conducted a 6hr 15min anti-submarine patrol and a 5hr 46min convoy escort patrol. These were the only aircraft assigned to the Squadron at this time. The 362nd Bomb Squadron, 25th Anti-submarine Wing (redesignated as the 18th Antisubmarine Squadron the next day), also had two 'B-18Rs' and conducted one 5hr 18min convoy escort mission.

29 November 1942: Lt Martus and crew of the 1st SSAG, flying B-18B AC37-464, flew a 3hr 30min 'killer search' without result.

30 November 1942: Two crews from the 1st SSAG based at Langley Field flew two 'killer searches' on this date. Capt Zinn in B-18B AC37-464 flew 3hr 20min without result and Lt Hafner flew 6hr 3min, also without result, in AC37-548.

December 1942: The 10th Bomb Squadron, fully equipped with B-18s, completed fourteen convoy coverages, fifteen convoy sweeps, forty-one anti-submarine sweeps and hunts, and forty-nine patrols and bauxite convoy escorts during the month.

1 December 1942: The 4th Antisubmarine Squadron (ASRON), formerly the 40th Bombardment Squadron (M), was activated at Mitchel Field, NY.

3 December 1942: The 7th Antisubmarine Squadron (ASRON), formerly the 78th Bomb Squadron (M), was activated at Jacksonville, FL.

6 December 1942: A 'B-18R' of the 4th Antisubmarine Squadron flew a 5hr 46min convoy escort mission covering shipping lanes from 44N southward along the east coast to Jacksonville, FL. The unit had a total of five 'B-18Rs' at this time.

9 December 1942: The 3rd Sea Search Attack Squadron (H), 1st Sea Search Attack Group, was activated. The cadre, consisting of nine officers and thirty-nine enlisted men, was drawn from the existing 2nd Sea Search Attack Squadron.

12 December 1942: Two 1st SSAG crews flew 'killer searches' this date without result: Lt McIntosh in B-18B AC37-621 (5hr 20min) and Lt Rockwood in AC38-587 (7 hours).

13 December 1942: Lt LeVan and his crew, flying B-18B AC38-605 of the 2nd Sea Search Attack Squadron, picked up three MAD indications but had negative results. Their mission lasted 6hr 45min.

The same day, veteran anti-submarine skipper Capt Kenneth B. Carlson and his 35th Bomb Squadron crew, operating from Trinidad, engaged in what was, according to the sole AAF survivor of the action, Pt Lingafelt, one of the most incredible actions that any B-18 was to experience. The aircraft apparently engaged a submarine fully surfaced and, after expending all of its droppable ordnance, continued to circle the submarine with the onboard gunners firing the dorsal turret and tunnel guns, out of range for the most part. In turn, according to the survivor, both engines were shot completely off the aircraft and it was forced to ditch. It alighted safely not far from the submarine, and continued to exchange fire from the rear turret, mainly to cover the surviving crew, who were attempting to avoid the murderous fire from the submarine's deck guns and escape the aircraft. Apparently the B-18's radios had become inoperable early in the action, unbeknown to the crew, who believed that help was on the way; the aerial was apparently shot away. The aircraft apparently sank not long afterwards and Pt Lingafelt was rescued from the only remaining life raft on the 16th (see below). This account, in fragmentary form, was located in the records of the Sixth Air Force.

14-21 December 1942: The 35th Bomb Squadron, Sixth Air Force, stationed at Zandery Field, Surinam, used every available aircraft (five B-18Bs and one B-18) to search for Capt Carlson and his B-18B crew (AC37-483), which went missing on the 13th (see above). Pt Lingafelt, the radar operator, was rescued from a life raft on 16 December, the sole survivor.

By the end of 1942 and through to the end of the war in the Pacific, the area of operations covered by the Seventh Air Force in the Pacific was staggering. B-18s had been relegated to second-line status, but no fewer than fourteen of the fifty-two B-18s that had been assigned there since 1938 remained fully operational. Additionally, for reasons that have not been uncovered, AC36-336 was assigned TO HOLLY (Canton Island, also known by code name MYTHOLOGY) on 3 December 1942, and another was assigned to HAEMATITE (Funafuti, in the Ellice Islands) as late as 28 December 1943. *USAF*

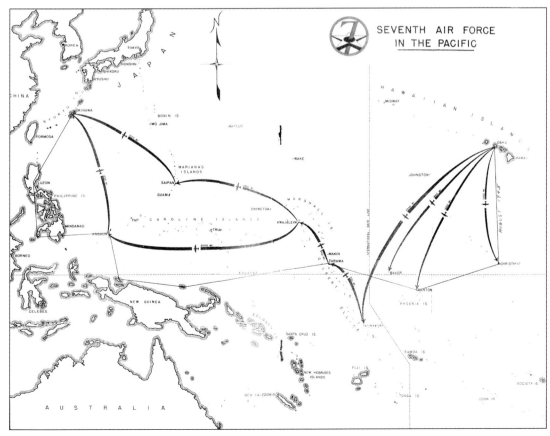

Tactical Radio Call Signs 25th Antisubmarine Wing Units – 15 December 1942

Unit	Mobile Ground Station	Primary Aircraft Assigned	Individual Aircraft Call Signs
304th Bomb Group	JV93	B-18, B-17, DB-7, A-20, OA-12	Y7K, S3J, 32Q, 04W, 4B7, U6E
3rd Antisubmarine Squadron	KH64	B-18, B-25, A-29	97H, B2T, 2X4, M8N, N1L, T5Y, G9C, 79W, 3V3, R70, H3B, 12L, S41, 1P7, 54D, A5L, D1C, F8D
4th Antisubmarine Squadron	3WJ5	B-18	65F, Z4F, N7Q, 9S8, V9X, 5C5, 26Q, F6Y, T2K, 6B1, A3A, 34H, D5J, C1S, X8E, 95E, P8B, 13Y
5th Antisubmarine Squadron	UJ39	B-18, B-25, A-29	V6S, 1U9, A2X, Q5S, 8Q3, E3H, 89O, 01M, B7F, F9V, 48D, E4N, 7S2, K8L, 51F, P6J, 9C6, D2Q
6th Antisubmarine Squadron	3ZJ6	B-18, B-25, A-29	4N4, J8C, 37V, W3T, 2J1, Z1V, S7E, 96G, X4Y, B9N, 3U7, 02R, Z5H, 72Y, J6H, 1Q4, Y8S, 17O
7th Antisubmarine Squadron	3OJ9	B-18, DB-7, A-20	G3M-8D1-55U-NE-9-H6G-9E5-17L-68B-G2D-T8M-5Y2-M5G-U4B-24V-M3V-6N8-N37-35G
11th Antisubmarine Squadron	9KV9	B-18, B-25, O-47, O-52	J9R, T6T, 4J5, A7Y, 1K3, F5O, H9D, 19R, Y4U, D8V, 8F7, A60, M2B, 82Z, 7E6, I1G, 41U, Q7J
12th Antisubmarine Squadron	V957	B-18B	F3K, 9Y9, X51, T9E, 53B, R4A, W7Z, 4R1, N4H, K1R, 2W8, Q6W, 36S, V3N, 94C, A9B, K5X, 3K4
13th Antisubmarine Squadron	7HH3	O-47	X2S, S8O, 77R, G7U, 1F1, V4C, NB4, 8O8, Q9A, 58X, 9L2, P2C, G6F, 61K, Y1E, Z8Q, 5A6, J5P
14th Antisubmarine Squadron	7KH1	O-47, O-52, B-25	25S, M7H, J3E, 6R5, B4M, 09S, 38C, 4W2, K2Z, Z6N, AN1, 9UD, JN1, KH5, Q62, 6WQ, OJ1, 60Q
15th Antisubmarine Squadron	PL61	B-23, O-47, B-25, B-34	1AJ, 5MV, EH9, 9HH, MV5, H93, VL8, 5JH, DH5, 9MD, UN1, 1WJ, UJ1, 1ZJ, 1NJ, LJ1, H97, 5GV
16th Antisubmarine Squadron	EL65	O-46, B-34	ZV5, 5RV, QH9, 7KN, TH5, 1N1, YN1, ZH5, 1RJ, WQ6, 6UQ, J15, 10J, 5ZV, HH9, 9YH, V57, 9KH
18th Antisubmarine Squadron	AL64	B-18B, B-17E, A-20C, B-24D	PL8, 1TN, 5DH, MH5, TN1, Q66, 6QQ, 1TJ, 6LQ, 1FJ, EV5, 5CV, AH9, H98, 5FV, 7MN, H56, SH5
19th Antisubmarine Squadron	L696	B-17	5CH, ON1, GJ1, RL8, 6VQ, 1UJ, 1IJ, RH, 9, 9QH, V58, 5NV, CV5, L87, 1XN, LN1, 1JN, FH5, J14
46th Bomb Squadron	V991	B-18, A-29, B-17	QV5, WJ1, 61Q, PQ6, VH9, 9XH, KV5, 9SH, 7ZN, RN1, H51, IH5, 9BM, 1MJ, 9VH, 1EJ, 6YQ
1st Sea Search Attack Group	UV96	B-18B, B-18C	J19, 5KV, 9PH, JH9, 5PV, GV5, EN7, BN1, 5BH, H52, FN1, BJ1, XJ1, XQ6, 6AQ, PH9, V55, 5EV

27 December 1942: The Army Air Forces Antisubmarine Command (AAFAC) consisted of the 25th Antisubmarine Wing with two subordinate units: the 4th Antisubmarine Squadron (ASRON) at Mitchel Field, NY, with ten B-18Bs, and the 18th ASRON at Langley Field, VA, with one Douglas A-20C, thirteen B-18Bs, five Consolidated B-24Ds, two Lockheed B-34s, and five North American B-25Ds.

At 0936 on this day a B-18B operating in the Trinidad area of the Caribbean sighted a submarine at conning-tower depth at 1055N 5715W and an attack was made with three depth charges dropped well to the rear and to the port side of the submerging craft. The closest depth charge exploded at least 110 feet away from the pressure hull. The fourth depth charge failed to release, despite two more runs. The same day, at 1806 hours, another B-18B operating from Trinidad, while on a 'killer hunt', sighted a fully surfaced U-boat at 1035N 5753W. Three attacks were made but in all cases the depth charges failed to release. This was almost certainly the aircraft commanded by Lt L. J. Cormier and his crew, consisting of Lt R. T. Shaw (co-pilot), Lt J. P. Stampon (navigator), Sgt H. V. Page (bombardier), PFC A. S. Guthrie (radar) and PFC R. Bush (gunner) of the 80th Bomb Squadron.

31 December 1942: A B-18B operating in the Trinidad area on a 'killer hunt' sighted a submarine at conning-tower depth at 0605. An attack was made and the depth charges were dropped approximately 2 minutes after the periscope submerged, and exploded 70, 130, 180 and 220 feet ahead of the swirl. The fourth depth charge was estimated to have exploded 945 feet behind the conning tower. This was almost certainly the crew of 2Lt H. E. Thomas, which included 2Lt Ray Wilson (co-pilot), 1Lt M. D. Zick (navigator), Sgt H. G. Greene (bombardier), Sgt H. A. Smith (radar), and Sgt J. W. Swinney (radio operator) of the 80th Bomb Squadron.

1943

January 1943: The 10th Bomb Squadron, completely equipped with B-18s, racked up six convoy coverages, thirteen convoy sweeps, no fewer than sixty-five anti-submarine sweeps and hunts, and thirty-one bauxite convoy escorts and patrols during the month.

1-9 January 1943: The 12th Bomb Squadron, 25th Bomb Group based at Dakota Field, Aruba, was truly a cosmopolitan outfit, as at this date, besides its primary equipment of eight B-18Bs, the unit also had a Douglas A-20A (attached from the 59th Bomb Squadron) and two Bell P-39Ds (attached from the 22nd Fighter Squadron)! During this week the unit conducted no fewer than two patrols, one sub-search and six convoy escorts, and amassed 291hr 5min of combat flying on B-18s alone.

The Dutch islands of Aruba and Curacao feature frequently in accounts of B-18 wartime actions, as they were in the very center of the Axis submarine target areas, with large oil refining and bauxite transhipment facilities. This wartime map shows the relative location of Dakota Field, on the south-western shore. *USAAF*

3 January 1943: A B-18B, AC37-519 of the 12th Bomb Squadron (M), commanded by 1Lt William A. Smith and his crew, 2Lt Ivan N. Bernson (co-pilot), 1Lt Francis N. Davies (navigator), S/Sgt David P. Reese (bombardier), Sgt Harrell M. Hudson (engineer), Sgt R. L. Selbe (radio operator), and Cpl L. J. Stalhauske (radar), made an attack on a sub at 1223N 6717W while on a search in a suspected area. The sub was sighted at 0640 and three depth charges were salvoed at intervals of 30 seconds from the time of sighting. On a repeat run, a fourth depth charge was released on the still-surfaced sub in a level run. By then the first flare dropped had burned out and visibility was significantly impaired. A second flare dropped hit the surface before igniting. There was no further contact.

4 January 1943: The 12th Antisubmarine Squadron (ASRON) made its first operational flights with B-18s, having previously been equipped with North American O-47As. The unit apparently received B-18Bs that had been fitted with radar and MAD gear, but with scant attention being paid to the rest of the aircraft, which were very high-time. Their first two aircraft, AC37-534 and 37-628, had been previously assigned to the 18th Antisubmarine Squadron at Langley, which had apparently handed over its two highest-time aircraft – a time-honored tradition in the service! The unit reported that '…the aircraft were flown overloaded with special equipment and therefore caused much excess maintenance. When received, they were in terrible condition and had to be given maintenance before they could be flown on patrol. Some had to have engine changes, replacement of control cables, repair of leaking fuel tanks, etc. On the average it required nearly one week for each plane before being able to use it on patrol.' Ironically, this first echelon and unit maintenance for 'new' unit aircraft was actually far below the norm for typical USAAF units as of January 1943, and units receiving 'new' combat types, such as Martin B-26 Marauders, had a much longer period of maintenance before operations could begin. During the eight months that the unit operated B-18Bs, operational availability was never lower than 60%, and for three months was above 80% – again, far above that attained by a normal line tactical squadron. They managed to amass no less than 5,236 hours of combat patrols and training during the period, with peak strength being twelve B-18Bs in February, May and June.

6 January 1943: 1Lt Harry B. Greene and his B-18 crew of the 59th Bomb Squadron (L) were credited with engaging a submarine in combat in the Caribbean.

8 January 1943: Illustrative of the rather ad hoc nature of the Army Air Forces' commitment to the anti-submarine war in the Caribbean region, by this date Zandery Field, Surinam, was home station to C and D Flights, 417th Bomb Squadron, attached at the time to the 35th Bomb Squadron (M) (but only A and B Flights) at Zandery, and three B-18Bs and crews of the 80th Bomb Squadron were also on station on detached service from 27 to 30 January.

9 January 1943: Capt Charles Ross and his B-18 crew from the 35th Bomb Squadron (M) affected the rescue of at least forty-two survivors of a vessel sunk by Axis submarines by flying over an area at less than 50 feet for not less than 6 hours, pointing out the locations of survivors afloat in life rafts, wreckage, etc, to the Commander of US Navy PC-577. This was accomplished in the face of extremely poor weather in the area.

13 January 1943: The 12th ASRON made its first armed patrol with B-18s.

21 January 1943: Two crews from the 1st SSAG, Lt Quinette's in B-18B AC38-605 and Lt McGehee's in AC38-590, conducted a joint patrol/'killer search' lasting, jointly, 7hr 30min, the only missions flown by this unit this month. The unit had been alerted at 1630 hours by Anti-Submarine Control, which advised that a sound contact had been made at 1520 hours by a PC boat at 3827N 7448W.

23 January 1943: 1Lt Duane C. Treeman and his crew, consisting of Major Norman L. Ballard (co-pilot), 1Lt William W. Weinzirl (navigator), 2Lt Charles R. McDowell (bombardier), Sgt Macon A. Rathburn (engineer), T/Sgt Weldon S. Johnson (radio operator), Pt Harold L. Johnson (radar), Sgt John Budagher (gunner) and Cpl C. Catching of the 417th Bomb Squadron (L) were credited with engaging a submarine in combat in the Caribbean on this date.

25 January 1943: While on a convoy sweep mission, a B-18 of the 35th Bomb Squadron (M) stationed at Zandery Field, Surinam, sighted a submarine from 5,000 feet at 0730N 5700W. The sub dived before an attack could be made. 'Killer' tactics were immediately invoked.

February 1943: B-18B AC38-593 was assigned to 1110th AAF Base Unit, Air Transport Command, Zandery Field, Surinam, for unspecified duties, one of the first B-18s assigned to ATC. Elsewhere in the same region, the 10th Bomb Squadron amassed twenty-two

Seldom illustrated, this is the Weekly Status and Operations Report for the 12th Bomb Squadron, 25th Bomb Group, Sixth Air Force, for 14-20 February 1943, while stationed on Aruba. Unfortunately, most of these reports no longer exist, making accounting for all B-18 missions flown, and as reported herein to the extent documented, problematic. *USAFHRA*

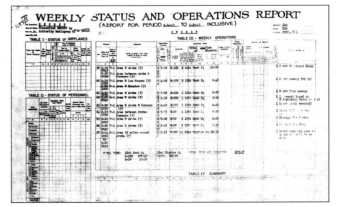

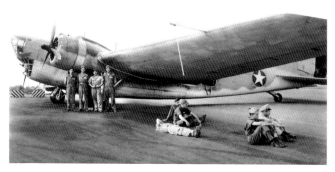

By early 1943, long after all previously published accounts report B-18As as having been 'relegated to training duties', a number that had not been converted to B-18B or B-18C configuration soldiered on in combat units. This B-18A of the 1st Reconnaissance Squadron, Sixth Air Force, operating from Albrook Field, Canal Zone, was named 'Solitary', as it was the sole remaining B-18 in the unit! Note the distinctive white 'cloud' splotches on blue on the undersides, unique to Sixth Air Force aircraft engaged in anti-submarine work. *Ed Dalton via George L. Redheffer*

convoy coverages, seven convoy sweeps, an astonishing seventy anti-submarine sweeps and hunts, and thirty-six patrols and bauxite convoy escorts during the month, all on B-18s.

This month the 25th Antisubmarine Wing had a total of twenty-two B-18s assigned, second only to forty North American B-25s, with an 82% 'in-commission' rate, better than the B-25s, with 80%. A total of 40 hours were flown by the B-18s in February.

1 February 1943: Two B-18Bs with complete combat crews from the 10th Bomb Squadron and three B-18Bs and crews from the 80th Bomb Squadron, which had been attached for operations to the 35th Bomb Squadron (M) at Zandery Field, Surinam, were returned to their parent units.

Readers who check such things as serial numbers will be puzzled by the serial on this 1st Reconnaissance Squadron, Sixth Air Force, RB-18A until receiving the information that the last digit of the serial ('4') has been overpainted on a newly recovered rudder! The actual serial was AC37-624, one of the last five B-18s in the Canal Zone area by February 1943, all others having gone to anti-submarine units in the Antilles. T/Sgt W. W. Wieble works on the still functional dorsal turret. *USAFHRA*

7-14 February 1943: The 1st SSAG conducted not less than 229hr 10min of intense training, including pilot transition, bombardment practice, gunnery practice, night transition training, night navigation, special equipment transition, compass swinging, instrument training and thirty-one test flights. B-18B AC37-464 was returned to the unit from California (where it had been used in unspecified tests), and AC38-590 returned from Quonset Point. This aircraft had been at the Navy station with Lt Hafner and his crew and, while there, had the unusual experience of being asked by the Navy to participate in a search. Due to the fact that the Bell Lab had just installed a 'special' MAD device in his aircraft, Lt Hafner felt that this would be an excellent opportunity to test the new equipment on 'live bait'. The Navy made one definite sound contact, one probable approximately 25 miles off Block Island, off Long Island. Lt Hafner took off at 1730 on the 9th (see below) and flew a MAD search at 300 feet between the two sound contacts but without result.

8 February 1943: The 421st Bomb Squadron (H) was redesignated as the 20th Antisubmarine Squadron and assigned to AAFAC.

9 February 1943: There were a total of sixty-four B-18Bs with ASV-S assigned to elements of the Army Air Forces Antisubmarine Command (AAFAC), and forty-five assigned to the Caribbean Defense Command. A B-18B, AC38-590 of the 1st SSAG commanded by Lt Hafner, flew a 2-hour patrol on this date, without result.

11 February 1943: Lt Hickman and his crew of the 1st SSAG flying B-18B AC37-565 flew a 3hr 25min 'killer patrol' this date, without result. He was responding to an Anti-Submarine Command Control advisory that the Navy had made a visual sighting at 1430 hours on 10 February at 3650N 7525W, but that a Navy scout aircraft had lost the target. He was ordered back to base and landed at 1010 hours due to extremely foul weather.

14-20 February 1943: The 12th Bomb Squadron, still stationed at Dakota Field, Aruba, now had one B-18 (AC36-316) and six B-18Bs organic (AC37-462/519/560/589/617 and 39-12), two P-39Ds attached from the 22nd Fighter Squadron, and one B-18 (AC36-302) attached from the 59th Bomb Squadron. It conducted six convoy escorts, one patrol and one sub search during this period and amassed 177hr 40min on the B-18Bs and 13hr 10min on the B-18s.

22 February 1943: Two 1st SSAG crews, flying B-18Bs AC38-586 (Capt Herrick) and 37-465 (Capt Lehti), made 'killer searches' lasting 2hr 15min and 2hr 40min respectively, without result. These were as a result of an Anti-Submarine Control sighting of a submerged sub approximately 113 miles from Langley at 3616N 7429W. Both crews returned due to extremely poor visibility.

24 February 1943: The 108th Observation Squadron, Sixth Air Force, conducted its one and only B-18 mission of the war 'over the Pacific coast of Colombia'.

26 February 1943: Lt Dustin and his 'B-18BR' crew of the 4th Antisubmarine Squadron out of Mitchel Field, NY, reported a MAD contact at 1342 hours at 3840N 7400W. Three sweeps were made and an object was detected at the same position on each. An oil slick was observed in the same position. No other visual observations were reported. Bubbles were also observed at the end of the slick and the aircraft stayed on station for 3 hours observing the area. The same unit conducted three reconnaissance patrols this date totaling 11hr 11min.

28 February 1943: A 4th Antisubmarine Squadron B-18 ground-looped at Mitchel Field, NY, while returning from a patrol.

At Zandery Field, Surinam, the 35th Bomb Squadron was conducting intensive operations with four assigned B-18Bs and one B-18, and five additional B-18Bs attached from other units.

B-18 AC36-294 is a long way from home station, shown here on the tarmac on the Galapagos Islands. Assigned to the 108th Reconnaissance Squadron (Special), Sixth Air Force, at the time, it had probably flown in from Salinas, Ecuador or Talara, Peru. The camouflage shown here, including the almost white under surfaces, was unique to aircraft of the Sixth Air Force. *via John Woram*

28 February–6 March 1943: The 12th Bomb Squadron, 25th Bomb Group, based at Dakota Field, Aruba, had six B-18Bs and one B-18 organic, and two P-39Ds attached from the 22nd Fighter Squadron. It flew six convoy coverage missions and patrols around Aruba twice daily, and one search for a missing aircraft during this period, totaling 35 hours. The unit had only three qualified bombardiers, although it was noted that it also had 'fifteen students'.

March 1943: The air echelon of the 7th Antisubmarine Squadron deployed from Jacksonville (actually Fernandia, 29 miles north-east of Jacksonville), FL, to Edinburgh Field, Trinidad, with ten B-18s, carrying crews of four officers and four enlisted ranks each. All had arrived on Trinidad within the last ten days of the month. By 1 April the unit had eight B-18Cs and one B-18B. This is believed to have been the highest concentration of B-18Cs in any single operating squadron. This increased to nine B-18Cs and one B-18B by 1 May. The unit, while in Trinidad, had a total of thirty-four pilots, eleven bombardiers and one solitary navigator! The unit was attached to the 25th Bomb Group for tactical duties. Tactical flying was divided between 'sweeps' and 'coverages'. Sweeps were made to the west, north-east and east of Trinidad, while coverages were provided for convoys going and coming west of the island and for convoys going and coming to the south-east along the South American coast. Coverages were also provided for the bauxite ships, shallow-bottom boats carrying bauxite ore plying between Surinam and Port of Spain. This lane was often covered at night because poor weather was frequently experienced in the region. The squadron acquired a special Gremlin pilot – 'Duffy' – who maintained a constant vigil on the bauxite lane. The unit maintained nearly 100% operational status on its ten aircraft during its stay in Trinidad and flew 1,141 combat patrol hours.

The same month, the 10th Bomb Squadron, in the Caribbean, flew twenty-four convoy coverages, nine convoy sweeps, fifty-two anti-submarine sweeps and hunts, and forty-three patrols and bauxite convoy escorts – all on B-18s. Also, the problem of the 'neutralised' Vichy French 'fleet-in-being' at Guadeloupe and Martinique (see entry for 9 May 1942) once again surfaced when it was suspected that Vichy French Admiral Robert intended to use his small but potentially influential fleet to support a pro-Vichy Government in French Guiana. A force of AAF B-18s was concentrated at Beane Field, St Lucia, for the express purpose of preventing such a move. On 19 March the B-18s were sent back to their normal anti-submarine duties when Admiral Robert disclaimed any intention of using his forces in French Guiana. See the entry for June 1943.

1 March 1943: ASV-equipped B-18s in the inventory of the AAF as of this date were deployed as follows:

Antisubmarine Command

(Trinidad, on detached service from Miami)	10
Antisubmarine Command (Mitchel Field, NY)	11
Antisubmarine Command (Langley Field, VA)	6
Antisubmarine Command (Atlantic City, NJ)	8
Caribbean Defense Command (Panama Canal Zone and Caribbean)	35
1st Sea Search Attack Group (Langley Field, VA)	12

2 March 1943: A B-18C of the 9th Antisubmarine Squadron (ASRON), piloted by 1Lt R. Wilson Jr, attacked a submarine (U-156, which was damaged) at 1400 hours in the vicinity of Trinidad (1059N 6205W) from 100 feet, dropping two 650lb and two 325lb depth charges. Another B-18C from this unit, possibly the same aircraft, and also commanded by Lt Wilson, apparently attacked the same target at 2307 hours at 1059N 6205W, dropping the identical ordnance, this time with 'excellent' results. Another B-18B, from an unidentified unit (but probably the 80th Bomb Squadron), was approaching a submarine in an attack at 1102N 6155W as 2340 hours when the surfaced U-boat fired on the landing lights of the aircraft with tracers from at least two guns. The sub crash-dived before a second run could be made.

3 March 1943: A B-18B of the 9th ASRON flown by 1Lt L. J. Cormier attacked a surfaced sub at 0325 hours at 1102N 6155W from 200 feet with four depth charges, but no claims were noted. The same submarine had been attacked by another aircraft 2 hours earlier. Cormier and his crew visually spotted the U-boat at three-quarters of a mile and turned on his landing lights, and was immediately met by anti-aircraft tracer fire. The landing lights were turned off immediately and a second pass was made, but the sub disappeared. After a 2-hour square search, four more contacts were made and depth charges were released on a visual sighting on the fourth run, straddling the U-boat; at least two explosions were within lethal range. This may have been the aircraft that attacked the U-161, which itself had attacked a freighter 200 miles north-west of Trinidad. If so, U-161 was badly shaken up and all of her lights went out. Her skipper complained to U-boat Command about operating in the bright moonlight.

7–13 March 1943: The 417th Bomb Squadron with five B-18Bs, flying from Vernam Field, Jamaica, flew six missions – three convoy escorts and three anti-submarine searches, totaling 27 hours combat time. Their activities were directed from the Naval Operating Base, Camaguey, Cuba.

8 March 1943: The 128th Observation Squadron was redesignated as the 21st Antisubmarine Squadron (ASRON), the 46th Bomb Squadron (M) was redesignated as the 22nd ASRON, and the 76th Bomb Squadron was redesignated as the 23rd ASRON; all were assigned to the AAFAC from this date. At Zandery Field, Surinam, two B-18Bs of the 10th Bomb Squadron were attached to the 35th Bomb Squadron (M) for operations.

9 March 1943: Three B-18Bs from the 9th Antisubmarine Squadron were attached to the 35th Bomb Squadron (M) at Zandery Field, Surinam, for operations.

14 March 1943: Capt Reynolds of the 1st SSAG took off at 1820 hours in response to an Anti-Submarine Control report that there was a strong possibility of three enemy submarines operating between 70 miles out from Carrituck Beach South to 20 miles below Cape Hatteras, and from Carrituck North to Atlantic City. He was forced to return at 1850, however, due to engine trouble. Lt Herrick then took off in AC37-561 and returned at 0120 the next morning with negative results. Capt Reynolds had taken off again at 1910 in B-18B AC37-538 and returned at 2340.

15 March 1943: A B-18B, AC37-470, commanded by Lt Harris of the 2nd Sea Search Attack Squadron, picked up an ASV contact but had negative results during a 6hr 30min patrol. The same unit flew three other missions this day. Lt Reynolds, in B-18B AC37-538, flew a 4hr 30min patrol, while Lt Herrick, in AC37-561, flew a 7-hour 'killer search' and Lt Bacalis, flying AC37-621, flew for 3hr 15min, all without results.

By mid-March 1943 six dedicated Antisubmarine Squadrons (called ASRONs) were operational along the east coast of the US and throughout the Caribbean, and engaging the enemy with a variety of radar gear. This chart summarises their operational altitude, number of missions flown and the relative effectiveness of the equipment. *USAFHRA*

CONFIDENTIAL

RADAR EQUIPMENT OPERATIONAL PERFORMANCE

ARON	Type Equipment	Average Altitude	Number of Missions	Average Land	Average Other (Ships,etc)	Operational Effectiveness of Equipment
7th	517A	1325	95	28	22	84%
7th	517C	1225	173	41	26	78%
8th	517C	1300	64	35	28	60%
8th	521	1300	16	30	22	50%
8th	717A	1300	97	67	38	81%
9th	517A	800	3	23	20	66%
9th	521	1400	25	26	14	67%
9th	717A	1800	29	64	32	79%
10th	521	1900	55	39	11	97%
15th	521	3300	100	35	17	98%
17th	517A&C	1550	100	27	15	62%

CONFIDENTIAL
- 116 -

16 March 1943: Lt Hafner and his crew, flying B-18B AC38-587 of the 2nd Sea Search Attack Squadron, picked up ASV contacts but had negative results during an 8hr 55min patrol. The same unit flew four other missions the same day. Lt Lehti (AC37-465) flew a 6hr 45min patrol, Lt McIntosh (AC37-470) flew a 7hr 50min patrol, Capt Zinn did 7 hours in AC37-621, and Lt Biddison flew 7hr 40min in AC37-470, all without result.

17 March 1943: Two 1st SSAG crews flew patrols on this date, led by Lt LeVan in B-18B 37-464 (5hr 50min) and Lt Reynolds in AC-37-538 (5hr 45min) without result.

19-20 March 1943: Two 35th Bomb Squadron (M) B-18Bs were specifically tasked to watch the every movement of the Vichy French gunboat *Mouttet*.

22 March 1943: The 35th Bomb Squadron (M) at Zandery Field, Surinam, detached three B-18Bs to Cayenne, French Guiana, to cover Convoy BT-7; they returned to their home station the next day.

23 March 1943: A 'B-18BR' of the 4th Antisubmarine Squadron out of Mitchel Field, NY, dropped depth charges at 3810N 7225W to lighten the aircraft and gain altitude because of engine trouble. The depth charges were armed and set for 25-foot detonation.

24 March 1943: A B-18B of the 12th Antisubmarine Squadron made a 'special equipment' contact at 22 miles at 3552N 7353W, but the contact disappeared at 15 miles in very deep water. There were no reported wrecks in the vicinity. The pilot reported that, if it was a submarine, '…it must have detected the plane with special equipment' as visibility was very bad. The area was searched with negative results.

26 March 1943: Lt Zinn of the 1st SSAG flew a 5hr 30min 'killer search' with his crew in B-18B AC37-465 without result. Lt Zinn was promoted to Captain by 28 March and transitioned to the first of the unit's Consolidated B-24Ds.

28 March 1943: Four B-18Bs of the 35th Bomb Squadron (M) at Zandery Field, Surinam, were detached to Cayenne, French Guiana, to cover Convoy TB-9, returning to their home station the following day.

29 March 1943: Lt LeVan and crew of the 1st SSAG flew a 4hr 30min patrol in B-18B AC37-561 without result.

30 March 1943: Lt Harris and crew of the 1st SSAG flew a 6-hour patrol in B-18B AC38-590 without result.

31 March 1943: Lt Quinette and crew of the 1st SSAG flew a 3-hour patrol in B-18B AC38-590 without result.

During March 1943 this unit flew sixteen missions totaling 96hr 20min of combat flying.

Elsewhere, two B-18Bs of the 35th Bomb Squadron (M) at Zandery Field, Surinam, were sent to La Gallion Field, French Guiana, to cover Convoy BT-8.

April 1943: The 10th Bomb Squadron, operating exclusively in the Caribbean with B-18s, flew forty convoy coverages, two convoy sweeps, forty-eight anti-submarine sweeps and hunts, and forty-six patrols and bauxite convoy escorts during the month.

1 April 1943: Lt McIntosh of the 1st SSAG in B-18B AC37-561 took off on a routine patrol mission at 1705 and landed at 2135 with negative results.

Elsewhere a B-18 of the 4th Antisubmarine Squadron out of Mitchel Field, NY, dropped four depth charges on this date, but not in connection with an attack. The aircraft had taken off from Langley Field, VA, bound for Mitchel but could not land because of very poor weather. After being unaccounted for, it landed at Cape May, NJ at 0010 the next morning. The crew had jettisoned three of the depth charges and knew more or less where they were dropped, but did not see where the fourth one went! The aircraft exhausted all fuel while taxiing.

Much further south the 35th Bomb Squadron (M) at Zandery Field, Surinam, dispatched five of its B-18Bs to La Gallion Field, French Guiana, to continue coverage of Convoy AFD-24 and BT-8. Two of these recovered to Zandery on 3 April and the other three on the 5th.

5 April 1943: Lt McGehee and crew in 1st SSAG B-18B AC37-470 took off on a routine patrol mission at 1710 and landed at 2020 with negative results.

8 April 1943: Two crews of the 1st SSAG flew a 5hr 45min 'killer search '(Lt Wood in B-18B AC37-464) and a 3-hour patrol (Capt Reynolds in AC37-538) without result. The 35th Bomb Squadron (M)

USAAF B-18 Status, Service-Wide as of 5 April 1943

Station or Unit	B-18	B-18A	B-18B
Alaska	1	8	
Antigua, BWI	1		
Aruba, NWI		1	9
Brazil	2		
Canton Island	1		
Caribbean (unspecified)			3
Cuba		2	5
Hawaii	6		
Iceland		1	
Netherlands West Indies	1		7
Newfoundland		1	
Panama Canal Zone	9	1	1
Puerto Rico	5		7
Trinidad, BWI	1	1	9
'Other foreign' (unspecified but probably Sixth Air Force units)			13
1st SSAG, Langley Field, VA			4
2nd SSAG, Langley Field, VA			2
3rd SSAG, Langley Field, VA			2
13th Bomb Group (M), Westover Field, MA			2
25th Bomb Group (M), Borinquen Field, PR		1	1
42nd Bomb Group (M), Stoneman, CA		1	
45th Bomb Group (M), Dover, DE			2
83rd Air Base Group, Midland AAF, TX		1	1
319th Air Base Group, Boca Raton AAF, FL			2
645th AFT, Boca Raton AAF, FL			1
1st ASU, Langley Field, VA			1
4th ASU, Mitchel Field, NY			4
5th ASU, Westover Field, MA			1
7th ASU, Jacksonville FL			2
8th ASU, 36th Street Airport, Miami, FL			4
8th Tow Target Squadron, McChord Field, CA		1	
9th ASU, 36th Street Airport, Miami, FL			2
12th ASU, Langley Field, VA			13
15th Ferry Squadron, Morrison Field, FL			1
Middletown Air Depot, PA			2
AAF Sub-Depot, Boca Raton AAF, FL			1
AAF Materiel Command, Wright Field, OH			1
4th BCN, Patterson Field, OH			1
4th BSN, March Field, CA		1	
'Unaccounted for'			2
TOTAL ACTIVE IN AAF	**27**	**20**	**106**

at Zandery Field, Surinam, sent five B-18Bs to La Gallion Field, French Guiana, to continue coverage of Convoy TB-10; they recovered to Zandery on the 10th.

9 April 1943: Lt Coleman of the 1st SSAG took off on a routine patrol in RB-18B AC37-470 at 1700 and landed at 2110 without result.

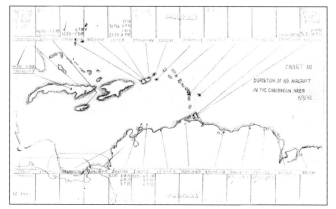

This map of 9 April 1943 shows the ring of airfields and dedicated anti-submarine assets in the Caribbean region as of that date. The thirty-five B-18 series aircraft are the most numerous type, followed closely by twenty-nine assorted Navy Consolidated PBY Catalina series aircraft. *USAFHRA*

10 April 1943: Lt Wood and crew of the 1st SSAG flew in B-18B AC38-587 on a 7hr 15min 'killer search' patrol without success. The previous day, the 12th Antisubmarine Squadron at Langley had a radar contact at 21 miles, at 3643N 7311W, disappearing at 5 miles, and at 3621N 7305W at less than 2 miles. Missions were scheduled by the 1st SSAG to cover this area on this night. Lt Wood took off at 1805 in RB-18B AC38-587 and landed at 0115 without success.

12 April 1943: A B-18B of the 25th Antisubmarine Wing (squadron not cited) made a radar contact at 1417hrs at 3709N 7424W at 7 miles, but lost it at a half a mile out. From Zandery Field, Surinam, the 35th Bomb Squadron (M) sent four of its B-18Bs to La Gallion Field, French Guiana, to cover Convoy BT-9. They returned home on the 13th.

13 April 1943: Two B-18B crews from the 1st SSAG flew 7hr 25min (Lt Herrick in AC38-587) and 6hr 15min patrols (Lt Rockwood in AC37-465). Lt Brown and crew, in RB-18B AC37-621, also took off at 1410 in the same search but, due to a severe storm in the area, he was forced to make a crash-landing with wheels up at Cape Hatteras. Since the landing was made on a sandy beach, the crew suffered no injuries, and the only damage to the aircraft was bent props and damaged bomb bay doors. The aircraft was recovered and moved to Pope Field, where it was returned to service!

14 April 1943: B-18B AC38-587 of the 1st SSAG commanded by Lt Hafner flew a 4-hour patrol without result.

15 April 1943: Lt Quinette of the 1st SSAG took off at 0850 on a routine patrol in RB-18B AC38-587 and returned at 1500 with negative results.

18 April 1943: A 35th Bomb Squadron (M) B-18 from Zandery Field, Surinam, was sent to La Gallion Field, French Guiana, to assist a rescue party there in locating a downed B-25. It returned to base on the 28th. The same day, the same unit sent four of its B-18Bs to La Gallion to continue coverage of Convoy TB-11; they returned on the 20th.

20 April 1943: The 1st SSAG conducted three patrols on this date. Lt Brown in B-18B AC37-621 found no results after no less than 8 hours, nor did Major Pohan in AC38-590 (4hr 15min) or Lt LeVan in

Three aircraft of the 417th Bomb Squadron Detachment at Camaguey, Cuba, are shown on the line on 20 April 1943, with a resident Cessna UC-78. The near aircraft, AC37-474, was lost at sea on 6 June 1943 and, although officially carried as a B-18A at the time, is clearly a B-18B, as are the other two aircraft visible, AC37-559 and 39-24. Note the variation in the size of the national insignia. All three aircraft have some form of nose art, but they cannot be distinguished. They bear the very late, nearly all-light-gray anti-submarine scheme. *DIA*

By the time of this photo, at San Antonio de Los Banos, Cuba, B-18C AC37-513 was assigned to the 9th Antisubmarine Squadron and was a veteran of the anti-submarine campaign, having served previously with the 80th Antisubmarine Squadron. Barely visible is the upper-surface gray camouflage, some of which can be seen on the engine cowl, some sort of nose art, and a dark gray B-18B or B-18C, also with some form of nose art, just behind the egg-white B-18C on 30 April 1943. *DIA*

The quartet of B-18s that survived the US collapse in the Philippines continued to serve in Australia well into 1943. Here VHCWB (probably AC37-16), bearing unique nose art and nicknamed 'Goober Dust', makes an approach to land somewhere in Australia. The aircraft was not finally salvaged until 7 October 1944. It was flying for the Allied Directorate of Air Transport (ADAT) by this time, having previously served with the 21st Troop Carrier Squadron. *via Buz Busby*

AC37-538 (4 hours). Altogether, during the month of April 1943 this unit flew ten combat missions totaling 57hr 35min.

Operating Bases of AAFAC Units 30 April 1943

Unit	At Time of Activation	As of 30 April 1943
1ST ARON	Langley Field, VA	North Africa
2nd ARON	Langley Field, VA	North Africa
3rd ARON	Dover, DE	Fort Dix, NJ
4th ARON	Mitchel Field, NY	Mitchel Field, NY
5th ARON	Westover Field, MA	Westover Field, MA
6th ARON	Westover Field, MA	Newfoundland
7th ARON	Jacksonville, FL	Trinidad, BWI
8th ARON	Miami, FL	Miami, FL
9th ARON	Miami, FL	Miami, FL
10th ARON	Galveston, TX	Galveston, TX
11th ARON	Fort Dix, NJ	Fort Dix, NJ
12th ARON	Atlantic City, NJ	Langley Field, VA
13th ARON	Grenier Field, NH	Grenier Field, NH
14th ARON	Otis Field, MA	Otis Field, MA
15th ARON	Jacksonville, FL	Jacksonville, FL
16th ARON	Charleston, SC	Charleston, SC
17th ARON	Lantana, FL	Boca Chica AB, Key West, FL
18th ARON	Langley Field, VA	Langley Field, VA
19th ARON	Langley Field, VA	Newfoundland
20th ARON	APO #865	Newfoundland
21st ARON	New Orleans, LA	New Orleans, LA
23rd ARON	Tampa, FL	Cuba
HHS AAFAC	Mitchel Field, NY	Mitchel Field, NY
338th Signal Co. (Wing)	Mitchel Field, NY	Mitchel Field, NY
HHS, 26th Antisubmarine Wing	Miami, FL	Miami, FL
323rd Signal Co. (Wing)	Miami, FL	Miami, FL
30th Antisubmarine Communications Squadron	Mitchel Field, NY	Mitchel Field, NY

May 1943: The 10th Bomb Squadron, by this time one of the premier B-18 operating units in the Caribbean, completed twenty convoy coverages, seven convoy sweeps, nineteen anti-submarine sweeps and hunts, and forty-nine patrols and bauxite convoy escorts during the month.

1 May 1943: C and D Flights, 417th Bomb Squadron, were transferred to the 35th Bomb Squadron (M) at Zandery Field, Surinam.

2 May 1943: A B-18B of the 12th Antisubmarine Squadron flown by Lt Taylor and crew made a radar and MAD contact at 2215 hours at 3722N 7539W at 3 miles from 500 feet, but it disappeared at 1 mile.

7 May 1943: A B-25 based on Trinidad spotted a 'dull red object' at 6 miles, 4 miles east of Galera Point, which it believed to be the bow of a submarine. The aircraft passed within a mile of the object and a definite wake was reported as sighted, moving at between 10 and 15 knots. Two Bell P-39s were dispatched to the scene followed by a number of Trinidad-based B-18s, Navy Consolidated PBYs and a blimp, which maintained continuous night and day coverage over the location, but results were negative. At 1620 hours the same day the Galera Point Observation Post reported that the 'radar devices' had been picking up an unidentified surface target about 6 miles east. P-39s were again dispatched but the target disappeared, and when they left the target reappeared. B-18s on a sub hunt in the area of the B-25 sighting carried out a localised concentrated search of the vicinity but no more positive contacts were made.

8 May 1943: Lt Hafner and crew of the same unit, also flying B-18B AC37-470 of the 1st SSAG, picked up four definite and four doubtful MAD contacts but also had negative results during a 7hr 45min patrol. He had taken off at 1145 and returned at 1910. At 1407, at 3427ZN 7336W, the radar operator changed from 100-mile range to 20-mile range and immediately saw an object, which appeared to be a sub, at 5½ miles, 15 degrees. A MAD contact was made at 1440 in the area and the pilot then flew a clover-leaf pattern over the contact and had three more good contacts in searching until 1625. The MAD operator, Mr Webster, was quite certain that a submarine was at the point of contact and that it was zig-zagging in a generally westerly direction at 2½ knots. The same unit flew two other B-18B missions on this date: Lt Coleman (AC38-587) flew 5hr 30min, and Lt Harris (AC37-538) flew 5hr 30min.

24 May 1943: The 9th Antisubmarine Squadron flew its last RB-18B missions on AC37-487 and another unidentified aircraft, both local patrols out of Edinburgh Field, Trinidad, lasting 0600 to 1200 hours and 1435 to 2035 hours respectively, commanded by Lt Newman and Capt Uhle, with crews of five others. The unit was replaced at Edinburgh Field by the 7th Antisubmarine Squadron.

26 May 1943: Three US Marine Corps Naval Aircraft Factory OS2N Kingfishers and an Army B-18 were dispatched to the area of 1450N 6115W to follow up on an earlier OS2N report that a submarine had surfaced in the vicinity of the Vichy French gunboat *Gouverneur Mouttet*, but saw no submarine. The French vessel weighed anchor

By 18 May 1943, besides Sixth Air Force and Antilles Air Command units engaged in anti-submarine activities, units of the 26th Antisubmarine Wing were ranging widely throughout the Caribbean. This is their plan for coverage out of Batista Field, Cuba, called 'Plan Able Sugar I Batista' as of that date, using B-18B aircraft. *USAFHRA*

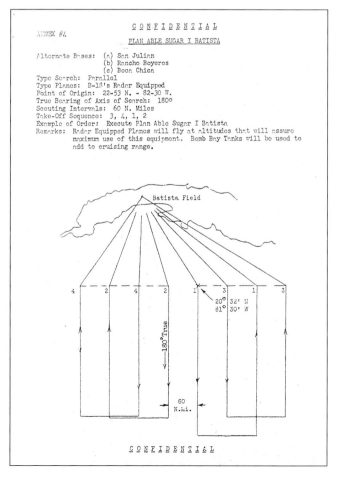

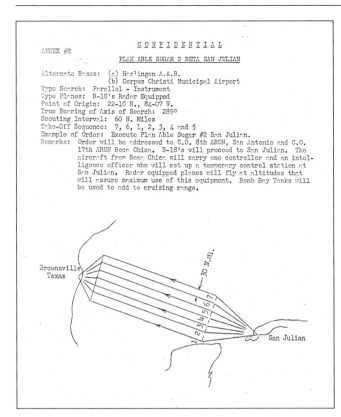

CONFIDENTIAL

ANNEX #8

PLAN ABLE SUGAR 2 BETA SAN JULIAN

Alternate Bases: (a) Harlingen A.A.B.
                 (b) Corpus Christi Municipal Airport
Type Search: Parallel - Instrument
Type Planes: B-18's Radar Equipped
Point of Origin: 22-10 N., 84-07 W.
True Bearing of Axis of Search: 289º
Scouting Interval: 60 N. Miles
Take-Off Sequence: 7, 6, 1, 2, 3, 4 and 5
Example of Order: Execute Plan Able Sugar #2 San Julian.
Remarks: Order will be addressed to C.O. 8th ARON, San Antonio and C.O.
       17th ARON Boca Chica. B-18's will proceed to San Julian. The
       aircraft from Boca Chica will carry one controller and an intel-
       ligence officer who will set up a temporary control station at
       San Julian. Radar equipped planes will fly at altitudes that
       will assure maximum use of this equipment. Bomb Bay Tanks will
       be used to add to cruising range.

This diagram shows the patrol coverage known as 'Plan Able Sugar 2 Beta San Julian' for B-18B-equipped units of the 26th Antisubmarine Wing operative over the Gulf of Mexico from San Julian, on the extreme western tip of Cuba, as of May 1943. *USAFHRA*

and put in to Le Carbot, a harbor on the west coast of the island in question. Two Navy PBYs covered the area during the night of 26/27 May and also patrolled the vicinity of the sighting during daylight on the 27th. Four B-18s operating from Beane Field, St Lucia, were available for coverage of the locality, and two of these were in the area continuously during daylight on the 27th.

27 May 1943: The 17th Antisubmarine Squadron was ordered to move to Batista Field, Cuba; at this time its equipment consisted of seven 'B-18Rs', four North American B-25Ds and unspecified 'attached aircraft'. They replaced the 23rd Antisubmarine Squadron there.

30 May 1943: At 0528 hours 'MO' radio signals were received by 26th Antisubmarine Wing (radio call sign '5KB') from Douglas B-18C AC37-577 flying out of Los Banos, Cuba. The aircraft, assigned to the 9th Antisubmarine Squadron, continued to send 'MO' until 0549, when the land station sent a triangulated position to the aircraft, which acknowledged same at 0553. The aircraft started sending 'MO' again at 0605, and at 0615 the ground station requested by voice transmission the plane's heading, which was given as 90º. At 0635 the aircraft reported that it had only 15 minutes fuel remaining, and '5KB' advised it to tie down the transmitter key, have a Very Pistol ready, and prepare for a forced landing at sea. The aircraft was also informed that an alert

Status of AAFAC as of 17 May 1943

Unit	Station	Aircraft on hand
7th Antisubmarine Squadron (H)	Trinidad	Douglas B-18B – 11
8th Antisubmarine Squadron (H)**	Miami, FL	Consolidated B-24D – 2 (at Batista Field, Cuba)
		Douglas B-18B – 6 (at Batista Field)
		Lockheed B-34 ("RM-37") – 1 (at Batista Field)
		Lockheed B-34 – 3 (in depot)
12th Antisubmarine Squadron (H)	Langley Field, VA	Douglas B-18B – 11 (plus one in Depot)
17th Antisubmarine Squadron	Flight echelon transferred from Boca	Douglas B-18R* – 7
	Chica AAF, FL to Miami (APO 632)	North American B-25D – 4
	this same day	
18th Antisubmarine Squadron (H)	Boca Chica, FL	North American B-25D – 8
		Lockheed B-34 – 2
		Douglas B-18B – 4
HQS Antisubmarine Squadron	Miami, FL	North American B-25D – 6
		Douglas B-18B – 7
		Cessna UC-78 – 3
		Lockheed A-29 – 1
HQS Antisubmarine Squadron	Mitchel Field, NY	North American B-25D – 1
		Lockheed C-60 – 1
		Cessna UC-78 – 2
		Northrop A-17 – 1
		Douglas B-18B – 1
		North American BT-14 – 1

Note: By this date, all B-18Bs in AAFAC were equipped with ASV-S standard gear. In addition to the B-18Bs assigned to AAFAC, the Caribbean Defense Command had 35 and the 1st Sea Search Attack Group at Langley Field, VA had 12.

* This designation is often noted in official correspondence as a form of local shorthand for ASV equipped B-18Bs.

** Between May 16th and 22nd, 1943, the 8th ASRON flew a total of 20 missions, 16 of them with its B-18Bs and the other four on the B-24Ds, most of them over the Yucatan Channel and the Caribbean southwest of Cuba.

As the end of the war approached, B-18s of all series remaining in the inventory were relegated, finally, to various support tasks, such as AC37-504, by this time officially an RB-18B (but with radar gear removed) assigned to the Caribbean Wing of the Air Transport Command. She still appears very smart for an aircraft that was delivered on 26 June 1939. This aircraft was formally salvaged in Puerto Rico on 28 August 1945. *Col Ole Griffith*

plane was being dispatched to the scene of the action. The aircraft acknowledged that last transmission at 0650 and one short dash was heard by the ground station at 0653, which correctly assumed that the aircraft had ditched. The alert aircraft took off at dawn and had not located the aircraft by 1125, but it had been located by surface units. The entire crew was rescued.

30 May–6 June 1943: The 417th Bomb Squadron (which at this point actually consisted of Flight D, 12th Bomb Squadron), supported by three Navy OS2N-3 Kingfishers and equipped with an old RB-18 (AC36-324) and two RB-18Cs (AC37-508 and 37-504) flew an incredible total of 105 combat hours during this period in anti-submarine searches and coverages of the Mona Passage.

June 1943: The 10th Bomb Squadron, stationed at various locations in the Caribbean and flying B-18s, completed twenty-three convoy coverages, two convoy sweeps, only three anti-submarine sweeps and hunts, and twenty-six patrols and bauxite convoy escorts during the month.

A Martinique Task Force (see entry for March 1943) was formed for the purpose of invading and ending, once and for all, the Vichy French 'thorn in the side' at the French islands. The 10th Bomb Squadron (M), two Flights of the 7th Antisubmarine Squadron, which were on duty in the Caribbean at the time, the 59th Bomb Squadron (L) and the 39th Observation Squadron, all based at Beane Field, St Lucia, were designated to support Army landings on Martinique. The 10th Bomb Squadron and the Flights of the 7th Antisubmarine Squadron were to be on alert 45 minutes before 'H' hour near the Trinidad convoy transporting the invasion force, at altitudes of 1,500, 2,000 and 2,500 feet. The 59th Bomb Squadron was to have a flight of three B-18s on air alert near the Puerto Rico convoy at 'H' minus 30 minutes. Both of these B-18 elements were to attack targets as called for by the respective Task Force Commanders. Another aircraft of the 59th Bomb Squadron was to be on air alert with the Trinidad force for the purpose of laying smoke or destroying searchlights. None of this plan was put into effect as negotiations apparently quelled the French Admiral once again and he and his nationalist entourage were forced to return to mainland France.

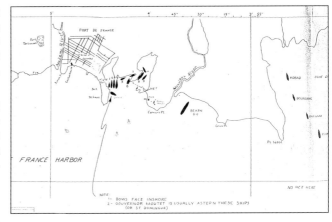

In June 1943 the issue of the Vichy French 'fleet-in-being' and garrison on the Caribbean island of Martinique once again came to the forefront, and B-18-equipped units were assembled into the Martinique Task Force and assigned targets for what would have been a pre-emptive strike. Negotiations ended the crisis and the B-18s again missed an opportunity to show their abilities against surface vessels. This map shows the locations of the French Navy surface vessels that would have been attacked, including an aircraft carrier and a cruiser. *USAFHRA*

1 June 1943: Two 1st SSAG B-18B crews flew a 5hr 45min patrol (Lt North in AC37-593) and a 6hr 30min 'killer patrol' (Lt McGehee in AC38-585) without result.

2 June 1943: Two patrols were flown by B-18Bs of the 1st SSAG on this date. Major Pohan led the crew of AC37-561 on an 8hr 15 min patrol while Lt Biddison flew 6 hours in AC37-538 without result.

3 June 1943: Lt LeVan of the 1st SSAG flew a 7hr 30min patrol in B-18B AC37-561 without result.

4 June 1943: Orders were issued directing that all twelve B-18Bs then in the possession of the 12th Antisubmarine Squadron at Langley Field, VA, be fitted with retro-rocket rails. On the same date, a B-18B from this unit made a radar contact at 0925 hours at 1,000 feet at 3705N 7350W at a distance of 4½ miles. The contact was lost at 1½ miles at 700 feet due to poor visibility.

10 June 1943: Two 'killer searches' were conducted by B-18B crews of the 1st SSAG. Lt Burghoff flew 6 hours in AC37-574 and Lt McGehee flew 7hr 20min without any sightings. Burghoff's crew had taken off at 0910 and later passed over what the crew were reasonably certain was a submarine at 3641N 7445W. They saw a propeller screw was just under the surface of the water. They returned and landed at 1510 without results, however. The same day, Lt LeVan and his crew, flying RB-18B AC37-538, departed on a search at 1450 and made several MAD contacts, one of which was good. At 3652N 7435W they dropped eight slicks and flew a 'trapping' circle in a clover-leaf pattern, but returned to base at 2155 without results. Lt McGehee's crew, likewise, after their 1000 hours launch, also made three MAD contacts, but they proved to be too far apart to be of any value. They returned to base at 1715.

11 June 1943: The 1st SSAG flew four missions on this date, two patrols and two 'killer searches', using B-18Bs AC37-538 (Lt LeVan, 7hr 10min), AC37-484 (Lt Quinette, 6hr 45min), AC37-593 (Lt Biddison, 6hr 25min) and AC37-561 (Lt McIntosh, 6hr 15min) without result.

13 June 1943: Lt Biddison and his crew of the 1st SSAG flew a 4hr 30min patrol in RB-18B AC37-574 without result. This mission was as the result of a Navy PBM having sighted a periscope wake at 3438N 7427W. Biddison and his crew responded at 2100 hours to cover the position and returned to base at 0130 the next morning without results. Lt Burghoff and his crew were scheduled to take up the search the next morning but a 65mph gale came up and the mission was cancelled.

14 June 1943: The 1st SSAG flew two patrols and one 'killer search' on this date on RB-18B equipment. Lt LeVan put in 8hr 10min in AC37-593 while Lt Harris did 5hr 40min on AC37-538 and Lt Burghoff completed 7hr 5min on AC37-470 without result. These missions were in response to the 13 June PBM sighting noted above. During Lt LeVan's mission, which departed at 0500, a sonic buoy was deployed and engine sounds were heard. Tracking procedures with the MAD gear were commenced and eight contacts followed. The left MAD unit went unserviceable, however, and no attack was made.

15 June 1943: Two patrols and one 'killer search' were completed on this date by B-18B crews of the 1st SSAG. Lt McGehee flew 4 hours on AC37-464 while Lt Biddison did 6hr 35min in AC38-590. A new pilot, Lt Ring, and his crew flew 6hr 40min on AC37-593, all without result.

19 June 1943: Lt Burghoff and crew of the 1st SSAG flying RB-18B AC38-590 flew a 4hr 10min patrol without result, while Lt Quinette in AC37-538 flew 5hr 20min. These missions were in response to another Navy PBM sighting of a periscope at 3700N 7400W, and a sound contact made by a Navy gunboat at 3710N 7350W. Lt Quinette and his crew took off at 1700 to cover this last sighting and returned to base at 2225 without result.

20 June 1943: A 17th ASRON RB-18B is lost at sea at 0545 under unknown circumstances. This may have been AC37-526.

24 June 1943: The 7th Antisubmarine Squadron (7th ASRON), 26th Antisubmarine Wing, was stationed at Trinidad with ten B-18Bs. The 8th ASRON was at Batista Field, Cuba, with ten B-24s and one B-18B. The 12th ASRON was at Langley Field, VA, with eleven B-18Bs, and the 17th ASRON was also at Batista Field, Cuba, with three B-25Ds and eleven B-18Bs. The 417th Bomb Squadron (M) by this date was operating from Miami, FL, with one RB-18 and five B-18Bs. The unit completed five missions between 24 June and 3 July, all on B-18Bs, over the Old Bahamas Channel, a sweep from Caibairien to Nuevitas, and three convoy coverages, totaling 24 hours combat time.

2X June 1943: The 17th Antisubmarine Squadron (ASRON) was assigned to the 26th Antisubmarine Wing at Miami, FL, with three RB-18Bs and four North American B-25Ds, and conducted anti-submarine patrols over the straits of Florida. Unit strength had increased to ten RB-18BRs (a designation often reported in official correspondence) and four B-25Ds by 13 June. Strength peaked at eleven RB-18Bs and three B-25Ds by 20 June, but dropped to just three RB-18Bs and eight B-25Ds by 4 July.

30 June 1943: RB-18B AC37-593, of the 1st SSAG at Langley, flown by Lt LeVan, made a MAD contact at 1730 hours at 3524N 7430W at 100 feet and made an attack on an oil slick, followed by a second run. He had a second contact at 1732 hours and made another attack from 100 feet. The weather closed down and the aircraft was forced to withdraw with no claim. This was the last B-18 mission flown by this Group. During June 1943 the Group flew a total of twenty-two combat patrols totaling 141hr 5min.

This same day, B-18B AC37-526, of the 17th Antisubmarine Squadron, commanded by Lt Mason out of Batista Field, Cuba, made a forced landing 100 feet offshore of Havana. No one was injured, and the seaworthiness of the B-18 was once again hailed by the crew.

July 1943: The 10th Bomb Squadron, still B-18-equipped, but adding its first two North American B-25Ds this month, completed twenty convoy coverages, three convoy sweeps, twenty-four anti-submarine sweeps and hunts, and no fewer than eighty-three patrols and bauxite convoy escorts during the month.

The red outline of the national insignia on B-18A AC37-540 stationed in Iceland dates this photo, most likely, to between June and August 1943, and this is the only known photo of a USAAF B-18A with this marking. The crews also appear to have added sealant around the cabin windows of the aircraft, probably to help deal with the extreme weather conditions encountered there. *via Ragnar Ragnarsson*

1 July 1943: AAFAC advised one of its subordinate units, the 12th ASRON, that all RB-18s assigned were to be grounded. The unit conducted its last B-18 patrol that day. On 3 July three North American B-25Ds arrived and, on the 14th, all B-18s assigned to the unit (a total of eight aircraft, AC37-527, 37-502, 37-524, 37-505, 37-543, 37-548, 37-568 and 38-608) were transferred to the 51st Sub Depot. It is noteworthy that this unit, even until this time, actively conducted training on both the dorsal gun turret and the tunnel guns mounted in its B-18B aircraft.

The same day, 17th ASRON RB-18B AC37-585, piloted by 2Lt William P. Ballard operating out of Miami, crashed at sea at 1721 hours. It had been on a routine patrol of the western area. At 1715 hours the left engine seized for no apparent reason. The entire crew, due to the superb flotation qualities of the B-18, were rescued at 0305 the next morning. They had salvaged all radar and radio gear.

1-10 July 1943: The 417th Bomb Squadron (M) was by now reduced in strength to one RB-18 and two RB-18Cs, but continued with no fewer than thirteen combat missions on the RB-18Cs over the Mona Passage during this period, totaling 83hr 55min. RB-18C AC37-508 was forced to be removed from combat status, however, as she was just worn out.

By 1 July 1943 the 12th ASRON, with eight B-18Bs, including AC37-543, shown here after the removal of its radar gear, was stood down from anti-submarine duties and the B-18s replaced by North American B-25D Mitchells, far less comfortable – but more modern – mounts. This aircraft had a nickname (overpainted) and a 'rooster' emblem on the port nose, as well as the silhouette of two submarines, indicating at least two claimed 'kills'! *via Leo J. Kohn*

18 July 1943: The Commander of the 35th Bomb Squadron (M) formally requested, through channels, that B-18B and B-18C series aircraft be fitted with .50 caliber forward-firing machine guns for use against enemy submarine deck gun crews. Apparently a number of B-18B and B-18C operating units had already made such 'field' modifications to their aircraft, usually one gun in the lower starboard (right) side of the fuselage, fired by the pilot using a 'ring-and-bead' sight!

19-30 July 1943: The crews of the 35th Bomb Squadron (M) in particular, and other B-18 operating units in the Caribbean, experienced a totally new trial by German and Italian submarines involving new tactics in remaining on the surface and fighting off air attacks. During this period there were numerous separate attacks in the general area from 04° to 08° North and from 49° to 56° West.

19 July 1943: A B-18B of the 35th Bomb Squadron (M), commanded by 1Lt Paul R. Crandall and his crew, 2Lt J. E. Kinney (co-pilot), 2Lt Stanley Fleischer (bombardier), S/Sgt Joseph I. Hasbrouck (engineer), Sgt Albert F. Sager Jr (radio operator), and Pt Robert W. Seach (radar), sighted a surfaced submarine at 2110 hours, which appeared to be disabled at 0448N 4910W. The B-18 made an attempt to attack and was met by anti-aircraft fire. The B-18 circled the sub, while the rear turret gunner fired at it non-stop. The B-18 then made a second attempt to attack, but was fired upon very intensively again. The B-18 resumed circling and again the sub attempted to submerge. The B-18 immediately swung around and dived to the attack. By then the sub was under for 30 seconds and the aircraft bombed 30 yards from the end of an oil slick at 2140. The aircraft circled for some time but no wreckage appeared.

20 July 1943: An 8th ASRON B-18B, operating from Gallion Field, French Guiana, was dispatched at 1710 hours to the area of a submarine attack started by Navy aircraft, and sighted the sub on the surface from 8 miles at 0448N 4910W. The B-18 started two attacks but was forced to withdraw out of range because of very intense anti-aircraft fire, which kept turning continuously towards the aircraft. The B-18 circled out of range for 30 minutes, then the sub suddenly started to dive. The aircraft dived at 140mph and dropped five Mk 44 depth charges on the course of the sub from 25 feet, spaced at 100-foot intervals with a 25-foot setting. The first one fell 100 feet ahead of the swirl about 30 seconds after the sub dived and all of the depth charges exploded. There were no visible results.

23 July 1943: A B-18C of the 35th Bomb Squadron (M), operating from Zandery Field, Surinam, and commanded by Lt Crandall, was launched on a 'killer search' for a sub that had been sighted by a Navy Consolidated PBY Catalina at 1054 hours. The PBY dropped depth

charges, which caused the sub's bow to rise some 30° out of the water, and it then rolled over on its starboard side and disappeared. The B-18 navigator, Capt Cohen, sighted the sub's conning tower breaking water at 5 miles at 1725 hours at 0710N 5131W and attacked with five Mk 44 depth charges with 100-foot spacing on a 40° true course. The first one exploded at the outer edge of the swirl after the sub had been submerged for 15 seconds. Oil and bubbles arose some 50 feet ahead of the last explosion. The B-18 remained on station for 2 hours. Three additional B-18s and a B-24D were dispatched from Zandery to follow up.

24 July 1943: 1Lt James Thomas and his crew of the 12th Bomb Squadron, 25th Bomb Group, flying B-18C AC37-519, took off at 1800 hours on a 7hr 45min convoy escort mission. They found their convoy at 2353 hours, climbed to 3,000 feet and criss-crossed the convoy until 0330, then turned for home. At 0430 their radar picked up an indication at 8 miles, so they made an attack run on it and dropped flares on a second run, but observed negative results. Their radio compass then failed completely and, in trying to take a bearing for home to Dakota Field, they became lost and eventually exhausted their fuel and ditched at sea. The crew did not include a rear gunner. They were picked up by a Colombian Navy gunboat and taken to Rio Hatche, where they were picked up by B-18 AC36-315 from their parent unit on 26 July. Incredibly, their B-18C was found still afloat and spotted by the skipper of the SS *F. Q. Barstow*, a tanker, at 1810 hours on the 26th, between Cristobal, Canal Zone, and Aruba, at 1234N 7159W, about 102 miles from Aruba, and the water inside the aircraft was only ankle deep. The tanker sent a launch to the aircraft and recovered 'confidential papers', knives, a Thompson sub-machine gun (!), a parachute, octant and first-aid pack. Subsequently, a US Navy destroyer was sent to locate the aircraft and sink it. After firing more than twenty rounds of 5-inch shells, it sank! This may have been the aircraft commanded by 1Lt Paul R. Crandall, which was formally noted as assigned to the 35th Bomb Squadron (M).

On the same day, a B-18C of the 8th Antisubmarine Squadron commanded by 1Lt G. W. Richmond was credited with damaging the U-466 in the Caribbean.

25 July 1943: A B-18B of the 35th Bomb Squadron (M), operating from Zandery Field, Surinam, obtained a radar contact at 2114 hours at 0724N 5028W, homed on the target and dropped flares, but did not spot the sub until it fired on the aircraft, inaccurately. Another flare was dropped, but it extinguished before another attack could be made and the sub dived.

25-31 July 1943: The 417th Bomb Squadron was reinforced, and now had one RB-18, three RB-18Cs and one North American B-25D; it managed nine combat missions over the Mona Passage, all on RB-18Cs, totaling 78hr 15min. The old RB-18 even managed 8hr 20min on training.

26 July 1943: A B-18B of the 35th Bomb Squadron (M), operating from Zandery Field, Surinam, sighted a submarine at 0110 at 0724N 5028W by radar at 9 miles. At 0114 the aircraft was over the target, circled twice and at 0118 dropped a flare from 1,500 feet. This was met by one burst of tracer anti-aircraft fire, directed at the flare, followed by another aimed at the aircraft, which fortunately broke 100 yards to the rear. At 0125 the B-18 dropped a second flare on the sub from 1,000 feet; its conning tower was about 20 per cent fully surfaced, then it disappeared.

28 July 1943: B-18C AC37-499 of the 35th Bomb Squadron (M) operating from Zandery Field, Surinam, and commanded by Capt Berry, made a radar contact on an enemy submarine at 11 miles, 90 degrees right at 0812N 5445W from 1,500 feet. On the first run, the aircraft failed to sight the target in time for an accurate attack, as the completely surfaced sub, with its anti-aircraft guns blazing, passed just under the left wing in full view of Lt Spells, the bombardier. After a second run at 500 feet, with no radar sighting, a second contact occurred at 1,500 feet at 0325 hours at 0803N5315W on a course of 280 degrees. After Capt Berry turned 35 degrees to the left directly towards the target, radar contact was lost. Still turning, the aircraft dropped a flare from 1,500 feet, climbed on up to 1,800 feet, sighted the submerged sub, and Lt Spells dropped five Mk 44 depth charges from 1,500 feet. The results were unobserved, and the aircraft recovered to its home station with no damage.

29 July 1943: B-18B AC37-499 of the 35th Bomb Squadron (M), the same aircraft involved in the action on the 28th, operating temporarily out of Atkinson Field, British Guiana, spotted a submarine at 2330 hours at 0615N 5536W. This time the aircraft was commanded by Capt Richard P. Mansfield. After twice passing over the fully surfaced sub for the purposes of positive identification, two flares were dropped on the third run. Immediately after the flares were released, the sub opened heavy and concentrated fire, and continued a fusillade of tracers at the plane as long as she remained in range. The B-18C circled back, executed a run at 300 feet and Lt Noble, the bombardier, made his attack with five Mk 44 depth charges in train. In passing over the target in the final run, a terrific but very brief burst of machine gun fire was met. Fire from the sub ceased after the attack and a large oil slick was noted at the site the next day. The aircraft returned to Zandery with slight damage in both wings and fuselage. The sub appeared to be of a very large type and, as it was very close inshore, was believed to be engaged in mining.

The same day, at 2040 hours, a B-18B operating from Curacao attacked a surfaced sub at 1340N 7020W. The submarine again fired on the aircraft but the fire was poorly directed, indicating that the crew could hear the aircraft but not see it. The attack was rated as a good one, and damage was probable. The same day, yet another B-18 operating from Zandery Field, Surinam, attacked a surfaced sub at 2340 hours at 0615N 5526W, but no other details are available. This may have been the aircraft commanded by Capt Erskine G. Berry of the 35th Bomb Squadron (M), which was credited with engaging a submarine in combat on this date. The Commander of the 35th Bomb Squadron (M), in one of his weekly combat summaries, noted that the unit had a 'dire need for binoculars'.

Also in the Caribbean on this date, 1Lt Thomas L. Merrill and his B-18 crew of the 12th Bomb Squadron (M) were credited with engaging in combat with a submarine (the U-653).

30 July 1943: A 2nd Sea Search Attack Squadron RB-18B made an instrument contact at 1626 hours at 3812N-7358W at 8 miles, but lost the signal at 3 miles. The aircraft held station for 4 minutes, but no new signal was detected. Elsewhere, Lt Thomas L. Merrill, flying B-18C AC37-512 of the 12th Bomb Squadron, operating from Dakota Field, Aruba, attacked a sub at 1340N 7020W while on a routine search patrol. A radar contact had been made at 0040 and, on reaching the position, a flare was dropped. The sub was in full view and fully surfaced. Bombs were released at 0045 from 100 feet at 140 knots. A geyser resulted from an explosion and tracer bullets from the sub's anti-aircraft weapons passed just to the left and outboard of the port engine. Evasive action was immediately taken but there was no further radar contact.

The same day, at 0240 hours, a B-18 commanded by Capt Richard P. Mansfield of the Detachment, 35th Bomb Squadron (M), made four runs on a submarine (probably the U-406), and took a number of anti-aircraft hits in the process.

August 1943: The 10th Bomb Squadron, by then one of the most experienced B-18 operating units in the AAF, but also partially equipped with B-25Ds, continued its work in the Caribbean, completing twenty-seven convoy coverage missions, one convoy

sweep, fifteen anti-submarine sweeps and hunts, and seventy-eight patrols and bauxite convoy escorts during the month.

5 August 1943: Two B-18s of the 7th Antisubmarine Squadron, together with two Martin PBM Mariners of VP-204 and a Lockheed PV-2 of VB-130, participated in a very intense combat with the U-615 in the Caribbean on this date.

7 August 1943: A B-18 of the 10th Bomb Squadron, nicknamed 'Robust Mon', attacked a submarine while commanded by Lt Milton L. Wiederhold and his crew, consisting of Lt Paul E. DeWeendt (co-pilot), Lt Edwin I. Boyd (navigator), Lt William F. Abrams (bombardier), S/Sgt Edward J. Jaskulski (radio operator), Sgt James R. Edwards (gunner) and Sgt Robert E. Medley (engineer). The same sub had successfully withstood attacks by several US Navy aircraft, fighting on the surface, when it was sighted again at dusk by 2Lt Abrams, the B-18's bombardier. Working with a Navy Martin PBM Mariner, the B-18 dropped five depth charges from 20 feet by moonlight. The submarine was claimed as sunk and the USS *Walker* picked up survivors the next day. The entire crew of this B-18 were awarded Distinguished Flying Cross medals including 2Lt Paul E. DeWeendt (co-pilot), 1Lt Edwin I. Boyd (navigator), 2Lt William F. Abrams Jr (bombardier), S/Sgt James R. Edwards (gunner), Sgt Robert E. Medley (engineer) and T/Sgt Edward J. Juskulski (radio). The submarine was the U-615, and it was officially listed as a 'shared' credit with US Naval aircraft.

Master Sergeant Diamentini of the 10th Bomb Squadron conducts an open-air, 50-hour check on one of the unit's nine B-18Bs (they also had one 'straight' B-18) in early August 1943. The unit was a veteran of the anti-submarine war, and very experienced at working on a shoestring. The aircraft of the 10th Bomb Squadron all had nicknames, and this one was probably 'Sad Sack'. Note that although the aircraft shows signs of great wear, the port propeller is almost brand-new. *USAFHRA*

The triumphant crew of a B-18 of the 10th Bomb Squadron named 'Robust Mon' pose by their aircraft on 7 August 1943 after a successful attack, shared with Navy aircraft and other B-18s, on U-615, a Type VIIC sub. The aircraft commander, Lt Milton L. Wiederhold (rear, extreme right) together with his co-pilot Lt Paul E. DeWeerdt, Navigator Lt Edwin I. Boyd, bombardier Lt William F. Abrams (also in the back row, but in unknown order) and radio operator S/Sgt Edward J. Jaskulski, gunner Sgt James R. Edwards and engineer Sgt Robert E. Medley (believed right to left, kneeling) were stationed at Edinburgh Field, Trinidad, at the time. The entire crew received DFCs. *USAFHRA*

22-28 August 1943: The 417th Bomb Squadron (M) operating from APO#848 (Ponce Field, PR) now had two RB-18Cs remaining on strength, two North American B-25Ds and one new B-25G. The unit conducted ten sweeps and coverage missions over the Mona Passage during the period, all but two of which, totaling 55hr 10min, were flown on the RB-18Cs.

September 1943: The 10th Bomb Squadron in the Caribbean, in its final month operating from Trinidad, amassed thirty-five convoy coverage missions, two convoy sweeps, nineteen anti-submarine sweeps and hunts, and sixty-five patrols and bauxite convoy escorts during the month, on a mix of B-18s and B-25Ds.

One of the last, if not the very last, 'straight' B-18s assigned to an operational unit, this example was with the 10th Bomb Squadron at Edinburgh Field, Trinidad, and is shown here being loaded with practice bombs in August 1943. It appears to be named 'Shack Job' on the forward starboard nose. Note the severe weathering of the camouflage. *USAFHRA*

5-11 September 1943: The 417th Bomb Squadron (M) at Ponce Field, PR, still retained two RB-18Cs on strength (in addition to one B-25C and two B-25Gs), but of eleven sweeps and coverages flown over the Mona Passage during this period only two were flown on RB-18Cs.

7 September 1943: The 1st Sea Search Attack Group (H) was redesignated as Headquarters, 1st Sea Search Attack Unit.

4 October 1943: The veteran 35th Bomb Squadron (M), by this time stationed at Vernam Field, Jamaica, neared the end of its very eventful association with its trusty B-18s when six B-18Bs were transferred out. One went to the 24th Air Depot Group, four to the 59th Bomb Squadron and one to the 349th Air Base Squadron at Zandery Field, Surinam.

18 October 1943: The final two B-18s with the 35th Bomb Squadron (M) at Vernam Field, Jamaica, both B-18Cs, were transferred to the parent 25th Bomb Group. The 35th had re-equipped with nine North American B-25Gs.

28 December 1943: The Headquarters and Headquarters Squadron, VII Fighter Command (Flight Section), Seventh Air Force, still had two RB-18s on strength, survivors of the Pearl Harbor attack, and also operated one Republic P-47D-11 Thunderbolt, two Curtiss P-40Es, two P-40K-1s and single examples of the Douglas A-24B and Grumman OA-9 at Hickam Field.

From April 1943 into early 1944, some of the surviving RCAF Digbys were still operational in rather ragged all-white camouflage with 161(BR) Squadron, including what appears to be No 741/U (painted just under the bombardier's position) shown here. *via Carl Vincent*

1944

3 February 1944: A B-18C of the 4th Tactical Reconnaissance Squadron flew from Borinquen Field, PR, to Curacao, piloted by Col Howard A. Cheney, A-3 of the Antilles Air Command, to test the efficiency of the Air Warning Service (AWS) at that base. At the time this Squadron had a very eclectic assortment of aircraft on strength, including three North American B-25Ds, three B-25Gs, one RB-18, one B-18C, three Bell P-39Ns and three P-39Qs!

28 February 1944: The 24th Service Group at APO 811 (Hato Field, Curacao), Trinidad Wing, Antilles Air Command, still had one B-18B on strength (as well as two Cessna UC-78s, and one Piper L-4A), one of the last remaining B-18s in this formerly very active area.

21 May 1944: 2Lt Gerald E. Brissette (pilot) and 2Lt Leonard J. Sherron (co-pilot) of the 4th Tactical Reconnaissance Squadron departed APO#845 (Borinquen Field, PR) for Waller Field, Trinidad, with a unit B-18 on a tracking mission, which was completed on the 22nd. This may well have been the last operational B-18 mission in the Caribbean. The same day, 2Lt Samuel W. Cocks and his crew, from the same unit, departed APO#845 for Waller Field, also in a B-18 on a calibration mission.

August 1944: The 4007th AAF Base Unit, Air Transport Command, at Brookley AAF, AL, had RB-18 AC37-29. It was transferred to the ATC's 4119th AAF Base Unit at Greenville AAF, SC, by October.

September 1944: The 1103rd AAF Base Unit, Air Transport Command, at Morrison AAF, FL, had RB-18B AC38-593, apparently stripped of her ASV gear.

1945

31 March 1945: Three RB-18s are still assigned to the Panama Air Depot but in a 'miscellaneous' status.

CHAPTER TEN

Naming the B-18

Astute readers will have noted by now that up to this point not a solitary mention has been made in this account of the so-called 'popular' name that has come to be associated with the B-18 series over the years – Bolo.

Like the reputation that the series seemed to gain long after it had passed from the active inventory, the origins of the 'popular' name assigned to the series have been guessed at and speculated upon on numerous occasions – often without any basis in fact whatsoever.

One authoritative history of bombardier training stated, unequivocally, that the aircraft was named Bolo '…because the fuselage profile resembled that type of knife'. Another highly respected historian, writing of the B-18 and its prominence between 1937 and 1941 in the USAAC inventory as making up more than half of the bombardment strength, confidently stated that the aircraft was named Bolo during that period because it was a term gaining prominence within the burgeoning Army basic training establishment that was applied to troops who could 'not qualify on the rifle range', apparently implying that the B-18 series would, when called upon to shoot, similarly not be able to shoot straight. In fact, the aircraft was not named at all during the period he described.

The quest to discover the real sequence of events leading to the selection of this seemingly out-of-character, if not non-standard, term became a quest for this scribe, as, at least in part, the origins of the term seemed to require clarification, one way or the other, once and for all. The inevitable connotation that the name seemed to imply to even the most casual observer seemed slightly derogatory, and even frivolous, compared to the proud and fearsome names applied to its contemporary brethren.

What followed proved far more challenging then might be expected.

Mr John D. Biggers, then with the Federal Office of Production Management, wrote a letter on 23 June 1941 to Merrill C. Meigs, suggesting the use of names for American aircraft. This is the earliest dated document that could be located in official Army Air Corps records pertaining to this issue. As of that date, some US service aircraft had, in fact, acquired 'popular' names – but these were all completely incidental and, usually, had been unofficially attributed to certain aircraft series based on what the original manufacturer called the aircraft, for marketing purposes. The new B-17 series, for example, had been nicknamed the Flying Fortress not by the Army Air Corps but, rather, by Boeing marketing folks and the aviation press of the day, and the name gained a life of its own. As of the date of Mr Biggers's letter, the B-18 series, production of which had been completed, had no popular name attributed to it – by either Douglas or the Army – and as of that date the only 'official' name attached to any variant of the basic design was 'Digby', assigned by the British Commonwealth for the Canadian-acquired DB-280s.

At this juncture the Chief of the Intelligence Division, Office of the Chief of the Air Corps (OCAC), recommended the adoption of Mr Biggers's idea – but the Chief of the AAC Materiel Division opposed it on the grounds that the British system was causing considerable confusion and that if press releases were couched in terms of official American designations, they would be equally as popular from a news standpoint. General Scanlon and General Cousins opposed the idea on the grounds that, at that time, it would be necessary to follow British names, but there was considerable variation between the British and American models of the same type. Hence, confusion would result.

Ultimately, the Chief of the Air Corps, General Arnold, ruled on 15 August 1941 that 'Army planes will not be officially named for the present.' However, the Intelligence Division recommended, on 11 July 1941, that a Board of three officers be appointed to name airplanes and motors then in use, and also to name those that were to be accepted for future use. They suggested that types be named for popular reference, and made the following, apparently poorly thought out, suggestions.

Trainers – would be named for small, harmless birds, such as Fledgling, etc.
Transports – would be named for large animals, such as Elephant, etc.
Pursuit and Attack Aircraft – would be named for poisonous snakes found in North America, such as Copperhead, etc.
Observation Aircraft – would be named for sharp-eyed birds of predatory instincts, such as Hawk, etc.
Bombers – would be named for large, heavy, powerful animals, ugly when aroused, such as Behemoth, Rhino, etc.

Clearly, had the Intelligence Division's recommendations been adopted, the lexicon of aviation enthusiasts' language regarding aircraft would be very, very different!

The press of events following Pearl Harbor pushed this rather trivial matter to the back burner and, in the meantime, the manufacturers themselves did a very good job of promoting 'popular' names for their products, which by then were sorting themselves out on the fighting fronts. Warhawk, Tomahawk, Airacobra, Mitchell, Marauder, Liberator, Mustang, Thunderbolt, Texan and a host of other 'popular' names, which have become commonly accepted terms for entire series of aircraft, were in fact names promoted and adopted by manufacturers for their products, and only became 'official', through force of circumstances, much later.

It was, in fact, not until the publication of Army Air Forces Regulation (AAF Regulation) No 200-3 of 25 June 1943, 'Miscellaneous: Naming of Army Aircraft Types', that the AAF finally adopted not only an 'official' procedure for naming its aircraft, but made those in actual common use 'official'. The Regulation provided for the appointment of a committee, to be known as the Army Air Forces Aircraft Naming Committee, appointed by the Commanding

General, to make recommendations for naming types of Army aircraft and other types of aircraft used by the Army and the Navy. It was to be composed of three officers from Headquarters, AAF, including at least one officer representing the Assistant Chief of Air Staff, Materiel, Maintenance and Distribution. One of the members was also to be a permanent recorder for the committee (with a vote). Significantly, names were only to be applied to aircraft 'in mass production or previously procured in large numbers'. The names selected were not to duplicate, or permit confusion with, names already in use by the Army, Navy, Coast Guard, or any United Nations allies using 'popular' names for types of aircraft. Another interesting part of the regulation was Paragraph 11, which stated that '...the committee will consider names selected from suggestions submitted by aircraft manufacturers through their AAF resident representatives.'

The Committee held its very first meeting on 28 August 1943 – which, for the purposes of our story, was almost at precisely the time that the definitive versions of the B-18 – the B-18B and B-18C – were nearing the end of their useful combat lives. Shortly thereafter, in conjunction with the Joint Aircraft Committee, they produced a 'Standard List of Names for Army, Navy and British Aircraft'.

The list produced included, for the very first time, the name 'Bolo' for the Douglas B-18 series – which seemed to fly in the face of the rules that had been set down by AAF Regulation 200-3 and the guidance from the Commanding General, since the DB-280, already long since in service, had been named 'Digby' by the British Commonwealth system. The list also included Dragon for the Douglas B-23, Grasshopper for not only the Piper L-4 (O-59) but also for the Taylorcraft L-2 (O-57) and Aeronca L-3 (O-58). It also denoted the Beech AT-11 as Kansas (not Kansan), the Boeing AT-15 as Crewmaker, the Fleetwing BT-12 as Sophomore, and the Boeing-Stearman PT-13, PT-17 and PT-18 series as Caydet (not Kaydet).

So how did the Committee arrive at the name 'Bolo'? The Minutes of the Committee and their deliberations have not been located. However, in early 1942 the Douglas in-house publication *Airview* published an article honoring the valiant last-ditch defenders of the Philippines, which were then very much up against the wall, entitled 'In the Land of the Bolo'. This, of course, referred to the fearsome machete-like knives wielded with such ferocity by natives of the Philippines during the period of US occupation. It was the first and only connection to the term Bolo that could be located in any Douglas documents.

It is therefore the conclusion of this writer that the 'popular' name for the B-18 series, adopted by the Committee only in August 1943, was in fact nominated to the Committee by Douglas, and appears to have had its genesis in the last-ditch stand made by US forces in the Philippines.

STANDARD LIST OF NAMES FOR ARMY, NAVY AND
BRITISH AIRCRAFT AS APPROVED BY THE
JOINT AIRCRAFT COMMITTEE

*Names contained within parentheses are British designations used in their official records, publications and communications.

BOMBERS	Model		Approved
Manufacturer	Army	Navy	Name
Boeing	B-17		Fortress
Douglas	B-18		Bolo
Douglas	B-23		Dragon
Consolidated	B-24	PB4Y	Liberator
North American	B-25	PBJ	Mitchell
Martin	B-26		Marauder
Vega	B-34	PV	Ventura
Douglas	A-20 (P-70)	BD-1	Havoc (Boston)*
Douglas	A-24	SBD-1	Dauntless
Curtiss	A-25	SB2C-1	Helldiver
Douglas	A-26		Invader
Lockheed	A-29	PBO-1	Hudson
Martin	A-30		Baltimore
Vultee	A-31		Vengeance
Vultee	A-35		Vengeance
Brewster	A-34	SB2A-1	Bermuda
North American	A-36 (P-51)		Mustang
Consolidated	OA-10	PBY	Catalina
Boeing		PB2B	Catalina
NAF		PBN	Catalina

-1-

ATTACHMENT B

This is a copy of the actual first page of the Joint Aircraft Committee report of late August 1943 in which both the B-18 and B-23 series were officially named 'Bolo' and 'Dragon' for the first time. No earlier references can be located and, although many crews were interviewed for this work, not a solitary one ever referred to the B-18 as Bolo during the war. *USAFHRA*

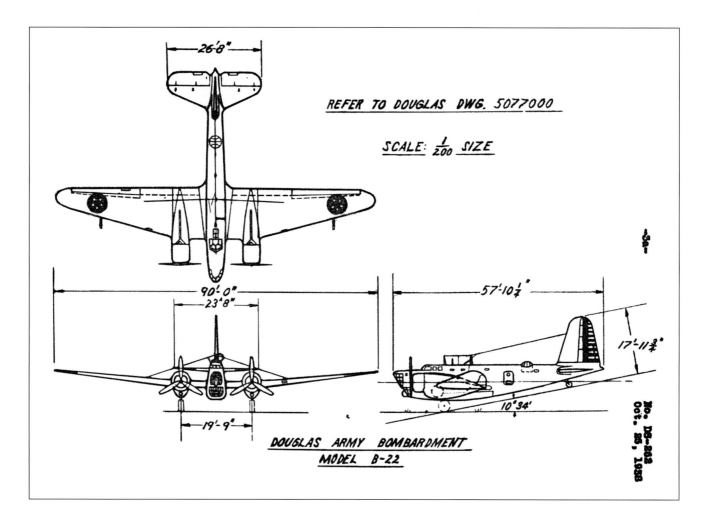

Inside the drawing:

26'8"

REFER TO DOUGLAS DWG. 5077000

SCALE: 1/200 SIZE

90'0"
23'8"

57'10½"

17'11¾"

19'9"

10'34'

No. DS-262
Oct. 25, 1938

DOUGLAS ARMY BOMBARDMENT
MODEL B-22

CHAPTER ELEVEN

The Douglas XB-22 (DS-262)

Little more than a footnote in most publications, and uncommonly difficult to document, the elusive XB-22 very nearly became an 'off the shelf' production aircraft.

Basically, the XB-22 was a B-18A look-alike, with vertical tail surfaces reminiscent of the next aircraft in the scheme, the B-23. It was laid down as Detailed Specification DS-262 on 25 October 1938, concurrent with the B-18A production. It was to have the same defensive armament capability, with the exception that late provision was added in the specification, as of 29 September 1938, for installation of a tail gun position. The aircraft was to be powered by Wright GR-2600-A71 (Army designation R-2600-3) Cyclone engines of 1,600hp. It offered a Douglas guaranteed maximum speed of 246mph, a cruising speed of 220mph, a service ceiling of 25,000 feet, and an endurance at operating

As originally conceived, and in the first of two distinctly different configurations, the proposed Douglas XB-22 was basically an improved B-18A, with different engines, nacelles, and a vertical fin and rudder that appears nearly identical to that of the B-23 that followed. This concept drawing is dated 25 October 1938, barely a month after delivery of the first production B-18As. *Douglas Drawing 5077000*

speed of 7.3 hours guaranteed. The undercarriage was also fully retractable, an advantage that was enabled by the larger cowlings and fairing nacelles allowed by the R-2600 engines. The addition of some 13 square feet of vertical tail surface was also predicted to significantly improve handling.

Although the Douglas Specification was dated 25 October 1938, by the 14th Douglas had already requested early delivery of two R-2600s 'for installation in the first B-22 aircraft', which clearly seems to indicate that the project had been moving forward for some time even prior to the publication of the Specification. The Materiel Division at Wright Field commented, the same day, that 'the exact quantity of B-22 aircraft to be procured is not yet known', which again seems to suggest that movement on acquisition of this design had reached an advanced stage.

As it turned out, the XB-22, as initially conceived, was found by the Materiel Division to be '*in many aspects unsatisfactory and overly optimistic*' [emphasis from the original Air Corps document], and Douglas very quickly returned to the drawing boards to see what could be salvaged from the program. The result was the B-23, about which more later.

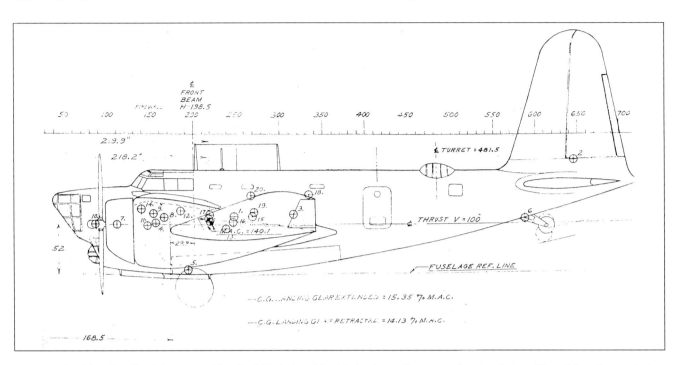

An even earlier inboard profile of the proposed Douglas B-22 deals mainly with the changes in power and stations that would result from the new design. The Air Corps had actually come close to ordering these improved aircraft off the drawing board. *Boeing Archives*

By 9 January 1939, at the urging of the Air Corps, Douglas had all but abandoned the original B-22 concept of a modified B-18A, and had commenced the mock-up of an entirely different aircraft, but which they still referred to internally as the B-22. This is the bombardier's station, and the nose configuration will be quickly recognised as nearly identical to the definitive B-23. *Boeing Archives SM-14404*

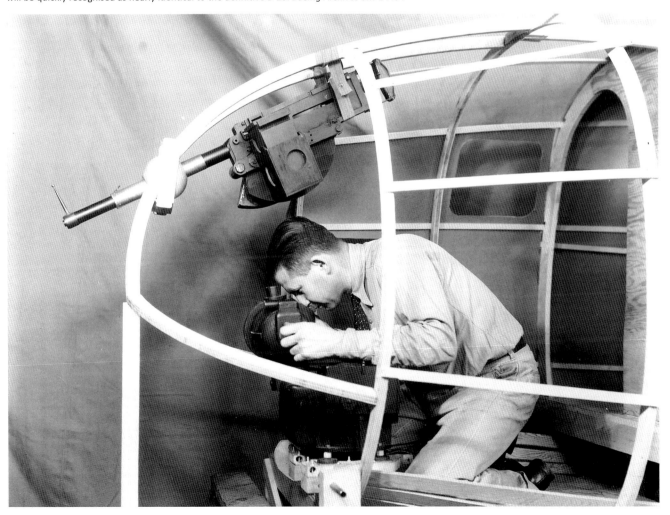

This was the proposed ventral gun position for the Douglas B-22 as seen in mock-up as of 9 January 1939. Although the gun had 360-degree rotation ability, exactly how the gunner was supposed to see a moving target is difficult to imagine. Even for stationary ground targets, the concept was a reach. Although the original caption describes this as a .30 caliber weapon, it appears to be a .50 caliber gun. *Boeing Archives SM-14405*

The XB-22 featured an additional forward ventral gun position, as shown here in this mock-up view from 17 January 1939. Again, the practicality of this installation must have been questionable to one and all, but power turret development had not yet advanced to the point that the aircraft could seriously be considered for such an installation. Note also the large camera gear position on the left. *Boeing Archive SM-14479*

The same gunner who manned the dubious ventral gun on the mock-up B-22 also had charge of the exceptionally demanding waist and dorsal gun, which was mounted on a pivoting pedestal that allowed it to be fired out of either the starboard or port-side hatch, or out of the dorsal hatch as shown. The gunner would have had to be an exceptional athlete.
Boeing Archives SM-14411 and SM-14408

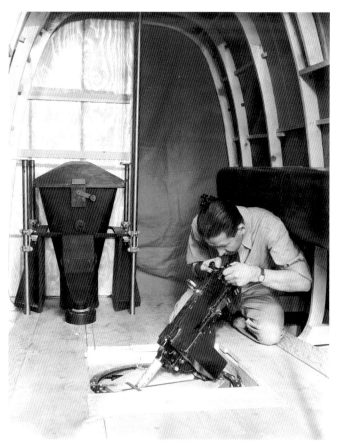

The cockpit mock-up of the definitive B-22 clearly links it with the definitive B-23, which was nearly identical. *Boeing Archive SM-14476*

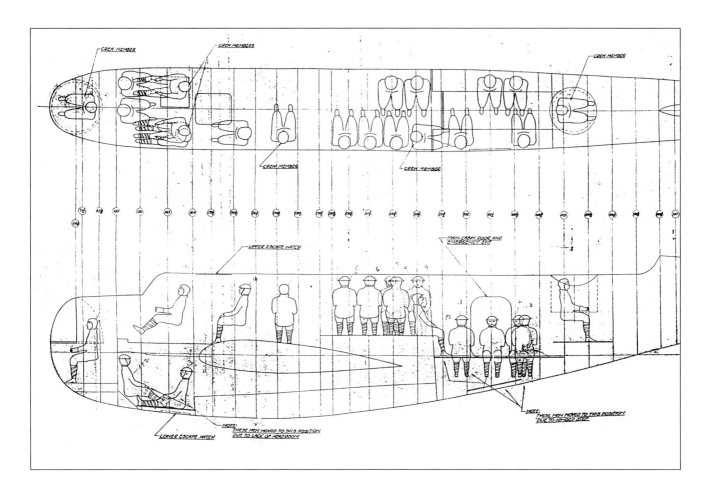

CHAPTER TWELVE

The Douglas B-18AT and C-58

It was perhaps inevitable that a number of B-18 series aircraft were destined to be converted to transport configuration.

Indeed, as early as 11 January 1937 Douglas had provided the Air Corps with detailed calculations covering the estimated weight and balance of a standard B-18 'as a troop carrier'. These calculations allowed for a total of thirteen 'passengers' in addition to a standard crew of six, with all normal crew members, except the lower rear gunner, in their normal positions. This configuration was referred to as the Troop Transport Condition.

In retrospect, given that the series was amongst the most numerous of types in the inventory, possessed a commodious interior

As early as 11 January 1937 Douglas had provided the Air Corps with a detailed breakout of exactly how to configure a standard B-18 as a troop carrier capable of carrying one fully equipped Infantry Squad of thirteen troopers. This Douglas diagram shows the aircraft crew and all thirteen troops in their chummy, but certainly tolerable, positions. There is ample evidence that far more than thirteen passengers were carried by B-18s in the Philippines. *Boeing Archives*

that lent itself well to modification, and was possessed of good handling qualities and a very respectable range when lightly loaded, Air Corps leaders quickly recognised the possibilities.

As early as 28 February 1940 instructions were issued to release one B-18A from GHQAF assets (AC37-502 from Hamilton Field was chosen) and to equip it with fully feathering propellers for exclusive assignment to Bolling Field, DC, for the exclusive use of Major General Jacob E. Fickel, who had been appointed as Assistant Chief of the Air Corps that month. The aircraft was to have removable, adjustable arm rests on both the pilot's and co-pilot's seats, suitable markings for the Assistant Chief of the Air Corps, and 'other work' performed on it. It was to be equipped similarly to the B-18A (AC37-546) that had been outfitted for Major General George H. Brett, who became the Acting Chief of the Air Corps between November 1939 and May 1941, when Arnold was serving as Acting Additional Deputy Chief of Staff (Air) on the Army's General Staff.

Work on General Fickel's aircraft included the following known modifications and alterations:

* a new nose to replace the lower front gun sphere (a very recognisable feature in photos)
* a completely revised navigator's table
* covering of the floor corrugations in the cabin walkway with sheet metal
* complete removal of the dorsal turret and covering of the hole with sheet metal
* installation of a clothes closet in place of the rear turret, to include a door, and a rack for storage of hats and a rod for hanging clothes
* construction and installation of a removable floor to cover the 'tunnel' gun aperture
* installation of extra parachute racks
* installation of containers for two 1-quart Thermos bottles and a 1-gallon jug
* replacement of the navigator's seat with another pilot's chair
* installation of a cabinet immediately to the rear of the entrance door for storage of maps
* installation of bomb bay fuel tanks as a permanent installation
* installation of extra oxygen bottles and changed lines enabling each person on board in the cabin to have a separate supply
* installation of a frame on the vertical fin for insertion of the General Officer's insignia
* installation of new steps for the entrance door
* installation of tool boxes in the former bombardier's compartment
* installation of two upholstered passenger seats behind the pilot's and co-pilot's seats, taken from the cabin of a Grumman OA-9

This detail work was accomplished at the Middletown Air Depot around 4 April 1940, and the aircraft was immediately redesignated, for lack of a better descriptor, as a B-18AM.

In the meantime, while work on General Fickel's aircraft was ongoing, Wright Field received what was apparently an interim request from the Chief of the Air Corps to install 1,100hp Cyclone G-202 engines in the two B-18As then assigned for staff use. Wright Field responded by suggesting that a much more practical engine for this purpose would be the R-1820-59, as installation of the G-202s would require a major redesign of the engine mounts. It is not clear if either of these installations was in fact accomplished

Technical Order T.O. 01-40E-107, dated 6 February 1941 and entitled 'Installation of Bomb Bay Freight Racks', provided for the installation of bomb bay freight racks, secured through the use of standard bomb shackles, when either B-18 or B-18A series aircraft were to be engaged in carrying baggage or freight. These could be '…dropped in the same manner as the normal bomb load in cases of emergency.' No actually instance of such an installation has been identified.

Technical Order T.O.01-40E-108, dated 26 May 1941, required the reinstallation of bomb shackles on B-18 and B-18A series aircraft and the removal of the symbol 'M' from the model designations after the shackles had been reinstalled. In the case of the two radically modified 'staff transports' noted above, the changes that had been made were regarded as so extensive as to preclude the reinstallation of armament. It was, accordingly, requested that necessary action be taken to redesignate these aircraft as type 'B-18AT … or such other symbol as may be necessary to indicate that they had been converted to transport airplanes.' The 2nd Endorsement to this Memorandum, from Wright Field, dated 11 June 1941, instructed that these two aircraft had been formally redesignated as Model C-58 transport types.

As noted elsewhere in this account, standard B-18 and B-18A series aircraft had, since initial concept, been regarded as ad hoc transports in emergency situations. In a Memo dated 17 July 1941, entitled 'Troop-Carrying Provisions for Bombardment Type Airplanes', Wright Field observed that '…it was found that the normal bomb load of an aircraft could be replaced by the equal weight in troops. The B-18A, in present condition, provides for [normal] crew and at least seven troops. Seats for two remaining troops must

The two aircraft shown here are believed to be the two B-18s converted to B-18AT status as dedicated VIP transports commencing in November 1939. Note the Brigadier General's placard on the rear fuselage just aft of the crew access door. *Authors' collection*

be provided in the lower forward gunner's compartment.' In a number of pre-war exercises, and in the Philippines and Caribbean theaters, this capability was frequently engaged and exceeded – although these aircraft were not redesignated in the Cargo category, and retained their bombardment designations.

There has been much speculation regarding precisely which aircraft were formally redesignated as type C-58. While a number of B-18s are known to have been subjected to 'field' conversions to dedicated transport roles, only the two aircraft noted above were formally redesignated. This is confirmed by a document issued on 28 February 1943 by the Technical Data Laboratory, Engineering Division, at Wright Field, which noted on the 'Airplane Characteristics & Performance' data sheet of that date that designation C-58-DO pertained to '…two B-18As with R-1820-53 engines converted by removal of armament and used for transport.'

MONTHLY CHART

AIRPLANE CHARACTERISTICS & PERFORMANCE

CONFIDENTIAL — TRANSPORT — PAGE 22 — DATE Feb. 28, 1943

MODEL & MFR. ENGINE — CONT. NO. PLANES	ENG. RATINGS (NORMAL/ALT. MIL./CRIT.ALT. TAKE-OFF/S.L.)	SPEEDS (HIGH/ALT./H.P. LANDING)	CLIMB (TIME TO/FT. SERV. CEIL. CEIL—1/2 ENGS. OUT)	T.O. & LAND (T.O. OVER 50' OBS. LAND OVER 50' OBS.)	RANGE @ SPEEDS % POWER (MAXIMUM NORMAL)	FUEL MAX NORMAL	PERSONNEL PLACES & CREW	WEIGHTS (WT. EMPTY WEIGHT DESIGN GROSS)	DIMENSIONS (SPAN LENGTH WING AREA)	ARMAMENT (NO. OF GUNS CAL—RDS. AMM.)	COMBAT PROT. TYPE	REFERENCE
C-54-DO Four R-2000-3 AC-19441 9	A 1100/7000 1000/14000 1350/S.L.	A 282/15400/ 1930 81	A 13.5/10000 A 22200 A 16200 [On 3 Engines]	(At 63000#) A 3050 A 1780 (At 52000#)	3800/182/ - 2080/188/ -	3170 1860	15 & 6 24 & 6	36202 62000 52000	117'6" 93'10" 1461 Sq.Ft.	None	None	Spec. 449 A PHQ-M-19-1382-A.
C-54A-DO Four R-2000-3 ** DA-877 15 AC-20284 127	1100/7000 1000/14000 1350/S.L.	282/15400/ 1930 81	13.5/10000 A 22200 A 16200 (On 3 engines)	(At 63000#) A 3050 A 1780 (At 52000#)	(3700 gal. max.) 3800/182/ - 2080/188/ -	3170 1860	15 & 6 50 & 6	37319 62000 62000	117'6" 93'10" 1461 Sq.Ft.	None	None	Spec. 450 A Estimated on C-54 test.
C-55-CU Two R-2600-17A AC-19164 1	1350/15000 - 1700/S.L.	C 235/10400/ 2360 -	11.0/10000 25000 12500	2500 2500	C 1055/201/61% C 2120/201/61%	2600 1360	24 & 3	C 27599 50000 C 39206	108'0" 76'4" 1360 Sq.Ft.	None	None	Spec.20-2-51 C PHQ-M-19-1264-A.
C-56-LO Two R-1820-79 AC-19352 1	900/6700 - 1100/S.L.	251/7900/ - 65	- 23600 10800	1750 1750	- -	644 -	18 & 2	12082 - 17500	65'6" 49'10" 551 Sq.Ft.	None	None	Spec. 2109
C-56E-LO Two R-1820- 2	1000/6900 1200/14100 1200/S.L.	253/8200/ 2000 65	7.1/10000 23300 -	1870 1750	1660/200/ - 1290/209/ - 994/206/ -	644 525 425	18 & 2 8 & 2 15 & 2	11646 21500 Max. 17500 Des. 18500 Alt.	65'6" 49'10" 551 Sq.Ft.	None	None	Spec. 2725
C-57-LO Two R-1830-S1C3-G AC-19352 10	1050/7500 - 1200/S.L.	263/8800/ - 65	- 26100 12800	1625 1750	1175/224/51% -	644 -	14 & 2	12386 18500 17500	65'6" 49'10" 551 Sq.Ft.	None	None	Spec. 2097
C-57B-LO Two R-1830-S1C3-G 7	1050/7500 - 1200/S.L.	256/18800/ 2100 65	6.6/10000 24000 -	1870 1750	1660/200/ - 1290/209/ - 994/206/ -	644 525 425	18 & 2 7 & 2 14 & 2	11911 21500 Max. 17500 Des. 18500 Alt.	65'6" 49'10" 551 Sq.Ft.	None	None	Spec. 2724
C-58-DO Two R-1820-53 - 2	TWO B-18A'S CONVERTED BY REMOVAL OF ARMAMENT AND USED FOR TRANSPORT.											
C-59-LO Two R-1690-S1E3-G DA-53 2	750/ - 800/7000 850/S.L.	236/7000/ - 65	- 20400 7600	1825 1750	1740/168/50% 1293/197/60%	644 525	15 & 3 9 & 3	11518 19000 17500	65'6" 49'10" 551 Sq.Ft.	None	None	Spec. 2313
C-60,A-LO * Two R-1820-87 DA-1039 (C60) 15 DA-1039 (C-60A) 52 AC-29618(C-60A) 240	900/15200 1000/14200 1200/S.L.	C 266/17150/ 1850 65	C 6.6/10000 C 30100 16300	C 1400 1750 (T.O. over macadam)	1660/200/ - 1290/209/ -	644 525	18 & 3 6 & 3	12875 21500 17500	65'6" 49'10" 551 Sq.Ft.	None	None	Spec. 2400 C PHQ-M-19-1451-A.

(3000 mi. range/170 mph./1040 gal. fuel with 9 & 3 places)

NOTES   * C-60A; AC-33349---691   ** C-54A; AC-27311---675

AC AIR CORPS
DA DEFENSE AID
PO PURCHASE ORDER

A—ACCEPTANCE PERFORMANCE TEST RUN AT FACTORY
B—OFFICIAL PERFORMANCE REPORT NO.
C—PRELIMINARY FLIGHT TEST

Prepared by Tech. Data Lab., Engr. Div.

CONFIDENTIAL

This chart, prepared on 28 February 1943, clearly identifies that two B-18As had, by that date, been reconfigured as transports and designated as type C-58-DO. *NMUSAF*

CHAPTER THIRTEEN

B-18 series aircraft engaged in test work

While the wartime contributions of B-18 series aircraft to training and anti-submarine warfare, outlined in detail earlier in this study, will by now have been clearly far more significant than has been previously recorded, the use of B-18s and B-18As in an enormous range of equipment tests – yet another aspect of the versatility of the basic design – has been unreported entirely.

Of course the spectacular trials with a 75mm Howitzer, outlined earlier, probably constituted the most radical transformation. However, many others that followed – well into the war years – deserve mention in this account, as they contributed significantly to the thorough testing and preparation for fielding of a number of very important systems – and the elimination of others through thorough testing.

Some of these systems remain obscure and, despite a concerted effort, details of some have not been located. It is hoped that this chronological summary might provide the grist for further research by students of, in particular, electronics systems.

15 April 1938: A Mr Marvel and Mr Beibach of C. F. Norden & Co were authorized to fly on B-18 AC36-316 between 15 and 22 April 1938 to test a bombsight made by that company.

Although pictured earlier, the radical transformation of the 75mm cannon-configured B-18X, AC37-51, from this perspective, appears almost indistinguishable as either a B-18 or the DB-1. Here, the pilot's gunsight has apparently not yet been installed and the extent of the fairing modifications under the rear bomb bay area and additional vents is evident. *NMUSAF Wright Field 66015*

19 October 1938: B-18 AC36-284 was extensively tested by the NACA to investigate the flight characteristics of the type.

27 December 1938: B-18 AC37-34 and B-18As AC37-458 and 37-469 were at Wright Field being tested with de-icers on their wings.

27 February 1939: Authorisation was issued for the removal of a special turret installed in the rear cockpit of B-18 AC37-34 and the reinstallation of a standard turret in that location. It involved the use of something called the Alkan gunsight.

16-29 August 1939: B-18 AC36-285 was made available to the NACA for three days on 17 August 1939 to test new outer wing panels. B-18 AC36-286 was 'loaned' to the NACA from assets at Barksdale Field, LA, for six months from 29 August 1939 for unspecified tests.

5 March 1940: B-18 AC37-51, the same aircraft used to test the 75mm cannon, was being fitted with a new 'range finder device' at Wright Field by this date, which required cutting holes in the fuselage skin and installing two protruding ends of the range finder, extending forward at the leading edge of the wing. The work was actually accomplished at Aberdeen Proving Ground, MD.

18 July 1940: B-18A AC37-476 was being used by the Equipment Lab at Wright Field for parachute testing.

20 November 1940: Project MX-68 covered installation of AI equipment in B-18A aircraft. This project has eluded documentation.

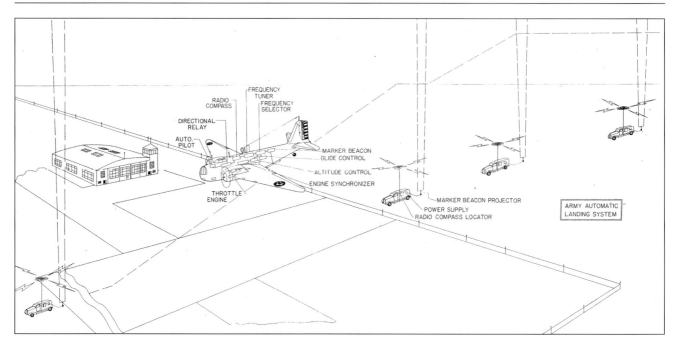

Above: This aspect of the B-18X shows more details of the special housing placed over the former bomb bay area for the 75mm cannon installation, the fact that the Wright Field 'arrow head' was indeed painted on the rear fuselage, and that the dorsal turret had been faired over, aside from a square aperture. The triangular housing for the test cameras atop the forward fuselage is also more apparent. This aircraft was the original DB-1. *NMUSAF Wright Field 66016*

Below: Unusual in wearing the last three digits of its Air Corps serial on the vertical fin in the pre-war period, this is B-18A AC37-596, the very first aircraft, delivered from the factory with a standard M-1 bombsight and associated flight control equipment installed. It went directly to Wright Field (note the Wright Field 'arrow head' on the rear fuselage) but, by March 1940, was assigned to the 15th Bomb Squadron (L), 27th Bomb Group (L), at Barksdale Field, LA. The aircraft ended its days with the Brazilian Air Force Technical School. *NMUSAF Wright Field 66305*

Above: A B-18 served as the test platform for the first Automatic Landing System successfully demonstrated by the USAAC. This schematic illustrates the rather elaborate system of trucks necessary to facilitate this early system. It is not clear which B-18 served as the platform for the tests in 1939-40, but it was probably AC36-264. *NMUSAF Wright Field 59111*

Below: Commencing in July 1940, B-18A AC37-476 was detailed to Wright Field for tests of parachute-droppable items of equipment that could be accommodated in the large bomb bay of the type. Here, looking aft, a complete 75mm pack howitzer is slung just aft of a large parachute bag, visible in the foreground. *NMUSAF Wright Field 81678*

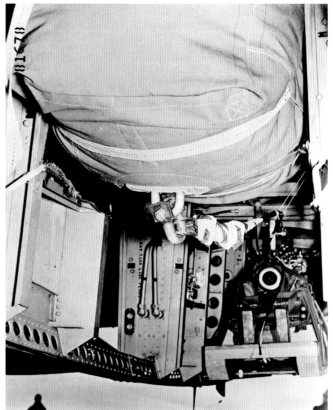

December 1940: A very classified airborne radar system developed by the Bell Laboratories, known at the time as the 'S-band (10-cm) radar' (which became the SCR-519-T3) was tested aboard an unidentified B-18 at the Atlantic Highlands test site between December 1940 and January 1941.

30 July 1941: B-18A AC37-511 was used to conduct extensive sound level tests in the aircraft cabin.

3 October 1941: B-18A AC37-469 was provided with two installations of the North American Scanning Lens, one of these being installed in the side entrance door on the left side of the aircraft and the other in the lower machine gun tunnel emplacement.

Identified by its GHQAF unit identifier code AC 80 (indicating that the aircraft had been assigned, oddly, to the 3rd Attack Group at Savannah, GA), this B-18 certainly experienced one of the most bizarre test periods of any of the series. Shown initially at the NACA at Langley Field on 20 April 1941, the aircraft was being used to test boundary layer transition at high Reynolds numbers, tests that continued into mid-June 1941. The final image confirms that the aircraft retained the painted engine cowlings of the parent unit, but by 5 November 1941 had acquired a long nose probe and what appears to be an airfoil attached on a mast on the rear spine. *Rich Dann and NMUSAF*

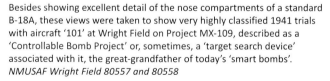

Besides showing excellent detail of the nose compartments of a standard B-18A, these views were taken to show very highly classified 1941 trials with aircraft '101' at Wright Field on Project MX-109, described as a 'Controllable Bomb Project' or, sometimes, a 'target search device' associated with it, the great-grandfather of today's 'smart bombs'. *NMUSAF Wright Field 80557 and 80558*

c9 October 1941: An unidentified B-18 had been tested by the NACA at Langley Field, VA, until this date, when it was removed, with a large 'glove' on the wing, on which pressure distribution and wake surveys were tested at high Reynolds numbers.

25 February 1942: B-18A AC37-528 was assigned to Wright Field for two weeks for use in testing air pick-up and delivery equipment developed by the All-American Aviation Corp. These tests stretched into the end of June 1942, however, and also involved installing the All-American Corp glider pick-up winch in the subject aircraft.

8 July 1942: One Lockheed C-40 and one B-18A were delivered to United Airlines at Mills Field for installation of carburetor air filters, then delivered to Wright Field for observation for three days.

19 August 1942: B-18A AC39-12 was assigned to Douglas (Santa Monica) under the supervision of the National Defense Research Committee at California Tech for a 'special project' to be installed. It was flight-tested at Muroc on 24 August. The aircraft is known to have had electric stabilising and gyro equipment for the Norden bombsight.

30 October 1942: An unidentified B-18B was used in conjunction with the MX-241 Project involving the installation and trials of a Rocket Gun.

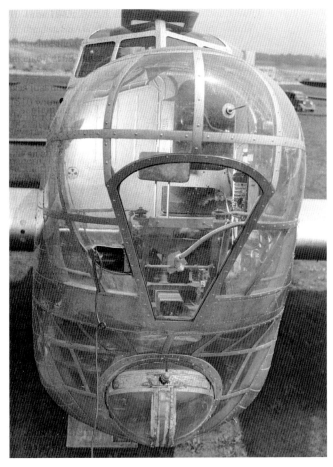

Two B-18As, AC37-469 and 37-555, were modified at Wright Field to test the Type S-1-P.D.I bombsight systems around 9 June 1942. The B-18 afforded the technicians at Wright Field an excellent test platform, with modern performance and room to move about. Note that the chin gun blister has been heavily taped to seal it against draughts. *NMUSAF*

9 December 1942: B-18 AC36-262 was used extensively commencing around this date in testing the LAB Low Altitude Radar Bombing Equipment.

25 January 1943: B-18B AC37-567 was returned to Wright Field for six days for tests of the mock-up of the RC-221 and RC-222 upon completion of armament installations by the Air Service Command at Fairfield Air Depot. It was also used to test-drop D-18 Mark II (RC-222) receiver equipment and radio beacons.

23 February 1943: B-18B AC36-262 was at Wright Field for installation and tests of SCR-622 equipment as well as SCR-620 Interim and SCR-620-T1 by 2 April 1943. The same aircraft was being used by 24 April 1943 for tests with the Phantom Target TS-4/AP equipment.

23 June 1943: B-18B AC37-532 was at Wright Field for use on tests with the SCR-537-T1 airborne radar equipment.

3 August 1943: RB-18 AC37-600 was at Wright Field being used to test radio sets AN/CPN-6, AN/CPN-8 and AN/APN-6, but was damaged beyond repair in the process.

5 August 1943: RB-18B AC37-567 was at Wright Field being used for developing CU-6 and the launching mechanism for the CRT-1 transmitter.

3 December 1943: Tests were inaugurated to determine the feasibility of using a B-18A as a glider tug for one or two fully loaded Waco CG-4As. It was found to have a 'negative margin of safety in trying to tow two CG-4s' but when towing one it was 'not critical'.

9 February 1944: RB-18 AC37-533 was at Wright Field for flight tests of the AN/APS-16. The same month RB-18 AC36-286 was used at the AAF Proving Ground, Eglin Field, FL, to test the Vertical Bombing System, Project (M-5) 108. This system consisted of two types of bomb launchers on the aircraft. Each launched, by rocket power, 60lb Mark XX bombs (also known as VARs – Vertical Anti-submarine Rockets). The rocket motor provided sufficient rearward velocity to the bomb to compensate for the forward velocity of the aircraft. The bomb back rack type installation was a unit to which were attached four sets of rails for launching four bombs. It was extended, by hydraulic power, beyond the aircraft airframe to fire the rockets, but was normally retracted into the bomb bay, at which position the rails were loaded. The bombs were fired manually by the bombardier but, with the installation of MAD equipment, they could be fired automatically when the aircraft was directly above a water target.

18 January 1945: RB-18 'AC37-352' (obviously in error) was assigned to the Federal Telephone & Radio Corporation at Rye Lake Airport, Port Chester, NY, for unspecified research work.

B-18 and B-18A series aircraft were found to provide exceptionally stable camera platforms for aerial photography and, besides the standard aperture built into the rear fuselage of each aircraft, very large hand-held cameras, such as this K-15A, were also tested. The operator, in this case, is Col George W. Goddard. *NARA RG342FH K4849*

CHAPTER FOURTEEN

US B-18 series colors, markings and camouflage

A casual glance through the images presented in this volume in the opening chapters, describing the introduction of production B-18 and B-18A series aircraft into the Air Corps inventory, could easily give the impression that the aircraft were a rather monotonous aftermath of shiny aluminum, following in the wake of the wonderful blue fuselages, glittering national insignia and rudder striping and yellow wings of their immediate predecessors.

Markings historian Dana Bell, in his classic three-volume series from Squadron/Signal publications, *Air Force Colors*, Vols 1, 2 and 3 (Carrollton, TX, 1979, ISBN 0-89747-091-5), illustrates and describes in authoritative detail the economic motivation for the abandonment of the overall color schemes in favor of so-called 'natural metal' finishes. He also details the advent of special markings to denote leadership within the Air Corps tactical hierarchy of Wing, Group and Squadron, and the bare bones of the General Headquarters Air Force (GHQAF) designator system.

B-18s R-65 and R-64 (the codes were given with the 'dash' in unit documents, although not painted that way on the aircraft) of the 88th Reconnaissance Squadron (L/R) prior to April 1940, operating from Hamilton Field, CA, very nearly epitomise the pre-war GHQAF colors and markings guidance. R-64 was actually AC37-14, while the number R 65 was later reassigned to a B-18A of the same unit. The Squadron insignia is painted on the mid-fuselage, and R-65, with the unusual, segmented double band around the rear fuselage, is the Squadron Commander's aircraft. The engine cowls were chequered yellow and black, as were the fuselage bands. *NMUSAF*

Between the acceptance of the first B-18s and B-18As and the emergence of these identification systems, however, there existed an interim period. The first of these occurred from 15 November 1937, when the service issued the first coordinated system for aircraft markings and radio call lettering. Since the first production B-18 had been delivered a scant seven months previously, as they were accepted and delivered to tactical units they were amongst the first Air Corps aircraft to have never been previously adorned with earlier systems. Available evidence seems to suggest that the scant thirty-two B-18s actually accepted prior to the promulgation of this directive, and which were widely scattered throughout the service, operated initially without benefit of any special markings or field numbers, and indeed wore nothing more than standard national insignia and such organisation special insignia as was appropriate for the period.

The November 1937 order effectively standardised squadron 'colors' and command markings and designators. Three colors, initially, became the only authorized squadron colors for most Air Corps attack, bombardment and pursuit units, and these were white, yellow and red, although in some instances, if a Group was large enough to have a fourth subordinate squadron, blue was also used. The technical order dictated that a 'suitable depth of the front portion of the engine nacelles' would be painted with one of these four colors, uniform to each squadron and, by 1940, this was amended slightly to permit Groups to select any of the four.

The cowlings of Group Headquarters and Headquarters Squadrons (HHS), to distinguish them from the 'line' units, were divided into sections making use of the subordinate Squadron colors. Reconnaissance Squadrons, which during this period were attached to Groups and retained a certain amount of autonomy, were assigned colors by the several Wing commanders, most of whom selected exotic colors and presentation, such as chequered squares. Wing headquarters and the aircraft assigned to the GHQAF itself were not permitted to 'wear' colors on their cowlings, instead relying for recognition on low numbers, to distinguish them from the tactical units.

Command recognition markings changed also, and are frequently noted on B-18s in photos from the period. Consisting of 5-inch stripes in the Squadron color (but with black replacing white on aluminum fuselages), these were painted on the Squadron Commander's aircraft (two equal-distance stripes) around the waist, while Flight Commanders' aircraft within the Squadron (usually 'A', 'B' and 'C' Flights) wore a vertical band around the waist, either diagonal front-to-rear or diagonal rear-to-front. These were sometimes stylised or edged in actual practice. Similar stripes for Group and Wing Commanders were never actually proscribed in orders, but a number are known to have made use of them on B-18s.

The major uniform change, however, were the so-called Designators. These were marked on the vertical fins of each unit aircraft (in two lines) and above and below each wing (on one line in this case), in vertical type not larger than 18 inches high or strokes wider than 3 inches. The first of (usually) two letters identified the type of unit (with, in the case of B-18s, 'B' for 'Bomber' and 'R' for 'Reconnaissance'), while the second letter indicated the number of the unit ('B', for instance, being the 2nd Bomb Group, 'B' being the second letter in the alphabet, and so on). These two characters were then positioned on the fin and wings above a numeric digit, indicating individual aircraft within that unit. Normally, most three-squadron Groups reserved the numbers 1 to 9 for the Headquarters and Headquarters Squadron aircraft (although they seldom had that many aircraft), with the 'line' Squadrons being issued numbers in blocks, such as 10 to 39, 40 to 69, 70 to 99 and so on. Unfortunately, units of the GHQAF took a rather liberal interpretation of this in applying the designators to B-18s, and as a result some of these relationships are extremely elusive. This system was used by the GHQAF until about November 1939, when it was extensively modified for use throughout the rapidly expanding Air Corps. Air Corps units in the Philippines, Hawaii and Panama, not being part of the GHQAF, adopted similar systems, which have challenged aviation historians ever since, but they were not required to do so, and only commenced their systems when B-18s were received from GHQAF units in the US – this almost certainly being the impetus for them adopting such a system.

The first GHQAF subordinate organisation to report a designator to the senior command was Headquarters and Headquarters Squadron, 3rd Wing, at Barksdale Field, LA, which noted that as of 17 January 1940 its single B-18A, AC37-597, which had been issued the designator SR1, was being transferred to the 90th Bomb Squadron (L) – but that it was retaining that designator for future use. The last subordinate organisation to report was the Base Headquarters and 4th Air Base Squadron (Double), March Field, CA, on 27 August 1940, which had two B-18s (AC36-304 and 36-306) with designators 4AB11 and 4AB12, one B-18A (AC37-540) with designator 4AB10, and a single Northrop A-17 (AC35-77) with designator 4AB1. In both systems, it was common for B-18s to also have the number-within-unit also repeated on the forward fuselage, sometimes just under the nose gun turret, and sometimes on both sides just under the nose turret. All known designators are noted in the individual Production List historical aircraft sketches in Annex 1.

Even while the units of the GHQAF were issuing and painting the new designators on their aircraft, however, as of May 1940 the system was expanded to include all Air Corps organisations. In the new system individual organisations were identified by a unit number, rather than a corresponding letter. The impetus behind this was, of course, the massive Air Corps expansion program known generally as the 41 Group Program. Since the number of proposed Groups exceeded the number of letters in the alphabet, it was obvious that a new system was needed. The new method of presenting these revised designators on the aircraft was very similar in appearance to the original system; however, the unit designator was now placed below the individual aircraft number, rather than above it.

Besides the designators and standard national insignia placement of the period, unit distinctive insignia were also nearly always painted on B-18s and B-18As. There was apparently little standardisation in the placement of these. Some aircraft in the B-18 series wore them high at mid-fuselage on either side, while others had them on the nose of the fuselage, just ahead of and midway on the fuselage from the windscreen on either side. Others had them in the center of the nose, just on the 'chin' of the fuselage, under the nose turret.

As far as interior colors of the B-18s were concerned, the Air Corps had stipulated to Douglas, with great precision, exactly how the aircraft was to be completed, and these details have often been the source of assumption and outright erroneous claims by many students of the subject – often based on 'interpretation' of existing black and white photographs.

As originally built, the Air Corps stipulated that all interior metal surfaces that were exposed to view (other than the cockpit and radio operator's area, as noted below) were to be finished with aluminised spar varnish. The exposed metal surfaces in the cockpit and radio operator's station were seven basic colors (or lack thereof) as follows:

Pine Green 246-30966: The radio table, radio operator's and navigator's seats, the brackets below the level of the radio table, the oil tank and wobble pump handle, all corrugated floors, the hand rails and assist handles inside the fuselage. The parts of the cockpit that were finished in green were given one coat of primer and two coats of Pine Green lacquer as a final finish.

No Finish: The top of the radio table, the oil wobble pump, the dome light frames, and conduits were left their natural finishes.

Light Gray Duco 258-38141: The brackets and junction boxes above the radio table, the warm air ducts, the loop brackets and doors, the flight report holder, the emergency exit hatch in the roof of the cabin, the exposed surface of the dome light box, and the trailing antenna reel bracket were painted this color.

Dark Gray Duco 258-38142: The drinking cup container and vacuum bottle support, the flare brackets, the oscillator case, trim strips and window frames, the map case, and the horizontal metal panel in the curve between the side wall and ceiling were painted this color.

Chromium Plate: The loop tubes were installed finished in this way.

Yellow: The solitary bright color in the cockpit, the oil wobble pump handle was yellow.

Dull Black: The instrument panels and instruments and such parts as the control wheels and control handles were painted dull or flat black.

Camouflage

Experiments with camouflage on B-18 series aircraft, at first in connection with various maneuvers, commenced as early as 25 April 1938, when the 5th and 7th Bombardment Group B-18s were adorned with both upper-surface, water-soluble paints (brushed on with long-handled brushes rather crudely). Five 7th Bomb Group, First Wing, B-18s received this treatment, which consisted of random applications of dark green (AC36-1782-P), olive-drab (Spec 14057A) and neutral

gray (AC37-3539-P) on the upper surfaces (described as 'day ground'), and light blue undersides (AC33-5790, described as 'sky camouflage'). Some 5th and 19th Bomb Group B-18s, particularly five of the subordinate 31st Bomb Squadron, had their undersurfaces painted matte black (AC36-3162-P). Some sources state that the entire aircraft were painted black for night bombing trials to test the effectiveness of such paint against searchlights (the aluminum apparently shone through and was visible). At least two B-18s, on opposite sides of the Continental United States, are known to have been painted black overall during this period as well, although the reasons for this have not been isolated to the satisfaction of this writer.

The so-called McClelland-Barclay camouflage scheme was first cited in Air Corps documents on 2 September 1938, and appears to have been a US effort to test the effectiveness of similar schemes then starting to appear on military aircraft in Europe. This scheme was developed by Mr Barclay, a well-known artist of the day, who in fact submitted drawings of his proposals to the Air Corps via R. T. Hurley of New York. Although certainly exotic and somewhat effective, and based on deception principles, they apparently proved to be labor-intensive to apply and maintain compared with the perceived benefits.

The first known instance of B-18s receiving camouflage was during the May 1938 East Coast maneuvers. Here, crewmen swab a mixture of White #25, Light Blue #27, Sea Green #28, Dark Green #30, Dark Olive Drab #31 and Neutral Gray #32 in completely random patterns on a 7th Bomb Group aircraft. Some areas were left 'natural metal' as well. The work was being done at Westfield, MA. *NARA RG342FH 14688AC*

The water-soluble paints used on the B-18s during the 1938 maneuvers eroded rather quickly, through a combination of slipstream effect, rain and night-time and early-morning moisture accumulation. The pre-war rudder striping can just be seen on this 21st or 31st Reconnaissance Squadron aircraft, which oddly appears to have its engine cowlings painted a dark color. *via Dana Bell*

Four camouflaged B-18s wing along in company with an uncamouflaged Martin B-10B over Massachusetts during the May 1938 maneuvers. Note the wide variation in the random application of the colors. Although this image has been previously published, what is not normally noted is that the second aircraft in the step-down formation is wearing the first of the so-called Barclay camouflage schemes; as described in the text, this aircraft crashed and was replaced by another B-18 with a far more garish scheme. *NARA RG342FH 14692AC*

This B-18, also taking part in the 1938 maneuvers, appears to have had its entire underside painted a single color, possibly light blue. Note that the propeller is uncamouflaged, and that the prop-spinner has retained the squadron color, probably blue. *NARA RG342FH*

An exceptionally weathered B-18 at the conclusion of the 1938 maneuvers, which some wag has labelled 'Ye Westfield Zephyr'. It was Field Number 162. The B-18s operated effectively during the maneuvers from very crude grass aerodromes. *R. W. Harrison via Dave Menard*

This perspective gives a good appreciation of the effectiveness of the temporary May 1938 maneuver camouflage shortly after being applied. The antenna array is noteworthy in that, in addition to the wiring between the masts and the vertical fin, at this time wires also went outboard to the starboard wing from the aft mast and to the port wing tip from the leading mast. This is probably a 7th Bomb Group aircraft. *via Rich Dann*

The experiments with camouflage during the 1938 maneuvers, and with an eye on the use of camouflage then taking place in the Spanish Civil War, prompted the Air Corps to continue to develop the theme into the Anti-Aircraft Air Corps Exercises held at Fort Bragg, NC, in October 1938. The scheme worn on this B-18 was the definitive Barclay scheme. *via Dana Bell*

At the conclusion of the 1938 maneuvers, the wear on the temporary camouflage of the B-18s is evident in this photo. Besides the fact that some GIs took the opportunity to post some graffiti on the aft fuselage in the chalk-like paint, it is also worth noting that, when the camouflage paint was applied to the underside of the wing (a combination of white and light blue), it was positioned so as to cover the national insignia and the large black 'U.S. Army' there – with some areas remaining bare natural metal. *William F. Yeager Collection, Wright State University*

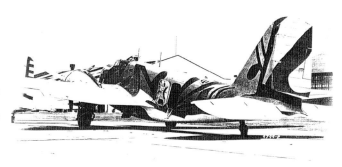

Seen on 15 January 1940, this may well be the same B-18A that was in line at Bolling Field, DC, on 18-19 January. However, in this view it is clear that the undersides, besides being painted light blue, also have white 'splotches' dabbed on, to simulate cloud, it is assumed. The props remain highly polished, however! *NASM 2006-26071*

This aircraft is something of a puzzle. The GHQAF codes 'BG' are barely visible on the vertical fin, indicating that this was a 7th Bomb Group aircraft photographed in January 1939. It appears to be overall matt black, to include the nose turret and the propeller blades! This may have been the aircraft used to test the effectiveness of so-called 'night' camouflage against searchlights, as described in the text. *William F. Yeager Collection, Wright State University*

Experiments with water-based camouflage schemes did not end in 1938 and 1939. This B-18A, shown at the Aeronautical Exhibition at Bolling Field, DC, on 18 and 19 January 1940, is in a line-up of similarly painted aircraft, including the XB-15. *NARA RG342FH 19607AC*

B-18 Barclay Artwork by Rich Dann

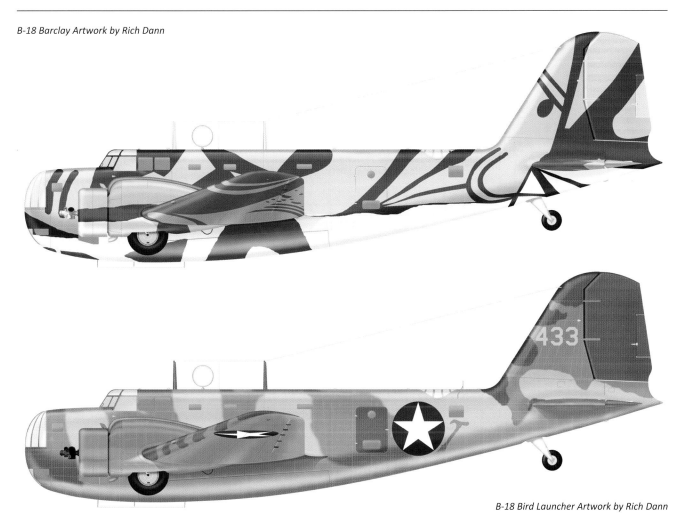

B-18 Bird Launcher Artwork by Rich Dann

Barclay proposed to apply one of his finishes to the undersurfaces of a standard B-18 for $500 (provided the Air Corps provided the necessary paint and labor!). The Materiel Division suggested that the scheme be tested during the Fort Bragg, North Carolina, maneuvers scheduled for that autumn, over an anti-aircraft battery during daylight hours. The test was to involve one B-18 painted with the Barclay scheme, one with no camouflage, and one with what was described as an 'Air Corps scheme' (this consisted of light pastel shades). The aircraft selected for the Barclay scheme was actually painted at Mitchel Field, NY, and initial instructions were to apply the scheme only to the undersurfaces of the wings, fuselage and empennage. In the initial tests it consisted of neutral gray, non-reflective paint on the sides of the fuselage and the vertical fin, and vivid ultramarine blue employed on the undersides of the wings. The aircraft was flown, and observed by Mr Barclay, in flights up to 10,000 feet from Mitchel Field, and color motion picture film was taken of the flight – possibly a first for the Air Corps.

The tests revealed that the 'Air Corps scheme' of pastels 'was always easily visible and indeed served as a reference point for locating the entire formation.' The uncamouflaged aircraft was found to be 'only slightly more visible than the McClelland-Barclay example.' The test evaluators were of the opinion that the Barclay scheme was 'approximately 20% more effective in reducing the visibility of the airplane than the uncamouflaged example...', but that 'both of these were markedly superior to the Air Corps system of camouflage as exemplified by the third plane.'

Another series of tests were conducted at Pope Field, Fort Bragg, NC, between 3 and 19 October 1938, this time involving four B-18s – two from the 21st Reconnaissance Squadron, reinforced by two others

from the 2nd Bomb Group. Again, one aircraft was completely without camouflage, while another had what was described as 'standard Air Corps scheme of camouflage' (R-20 of the 21st Reconnaissance Squadron, Langley Field), one had a 'special Air Corps scheme of camouflage' (BB-16 of the 2nd Bomb Group, Langley Field, consisting of uniform gray on the horizontal portions of the aircraft and uniform dark blue on the vertical surfaces), and the fourth (AC36-296 of the 18th Reconnaissance Squadron, coded R-5) a modified McClelland-Barclay scheme, applied at Langley Field.[38] Additionally, three B-18s (BS-12, BS-14 and BS-21) of the 2nd Bomb Group, Langley Field, received 'night sky camouflage' during this period for tests at Pope Field as well. The props were also painted, but not, for some reason, the vertical tail surfaces. The night camouflage was found to be 'much less effective than had been anticipated'.

Following rather pointed guidance from General Arnold, Chief of the Air Corps, as early as May 1939, the service once again investigated camouflage and, by early 1940, a service standard was finally adopted that, finally, in July 1941, was formalised with issuance of the seminal 'Study #42, The Shadow Shading of Aircraft'. This was the guidance that gave rise to the introduction of the now universally familiar AAC system of employing dark olive-drab on upper surfaces and 'Neutral Gray' undersides. The separation of the two colors was to be blended rather than show a distinct line of demarcation. In July 1940 the Air Corps Board, in line with the obvious intent to cloak the aircraft to the most effective extent possible, issued a Memo suggesting the removal of one upper and one lower wing national insignia and all of the classic rudder striping, and the addition of the national insignia to each side of the rear fuselage. At first, unit insignia and designators remained unchanged but, as the world situation grew ever more bleak, these also

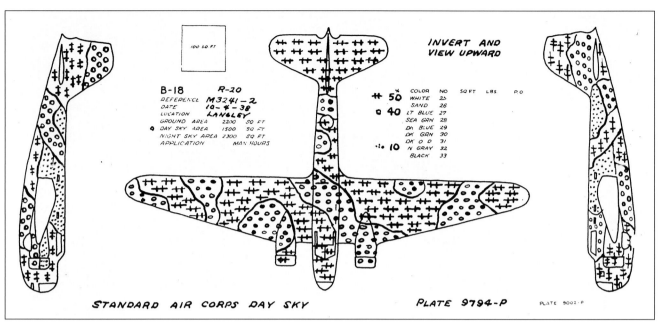

STANDARD AIR CORPS DAY SKY   PLATE 9794-P

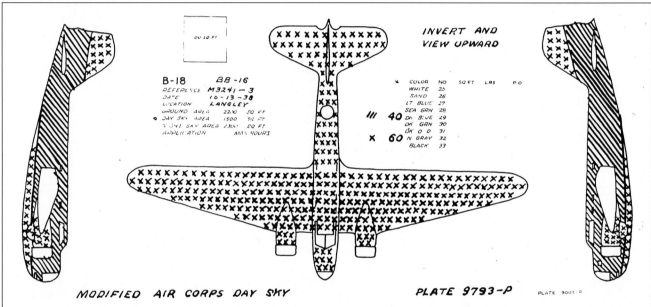

MODIFIED AIR CORPS DAY SKY   PLATE 9793-P

soon began to be removed. Designator colors were actually specified to be applied in yellow on the aircraft but, again, as the crisis worsened many units repainted these in black to further enhance the camouflage qualities. Many of the same units unilaterally dropped the unique unit designators, leaving only the 'aircraft-within-unit' numbers on their aircraft, a curse to future airpower historians!

Thus, as it transpired, between mid-1940 and well past 7 December 1941 organisations equipped in whole or in part with B-18s and B-18As attempted to carry out the Air Corps directives on camouflage and markings to the best of their ability. Units that were served by dedicated Air Corps Depots can probably be said to have been provided with the most uniform application of the guidance provided, as aircraft were painted when they came due for any form of Depot maintenance. Otherwise, however, units were left to their own resources to carry out this very labor-intensive activity, and perhaps not surprisingly the results reflected a rather wide range of differences.

Overseas, in Panama, the Caribbean Air Force is known to have found that aircraft based with units at Albrook Field on the Pacific side of the Isthmus were painted differently from the majority of others in

These two schemes reflect the general outline and colors used during Anti-Aircraft Exercises in October 1938 on R-20 and BB-16. Unfortunately, no photos of either have thus far surfaced. via Dana Bell

the command, which were based for the most part at France Field on the Atlantic side – and adjacent to the Panama Air Depot of that era. At least one known color image (enlarged in this volume) shows two B-18s from each side of the Isthmus side by side. One appears to be painted in some form of blue-gray, topside, while the other appears to be a decidedly 'olive' form of olive-drab! In Hawaii it appears that the command there may have intentionally started very late with this task, as a number of the aircraft caught on the ground at Hickam Field had only the undersides painted gray, while the topsides remained natural metal. It is possible that the bomber units were intentionally delaying implementation of the camouflage directives by waiting for the slow depot maintenance schedule in order to keep the aircraft as cool as possible in the tropics. The aircraft shipped from Hawaii to the Philippines all arrived still in natural metal schemes, and were camouflaged – rather more crudely than anywhere else in the Air Corps – as the hard-pressed single spray gun would allow.

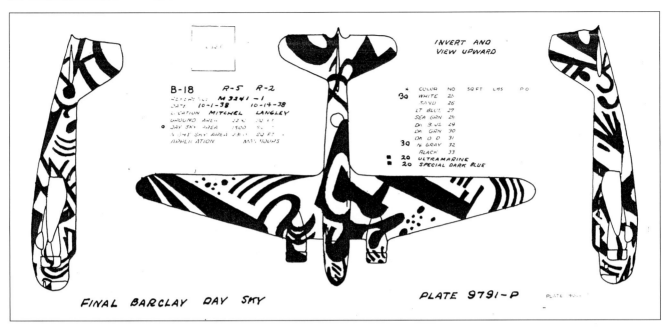

FINAL BARCLAY DAY SKY

PLATE 9791-P

Certainly qualifying as one of the most spectacular camouflage schemes ever applied to a US service aircraft, this was the definitive Barclay scheme painted on two Reconnaissance Squadron aircraft, R-5 and R-2, in October 1938. *via Dana Bell*

This is one of the B-18s that survived the Japanese onslaught in the Philippines, almost certainly AC36-343. In typical GI fashion it has received a lighthearted rendering at Eagle Farm, Australia, of Donald Duck with the classic contraction of the universal phrase of the day, 'Damn If I Know'. Note how low on the forward fuselage the underside neutral gray starts compared to other aircraft pictured herein. This B-18 was with the 21st Troop Carrier Squadron at the time this photo was taken. *via Buz Busbyv*

B-18 Olive Artwork by Rich Dann

As the events of 1941 unfolded, the US Army hastened to camouflage its aircraft in the soon to become familiar and relatively simple scheme of olive-drab upper surfaces and neutral gray undersides – although there remained a considerable variation, from station to station, as to how this was applied. This B-18, showing only Field Number 2 (probably in yellow), was based at Mitchel Field, NY, and was typical for late 1941. *Cradle of Aviation Museum*

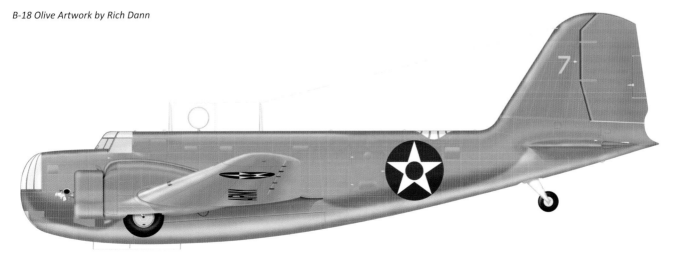

When war arrived, with its inevitable rush to accomplish even the most mundane tasks, and with the rapid elimination of pre-war budget and manpower restrictions, nearly every B-18 and B-18A, with the exception of those assigned to bombardier training duties at several locations, were very quickly camouflaged in accordance with the best information available to local crews – resulting in yet more variations locally. The orders to carry out this obvious wartime requirement were often rather later in being issued than might be expected. The Commander of the First Air Force and the Eastern Theater of Operations, for example, issued a directive entitled 'Camouflaging of Airplanes' only on 1 January 1942, with the simple sentence, 'It is desired that necessary action be taken immediately to have the prescribed camouflage paint applied on all airplanes.' This message was directed specifically to I Bomber Command, 34th Bomb Group, 43rd Bomb Group, 13th Reconnaissance Squadron and 2nd Bomb Group, suggesting that, even three weeks after Pearl Harbor, some aircraft had still not been camouflaged. By 10 January there was still rather spirited communications being exchanged on the issue within the First Air Force, centered on the apparent scarcity of the necessary Army issue paints to accomplish the requirement!

Although of marginal quality, this image reveals the colorful markings associated with bombardier training establishments at the B-18 and B-18A aircraft they utilized very heavily throughout 1942, especially at Albuquerque, NM and Midland, TX. *Author's Collection*

This B-18A sports most unusual white 'swirl' paint on the outer wing panels (possibly to cover up the Mandarin red wing panels that had been there before) and on the bronze green anti-glare panel of this aircraft based at the Alaska Artic Test Center at Ladd Field. Like the late Canadian Digbys, it appears to have otherwise been rather crudely painted white overall. *USAF via Dana Bell*

Between 1 January and 9 April 1942, as witnessed by the summaries earlier in this account, a large percentage of the AAF B-18 fleet was engaged in very intensive coastal, anti-submarine and maritime patrol activity.

The First Air Force, in conjunction with its Royal Canadian Air Force counterpart, the Eastern Air Command, which were jointly primarily responsible for the anti-submarine activities on the Atlantic coast, was the first AAF activity to observe that the 'standard' AAF camouflage scheme for bombardment aircraft might not be ideal for anti-submarine activities – and became the first to experiment, following the RCAF's lead, after the US entered the war, with attempts to deal with this issue.

The first practical test of a solution by Eastern Air Command, involving Royal Canadian Air Force Catalinas painted all white, took place about 15 miles off Halifax harbor, Nova Scotia, on 9 April 1942, around noon. These tests proved, to the satisfaction of the RCAF, that 'unquestionably the effectiveness of white paint on planes used for anti-submarine work on sunny days is excellent.' The paint used was not 'flat' enough (shine) and therefore a 'just off-white' was recommended. The paint did add some 350lb to the weight of the aircraft, however, although the older camouflage beneath the white had not been removed. While the AAF made special note of these tests via a liaison officer, and forwarded comments to the Commanding General of the AAF, official US action on these findings did not enter the US discussion until 29 June 1942.

On that date I Bomber Command, acting on the valuable tests conducted by the RCAF, requested authority from First Air Force to 'camouflage aircraft engaged in patrol operations' in accordance with the RCAF experience, '…until such time as an official camouflage paint is adopted by the Air Service Command.' The Command specifically requested what it described as '#1 White' or, stated otherwise, 'just off-white', be authorized for application to all of its patrol aircraft, including a sizeable proportion of B-18s. The AAF Materiel Center delayed approval of the request because it was awaiting a satisfactory paint for the de-icer boots fitted to many of the aircraft operating over the North Atlantic, and had asked the Goodrich Tire & Rubber Company to rush a solution. The company suggested that, as an interim measure, I Bomber Command units could concoct an 'oyster gray' paint finish for the metal and fabric-covered surfaces of its aircraft locally by simply tinting Shade 46 White Camouflage Enamel with Black Camouflage Enamel of the same specification. It also suggested, as an interim measure, that water paints could also be tried, in accordance with Specification 14057, but that these would probably only suffice for tests. By 23 July 1942 I Bomber Command had moved forward to actually paint thirteen B-18s of the 13th Bomb Group at Westover Field, three B-18s of the 2nd Bomb Group at Langley, twelve B-18s of the 2nd Sea Search Attack Squadron at Langley, and six B-18s of the 80th Bomb Squadron at Miami (as well as a number of B-34s, B-25s, B-17s and A-29s at these locations) with the new experimental patrol camouflage. The Command also requested that B-18Bs due into these units from depots also be painted in this manner before arrival at their operating units, and emphasised the urgency of '…having this work accomplished at the earliest practical time, with the most suitable paint available which meets the original requirements as closely as possible.'

Actual tests of the Canadian 'off-white' scheme turned up some interesting results, however. On 28 August 1942, using two B-17Es and two B-34s, one of each being painted 'off-white' and one 'brown', on every pass, from numerous angles, the observers invariably sighted the 'off-white' aircraft before the 'brown' one! However, in tracking the aircraft after being sighted, the 'off-white' examples were lost before the 'brown' ones. The conclusions reported, on 31 August, were that there was a '…definite advantage in the "white" airplanes over the

In a staged photo, Lt Herschel Chenoweth is shown releasing a courier pigeon from the upper hatch of a camouflaged Seventh Air Force B-18 in January 1943. This scheme was unique to Seventh Air Force aircraft, and details are lacking. *15th AWW via Rich Dann*

On the home front, most of the B-18s and B-18As were assigned to training activities, like AC38-585 shown here, which arrived at Albuquerque, NM, for the Bombardier Training School on 21 January 1942. Here, it is marked in an unusual manner in having both the radio call number and unique Field Number, Q-133, in yellow on the vertical fin. The aircraft moved to Midland, Texas, on 27 March, so wore this scheme only very briefly. *via Harry Davidson*

"brown" airplanes in anti-submarine operations', and recommended that '…with the least practical delay, paint all aircraft in this Command a shade of "off-white" with a shade a little more "off-white" than those used in the tests believed preferable.'

This was not the final solution to this question by any means, however. The 1st Sea Search Attack Group, in Project SS#28, had painted one B-18 as early as 14 August 1942 '…white on the underside and a "dirty water color" on the top' as a preliminary step in the project. Continuing on, the 1st SSAG, by 14 September 1942, was deeply involved in yet another related Sea Search Project 10 (SS#10), which involved determining the ideal camouflage for anti-submarine aircraft. The unit was coordinating its experiments with the co-located 2nd Bomb Group and, at a conference with Dr Arthur W. Kenny of the National Defense Research Committee (NDRC), Major Randall and Capt Heckle of Eglin Field, and line officers of the 1st SSAG and 2nd Bomb Group, concluded that 'a white aircraft has advantages only under certain circumstances'. They proposed the following experiments:

(1) Paint the top side of a test B-18 with the blue-gray now used on the under section, and retain the natural aluminum color on the underside
(2) Paint a B-18 on the top with blue-gray and the undersides white

They also reported that, at that time, the 2nd Bomb Group was experimenting, on its own initiative, with 'various other combinations using a water color paint'.

One of the largest concentrations of B-18As stateside during the war was at the Bombardier Training School at the Midland Army Air Field, Texas. Here AC37-511, with Field Number 301, which arrived from Albuquerque on 2 September 1942, shares the line with AC37-471, which had arrived twenty-four days later. Note the differences in the style of numbers used on all three aircraft visible, and that the fourth aircraft has been camouflaged. The B-18A is a hands-down favorite amongst trainees over the cramped AT-11. *American Airpower Heritage Museum*

A surprising number of B-18s survived the war years. AC37-537 was assigned to Alaska in March 1941 and remained there until 24 March 1943. Since the national insignia shown here, with the radio call number repeated on the underside of the lower wing (only on aircraft in the Continental United States), was adopted after November 1944, this image, with a number '6' painted above the number on the fin, must have been taken not long before it was passed to the Reconstruction Finance Corporation (RFC) for surplus disposal at Muskogee, OK, on 7 December 1944. The aircraft became NC-64735 in the post-war period, but its fate is unknown. *via David W. Ostrowski*

Looking almost brand-new, B-18A AC37-624 spent most of the war years in the Sixth Air Force and Caribbean region. It returned to the US by 5 August 1944, and this image must have been taken shortly before that movement in Panama. The size of the national insignia is smaller than usual for the period, and the radio call numbers on the vertical fin and rudder were of a style common to the Panama Air Depot. *Major Charles E. Snyder Jr, USAF (Ret)*

Finally, on 19 November 1942 none other than the Director of Bombardment himself, BG E. L. Eubank, reported to the Commander of Anti-submarine Command that the AAF had determined that 'the best type of camouflage for general use on airplanes engaged in submarine search' involved painting all undersurfaces and the surfaces of the aircraft that were in shadow with Insignia White No 46, and all other surfaces Neutral Gray No 43. General Eubank left the door open for AAFASC to develop its own, in-house solution,

B-18B AC37-573, unit unknown, nicknamed 'Ruptured Duck', was forced to ditch while operating out of Dakota Field, Aruba, on 13 October 1942 due to engine failure. A version of the dark green and faded olive-drab upper camouflage scheme is visible on the aircraft as it floats, the crew having been rescued. An unsuccessful attempt was made to salvage the aircraft by towing it, backwards, on the surface, with the resultant damage. The flight and ground crews are shown prior to the mission. *N. Doug Meadowcroft via Lumpy Lumpkin*

however – and this 'exception' was apparently exercised liberally in the months to follow.

The 1st SSAG continued its camouflage project, SS#28, well into late January 1943, and this resulted in some truly amazing appearances. Five B-18Bs (AC37-464, 37-465, 37-621, 37-561 and 37-574) received various specially developed camouflage schemes, as described elsewhere in this account and in the individual aircraft summaries in Annex 1.

By 9 July 1943 all AAF aircraft engaged in anti-submarine operations were being painted in accordance with T.O. 07-1-1, which had taken effect on 15 June 1943. This called for white paint on undersurfaces and all leading edges, and olive-drab on all upper surfaces. Special paint, described as 'oyster white', was to be used for the de-icers.

Meanwhile, in the Pacific, the Seventh Air Force did not issue a teletype message to its far-flung units until 8 May 1942, to remove, effective from 15 May, 'the red circle in the national insignia on all aircraft' and that the area of red removed be '…painted white, and the horizontal red and white stripes on the rudder on all aircraft be eliminated. Painting on the rudder will conform to the general camouflage scheme of the aircraft.' This of course included all of the surviving B-18s in the Command.

In the primary operating theater for the B-18 series, however, the Caribbean, a wide range of camouflage practices has been noted, especially amongst the aircraft of the Sixth Air Force, headquartered in the Panama Canal Zone, which adopted its own unique camouflage schemes and regulations in late May 1942. Initially, VI Bomber Command was authorized to paint its aircrafts' undersurfaces 'light bluish gray with white puffs' while the upper surfaces were to be 'greenish blue'. Some aircraft retained this unique scheme, while others adopted a more conventional upper surfaces scheme reminiscent of some RAF camouflage schemes. Throughout this volume, an effort has been made to illustrate as many of these variations as possible, although nearly all have eluded institutionalised documentation. Likewise, in the primary operating theater, unlike other overseas combat arenas, little attention was paid to such things as Squadron and Group codes actually painted on aircraft, since formation flying and recognition by other 'friendlies' was practically unknown. Anti-submarine duty was a solitary way of going to war and, as a consequence, individual aircraft acquired reputations and nicknames of a much more intimate nature than the often pooled aircraft of, for instance, the Eighth Air Force. Crew mix certainly was fluid, as elsewhere, but generally speaking many aircraft commanders had their 'favorite' aircraft and crew composition and, depending on serviceability and the mission at hand, this was usually entertained.

This B-18B exhibits some very unusual markings, including the seldom seen camouflage 'cloud' splotches unique to aircraft assigned to the Sixth Air Force or Caribbean Air Command. It also appears to have yellow engine cowls and the leading edges of each wing stripped of de-icer boots. *Rich Dann collection*

B-18B. Artwork by Rich Dann

B-18B Sad Sack. Artwork by Rich Dann

B-18 Jonah. Artwork by Rich Dann

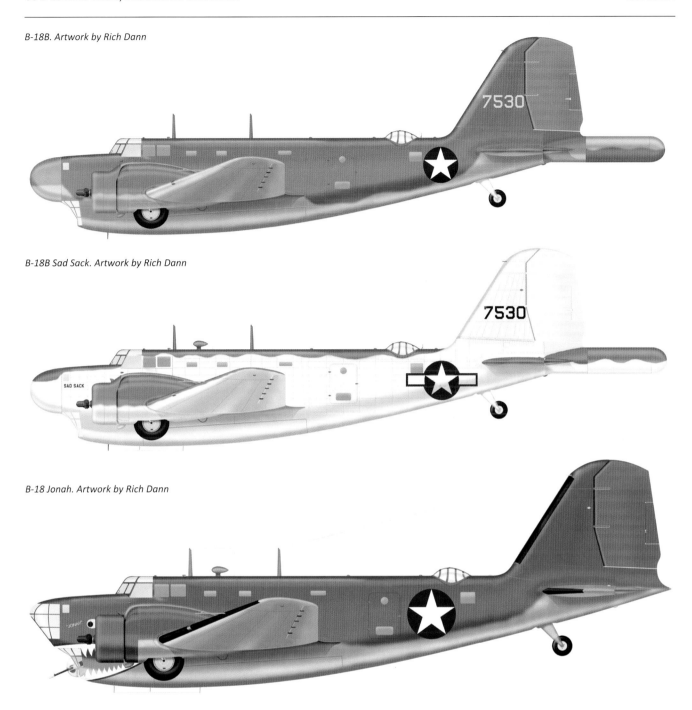

Anti-submarine mission markings

Last but not least, and published here for the first time in a public forum, the War Department actually issued instructions on 12 December 1942 entitled 'Joint Army-Navy Agreement for Awards to Air Personnel on Antisubmarine Duty'. Besides outlining individual and crew awards, citations and medals, and the eligibility for various claims, paragraph five specifically cited the following:

'5. Insignia will be authorized as follows for each aircraft of a squadron, the personnel of which have participated in attacks on submarines:

a. The insignia to be silhouettes of a submarine painted on the left side of the fuselage in the vicinity of the cockpit.

b. A white silhouette for each attack classified as 'A' [confirmed sinking]

c. A red silhouette for each attack classified as 'B' [damaged or disabled]

d. An appropriate symbol to be superimposed in the center of the silhouette indicating the nationality of the submarine'

This B-18A, named 'Flo', and unusual in having its Field Number, 6V85, in segmented characters on the nose, is almost certainly AC37-494. The original photo was taken at Coffeyville Army Air Field, Kansas, and the national insignia dates it as some time in very late 1943 or 1944. It was probably assigned to the 2532nd Air Base Squadron at Hardin Field, Baton Rouge, LA, at the time. Note that the area aft of the cowling has been painted glossy black, probably to facilitate maintenance. *Kevin Gray via Rich Dann*

Even B-18s assigned to training installations were not exempt from forms of 'nose art'. Bombardier trainees at Albuquerque, NM, as of July 1942 placed implicit trust in 'Cockeyed Willie G' to lead them true!
NARA RG342FH 22200AC

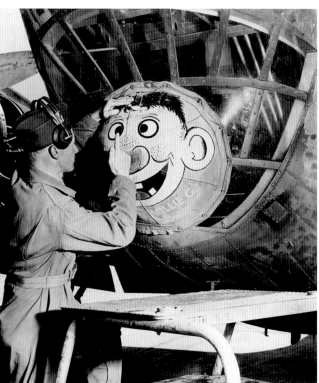

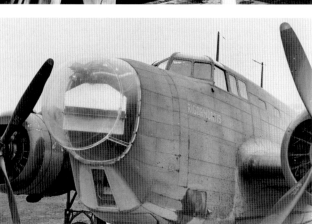

This close-up of AC37-458, an RB-18B of the 35th Bomb Squadron (M) at Zandery Field, Surinam, was probably taken very near the time it returned to the US on 1 June 1944. Although the aircraft appears natural metal, it is actually oyster white, and the gray upper surfaces can just be seen on top of the canopy area and the starboard upper engine cowl. *Brigadier General Charles E. Williams Jr, USAF (Ret)*

These two views show the definitive anti-submarine color scheme worn by most of the RB-18Bs assigned to the veteran 35th Bomb Squadron (M) based out of Zandery Field, Surinam, from 16 October 1942. Here AC37-458, named 'Sad Sack', displays the oyster white lower surfaces and gray upper surfaces (wavy along the fuselage top) unique to the Caribbean campaign at this time. This aircraft returned to the US on 1 June 1944, and went on to see action with the Caribbean Legion in Costa Rica in 1948. *Brigadier General Charles E. Williams Jr, USAF (Ret)*

This highly modified B-18B, photographed at East Boston Airport, Massachusetts, on 22 November 1943, wears the nickname 'Rigormortis', probably referring to the elderly character of the airframe by that time. Although camouflaged, the leading edges of the engine cowls appear to have been painted. *MIT Museum RL-H2K-3*

Above: 'Satan's Chariot' was B-18C AC37-473, and shows evidence of the removal of most of her camouflage. This aircraft survived to be surplused, and ended her days as a tramp freighter in Mexico as XA-LUO. *Peter M. Bowers via The Museum of Flight*

Right: While most 'nose art' discovered to date associated with B-18s was humorous or derisive, there were also a few instances of scantily clad ladies. 'Bashful Betty' adorns a very nicely scrubbed B-18B seen at Base 0109, but the location has been elusive. *via David W. Ostrowski*

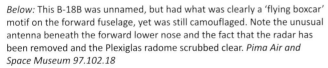

Below: This B-18B was unnamed, but had what was clearly a 'flying boxcar' motif on the forward fuselage, yet was still camouflaged. Note the unusual antenna beneath the forward lower nose and the fact that the radar has been removed and the Plexiglas radome scrubbed clear. *Pima Air and Space Museum 97.102.18*

Known to have been operational in the anti-submarine campaign in the Caribbean, the unit and crew names of B-18B 'Roving Cock' were unfortunately not recorded. Note that the top of the starboard (right) engine cowling has been painted a dark color, but the port (left) engine cowl has not. *San Diego Air & Space Museum*

Another anonymous B-18C anti-submarine warrior and crew (note the forward-firing .50 caliber gun just visible protruding from the starboard side of the gunner's area) displays yet another variation on the camouflage scheme, especially the undersurfaces. *via Lumpy Lumpkin*

Although AC37-458 of the 35th Bomb Squadron (M) was known to have been named 'Sad Sack' (see the earlier images), this aircraft is a completely different example, probably of another unit, and was named 'The Sad Sack' – apparently a popular name for the portly B-18Bs. Note again the application of the gray undersides under the nose and that the leading edges of the engine cowls have been painted. The crew names and operating unit are, unfortunately, not known. *San Diego Air & Space Museum*

RB-18 AC36-295 was in use as a utility transport with the Antilles Air Command and nicknamed 'Ye Ancient Ox Cartte' by June 1943. The aircraft survived the war and ended her days in Mexico as XA-GEO. *Authors' collection*

This B-18, AC36-274, nicknamed 'Watsername' while commanded by Capt Grant K. Chapman, ran out of fuel and made a forced landing with nine passengers and crew on the Overturf farm, 10 miles north of Portsmouth, OH, on 30 August 1943. She survived the war only to disappear in Peru as OB-TAH-306 on 24 November 1954. *NARA RG342FH 123079*

This B-18A, named 'Bird-o-Prey XV' and bearing the number '1' under the bombardier's position, was one of the wartime mounts of (then) Major General Clarence Tinker, center. He commenced naming his personal aircraft 'Bird-o-Prey' with a Curtiss A-3A in 1929! *Authors' collection*

CHAPTER FIFTEEN

The B-18 in the movies and media

Although it never achieved the 'star' status bestowed upon its four-engined brethren, a number of B-18 series aircraft did appear prominently in the company with some 'name' actors in support of the war effort.

The earliest known B-18 cameo in a motion picture did not involve an actual aircraft. In 1940-41 MGM released a cartoon entitled *Flying Bear*, and in the background of one scene appears the unmistakable likeness of a B-18A, taxiing behind the heroes of the comedy, Barney the Bear and a little aircraft that was apparently inspired by the diminutive Curtiss-Wright CW-1 Junior.

Ironically, the first known instance in which an actual B-18 series aircraft appeared was in the award-winning 1941 British propaganda film *49th Parallel*, in which the roster of stars included the likes of Leslie Howard, Raymond Massey, Lawrence Olivier, Anton Walbrook, Glynis Johns and Eric Portman. The aircraft featured were

Above: This 5th Bomb Group B-18, RE 9, probably of the 4th Reconnaissance Squadron, had the delightful duty of giving Dorothy Lamour a ride over the island paradise during her 1938 vacation there, while piloted by Captain Ralph Rhudy. She reportedly moved about the aircraft, and even into the nose turret, during the flight. *S/Sgt David Miller via Bill Stewart*

Right: Actress Dorothy Lamour (her real name) poses beside a Hawaii-based B-18, unusual in bearing the four fuselage colored bands of a Group Commander's aircraft. Since the first B-18s did not arrive in Hawaii until March 1938, and her last 'sarong' movie, *Jungle Princess*, was made there in 1936, she must have been on vacation when photographed. *via Rich Dann*

Even mighty Douglas could not pass up the opportunity to situate a winsome lass to help market its new aircraft, a widespread practice during the late 1930s. The identity of the beauty is, unfortunately, unknown at this writing. *via Rich Dann*

RCAF Digbys and Hudsons searching for and 'destroying' a German U-boat, with major attack scenes rather surprisingly well done, showing the Digbys attacking a submarine. For the purposes of this study, it offers one of the easiest ways for the average observer to actually see a B-18 series aircraft manoeuvring and in flight.

The National Broadcasting Company (NBC) organised a series of special radio broadcasts in September 1942 entitled 'This Nation at War'. One instalment, under the direction of NBC Special Events Director Bill Baldwin, was at Kirtland Field, Albuquerque, NM, and featured a live radio interview with the pilot, co-pilot and student bombardier in a B-18A cockpit just prior to a live bombing 'mission'. The type of aircraft used in the broadcast was not mentioned, merely being described as a 'huge, modern Army bomber'.

It was not until 1943 that RKO released *Bombardier* staring Randolph Scott and Pat O'Brien, which includes a story line comparing 'precision' bombing opposed to dive-bombing. The B-18A in the film, which appears in several scenes marked differently (but always with the fictitious 'Field Number' Q-111), is remarkably well-marked, but what most viewers miss is the fact that the lower nose gunner's barbette had a representation of a frowning Donald Duck! In the case of this film, the irony is that it was intended to perpetuate and enhance the impregnability of the 'flying fortress' concept.

The NBC radio network broadcast a series entitled 'This Nation at War', and the 30-minute segment for 22 September 1942 featured bombardier trainees at Kirtland Army Air Field, Albuquerque, NM, who broadcast during an actual bombing training mission. From left to right, they are Lt Howard K. Finch (Kirtland PR officer); Lt Richard Bulgin (pilot); Bill Baldwin (NBC Special Events Director); Lt Robert French (co-pilot); and Aviation Cadet Henry Morris (bombardier trainee). *via Harry Davidson*

The 1943 movie *Bombardier*, starring Randolph Scott and Pat O'Brien, made heavy use of B-18A AC38-596, marked as Field Number Q-111 (technically, a correct Albuquerque Field number, but believed to have been adopted for easy recollection by viewers), which had been assigned to Albuquerque from February 1942. The scenes even included one in which the aircraft was lowered onto its belly, complete with bent props. The aircraft survived the war and ended up in Costa Rica under dubious circumstances. *via Allan Janus*

B-18A AC38-596 was returned to full service after the completion of the RKO movie *Bombardier*, which was filmed in 1942 and released in 1943. The engine cowls are believed to have been yellow, as were the Field Number Q-111 and radio call number on the vertical fin. *Wright State University*

Painted on during the making of the movie, but seldom noted in the close-up photography in the RKO film *Bombardier*, B-18A AC38-596, Field Number Q-111, has a fierce-looking Donald Duck caricature covering the nose gun blister, with the script 'Fit'in 56th'. This was in fact an accurate reference to the 56th Bombardier Training Squadron, which had been transferred to Albuquerque from Barksdale Field, LA, a few days after Pearl Harbor. *Peter M. Bowers Collection, The Museum of Flight*

CHAPTER SIXTEEN

Surplus, civil and survivors

It is interesting to compare the survivability of major aircraft types used in squadron strength by the wartime Army Air Forces during the Second World War.

Most combat types clearly possessed characteristics that would make them less than attractive as efficient civilian, demilitarised aircraft after the war, and as a result the vast majority of B-17 and B-24 series aircraft went to the smelter. Efficiency was only part of the reason for this vast purge, however. Post-war politics and the very strict rules that were placed into effect by the War Assets Administration (WAA), Foreign Liquidation Commissioners (FLC) and Reconstruction Finance Corporation (RFC) as to who had first priority on surplus aircraft also factored into this equation. Generally speaking, at least initially, veterans had first preference, followed by established commercial operators. As time wore on and the surplus stocks were depleted, these rules were modified and, finally, abandoned altogether.

We know that between May 1937 and February 1940, the Army Air Corps accepted and placed into service 351 B-18 and B-18A

series aircraft (including the DB-1 and DB-2 reconfigured). By August 1944, after pre-war losses to accidents and combat losses in the Philippines, Hawaii and the Caribbean, no fewer than 120 B-18, B-18A, B-18B and B-18C series aircraft – more than one-third of all aircraft built – still remained active in the inventory. Very few wartime combat aircraft series, let alone pre-war production aircraft, could make such a claim.

August 1944 marked the beginning of the end for active service for the B-18, however, as the first three aircraft were declared surplus and passed to the Reconstruction Finance Corporation (RFC) for surplus disposition. By November 1944 the twenty-three RB-18s (as

Above and right: Nicknamed 'Sweet Sue' and bearing what appears to be a baby elephant's head on the forward nose, AC37-2 (marked, to the befuddlement of many observers, by this time as '702') was a Hawaiian survivor of the 5th Bomb Group, and was declared surplus at the Hawaiian Air Depot (HAD) and scrapped some time after 21 March 1944. The aircraft appears to still bear remnants of the red outline on the national insignia from the brief period when this was authorised between June and August 1943. *via Rich Dann*

they had all been reclassified) remaining active in the inventory, having amassed 284 flying hours. By 28 February 1945 a total of sixty had been declared surplus, but thirteen were still flying actively, and amassed 106 flying hours during that month alone. By 1 August 1945, the last month in which B-18 series aircraft were still shown on the AAF inventory, seventy-nine had been transferred to the custody of the RFC, eight others had been scrapped while in RFC custody, and eleven more were either surveyed or declared Class 26 (instructional airframes), for a total of ninety-eight aircraft. By the end of August, two more had been salvaged by the RFC and two others declared surplus, for a total of 102 aircraft.

In Canada, of the twenty DB-280 Digbys acquired commencing in December 1939, six survived what can only be described as very intensive use throughout the war years, to be surplused after VE Day. Oddly, unlike their US counterparts, not a single one is known to have been acquired for post-war civil use – possibly due to the extremely heavy wartime use that they had experienced, but also probably influenced by the fact that, when the Digbys were withdrawn from airworthy service, they commenced deteriorating even further almost immediately due to the elements.

At this point, an analysis of the ultimate fates of all B-18 and B-18A series (and modified B-18B and B-18C) aircraft is in order. Amazingly, both the original DB-1 (redesignated after acceptance as a B-18) and the DB-2 (also redesignated after acceptance) survived to pass, respectively, to Class 26 (Ground Instructional Airframe, in the case of the former DB-1 on 15 February 1944) and to ultimate survey and scrapping (in the case of the DB-2). For the remainder of the fleet, see the accompanying table.

So far as can be determined, the very last B-18 series aircraft struck from the AAF inventory was B-18A AC37-564, surveyed and scrapped on 31 March 1946.

Although a surprising number of B-18 series aircraft survived the war, nearly one-third of those built, the oldest and most weary, were simply stripped of useful components and smelted down, like Field Number 68 shown here. *via Rich Dann*

Since a number of B-18s are known to have been placed on the civil aircraft registers in several Latin American nations, and no known former US civil registrations are known, it would appear that these aircraft either (a) had a US registration or temporary licence that remains untraced, (b) they were sold surplus directly to a foreign buyer via the FLC, or (c) they were acquired by a US owner, never registered in the US and exported illegally without documentation.

Disposition of Aircraft Built as Type B-18

Disposition	Number of Aircraft
Class 26 (Ground Instructional Airframes)	6
Surveyed or Scrapped in Service due to all causes, including age, wear-and tear	45
Crashed or damaged sufficiently to be declared written off in service	27
Destroyed as the result of Enemy Action (Hawaii, Philippines)	30
Surplused to civil owners for which no known subsequent identities are known	2
Surplused to U.S. or foreign civil owners where registrations are known	15
To Brazilian Air Force under Lend-Lease	3

Disposition of Aircraft Built as Type B-18A

Disposition	Number of Aircraft
Class 26 (Ground Instructional Airframes)	20
Surveyed or Scrapped in Service due to all causes, including age, wear-and-tear	45
Crashed or damaged sufficiently to be declared written off in service	69
Destroyed as the result of Enemy Action (Caribbean, Atlantic)	5
Surplused at Stillwater, OK, no subsequent identity known	1
Surplused at Rome, NY, no subsequent identity known	1
Surplused at Ontario, CA, no subsequent identity known	1
Surplused at McKellar Field, TN, no subsequent identities known	22
Surplused at Bush Field, GA, no subsequent identities known	5
Surplused to U.S. or foreign civil owners where registrations are known	38
Surplused to RFC and scrapped while in their custody	8
To Brazilian Air Force under Lend-Lease	1

While appearing unutterably tired and worn, RB-18 AC36-279, originally accepted on 17 September 1937, the nineteenth B-18 delivered, still manages to sit proudly, like an old veteran in its vintage uniform, at McKellar Field, TN, around November 1944. Last operated by the 41st Sub Depot at Hamilton Field, CA, she had originally served overseas in Panama with the 19th Bomb Group, but spent most of the war in California. She became NC-63113 but was cancelled in January 1949 and her fate is unknown. *via Rich Dann*

US civil-registered B-18 series aircraft

As noted in the tables, at least fifteen B-18s and thirty-eight B-18A, B-18B or B-18C series aircraft – a total of no fewer than fifty-three aircraft – are known to have gained US civil registration markings and, where known, these are noted in the individual aircraft production listings in Annex 1. Although no Approved Type Certificate (ATC) was ever issued for B-18 series aircraft, they were authorized to gain US civil aircraft registrations on the basis of a Group 2 Category approval (No 2-577). Ironically, of the B-18s that survive to this day in US museums or private hands, every one of them owes its continued existence to the fact that it survived the war to gain US civil marks as a surplused aircraft. The AAF, under the guidance of General Arnold, set aside examples of many service types for one of the pet ideas of the wartime leader, a National Aviation Museum – but the B-18 did not figure in his listings of aircraft tagged for salvation.

The B-18 series had, in fact, been the subject of one earlier 'near miss' at entering civil, commercial service, and in a most unlikely set of circumstances. Had it happened, it would have been the first civil application of the type. During the war the US State Department and AAF officials grappled with the Central American creation of New Zealand adventurer Lowell Yerex, known as TACA (Transportes Aéreos Centro-Americano SA), which, the US finally conceded, was in actuality providing outstanding services through its several local national subsidiaries throughout Central America and the Caribbean and, more importantly, did not pose a significant threat to US defense interests in the region. Pan American Airways, of course, took a different view, from a strictly commercial standpoint, and worked tirelessly to defeat the TACA network.

One of TACA's primary difficulties during the war was acquiring replacement equipment for its decidedly weary fleet, which consisted for the most part of second- and third-hand aircraft of an amazing array of sources, the majority consisting of Ford Tri-motors. The one bright spot was a small number of Lockheed 14s that no one else seemed to want, and which Yerex acquired with his well-known aplomb.

One of his subsidiaries was British West Indian Airways (BWIA), which, while providing very good service to British territories in the Antilles and Caribbean region, was beset by the added difficulty of being viewed by the US as a strictly British problem and, by the hard-pressed British, as a convenient but rather unruly asset that they apparently would have preferred to see the US support. BWIA was also beset by equipment shortages, and late in the war Yerex appealed to Britain for help in acquiring, through whatever means, either more Lockheed 14s, DC-3s or demilitarised Hudsons or Lodestars, similar to the Lockheed 14s already on hand. The British, probably to the consternation of all concerned, offered him second-hand Vickers Wellington twin-engine bombers, which he was quick to point out had notoriously poor single-engine performance, not a desirable characteristic for an airline that flew the vast majority of its routes over shark-infested waters. Yerex, probably wisely, refused this offer.

The British then appealed to the US to render aid to BWIA, and, out of nowhere, the US made arrangements to propose the 'loan' to BWIA of two B-18s until such time as the Wellingtons could be converted and delivered to him, not knowing that Yerex had already declined the aircraft. It is not clear what B-18s the US had in mind for this extraordinary offer, but it does not require much imagination to consider that it may have been either several demilitarised early B-18s then in the hands of the AAF Air Transport Command Caribbean Wing, or even the two formally converted VIP C-58s. The entire matter quickly passed into obscurity, as Yerex would have been hard-pressed to convert B-18s to adequate passenger configuration, given the very limited wartime circumstances of firms capable of such work.

A combat veteran of numerous anti-submarine actions, noted in the earlier chronology, B-18C AC37-473, named 'Satan's Chariot', was photographed here after being surplused, probably at Chicago, when she became NC-4611V some time after November 1944. The aircraft later went to Mexico as XA-LUO.
Art Krieger via Brian R. Baker

Showing vestiges of her mottled dark green over olive-drab wartime camouflage, RB-18A AC37-554 was surplused at McKellar Field, TN, on 11 November 1944 and became NC-66809, which was finally cancelled in May 1965! The fate of the aircraft remains unknown. *via Rich Dann*

When the AAF started withdrawing B-18s from active service, the decision was apparently taken to concentrate the majority of these at two RFC storage locations: Bush Field, near Augusta, GA, and McKellar Field, near Jackson, TN, where the majority of them ended up. Precisely why these locations were selected remains a mystery, although the fact that the vast majority of B-18 series aircraft still airworthy were coming back from the Caribbean probably had a hand in the decision.

On 25 April 1946, not quite one month after the last B-18 was struck from the AAF inventory, the Civil Aeronautics Authority (CAA) approved all B-18, B-18A, B-18B and B-18B (Special) aircraft for a Group 2 Certification, No 2-577. The precise meaning of the description 'B-18B (Special)' is unknown but, since the B-18C was not included in the approval, it was probably intended for those few aircraft.

As will be noted in the individual aircraft summaries in Annex 1, the fifty-three aircraft that gained US civil registrations under the Group 2 approval were snapped up fairly quickly in the immediate post-war rush by any number of entrepreneurs, initially (by law) being veterans, who were given preference in acquiring war-surplus aircraft via the RFC and the War Assets Administration (WAA). Incredibly, the aircraft, although appearing tired and worn, were in remarkably good condition but, what was more important to the surplus buyers, the RFC and WAA had tagged

RB-18A AC37-572 has been stripped down after serving last with the 263rd Air Base Squadron at Baton Rouge, LA, where she was surplused in December 1944. Although sold, no civilian identity has been traced. *Ben L. Brown via Dave Menard*

Another anti-submarine campaign veteran, having been assigned to both the 7th and 9th Antisubmarine Squadrons, RB-18B AC38-591 shows the remnants of her dark sea gray over oyster white maritime camouflage to good advantage. The aircraft became NC-67274 after September 1944. *NASM 117042*

This post-war RB-18B was acquired by an unknown aerial spraying outfit, which took the trouble to paint nose art on the aircraft, a waif-like female form holding a huge insect in one hand and a bomb in the other, and nicknamed 'Miss Misty'. This is the aircraft now with the McChord Air Museum, and was thus AC37-505 and NC-67947. The scantily clad form was apparently repainted at some later date, as the restorers at McChord found far more 'clothing' on her later version! *via David W. Ostrowski*

A surprising number of B-18s were converted to huge crop-dusters, a duty that their 'Cadillac' handling characteristics and reliability made them peculiarly suitable for at cut-rate prices. This RB-18B has plumbing under both wings and twin propeller mixers under the nose. She has also been fitted with a third antenna blade on the upper nose. *via David W. Ostrowski*

So far as can be determined, the very first B-18 series aircraft to be approved for a CAA operating manual was NC-63056, RB-18 AC37-14, as of 17 January 1947. The aircraft was operated briefly by the CAA for unspecified duties as early as 2 December 1944, and may well have been the first B-18 with a civil registration. *Robert L. Taylor*

Probably the very last B-18 series aircraft authorised to fly with a civil registration in the US was N52056, formerly RB-18 AC37-29, shown here at Lambert Field, St Louis, MO, in April 1957. Identified at the time as a sprayer, there does not appear to be any visible evidence of spraying gear. *Bob Burgess via Brian R. Baker/Rich Dann*

them at between $1,000 and, at most, $3,000 each, complete! This was an astonishing bargain, as even surplus North American AT-6 Texan series aircraft were going for $1,500 each. It is important to note that, even though DC-3s and C-47s were by far the preferred aircraft, they came in at an average gross weight of 26,900lb, while the former B-18s, stripped of their military equipment and fitted with a variety of cargo-capable compartments and flooring arrangements, came in at only 21,000lb gross weight, which meant better economy of operation with only a relatively modest loss of interior capacity.

The vast majority of the B-18s acquired by surplus owners were almost immediately converted to freighters, and nearly all of these were placed into relatively intensive service by the myriad of non-scheduled operators that blossomed briefly in the immediate post-war boom. A number, however, were described in post-war government documents as '9PCLM' (meaning nine-place, cabin land monoplanes), which indicates that at least four were modified in some undocumented manner as passenger transports! By 31 December 1947, of the fifty-three surplused B-18s, only five were identified by the CAA as still being operated by non-schedule air carriers. The remainder had, for all intents and purposes, been reduced to 'tramp' freighter status.

So far as can be determined, the first B-18 to be approved for a CAA Approved Operating Manual was NC-63056, MSN 1875, formerly B-18 AC37-14, which was approved on 17 January 1947. This is perhaps not surprising, as, for reasons that are unclear, this aircraft had been transferred from the AAF to the Civil Aeronautics Authority (CAA) on 2 December 1944 for unspecified duties. The aircraft was subsequently acquired by a broker and converted, somehow, to one of the nine-place aircraft with passenger seats noted earlier, one of the few to be so converted. The last registered and active B-18 is a bit more difficult to determine, but was probably RB-18 AC37-29 (MSN 1890) as N52056, which was sold via a Wyoming firm in 1979 and is now on display at the Castle Air Force Base Museum in California.

The long-lived N52056 provides a convenient example of the multitude of tasks that were handed to surplus B-18s after the war – and the fact that the modifications made to them to accomplish these functions were amazing. N52056 last served with a fire suppression outfit in Wyoming, but not as a 'mud' dropper, as the aircraft was not legally cleared for that exacting duty. Instead, it was used for the less glamorous task of re-seeding burned areas from the air. A Volkswagen engine turning a GMC-6-71 blower was fitted in the rear fuselage, piped out via nozzles in and under the wings, and a huge hopper installed in the mid-section that held the seed, with even more in the former bomb bay area. The aircraft was sent into burned areas while the ground was still hot from the fast-moving fires, as better germination was achieved in that way. Unfortunately, there is no accurate account of how many hours N52056 flew on this low-altitude type of mission, but the aircraft was described as being nearly ideal for the task.

Above: N52056 with Fire Number B20 at Graybull, Wyoming, in October 1980. *via Guido E. Buehlmann 23597A HK-519*

Some civil operators acquired small 'fleets' of surplus B-18s, and these were mainly concentrated in California, Florida, Illinois, Philadelphia and New York, although odd examples turned up in strange places, such as Beckley, West Virginia, and Willow Run, Michigan. Unaccountably, at least twenty B-18s stored at McKellar Field, Jackson (Madison), Tennessee, for surplus disposal appear not to have gained any known civil marks, although some of them may have gone overseas to some of the otherwise undocumented civilian registrations known in Mexico, Honduras, Colombia, Peru, Brazil and elsewhere. For a listing of known aircraft registrations in these nations, see Annex 4.

Surviving B-18 series aircraft

Five B-18 series aircraft are known to still exist in museum collections, and possibly a sixth and seventh aircraft are derelict in Alaska and Hawaii. Ironically, but perhaps in keeping with the tradition of modification and adaptation witnessed throughout this account, every single one of the aircraft, except the derelict example in Hawaii, has been assembled or restored using parts of other aircraft, and none are completely 'original' in the truest sense of the term.

Thus the oldest existing B-18 still basically intact on the planet is B-18 AC36-446, which still apparently resides in a jungle-enveloped gully in the Kohola District, Waimanu, Hawaii, where it crashed on 25 February 1941.

It seems fitting that a part of the Hawaiian B-18 should be used in the restoration of a museum example and, after what can only be described as Herculean efforts, the all-volunteer B-18A Restoration Crew at the McChord Air Museum at McChord Air Force Base, Washington, managed to wrestle the extremely rare dorsal turret out of the Hawaiian B-18 and mate it with their aircraft. As many will note, the turret they retrieved at such personal cost was not correct for a B-18A, but given the fate that would certainly otherwise have befallen the turret had it been left on the original B-18 airframe in tropical Hawaii, perhaps this can be forgiven.

The authors had the pleasure of inspecting the McChord aircraft 'up close and personal' in mid-2007 in company with three members of the volunteer restoration crew, led by Herb Tollefson of Tacoma. This is of course B-18A AC37-505 (see Annex 1 for a complete service history synopsis), which survived the war to become NC-67947, then was sold into Mexico as XB-LAJ, where it had been flown extensively flying

AC36-446 was in remarkably good condition when photographed, and the insignia of the 50th Reconnaissance Squadron, to which it was assigned at the time of its accident, are still visible. The dorsal turret was removed and is now in place on the B-18A at the McChord Air Museum. *Gary Larkins, AirPirates.com*

The nineteenth B-18 lost after the aircraft series entered service, AC36-446 was mushed in under the command of Capt Boyd Hubbard Jr on 25 February 1941 near Waimanu, Kohola District, Hawaii. All aboard survived, and the aircraft remains in this jungle gully to this day, although rumors abound that it has been recovered. *Gary Larkins, AirPirates.com*

XB-LAJ, RB-18B MSN 2505, after her return from Mexico but before being registered as N18AC. *Eddy Gual*

The B-18A at the McChord Air Museum (AC37-505) was being stripped of the garish color scheme last worn while in Mexico, when the alert crew member noted the outline of what appeared to be nose art on the starboard side of the nose. The crew restored "Miss Misty" as best they could. *McChord Air Museum*

shrimp to market (with extensive corrosion in her guts as a direct result) and returned to the US as N18AC. It flew for the very last time in April 1971, when it was ferried from Watsonville to Tucson via Palm Springs by aircraft entrepreneur Keith Larkin.[39] Along the way, the aircraft passed through several temporary custodians including the AMARC facility at Davis-Monthan AFB, AZ, where the aircraft was held briefly on behalf of the National Air & Space Museum, before passing to the collections of the Pima Air & Space Museum, across the road from AMARC. Pima's staff, basically, excised what was needed from the airframe to aid in the restoration of their own B-18B (see below) before passing the hulk to the McChord group around October 1986.

"Miss Misty" is the revitalized nose art discovered during the paint stripping of the McChord Air Museum's B-18A. Although essentially accurate, the original female form had only a bearskin across her lap, and was apparently a civilian acquired nose-art item – not military. *Ted Young*

An absolutely outstanding restoration effort, carried out entirely by volunteers, B-18B AC37-505 has been returned to very near its original B-18A configuration with loving care. That said, it is rather a composite aircraft, with a B-18 dorsal turret, R4D wings, missing her distinctive over-the-cowling exhausts, and nose art actually worn in its former civil configuration as a sprayer as NC-67947. Otherwise the aircraft is immaculate in 17th Bomb Group livery. *Ted Young*

Still missing a number of internal equipment items, the McChord Air Museum B-18A, AC37-505, has been masterfully restored – to include fully functional bomb bay doors operated by Hagedorn Sr! The nose art, 'Miss Misty', was discovered during the removal of the former Mexican civil color scheme, and actually dates back to a US civil application on NC-67947, but in the most recent form. *Ted Young*

Between May 1983 and October 1994 the all-volunteer McChord B-18A Restoration Crew invested at least 25,214 man-hours in the airframe (the actual number was much higher than this, since no logs had been kept between May 1983 and October 1986). By February 1995 the complex lower section of the interior of the nose section had been dismantled and, to the surprise of the crew, the original bombardier's controls, cables and associated systems were all basically still intact. An enormous amount of energy went into reconstruction of the articulated bomb bay doors of the aircraft, which of course had been removed when the aircraft was converted to civilian use at some point after passing to civilian registry. The bomb bay door actuating cylinders were rebuilt by Northwest Hydraulic Systems in Tacoma.

By the time we inspected the aircraft in 2007, the McChord crew had invested not less than 40,000 man-hours in the effort, and still had a considerable amount of work left to perform. Their outstanding efforts were chronicled faithfully by *The Rip Chord*, the newsletter of the McChord Air Museum Foundation, starting as early as the July-September 1986 issue. Starting in historic Hangar 3, and by December 1986 numbering some 300 retirees who brought an enormous bounty of mechanical skills to the project, the crews started off working 5-hour shifts, convening at the time typically on Wednesdays, with usually up to fifteen crew members swarming over the sad aircraft. The first order of business was the nasty job of replacing corroded aluminum with new metal – a task very familiar to the crews, many of whom had been based at rainy McChord. The aircraft, as received, had lost most of her nose to the Pima museum. From the outset the intention was to mark the aircraft in the colors of the 73rd Bomb Squadron, 17th Bomb Group, the aircraft having actually served with the Group during 1942, based mainly at Geiger Field, Spokane, WA, but frequently operating in and out of McChord. By December 1986 the crew was actually led by two full-time USAF technicians, S/Sgt Bill Miranda and T/Sgt Tim Louden, and included retirees Cliff Bouchee, Al Birchman, Willy Bledsoe, Al Kamcheff, Glenn Lundberg, Glenn Morgan, Paul Morasch, Wes Reed, Jim Schmoker, Dillard Stevens, Herb Tollefson, Dale Turner, John Wilsco, Daryl Trent, Gordon Gisler, Carl Bell, Jim Midgette, Larry Moore, A. Scornaienchi and Don Beyl.

By June 1988 the McChord crew was engaged in the task of restoring the nose of their aircraft to B-18A configuration (it had been modified to a B-18B in January 1943 and retained that configuration even into post-war civil service, having the nose lopped off at Pima for their aircraft), and an extra work shift each week literally did 'nasal reconstruction surgery' for the aircraft, using original Douglas engineering drawings. They also faced the daunting task of fabricating a completely new bomb bay keep stiffener, in order to enable the crew to have sufficient strength to be towed. The original keel had been removed when the aircraft was converted to a freighter after the war. The aircraft also had been fitted, probably while in Mexico, with the wings from a Douglas R4D transport, which are not quite correct for a B-18 – but which fit almost perfectly when joined to the fuselage. Navigation and functioning landing lights were installed and all new cockpit glass was fitted.

In July 1989 the McChord Restoration Crew obtained a complete aft B-18 fuselage in Oregon (the origins of this aircraft are unknown), which was in remarkably good condition, and helped enormously with the corrosion problems associated with the original aft fuselage. By December the crew were working mainly in Hangar 1 and were devoting almost all of their time to finishing the keel, forming Plexiglas panels for the complex bombardier nose, making flooring and forming small parts for the fully restored bomb bay. Dennis Nyland of Creative Casting in Tacoma donated his time and materials to cast about forty of the unique bomb bay castings.

By June 1991 the McChord volunteers had constructed wooden forms in Hangar 4 to create the custom-built bomb bay doors for the aircraft (fully functional, and actuated by Dan Senior during his visit!), the brainchild of Milt James, working with other volunteers including Carl Schuler and Don Tracy. They matched the original Douglas blueprints exactly.

By March 1995, well into the ninth year of the McChord B-18A restoration, detail work on the nose section and the bomb bay doors continued, and the crew entry door had been rebuilt, using parts from one donated from an owner in Oregon. The main cabin interior floor over the bomb bay had been restored, but radio racks, seats and miscellaneous plumbing still lay ahead. Glenn Morgan was the crew chief.

Well into the eleventh year of the project, by June 1997 LTC Don Tracy, USAF (Ret), who had for some time been the solitary machinist on the team, was joined by Len Vail and Bob Meeker, and an expedition to Tucson in 1995 had netted a much-needed rudder post for the aircraft. Len Vail also produced very faithful replica .30 caliber machine guns for the aircraft and, between the active USAF 446th Maintenance Squadron and Clover Park Technical College, all of the complex flight control cables had been installed and rigged.

A close look at the instrument panel in the McChord B-18A reveals that at least six of the flight instruments on the starboard (right/co-pilot's) side of the cockpit are turned 90° to the right, including the Manifold Pressure Gauge, RPM Indicator, Carburetor Temperature Gauge and Oil Temperature Gauge. This standard configuration for a B-18A instrument panel is obscure but accurate, but the precise reasons for this arrangement are unknown. At least six of the co-pilot's instruments – but not all of them – were so arranged.

When the McChord team stripped the rather garish former Mexican color scheme from N18AC/XB-LAJ (on which some wag had spray-painted the name 'B-18 Bummer' while at AMARC, devoid of wings), they were surprised to find the remains of 'nose art' on the starboard forward fuselage. The provenance of the female image, perched on a cloud and named 'Miss Misty', is unknown, but may well date from her wartime service. Although the exact colors are unknown, the crew have attempted to reconstruct the image to the best of their ability and – although incorrect for the pre-war color scheme selected – retain the artwork as an integral part of the history of the aircraft.

The outstanding National Museum of the United States Air Force (NMUSAF) at Wright-Patterson Air Force Base, Ohio, has actually had two B-18 series aircraft in its collections. The first was B-18A AC39-25, which came to the museum via a rather curious set of circumstances. At some point in her post-war civil career as NC-62477, the aircraft had a truly ugly fiberglass nose grafted over the former 'shark mouth' nose and, as late as October 1958, had been for some time involved in ferrying arms and ammunition, quite illegally, to the embattled Batista regime in Cuba – all the while still carrying her US civil registration, which by that time was painted as simply N62477. Nominally, the aircraft was operated

The very oddly modified B-18 that the (then) U.S. Air Force Museum displayed outside at its old facility at Wright-Patterson AFB, OH, as it appeared as of June 9, 1963. This is one of the first color slides ever taken by your scribe! The markings are a complete fiction, aside from the modernized serial number, AC39-25. *Author*

by crews of the Cuban Fuerza Aérea de Ejercito de Cuba (Cuban Army Air Force), and was thus shown on Cuban Air Order of Battle documents for the period, although she never wore Cuban insignia at the time. The aircraft was seized by the US Customs Service in Florida and eventually turned over to the (then) USAF Museum at its old facility at Wright Field. There it was displayed with completely spurious post-war-style USAF insignia. The aircraft was practically gutted and resembled an actual B-18 in a cosmetic sense only. When the USAF finally acquired a more complete aircraft in the 1980s, AC39-25 was transferred to Cannon Air Force Base Memorial Park, New Mexico. Still later, when the Wings Over The Rockies Air Museum was formed at the former Lowry Air Force Base near Denver, CO, the staff there somehow managed to reconfigure the aircraft to a very handsome B-18A configuration, and she is now comfortably ensconced in their hangar there.

The first of two B-18s that joined the collections of the National Museum of the United States Air Force was B-18A AC39-25, which was surplused to become NC-62477 in very stock configuration as shown here in the 1950s. *via Rich Dann*

By the time the first B-18 joined the collections at the National Museum of the United States Air Force, it had experienced a rather spotty post-war career, including a stint running guns to the beleaguered Batista regime in Cuba in the late 1950s as N62477, and had been heavily modified with a truly ugly fiberglass nose. The NMUSAF staff dutifully marked it with 'U.S. Air Force' markings, post-war national insignia, and a 'correct' post-war presentation of the radio call number, 90025! The aircraft subsequently was fully restored to B-18A configuration and is now at the Wings Over The Rockies Air & Space Museum in Denver. *Art Krieger via Brian R. Baker*

The NMUSAF then acquired B-18A AC37-469 some time in 1994, which had somehow survived extensive use as NC-56847 and, in Mexico, as XB-KEA. The NMUSAF restoration crew did an outstanding job of restoring the aircraft to full exterior B-18A configuration. Former Research Team Leader at NMUSAF and noted aero-historian Dave Menard, who took part in the restoration, confessed, however, that many of her interior systems defied full restoration. The aircraft is marked in the colorful pre-war markings of the 38th Reconnaissance Squadron, although no evidence has been found linking this particular aircraft with that unit. The aircraft was assigned to Wright Field for a protracted period between December 1938 and 1942 for test purposes, however.

B-18A AC39-25 as she appears today in a place of honor at the Wings Over The Rockies Air & Space Museum at the former Lowry AFB, Denver, CO. The restoration crews faced a daunting task reconfiguring the former civilly installed fiberglass nose, and while the results are not 100% accurate, given what they had to work with, it is very respectable. *Photo reprinted courtesy of Wings Over The Rockies Air & Space Museum, Denver, CO*

The second B-18 to join the collection at the National Museum of the United States Air Force was AC37-469. After extensive wartime use in the US, including a number of test functions, the aircraft passed to civil status as NC-56847, and is pictured here very late in her civil life as merely N56847 before going to Mexico as XB-KEA. *via Dave Ostrowski*

Although nice to look at, the checkered engine cowl paint job on 38th Reconnaissance Squadron, 19th Bomb Group B-18s stationed at March Field, CA in the pre-war days must have been a maintenance headache. *NMUSAF 00018)*

B-18A AC-37-469 is painted to represent R-33 of the 38th Reconnaissance Squadron, although it is not clear if it was ever actually assigned to that unit at Albuquerque, NM. Although immaculate, like the McChord Air Museum B-18, it has the incorrect dorsal turret. *Boeing/McDonnell Douglas HG83162*

The B-18 now at the Castle Air Museum in California is AC37-29, where it is marked as R 38 and displayed outdoors, the one and only 'straight' B-18 on display anywhere. A former 9th, 2nd and 29th Bomb Group aircraft, its description at the Castle Air Museum states that it was 'equipped with airborne radar and submarine detection gear' and that it was engaged in 'anti-submarine patrol along the east coast of the United States and the Caribbean'. So far as your scribe can determine, this aircraft was never fitted with any ASV or MAD gear, although it may have participated in anti-submarine patrols as a 'straight' B-18 along the east coast early in the war. After the war, it became NC-52056 and was flown by Southern Air Express of New Smyrna Beach, FL, as a freighter. The engines were changed to Wright R-1820-53s in April 1947, a change made on many post-war B-18s. Much later, it passed to Christler & Avery Aviation in Graybull, WY, where it was outfitted as an aerial sprayer for both agricultural and pest spraying – certainly one of the largest aircraft ever configured in that way. It was last operated by the famed Hawkins & Powers Aviation of Graybull. This owner than traded the aircraft to the NMUSAF for unspecified items, and the NMUSAF ceded it to Castle. The Castle Air Museum quite rightly claims that the aircraft made the very last flight of a B-18, on 26 October 1981.

The Castle Air Museum aircraft is very nearly a textbook case of how the provenance of museum-owned aircraft can become obscured through what this writer terms the Law of Unintended Consequences! As might be expected, it did not have bomb bay doors by the time of its last flight. Meanwhile, the Pima Air & Space Museum at Tucson, AZ, had acquired a second B-18A, which had nominally been on the books of the NMUSAF as of the early 1980s. This was AC37-505, now in the custody of the McChord Air Museum noted above. When it passed AC37-505 to McChord, the NMUSAF sent its damaged right and left (upper) bomb bay doors to Castle, which is why the team at McChord were obliged to hand-craft replacements. Then, some time in 1984, the Pima Air & Space Museum loaned its B-18B's (see below) bomb bay doors to Aero Nostalgia in Stockton, CA, which used it as a template to make a 'new' right bomb bay door out of fiberglass for the Castle aircraft. The left door was never made, due to financial challenges, and thus remained open to the elements until 1992.

The forward turret in the Castle aircraft was only 50% complete when it arrived, having at some point been crudely reversed and sealed for civilian configuration. The Castle crew were thus obliged to essentially reconstruct the entire turret.

However, pride of place for extant B-18 series aircraft must go to the Pima Air & Space Museum at Tucson, and in particular to the dedication of 'Lumpy' Lumpkin, who spearheaded the restoration of AC38-593 to full B-18C configuration. Dan Hagedorn Sr was afforded the privilege of examining this aircraft in every detail, and found both the exterior and interior detailing exceptionally well detailed in late 1942 and early 1943 configuration. Although the

The B-18 at the Castle Air Museum in California, AC37-29, is the only 'straight' B-18 on public display anywhere, although rather inaccurately painted and marked. The unit designator and individual aircraft number on the vertical fin, at one time R-38, has also been BI-24, as shown, suggesting that it represents a 9th Bomb Group aircraft. The overall gray paint scheme is unfortunate but, given that it is displayed in the open air, hopefully helps protect it from the elements. It holds the distinction of having been the last B-18 to fly, on 26 October 1981. *via Al Hensen*

This is B-18C AC-38-593 as she appeared on 18 January 1991, just before extensive restoration commenced, but after having been acquired by the Pima Air & Space Museum, Tucson, AZ, from Roberts Aircraft Co on 11 February 1976 as the former NC-66267. *Sam Smith*

'official' record does not address it, this aircraft, with the fixed forward-firing .50 caliber gun properly located in the lower-right fuselage, entitles it to be designated as a B-18C. Unfortunately, the magnificent restoration carried out by the Pima crew is being endangered by its continued exposure to the extremely harsh Arizona heat and sunlight, and the aircraft would benefit enormously by being housed under cover as soon as possible. It had been NC-66267 in its civil career, and was acquired by the Museum in February 1976 and, after a number of rather confusing exchanges, noted in part above, was restored in 4th Antisubmarine Squadron markings by 1994.

The fate of the last three B-18s on the US Civil Aircraft Register remains something of a mystery. N1043M, MSN 2624, was last registered to William L. Rausch of 15 52nd Street, Hasbrouck Heights, NJ, while N62477, MSN 2673, was with an unknown owner in Oklahoma City, OK, with, according to the FAA, 'sale reported'. N67931, MSN 1883, identified in FAA records as type 'Douglas B-18 Special', was last known owned by Aero Enterprises Inc, Anchorage, Alaska, as of 1971.

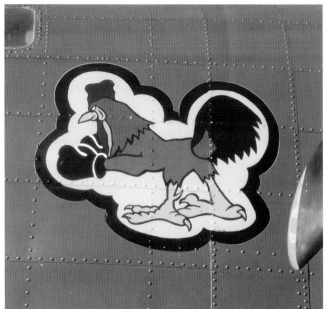

A close-up view of the unit insignia of the 4th Antisubmarine Squadron (ASRON) as worn on the Pima B-18C in November 1996, not long after painting. The color scheme selected is probably open to debate. *via Robert Dorr*

The Pima Air & Space Museum can take justifiable pride in the remarkable restoration it performed, both externally and internally, on B-18C AC38-593, the former NC-66267. Here, the aircraft is essentially complete but awaiting the installation of her bomb bay doors, and gives a unique opportunity to appreciate just how long they were. *Robert L. Taylor*

The only B-18 or B-23 series aircraft preserved outside the United States, this former Ecuatoriana aircraft was HC-APV, MSN 2717 and AC39-31. Converted to UC-67 configuration during the war, Ecuatoriana acquired her in December 1968. She is now in the Ecuadorian Air Force Museum at Guayaquil minus any identifying marks. *Dick Lohuis*

What makes a B-18C different from a B-18B? Note the forward-firing .50 caliber machine gun barrel protruding from the forward lower nose. Some B-18Cs had the single gun positioned just inside the lower right Plexiglas area. The pilot was provided with a 1920s ring-and-bead sight forward of his windscreen! *Author*

Below: Identified in Federal Aviation Administration records as a 'Douglas B-18 Special', N67931 was MSN 1883 was last reported registered to Aero Enterprises Inc of Anchorage, Alaska, as of 1971. Her fate is unknown. Note the RDF loop on the forward fuselage. *via David W. Ostrowski*

CHAPTER SEVENTEEN

Foreign B-18 use

Besides the sterling service provided by the Canadian DB-280 Digbys noted earlier in this account, a small but surprising number of B-18 series aircraft saw both military and civil service in foreign settings.

Australia

Although cited elsewhere in the text, at least four (and possibly five) survivors of the ill-fated B-18 fleet stationed in the Philippines at the time of the Japanese onslaught managed to reach Brisbane, Australia, where they were operated, once conditions stabilised somewhat, as part of the thrown-together 21st Troop Carrier Squadron. This ad hoc unit, officially organised on 28 January 1942 at Amberley Royal Australian Air Force Station near Brisbane, was issued a simple directive: to 'ensure all US transport airplanes now in Australia, and all combat airplanes flyable but unfit for combat, will be part of Air Transport Command.' It is seldom mentioned that, at least initially, the unit was referred to simply as the Air Transport Command, Archerfield, and was not formally designated by USAAF order as the

On the orders of none other than General 'Hap' Arnold himself, the Caribbean Defense Command in Panama was directed to supply the Força Aérea Brasileira (FAB) with two B-18s 'without delay' in January 1942, and this image shows the aircraft arriving, bearing 9th Bomb Group unit designators. There is only one problem with this image: the first two aircraft acquired by Brazil, officially handed over on 4 April 1942, were both 'straight' B-18s, while the aircraft shown here are both B-18As! *Pan Am Archives, University of Miami*

21st Transport Squadron until 3 April 1942 and, finally, the 21st Troop Carrier Squadron on 26 July 1942.

The unit, in fact, operated as the US element of the Allied Directorate of Air Transport, known by the acronym ADAT, which had also been assembled to coordinate the nearly desperate need for Allied air transport in the Southwest Pacific.

The first aircraft assigned to the 21st TCS were three B-18s, a Douglas C-39, a Boeing B-17C, five nearly brand-new Douglas C-53s ('found' aboard a ship in the first convoy that had started for the Philippines, but which had wisely docked at Brisbane on 22 December 1941) and three Consolidated LB-30 Liberators. The unit also inherited nearly all of the aircraft of the former Dutch KNILM airlines that survived the Japanese onslaught, and by March 1942 these consisted of three Lockheed 14s, eight Lockheed Model 18s (which the USAAF referred to as C-56s), three Douglas DC-5s, two Douglas DC-3s and two Douglas DC-2s. Between January and July 1942 the motley assortment of transports reportedly flew some 5 million air miles in support of the Allied defenses in the region, a truly amazing testament to a little-known organisation.

Of the B-18s assigned, only two were initially identified. One was AC36-343, which had been issued the Australian quasi-civil radio call sign VH-COB (according to the official USAAF history of the unit) by February 1942, and which was later transferred out of the unit on 10 October 1942). The other was AC37-16, which became VH-OWB (again, according to the official USAAF history) in January 1942, also being transferred in September 1942.

B-18 36-343 Artwork by Rich Dann

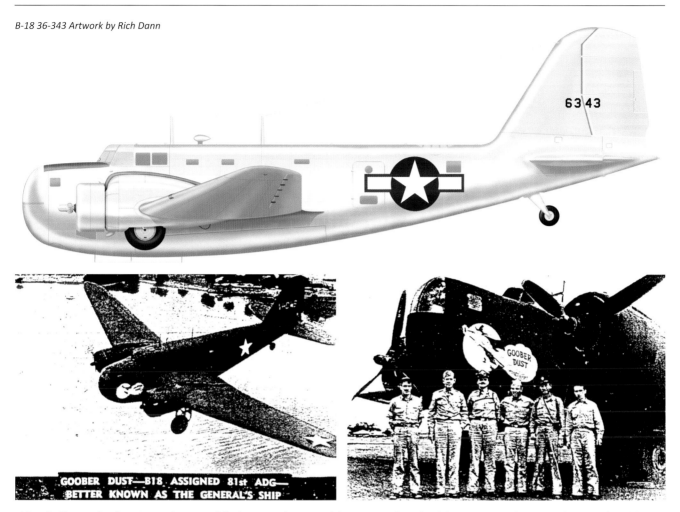

GOOBER DUST—B18 ASSIGNED 81st ADG—
BETTER KNOWN AS THE GENERAL'S SHIP

Although of low quality, these images show one of the four B-18s that survived the US retreat from the Philippines to Australia, VHCWB, bearing rather elaborate nose art and the nickname 'Goober Dust' while flying with the 81st Aerodrome Defense Group as a General's hack. This was almost certainly AC37-16, which had previously served in California, Hawaii, the Philippines, Java and finally Australia – certainly a record for international assignments for the type! *via Buz Busby*

In fact, the Australian radio call signs for these aircraft were apparently corrupted somewhere along the line before being recorded in the 'official' histories, as the correct call signs for the first two aircraft were actually VH-CCB and VH-CWB (given in some documents, for reasons unknown, as VHC-CB and VHC-WB, although CHC-CB is known to be an error for VHC-BB). These radio call signs were painted in rather prominent white characters over the camouflage finishes of the aircraft on either the vertical tail surfaces or rear fuselages. VHC-WB, while assigned later to the 81st ADG, carried a rather prominent example of 'nose art' and was nicknamed 'Goober Dust', but as it was apparently used almost exclusively as a VIP transport for General Connell, it was usually just cited as 'The General's Ship'. This aircraft, incredibly, survived until at least the end of the war on the Seventh Air Force Order of Battle.

The third B-18 utilised by the ADAT, possibly AC36-434, has frequently been cited as VHC-WA, but this has now been confirmed as having been a C-53, although radio call signs VHC-BB (or VHC-BR, reported by some sources as being AC36-343 between February and October 1942) and VHC-DX have also been associated with B-18s in Australia, and it has been suggested that these were used on AC37-16.

Seldom noted is the fact that the 21st TCS was augmented on 3 April 1942 by the creation of a second Troop Carrier Squadron, the 22nd TCS, formed by a cadre of 21st TCS personnel. By 21 May 1942, this unit, also operating under the ADAT umbrella, possessed one Boeing B-17, no fewer than eleven Lockheed Model 18s (C-56s), two Douglas C-39s, one Douglas C-47 and one Lockheed 14, and was temporarily assigned one of the B-18s and one C-53.

Brazil

None other than General Henry H. 'Hap' Arnold himself, acting on instructions from President Roosevelt, sent an urgent telegram to the Commanding General of the US Caribbean Defense Command on 22 January 1942, less than two months after Pearl Harbor. In it, he issued the following unequivocal orders:

'You will issue necessary orders moving two B-18s and 10 P-36s now in the CDC to Fortaleza, Brazil, to accomplish the following: transfer two B-18s and 10 P-36s from CDC without delay to the Chief of Military Aviation Mission to Brazil.'

It must be observed that this extraordinary order came as a direct result of the very high anxiety amongst the US leadership regarding Axis influence in Latin America and, as a minimum, the sincere hope that these erstwhile Western Hemispheric 'neighbours' might at least sever diplomatic relations, a crucial question at the Rio de Janeiro Conference of Foreign Ministers of earlier that month. Roosevelt telephoned General Marshall, the US Chief of Staff, on 19 January and asked him point-blank what munitions could be made '… immediately available to the South American nations, particularly to Brazil, to reassure them of the determination of the United States to guard the Americas against external attack.' General Marshall dutifully gathered together a list of some 150 coastal artillery pieces and mortars of various calibers. But this listing fell on deaf ears; what the South American nations wanted was modern equipment, and in particular combat aircraft and modern anti-aircraft guns.

B-18 AC36-300 was the first ex-USAAC aircraft officially' turned over to Brazil, via the US Military Aviation Mission, on 4 April 1942. It is pictured here at Campo dos Afonsos, still bearing its US radio call number, which was adopted as the FAB serial, 6300, on 12 June 1942. Brazilian sources state that this was the 'arrival' of the aircraft 'after a long flight from the US', but this seems at odds with known delivery and turn-over dates. The unique Brazilian 'star' national insignia was rather crudely painted over the US insignia. *Jose de Alvarenga*

The individual aircraft number '32' on the nose of this B-18 identifies it as AC37-32, the second B-18 supplied to Brazil by the US. The unusual camouflage scheme is noteworthy, and the national insignia has obviously been more artfully applied, suggesting a much later than delivery image. This picture was probably taken at Recife Air Base, Pernambuco, in 1943 or early 1944. *Jose de Alvarenga*

The starboard side of Brazilian B-18 AC37-32, probably at Recife Air Base, Pernambuco, Brazil in 1943 or early 1944. *Jose de Alvarenga*

This aircraft carries a rarity, a wartime Brazilian nickname 'Vira-Lata', which translates, roughly, as 'ownerless dog that turns over rubbish cans to get food'! The significance of the numeral '6' on the extreme nose probably indicates that this is FAB 5026, the late Brazilian serial number for the former AC36-300. *Jose de Alvarenga*

Brazil had, as of this date, not yet been included in the umbrella of the Lend-Lease program, although the immediate predecessor of Lend-Lease, the Defense Aid program, was 'made to fit', and, retrospectively, for fiscal reasons, two of the four B-18 series aircraft eventually offset to Brazil were in fact covered by Lend-Lease Project B-54220. These two aircraft (former Sixth Air Force B-18s AC36-300 and 37-32) were 'officially' handed over on 4 April and 8 May 1942, although in fact they had arrived at Recife in February.

This was a highly significant event, as it marked the first instance in which the United States had transferred modern, multi-engine bombardment aircraft to any nation other than Great Britain in a strictly government-to-government arrangement. Indeed, Brazil remained the solitary Latin American nation to receive bombardment aircraft during the war under Lend-Lease, Mexico not receiving a trio of B-25Js until after VE Day.

Although initially bearing US marks as '6300' and '7032' and flown by mixed US and Brazilian crews, mainly on the north-east 'hump' of Brazil, the aircraft eventually had Brazilian national insignia painted on and were issued Força Aérea Brasileira (FAB) serial numbers FAB-5026 and 5027.

In April 1944 a third B-18, AC36-286, which by then had been converted to B-18B configuration, was offset on a special program for delivery to the Brazilian Air Force Mechanics Training School. Several accounts allege that this aircraft was totally wrecked in Guatemala on its delivery flight. If so, it must have been replaced by another aircraft, as FAB Air Order of Battle data clearly show the service with a total of four B-18s as of 14 June 1946; one B-18B series aircraft was in fact delivered to the school and at least one photo shows it with the lower half of its nose radar radome scrubbed clear, suggesting that the radar gear was not delivered with the aircraft. The identity of this aircraft, if not AC36-286, remains unknown, and the aircraft was not issued an FAB serial number. This was one of the very few 'straight' B-18s converted to B-18B configuration.

A fourth B-18, in this case B-18A 37-596, was apparently issued as a replacement for AC36-286, and was officially handed over on 10 April 1944, gaining FAB serial 5073.

B-18s were last reported on the Brazilian Order of Battle for 14 June 1946, when a total of four were reported.

As noted below in the discussion of Cuban B-18s, at least two and possibly three B-18s had Brazilian civil aviation connections, although these are rather tenuous.

US entrepreneur Harold Wemmer, who owned three aircraft, RB-18 NC-66115 (MSN 1701), and RB-18As NC-66114 and NC-66116 (MSN 2607 and 2628), ostensibly 'sold' at least two of these, MSN 2607 and 1701, to a Brazilian freight airline, SAVAG, where they were to have become PP-SBB and PP-SBC respectively. In fact, the aircraft

Brazil B-18 Artwork by Rich Dann

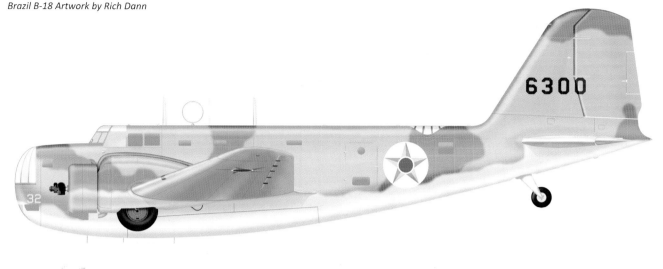

This photo of a Brazilian B-18, while of marginal quality, holds a number of interesting oddities. First, the nose turret gun is in place. Second, the engine cowlings appear to have been painted a bright color, and third, of course, the unusual insignia, possibly associated with the Parque de Aeronautica de São Paulo, a depot organisation. *Jose de Alvarenga*

The Brazilian Air Force also received one B-18B, AC36-286, apparently minus its radar, for use as a training aid, and students and faculty at the Mechanics Training School pose here with the aircraft, which has apparently had the lower portion of its Plexiglas radome scrubbed clear. *Jose de Alvarenga*

This post-war photo is unique, as it shows Brazilian B-18 FAB-63 (probably the former AC36-300) stripped to bare metal and sitting alongside Lockheed C-60s, another B-18 and a host of BT-13s and Vultee A-35s at the Parque de Aeronautica de São Paulo. *Jose de Alvarenga*

A very rare photo, even if of low quality. Brazil received only one B-18A, AC37-596, for use by the Mechanics Training School as an airworthy training aid. It is pictured here with a somewhat modified bombardier glazing area. *Jose de Alvarenga*

appear instead to have been intended for use by the short-lived and ill-fated revolutionary attempt to invade and topple the regime of Rafael Trujillo in the Dominican Republic from the Cuban launch point at Cayo Confites. The aircraft apparently did make it to Cuba, and available evidence seems to suggest that they were entered onto the Cuban civil register by 1951 (qv). The third aircraft, however, MSN 2628, is also known to have had connections with Mexican civil registration XB-BUR (qv), although the order is not clear.

This entire scenario is confounded, however, by yet another Brazilian operator, Transportes Aéreos Sul-Americanos (TASA), of São Paulo, RG, which is also known to have reserved registrations for the same two aircraft noted above – MSN 2607 (as PP-SVB) and MSN 1701 (as PP-SVC) – on or about 16 August 1948. TASA had been founded in February 1948, and did in fact acquire a DC-3 (PP-SVA), but had disappeared by January 1949, which may not be coincidental. The proximity of that reservation date to the aborted Cayo Confites revolutionary activity, and the similarity of the reserved Brazilian registrations, PP-SBB vice PP-SVB and PP-SBC vice PP-SVC, cannot be ignored. In any event, reputable Brazilian aviation historians Captain Carlos Dufriche and Alvaro Avarenga report that these aircraft apparently never reached Brazil and, if they did in fact don the provisional registrations noted, no photos of either have ever surfaced – nor have any photos of NC-66114 to -66116 nor the three Cuban civil registrations ever turned up.

The first of two aircraft known to have gone to Colombia, N1037M was B-18B AC37-527, shown here at Miami before heading south in 1954. Note how the dorsal gun turret location has been permanently faired over. *David W. Ostrowski*

The former B-18B AC37-527 and N1037M is seen after arrival in Colombia and receiving registration HK-367 with La Urraca/Alvaro Henao Jaramillo. The aircraft was lost in an accident on 22 January 1965. Here it appears to have had its fuselage painted a dark color and the wings a light color, and is due for some rather heavy maintenance! *via Gustavo Arias*

The second B-18 known to have gone to Colombia was N1692M, shown here as a sprayer with its US operator ACE – note the tail-mounted spray apparatus. What appears to be a protuberance over the rear fuselage is the tail fin of another B-18 in the background. *Doug Olson via Brian R. Baker*

The identity of the second B-18 to go to Colombia was AC37-534, also a converted B-18B. Here it is shown operating in 'el campo' under very harsh conditions with the bush airline La Urraca, registered HK-537, with its logo just visible on the heavily modified nose. *via Gustavo Arias*

Colombia

At least two B-18 series aircraft gained civil registrations in Colombia.

The first of these was HK-367, MSN 2527, which was NC-1037M and which was cancelled in September 1954 as sold to the Alvaro Henao-Jaramillo brothers' Lineas Aéreas La Urraca, based at Villavicencio. It apparently also carried the suffix 'E' as HK-367E at some point, which indicates that it was regarded as an oil exploration support aircraft. It was lost between Parana and Pichuna on either 22 or 26 January 1965.

The second Colombian aircraft was MSN 2534, the former NC-/N1692M, which was also acquired by Lineas Aéreas La Urraca. It was apparently acquired some time around October 1958 as HK-537 and some reports suggest that it survived as late as 1968. Little is known about the use of these aircraft in Colombia.

This is probably the nose of Lineas Aéreas La Urraca B-18B HK-537, again very heavily modified. It is possible that this is yet a third, unidentified, B-18 acquired by the bush operator. *Authors' collection*

Colombian B-18B HK-367-E is seen in happier days with La Urraca lettered on the extreme nose and the line's distinctive bird insignia on the starboard nose. The 'E' suffix to the registration is for 'Exploración', indicating that the aircraft was engaged in oilfield support duties at the time. *Harold G. Martin Collection, Kansas Aviation Museum*

An extraordinarily rare photograph, this is the Caribbean Legion B-18B that became TG-CIL-54, nominally registered to Leopoldo T. Castillo and, later, Luis Arenas Barrera, which crashed en route to Mexico on 8 February 1958. It is keeping company, in the Fuerza Aérea Guatemalteca area at Guatemala City's La Aurora airport, with an FAG C-47 and the Caribbean Legion's Lockheed 14! On the original photo, a circular insignia can be seen to have been scrubbed off the rear fuselage of the B-18B. *NARA RG342 IR-43-53*

Guatemala

In mid-December 1957 a single RB-18B (although listed officially as type RB-18A) was entered on the civil register of Guatemala as TG-CIL-54 to Leopoldo T. Castillo; it was MSN 2458, the former AC37-458 and NC-/N67946. This aircraft is often linked with the elusive Costa Rican aircraft, TI-205, but does not appear to have been the same airplane. By 14 February 1958 the registered owner was given as Luis Arenas Barrerea. The aircraft reportedly crashed on 8 February 1958 27 miles north-east of Ixcan and was written off en route to Mexico, with the three crew members on board suffering injuries. Oddly, another owner is also cited for the Guatemalan sojourn of this aircraft, one J. L. Crenar.

Haiti

Although an instance of circumstance, it appears from available evidence that the Government of Haiti acquired title to a single Douglas RB-18B, AC37-495, via a rather curious route.

This aircraft had in fact crashed at sea on 31 March 1944, just offshore of Roche-a'Bateau, Haiti, while under the command of Robert Alan, 35th Bomb Squadron, operating from distant Atkinson Field, British Guiana. It was apparently regarded as uneconomical to recover and the Army finally condemned it at the crash site.

On 7 June 1944 the USAAF received a formal request from the Haitian Government for the aircraft. In fact, what the Haitians wanted were the engines and props, as well as other salvageable items. Exactly what they intended to do with them is unclear, as they had no aircraft capable of mounting such engines or props, so it can only be surmised that they apparently intended to sell them for profit! Thus, adding Haiti to the 'owners' of B-18 series aircraft is only in the academic and legal sense.

Honduras

One former RB-18B, MSB 2574, became XH-016 on the early Honduran civil register as late as 21 September 1949, and was formerly NC-66281. Virtually nothing is known about the Honduran tenure of this aircraft, although it has been suggested that it was used by Transportes Aéreos Nacionales (TAN) airlines. Although reportedly sold into Mexico, it is also reliably reported to have crashed in January 1948 at Catacamos, killing three on board. By all accounts, it may have been TAN's first aircraft.

Costa Rica

An exceptionally well-travelled B-18 played the starring role in an epic that had all of the hallmarks of stereotypical 'Banana Republic' intrigue in the early post-war years.

The arrival of the aircraft in question at La Sabana Airport, San Jose, Costa Rica, intended for delivery to the local airline TAN, resulted in an accident on 15 October 1947. It was being flown by none other than the legendary Jimmy Angel and Arlington Willaur at the time, and was clearly identified as RB-18A NC-67852 (MSN 2646), formerly AC38-596.

The aircraft was subsequently repaired in the local TACA shops, but by that time Costa Rica had been subjected to internecine civil strife and a change of government and, for the first time, had set about organising an Army for national defense against exile forces organising in Nicaragua – as well as a small air arm.

On 16 August 1948 the sitting Costa Rican government, in the person of General Figueres, had formally requested export authorisation for five Lockheed P-38 Lightnings, a single Douglas A-24 Dauntless, and one Douglas B-18. The P-38s and the A-24 were located in California (only two of the P-38s and the A-24 were actually acquired there, and one of the P-38s and the A-24 crashed before they could be delivered). These aircraft had been acquired with the aid of some $40,000 contributed by General Juan Rodriguez, and were intended from the outset to be brought to Costa Rica for later use by the Caribbean Legion. The B-18, on the other hand, was already in Costa Rica and

Believed to have been RB-18A NC-67852, this was one of at least two B-18s that became involved with TAN airlines of Costa Rica, the Caribbean Legion and the little-known 'Costa Rican Air Force'. According to a participant, the aircraft had one .50 caliber gun mounted in the nose, and Legionnaires aboard fired sub-machine guns from the fuselage windows during the civil war. *Harold G. Martin*

marked locally as TI-205; it was nominally owned by Leon Pacheco, a professor at the Universidad Nacional de Costa Rica, who had gained title to the aircraft, somehow, from the new government around June or July 1949. This was undoubtedly NC-67852, ownership of which was tied up in a legal dispute, as TAN had gone bankrupt and the TACA shops had a mechanics lien against the aircraft for the work they had performed. Pacheco had, in the meantime, gone ahead and provisionally registered the aircraft in Costa Rica.

A US intelligence report, dated 30 November 1949, suggested that the Pacheco B-18 had actually been turned over to him only nominally, and that the aircraft had '…actually been sold to a Nicaraguan revolutionary of the Conservative party, General Carlos Pasos, but concealed the true buyer because of restrictions imposed upon the Costa Rican government by the original Export License granted in the US.' Immediately following the inauguration of President Ulate on 8 November, the B-18 was flown to Guatemala (apparently on the 11th) where it was apparently turned over to the custody of the Fuerza Aérea Guatemalteca (FAG, but see below). The intelligence report suggested that General Pasos did this in order to keep the aircraft, it being known that President Ulate would not support or permit any revolutionary activities in Costa Rica, or else that he sold the aircraft outright to the Guatemalan government.

But that is not the end of the Costa Rican connection. Pioneer Costa Rican aviator and airline entrepreneur Roman Macaya, in a letter to the author, revealed that this aircraft, while being repaired by the TACA shops, had been fitted with a heavy machine gun in the area of the former .30 caliber ball mount under the nose, and had in fact been painted in 'Costa Rican Air Force' markings at the time. This was, of course, before the new government essentially disbanded the 'air force'.

But as early as the afternoon of 22 April 1949, long before the aircraft had been flown out of Costa Rica to Guatemala, TI-205, in company with none other than two fully marked FAG Douglas C-47s, had been very actively engaged in transporting Caribbean Legion arms from Costa Rica, where they had failed to topple the government, to Guatemala. The blatant use of fully marked FAG aircraft was occasioned by the fact that the Guatemalan government had loaned the arms to the Legion and that the aircraft, including the B-18, were carrying not only Legion arms actually the property of the Costa Rican government, but also other arms exclusively the 'property' of the Legion. These included .30 and .50 caliber machine guns, rifles and pistols. FAG officers taking part in this extraordinary airlift included Teniente Coronel Julio Archila and Eduardo Weymann, as well as Mayor Carlos H. Sarti and Luis Urrutia de Leon. Apparently the airlift was carried out with the full knowledge and consent of the Commander of the FAG, Teniente Coronel Francisco Cosenza G.

During May 1949, after the airlift was completed, and while the Caribbean Legion was making preparation for the aborted attack against Trujillo in the Dominican Republic (known as the Luperon Incident), Figueres had promised to assist the Legion by contributing the B-18 and the solitary P-38. The B-18 was in fact flown back to Costa Rica, where it picked up no fewer than twenty-one Legion troops, and was flown back to Guatemala by a pilot named Velazco, with the intention of flying these men on to take part in the 'invasion' of the Dominican Republic. A few days later the B-18 again flew into Costa Rica and picked up yet more troops and equipment. It was held at San Jose, however, by the Chief of Security there, and not allowed to depart.

Some time late in 1949 or early 1950, Arevalo used his influence with Figueres, and the B-18 was again returned to Guatemala, where it was parked beside the Lockheed Model 14 also 'owned' by the Legion on the west side of the FAG's main maintenance hangar.

Little is known of the status of TI-205 between these heavily laden transport flights and the May 1949 aborted invasion of the Dominican Republic and late June 1952, but it must be assumed that the aircraft was nominally on the strength of the FAG during that period, or at the least

under its protection and maintenance. The US National Intelligence Survey of Guatemala for August 1950 noted that '…the Guatemalan Air Force also has available for use a B-18, although it has not been flown for more than a year.' In June 1952 the aircraft was 'sold' and the Bill of Sale transferred ownership from none other than Juan Jose Arévalo, lately President of Guatemala, to Eufemio Fernandez, a Cuban exile then in Guatemala; on 5 July 1952 he in turn sold the aircraft to Pelin Mendoza. It was reportedly undergoing extensive overhaul at the time in the FAG shops and was to be flown to Mexico for use by ex-President Prio. Pelin Mendoza had also acquired a Lockheed Model 14 that had been keeping company with the B-18 (often erroneously reported as a Model 18 Lodestar) as well as two other aircraft, also on behalf of Prio.

By August 1954 the B-18 and its mate, the Lockheed 14, were undergoing, once again, extensive maintenance by mechanics of the FAG in conjunction with Aviateca personnel. The Model 14 was declared airworthy, but two Mexican pilots sent to take delivery of it refused to fly it. It had been painted navy blue and white by this time and registered in the private Mexican civil series as XB-XEN. The B-18 had been masked for painting as well and was to become XB-XEM, both registrations being provisionally issued to Leopoldo Garcia E. The Commander of the FAG at the time stated correctly that the aircraft had been the property of Pelin Mendoza but that he believed that they had been turned over to 'a Mexican General, who he could not identify'. He further stated that he was 'under orders from the General Staff not to release the aircraft to anyone.'

Incredibly, the FAG was finally issued authority to dispose of the B-18 and the Lockheed 14 around 14 May 1956. The Lockheed was, as noted, sold to a Mexican General, while the B-18 was sold, for not less than $17,000 to Luis Arenas, a Guatemalan citizen, who told the FAG that he intended to use it for hauling freight.

Cuba and the Cayo Confites expedition

Based on available evidence, it appears that there is a distinct possibility that US owner Harold Wemmer was directly involved in the procurement of one RB-18 (MSN 1701, NC-66115) and two RB-18As (MSN 2607, NC-66114, and 2628, NC/NX-66116) on behalf of a 'Brazilian' airline known as SAVAG, and that two of these were issued preliminary Brazilian civil registrations as PP-SBB (NC-66114) and PP-SBC (NC-66115).

In fact, these aircraft were destined for the ill-fated Fuerza Aérea del Ejercito de Liberacion Americana, which was organised to invade and oust the Trujillo regime in the Dominican Republic, based at Cayo Confites in Cuba. To what extent Wemmer was culpable in these movements remains unknown, as the aircraft cited apparently never reached either the revolutionaries or Brazil. They may, however, account for the otherwise untraced B-18s on the Cuban civil register, which just happen to total three aircraft – CU-P471, CU-P477 and CU-P486 – all registered by April-July 1951 (see Annex 4).

Mexico

The use of B-18s in Mexico is clouded in uncertainty. At least eighteen Mexican civil registrations have been associated with B-18s, but this does not indicate, by any means, the total number of actual aircraft, since at least one RB-18 (MSN 1665, AC36-277, formerly NC-1045M) alone is known to have worn at least four different Mexican registrations!

Similarly, the operators of these aircraft are equally obscure, although the majority almost certainly were relatively small freight and mixed passenger operators seeking low-cost, relatively high-yield aircraft for clientele who were not particularly discriminating. A brief survey of the aircraft at this juncture will, it is hoped, aid further research – see the accompanying table.

Mexico was by far the most significant foreign user of B-18 series aircraft. B-18B NC-66191, shown here with 'Yucatan' titles on the rear fuselage, became XA-KEX with Lineas Aéreas del Pacifico by October 1952. It has an acronym on the nose, but it is not entirely visible. *via David W. Ostrowski*

Appearing very down at the mouth, this B-18B was formerly 'Satan's Chariot' and had a combat record during the war. Here, as N4611V, she awaits grooming to go to Mexico as XA-LUO with Moises Rasilio Garcia, doing business as Transportes Aéreos de Carga SA in April 1957. *Pima Air & Space Museum 95.91.3A*

The photographer who took this picture claimed it was 'the last USAF B-18, being used as a General's VIP transport, landing at Bolling Air Force Base in 1948'. In fact, it is NC-1045M, formerly B-18 AC36-277, which went to Mexico, initially, as XB-VAK, returned to the US as N2801D, then went back to Mexico as XB-MAP and XA-NIS! *Jim Pyle via Kevin Grantham*

Manufacturer's Serial Number 1665, a B-18B, is seen after returning to the US as N2801D with Skyspray from Mexico as XB-VAK and just prior to its return to Mexico as XB-MAP. It is pictured here at Rapid City, SD, on 5 July 1959. *Bob Burgess via David W. Ostrowski*

At first glance the Mexican registration on this rather oddly nosed B-18B appears to be XB-UIW, but in fact it is XB-JIW, formerly NC-69002, which went to LAGOSA around 1951. It later became XA-KAP. It was named *Isla de Triz* while with LAGOSA. *Ing José Villela Jr via Dr Gary Kuhn*

XB-NOC was B-18 AC36-277, MSN 1665, and during her civil career, had not less than five different Mexican and U.S. registrations! She was probably owned by C. Cambera/Cia. Impulsora de Aviación when photographed around 1973. *Wings of Progress*

Based on an analysis of the table, it can be seen that at least thirteen individual RB-18, RB-18A or RB-18B aircraft entered the Mexican civil register, with a further five unknown, but probably amongst the thirteen known as re-issues. MSN 2574 is known to have been exported to Mexico, and is certainly one of the aircraft noted in the table.

Besides the identified operators, at least one B-18 is also known to have been operated by Transportes Aéreos de Jalisco, flying the Guadalajara-San Martin de Bolaños route over very rugged terrain indeed, probably in 1954. This route was known locally as the 'Aircraft Carrier Route' due to the nature of the crude airfields hacked out along the route.

Photographed at San Diego, California in 1953, XB-VAK was MSN 1665 in yet another guise, and rather elaborate cheat lines for a Mexican civil operator. *Chalmers A. Johnson via Charles N. Trask*

Mexican Civil Registered B-18s

Mexican Markings	MSN	Previous Identity	Mexican Operator	Fate
XA-GEO	1683	NC-56568	Manuel Contreras Farfan dba Aerovias Contreras Tijuana, Mexico c. Dec 47 as a 16PCLM!	Fate unknown
XA-HAL	2636	NC-75845	c. Jul 48	
XA-HES	2555	NC-5487N	Servicios Aéreos de Chiapas c. Jan 49-Oct 49	
XA-KAP	2633	NC-69002, XB-JIW		To XB-PIL by Feb 55. Also reported in some sources as XB-KAP, but XA-KAP believed correct
XA-KEX	2567	NC-66191	Lineas Aéreas del Pacifico c. 28 Oct 52; Impulsora de Aviación 22 Feb 63	To XB-POI 21 Feb 63 and back to XA-KEX 22 Feb 63.
XA-LUN	1702	NC-48584 (Canc. 16 Apr 47)	Moises Rasilio Garcia dba Transportes Aéreos de Carga. Bgt. Jan 57	Cancelled 21 Jun 63 no C of A
XA-LUO	2473	N4611V	Moises Rasilio Garcia dba Transportes Aéreos de Carga Bgt. 29 Apr 57	Cancelled 21 Jun 63 no C of A
XA-NIS	1665	NC-1045M, XB-VAK, N2801D, XB-MAP	Unknown. Rgt. 21 Feb 62	To XB-NOC 22 Aug 62
XB-BUR	2628	NX/NC-66116	Last operator was Federación Regional Soledades Cooperativas de la Industria Pesquera "Baja California" FCL.	Derelict at Ensenada, BC 14 Oct 69
XB-DON	Unknown	Unknown	Jack Gill	Formerly Air-Sea For warders in the U.S. application to export to Mexico dated 17 Sep 51
XB-JEN	2506	NC-75842	Ventura Marin; Jaime R. Paullada Rgt. Apr 48	To XB-KOX?
XB-JIW	2633	NC-69002	LAGOSA (Lineas Aéreas Guerrero-Oa-xaca, S.A.) c. 1951	Named Isla de Triz. To XA-KAP
XB-JOW	Unknown	Unknown		Reported but not verified
XB-JUO	Unknown	Unknown	Marco Ayala c. Feb 55 as 16PCLM; later Empresa Rodriguez Otegui y Cia.	Cited in some Mexican publications as a Douglas "B-22"!
XB-KEA	2471	NC-59680 (Canc.7Oct48)	Alfonso Huitron, 2PCLM by Feb 55	Also cited as MSN 2469
XB-KOX	2506?	NC-75842, XB-JEN?	Nacional Financiera S.A.	Canc. 22 Aug 69
XB-KUX	Unknown	Unknown	c. 27 Dec 63	
XB-LAJ	2505	NC/N-67947. Canc. 19 Oc 66	Federación Regional la Cooperativas de la Industria Pesquera "Baja California" FCL	To N18AC 26 Feb 71
XB-LAW	Unknown	Unknown		Derelict at Ensenada, BC by 14Oct69
XB-LUI	Unknown	Unknown	Gilberto Contreras A. c. Feb 55	
XB-MAP	1665	NC-1045M, XB-VAK, N2801D (Canc. 12 May 60)	Unknown	To XA-NIS 21 Feb 62
XB-NOC	1665	NC-1045M, XB-VAK, N2801D, XB-MAP, XA-NIS	C. Cambera Rgt. 22 Aug 62. Later Cia. Impulsora de Aviación	Last reported 1977
XB-PIL	2633	NC-69002, XB-JIW, XA-KAP		Crashed Nov 1955
XB-POI	2567	NC-66191, XA-KEX	Rgt. 21 Feb 63	To XA-KEX 22 Feb 63
XB-VAK	1665	NC-1045M	Marcelo Gaume Dumas as 2PCLM Rgt. 7 May 53	To N2801D 12 May 60
XB-XYZ-504	2499	AC37-499	Unknown	To NC-68147 Feb 48

The solitary B-18 to be registered in Peru, OB-TAH-306 was operated as a freighter by CAMSA from June 1953 until it disappeared in the Peruvian wilderness on 24 November 1954. *via Tony Beale*

Peru

RB-18, MSN 1662, formerly NC-1044M with Latin-American Cargo Inc of Philadelphia, and Harry R. Wheeler Inc of Miami, was acquired by Cia Aéreo Mercantil SA (CAMSA) of Tingo Maria, Peru, on 26 June 1953, but had been placed on the Peruvian civil aircraft register as OB-TAH-306 as early as 28 March 1953. This aircraft disappeared on a flight between Tingo Maria and Juanjui on 24 November 1954. The crash site has also been reported as Mojarsyacu. This little-known operator also reportedly acquired RB-18A MSN 2624, AC37-624, ex-NC-1043M, but the aircraft was last reported in Jamaica and may have had Caribbean Legion connections. To round out its brief existence, CAMSA also acquired a Fairchild C-82A by around 1956.

CHAPTER EIGHTEEN

The Douglas B-23, DC-266 and DB-320

The earliest identified official mention of type B-23, and Douglas Specification DS-266, was 5 December 1938, when Air Corps Specification No 98-204-3A was issued embodying the original specification, which was later revised on 15 May 1941.

As noted in Chapter 11, and contrary to most accounts, it is clear that the B-23 was a rather hasty development of the short-lived XB-22, a compromise between demands for improved performance from the Air Corps and add-on features to the basic B-18A design engineered by Douglas to meet those demands.

General Arnold himself had sent a letter to Wright Field on 5 December titled 'Modernization of B-18A Airplanes', with the subtitle 'References will be B-22 Specifications DS-262 and Douglas Letter dated October 25, 1938'.

He noted that, as of that date, the Materiel Division was proceeding with the preparation of a Change Order on the last B-18A contract, which was '...based on modernising as many of the B-18A airplanes as funds will permit in conformance with Detailed Specification DS-262 dated October 25, 1938'.

This, fundamentally, accounts for the small production run of B-23s, and the confusing series of events that led from the B-18A, through the XB-22, to the B-23 as we know it.

Believed to be the first B-23 (there was no XB-23), unique in having a 'solid' nose instead of a bombardier nose, AC39-27 was accepted on 13 October 1939, following a first flight on 27 July. In this view, the Air Corps markings have, for some reason, been airbrushed out. It survived until March 1942 when it was condemned for unspecified reasons and scrapped. *Douglas*

On 29 November 1938 Douglas had suggested certain revisions to the XB-22 that would improve its performance and general usefulness. General Arnold, in his letter, stated that '...the airplane resulting from [the] suggested changes in the B-22 Specification, will be referred to as the B-23 airplane.' Thus, by directive from the Commanding General, the DS-266 was born and the B-23 designated. He went on to state that 'the airplane resulting from the suggested changes in the B-22, is superior to the B-22.' Concurrently, he directed that negotiations for a change on the DS-262/XB-22 be halted immediately and that DS-262 be revised to include the data that would bring the aircraft to DS-266 and the definitive B-23.

That same day, a conference was held at Douglas concerning the newly evolved B-23. The major points discussed had a great deal to do with what, in retrospect, came to be the distinguishing characteristics of the B-23, as distinct from its lineal forbears, the B-18A and XB-22. These are itemised as follows:

Item 1: A side-by-side seating arrangement was to be furnished for the pilot and co-pilot, but, in the British style, with only flight controls for the pilot. The seats were to be arranged, however, so that the pilot and co-pilot could readily move from one seat to the other – a feat perhaps easier said than done in flight.

Item 2: The radio equipment on the B-23 was to consist of the SCR-183 set, the SCR-187 set, a radio compass, an inter-phone and a marker beacon receptor – except that the number

This Douglas image, dated 26 July 1939, shows the first aircraft, AC39-27, nose-to-nose with a B-18A as it undergoes final assembly. *Douglas 15524*

of coil boxes provided for the SCR-187 set would be limited to not more than four in the aircraft at any one time. Oddly, individually lighted instruments were not to be used.

Item 3: This discussion dealt with detailed equipment, and included some rather strange requirements. For example, the aircraft were to be supplied without de-icer boots, would have no life preserver cushions, no cabin lining (sound-proofing) or carpeting, as 'simple a heating system as possible', no signal pyrotechnics installed aside from landing flares, as 'simple a refueling system as practicable, consisting only of a place to attach a hose and refueling pump', no bunks or troop-carrying equipment, and, perhaps worst of all for B-18 crews by now spoiled by standard amenities, no toilet facilities!

These, and a number of other decisions made at the 5 December 1938 conference between Arnold himself and Donald Douglas, were clearly made, and without reservation, in the interests of expediting the procurement of the aircraft, and with little or no consultation with the Materiel Division at Wright Field. The correspondence stated, essentially, and rather bluntly, that if the Materiel Division had any problem with the decisions made by General Arnold, they should be referred to Arnold 'personally' upon his return to Washington!

Wright Field was faced with what amounted to a Command Decision and had little alternative other than to comply with 'Hap' Arnold's unilateral decisions. However, the Bombardment Branch had apparently organised a position on the B-23 by 25 February 1939,

had convened a conference of its own between representatives of the NACA, Douglas and the Air Corps leadership, and had somehow hammered out a remarkable conclusion. It stated that:

> '...the improvements in performance offered by the Douglas Aircraft Corp are not sufficiently increased to warrant award of a contract for B-23 aircraft in large quantities, because such performance would be below the requirements of the service, and below that expected from up-to-date aircraft.'

In what in retrospect was a bit of accounting sleight-of-hand, the small production batch of B-23s that could be afforded as the 'tail end' of the last B-18A contract was initially issued with Douglas Manufacturer's Serial Numbers 2675 onwards, continuing from the final B-18A built as such, although it is the belief of this writer that these numbers had actually been forecast by Douglas for assignment to the still-born B-22s.

The third production B-23, AC39-29, shows the forward fuselage, usually obscured in most photos by the high-set engine cowlings. The cockpit enclosure was a noticeable improvement over the B-18 series, but the large aircraft was fitted with only one set of primary flight instruments. This aircraft crashed on 31 May 1943 in bad weather. *Douglas 17913*

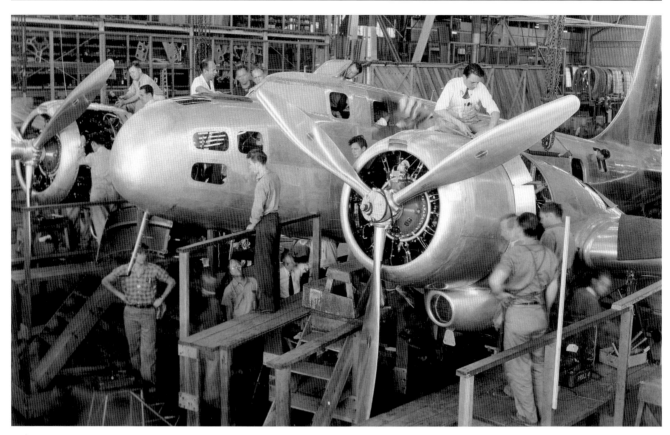

Douglas line workers swarm over the first B-23, AC39-27, as it nears readiness in this 26 July 1939 view. The nose was fitted with a 'solid' dome to accommodate test gear. Note the mast protruding below and to the starboard side. *Douglas 15525*

However, a hand-written note in the ledger states: 'See Purchase Sections Numbers for planes 2713-2750 inclusive. They are duplications of those noted for 2675-2712 inclusive.'

The total production run of B-23s was only thirty-eight aircraft, with first deliveries made on 13 October 1939 (to Wright Field) following not long after the first flight of the type at Clover Field in Santa Monica, CA, on 27 July 1939, and the final aircraft on 20 September 1940 (to McChord Field). Initial delivery assignments saw the first four to Wright Field, one to Bolling Field, DC, one to Lowry Field in Denver, sixteen to Maxwell Field, AL, and the remaining eighteen aircraft all to McChord Field, WA.

The aircraft was officially described as a low-wing monoplane of all-metal construction, with an overall span of 92 feet (compared with the 89ft 6in of the B-18), a length of 58ft, 4 3/8in, and a height of 18ft 5½in. The normal crew complement consisted of six, including a bombardier/nose gunner, pilot, avigator, radio operator/gunner,

Dated 6 November 1939, this appears to be the first B-23 again, AC-39-27, posed to show off the moderately more modern lines of the B-18 derivative – including America's first purpose-built modern tail gun position. The size and length of the anti-glare panels on the inboard sides of the cowlings is of interest. *Douglas 16213*

cameraman/gunner and, a first, a dedicated tail gunner. Armament, incredibly, still consisted of but three .30 caliber guns (one in the nose, one in a very awkward ventral floor mounting, and another on a complex waist mounting capable of being fired out of either side or upwards through a swing-down dorsal hatch) and a single .50 caliber tail gun, the first enclosed tail gun position designed into a US Army aircraft as part of the basic design. The aircraft was also, reputedly, fitted with a wing that was very nearly the same as that on the commercial DC-3, which was regarded as somewhat stronger than the B-18 wing, but with flotation qualities retained as on the B-18. This accounts for the markedly different plan-form for the B-23 when noted from above, compared to the B-18 and B-18A. The crew, while enjoying many of the 'roomy' qualities of the familiar B-18 series (the navigator, seated immediately behind the pilot, had a plotting board large enough to hold a 3 feet by 3 feet chart, the radio operator was seated just aft of the navigator, and there was excellent intercommunication), found the fuselage much shallower. The very first B-23 apparently had an unglazed nose, at first, although this was later converted to the standard 'glass' nose. The common wisdom, although unsupported by Douglas or Air Corps documents, has always been that the much higher operating speeds of the B-23 would render it less likely to encounter head-on attacks from defenders, hence the single .30 caliber nose gun versus a dedicated, power-operated turret.

Seldom viewed from below in flight, this pre-war postcard, offered for sale in numerous Air Corps Post Exchanges, convinced many GIs that the aircraft was a B-18! The ventral gun aperture can just be detected on the rear fuselage. *e-Bay*

were literally cast to the winds, and the aircraft seemed to be turning up everywhere – but not without attendant problems. A number of previously published accounts have recorded that B-23s were assigned to the 17th Bomb Group while it was still at March Field, CA, but this is absolutely incorrect. All went new directly from the factory to the stations noted above.

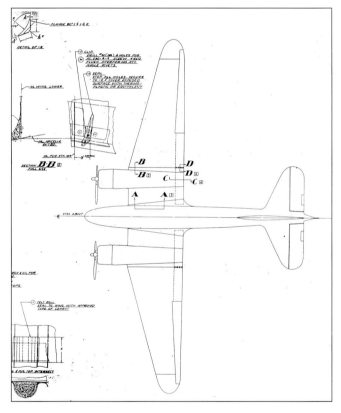

The lineage of the B-23, viewed from the underside, in spite of the streamlining and other improvements, was unmistakable. *NASM EDM*

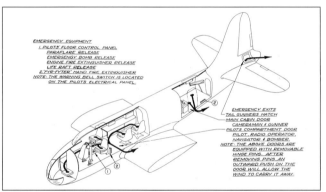

This crew emergency egress diagram also conveys the relationships of the work stations and the fact that the tail gunner would need to be a compact GI! *T.O. 01-40EC-1*

This drawing shows the travel of the B-23 nose gun and details of its components. *NASM EDM*

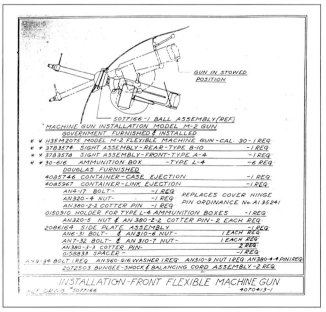

Contrary to many published accounts, the production B-23s were in fact assigned to tactical units in some numbers, including, initially, the 23rd Composite Group (also known throughout the Air Corps as 'The Demonstration Group') and the 17th Bomb Group, which apparently mixed the aircraft with B-18s in its 34th, 37th and 95th Bombardment Squadrons (M), and the attached 89th Reconnaissance Squadron at McChord. Later, when the mission of the 23rd was overtaken by events and the 17th Bomb Group re-equipped, its B-23s

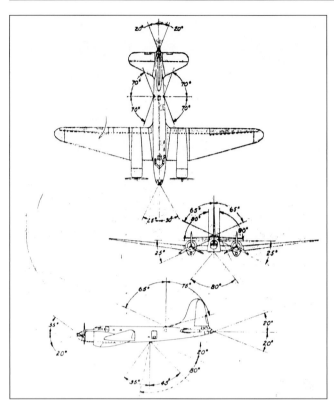

This sketch showed the rather optimistic fields of fire for the four defensive guns. In reality, the manner in which the guns were mounted would have made the B-23 extremely difficult to defend in aerial combat. *NASM EDM*

Although celebrated as the first modern application of a tail-gun 'stinger' in a US Army aircraft, in fact the .50 caliber installation was the source of numerous complaints by operational crews. The gunner was extremely cramped, and access was only by great exertions; escape in an emergency would have been very problematical, as the gunner's parachute could not possibly have been accommodated with him in the position. No information has been located describing effects on the directional stability of the aircraft with the position clam-shell aperture open. *Douglas 17819*

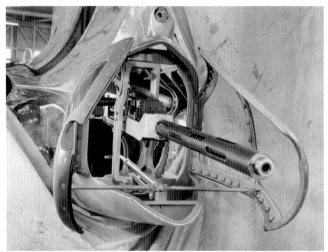

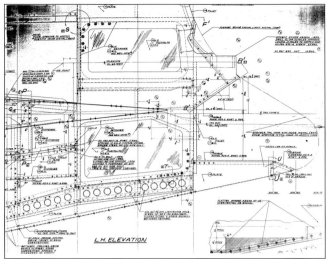

Douglas experimented with several configurations for the B-23 tail gun position, and this appears to have been the earliest. It includes what appears to be a large-format telescopic sight and less window area than the definitive version. *NASM EDM*

The principal pre-war operator of the B-23 was the 17th Bomb Group at McChord Field, WA. Here, 17B38, bearing the insignia of the 34th Bomb Squadron, seems to be popular with an open-day crowd. *via Rich Dann*

As early as 28 November 1940 the Commander of the 23rd Composite Group at Maxwell Field, Alabama, which had received the first of sixteen aircraft on 28 June 1940, was reporting that it was having 'difficulties in keeping any great number of the B-23s operating', mainly because of the haste with which the aircraft had been procured, the economies of the situation, which basically dictated that there was no money for spares, and finally because the Air Corps supply system was experiencing enormous difficulties in locating even the most fundamental spares to repair the comparatively small number of aircraft in the inventory.

Entry of the comparatively small number of B-23s acquired into line service was not without incident, although the numbers of Unsatisfactory Reports (U/Rs) for the type was comparatively low. As an example, the entire fleet was grounded temporarily on 27 August 1941 when failures in the right tail wheel support fittings were discovered. This was rectified relatively quickly, however.

One actual Unsatisfactory Report, dated 5 May 1941, and involving AC39-62, named the 'Part Number of the Defective Part' as 'Passing Lights and/or Tail Lights of Subject, Duck' and was duly entered into the Air Corps record exactly as written. The aircraft was assigned to the 95th Bombardment Squadron, Felts Field, WA, at the time. The 'Description of Trouble' is quoted exactly as submitted:

B-23 17B3 was probably assigned to the Headquarters and Headquarters Squadron of the 17th Bomb Group, while B-18A 17B77 was probably with the 95th Bomb Squadron. The biplane appears to be a PT-17, but the location of the photo is unknown. *via David W. Ostrowski*

The principal operating base for the largest concentration of B-23s at any one time was McChord Field, WA. Here, B-23 89R6 of the 89th Reconnaissance Squadron is on the ramp in front of Hangar 2 alongside three apparently brand-new Boeing B-17Cs, which have not yet received unit designators. The photo is dated 10 December 1940. *USAAC*

Two 89th Reconnaissance Squadron B-23s, 89R8 and 89R9, adorn the ramp at McChord Field, WA, on 4 October 1940, while the focus of the photographer was on the far more photogenic B-17Bs on the right and the B-17C on the far left, with a North American BC-1A thrown in for good measure. *USAAC*

'While cruising at 6,500 feet on a routine night flying mission in B-23 airplane AC39-62, the following described difficulty was encountered: Immediately after passing over the Spokane radio station cone of silence and entering the westerly "A" quadrant, said airplane had a direct head-on collision with a one pound, twelve ounce specimen of Aves Aquavinius Quackus, more generally known as a Bluebill Duck. As far as could be determined, said duck was flying east directly on the beam and without passing or riding lights of any sort, thus giving the pilot absolutely no opportunity to duck the duck. The immediate result of the accident was the appearance of a hole in the starboard windshield approximately six inches wide, and directly above the pilot's head, following which the wind blew and duck flew inside the cabin. After a short delay, during which the pilot was separated from the duck and the ship's engineer was tied in his seat, a deferred forced landing was made at the Spokane airport. Upon examination after landing, the duck was found to be dead, subject demise being patently due to suffocation caused by its head being driven through its tail empennage. Subject duck was not carrying a log book, consequently flying time is unknown.'

Apparently the B-23 crews had a sense of humor, although the response of Army officialdom could not be located.

B-23 myths and legends

Few would dispute that, from a purely aesthetic viewpoint, the B-23 was a much more attractive aircraft than its portly cousin, the B-18 series. It was very nimble, as well, and for a relatively large aircraft was described as a pleasure to fly with only one pilot actually at the controls.

But describing the B-23 as a 'development' of the B-18, other than the rather convoluted trek from the B-18A to the XB-22, is patently absurd. There were virtually no components of the B-23 compatible with the B-18 series, other than perhaps the ease of movement between crew positions (and that wonderful navigator's and radio operator's table), and it was very much a case of making a 'silk purse out of a sow's ear' to many Douglas engineers.

The common wisdom has always been that the B-23s didn't do much for the war effort. In fact, one of the largest concentrations of the type was selected to provide the bulk of the defensive bombardment force guarding none other than the Boeing facilities in and around Seattle, WA, as well as the important naval bases and shipping facilities there, while the Air Corps elite Demonstration Group at Maxwell Field, which was a showcase for tactics development and foreign dignitaries, was quick to capitalise on the modernistic lines and mystique of the B-23 – but without revealing its relatively weak defensive armament, and often suggesting a performance that was, while impressive for the time, to be honest, rather stretching the facts a bit.

But that utility, like the steadfast example of the B-18 force, lasted only until such time as more B-17s, B-25s and Martin B-26s started to arrive on the scene. The small numbers of B-23s available throughout the Air Corps (their numbers were never revealed in pre-war news releases) quickly resulted in them being side-lined. But that dispersion was, in itself, an Air Corps ruse. Air Corps documents exist clearly indicating that at least part of the rationale for rationing out B-23s to far-flung units all over the nation in small numbers was to cloak exactly how few of them there actually were in the service, and at the same time give the impression that there were far more. In this way, the B-23s provided a most valuable propaganda service at a crucial point in the war.

Although often cited as a myth, in fact Colonel (later General) 'Jimmie' Doolittle did indeed initially propose that his attack on Tokyo be made using B-23s versus the North American B-25Bs actually selected. However, the reasons for the initial selection of the B-23 for this daring mission were based on factors that have been largely ignored. The irony is that the mix of Doolittle, his crews and the B-25 gained immortality primarily because the B-25Bs could, with some exertions, be launched from the USS *Hornet* (CV-8). With several February 1942 trials and a lot of practice, and a wing span of just 67ft 6in, with lightened loads and minimal crews, B-25Bs could get by the starboard-side 'island' structure with some breathing room to spare.

In fact, even though the B-23 has almost consistently been stated to have been turned down for this mission because of its wingspan of an even 92 feet (actually 4 feet shorter than the similar DC-3 wing, and heavily reinforced; many sources claim it was the same wing, but it was not), if placed just right it could in fact have been launched – although not nearly as many could have been marshalled on the aft deck of the *Hornet*, nor as compactly.

Doolittle was serious about selecting the B-23 for several reasons. First, B-25Bs were in short supply as of early 1942, and were needed everywhere. B-23s were considered virtually expendable. Second, the B-23 could, with R-2600-3s (1,275hp) – the B-25Bs used uprated versions of the same engines, R-2600-9s, at 1,350hp – take off at normal take-off power and clear a 50-foot obstacle in 1,465 feet, whereas normally the B-25B required 2,130 feet to do the same; this was a very significant factor, and all attributable to that wonderful B-23 wing. Third, the B-23, with maximum bomb load and 30% power, could do 172mph and not less than 3,600 miles in range, versus the B-25B's 200mph at 33% power and a maximum range of 2,600 miles. Additionally, the B-23s could have retained their .50 caliber tail guns and all three .30 caliber guns for the mission, even though as it turned out they would not have been needed. It does not require extensive calculations to conclude that, not only could the B-23s have carried out the mission, although not in the same numbers, but they could also have almost certainly all reached their safe-haven destinations in China safely, and without the frightful loss of crews and aircraft that the B-25Bs suffered (all were lost, mainly due to fuel starvation).

Like the B-18, the matter of the 'popular' naming of the B-23 deserves comment. Although almost universally cited in post-war publications as being named 'Dragon', by January 1943 this name had in fact been adopted by the AAF committee charged with that responsibility. However, not a solitary reference to the name can be located prior to that time, and not a single crew member interviewed every recalls using that name in referring to the aircraft during the war years.

Douglas also had a projected export version of the B-23, which it promoted very briefly in December 1939 as the DB-320. Although the French are said to have evinced interest, no orders materialised.

While much has been made of the B-23's performance, some of it justified, a fully equipped aircraft turned in almost exactly the same maximum speed at 12,000 feet as the standard North American B-25B and B-25C, although, as noted, with a substantially greater range at cruise.

Only two B-23 series aircraft are known to have ever been stationed or operated extensively outside of the Continental United States. AC39-63, converted to a C-67, was assigned to the Headquarters and Headquarters Squadron Sixth Air Force, Albrook Field, Canal Zone, on 7 October 1944. By 31 March 1945 it had been 'promoted' to the Caribbean Defense Command-Panama Canal Department (CDC-PCD) Flight Detachment at Albrook, where it remained until being surplused in theater on 17 July 1946 – very possibly the last B-23/C-67 in the USAAF inventory. Major General Clements McMullen, chief of the wartime Air Service Command, which had worldwide responsibilities, is known to have made use of a C-67 nicknamed 'Burma Roadster' extensively on long-range survey flights throughout the Pacific and into the CBI. This qualifies this aircraft as the only B-18/B-23 series aircraft to operate in the CBI.

Although nearly every B-23 still in the inventory after Pearl Harbor received standard olive-drab over neutral gray camouflage, not a single example has thus far been reported as having worn any form of 'nose art', and only one, cited above, a nickname. This may qualify it as the solitary wartime US combat category aircraft type not to have gained such a personalisation from crews.

Finally, as pointed out earlier, B-23s did in fact take part in a large number of coastal patrol and anti-submarine missions, both in the Pacific Northwest and off the east coast, and at least one aircraft, commanded by Major W. A. Keenan and his crew, engaged a submarine on 30 June 1942. It appears that the aircraft involved may have been either AC39-37 or 39-63.

Conversions to C-67 and UC-67

Most sources cite between eleven and eighteen standard B-23 aircraft as having been converted to transport configuration and redesignated as (initially) C-67 or later UC-67 (Utility Cargo) configuration. This writer can only account for sixteen such conversions that are clearly defined as such on the actual Individual Aircraft Record Cards.

By the time this photo of AC39-31 was taken, the fifth aircraft off the production line had long since been converted to UC-67 transport configuration. Notice the additional slit windows in the mid-fuselage area. It became NC-51436 with Pan American, then went to Ecuador, where it survives in a museum. *Harold G. Martin, Kansas Aviation Museum*

AC39-38 was surplused as an RB-23 in May 1945 with a scant 992 hours total time. It, too, survives today in the collections of the Commemorative Air Force after passing through a number of civil owners. *Harold G. Martin, Kansas Aviation Museum*

It did not take long for the Air Corps to commence the practice of parcelling out the small production run of B-23s to support units. This aircraft, 10AB63, was operated by the 10th Air Base Squadron, Air Corps Technical School, at Scott Field, IL, and had been converted to UC-67 configuration. *via Warren Bodie*

Most, but not all, B-23s and UC-67s that survived into the war years received standard AAF camouflage, including AC39-36, Field Number 88, which appears to have had temporary camouflage scrubbed off, but not completely. Officially, this aircraft was not redesignated as a UC-67 until around July 1944, but this image was obviously taken much earlier, probably in late 1942. The tail gun is still in place, and the trailing antenna gear fairlead can just be seen under the fuselage by the entry door. One source claims that this was the C-4 tow-target lead, but no definitive description of this installation could be located. *USAAC*

Usually, such conversions of standard category combat aircraft take place some time after the aircraft have been removed from squadron service as combat types. In the case of the B-23s, however, this was clearly not the case, and at least five such conversions had already been accomplished by 23 December 1941, with three more following during January 1942. For the remaining eight known and confirmed conversions, these occurred at odd intervals until the last was accomplished in mid-February 1943.

These conversions, so far as can be determined, were completed for the most part at the San Antonio Air Depot (SAAD), but no 'standard' configuration or pattern seems to have been established. On most of the aircraft, the removal of all military equipment and armament, as well as sealing of the bomb bays and removal of all racks, was part of the work carried out. The equipment for the bombardier and the tail gunner was entirely removed and, on some, the large navigator's and radio operator's table was also deleted and replaced by smaller stations more akin to those found on C-47 and C-53 transports. On some C-67s, C-5 windlass kits for target-towing duties were retained, as this very necessary but mundane duty was one that the standard B-23s and C-67s were uniquely suited to perform, especially when towing at relatively high speeds for pursuit interceptor training. C-5 gear had already been installed on three standard B-23s as early as 17 July 1941, and the Air Corps had been thinking ahead, as it had acquired a total of thirty-eight additional C-5 sets for the remainder of the B-23 fleet, including some spare units.

The majority of the C-67s, however, and even some B-23s (redesignated for the most part as RB-23s to indicate 'obsolescent' status by 1943), were very highly prized as VIP transports, and this was the fate of the majority of the aircraft.

Test work

Like their B-18 brethren, the relatively small number of B-23s and C-67s, mostly after but even before replacement in unit service, rendered exceptional service to the AAF through use in an amazing array of test work.

B-23s were detailed to test duties early in their service lives. One was being used by 26 April 1941 to test both 700lb and 1,200lb parachute-delivered 'aerial mines' dropped from the bomb bay. Not long afterwards, AC39-28 was engaged in tests of the so-called MX-104 system, ST.961A as of 16 July 1941, although the nature of this system has eluded definition. By 9 August 1941 a B-23, possibly also AC39-28, was being used as the launch platform for the little-known RF1 controllable glide bomb, suspended fully beneath the aircraft.

As early as 30 November 1941, the 24th Bomb Squadron (L), which was stationed at the time at the Air Corps Proving Ground Detachment at Eglin Field, FL, was actively engaged in supporting the activities of the proving ground with a truly cosmopolitan assortment of aircraft, which included four B-23s, three Boeing-Stearman PT-17s, and single examples of the Lockheed C-36 Electra, Curtiss A-18 and Bell YFM-1A. Also stationed at Eglin at the time, and engaged in similar activities, was the 54th Bomb Squadron (M), which had one B-23 on its ramp, serving alongside three brand new Martin B-26 Marauders and a Grumman OA-9 Goose.

One B-23 was bailed to Hamilton Standard for tests with three-bladed, constant-speed, contra-rotating propellers – the first such installation on any US aircraft. The two masts protruding below the nose are also non-standard additions. *Hamilton Standard*

The Air Materiel Command at Wright Field also made intensive use of B-23s for assorted work. AC39-28 was engaged, as early as 16 March 1942, in extensive tests measuring the noise levels inside the aircraft while in flight, and it was found to possess 'unusually low overall noise levels for an aircraft of this type'. However, evaluators also commented that 'air leakage in the cabin of the aircraft was [also] found to be unusually high,' probably yet another manifestation of the 'quick-and-dirty' completion criteria for the aircraft originally set down by 'Hap' Arnold when he hammered out the contract with Douglas.

The Army's Aberdeen Proving Ground in Maryland used AC39-28 to test aerial delivery of the 4,000lb T-1 bomb as early as 15 November 1941 while by January 1943 another B-23 was engaged in towing trials

Because of their speed, power and accommodation, B-23s and UC-67s were engaged in numerous equipment tests. AC39-28, the second aircraft built, was used as the tow plane for a number of glider tests in and around Wright Field during the war, and the tow gear, apparently monitored by a crewman in the tail 'stinger' position, is shown here. The external stiffener along the port side of the fuselage is non-standard, as is the RDF bullet on the forward fuselage. *NARA Wright Field 113977*

B-23 AC39-28 was also used at Aberdeen Proving Ground to test the 4,000lb T-1 bomb as early as November 1941, and this view shows the very generous bomb bays of the aircraft. The manner in which the 'Army' logo under the port wing had been back-painted is unusual. *USAAC*

with the Waco CG-3A glider. It was established, during the latter, that it was possible to tow one of these substantial gliders with a B-23 some 1,408 miles, while consuming 880 gallons of fuel to do so. Yet another B-23, AC39-28, was intensively utilised, with appropriate modifications, to test an adaptation of the All-American Aviation-designed glider pick-up apparatus. This process involved a very low approach to a trapeze arrangement and, using retrieval gear located near the former tail gun position, 'snag' the tow line and proceed to tow a grounded glider aloft. The same aircraft was used to test a number of Emerson-designed remotely controlled gun turrets, although oddly no photos of these installations have surfaced.

B-23 AC39-32 was bailed to Pratt & Whitney at a very early stage on 20 August 1940, to serve as the test bed for installation of R-2800-5 engines, which were intended for the Martin B-26 Marauder and the short-lived XB-28 program. Much further west, AC39-53 was engaged as the 'mother' or controller aircraft in tests of the remotely controlled Culver PQ-8 drone at Muroc Dry Lake in California.

An unidentified B-23 or C-67 was also bailed to Hamilton Standard some time prior to February 1943 for tests with three-bladed, constant-speed, contra-rotating propellers – the very first such installation to ever fly successfully in the US. The tests were conducted from Rentschler Field in East Hartford, CT.

Yet another B-23, AC39-50, was bailed to a joint program being carried out by American Airlines and General Electric on 20 February 1942, which used the aircraft to test a specially designed pressurised cabin that would ultimately be applied to the Boeing B-29. The conversion was accomplished at La Guardia Field in New York and, during the tests, the aircraft carried the nickname 'Robert E. Lee'. Although frequently cited as having been designated as an XB-23 during the course of this work, no documentation has been found establishing this. This same aircraft was then handed over, under unknown circumstances, to none other than Pan American Airways some time after 27 December 1942 at the airline's Brownsville, Texas, base, and remained with the carrier until at least 7 May 1946 on unspecified duties, when it was salvaged.

Surviving B-23s and UC-67s

Of the total of thirty-eight B-23s built, no fewer than twenty-five survived the war intact – and probably more, if one counts the eight examples that passed to Class 26 Instructional Airframe status but were subsequently scrapped. Of the twenty-five surviving aircraft, twenty-two are known to have acquired either United States or foreign civil registration marks, and these are detailed insofar as they are known, with ownership details, in Annex 1. Three B-23/C-67 aircraft that were definitely passed to the custody of the Reconstruction Finance Corporation (RFC) for surplus sale, one on 18 November 1944 (AC39-35) and two on 2 June 1945 (AC39-32 and 39-39), were offered for sale, but have no known foreign or domestic civil identities and are presumed not to have been sold.

The Army Air Forces commenced declaring the B-23/C-67 surplus as early as 2 September 1944 (AC39-31), and this was very much a reflection of the increasingly difficult spares problem rather than any lack of demand for the fleet-footed aircraft. Only five aircraft are known to have been lost to accidents during the war, a remarkably low attrition rate.

Conversions of post-war B-23s to high-speed VIP or business transports is a story in itself, and it is safe to say that no two were exactly alike, being outfitted with often spectacular interior fittings for the day. The CAA had actually approved the type for a Group 2 airworthiness certificate as early as 28 November 1945, and apparently used UC-67 AC39-31 to arrive at the calibrations for operation. By 1947 the aircraft were highly sought after, as conversions could boast a cruising speed in excess of 200mph at 10,000 feet and could maintain altitude at 8,000 feet with single-engine performance indicating 160mph at cruising power, with either prop capable of being feathered. The aircraft could land, with gear and flaps down, at between 55 and 60mph, suggesting a ratio between top speed and stall speeds probably greater than any other large aircraft flying at the time. The CAA licensed B-23s and C-67s for a gross weight of 27,000lb, whereas the wartime B-23 grossed at 33,000lb. Some conversions, with ultra-luxurious appointments, could seat as many as fifteen very comfortably.

At least six B-23 series aircraft survive in museum settings. The National Museum of the United States Air Force has AC39-37 at its beautiful facility at Wright-Patterson Air Force Base, OH, while the Castle Air Museum in California has AC39-45 staked down out of doors and marked as '112/MD' with a faired-over nose cone. AC39-36 has been nicely displayed by the McChord Air Museum at McChord Air Force Base, WA, and AC39-51 is awaiting restoration by the Pima Air & Space Museum in Tucson, AZ. The Commemorative Air Force (formerly the Confederate Air Force) has AC39-38 on display at its Midland, Texas,

Never redesignated as a UC-67, N747M shown here was surplused as an RB-23, formerly AC39-33, one of the oldest B-23s to enter the civil market. It is shown here while owned by The Oxford Group/Moral Rearmament Inc, a New York-based organisation, as of 26 January 1965, and is believed to be still extant. *Authors' collection*

facility. Finally, the Fantasy of Flight (better known as the Kermit Weeks collection) attraction at Polk City, FL, has AC39-57.

A number of enterprising aircraft modification firms, hedging their bets that there would be a post-war demand for high-speed corporate aircraft – not least of which the Hughes Aircraft Company of Culver City, California – commenced specialised conversions of a number of wartime aircraft, including former B-23 and UC-67 variants, by the autumn of 1945.

The first conversion had been completed by 15 September 1945 – barely a month after VJ Day – and delivered directly to the Hughes Tool Company for use by officers of the parent organisation from its Houston, Texas, headquarters. A second aircraft was similarly converted for that company. By the end of September, no doubt under the direct guidance of Howard Hughes himself, his enterprise had secured orders for converted B-23s and UC-67s from the United Drug Company, the General Motors Corporation, Gar Wood Industries Inc (for two aircraft), and the redoubtable partner in the HK-4 Hercules (aka 'Spruce Goose'), Henry J. Kaiser. To no one's surprise, Hughes had very close connections with all of these customers.

Although the conversions were specific to the customers' specifications, the two for Gar Wood Industries might serve as examples of how these luxurious aircraft were outfitted. Finished in a gray, navy blue and oak combination, the interior passenger compartments featured deep napped rugs of gray curled mohair opposite gray gabardine head-liners, which provided a background for navy Bedford cord side walls complete with book cases and panelling of oak. The furnishing consisted of pigskin armchairs of contemporary lines, several fold-away tables and movable lounge chairs, which could be made up into beds. The extra large-format windows cut into the fuselage at eye level when seated were shaded by white Venetian blinds with blue webbing. The aircraft were provided with galleys that consisted of a combination stove, sink and refrigerator.

Hughes of course completely sealed up the bomb bays (the Army Air Forces modifications converting the aircraft from B-23 to UC-67 configuration were widely variable), and gave each aircraft a complete factory-level overhaul, including engines, all instruments, props, the

airframe itself and customer-specified accessories, such as radios, heating and ventilation systems. The cabin was outfitted with a lightweight, Duramold flooring material (Hughes had a wartime interest in the development of Duramold) in the main cabin, and the passenger compartment walls were soundproofed with fiberglass. Typically, the cabins were configured to accommodate from eight to twelve persons, although some were reportedly outfitted to accommodate as few as two. A typical conversion took about sixty days.

After conversion, the UC-67s were hotrods, and were advertised to cruise at 240mph and have an unrefuelled range of 1,600 miles. The Civil Aeronautics Administration (CAA, forerunner of the FAA) issued CAA Report No 25 (which became STC363CE) on 14 January 1946 and, in its Approved Operating Manual, classed all eligible aircraft as type UC-67. It is interesting to note that, as of 25 May 1950, the CAA removed the requirement for carrying a co-pilot in converted UC-67s, reducing the crew, officially, to just one pilot.

The detailed production listing appended to this volume details the surprising number of civil operators of B-23 and UC-67 conversions, and the accompanying photographs, with their captions, give some idea of the extent of these conversions and the breadth of civil operators who enjoyed the unique services of this limited series of specialised aircraft for nearly three decades after the war.

The second B-23 built, N54584, was MSN 2714 and is pictured here some time between May 1946 and March 1951, probably while being operated by the National Distillers & Chemical Products Corporation of New York. It became N100P on 8 March 1951. *via Norm Taylor*

An almost identical view of MSN 2714, previously N54584, after being re-registered as N100P on 24 October 1952. This view, however, reveals the passenger windows in the rear fuselage, complete with curtains, and the addition of the National Distillers logo on the vertical fin. Two radio antenna probes have also been added to the extreme nose, as well as a navigation beacon at the tip of the vertical fin. *via Norm Taylor*

N49892 was MSN 2716, and was being operated when photographed here by the International Harvester Company of Chicago, Illinois, and carried that company's titles on the fuselage. IH acquired the aircraft on 22 July 1947. It was very highly polished and was sold to the General Tire & Rubber Company of Akron, Ohio, on 2 January 1952. The aircraft had the script name 'Harvester' on the nose.

Gleaming with a highly polished finish, Standard Oil of Texas's N52327, MSN 2722, was operated between 18 July 1960 and March 1970. It is seen here at Houston on 20 January 1964. Note the air-stair on the port side of the rear fuselage. *via Norm Taylor*

N41821, MSN 2723, was originally registered on 29 March 1945, and was unusual in having a rather truncated forward fuselage and basically the same cabin window arrangement original to the aircraft as a B-23, with just two small windows added aft of the flight deck. Seen here at San Antonio, Texas, in 1964, it was last operated by Carpet Mills Inc of Chicago, which owned the aircraft briefly between June 1962 and February 1963. By the time of this image it was probably registered to A. J. DeWitt of Chicago, who shortly re-registered it as N80N. *via Norm Taylor*

Wearing full Ecuatoriana colors and markings, MSN 2717, as HC-APV, saw service with the Ecuadorian flag-carrier from December 1968, and was formerly NC400W. Seen here at the unit's base at Quito, the author saw this aircraft there semi-retired from service in May 1969. It was apparently used sporadically for charters and VIP flights, but saw comparatively little service. Now at the FAE Museum at Guayaquil, it bears fictitious air force markings. It was the solitary B-23 to wear foreign markings. Note the panoramic windows at mid-fuselage and just aft of the flight deck. *Capt George G. Farinas*

N747M, MSN 2719 and formerly AC39-33, the aircraft used extensively in Air Corps service at Aberdeen Proving Grounds for bomb ballistics tests, was registered as such 7 June 1965 and was formerly NC747. It bears no evidence of its operator at this point, which was, ironically in view of its previous usage, The Oxford Group/Moral Rearmament Inc, based in New York. *Robert F. Dorr*

A rather sad-looking RB-23, AC39-38, MSN 2724, as she appeared at an RFC disposal station in California as of 4 August 1945. This is one of the aircraft acquired by the Hughes Aircraft Company that same month, becoming NC-56249. At this point it was very much a stock B-23. *Jim Hawkins*

Here is MSN 2724 again much later, at Houston, Texas, on 27 May 1963, while being operated by John W. Mecom of that city as N62G. Formerly NR-56249, it was registered as N60G on 25 March 1963 and was one of the first four B-23 series aircraft converted by the Hughes Aircraft Company in 1945. It survives today with the Commemorative Air Force collection in Midland, Texas. *via Norm Taylor*

Gleaming in the sunlight, MSN 2727, as NC-61666, was owned when photographed by the giant General Motors Corporation from 31 July 1945, and was operated with the basic UC-67 Army Air Forces interior, with relatively minor improvements for most of its service life. Note that even the tail gun position has just been crudely faired over and that the nose glazing remains. The aircraft ended its days as a contraband runner in Argentina by 1967. *via Norm Taylor*

By the time of this 22 March 1963 photo at Daytona Beach, Florida, MSN 2727 was still N61666 but was operated by this time by the General Electric Company between November 1954 and September 1965. *via Norm Taylor*

N53253 was MSN 2732 and was operated as shown here by the A. C. Price Company, Pipeline Construction (note the small logo on the vertical fin and on the engine cowling) between October 1953 and October 1961. This aircraft had a specially configured interior and, by the time of this photo, was starting to show the ravages of time. The aircraft was reportedly stolen (!) circa 1970 and used to run contraband from Paraguay into Argentina. *via Norm Taylor*

Another 'short-nose' conversion, N6700 was MSN 2734, formerly AC39-48, and had been converted by Hughes in July 1946 for the Pacific Lumber Company of Oakland, California, with which it is pictured here. The aircraft crashed on 29 March 1954 at Akron, Ohio, while landing after a flight from New York, although all six on board survived. Oddly, the photographer who took this image claims it was shot at Denver, Colorado, in 1963! *via Norm Taylor*

Another 'long-nose' conversion, probably by Hughes, N49811, MSN 2730, is seen here in 1962 while being operated by the Winn-Dixie Stores Inc, a southern grocery retail chain of Greenville, South Carolina, which acquired it in June 1960. The aircraft allegedly became N141WD on 24 June 1960, but this photo indicates that this was apparently not actually painted on the aircraft for some time. *via Norm Taylor*

Not long out of surplus, NR-53253, MSN 2732, was photographed on Long Island, New York, on 4 August 1945 while still owned by the Hughes Tool Company, which had acquired it from the RFC for $20,000. Precisely why it was registered in the 'Restricted' category is unknown. As shown here, it is basically in UC-67 configuration. *Jim Hawkins*

B-23s saw extensive use during the war years in various test and experimental settings, and B-23 AC39-51, MSN 2737, seen here in full early wartime camouflage on 2 October 1942 at Eglin Field, Florida, was assigned to the 54th Bomb Squadron (M) at the time with Field Number '91'. It survived to become NC-46977 and N61Y. Note how the cabin hatch opened upwards and that the .50 caliber tail gun was installed. *USAAC*

The same aircraft, MSN 2737, after surplus as N61Y while owned and operated by none other than the Roscoe Turner Aeronautical Corporation in Indianapolis, Indiana, some time prior to March 1954, when it became N34C. That company had converted the aircraft to Wright Cyclone engines after acquiring it in November 1946. The text over the cabin door reads 'Hoosier Legionnaire'. Note the oddly spaced cabin window and the two circular portholes. *via Dick Phillips*

Serial Number 2737 once again, this time as N534C with The Ohio State University, which acquired the aircraft on 27 December 1965. It sold it to N230SU in June 1966. Note that, by the time Ohio State acquired the aircraft, the cabin window arrangements had been radically reconfigured and a long nose added. *via Norm Taylor*

B-23 and UC-67 series aircraft saw far more of the world in post-war civil use than during the war. N86E, MSN 2745, formerly NX-49891, is shown here at London, England, in 1964, while being operated by John W. Mecom of Houston, Texas, in connection with his oil interests in Oman. He had acquired the aircraft in January 1963. Although there is no known connection, it is noteworthy that a surprising number of B-23 civil conversions featured some form of a 'vic' on the vertical tail surfaces. *via Norm Taylor*

N777LW, MSN 2749, was the former Sixth Air Force wartime aircraft (the sole example stationed permanently overseas during the war years), formerly NC-47994. It was registered to the Le Tourneau-Westinghouse Company of Peoria, Illinois, when pictured, having been registered by that company in November 1958. *via Norm Taylor*

The last B-23 built, MSN 2750, became AC39-64 and is pictured here during its long sojourn with the General Electric Company of New York City as N33311; that company operated the aircraft between 5 December 1949 and 20 July 1962. It was donated to the Los Angeles, California, Board of Education to be used as an instructional airframe by the Los Angeles Trade & Technical College, but was vandalised and destroyed by fire in late 1968. *via Norm Taylor*

Sold surplus before the war was over on 28 February 1945 to the Hughes Tool Company, here is photographic evidence that B-23 msn 2730 (AC39-44) did in fact wear Restricted marks NR49811 – but precisely what the nature of the restriction was has not surfaced. *R. L. Taylor*

NC56249, msn 2724 (AC39-38), although bearing the logo of Chevron Aviation on her vertical fin, is not known to have been amongst the registered operators post-war! Passing through numerous private and corporate owners between August 1945 and October 1973, the aircraft is now part of the Commemorative Air Force collection *via Dr. Gary Kuhn*

Sporting a handsome custom color scheme, and with a 'radar nose,' NC54584 was msn 2714 (AC39-28), the second B-23 built. She was sold 3 June 1945 to Michael Efferson, care of the Laister-Kauffman Aircraft Corp. in St. Louis, for a bargain $17,500. They intended to use her as a tow aircraft for their CG-10A "Trojan Horse" glider on a Latin American sales tour! *via Dr. Gary Kuhn*

Another view of msn 2730 (AC39-44), now as N49811, which she had become by 24 June 1955, when owned by Container Corporation of America (note logo on the tail), a Chicago-based firm. *R. L. Taylor*

NC54584 (msn 2714) again, apparently photographed at the same time as the image on the previous page, but showing the addition of the two passenger windows on the port side. There is no evidence of any owing apparatus. *via Dr. Gary Kuhn*

N86E was msn 2745 (AC39-59), registered as such by June 1958, and apparently owned by the Houston Chemical Corp. at the time. She ended her days derelict at Athens, Greece, being broken up there during the summer of 1986 with Greek titles on the rear fuselage. *via Dr. Gary Kuhn*

When photographed registered as N100P at National Airport, Washington, DC 31 July 1946, msn 2714 was probably owned by Daniel Peterkin, Jr. (of Morton Salt fame). She was previously NC54584 and had been re-engine with Wright R-2600-3 engines of 1,600hp. *via Dr. Gary Kuhn*

Pictured in this and the next two views at Midland, Texas, N53237 was msn 2722 (AC39-36) and she was owned at the time by Standard Oil of Texas (Houston), and represented the epitome of business aircraft prior to the advent of business jets. The aircraft appears to have had an observation dome grafted onto the extreme rear fuselage, allegedly a skylight for the lavatory! *via Dr. Gary Kuhn*

Often quoted erroneously as msn 2722, Converted, like other B-23s, to mount Wright R-2600-3 engines, N61666 (msn 2727, AC39-41) was photographed 20 February 1956 while still owned by the General Electric Co., Note that the rear cabin windows have been positions rather lower on the fuselage than on other known conversions. *via Dr. Gary Kuhn*

Pictured at Hutchinson, Kansas 17 July 1948, these two views of N33310 (msn 2748, AC39-62) show the aircraft when she was nominally still owned by Pan American World Airways, which had procured her surplus 11 October 1944 with a scant 771 hours total time. *via Dr. Gary Kuhn*

Often quoted erroneously as msn 2722, N53253 was actually msn 2732 (AC39-46) and had numerous corporate owners between July 1945 when registered as NR53253, and 1970 when, like N61666, she was seized in Argentina for smuggling. *via Dr. Gary Kuhn*

Footnotes

Chapter 1

[1] "Buying Aircraft: Materiel Procurement for the Army Air Forces," United States Army in World War II, Special Studies, Irving B. Holley Jr., pp49.determine, from the existing records, whether Congress this as an actual ceiling, based on War Department requests, as being adequate. Whatever the actual situation, this number remained the "official" ceiling on the size of the Air Corps until 1939, when the rush of world events once more forced a reopening of the entire question.

[2] For reasons unknown, nearly every historical discussion of the evolution of the B-18 subsequently gave the date for opening of these bids as 1936, rather than 1935.

[3] This aircraft has been almost invariably mis-identified as the Model 145, XB-16 or XB-16A in every published account of the competition prior to this time.

[4] Even at that, the Martin Model 146 was smaller dimensionally than the competing DB-1, which had a wing span 13 feet, six inches greater and a length five feet longer.

[5] Comparisons between the Y1B-17 and the B-18 appear to have been rather intentionally slanted, depending on who was drafting the data. The Office of the Chief of the Air Corps, for example in a report to The Adjutant General of the War Department, dated June 9, 1937, claimed that the Y1B-17 had a tot speed of 256mph at 14,000 feet, while stating that the high speed of the B-18 at 10,000 feet was 214mph, with "full load ranges" of 1,327 and 690 miles, respectively. The same report stated that the Y1B-17 could tote 10,500 pounds of bombs and the B-18 only 6,500. These figures, in fact, left a decidedly biased impression, since the actual maximum bomb load of the Y1B-17 was 8,000 pounds and the actual range of the B-18 at operating speed, with a full load, was 1,082 miles, nearly 400 miles longer than the OCAC reported.

[6] The first B-18, A.C.36-262, to be fair, actually cost $83,790.04, while the first A-20A's cost $94,080 each.

[7] J. H. Kindelberger's factory was in Baltimore, General Aviation Corporation (later to evolve into North American). He was widely known to be unhappy there, and the aircraft that was to become the XB-21 was designed there, but actually built in California when the firm moved, lock, stock and barrel. The XB-21 was actually recommended by one faction in the Air Corps, but was overruled by another which favored the B-18. Ironically, the XB-21 was named the Dragon, which was later adopted official for the successor to the B-18, the Douglas B-23. The XB-21 did have a number of merits, including the first power operated gun turrets on a U.S. bomber, 20mm cannon, supercharged engines and a decent bomb load. Kindelberger and NAA were left with a $550,000 investment but the aircraft showed sufficient innovation that the Air Corps bought it for extensive experimental testing. The XB-21 cost $122,000 as compared to $64,000 for a production B-18A. Five YB-21s were in fact ordered, but later cancelled.

[8] Although the company had guaranteed 215mph at a gross weight of 20,035.5 pounds, thy submitted a Revised Performance Guarantee on August 7, 1936, which notched this down to 214mph, with the cruise/operating speed remaining the same, no change in endurance, same time-to-climb to 10,000 feet and changes in ceiling with one engine and take off over a 50-foot obstacle. This was due to a weight change in Change No.2, Serial No.2076 to Contract W535-ac-8307 of plus 30 pounds for an additional five gallons of fuel required to meet the minimum endurance at normal gross weight. Interestingly, this report was entitled "Revised Performance Guarantees for the B-18 (DS-148)" with no mention in the title of type DB-1!

[9] The cost originally quoted, and often repeated over the years, of $58,500 did not include the engines or other specialized equipment. It is assumed that this was also true for the Boeing X-299 as well.

[10] A Confidential USAAF "Airplane Characteristics & Performance Chart" issued monthly during the war years invariably showed the total of Douglas B-18-DOs acquired as 133, obviously including the DB-1 and DB-2 in the total.

[11] By way of comparison, and even allowing for wartime inflation, a brand-new Republic P-47C Thunderbolt cost the USAAF $82,997 per item as of 1942.

[12] The Murray Green Collection Interviews, and incredible collection of extremely detailed notes, cross-references and question-and-answer interview transcripts, were examined by the authors at the USAF Academy Library.

[13] Murray Green citations are quoted from his collection held by the U.S. Air Force Academy Library, Clark Special Collections Branch, known as The Murray Green Collection.

[14] This was the wording of a Memo by Major Hoyt to Arnold dated March 11, 1936, including the extract from the Pratt-MacArthur agreement, located in AAG (Classified) 370.3 Coast Defense at the National Archives, RG18. An article on the agreement was also found in the Army-Navy Journal for January 17, 1931.

[15] Futrell, "The Army and the Strategic Bomber, 1930-1939" Vol. I, pp 75-79 and Military Affairs, Vol. XXII No.4, Winter 1958-59, pp208-211.

[16] At least one Douglas-originated drawing of a B-18A configured aircraft showed both a rear and a forward dorsal turret, the forward one being in approximately the same area as the crew escape hatch.

Chapter 2

[17] There is a Douglas drawing of a B-18 variant with R-2600 engines and a vertical fin and rudder closely resembling that developed for the B-23, which Douglas arbitrarily labeled as the "B-18B". This aircraft was projected to be capable of a maximum speed of 246mph at 10,000 feet and have an endurance of 7.3 hours. Nothing further has surfaced regarding this concept

[18] See the dedicated Annex listing (*Annex 4: pages 385-390*) all known accidents and losses in chronological order for full details.

[19] See pp336-339 of *Curtiss Fighter Aircraft: A Photographic History* by Francis H. Dean and this writer (Schiffer Publishing, ISBN978-0-7643-2580-9), 2007, for further details.

Chapter 3

[20] Often quoted, or so it appears, to add yet more glory to the B-17, for the 2nd Bomb Group's attitude towards the B-18, see the conversation held at the USAF Historical Research Agency, Maxwell AFB, AL, with Major G. D. Davies, quoted only in June 1944, by then the Assistant S-2 (Intelligence) for the I Bomber Command, flying B-24s, in which he recalled second-handedly the comments of Colonel R. W. Finn. The exact quotation was *"With the aid of a fairly strong tail wind, the B-18s made 150mph, even when climbing – pretty good for those 'old ducks'"* In fact, Colonel Finn's comments were clearly in admiration for the aircraft, if the entire except from the 2nd Bomb Group Diary is read in full.

[21] Exactly how the commander arrived at a total of 2 B-18s cannot be ascertained, since the only aircraft then extant was the DB-1, the first production B-18 not being handed over until May 25, 1937. It is possible that the aircraft was flown to Langley before formal hand-over to join the DB-1.

[22] The first incarnation of such a directive was actually dated November 15, 1937, and these differed rather markedly from those shown in the table for November 6, 1939, shown above. For an excellent description of these, see pp32 of *Air Force Colors, Vol.1 1926-1942* by Dana Bell (Squadron/Signal Publications, 1979, ISBN 0-89747-091-5).

[23] Notably the work of the late Peter M. Bowers and world-renowned authority of the subject, Dana Bell.

[24] The 37th Bombardment Squadron (M), activated on February 1, 1940 (and formerly the 37th Attack Squadron) was at Barksdale Field as of July 1, 1940 and was thus nominally a GHQAF unit, although not assigned to any of the tactical Groups then at Barksdale. It was moved on Temporary Duty to Lowry Field, CO nine days later and, on June 19, 1941, was again transferred to Pendleton Field, OR, where it finally became part of the 17th Bomb Group. It did in fact operate B-18s during the period prior to June 1941, when it started training on B-25.

Chapter 5

[25] The first known use of this popular name in an official Canadian document was a memo from the Canadian Director of Purchases to Douglas dated July 20, 1940, in which the aircraft were referred to as "Canadian Twin-engine Bombers *(Digby)*."

[26] There is only one known document in which the DB-280s were cited as "B-18A" type aircraft. This was the actual order, completed by the War Supply Board on behalf of the RCAF, dated November 3, 1939 in which the "Wireless Stores" for the aircraft were specified as "20 sets – radio equipment for "Douglas" B-18A Bomber Aircraft, each set consisting of the following: 1 Radio Compass Bendix Model MN-26; 1 Receiver Bendix Model RA-1; 1 Transmitter Bendix Model 3003; 1 eight-place Interphone System Bendix 3609; 8 Microphone Bendix Model MT.42A; 8 Headphones Bendix Model MR-8E; 1 Set additional Marker Beacon Indicators (R.H. and L. H.); 1 Marker Beacon Rauland Model BC.341."

[27] 10(BR) Squadron coded its *Digby's* in the RAF manner with fuselage codes on either side of the national insignia roundel. From April 1940 through about May 1942, the unit code was PB (thus, for example, aircraft serial number 748 was PB+V, with the "+" indicating the location of the national insignia roundel) while from May 1942 through about October 1942, the unit used code JK (an example being aircraft serial 751, which was coded JK+K). Similarly, 161 Squadron, which also flew *Digby's* used code TN from April 1943 through about May 1944, an example being 754, which was coded TN+G.

Chapter 6

[28] This apparently included one assigned to the 20th Air Base Group as 178/20AB, which was probably the Tow Target Detachment aircraft cited in the text.

[29] Some sources claim that the RAF had a full squadron of Vickers *Wellington's* at Reykjavik by this time, but this cannot be substantiated.

Chapter 7

[30] The reader is recommended to review any number of excellent books detailing the events leading up to Pearl Harbor. However, one of the most revealing is ***"And I WasThere": Pearl Harbor and Midway – Breaking the Secrets*** by Rear Admiral Edwin T. Layton, USN (Ret), Quill, 1987, ISBN 0-688-06968-1

[31] As related by author Robert F. Dorr based on a telephone interview with Major General Gordon Austin, USAF (Ret) in December 2002. While the precise time of the B-18s arrival is not recorded, the first USAAC aircraft known to have taken off in defense of the Hawaiian installations, four P-40s and two P-36s, got airborne at about 0830. These were followed by other fighter aircraft as quickly as ammunition and crews could be assembled, and these launched in nearly spontaneous, undocumented missions. These were followed by an O-47B from Bellows Field at 0950 and, at 1140 by four A-20As and two B-17s.

[32] Prior to this time, USAAC elements in the Philippines had been under the umbrella of the Philippine Department Air Force, headquartered at Nichols Field, Luzon.

[33] Not the 28th Bomb Squadron, as has been reported in numerous publications. The FEAF Tow Target Detachment had one B-18, three Martin B-10Bs, one ancient Thomas-Morse O-19E biplane, and one Douglas O-46A as of November 30, 1941, and these aircraft were the only FEAF aircraft fitted for target tug duties. It is believed that they were amongst the only aircraft still in the command as of that date that had not been camouflaged, in order to make them as highly visible as possible to both aerial and anti-aircraft unit gunnery training.

[34] T.B.A., or Table of Basic Allowances, also known as the T.O. & E. or Table of Organization and Equipment.

[35] This seems to be contrary to many published accounts that FEAF had constructed no revetments to protect aircraft on the ground.

Chapter 8

[36] The organization had evolved from the so-called Gulf Task Force of I Bomber Command from June 21, 1942.

[37] In more accounts, this equipment is usually referred to as Magnetic Anomaly Detector gear, but the original AAF documents invariably refer to it this way, and with this spelling of "Airbourne".

Chapter 14

[38] Another 18th Reconnaissance Squadron B-18, AC36-290, coded R-2, had also been painted with the modified Barclay scheme at Langley, following the crash of AC36-296/R-5. The modifications made to the scheme at Langley mainly involved changing the pattern on the right wing. This final Barclay scheme consisted of four colors: white, gray, ultramarine blue and a *"special dark blue."* All horizontal surfaces consisted of white and ultramarine blue, while the darker paints were used on all vertical surfaces. It was intended that many of the "irregular lines" in this pattern would result in straight line projection when viewed from below and from the front.

Chapter 16

[39] An amusing account of the last flight by Gary V. Plomp was published in the October-December 2002 issue of ***The Rip Chord.***

Line art

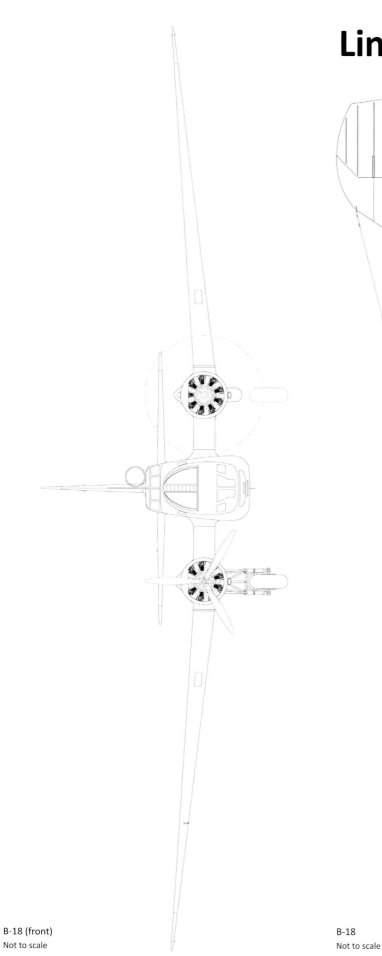

B-18 (front)
Not to scale

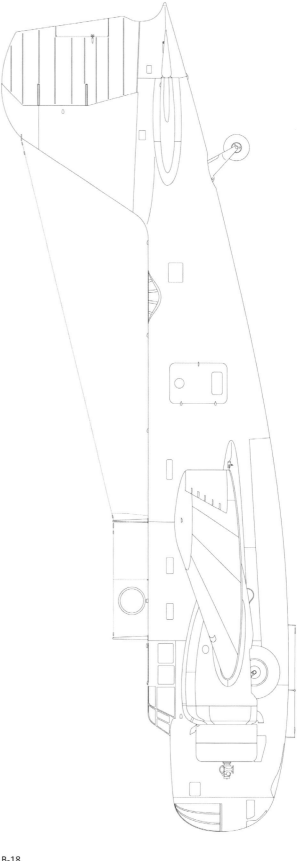

B-18
Not to scale

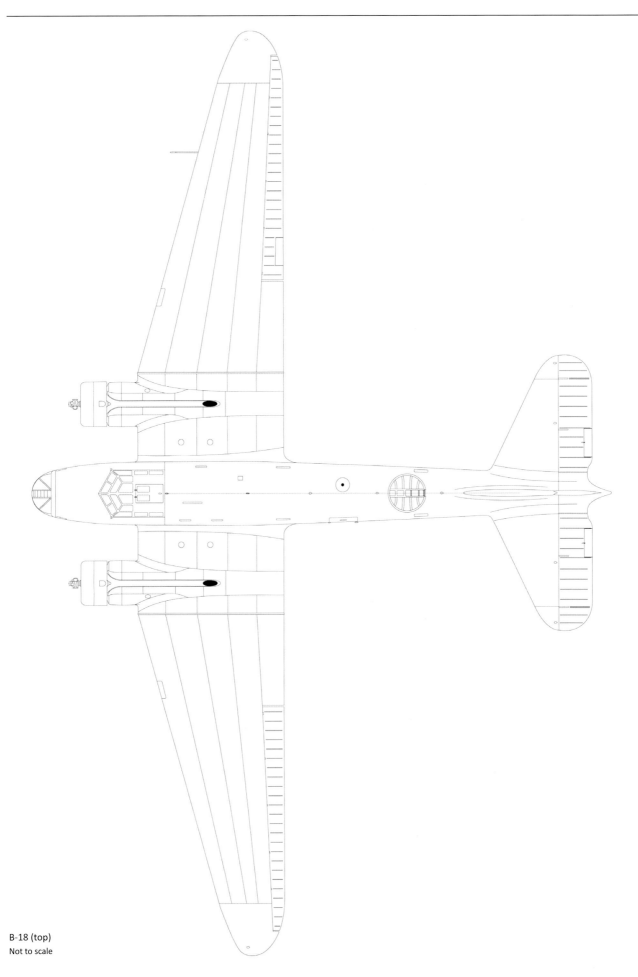

B-18 (top)
Not to scale

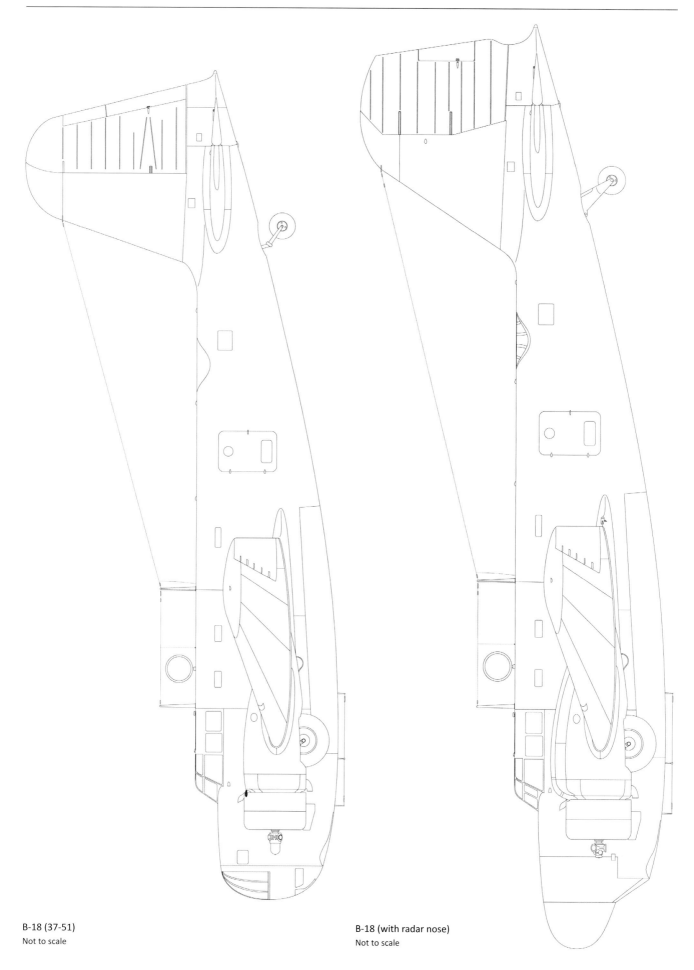

B-18 (37-51)
Not to scale

B-18 (with radar nose)
Not to scale

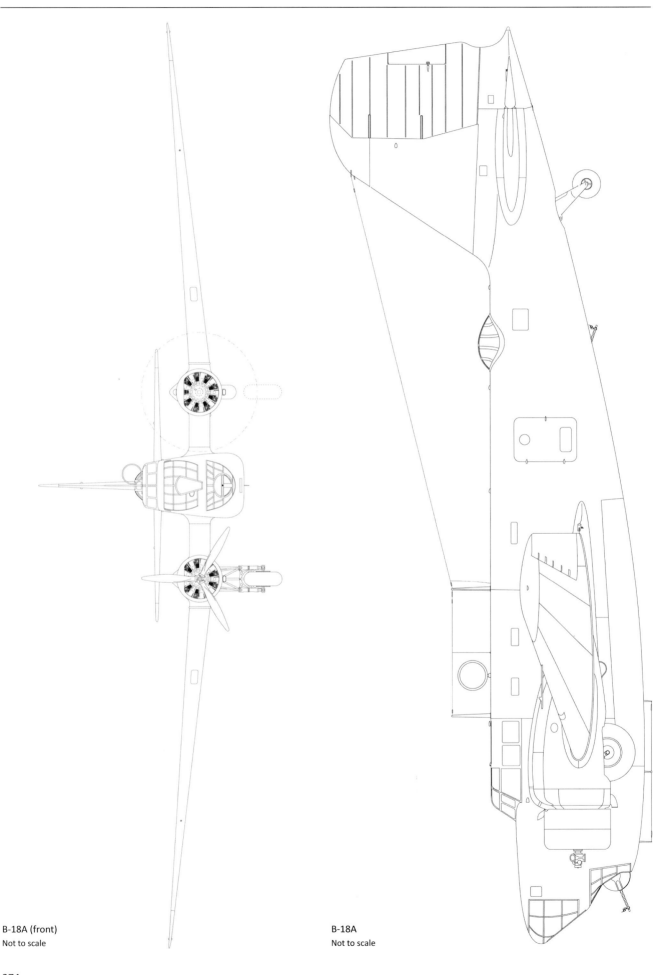

B-18A (front)
Not to scale

B-18A
Not to scale

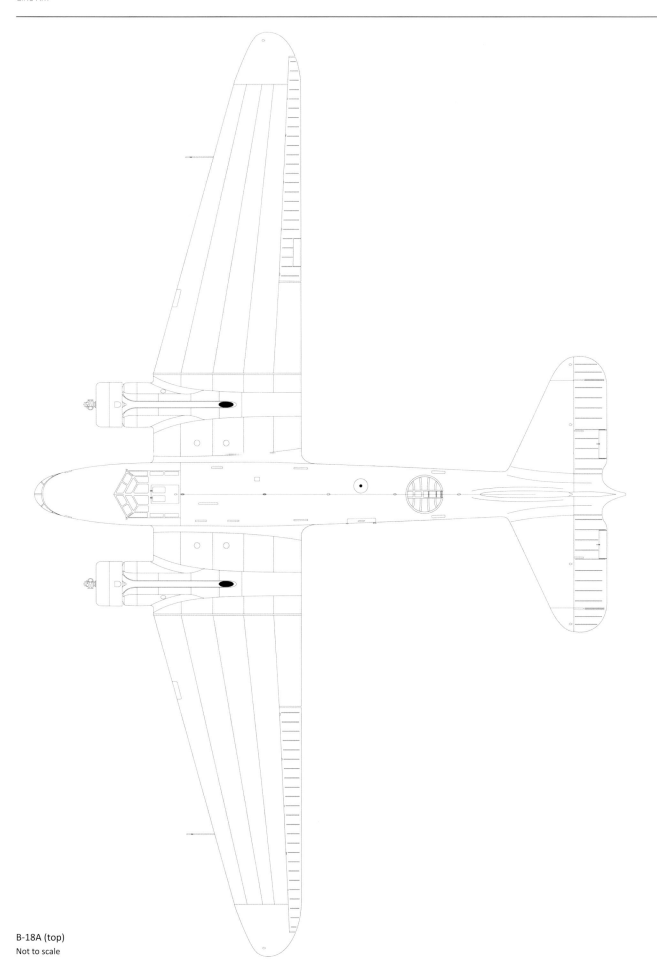

B-18A (top)
Not to scale

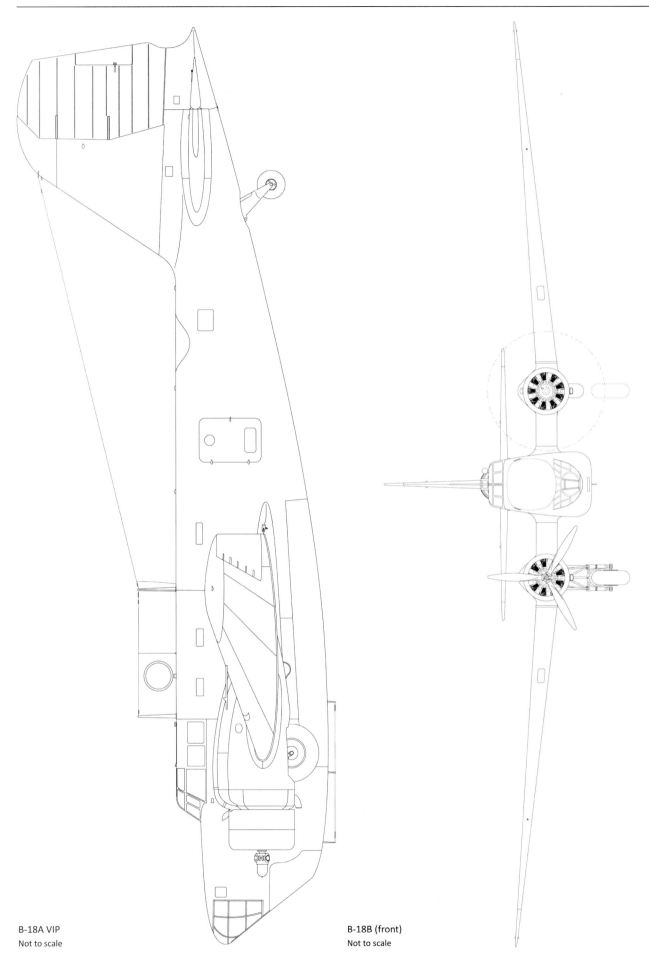

B-18A VIP
Not to scale

B-18B (front)
Not to scale

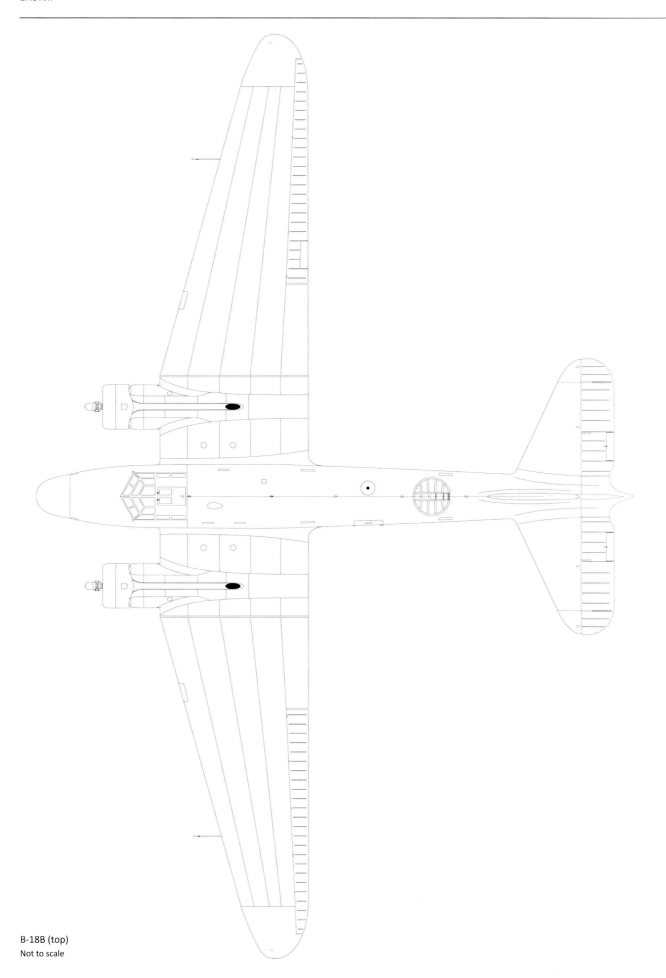

B-18B (top)
Not to scale

Index

Fields

General

Groups

Ships

Squadrons (all Bombardment Squadrons unless otherwise stated)